ICD-9-CM
Coding Handbook
with Answers

2012 REVISED EDITION

Faye Brown

REVISED BY Nelly Leon-Chisen, RHIA

CENTRAL OFFICE ON ICD-9-CM

OF THE AMERICAN HOSPITAL ASSOCIATION

HEALTH FORUM, INC.

An American Hospital Association Company

Chicago

At press time, additional guideline changes were anticipated for October 1, 2011, implementation. Please visit www.ahacentraloffice.org for guideline revisions.

Printed in the United States of America—08/11

Cover design by Cheri Kusek

ISBN: 978-1-55648-380-6

Item Number: 148048

Contents

List of Figures and Tables

About the Author and Contributors

IN MEMORIAM: **Faye Brown,** who was responsible for educating many generations of *ICD-9-CM* coders, died January 2, 2006. She was 86.

The first *ICD-9-CM Coding Handbook* was developed by the staff of the Central Office on ICD-9-CM of the American Hospital Association and published in 1979 by American Hospital Publishing, Inc., now AHA Press. Faye Brown authored and revised subsequent editions of the handbook from 1989 through the 2006 edition, which was published in the summer of 2005.

Faye Brown was a nationally known consultant in medical record management and data quality evaluation. She worked extensively for national and international health care organizations, including the American Hospital Association, the Institute of Medicine, the Pan American Health Organization, and the World Health Organization.

Ms. Brown was a member of the editorial advisory board for the *AHA Coding Clinic for ICD-9-CM,* which is published by the Central Office on ICD-9-CM of the American Hospital Association. She served as acting director of the Central Office in 1990. She also participated in several coding teleconferences presented by the AHA.

In addition to having broad hospital experience in medical record administration, she served as chair of the Medical Record Administration Department in the School of Allied Health Sciences at Loma Linda University, Loma Linda, California. She was president of the American Medical Record Association during 1970–1971 and was named the association's distinguished member for 1978.

Revisions of more recent editions of the *ICD-9-CM Coding Handbook* have been produced in collaboration with the Central Office, following the Faye Brown tradition. In tribute to her, the staff of the Central Office and AHA Press honor her legacy by carrying on her commitment to coding education through this and subsequent editions of the coding handbooks.

Nelly Leon-Chisen, RHIA, is the director of coding and classification at the AHA, where she heads the Central Office on ICD-9-CM and the Central Office on HCPCS. She represents the AHA as one of the *ICD-9-CM* cooperating parties and is responsible for the development of *AHA Coding Clinic for ICD-9-CM, ICD-9-CM Official Guidelines for Coding and Reporting,* and *ICD-10-CM and ICD-10-PCS Official Guidelines for Coding and Reporting.*

Ms. Leon-Chisen's *ICD-10* activities include membership in the ICD-10-PCS Technical Advisory Panel, past co-chair of the Workgroup for Electronic Data Interchange (WEDI) ICD-10 Implementation Workgroup, and numerous testimonies on *ICD-10-CM* and *ICD-10-PCS* before the ICD-9-CM Coordination and Maintenance Committee and the National Committee on Vital and Health Statistics. She was also the AHA lead project manager on the joint American Hospital Association–American Health Information Management Association (AHIMA) ICD-10-CM Field Study. She is a first-generation AHIMA-approved ICD-10-CM/PCS Trainer. She is the author of the *ICD-10-CM and ICD-10-PCS Coding Handbook,* published by AHA Press.

Ms. Leon-Chisen represented the AHA as a member of the Present on Admission Workgroup. In her role as the AHA representative to the *ICD-9-CM* cooperating parties, she participated in the development and approval of the present on admission (POA) guidelines and examples. She has lectured on the implementation of the POA indicator for American Hospital Association and American Health Information Management Association audioseminars and Healthcare Financial Management Association webinars, as well as for state hospital and health information management (HIM) associations.

Ms. Leon-Chisen has lectured on coding, data quality, DRGs, and *ICD-10* throughout the United States, Europe, and Latin America. She is also a speaker for the popular *AHA Coding Clinic* audioseminar series. She has broad HIM experience in hospital inpatient and outpatient management, consulting, and teaching. She has been an instructor in the HIM and Health Information Technology Programs for the University of Illinois and Truman Community College, both in Chicago. She is a past president of the Chicago Area Health Information Management Association and the recipient of its Distinguished Member Award. She is the recipient of the Professional Achievement Award from the Illinois Health Information Management Association. She is a member of the Advisory Board of the Health Information Technology Program of DeVry University in Chicago.

The Central Office on ICD-9-CM was created through a written Memorandum of Understanding between the AHA and the National Center for Health Statistics in 1963 to do the following:

- Serve as the U.S. clearinghouse for issues related to the use of *ICD-9-CM*
- Work with the National Center for Health Statistics and the Centers for Medicare & Medicaid Services to maintain the integrity of the classification system
- Recommend revisions and modifications to the current and future revisions of the *ICD*
- Develop educational material and programs on *ICD-9-CM*

The Central Office on ICD-9-CM is the publisher of the *AHA Coding Clinic on ICD-9-CM*. In addition, the Central Office provides expert advice by serving as the clearinghouse for the dissemination of *ICD-9-CM* information.

Janatha R. Ashton, RHIA, MS, is the author of the case summary exercises in appendix B. She is an associate professor emerita of informatics in the Health Information Administration Program in the School of Informatics at Indiana University, Indianapolis. In addition, she conducts *ICD-9-CM* coding workshops and provides consultation services to hospitals, long-term care facilities, physician office personnel, insurance companies, and government agencies.

Acknowledgments

Nelly Leon-Chisen gratefully acknowledges the invaluable contributions of Anita Rapier, Gretchen Young-Charles, and Denene M. Harper, members of the American Hospital Association's Central Office on ICD-9-CM, who assisted in the revision and review of the manuscript for the handbook as well as the case summary exercises.

Anita Rapier, RHIT, CCS, is a senior coding consultant with the AHA Central Office on ICD-9-CM. She is also the managing editor of *Coding Clinic for ICD-9-CM,* for which she is responsible for developing educational material. She has more than 25 years of experience in health information management and has held several positions in HIM, including education, quality, compliance, hospital-based outpatient and acute care, and long-term care. Ms. Rapier has presented numerous educational seminars and has authored articles on coding and compliance. She is also a speaker for the popular *AHA Coding Clinic* audioseminar series. She is a first-generation AHIMA-approved ICD-10-CM/PCS Trainer.

Gretchen Young-Charles, RHIA, is a senior coding consultant at the AHA Central Office on ICD-9-CM. In this role, she develops educational articles on official coding advice for publication in *Coding Clinic for ICD-9-CM.* She also served as the secretary to the AHA's Rehabilitation Coding Workgroup. Ms. Young-Charles has more than 20 years experience in the HIM field. She has worked in numerous HIM roles, including education, quality, hospital-based outpatient and acute care, and rehabilitation. She has also spent a number of years with the Peer Review Organization for the state of Illinois. She is also a speaker for the popular *AHA Coding Clinic* audioseminar series. She is a first-generation AHIMA-approved ICD-10-CM/PCS Trainer.

Denene M. Harper, RHIA, is a senior coding consultant at the AHA Central Office on ICD-9-CM. She is responsible for writing articles on official coding advice for publication in *Coding Clinic for ICD-9-CM.* Ms. Harper has more than 20 years of experience in the HIM field, including hospital-based outpatient and acute care, utilization review, and quality improvement. She is an AHIMA-approved ICD-10-CM/PCS Trainer.

Janatha Ashton gratefully acknowledges the dedicated efforts and significant contributions of many individuals, including Londa Bechert, RHIA, Danita Forgey, RHIA, Melinda Nicholson, RHIA, Ann Rugg, RHIA, Jamie Sadler, RHIA, Lenore Webb, RHIA, Mary L. McKenzie, RHIA, and Minette Terlep, RHIA. Indiana University Hospital and the HCA Coding Support staff are also thanked.

Finally, Jan wants to acknowledge the patience and understanding of her family during the months it took to develop the case summary exercises.

AHA Press National *ICD-9-CM* Coding Training Advisory Team

Marie T. Conde, MPA, RHIA, CCS
Program Director and Instructor
Health Information Technology
City College of San Francisco
San Francisco, California

Kathleen M. Craig, RHIA, CCS
Program Chair and Assistant Professor
Health Information Technology
Ivy Tech Community College
Bloomington, Indiana

Lisa DeLiberto, MS, RHIA
Program Chair and Assistant Professor
Health Information Technology
Passaic County Community College
Paterson, New Jersey

Betty Haar, RHIA
Program Director
Health Information Technology
Kirkwood Community College
Cedar Rapids, Iowa

Fanny C. Hawkins, EdD, CPHQ, RHIA
Program Director
Health Information Management
Texas Southern University
Houston, Texas

Susan Johnson, RHIA, CCS
Program Director
Health Information Technology
Rasmussen College
Green Bay, Wisconsin

Sherri Mallett, MEd, RHIA, CCS-P
Program Faculty
Health Information Management
Cincinnati State Technical and Community College
Cincinnati, Ohio

Patricia Pierson, RHIA
Program Faculty
Health Information Technology and Medical Coding
Collin College
McKinney, Texas

Cheryl A. Plettenberg, EdD, RHIA
Program Chair
Health Information Management
Alabama State University
Montgomery, Alabama

Nena Scott, MSEd, RHIA, CCS, CCS-P
Program Director
Health Information Technology
Itawamba Community College
Tupelo, Mississippi

Michelle Shipley, MS, RHIA, CCS
Program Director
Health Information Technology
Washburn University
Topeka, Kansas

Korene Silvestri, MA, RHIA, CCS, CPC, CPC-H, CPC-I
Program Director and Associate Professor
Health Information Technology
West Virginia Northern Community College
Wheeling, West Virginia

Corinne Smith, MBA, RHIA, CCS
Associate Professor, Clinical Coordinator
Montgomery College
Silver Spring, Maryland

Isaac Topor, EdD, RHIA
Program Chairman, Medical Informatics
College of Health Related Professions
SUNY Downstate Medical Center
Brooklyn, New York

Mary Worsley, MS, RHIA, CCS
Program Coordinator and Faculty
Health Information Management Technology
Miami Dade College
Miami, Florida

How to Use This Handbook

As with earlier editions, this revision is designed as a versatile resource:

- Textbook for academic programs in health information technology and administration
- Text for in-service training programs
- Self-instructional guide for individuals interested in learning coding outside a formal program or in refreshing their skills
- Reference tool for general use in the workplace

The general and basic areas of information covered in chapters 1 through 8 are designed to meet the requirements of various basic courses on the use of *ICD-9-CM*. They may also be used as a foundation for further learning and should be understood before moving on to the study of individual chapters of *ICD-9-CM*. Chapters 9 through 29 of the handbook include advanced material that is designed to be a learning tool for continuing education students and a resource for professionals in the field.

Throughout the chapters an icon (featured here in the margin) is used to indicate common coding pitfalls. These do not necessarily represent the most difficult or most important information in the book, but they do highlight situations in which coders often make mistakes or need to ask physicians for more information.

This handbook is designed to be used in conjunction with the three volumes of *ICD-9-CM*. The three volumes must be consulted throughout the learning process, and the material cannot be mastered without using them. The official versions published by the Government Printing Office are available only in CD-ROM format. Unofficial print versions are available from a number of publishers, often combined in one book with three divisions corresponding to the three volumes of the official version. There may be minor variations between the way material is displayed in this handbook and the way it is displayed in some of the printed versions.

The chapters in the handbook are not arranged in the same sequence as the chapters in *ICD-9-CM*. The first two sections of this handbook (chapters 1–8) provide discussions of the format and conventions followed in *ICD-9-CM* as well as basic coding guidelines and introductory material on the supplementary classifications (V codes and E codes). The next eight sections (chapters 9–29) progress from the less complicated *ICD-9-CM* chapters to the more difficult. Faculty in academic and in-service programs can rearrange this sequence to suit their particular course outlines.

Chapters 30–34 contain information on *ICD-10-CM* and *ICD-10-PCS*, the future replacements for *ICD-9-CM*. These chapters may be used as a reference tool in the workplace to prepare for future implementation. In addition, educators may feel a need to start informing their students about a potential replacement to the coding system they are currently studying.

Appendix A, "Reporting of the Present on Admission Indicator," contains information on the reporting of the Medicare requirement associated with the hospital inpatient reporting of all *ICD-9-CM* diagnosis codes.

Appendix B, "Case Summary Exercises," is included once again in this edition. The exercises are designed for students who have learned the basic coding principles and need additional practice applying the principles to actual cases. They are geared for beginning to intermediate levels of knowledge.

The case summaries are based on actual health records of both inpatients and outpatients. The patients described often have multiple conditions that may or may not relate to the current episode of care. Some exercises include several episodes of care for a patient in various settings.

Appendix C is the answer key for the case summary exercises. (Students using the handbook edition without answers will need to ask their instructors for this answer key.) After they have completed the exercises, students can check their answers against the key, which lists the appropriate codes for each exercise, with the codes for the principal diagnosis and principal procedure sequenced first. Explanatory comments discuss why certain codes are appropriate and others are not and why some conditions listed in the case summaries are not coded at all. They also indicate how the principal diagnosis and procedure codes were designated, and which symptoms are inherent to certain conditions and so are not coded separately.

The *ICD-9-CM Official Guidelines for Coding and Reporting,* referenced throughout this handbook, may be downloaded from the AHA Central Office Web site: www.ahacentraloffice.org.

To use this handbook effectively, readers should work through the coding examples provided throughout the text until they fully understand the coding principles under discussion. Readers should be able to arrive at correct code assignments by following the instructions provided and reviewing the pertinent handbook material until it is fully understood. Exercises in the body of each chapter should be completed as they come up in the discussion rather than at the end of the chapter or section. Most chapters provide a review exercise with additional material that covers the entire chapter. There is also a final review exercise toward the end of the book that offers additional coding practice. An answer key to these exercises is provided in the edition with answers.

The handbook follows three conventions:

- In some examples, a lowercase letter x is used to indicate a fourth or fifth digit that is required but cannot be assigned in the example given because certain information needed for assignment of these digits is not given. This is done to emphasize the concept and specific guideline without going too deeply into specific coding situations.
- The underlining of codes in text examples indicates correct sequencing; that is, the underlined code must be sequenced first in that particular combination of codes. When no code is underlined, there is no implicit reason why any of the codes in the series should be sequenced first. In actual coding, of course, other information in the health record may dictate a different sequence. This underlining convention is used in the handbook solely as a teaching device. It is not an element of the *ICD-9-CM* coding system.
- In the edition with answers, the underlining of words in exercise questions indicates the appropriate term to be referenced in using the alphabetic indexes. The underlining of codes in the answer column of the exercises indicates correct code sequencing, as it does in the examples in the main text.

CHANGES IN CODE USAGE

Official coding guidelines and official coding advice, approved by the four cooperating parties responsible for administering the *ICD-9-CM* system in the United States (American Hospital Association, American Health Information Management Association, Centers for Medicare & Medicaid Services, and National Center for Health Statistics), are published quarterly in the *Coding Clinic for ICD-9-CM* by the Central Office on ICD-9-CM of the American Hospital Association. Such advice becomes effective as of the date of printing, although in some cases the information is merely a clarification of coding practice that is already in existence, in which case the date does not necessarily apply. In other cases, this official information may provide new advice on coding specific conditions or procedures and therefore may require updating of some of the advice in this handbook or in previous issues of *Coding Clinic*.

Every effort is made to update the *ICD-9-CM Coding Handbook* with the most recently published *Coding Clinic* advice and current official coding guidelines. However, due to the publication schedule of the handbook and the release date of the official coding guidelines, it is not always possible to incorporate changes for the upcoming fiscal year. Readers should visit www.ahacentraloffice.org to download the updated guidelines.

Further information on *Coding Clinic* follows page xiv of this handbook.

AHA Coding Clinics – the Official Publications for Coding Advice from AHA Central Office

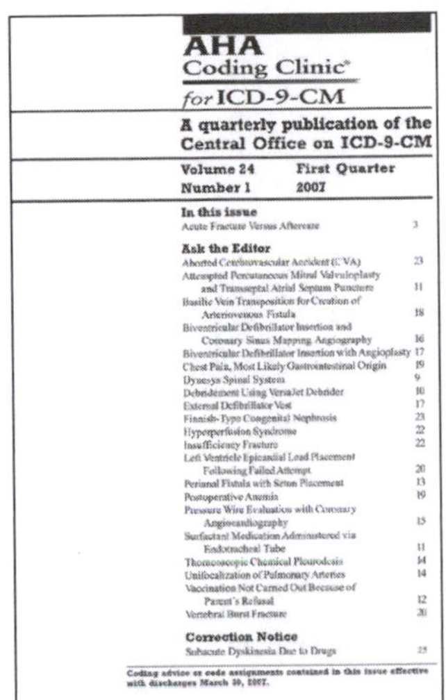

AHA
Coding Clinic®
for ICD-9-CM

A quarterly publication of the Central Office on ICD-9-CM

Volume 24 **First Quarter**
Number 1 **2007**

In this issue

Coding advice or code assignments contained in this issue effective with discharges March 30, 2007.

Improve Coding Accuracy and Your Organization's Bottom Line

AHA Coding Clinic® *for* ICD-9-CM

AHA Coding Clinic® for ICD-9-CM is the only official publication for ICD-9-CM coding guidelines and advice as designated by the four Cooperating Parties: American Hospital Association (AHA), American Health Information Management Association (AHIMA), Centers for Medicare & Medicaid Services (CMS), and the National Center for Health Statistics (NCHS).

An Annual Subscription includes an alphabetical index that is available in the first quarter.

Each issue features:

- Official coding advice
- Correct code assignments for new technologies and newly identified diseases
- Articles and topics offering practical information designed to help improve data quality
- A bulletin of coding changes and corrections to health care providers
- Actual examples from our coding advice service
- *AHA Coding Clinic®* continuing education quizzes for AHIMA Continuing Education (CE) credits offered 2 times a year

To subscribe, please call 800/621-6902
An Annual Subscription includes an alphabetical index published in first quarter
Non-Members: $290 — AHA Members: $196 — AHIMA Members: $250

AHA
Coding Clinic®
for HCPCS

Volume 7 • Number 1
First Quarter 2007

Use of modifiers 52, 73, and 74 and anesthesia reporting under OPPS

INSIDE:

AHA Coding Clinic® *for* HCPCS

Your essential tool for accurate, up-to-date outpatient codes

Maintain compliance and maximize outpatient reimbursement. *AHA Coding Clinic® for HCPCS* is required reading for compliance, finance, patient accounts, information systems, and medical records professionals.

This invaluable quarterly newsletter includes:

- Information on HCPCS reporting for hospitals HCPCS Level I (CPT-4 codes) and select Level II codes
- The latest code assignments for emerging technologies
- Real examples from our HCPCS coding advice service
- Practical tips for improving data quality
- Bulletins on coding changes and corrections
- Policy impacts on coding

To subscribe, please call 800/621-6902
Non-Members: $135 — AHA Members: $105 — AHIMA Members: $125

To subscribe, please see reverse side for order information

AHA CENTRAL OFFICE™

An American Hospital Association Service

AHA Central Office is the official clearinghouse for information on the proper use of ICD-9-CM codes, level I HCPCS codes (CPT-4 codes) for hospital providers, and certain level II HCPCS codes for hospitals, physicians, and other health care professionals.

www.ahacentraloffice.org

Order Form

	Non-Member Price	AHA Member Price	AHIMA Member	Quantity	Extended Price
AHA Coding Clinic for ICD-9-CM	$290	$196	$250		
AHA Coding Clinic for HCPCS	$135	$105	$125		
					Total Amount

Quantity discounts apply only to quantities shipped to ONE location.
Call 800-621-6902 for bulk pricing.

Payment Information

☐ **Payment Enclosed** Send this form with a check or money order payable to:
American Hospital Association
P.O. Box 92247 • Chicago, IL 60675-2247

☐ **Please Bill Me** Purchase Order Number________________

☐ **Credit Card Payment**

Credit Card Number ________________

Credit Card Type________________ Expiration Date________________

Signature ________________

Send Subscription To

Name________________

Organization________________

Department ________________

Address Line 1 ________________

Address Line 2 ________________

City, State, Zip ________________

Telephone________________

Email ________________

Place Your Order Today!

Mail: American Hospital Association
P.O. Box 92247
Chicago, IL 60675-2247

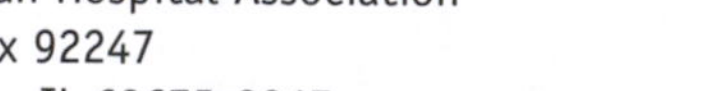

Online: www.ahacentraloffice.org/codingclinic

Phone: 1-800-621-6902 or
1-312-893-6800

Fax: 1-312-422-4799

Format and Conventions and Current Coding Practices for *ICD-9-CM*

Introduction to the *ICD-9-CM* Classification

CHAPTER 1

CHAPTER OVERVIEW

- *ICD-9-CM* is a medical classification system.
- Volume 1 is the Tabular List of Diseases and Injuries.
  - There are three-, four-, and five-digit codes.
  - Codes appear in numerical order.
- Volume 2 is the Alphabetic Index of Diseases and Injuries. There is a pattern to the indentations found in volume 2.
  - Main terms are flush to the left-hand margin.
  - Subterms are indented. The more specific the subterm the farther the indent.
  - Carryover lines are two indents from the indent level of the preceding line.
  - There are also strict alphabetization rules.
- Volume 3 is the Tabular List and Alphabetic Index of Procedures.
  - The format for the Tabular List and Alphabetic Index follows volumes 1 and 2 except for some slight modifications.
  - Main term entries are names of procedures and operations.

LEARNING OUTCOMES

After studying this chapter you should be able to:

- Explain the basic principles of the medical classification system *ICD-9-CM*.
- Describe the differences among the three volumes of the *ICD-9-CM*.
- Demonstrate understanding of the three-, four-, and five-digit subdivisions.
- Explain the alphabetization rules and indentation patterns.
- Differentiate between the codes in volumes 1 and 2 and the procedure codes in volume 3.

TERMS TO KNOW

E codes
codes used to indicate the external circumstances responsible for injuries

ICD-9-CM
International Classification of Diseases, Ninth Revision, Clinical Modification; a medical classification system used for the collection of information regarding disease and injury

V codes
codes used to indicate conditions not included in the main classification but that may be recorded as diagnoses

REMEMBER . . . The exclamation point icon (⚠) is meant to draw attention to a common pitfall in coding.

INTRODUCTION

The *International Classification of Diseases, Ninth Revision, Clinical Modification (ICD-9-CM),* is the medical classification system used in the United States for the collection of information regarding disease and injury. Volumes 1 and 2 consist of a clinical modification of the World Health Organization's *Manual of the International Statistical Classification of Diseases, Injuries, and Causes of Death, Ninth Revision (ICD-9). ICD-9-CM* is entirely compatible with *ICD-9* and maintains its statistical orientation. The clinical modification expands ICD-9 codes to facilitate more precise coding of clinical diagnoses. Volume 3 of *ICD-9-CM* is a classification of operations and procedures developed for use in the United States; it is not a part of the World Health classification. For statistical purposes, the procedure classification system follows the same organization and principles on which volumes 1 and 2 are based.

A classification system is an arrangement of elements into groups according to established criteria. In *ICD-9* and *ICD-9-CM* these elements are diseases, injuries, surgeries, and procedures, which are grouped into appropriate chapters and sections. Three-digit categories are used in volumes 1 and 2, and two-digit categories are used in volume 3. These groups are the common basis of classification for general medical statistical use. They help to answer questions about groups of related causes and provide the capacity for the systematic tabulation, storage, and retrieval of disease-related data. Each numerical code represents a counting unit, with the three-digit categories forming the basis for data tabulation. In *ICD-9-CM* many disease and injury categories have been expanded by fourth- and fifth-digits that provide for additional specificity but remain collapsible to the three-digit category.

ICD-9-CM is a closed classification system—it provides one and only one place to classify each condition and procedure. Despite the large number of different conditions to be classified, the system must limit its size in order to be usable. Certain conditions that occur infrequently or are of low importance are frequently grouped together in residual codes labeled "other" or "not elsewhere classified." A final residual category is provided for diagnoses not stated specifically enough to permit more precise classification. Occasionally these two residual groups are combined in one code.

Medical coders must understand the basic principles behind the classification system in order to use *ICD-9-CM* appropriately and effectively. This knowledge is also the basis for understanding and applying the official coding advice provided through the *Coding Clinic for ICD-9-CM,* published by the Central Office on *ICD-9-CM* of the American Hospital Association. It is important for coders in all health care settings to keep current with the official coding guidelines as well as *Coding Clinic for ICD-9-CM.* This official advice is developed through the editorial board for the *Coding Clinic* and is approved by the four cooperating parties for *ICD-9-CM,* which include the American Hospital Association, the American Health Information Management Association, the Centers for Medicare & Medicaid Services, and the National Center for Health Statistics. Revised codes and new codes are developed annually by the last two agencies and are implemented on October 1 of each year. Starting with Fiscal Year 2005, new *ICD-9-CM* codes may be implemented twice a year—April 1 and October 1 of each year. Only code proposals specifically requesting expedited approval and making a strong and convincing case for purposes of meeting the new technology process will be approved for April 1 implementation. There were no new codes implemented in April 2011.

ICD-9-CM is presented as three volumes:

- Tabular List of Diseases and Injuries (volume 1)
- Alphabetic Index of Diseases and Injuries (volume 2)
- Tabular List and Alphabetic Index of Procedures (volume 3) [Note: Volume 3 of the *ICD-9-CM* is intended for use only by hospitals for reporting of inpatient procedures.]

The official version of *ICD-9-CM* is available in CD-ROM format from the U.S. Government Printing Office. Write to the office at P.O. Box 979050, St. Louis, MO 63197-9000, call telephone number (866) 512-1800, or order online at http://bookstore.gpo.gov. Printed versions are also available from a number of commercial publishers.

TABULAR LIST OF DISEASES AND INJURIES (VOLUME 1)

The main classification of diseases and injuries in the Tabular List of Diseases and Injuries (volume 1) consists of 17 chapters. (See the table of contents reproduced in figure 1.1.) Approximately half of the chapters are devoted to conditions that affect a specific body system; the rest classify conditions according to etiology. Chapter 2, for example, classifies neoplasms of all body systems, whereas chapter 8 addresses diseases of the respiratory system only.

In addition, two supplementary classifications are included in volume 1. The first provides V codes that are used to code conditions that are not included in the main classification but may be recorded as diagnoses. The second provides E codes that are used as additional codes to indicate the external circumstances responsible for injuries and certain other conditions. V and E codes will be discussed briefly in chapter 8 of this handbook and in more detail in the chapters discussing the conditions to which they apply.

The variation in chapter titles in *ICD-9-CM*'s table of contents represents the compromises made during the development of a statistical classification system based partially on etiology, partially on anatomical site, and partially on the circumstances of onset. The result is a classification system based on multiple axes. By contrast, a single-axis classification would be based entirely on the etiology of the disease, the anatomical site of the disease, or the nature of the disease process. Each chapter in the main classification is structured to provide the following subdivisions:

- Sections (groups of three-digit categories)
- Categories (three-digit code numbers)
- Subcategories (four-digit code numbers)
- Fifth-digit subclassifications (five-digit code numbers)

The basic code used to classify a particular disease or injury consists of three digits and is called a category. Most categories are expanded into subcategories by the addition of fourth digits; many subcategories include fifth-digit subclassifications that provide more specificity in coding. A decimal point is used to separate the basic three-digit category code from its subcategory and subclassifications (for example, 842.13).

Listings of fifth-digit subclassifications appear at the beginning of the chapter, section, or three-digit category code to which they apply. Fifth-digit subclassifications must be assigned for all of the codes within the chapter, section, or category that follows the listing. In other cases, fourth-digit subcategory codes are expanded to display applicable fifth digits.

Codes in the Tabular List appear in numerical order. References from the Alphabetical Index to the Tabular List are by code number, not by page number. Code numbers and titles appear in bold type in the Tabular List. Instructional notes that apply to the section, category, or subcategory are also included in the Tabular List.

FIGURE 1.1 Table of Contents from *ICD-9-CM*

TABLE OF CONTENTS

In addition, volume 1 includes appendices that provide further information:

- Appendix A, Morphology of Neoplasms, provides optional codes indicating the histological type and behavior of neoplasms.

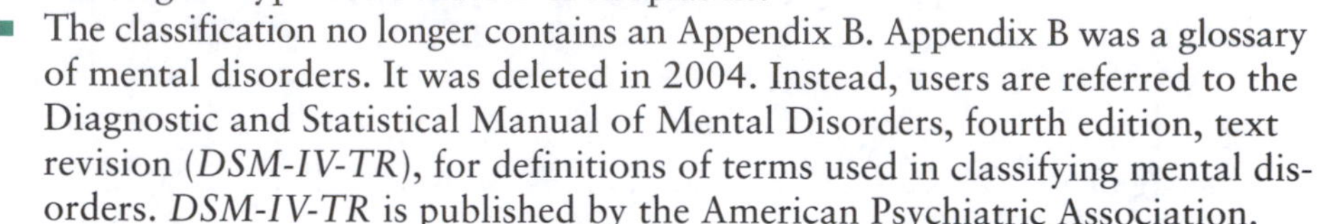

- The classification no longer contains an Appendix B. Appendix B was a glossary of mental disorders. It was deleted in 2004. Instead, users are referred to the Diagnostic and Statistical Manual of Mental Disorders, fourth edition, text revision (*DSM-IV-TR*), for definitions of terms used in classifying mental disorders. *DSM-IV-TR* is published by the American Psychiatric Association.
- Appendix C, Classification of Drugs by the American Hospital Formulary Service List Number and Their ICD-9-CM Equivalents, provides help in determining appropriate E codes for use with certain types of drugs.
- The classification no longer contains an Appendix D. Appendix D, Classification of Industrial Accidents According to Agency, was deleted in 2009.

The coder should become familiar with the location and format of the appendices because they often provide help in arriving at correct code assignment.

ALPHABETIC INDEX OF DISEASES AND INJURIES (VOLUME 2)

The Alphabetic Index of Diseases and Injuries (volume 2) includes entries for main terms, subterms, and more specific subterms. Main terms identify disease conditions or injuries. Subterms indicate site, type, or etiology for conditions or injuries. For example, acute appendicitis is listed under **Appendicitis,** acute, and stress fracture is listed under **Fracture,** stress. Occasionally, it is necessary for the coder to think of a synonym or other alternative term in order to locate the correct entry. There are, however, exceptions to this general rule, including the following:

- Congenital conditions are often indexed under the main term **Anomaly** rather than under the name of the condition.
- Conditions that complicate pregnancy, childbirth, or the puerperium are usually found under such terms as **Delivery, Labor, Pregnancy,** and **Puerperal.** They may also appear under the main term for the condition causing the complication by referencing the subterm "complicating pregnancy, childbirth, or puerperium." (An example of this type of entry appears under the main term **Diabetes, diabetic** in the Alphabetic Index.)
- Many of the complications of medical or surgical care are indexed under the term **Complications** rather than under the name of the condition.
- Late effects of an earlier condition can be found under **Late,** effect(s) (of).

A clear understanding of the format of the Alphabetic Index (volume 2) is a prerequisite for accurate coding. Understanding the indention pattern of the entries is a very important part of learning how to use the index. Now that a variety of vendors provide printed versions and others have computer programs for coding, the format is not as consistent as it was previously. In general, however, the following pattern is carried through:

- Main terms are set flush with the left-hand margin. They are printed in bold type and begin with a capital letter.
- Subterms are indented one standard indention (equivalent to about two typewriter spaces) to the right under the main term. They are printed in regular type and begin with a lowercase letter.

- More specific subterms are indented farther and farther to the right as needed, always indented by one standard indention from the preceding subterm and listed in alphabetical order.
- Carryover lines are indented two standard indentions from the level of the preceding line. Carryover lines are used only when the complete entry cannot fit on a single line. They are indented farther to avoid confusion with subterm entries.

In most printed versions, entries still continue to use two columns to a page, dictionary style. Most printed versions also use the basic three volumes, although they are now printed in one book rather than in three separate volumes. Printed versions for nonhospital settings (e.g., physician office, home health) usually consist of one book with only volumes 1 and 2 because volume 3 (procedure codes) does not apply to these settings.

The subterms listed under the main term **Rabies** in the following entry provide an example:

Rabies 071 [main term]
  contact V01.5 [subterm]
  exposure to V01.5 [subterm]
  inoculation V04.5 [subterm]
    reaction—*see* Complications, [more specific subterm]
        vaccination [carryover line]
  vaccination, prophylactic (against) V04.5 [subterm]

Each of the subterms (contact, exposure to, inoculation, and vaccination) is indented one standard indention from the level of the main term and is listed in alphabetical order. The fifth line is a more specific entry ("reaction") under the subterm "inoculation," and the sixth line is a carryover line indented two standard indentions from the preceding line.

Exercise 1.1

A reproduction of a page from volume 2 is shown below. Label the indicated lines as either main terms, subterms, or carryover lines.

1.	Main term	**Racket nail** 757.5
2.	Carryover line	**Radial nerve**—*see* condition **Radiation effects and sickness**—*see also* Effect, adverse, radiation
3.	Subterm	cataract 366.46 dermatitis 692.89
4.	Main term	sunburn 692.71 **Radiculitis** (pressure) (vertebrogenic) 729.2
5.	Subterm	accessory nerve 723.4 anterior crural 724.4 arm 723.4 brachial 723.4 cervical NEC 723.4 due to displacement of intervertebral disc
6.	Carryover line	—*see* Neuritis, due to, displacement intervertebral disc
7.	Subterm	leg 724.4 lumbar NEC 724.4 lumbosacral 724.4 rheumatic 729. syphilitic 094.89 thoracic (with visceral pain) 724.4 **Radiculomyelitis** 357.0 toxic, due to Clostridium tetani 037
8.	Carryover line	Corynebacterium diphtheriae 032.89 **Ramsay Hunt syndrome** (herpetic geniculate ganglionitis) 053.11
9.	Subterm	meaning dyssynergia cerebellaris
10.	Subterm	myoclonica 334.2 **Ranke's primary infiltration** (*see also* Tuberculosis) 010.0 **Ranula** 527.6 congenital 750.26 **Rape** (*see also* nature and site of injury) alleged, observation or examination V71.5

Alphabetization Rules

In order to locate main terms and subterms quickly and efficiently, it is important to understand the alphabetization rules followed in the Alphabetic Index. Letter-by-letter alphabetization is used both in volume 2 and in the alphabetical portion of volume 3. The system of alphabetization ignores the following:

- Single spaces between words
- Single hyphens within words
- The final "s" in the possessive forms of words

The following list shows an example of letter-by-letter alphabetization with these modifications:

- Beer-drinkers' heart (disease) 425.5 [ignores hyphen]
- Bee sting (with . . .) 989.5 [ignores space between words]
- Brailsford's disease 732.3 [ignores possessive form]
- Brailsford-Morquio disease or syndrome 277.5 [ignores hyphen]

Numerical Entries

Subterm entries for numerical characters and words indicating numbers appear first under the appropriate main term or subterm. These are listed in numerical order rather than being alphabetized in their spelled-out form. Such characters and words include Roman numerals, such as "II"; Arabic numerals, such as "2"; and adjectival terms, such as "second." For example, in volume 2, **Paralysis,** nerve, third, comes before, rather than after, **Paralysis,** nerve, fourth. Here are more examples:

Anomaly, anomalous . . .
  chromosomes, chromosomal 758.9
    13 . . .
    18 . . .
    21 . . .
Disorder . . .
  coagulation . . . 286.9
    factor VIII . . .
    factor IX . . .
    neonatal . . .
Disorder . . .
  nerve 349.9 . . .
    cranial 352.9
      first
      second
      third

Connecting Words

Words such as "with," "in," "due to," and "associated with" are used to express the relationship between the main term or a subterm indicating an associated condition or etiology. Subterms preceded by "with" or "without" are not listed in alphabetical order but appear immediately below the main term or appropriate subterm entries; subterms beginning with other connecting words appear in alphabetical order. Coders who fail to remember this feature of the alphabetization rules often make coding errors by overlooking the appropriate

subterm. Review the following subterm entries under the main term **Bronchitis** using the instructions at the end of this example:

Bronchitis (diffuse) (hypostatic) (infectious)
(inflammatory) (simple) 490
1 with
2 emphysema—*see* Emphysema
3 influenza, flu, or grippe 487.1
4 obstruction airway, chronic 491.20
with
acute bronchitis 491.22
exacerbation (acute) 491.21
tracheitis 490
acute or subacute 466.0
with bronchospasm or obstruction
466.0
chronic 491.8
5 acute or subacute 466.0
6 with
bronchospasm 466.0
obstruction 466.0
tracheitis 466.0
7 chemical (due to fumes or vapors)
506.0
8 due to
fumes or vapors 506.0
radiation 508.8
9 allergic (acute) (*see also* Asthma) 493.9
10 arachidic 934.1

1. Refer to lines 1, 5, 9, and 10 as indicated in the example. Note that the subterms preceded by the connecting word "with" immediately follow the main term **Bronchitis** and precede the subterms beginning with the letter "a" (lines 5, 9, and 10).
2. Refer to lines 6, 7, and 8 as indicated in the example. Note that the more specific subterms preceded by the connecting word "with" immediately follow the subterm "acute or subacute." In this case, the subterms beginning with the word "with" precede the subterms beginning with the letters "c" and "d" (lines 7 and 8).
3. Also note that, in both cases, the subterms indented under the connecting word "with" are listed in alphabetical order. For example, lines 2, 3, and 4 indicated in the example are in alphabetical order.

Index Tables

The main body of the volume 2 Alphabetic Index uses tables for the systematic arrangement of subterms under the main entries of **Hypertension** and **Neoplasm.** These tables simplify access to complex combinations of subterms.

Section 2 of volume 2 contains a Table of Drugs and Chemicals that begins with the code for poisoning and followed by E codes. The use of this table will be discussed later in this handbook in the chapter on poisoning and adverse effects of drugs (chapter 28).

The format and alphabetization rules used within the tables are the same as those followed in the rest of the Alphabetic Index. The use of these tables will be discussed in detail later in this handbook, but it would be useful for the reader to become familiar with the location and format of the tables at this point of the discussion.

TABULAR LIST AND ALPHABETIC INDEX OF PROCEDURES (VOLUME 3)

Volume 3 contains both the Alphabetic Index and the Tabular List for surgery and procedures. The format for the Tabular List section of volume 3 is the same as that for volume 1, except that procedure codes consist of two digits, followed by a decimal point and one or two additional digits (for example, 54.11). The format and alphabetization rules for the Alphabetic Index section of volume 3 are the same as those followed for volume 2, with the exception that subterms beginning with the words "as," "by," and "for" sometimes immediately follow the main term or subterm rather than appearing in the usual alphabetical sequence; otherwise, the words "with" and "without" remain in the first position. For example:

Arthrotomy 80.10
  as operative approach—*omit code*
  with
    arthrography—*see* Arthrogram
    arthroscopy—*see* Arthroscopy
    injection of drug 81.92
    removal of prosthesis (*see also* Removal, prosthesis, joint structures) 80.00
  ankle 80.17
  elbow 80.12

As the preceding example shows, subterms beginning with "as" and "with" precede the subterms "ankle" and "elbow." Main term entries are the names of procedures and operations, with many listed under more general terms such as "repair," "removal," "insertion," and so on.

Exercise 1.2

Without referring to the handbook material or any volume of *ICD-9-CM,* answer the following questions either true or false.

__F__ 1. The main classification consists of 17 chapters, which refer to types of conditions, anatomical systems, E codes, and V codes.

__T__ 2. In the Classification of Diseases and Injuries, three-digit code numbers are referred to as categories.

__T__ 3. For code numbers in disease classification, the decimal point appears between the third and the fourth digits, whereas in procedure classification, the decimal point appears between the second and the third digits.

__F__ 4. The Table of Drugs and Chemicals is found in volume 1 of *ICD-9-CM.*

__T__ 5. When the subterms "with" and "without" appear under a main term entry in the Index of Diseases and Injuries, they immediately follow the main term and precede all other subterms except numerical entries at the same indention level.

Incorrect answers to any of the questions in the preceding exercise indicate a need to go back and review the first section of this chapter of the handbook before proceeding further.

ICD-9-CM Conventions

CHAPTER **2**

CHAPTER OVERVIEW

- A variety of notes appear in all three volumes of *ICD-9-CM*.
  - *General notes* commonly provide information regarding fifth digits.
  - *Inclusion notes* and *exclusion notes* indicate when certain conditions are or are not included in a subdivision.
  - Additional instructional notes direct the coder to create a complete statement on the condition.
- Two main abbreviations (NEC and NOS) are used in *ICD-9-CM*.
- Cross-reference notes advise the coder to look elsewhere before assigning a code.
- Punctuation marks and relational terms have a specialized meaning in *ICD-9-CM*.

LEARNING OUTCOMES

After studying this chapter you should be able to:

- List the different types of instructional notes.
- Explain the importance of additional notes to the coding process.
- Describe the difference between the abbreviations NEC and NOS.
- Use your knowledge of cross-reference notes to navigate the *ICD-9-CM*.
- Define the specialized meanings of punctuation marks and relational terms in *ICD-9-CM*.

TERMS TO KNOW

NEC
not elsewhere classified; used in the Alphabetic Index to indicate that there is no separate code for the condition even though the diagnostic statement is specific

NOS
not otherwise specified; equivalent to the term "unspecified," used only in the tabular lists

REMEMBER . . . These conventions aren't just helpful; they're necessary to successful coding.

INTRODUCTION

ICD-9-CM follows certain conventions in order to provide large amounts of information in a succinct and consistent manner. Most conventions are used in all three volumes. Slight variations used in volume 3 are discussed in chapter 7 of this handbook. A thorough understanding of these conventions is fundamental to accurate coding. *ICD-9-CM* conventions include the following:

- Instructional notes
- Abbreviations
- Cross-reference notes
- Punctuation marks
- Relational terms ("and," "with," "due to")

INSTRUCTIONAL NOTES

A variety of notes appear in all three volumes as instructions to the coder. These include general notes, inclusion and exclusion notes, code first notes, and use additional code notes.

General Notes

Most general notes in the Tabular List of diseases provide information regarding fifth digits that must be used; a few provide general information on usage in a specific section such as code 250 that explains the fourth and fifth digits. General informational notes are used in a similar way in the alphabetic indexes for diseases and procedures. Index notes are usually enclosed in boxes and printed in italic type. For example, the main term **Fracture** in volume 2 includes an informational note that explains the diagnostic terms used to designate open and closed fractures. A similar note occurs in volume 3 under the main term **Examination.**

Inclusion and Exclusion Notes

Codes in a classification system must be mutually exclusive, with no overlapping of content. In *ICD-9-CM,* therefore, it is sometimes necessary to indicate when certain conditions are or are not included in a given subdivision. This is accomplished by means of inclusion and exclusion notes.

The location of inclusion and exclusion notes is extremely important. When this type of note is located at the beginning of a chapter or a section in *ICD-9-CM,* that advice applies to all codes within the chapter or section and is not repeated with individual categories or specific codes. The coder must keep in mind that instructional notes affecting the code under consideration may be located on a previous page.

Inclusion Notes

Inclusion notes are introduced by the word "includes" when placed at the beginning of a chapter or section; the word "includes" is not used when the inclusion note applies only to a category or subcategory code. Conditions listed in an inclusion note may be synonyms or conditions similar enough to be classified to the same code. Inclusion notes are not exhaustive; rather, they list certain conditions to reassure the coder, particularly when the title in the Tabular List may not seem to apply.

An example of an inclusion note can be found in volume 1, category **216, Benign neoplasm of skin.** The inclusion notes listed under category 216 apply to all codes listed from 216.0 through 216.9. Another list appears under code 216.5; here the additional terms apply to this code only.

Exclusion Notes

Exclusion notes are introduced by the word "excludes," and in most printed versions are usually enclosed in a box or shaded. Excluded conditions are listed in alphabetical order, with the code number or code range shown in parentheses.

Exclusion notes are the opposite of inclusion notes; they indicate that a particular condition is not assigned to the code to which the note applies. The basic message of an exclusion note is "code this condition elsewhere."

The most common type of exclusion note, and the most clear-cut, is an indication that another code must be used if there is a specific associated condition. An example can be found in volume 1, with the exclusion note under code **575.0, Acute cholecystitis.** This note indicates that code 575.0 is not assigned for acute cholecystitis when cholelithiasis is also present; code 574.0x should be used instead.

575.0 Acute Cholecystitis

Excludes *that with:*

acute and chronic choleystitis (575.12)
choledocholithiasis (574.3)
choledocholithiasis and cholelithiasis (574.6)
cholelithiasis (574.0)

A second type of exclusion note indicates that two conditions appearing to be similar actually have entirely different codes. For example, the same condition may have separate codes depending on whether it is acquired or congenital, or whether it occurs in an adult or a newborn. The correct interpretation in such cases is that one code or the other should be used but not both.

For example, observe the exclusion note under code **622.3, Old laceration of cervix,** in volume 1. The exclusion note indicates that code 665.3x should be assigned when the laceration is the result of current obstetrical trauma. Also, code **734, Flat foot,** excludes flat feet described as congenital, rigid, or spastic, and refers the coder to 754.61 for such conditions.

"Code First Underlying Condition"

The instructional note "Code first underlying condition" is used in the Tabular List to identify a code for a condition that is a manifestation of an underlying disease. It indicates that the code for the underlying condition must be sequenced before the code for the manifestation. In the Alphabetic Index this convention is indicated by listing the underlying code first, followed by the manifestation code in brackets. The code for the underlying disease will also have an instructional note in the Tabular List to "use additional code" for the manifestation. When the instruction notes and Alphabetic Index provide these instructions, the manifestation code must always follow the code for the underlying condition and can never be designated as a principal diagnosis. The use of two codes in this prescribed way is referred to as "dual classification" or "dual coding." The goal of this usage in *ICD-9-CM* is to maintain conformity with *ICD-9*.

Some instructions of this type indicate that a specific code must be assigned first. In volume 1, an example of this instructional note can be found under code ***484.5, Pneumonia in anthrax,*** which specifies that code **022.1, Pulmonary anthrax,** must be assigned before code 484.5. Other notes of this type provide a list introduced by the word "as"—meaning that any of the listed codes or any other appropriate code can be assigned first. Code ***595.4, Cystitis in diseases classified elsewhere,*** provides a list of conditions that may be the underlying condition.

"Use Additional Code"

The instruction to "use additional code" indicates that another code may be needed to include a complete statement of the condition. If the condition mentioned in the note is documented as present, the additional code should always be assigned.

For example, volume 1 includes an instructional note under category **595, Cystitis.** The note indicates that an additional code should be assigned to identify the organism responsible for the cystitis when it has been identified. Very occasionally, this instruction indicates that the manifestation should be listed first with an additional code for the underlying condition. The logic for this instruction is that a life-threatening condition should be listed before the chronic underlying condition. See code **337.3, Autonomic dysreflexia,** for an example of this instruction.

It is not necessary to report the code identified in a "use additional code" note in the diagnosis field immediately following the primary code. There is no strict hierarchy inherent in the guidelines or the *ICD-9-CM* classification regarding the sequencing of secondary diagnosis codes.

"Code, If Applicable, Any Causal Condition First"

The instruction to "Code, if applicable, any causal condition first" indicates that if a causal condition were present, it would be sequenced before the code to which this note is attached. In volume 1, an example of this instructional note can be found under subcategory **707.1, Ulcer of lower limbs, except pressure ulcer.** This instruction indicates that if a causal condition is documented, then the causal condition should be sequenced first (in this example, chronic venous hypertension with ulcer, postphlebetic syndrome with ulcer, etc.). However, unlike the instructional note "code first underlying condition," code 707.1x may be sequenced as a first-listed code or principal diagnosis if no causal condition is applicable or known.

ABBREVIATIONS

ICD-9-CM uses two main abbreviations:

- NEC for not elsewhere classified
- NOS for not otherwise specified

Although their meanings appear simple, these abbreviations are often misunderstood and misapplied by coders. It is very important to understand not only their meanings but also their differences, because they provide guidelines for correct code selection.

NEC

The abbreviation NEC (not elsewhere classified) is used in the Alphabetic Index to indicate that there is no separate code for the condition even though the diagnostic statement may be very specific. In the Tabular List, such conditions are ordinarily classified to the final digit 8 with a title that includes the words "other specified" or "not elsewhere classified." This permits the grouping of related conditions to conserve space and limit the size of the classification system. For example, a conduction disorder specified as atrioventricular (AV) or interference is included in code **426.89, Other specified conduction disorders.**

NOS

The abbreviation NOS (not otherwise specified) is the equivalent of "unspecified" and is used only in the tabular lists. Codes so identified are to be used only when neither the diagnostic statement nor the medical record provides information that permits classification to a more specific code. The codes in these cases are ordinarily classified to the final digit 9; conditions listed as both "not elsewhere classified" and "unspecified" are sometimes combined in one code. Note that a main term followed by a list of subterms in the alphabetic indexes usually displays the unspecified code; the subterms must always be reviewed to determine whether a more specific code can be assigned.

For example, the main term **Conduction disorder, unspecified,** displays code 426.9; subterms such as "heartblock, not otherwise specified" are provided for more specific conduction disorders. Code 426.9 should be assigned only when there is no information in the medical record to identify one of these subterms.

CROSS-REFERENCE NOTES

Cross-references are used in the alphabetic indices to advise the coder to look elsewhere before assigning a code. The cross-reference instructions include "*see,*" "*see also,*" "*see* category," and "*see* condition."

"See"

The "see" cross-reference indicates that the coder must refer to an alternative term. This instruction is mandatory; coding cannot be completed without following this advice. For example, the entry for **Hemarthrosis, traumatic,** uses this cross-reference to advise the coder to reference the entry for "sprain" by site.

"See Also"

The "see also" cross-reference advises the coder that there is another place in the Alphabetic Index to which the coder must refer when the entries under consideration do not provide a code for the specific condition or procedure. It is not necessary to follow this cross-reference when the original entries provide all the information necessary.

For example, the cross-reference for the term **Psychosis, schizophrenia, schizophrenic,** advises the coder to "*see also* Schizophrenia" when none of the specific subterms provides a code. If a coder is attempting to locate the code for catatonic schizophrenia, it would not be necessary to follow this cross-reference because there is a subterm catatonic under the subterm schizophrenic. If the diagnosis were undifferentiated schizophrenia, however, the code could be located only by following the "*see also*" reference.

"See Category"

The "see category" variation of the "see" cross-reference provides the coder with a category number. The coder must refer to that number in the Tabular List and select a code from the options provided there. For example, a cross-reference under the index entry for late effect of intracranial abscess refers the coder to category 326.

"See Condition"

Occasionally, the index advises the coder to refer to the main term of a condition. For example, if a coder references the main term **Arterial** for arterial thrombosis, the index advice is to "see condition" and the coder should then go to the main term **Thrombosis.** This cross-reference ordinarily appears when the coder has referenced the adjective rather than the term (in noun form) for the condition itself.

PUNCTUATION MARKS

Several punctuation marks are used in *ICD-9-CM,* most of which have a specialized meaning in addition to the usual English language usage.

Parentheses

Parentheses are used in *ICD-9-CM* to enclose supplementary words or explanatory information that may be either present or absent in the statement of diagnosis or procedure without affecting the code to which it is assigned. Such terms are considered to be "nonessential modifiers" and are used to suggest that the terms in parentheses are included in the code but need not be stated in the diagnosis or procedure. This is a significant factor in correct code assignment. Terms enclosed in parentheses in either the Tabular List (volume 1) or the Alphabetic Index (volume 2) do not affect the code assignment in any way; they serve only as reassurance that the correct code has been located.

For example, refer to the main term **Pneumonia,** which has numerous nonessential modifiers enclosed in parentheses. Unless a more specific subterm is located, this code will be assigned for pneumonia described by any of the terms in parentheses. Diagnoses of acute pneumonia and Alpenstich pneumonia, for instance, are both coded 486 because both terms appear in parentheses as nonessential modifiers. Pneumonia not otherwise specified is also assigned to code 486 because none of the terms in parentheses is required for this code assignment.

It is important to distinguish between the use of nonessential and essential modifiers. Essential modifiers are listed as subterms in the alphabetic indices, not in parentheses, and they do affect code assignment. However, words in parentheses are nonessential and do not affect the code assignment. For example, scoliosis described as acquired or postural is classified as 737.30 as these words are nonessential modifiers and do not affect the code; on the other hand, the term "congenital" is an essential modifier and the code for this term is 754.2.

Exercise 2.1

Referring only to the title and inclusion notes for code 490, mark an "X" in front of each of the diagnostic statements listed below that is included in code 490.

__X__ Catarrhal bronchitis NOS

_____ Chronic bronchitis

_____ Allergic bronchitis

__X__ Tracheobronchitis NOS

_____ Asthmatic bronchitis

Square Brackets

Square brackets are often used in the tabular lists to enclose synonyms, alternative wordings, abbreviations, and explanatory phrases that provide additional information—for example, paroxysmal atrial tachycardia [PAT]. They are similar in that they are not required of the statement of diagnosis or operation. Square brackets are also used to indicate that the number in the bracket can only be a manifestation and the other number must be assigned first for the underlying code. The code in the brackets in this situation indicates that both conditions must be used, and the code in the brackets can never be assigned as the principal diagnosis. In most printed versions of the manuals, both the brackets and the second code are printed in italics. In the following example from volume 2, the first code represents an underlying disease, and the second code enclosed in brackets manifestation:

Cystitis . . .
  actinomycotic 039.8 [*595.4*]

Colons

Colons are used in both inclusion and exclusion notes to indicate that one of the modifiers from the list indented below the entry must be present in order for the statement to apply. The exclusion statement under code 518.5 in volume 1 is an example of this usage; here the colon following the subterm "pneumonia" indicates that pneumonia described as aspiration pneumonia or hypostatic pneumonia is excluded.

518.5 Pulmonary insufficiency following trauma or surgery

Excludes *adult respiratory distress syndrome associated with other conditions* (518.82)
pneumonia:
  aspiration (507.0)
  hypostatic (514)
respiratory failure (518.81) (518.83–518.84)

Exercise 2.2

Referring only to the title and inclusion notes provided for the four-digit code 39.29, mark an "X" in front of each procedure listed below that is included in code 39.29.

X Brachial bypass

X Bypass graft of femoropopliteal arteries

X Vascular bypass, not otherwise specified

____ Bypass graft

X Popliteal bypass graft

RELATIONAL TERMS

Words such as "and," "due to," "with," "associated with," "without," and "in" are used to indicate various types of relationships expressed in *ICD-9-CM* and are used as subterms in the alphabetic indexes. These words have special meanings in *ICD-9-CM* and in the discussion of coding principles.

"And"

The word "and" should be interpreted to mean either "and" or "or" when it appears in a title. For example, code 415.1x in volume 1 includes pulmonary embolism and/or pulmonary infarction. In volume 3, code 38.5x includes ligation and/or stripping of varicose veins.

"Due To"

The words "due to" in either the alphabetic indexes or the tabular lists indicate that a causal relationship between two conditions is present. *ICD-9-CM* occasionally makes such an assumption when both conditions are present. In other combinations, however, the diagnostic statement must indicate this relationship. For example, certain conditions affecting the mitral valve are assumed to be rheumatic in origin, whether or not the diagnostic statement makes this distinction. In other cases, the Alphabetic Index provides a subterm "due to," which must be followed when the physician's statement indicates a causal relationship. The coder should be guided by the index entry.

"With"

Words such as "with," "with mention of," "associated with," and "in" indicate that both elements in the title must be present in the diagnostic or procedural statement. Although these terms do not necessarily indicate a cause-effect relationship, they occur together much of the time and the classification system indicates this relationship. The main term **Pneumonia** provides a good example of this use of the subterm "in" psittacosis 073.0. The word "with" should be interpreted to mean "associated with" or "due to" when it appears in a code title, the Alphabetic Index, or an instructional note in the Tabular List. The word "with" in the Alphabetic Index is sequenced immediately following the main term, not in alphabetical order.

Uniform Hospital Discharge Data Set

CHAPTER 3

CHAPTER OVERVIEW

- The Uniform Hospital Discharge Data Set (UHDDS) is used for reporting inpatient data.
- The following items are always found in the UHDDS:
  - — General demographic information
  - — Expected payer
  - — Hospital identification
  - — Principal diagnosis
  - — Other diagnoses that have specific significance
  - — All significant procedures
- The principal diagnosis is treated differently for an outpatient encounter than for an inpatient encounter.
- Following all the coding guidelines will ensure accurate and ethical coding.

LEARNING OUTCOMES

After studying this chapter you should be able to:

- Correctly identify a principal diagnosis.
- Understand the guidelines for assigning a principal diagnosis.
- Understand when other diagnoses have significance and should be reported.
- Explain the difference between a principal diagnosis and an admitting diagnosis.
- Explain the importance of accurate and ethical coding.

TERMS TO KNOW

MS-DRG system
Medicare severity-adjusted diagnosis-related groups system; a patient classification system used in hospital reimbursement

Other reportable diagnoses
conditions that coexist at the time of admission, develop subsequently, or affect patient care during the hospital stay

Principal diagnosis
the condition established after study that is chiefly responsible for admission of the patient to the hospital

UHDDS
Uniform Hospital Discharge Data Set; information used for reporting inpatient data

REMEMBER . . . The admitting diagnosis is not an element of the UHDDS.
. . . Diagnoses that have no impact on patient care or that are related to an earlier episode are not reported on the UHDDS.

INTRODUCTION

The Uniform Hospital Discharge Data Set (UHDDS) is used for reporting inpatient data in acute care, short-term care, and long-term care hospitals. It uses a minimum set of items based on standard definitions that could provide consistent data for multiple users. Only those items that met the following criteria were included:

- Easily identified
- Readily defined
- Uniformly recorded
- Easily abstracted from the medical record

Its use is required for reporting Medicare and Medicaid patients. In addition, many other health care payers also use most of the UHDDS for the uniform billing system.

DATA ITEMS

The UHDDS requires the following items:

- Principal diagnosis
- Other diagnoses that have significance for the specific hospital episode
- All significant procedures

The four cooperating parties responsible for maintaining *ICD-9-CM* have developed official guidelines for designating the principal diagnosis and for identifying other diagnoses that should be reported in certain situations. The UHDDS also contains a core of general information that pertains to the patient and to the specific episode of care, such as the age, sex, and race of the patient; the expected payer; and the hospital's identification.

The UHDDS definitions were originally developed in 1985 for hospital reporting of inpatient data elements. Since that time, the application of UHDDS definitions has been expanded to include all nonoutpatient settings. In addition to acute care, short-term care, and long-term care hospitals, the definitions for principal diagnosis and other (secondary) diagnoses also apply to psychiatric hospitals, home health agencies, rehabilitation facilities, nursing homes, and other settings. Guidelines for selection of principal diagnosis and other diagnoses discussed below apply to all these settings.

Principal Diagnosis

The principal diagnosis is defined as the condition established after study to be chiefly responsible for admission of the patient to the hospital. It is important that the principal diagnosis be designated correctly because it is significant in cost comparisons, in care analysis, and in utilization review. It is crucial for reimbursement because many third-party payers (including Medicare) base reimbursement primarily on principal diagnosis. It is ordinarily listed first in the physician's diagnostic statement, but this is not always the case; the coder must always review the entire medical record to determine the condition that should be designated as the principal diagnosis.

The words "after study" in the definition of principal diagnosis are important, but they are sometimes confusing. It is not the admitting diagnosis but rather the diagnosis found after workup or even after surgery that proves to be the reason for admission. For example:

- A patient admitted with urinary retention may prove to have hypertrophy of the prostate, which is causing the urinary retention. In this case, the prostatic hypertrophy is the principal diagnosis unless treatment was directed only to the urinary retention.

- A patient may be admitted because of unstable angina, and a percutaneous transluminal angioplasty may be carried out to clear arteriosclerotic blockage of the coronary artery in order to abort what appears to be an impending myocardial infarction. In this case, the coronary arteriosclerosis is the principal diagnosis because, after study, it was determined to be the underlying cause of the angina and the reason for admission.
- A patient was admitted with severe abdominal pain. The white blood cell count was elevated to 16,000, with shift to the left. The patient was taken to surgery, where an acute ruptured appendix was removed. After study, the principal diagnosis is acute ruptured appendicitis.
- A patient was admitted with severe abdominal pain in the right lower quadrant and an admitting diagnosis of probable acute appendicitis. The white blood cell count was slightly elevated. The patient was taken to surgery, where a normal appendix was found but an inflamed Meckel's diverticulum was removed. After study, the principal diagnosis is Meckel's diverticulum.

The circumstances of inpatient admission always govern the selection of the principal diagnosis, and the coding directives in the *ICD-9-CM* manuals, volumes 1, 2, and 3, take precedence over all other guidelines. The importance of consistent, complete documentation in the medical record cannot be overemphasized. Without such documentation, the application of all coding guidelines is a difficult, if not impossible, task.

There are special instructions related to the selection of principal diagnosis when a patient is admitted as an inpatient from the hospital's observation unit or from outpatient surgery. For example:

Admission following medical observation: A patient may be treated in a hospital's observation unit to determine if the condition improves sufficiently for the patient to be discharged. If the condition either worsens or doesn't improve, the physician may decide to admit the patient as an inpatient. The principal diagnosis reported would be the medical condition that led to the hospital admission.

Admission following postoperative observation: A patient undergoing outpatient surgery may require postoperative admission to an observation unit to monitor a condition (or complication) that develops postoperatively. If the patient subsequently requires inpatient admission to the same hospital, the UHDDS definition of principal diagnosis applies: "that condition established after study to be chiefly responsible for occasioning the admission of the patient to the hospital for care."

Admission from outpatient surgery: A patient undergoing outpatient surgery may be subsequently admitted for continuing inpatient care at the same hospital. The following guidelines should be followed in selecting the principal diagnosis for the inpatient admission:

- If the reason for the inpatient admission is a complication, assign the complication as the principal diagnosis.
- If no complication or other condition is documented as the reason for the inpatient admission, assign the reason for the outpatient surgery as the principal diagnosis.
- If the reason for the inpatient admission is another condition unrelated to the surgery, assign the unrelated condition as the principal diagnosis.

The following official guidelines for designating the principal diagnosis apply to all systems and etiologies. (Guidelines that apply only to specific body systems or etiologies are discussed in the relevant chapters of this handbook. To download a copy of the current version of the complete *ICD-9-CM Official Guidelines for Coding and Reporting,* please visit www.ahacentraloffice.org.)

1. *Two or more diagnoses that equally meet the definition for principal diagnosis:* In the unusual situation in which two or more diagnoses equally meet the criteria for principal diagnosis as determined by the circumstances of the admission and the diagnostic workup and/or therapy provided, either may be sequenced first when neither the Alphabetic Index nor the Tabular List directs otherwise. However, it is not simply the fact that both conditions exist that makes this choice possible. When treatment is totally or primarily directed toward one condition, or when only one condition would have required inpatient care, that condition should be designated as the principal diagnosis. Also, if another coding guideline (general or disease-specific) provides sequencing direction, that guideline must be followed.

   Example 1: A patient was admitted with unstable angina and acute congestive heart failure. The unstable angina was treated with nitrates, and intravenous Lasix was given to manage the heart failure. Both diagnoses meet the definition of principal diagnosis equally, and either may be sequenced first.

   Example 2: A patient was admitted with acute atrial fibrillation with rapid ventricular response and was also in heart failure with pulmonary edema. The patient was digitalized to reduce the ventricular rate and given intravenous Lasix to reduce the cardiogenic pulmonary edema. Both conditions meet the definition of principal diagnosis equally, and either may be sequenced first.

   Example 3: A patient was admitted with severe abdominal pain, nausea, and vomiting due to acute pyelonephritis, 590.10, and diverticulitis, 562.11. Both underlying conditions were treated, and the physician believed both equally met the criteria for principal diagnosis. In this instance, either condition may be listed as principal diagnosis.

2. *Two or more comparable or contrasting conditions:* In the rare instance where two or more comparable or contrasting conditions are documented as either/or (or similar terminology), both diagnoses are coded as though confirmed and the principal diagnosis is designated according to the circumstances of the admission and the diagnostic workup and/or therapy provided. When no further determination can be made as to which diagnosis more closely meets the criteria for principal diagnosis, either may be sequenced first. Note that this does not apply for outpatient encounters.

   Example 1: A patient with the same complaints as those outlined in example 3 above was admitted with a final diagnosis of acute pyelonephritis versus diverticulum of the colon. The patient was treated symptomatically and discharged for further studies. In this case, both conditions meet the criteria for principal diagnosis equally and either can be designated as the principal diagnosis.

   Example 2: The treatment of another patient with the same symptoms and the same final diagnoses was directed almost entirely toward the acute pyelonephritis, indicating that the physician considered this the more likely problem and that, after study, it was the condition that occasioned the admission. In this case, both conditions would be coded, but the acute pyelonephritis would be sequenced first because of the circumstances of the admission.

3. *A symptom followed by contrasting/comparative diagnoses:* When a symptom is followed by contrasting/comparative diagnoses, the symptom code is sequenced first.

However, if the symptom code is integral to each of the conditions listed, no additional code for the symptom is reported. Codes are assigned for all listed contrasting/comparative diagnoses.

Example 1: A patient was admitted for workup because of severe fatigue. The discharge diagnosis was recorded as fatigue, due to either depressive reaction or hypothyroidism. In this case, the symptom code for fatigue is designated the principal diagnosis, with additional codes assigned for both the depressive reaction and the hypothyroidism.

Example 2: The discharge diagnosis is stated as gastrointestinal bleeding, due to either acute gastritis or angiodysplasia. In this case, the diagnoses are coded as contrasting/comparative diagnoses and no separate code is assigned for the bleeding because the codes for both conditions include any associated bleeding.

4. *Original treatment plan not carried out:* In a situation in which the original treatment plan cannot be carried out due to unforeseen circumstances, the criteria for designation of the principal diagnosis do not change. The condition that occasioned the admission is designated as principal diagnosis even though the planned treatment was not carried out.

   Example 1: A patient with benign hypertrophy of the prostate was admitted for the purpose of a transurethral resection of the prostate (TURP). Shortly after admission, but before the patient was taken to the operating suite, the patient fell and sustained a fracture of the left femur. The TURP was canceled; hip pinning was carried out on the following day. The principal diagnosis remains hypertrophy of the prostate even though that condition was not treated.

   Example 2: A patient with a diagnosis of carcinoma of the breast confirmed from an outpatient biopsy was admitted for the purpose of modified radical mastectomy. Before the preoperative medications were administered the next morning, the patient indicated that she had decided against having the procedure until she was able to consider possible alternative treatment more thoroughly. No treatment was given, and she was discharged. The carcinoma of the breast remains the principal diagnosis because it was the condition that occasioned the admission even though no treatment was rendered.

Other Diagnoses

Other reportable diagnoses are defined as those conditions that coexist at the time of admission or develop subsequently or affect patient care for the current hospital episode. Diagnoses that have no impact on patient care during the hospital stay are not reported even when they are present. Diagnoses that relate to an earlier episode and have no bearing on the current hospital stay are not reported.

For UHDDS reporting purposes, the definition of "other diagnosis" includes only those conditions that affect the episode of hospital care in terms of any of the following:

- Clinical evaluation
- Therapeutic treatment
- Further evaluation by diagnostic studies, procedures, or consultation
- Extended length of hospital stay
- Increased nursing care and/or other monitoring

All these factors are self-explanatory except the first. Clinical evaluation means that the physician is aware of the problem and is evaluating it in terms of testing, consultations, and close clinical observation of the patient's condition. In most cases, a patient who is being evaluated clinically will also fit into one of the other criteria. Note that a physical examination alone does not qualify as further evaluation or clinical evaluation; the physical examination is a routine part of every hospital admission. No particular order is mandated for sequencing other diagnoses. The more significant ones should be sequenced early in the list when the number of diagnoses that may be reported is limited.

Reporting Guidelines for Other Diagnoses

The following guidelines and examples should be studied carefully in order to understand the rationale for determining other diagnoses that should be reported:

1. *Previous conditions stated as diagnoses:* Physicians sometimes include in the diagnostic statement historical information or status post procedures performed on a previous admission that have no bearing on the current stay. Such conditions are not reported. However, history codes (V10–V19) may be used as secondary codes if the historical condition or family history has an impact on current care or influences treatment.

   Example: A patient was admitted with acute myocardial infarction; the physician noted in the history that the patient was status post cholecystectomy and had been hospitalized one year earlier for pneumonia. At discharge, the physician documented the final diagnoses as acute myocardial infarction, status post cholecystectomy, and history of pneumonia. Only the acute myocardial infarction is coded and reported; the other conditions included in the diagnostic statement had no bearing on the current episode of care.

2. *Other diagnosis with no documentation supporting reportability:* If the physician has included a diagnosis in the final diagnostic statement, it should ordinarily be coded. If there is no supporting documentation in the medical record, however, the physician should be consulted as to whether the diagnosis meets reporting criteria; if so, the physician should be asked to add the necessary documentation. Reporting of conditions for which there is no supporting documentation is in conflict with UHDDS criteria.

   Example 1: A 10-year-old boy was admitted with open fracture of the tibia and fibula following a bicycle accident. On physical examination, the physician noted that there was a nevus on the leg and that the patient had a small asymptomatic inguinal hernia. All these diagnoses were documented on the face sheet. The fracture was reduced with internal fixation, but neither the nevus nor the hernia was treated or further evaluated on this admission. The nevus and hernia are not reported because there is nothing to indicate that they had any effect on the episode of care.

   Example 2: A patient was admitted with an acute myocardial infarction. The physician also included in the diagnostic statement a strabismus and a bunion noted on the physical examination. Review of the medical record revealed that no further reference to these conditions was made in terms of further evaluation or treatment; therefore, no codes for either the strabismus or the bunion would be assigned.

3. *Chronic conditions that are not the thrust of treatment:* The criteria for selection of chronic conditions to be reported as "other diagnoses" include: the severity of the condition, the use or consideration of alternative measures or an increase in nursing care required in the treatment of the principal diagnosis due to the coexisting condition, the use of diagnostic or therapeutic services for the particular coexisting condition, the need for close monitoring of medications because of the coexisting condition, or modifications of nursing care plans because of the coexisting condition.

Chronic conditions such as (but not limited to) hypertension, Parkinson's disease, COPD, and diabetes mellitus are chronic systemic diseases that ordinarily should be coded even in the absence of documented intervention or further evaluation. Some chronic conditions affect the patient for the rest of his or her life and almost always require some form of continuous clinical evaluation or monitoring during hospitalization and therefore should be coded. This advice applies to inpatient coding.

For outpatient encounters/visits, chronic conditions that require or affect patient care treatment or management should be coded.

Example 1: A patient was admitted following a hip fracture, and a diagnosis of Parkinson's disease was noted in the history and physical examination. Nursing notes indicate that the patient required additional care because of the Parkinsonism. Both diagnoses are reported.

Example 2: A patient was admitted with pneumonia, and the presence of diabetes mellitus was documented in the record. Blood sugars were monitored by laboratory studies, and nursing personnel also checked blood sugars before each meal. The patient was continued on his diabetic diet. Although no active treatment was provided, ongoing monitoring was required and the condition is reported.

Example 3: A patient was admitted with acute diverticulitis, and the physician documented in the admitting note a history of hypertension. Review of the medical record indicates that blood pressure medications were given throughout the stay. The hypertension is reportable, and the physician should be asked to add it to the diagnostic statement.

Example 4: A patient was admitted in congestive heart failure. She had known hiatal hernia and degenerative arthritis. Neither condition was further evaluated or treated; by their nature, the conditions do not require continuing clinical evaluation. Only the code for the congestive heart failure is assigned; the other conditions are not reportable.

Example 5: A 60-year-old diabetic patient was transferred from an extended care facility for treatment of a pressure ulcer. The physician noted in the history and physical exam that the patient was status post left below-the-knee amputation due to peripheral vascular disease. This condition required additional nursing assistance and is reported.

4. *Conditions that are an integral part of a disease process should not be reported as additional diagnoses, unless otherwise instructed by the classification.*

   Example 1: A patient was admitted with nausea and vomiting due to infectious gastroenteritis. Nausea and vomiting are common symptoms of infectious gastroenteritis and are not reported.

   Example 2: A patient was admitted with severe joint pain and rheumatoid arthritis. Severe joint pain is a characteristic part of rheumatoid arthritis and is not reportable.

   Example 3: A patient was seen in the physician's office complaining of urinary frequency and was diagnosed with benign prostatic hypertrophy. Although urinary frequency is a common symptom of benign prostatic hypertrophy, both conditions are reported because of the instructional note in the Tabular List under code 600.01 to use additional codes to identify symptoms.

5. *Conditions that are not an integral part of a disease process should be coded when present.*

   Example 1: A patient was admitted by ambulance following a cerebrovascular accident suffered at work. The patient was in a coma but gradually recovered consciousness. Diagnosis at discharge was reported as cerebrovascular thrombosis with coma. In this case, coma is coded as an additional diagnosis because it is not implicit in a cerebrovascular accident and is not always present.

Example 2: A 5-year-old boy was admitted with a 104-degree fever associated with acute pneumonia. During the first 24 hours, the patient also experienced convulsions due to the high fever. Both the pneumonia and the convulsions are reported because convulsions are not routinely associated with pneumonia. Fever is commonly associated with pneumonia, however, and no code is assigned.

6. *Abnormal findings:* Codes from sections 790–796 for nonspecific abnormal findings (laboratory, radiology, pathology, and other diagnostic results) should be assigned only when the physician has not been able to arrive at a related diagnosis but indicates that the abnormal finding is considered to be clinically significant by listing it in the diagnostic statement. This differs from the coding practices in the outpatient setting when coding encounters for diagnostic tests that have been interpreted by a physician.

The coder should never assign a code on the basis of an abnormal finding alone. To make a diagnosis on the basis of a single lab value or abnormal diagnostic finding is risky and carries the possibility of error. A value reported as either lower or higher than the normal range does not necessarily indicate a disorder. Many factors influence the values in a lab sample; these include the collection device, the method used to transport the sample to the lab, the calibration of the machine that reads the values, and the condition of the patient. For example, a patient who is dehydrated may show an elevated hemoglobin due to increased viscosity of the blood. When findings are clearly outside the normal range and the physician has ordered other tests to evaluate the condition or has prescribed treatment without documenting an associated diagnosis, it is appropriate to ask the physician whether a diagnosis should be added or whether the abnormal finding should be listed in the diagnostic statement. Incidental findings on X-ray such as asymptomatic hiatal hernia or a diverticulum should not be reported unless further evaluation or treatment is carried out.

Example 1: A low potassium level treated with intravenous or oral potassium is clinically significant and should be brought to the attention of the physician if no related diagnosis has been recorded.

Example 2: A hematocrit of 28 percent, even though asymptomatic and not treated, was evaluated with serial hematocrits. Because the finding is outside the range of normal laboratory values and has been further evaluated, the physician should be asked whether an associated diagnosis should be documented.

Example 3: A routine preoperative chest X-ray on an elderly patient reveals collapse of a vertebral body. The patient was asymptomatic, and no further evaluation or treatment was carried out. This is a common finding in elderly patients and is insignificant for this episode.

Example 4: In the absence of a cardiac problem, an isolated electrocardiographic finding of bundle branch block is ordinarily not significant, whereas a finding of a Mobitz II block may have important implications for the patient's care and would warrant asking the physician whether it should be reported for this admission.

Example 5: The physician lists an abnormal sedimentation rate as part of the diagnostic statement. The physician has been unable to make a definitive diagnosis during the hospitalization in spite of further evaluation and considers the abnormal finding a significant clinical problem. Code **790.1, Elevated sedimentation rate,** should be assigned.

Admitting Diagnosis

Although the admitting diagnosis is not an element of the UHDDS, it must be reported for some payers and may also be useful in quality-of-care studies. Ordinarily, only one admitting diagnosis can be reported. The inpatient admitting diagnosis may be reported as one of the following:

- A significant finding (symptom or sign) representing patient distress or an abnormal finding on outpatient examination
- A possible diagnosis based on significant findings (working diagnosis)
- A diagnosis established on an ambulatory care basis or during a previous hospital admission
- An injury or poisoning
- A reason or condition not actually an illness or injury, such as a follow-up examination or pregnancy in labor

If the admitting diagnosis is reported, the code should indicate the diagnosis provided by the physician at the time of admission. Although the admitting diagnosis may not agree with the principal diagnosis on discharge, the admitting diagnosis should not be changed to conform with the principal diagnosis. Examples of admitting diagnoses and subsequent principal diagnoses follow:

- Admitting: Gastrointestinal bleeding 578.9
  Principal: Acute duodenal ulcer with hemorrhage 532.00
- Admitting: Lump in breast 611.72
  Principal: Carcinoma of breast 174.9
- Admitting: Acute cholecystitis 575.0
  Principal: Acute cholecystitis with cholelithiasis 574.00
- Admitting: Congestive heart failure 428.0
  Principal: Acute myocardial infarction, anterior wall (initial episode of care) 410.11
- Admitting: Suspected myocardial infarction 410.90
  Principal: Dissecting thoracic aneurysm of aorta 441.01

PROCEDURES

The UHDDS requires that all significant procedures be reported. The UHDDS definitions of significant procedures and other reporting guidelines are discussed in chapter 7 of this handbook, along with other information on coding operations and procedures.

RELATIONSHIP OF UHDDS TO OUTPATIENT REPORTING

The UHDDS definition of principal diagnosis does not apply to the coding of outpatient encounters. In contrast to inpatient coding, no "after study" element is involved because ambulatory care visits do not permit the continued evaluation ordinarily needed to meet UHDDS criteria. If the physician does not identify a definite condition or problem at the conclusion of a visit or encounter, the coder should report the documented chief complaint as the reason for the encounter/visit.

ETHICAL CODING AND REPORTING

Whereas coded medical data are used for a variety of purposes, they have become increasingly important in determining payment for health care. Medicare reimbursement depends on the following:

- The correct designation of the principal diagnosis
- The presence or absence of additional codes that represent complications, comorbidities, or major complications or comorbidities as defined by the Medicare severity-adjusted diagnosis-related groups (MS-DRG) system
- Procedures performed

Other third-party payers may follow slightly different reimbursement methods, but the accuracy of *ICD-9-CM* coding is always vital.

Accurate and ethical *ICD-9-CM* coding depends on correctly following all instructions in the coding manuals as well as all official guidelines developed by the cooperating parties and coding advice published in the American Hospital Association's quarterly *Coding Clinic for ICD-9-CM*. Accurate and ethical reporting requires the correct selection of those conditions that meet the criteria set by the UHDDS and the official guidelines mentioned above. Over-coding and over-reporting may result in higher payment, but it is unethical and may be considered fraudulent. On the other hand, it is important to be sure that all appropriate codes are reported, as failure to include all diagnoses or procedures that meet reporting criteria may result in financial loss for the health care provider.

It is important for coders to abide by the AHIMA Standards of Ethical Coding, which are available for download at http://www.ahima.org/about/ethicsstandards.aspx.

Occasionally certain codes are identified by Medicare as being unacceptable as the principal diagnosis. This does not mean that the code should not be assigned when it is correct; it means that the third-party payer may question or deny payment. It is important to code correctly and then make whatever adjustment is required for reporting. Otherwise, the coder runs the risk of developing incorrect coding practices that will distort data used for other purposes.

Hospitals sometimes feel a need to code nonreportable diagnoses or procedures for internal use; this is acceptable if the facility has a system for maintaining this information outside the reporting system.

There are a variety of payment policies that may have an impact on coding, and many of those policies may contradict each other or be inconsistent with *ICD-9-CM* rules/conventions. Therefore, it is not possible to write coding guidelines that are consistent with all existing payer guidelines.

The following advice is intended to help providers resolve coding disputes with payers:

- First, determine whether it is really a coding dispute and not a coverage issue. For example, a payer may deny codes V72.5 and V72.6x for encounters for radiology and laboratory examinations. These codes are to be used only for routine examinations without signs or symptoms. Many payers do not provide coverage for routine tests, so such denials are not due to incorrect coding, but rather relate to noncoverage of routine tests; e.g., annual physical exams or screening tests without signs or symptoms. Therefore, always contact the payer for clarification if the reason for the denial is unclear.
- If a payer really does have a policy that clearly conflicts with official coding rules or guidelines, every effort should be made to resolve the issue with the payer. Provide the applicable coding rule/guideline to the payer. For Medicare claims, contact the fiscal intermediary (FI) or carrier contractor for clarification. If you are not satisfied with the answer you receive, follow up with the CMS regional office. The

FI or carrier should be able to provide you with information as to which regional office has jurisdiction over your area.

- If a payer refuses to change its policy, obtain the payer requirements in writing. If the payer refuses to provide the policy in writing, document all discussions with the payer, including dates and the names of individuals involved in the discussion. Confirm the existence of the policy with the payer's supervisory personnel.
- Keep a permanent file of the documentation obtained regarding payer coding policies. It may come in handy in the event of an audit.

The Medical Record as a Source Document

CHAPTER **4**

CHAPTER OVERVIEW

- The medical record is the source document for coding.
- Medical records contain a variety of reports. These include the following:
  - — Reason the patient came to the hospital
  - — Tests performed and their findings
  - — Therapies provided
  - — Descriptions of surgical procedures
  - — Daily records of patient progress
- The discharge summary provides a synopsis of the patient's stay.

LEARNING OUTCOMES

After studying this chapter you should be able to:

- Explain what is present in a medical record.
- Understand when it is appropriate to query a physician about his or her documentation.

TERMS TO KNOW

POA indicator
present on admission indicator; a data element that applies to diagnosis codes for claims involving inpatient care

Provider
a physician or any qualified health care practitioner (such as a nurse practitioner or physician assistant) who is legally accountable for establishing the patient's diagnosis

REMEMBER . . . The coder must make sure that the medical record documentation supports the principal diagnosis.
. . . Refer to appendix A for more information on the POA indicator.

INTRODUCTION

The source document for coding and reporting diagnoses and procedures is the medical record. Although discharge diagnoses are usually recorded on the face sheet, a final progress note, or the discharge summary, further review of the medical record is needed to ensure complete and accurate coding. Operations and procedures are frequently not listed on the face sheet or are not described in sufficient detail, making a review of operative reports, pathology reports, and other special reports imperative. The entire record should be reviewed to determine the specific reason for the encounter and the conditions treated.

Physicians sometimes fail to list reportable conditions that developed during the stay but were resolved prior to discharge. Conditions such as urinary tract infection or dehydration, for instance, are often not included in the diagnostic statement even though progress notes, physicians' orders, and laboratory reports make it clear that such conditions were treated. It is inappropriate for coders to assign a diagnosis based solely on physician orders for prescribed medications without the physician's documenting the diagnosis being treated. If there is enough information to make it likely that an additional diagnosis should be reported, the physician should be consulted; no diagnosis should be added without the approval of the physician. Because diagnostic statements sometimes include diagnoses that represent past history or existing diagnoses that do not meet the Uniform Hospital Discharge Data Set (UHDDS) guidelines for reportable diagnoses, a review of the medical record is required to determine whether these diagnoses should be coded for this encounter.

It is customary to list the principal diagnosis first in the diagnostic statement. Many physicians, however, are not aware of coding and reporting guidelines, and, consequently, this custom is not consistently followed. Because the correct designation of the principal diagnosis is of critical importance in reporting diagnostic information, the coder must be sure that medical record documentation supports the designation of principal diagnosis. If it appears that another diagnosis should be designated as principal diagnosis, or if conditions not listed should be reported, the coder should follow the health care facility's procedures for obtaining a corrected diagnostic statement.

CONTENTS OF THE MEDICAL RECORD

Medical records contain a variety of reports that document the reason the patient came to the hospital, the tests performed and their findings, the therapies provided, descriptions of any surgical procedures, and daily records of the patient's progress. Each report contains important information needed for accurate coding and reporting of the principal diagnosis, other diagnoses, and the procedures performed.

A number of standard reports can be found in almost any medical record, but other reports will appear depending on the condition for which the patient is being treated, the extent of workup and therapy provided, and the attending physician's style of documentation. For example, a physician may list final diagnoses on the admission record (face sheet), on progress notes, or on the discharge summary. Consultants occasionally record their consultation notes in the progress notes rather than on separate reports.

Review of the inpatient medical record should begin with the discharge summary because it provides a synopsis of the patient's hospital stay, including the reason for admission, significant diagnostic findings, treatment given, the patient's course in the hospital, follow-up plan, and final diagnostic statement. The history section usually indicates the reason for admission (principal diagnosis), which may require confirmation by review of the history and physical examination and admitting and emergency department records.

The section of the discharge summary that describes the course in the hospital usually indicates treatment given and any further workup that has been done. It is particularly useful in determining whether all listed diagnoses meet the criteria for reporting and identifying other conditions that may merit reporting.

Conditions mentioned elsewhere in the body of the discharge summary do not necessarily warrant reporting but may provide clues for more specific review to make a final determination. The medical record should be reviewed further to determine whether such conditions meet the criteria for reportable diagnoses as defined in the UHDDS. The medication record is often helpful in indicating that therapeutic treatment may have been administered, but the coder must not assume a diagnosis solely on the basis of medication administration or abnormal findings in diagnostic reports. In addition, recorded diagnoses do not always contain sufficient information for providing the required specificity in coding. For example, a diagnosis of pneumonia may not indicate the organism responsible for the infection; a review of diagnostic studies of the sputum may provide this information. The physician should be asked to confirm that the organism discovered on the positive culture is the causative agent. The physician should indicate confirmation by documenting in the medical record before a code identifying the specific type of pneumonia can be assigned. A diagnosis of fracture may indicate which bone was fractured but not the particular part of the bone, information that is necessary for accurate code assignment. The X-ray or the operative report should supply these data.

Some facilities may develop their own additional coding guidelines to provide assistance in determining when a physician query is appropriate. If the test findings are outside the normal range and the physician has ordered other tests to evaluate the condition or prescribed treatment, it is appropriate to ask the physician whether the diagnosis should be added. However, a facility's internal guidelines may not interpret abnormal findings to replace physician documentation or physician query.

The following examples illustrate diagnoses that are often recorded with less-than-complete information but can be coded more specifically by referring to diagnostic reports within the medical record and then obtaining the appropriate physician confirmation. Note the variation in code assignment when more information is available after physician confirmation:

- Diagnosis: Cancer of cervix 180.9
  Pathology report: Carcinoma, in situ, of cervix 233.1
- Diagnosis: Urinary tract infection 599.0
  Laboratory report: E. coli in urine 599.0 + 041.4
- Diagnosis: Fracture of femur 821.00
  X-ray report: Open fracture of subtrochanteric neck of the femur 820.32

Code assignment is generally based on the attending physician's documentation. It is also appropriate to base code assignment on the documentation of other physicians (e.g., consultants, residents, anesthesiologists, and so on) involved in the care and treatment of the patient so long as there is no conflicting information from the attending physician. A physician query is not necessary if a physician involved in the care and treatment of the patient, including consulting physicians, has documented a diagnosis and there is no conflicting documentation from another physician. If documentation from different physicians conflicts, the attending physician should be queried for clarification because he or she is ultimately responsible for the final diagnosis.

For inpatient coding, if the attending physician does not confirm the pathological or radiological findings, query him or her regarding the clinical significance of the findings and request that appropriate documentation be provided. Although the pathologist or radiologist provides a written interpretation of a tissue biopsy or an x-ray image, this is not equivalent to the attending physician's medical diagnosis, which is based on the patient's complete clinical picture. The attending physician is responsible for, and directly involved in, the care and treatment of the patient. A pathologist's interpretation of a specimen or a radiologist's interpretation of an image is not the same as a diagnosis provided by a physician directly involved in the patient's care. For example, if the attending physician documented "breast mass" and the pathologist documented "carcinoma of the breast," this would be conflicting information requiring clarification from the attending physician.

When coding outpatient laboratory, pathology, and radiology encounters in hospital-based as well as stand-alone facilities, it is appropriate to assign codes on the basis of the written interpretation by a radiologist or pathologist. However, it is inappropriate to report an incidental finding found on a radiology report when the finding is unrelated to the sign, symptom, or condition that necessitated the performance of the test for a patient being seen in the emergency department (ED). The ED physician would need to clarify that the finding was clinically significant and related to the visit in order for it to be coded.

In some institutions, there are midlevel providers, such as nurse practitioners and physician assistants, who are involved in the care of the patient and document diagnoses in the health record. It is appropriate to base code assignments on the documentation of midlevel providers if they are considered legally accountable for establishing a diagnosis within the regulations governing the provider and the facility. The *Official Guidelines for Coding and Reporting* use the term "provider" to mean physician or any qualified health care practitioner who is legally accountable for establishing the patient's diagnosis.

Not all reportable services or procedures during an encounter or admission are performed or documented by physicians. It is appropriate to assign a procedure code based on documentation by the nonphysician professional who provided the service. This applies only to procedure coding where there is documentation to substantiate the code. It does not apply to diagnosis coding. The documentation from the nonphysician professional who provided the service may be the only evidence that the service was provided. This is true of services such as infusions carried out by nurses and therapies provided by physical, respiratory, or occupational therapists.

Occasionally, provider documentation will include conditions listed with up and down arrows (for example, "↑ cholesterol" or "↓ potassium"). This does not mean that a code for hypercholesterolemia or hypopotassemia may be assigned. It is not appropriate to code a diagnosis on the basis of up and down arrows. Up and down arrows can have variable interpretations and do not necessarily mean abnormal. They could simply reflect a change, such as improvement, over past results. The provider should be queried for the meaning of the arrows and requested to document the clarification. This advice applies to both inpatient and outpatient records.

Outpatient records generally contain less information than inpatient records. Nevertheless, all available reports for the encounter should be reviewed prior to code assignment. Code assignment is dependent on the information available at the time of code assignment. For ambulatory records, an additional data element called "patient's reason for visit" (PRV) is usually reported. This data element has a dual use on electronic claims. For inpatient claims it represents the admitting diagnosis, while for outpatient claims it represents the PRV. On the revised paper claim, UB-04, "patient's reason for visit" is a unique data item separate from the admitting diagnosis.

The PRV is reported on unscheduled outpatient visits (e.g., emergency department or urgent care visits) to identify the main reason the patient sought treatment. The reason may differ from the physician's final diagnosis at the end of the encounter. Only one diagnosis code can be reported in this field on the electronic claim. If there are multiple conditions present, the code most likely to justify the patient encounter should be reported. This data element is now Form Locator 70a–c on the revised UB-04 paper claim. It allows for the reporting of three diagnosis codes.

The "present on admission (POA) indicator" is a data element approved by the National Uniform Billing Committee (NUBC) for inpatient reporting. The POA indicator applies to the diagnosis codes for claims involving inpatient admissions to general acute care hospitals or other facilities. Please refer to appendix A of this handbook for more detailed information on this topic.

Basic Coding Steps

CHAPTER **5**

CHAPTER OVERVIEW

- There are three basic steps for locating codes to be assigned.
  - — Locate the main term in the Alphabetic Index. Search for subterms, notes, or cross-references.
  - — Verify the code number in the Tabular List.
  - — Assign the verified code or codes.
- It is important to understand basic coding techniques before moving on to the harder, system-based chapters of this handbook.

LEARNING OUTCOMES

After studying this chapter you should be able to:

- Locate code entries in the Alphabetic Index.
- Determine the course of action when there are discrepancies between the Alphabetic Index and the Tabular List.
- Perform basic coding techniques.

TERMS TO KNOW

Alphabetic Index of Diseases and Injuries
volume 2 of the *ICD-9-CM;* includes entries for main terms (diseases, conditions, or injuries) and subterms (site, type, or etiology)

Tabular List and Alphabetic Index of Procedures
volume 3 of the *ICD-9-CM;* contains both the Alphabetic Index and the Tabular List for surgery and procedures

REMEMBER . . . You can't begin to code unless you've determined the principal diagnosis and other reportable diagnoses and procedures from the medical record.

INTRODUCTION

Once the medical record has been reviewed to determine the principal diagnosis and other reportable diagnoses and procedures, the following steps in locating the codes to be assigned should be undertaken, using the three volumes of *ICD-9-CM:*

1. Locate the main term in the Alphabetic Index.
   - Review subterms and nonessential modifiers related to the main term.
   - Follow any cross-reference instructions.
   - Refer to any notes in the Alphabetic Index.
2. Verify the code number in the Tabular List.
   - Read the code title.
   - Read and be guided by any instructional notes. Refer to other codes as instructed.
   - Determine whether a fifth digit must be added.
3. Assign the verified code or codes.

It is imperative that these steps be followed without exception; the condition or procedure to be coded must first be located in the Alphabetic Index and then verified in the Tabular List. Relying on memory or using only the index or Tabular List may lead to incorrect code assignment.

LOCATE THE CODE ENTRY IN THE ALPHABETIC INDEX

The first step in coding is to locate the main term in the Alphabetic Index. In volume 2, the condition is listed as the main term, usually expressed as a noun. General terms such as "admission," "encounter," and "examination" are used to locate code entries for the supplementary V code section. In volume 3, the main term may be the specific title of a procedure, or a general term such as "excision," "incision," or "removal." Some conditions and procedures are indexed under more than one main term. For example, anxiety reaction can be located in either of the following index entries:

Anxiety (neurosis) (reaction) (state) 300.00
Reaction . . .
  anxiety 300.00

In volume 3, adenoidectomy can be located by referring to the main term **Adenoidectomy** or by referring to the main term **Excision,** as follows:

Adenoidectomy (without tonsillectomy) 28.6
Excision . . .
  adenoids (tag) 28.6
    with tonsillectomy 28.3

If a main term cannot be located, the coder should consider a synonym, eponym, or other alternative term. Once the main term is located, a search should be made of subterms, notes, or cross-references. Subterms provide more specific information of many types and must be checked carefully, following all the rules of alphabetization. The main term code entry should not be assigned until all subterm possibilities have been exhausted. During this process, it may be necessary to refer again to the medical record to determine whether any additional information is available to permit assignment of a more specific code. If a subterm cannot be located, the nonessential modifiers following the main term should be reviewed to see whether the subterm may be included there. If not, alternative terms should be considered.

Exercise 5.1

Without referring to the Alphabetic Index of Diseases, underline the word in items 1–7 that indicates the main term for each diagnosis. In items 8–15, underline the main term for the procedure in the Alphabetic Index of Procedures. In some cases, more than one word in a statement of a diagnosis or procedure is to be underlined.

1. Acute myocardial infarction
2. Chronic hypertrophy of tonsils and adenoids
3. Acute suppurative cholecystitis
4. Syphilitic aortic aneurysm
5. Normal, spontaneous delivery, full-term infant
6. Drug overdose due to barbiturates
7. Urinary tract infection due to E. coli
8. Type II tympanoplasty, left ear
9. Incision and drainage of abscess, neck
10. Open fracture reduction, left femur, with nail
11. Scleral buckling, left eye
12. Magnet extraction of metallic sliver from right eye
13. Bowel resection with transverse colostomy
14. Right inguinal herniorrhaphy and right hydrocelectomy
15. Intracapsular cataract extraction, right eye

VERIFY THE CODE NUMBER IN THE TABULAR LIST

Once a code number entry has been located in the Alphabetic Index, the coder must refer to that number in the Tabular List; a code should not be assigned without such verification. In addition to the title for the code entry, it may be necessary for coders to review the title for the chapter, section, and category in order to be sure the correct code has been identified. Although the title in the Tabular List does not always match the Alphabetic Index entry exactly, it is usually clear whether it applies. For example:

- Appendicitis (541) has an additional modifier of "unqualified" in the Tabular List. This alerts the coder to look elsewhere when the type of appendicitis is stated in the medical record.
- Menorrhalgia (625.3) has the title **Dysmenorrhea** in the Tabular List. Although the title in volume 1 is not identical to the term in the Alphabetic Index, it is clear that it is the right code for this condition.

Any significant discrepancy between the index entry and the tabular listing should alert the coder to the need to review the Alphabetic Index for a more appropriate term.

All instructional terms and notes should be read and followed when they apply, with particular attention to exclusion notes. Ordinarily the code number listed with the main term entry in the index is for an unspecified condition. It is important to review other codes in the related area to determine whether a more specific code can be assigned.

CODING DEMONSTRATIONS

Follow the steps outlined above to determine the correct code for each of the diagnostic statements listed below:

- **Bunion, right great toe**
  Refer to main term **Bunion,** which provides a code of 727.1. Note that there are no subterms. Verify this by referring to code 727.1 in the Tabular List. In this case, the index entry and Tabular List title are identical, and code 727.1 should be assigned.
- **Sciatica due to herniated lumbar disc**
  Refer to the main term **Sciatica** in the Alphabetic Index and the subterms for displacement or herniation of nucleus pulposus. An inclusion note in the Tabular List indicates "lumbago or sciatica due to displacement of intervertebral disc," 722.10. If you are uncertain whether herniation and displacement are the same for purposes of coding, check the index for the main term **herniation.**
- **Acute bronchitis due to Staphylococcus**
  Look up the main term **Bronchitis** and then the subterm "acute." The code entry is 466.0. Read the "use additional code" note that advises you to also assign a code to identify the responsible organism. Look up **Infection,** staphylococcal, and find code 041.10, which is assigned in the Tabular List. The code title is Staphylococcal infection, unspecified. Review the medical record to see whether there is any mention of the specific type of Staphylococcus. If there is, consider 041.11, 041.12, or 041.19; if not, assign code 041.10 as an additional code.
- **Aberrant pulmonary artery**
  Refer to the main term **Aberrant.** Check the subterms, and note that there is no entry for pulmonary artery but that there is a cross-reference note to "*see also* Malposition, congenital." Follow the cross-reference advice and refer to **Malposition.** You immediately see a more specific subterm for "Artery, pulmonary," with code entry 747.3. The title for this code in the Tabular List is Anomalies of the pulmonary artery, and it is clearly the correct code for this condition.
- **Acute bronchopneumonia due to aspiration of oil**
  Locate the main term **Bronchopneumonia** in volume 2. Note the cross-reference instruction to "*see* Pneumonia, broncho." Follow the cross-reference by turning to the main term **Pneumonia** (acute) (Alpenstich) (benign). . . . Note that the term "acute" is a nonessential modifier enclosed in parentheses under the main term **Pneumonia.** This applies also to the subterm, and so this term has now been accounted for but does not directly affect code assignment. Refer to the following subterms listed under the main term:

  Pneumonia (acute) (Alpenstich) (benign) . . .
  broncho-, bronchial (confluent) (croupous)
  (diffuse) (disseminated) (hemorrhagic) . . .
  aspiration (*see also* Pneumonia, aspiration)
  507.0

  Search through the main term and subterms cited above and underline the component parts of the diagnostic statement that have been located so far. Note that all component parts of the diagnostic statement except "of oil" have been located. Refer back to the subterm aspiration and note the cross-reference to "*see also* Pneumonia, aspiration." When you refer to **Pneumonia,** aspiration, you see that there are additional subterms here under the connecting words "due to" with a subterm for oils and essences that takes you to code 507.1. Refer to code 507.1 in the Tabular List, and note that the title for this code is Pneumonitis due to inhalation of oils and essences. Although the title is not worded exactly the same as the diagnosis, there is such a close correlation that it is clear this is the code that should be assigned. Assign code 507.1 because it covers all elements of the diagnosis and no instructional notes contradict its use.

Review Exercise 5.2

Using the Alphabetic Indexes and the Tabular Lists, code the following diagnoses and procedures.

	Code(s)
1. Chronic hypertrophy of tonsils and adenoids	474.10
Tonsillectomy and adenoidectomy	28.3
2. Fibrocystic disease of breasts	610.1
3. Acute suppurative mastoiditis with subperiosteal abscess	383.01
4. Recurrent direct left inguinal hernia with gangrene	550.01
Herniorrhaphy	53.01
5. Acute upper respiratory infection with influenza	487.1
6. Benign cyst of breast	610.0
Aspiration of cyst, left breast	85.91

Basic Coding Guidelines

CHAPTER **6**

CHAPTER OVERVIEW

- There are basic principles that all coders must follow.
- It is important to use both the Alphabetic Indexes and the Tabular Lists during the coding process.
  - — Follow all instructional notes.
  - — Even if common codes have been memorized, refer to the Alphabetic Indexes and Tabular Lists.
- Always assign codes to the highest level of detail.
  - — All digits must be used.
  - — None can be admitted or added.
- NEC and NOS codes should be assigned only when appropriate.
- Combination codes should be used if they are available.
  - — Assign multiple codes as needed to fully describe a condition.
  - — Avoid coding irrelevant information.

LEARNING OUTCOMES

After studying this chapter you should be able to:

- Determine what level of detail to assign to a code.
- Understand how to use combination codes.
- Explain how to assign multiple codes to fully describe a condition.
- Determine what qualifications determine whether an unconfirmed diagnosis is coded as though it were an established diagnosis.
- Explain the difference between "rule out" and "ruled out."
- Code acute and chronic conditions.
- Code a condition labeled "impending," "threatened," or "late effect."

TERMS TO KNOW

Combination code
a single code used to classify two diagnoses, a diagnosis with a secondary condition, or a diagnosis with an associated complication

NEC
not elsewhere classified

NOS
not otherwise specified

"Rule out"
indicates that a diagnosis is still possible

"Ruled out"
indicates that a diagnosis once considered likely is no longer possible

REMEMBER . . . For the current version of the *ICD-9-CM Official Guidelines for Coding and Reporting* visit www.ahacentraloffice.org.

INTRODUCTION

The basic coding guidelines discussed in this chapter apply throughout the *ICD-9-CM* classification system. Following these principles is vital to accurate code selection and correct sequencing. Guidelines that apply to specific chapters of *ICD-9-CM* will be discussed in the relevant chapters of this handbook. To download a copy of the current version of the complete *ICD-9-CM Official Guidelines for Coding and Reporting,* please visit www.ahacentraloffice.org. Guideline changes are anticipated every year on October 1. Adherence to the guidelines when assigning *ICD-9-CM* diagnosis and procedure codes is required under the Health Insurance Portability and Accountability Act of 1996 (HIPAA). The instructions and conventions of the classification take precedence over guidelines.

USE BOTH THE ALPHABETIC INDEXES AND THE TABULAR LISTS

The first coding principle is that both the Alphabetic Indexes and the Tabular Lists must be used to locate and assign appropriate codes. The condition or procedure to be coded must first be located in the index, and the code provided there must then be verified in the Tabular List. The coder must follow all instructional notes to determine that more specific subterms or important instructional notes are not overlooked. Experienced coders sometimes rely on their memory for commonly used codes, but consistent reference to the Alphabetic Index and the Tabular Lists is imperative, no matter how experienced the coder is.

ASSIGN CODES TO THE HIGHEST LEVEL OF DETAIL

A second basic principle is that codes must be used to the highest number of digits available. This can be accomplished by following these steps:

- Assign a three-digit disease code only when there are no four-digit codes within that category.
- Assign a four-digit code only when there is no fifth-digit subclassification for that category.
- Assign a fifth digit for any category for which a fifth-digit subclassification is provided.

The same principles apply to the selection of a procedure code. No two-digit procedure codes are provided, and three digits can be used only when no four-digit code is provided.

All digits must be used. None can be omitted and none can be added. The one exception to this rule is that a zero (0) should be added as a fourth digit to the rare code that requires a fifth digit when no fourth digit is provided. The following examples demonstrate these basic coding principles:

1. Refer to volume 1, category **490, Bronchitis, not specified as acute or chronic.** Code 490 has no fourth-digit subdivisions; therefore, the three-digit code is assigned.
2. Refer to volume 1, category **540, Acute appendicitis.** This category includes fourth digits that indicate the presence of peritonitis or peritoneal abscess. Because fourth-digit subdivisions are provided, code 540 cannot be assigned.
3. Refer to volume 1, category **493, Asthma.** Category 493 has five fourth-digit subdivisions (493.0, 493.1, 493.2, 493.8, and 493.9). It also uses a fifth-digit subclassification

to specify whether there is any mention of status asthmaticus or acute exacerbation. Any code assignment from category 493 must have five digits to ensure coding accuracy.

4. Turn to the Tabular List in volume 3, code **50.4, Total hepatectomy.** This code is complete with only three digits because there are no subdivisions.
5. Turn to the Tabular List in volume 3, category **80, Incision and excision of joint structures.** Fourth-digit subdivisions to specify the anatomical site appear at the beginning of category 80, indicating that a four-digit code for the site will be required.

ASSIGN RESIDUAL CODES (NEC AND NOS) AS APPROPRIATE

The main term entry in the Alphabetic Index is usually followed by the code number for the unspecified condition. This code should never be assigned without a careful review of subterms to determine whether a more specific code can be located. When the coder's review does not identify a more specific code entry in the index, titles and inclusion notes in the subdivisions under either the three-digit or the four-digit code in the Tabular List should be reviewed. The residual NOS code should never be assigned when a more specific code is available. The following examples demonstrate this basic coding principle:

1. Refer to the Alphabetic Index in volume 2 for nontraumatic hematoma of breast, which is classified as 611.89. This is listed as "other" specified conditions of the breast. Even though the diagnosis is very specific, no separate code is provided.
2. Refer to the Alphabetic Index for phlebitis. Note that phlebitis, not otherwise specified, is assigned to code **451.9, Phlebitis, of unspecified site.** Further review of the medical record reveals that this is a phlebitis of the lower extremity and therefore is more appropriately assigned to code **451.2, Phlebitis of lower extremities, unspecified.**

ASSIGN COMBINATION CODES WHEN AVAILABLE

A single code used to classify either two diagnoses, or a diagnosis with an associated secondary condition, or a diagnosis with an associated complication is called a combination code. Combination codes can be located in the index by referring to subterm entries, with particular reference to subterms that follow connecting words such as "with," "due to," "in," and "associated with." Other combination codes can be identified by reading inclusion and exclusion notes in the Tabular Lists.

Only the combination code is assigned when that code fully identifies the diagnostic conditions involved or when the Alphabetic Index so directs. For example:

- Acute cholecystitis with cholelithiasis 574.00
- Acute pharyngitis due to streptococcal infection 034.0
- Bilateral recurrent femoral hernia with gangrene 551.03
- Glaucoma with increased episcleral venous pressure 365.82

Exercise 6.1

Code the following diagnoses.

	Code(s)
1. Influenza with pneumonia	487.0
2. Acute cholecystitis with cholelithiasis and choledocholithiasis	574.60
3. Meningitis due to *Salmonella* infection	003.21

Occasionally, a combination code lacks the necessary specificity in describing the manifestation or complication; in such cases, an additional code may be assigned. The coder should be guided by directions in the Tabular List for the use of an additional code or codes that may provide more specificity. For example, code 648.2x classifies anemia complicating pregnancy, delivery, or the puerperium. Because it does not indicate the type of anemia, an additional code can be assigned for this purpose.

ASSIGN MULTIPLE CODES AS NEEDED

Multiple coding is the use of more than one code to fully identify the component elements of a complex diagnostic or procedural statement. A complex statement is one that involves connecting words or phrases such as "with," "due to," "incidental to," "secondary to," or similar terminology. The coder should be guided by directions in the Tabular List for the use of an additional code or codes that may provide more specificity. When no combination code is provided, multiple codes should be assigned as needed to fully describe the condition regardless of whether there is advice to that effect.

Mandatory Multiple Coding

The term "dual classification" is used to describe the required assignment of two codes to provide information about both a manifestation and the associated underlying disease. Mandatory multiple coding is identified in the Alphabetic Index by the use of a second code in brackets. The first code identifies the underlying condition and the second identifies the manifestation. Both codes must be assigned and sequenced in the order listed.

In the Tabular List the need for dual coding is indicated by the presence of a "use additional code" note with the code for the underlying condition and a "code first underlying condition" note with the manifestation code. In printed versions of the manuals, the manifestation code is in italics. Manifestation codes cannot be designated as the principal diagnosis, and a code for the underlying condition must always be listed first except for an occasional situation where other directions are provided. A code in brackets in the Alphabetic Index can be used only as a secondary code for the specific condition or procedure indexed in this way. For example:

- Diabetic type 1, on insulin, polyneuropathy 250.61 + 357.2 + V58.67
  [Note: V58.67 is not required for type 1 diabetics. However, *Coding Clinic*, Fourth Quarter 2004, p. 55, indicated that V58.67 may be assigned for type 1 diabetics, if desired. The Editorial Advisory Board felt that although V58.67 was not required, it was useful information to capture. This handbook has followed that advice.]
- Arthritis due to mumps 072.79 + 711.50

Exercise 6.2

Code the following diagnoses according to the coding principles for correct sequencing of codes.

	Code(s)
1. Diabetic retinitis	250.50 362.01
2. Chondrocalcinosis of shoulder region due to calcium pyrophosphate	275.49 712.21
3. Arbovirus meningitis	066.9 321.2
4. Rheumatoid arthritis with polyneuropathy	714.0 357.1
5. Cataract due to chalcosis	360.24 366.34

Discretionary Multiple Coding

The "code, if applicable, any causal condition first" note indicates that multiple codes should be assigned only if the causal condition is documented as being present. For example, ulcer of lower limbs, except pressure ulcer (707.1x), requires that the code to identify postphlebetic syndrome with ulcer (459.11) be assigned as the first-listed code or principal diagnosis but only if it is documented as being the cause of the ulcer.

The instruction to "use additional code" indicates that multiple codes should be assigned only if the condition mentioned is documented as being present. Examples include the following:

- Raynaud's syndrome (443.0) requires an additional code to identify gangrene (785.4) but only when gangrene is mentioned in the diagnosis or documented in the medical record.
- Urinary tract infection (599.0) requires an additional code to identify the organism, if it is documented, such as positive culture of E. coli (041.49).

Exercise 6.3

Code the following diagnoses.

	Code(s)
1. Acute cystitis due to E. coli infection	595.0 041.49
2. Alcoholic gastritis due to chronic alcoholism	535.30 303.90
3. Diverticulitis of colon with intestinal hemorrhage	562.13
4. Diabetic neuritis due to type 1 diabetes mellitus, patient on insulin	250.61 357.2 V58.67
5. Reiter's syndrome with arthritis	099.3 711.10
6. Fulminant hepatitis, type A, with hepatic coma	070.0

Avoid Indiscriminate Multiple Coding

Indiscriminate coding of irrelevant information should be avoided. For example, codes for symptoms or signs characteristic of the diagnosis and integral to it should not be assigned. Codes are never assigned solely on the basis of findings of diagnostic tests, such as laboratory, X-ray, or electrocardiographic tests, unless the diagnosis is confirmed by the physician. This differs from the coding practices in the outpatient setting when coding encounters for diagnostic tests that have been interpreted by a physician. Codes should not be assigned for conditions that do not meet Uniform Hospital Discharge Data Set (UHDDS) criteria for reporting. For example, diagnostic reports often mention such conditions as hiatal hernia, atelectasis, and right bundle branch block with no further mention to indicate any relevance to the care given. Assigning a code is inappropriate for reporting purposes unless the physician provides documentation to support the condition's significance for the episode of care.

Codes designated as unspecified are never assigned when a more specific code for the same general condition is assigned. For example, diabetes mellitus with unspecified complication would never be assigned when a code for diabetes with renal complication (250.4x) is assigned for the same episode of care.

CODE UNCONFIRMED DIAGNOSES AS IF ESTABLISHED

When a diagnosis for an inpatient at the time of discharge is qualified as "possible," "probable," "suspected," "likely," "questionable," "?," or "rule out," the condition should be coded and reported as though the diagnosis were established. Other terms that fit the definition of a probable or suspected condition are: "consistent with," "compatible with," "indicative of," "suggestive of," "appears to be," and "comparable with." Note that the exception to this guideline is the coding of HIV infection/illness. Code only cases confirmed by physician documentation. The guideline regarding unconfirmed diagnoses does not apply to coding or reporting for an outpatient as if the diagnosis were established. For these patients the principal diagnosis is the highest degree of certainty, such as symptoms, signs, or abnormalities.

- Patient is admitted with severe generalized abdominal pain. The physician's diagnostic statement on discharge is: abdominal pain, probably due to acute gastritis (535.00). Only the code for gastritis is assigned as the pain is implicit in the diagnosis.
- Patient is admitted and discharged with a final diagnosis of probable peptic ulcer with a recommendation for additional workup 533.90
- Patient admitted as an inpatient and discharged with possible posttraumatic brain syndrome, nonpsychotic 310.2
- Patient is seen in the outpatient clinic with malaise. The physician's diagnostic statement is possible viral syndrome 780.79

Caution should be used in coding unconfirmed diagnoses of conditions such as epilepsy, AIDS, and multiple sclerosis as if they were established. Incorrect reporting of such conditions can have serious personal consequences for the patient, such as the inability to obtain a driver's license and possible social and job discrimination. Physicians are often unaware that official coding guidelines require a diagnosis qualified as unconfirmed to be coded as if established; therefore, the coder should consult the physician before assigning codes for such unconfirmed conditions.

Rule Out versus Ruled Out

It is important to distinguish between the terms "rule out," which indicates that a diagnosis is still considered to be possible, and "ruled out," which indicates that a diagnosis originally considered as likely is no longer a possibility.

Diagnoses qualified by the term "rule out" are coded as if established for inpatient episodes of care in the same way that diagnoses described as possible or probable are coded. A diagnosis described as "ruled out" is never coded. If an alternative condition has been identified, that diagnosis should be coded; otherwise, a code for the presenting symptom or other precursor condition should be assigned. Here are some examples of codes assigned according to this coding principle:

- Rule out gastric ulcer . . . 531.90 [condition is coded]
- Acute appendicitis, ruled out; Meckel's diverticulum found at surgery . . . 751.0 [code only the diverticulum]
- Rule out angiodysplasia of the colon . . . 569.84 [condition is coded]

Borderline Diagnoses

Care should be exercised with diagnoses documented as "borderline." Borderline diagnoses are not the same as uncertain diagnoses and are therefore handled differently. If the provider documents a "borderline" diagnosis at the time of discharge, the "possible/probable" guideline to code as if established would not apply in this situation. Instead, provider clarification is required for confirmation of the disease. If, after provider clarification, the disease is not confirmed, a code for abnormal findings may be appropriate, such as a code from subcategory 790.2, Abnormal glucose, for a documented diagnosis of "borderline diabetes." This advice is equally applicable to inpatient and outpatient coding.

ACUTE AND CHRONIC CONDITIONS

When the same condition is described as both acute (or subacute) and chronic, it should be coded according to the Alphabetic Index subentries for that condition. If separate subterms for acute (or subacute) and chronic are listed at the same indention level in the Alphabetic Index, both codes are assigned, with the code for the acute condition sequenced first. (Note that a condition described as subacute is coded as acute if there is no separate subterm entry for subacute.) For example, refer to the Alphabetic Index entry for acute and chronic bronchitis:

Bronchitis . . .
    acute or subacute . . . 466.0 . . .
    chronic . . . 491.9

Because both subterms appear at the same indention level, both codes are assigned, with code 466.0 sequenced first.

When only one term is listed as a subterm, with the other in parentheses as a nonessential modifier, only the code listed for the subterm is assigned. For example, for a diagnosis of acute and chronic poliomyelitis, the Alphabetic Index entry is as follows:

Poliomyelitis (acute) (anterior) (epidemic) 045.9 . . .
    chronic 335.21

The only code assigned in this situation is **335.21, Progressive muscular atrophy.**

In some cases, a combination code has been provided for use when the condition is described as both acute and chronic. For example, code 518.84 includes both acute and chronic respiratory failure. When there are no subentries for acute (or subacute) or chronic, these modifiers are disregarded in coding the condition. For example, refer to **Fibrocystic** disease, breast. Neither acute nor chronic is listed as a subterm, and so code 610.1 is assigned.

Exercise 6.4

Code the following diagnoses.

	Code(s)
1. Acute and chronic appendicitis	540.9 542
2. Subacute and chronic pyelonephritis	590.10 590.00
3. Acute and chronic cervicitis	616.0

IMPENDING OR THREATENED CONDITION

Selection of a code for a condition described at the time of discharge or at the conclusion of an outpatient encounter as impending or threatened depends first on whether the condition actually occurred. If so, the threatened/impending condition is coded as a confirmed diagnosis.

For example, the medical record shows a diagnosis of threatened premature labor at 28 weeks gestation. Review of the medical record indicates that a stillborn was delivered during the hospital stay. This is coded as **644.21, Early onset of labor, delivered,** because the threatened condition did occur.

If neither the threatened/impending condition nor a related condition occurred, however, the coder must refer to the Alphabetic Index to answer the following two questions: Is the condition indexed under the main term threatened or impending? Is there a subterm for impending or threatened under the main term for the condition? If such terms appear, the coder should assign the code provided. There are several subterms under each of the main terms **Impending** and **Threatened,** as well as several main terms with such subentries. For example, if a patient is admitted with threatened abortion but the abortion is averted, the code **640.0x, Threatened abortion,** is assigned, because there is an index entry for "threatened" under the main term **Abortion.**

When neither term is indexed, the precursor condition that actually existed is coded; a code is not assigned for the condition described as impending or threatened. For example: A patient is admitted with a diagnosis of impending gangrene of the lower extremities, but the gangrene was averted by prompt treatment. Because the gangrene did not occur and there is no index entry for impending gangrene, a code must be assigned for the presenting situation that suggested the possibility of gangrene, such as redness or swelling of the extremity.

REPORTING THE SAME DIAGNOSIS CODE MORE THAN ONCE

Each unique *ICD-9-CM* diagnosis code may be reported only once for an encounter. This applies both to bilateral conditions and to two different conditions classified to the same *ICD-9-CM* diagnosis code.

LATE EFFECTS

A late effect is a residual condition that remains after the termination of the acute phase of an illness or injury. Such conditions may occur at any time after an acute injury or illness. There is no set period of time that must elapse before a condition is considered to be a late effect. Some late effects are apparent early; others may make an appearance long after the original injury or illness has been resolved. Certain conditions due to trauma, such as malunion, nonunion, and scarring, are inherent late effects no matter how early they occur.

Late effects include conditions reported as such or as sequela of a previous illness or injury. The fact that a condition is a late effect may be inferred when the diagnostic statement includes terms such as the following:

- Late
- Old
- Due to previous injury or illness
- Following previous injury or illness
- Traumatic, unless there is evidence of current injury

Exercise 6.5

Write an "X" in front of each diagnostic statement given below that identifies a late effect of an injury or illness. For each such statement underline the residual condition once and the cause of the late effect twice.

__X__ 1. Hemiplegia due to previous cerebrovascular accident

__X__ 2. Malunion of fracture, right femur

__X__ 3. Scoliosis due to old infantile paralysis

_____ 4. Laceration of tendon of finger two weeks ago; admitted now for tendon repair

__X__ 5. Keloid secondary to injury nine months ago

__X__ 6. Mental retardation due to previous viral encephalitis

Locating Late Effect Codes

Codes that indicate the cause of a late effect can be located by referring to the main term **Late** and the subterm effects in the Alphabetic Index of Diseases and Injuries (volume 2). Note that *ICD-9-CM* provides only a limited number of codes to indicate the cause of a late effect:

- Late effects of tuberculosis 137.0–137.4
- Late effects of acute poliomyelitis 138
- Late effects of other infectious and parasitic diseases 139.0–139.8
- Late effect of rickets 268.1

- Late effects of intracranial abscess or pyogenic infection 326
- Late effects of cerebrovascular disease 438.0–438.9
- Late effects of complications of pregnancy, childbirth, and the puerperium 677
- Late effects of musculoskeletal and connective tissue injuries 905.0–905.9
- Late effects of injuries to the skin and subcutaneous tissues 906.0–906.9
- Late effects of injuries to the nervous system 907.0–907.9
- Late effects of other and unspecified injuries 908.0–908.9
- Late effects of other and unspecified external causes 909.0–909.9

Two Codes Required

Complete coding of late effects requires two codes:

- Residual condition or nature of the late effect
- Cause of the late effect

The residual condition is sequenced first, followed by the code for the cause of the late effect, except in a few instances where the Alphabetic Index or the Tabular List directs otherwise. If the late effect is due to injury, a late effect E code should also be assigned. For example:

- Traumatic arthritis of right shoulder due to old fracture of right humerus 716.11 + 905.2 + E929.9
- Paralysis of left leg due to old poliomyelitis 344.30 + 138
- Scoliosis due to poliomyelitis at age 12 138 + 737.43

There are three exceptions to the coding principle that requires two codes for late effect:

- When the residual effect is not stated, the cause of the late effect code is used alone.
- When no late effect code is provided in *ICD-9-CM* but the condition is described as being a late effect, only the residual condition is coded. Note that conditions described as due to previous surgery are not coded as late effects but are classified as history of or complications of previous surgery, depending on the specific situation.
- When the late effect code has been expanded at the fourth- or fifth-digit level to include the residual condition, only the cause of the late effect code is assigned. At present only category 438, Late effect of cerebrovascular disease, has been expanded in this way.

LATE EFFECT VERSUS CURRENT ILLNESS OR INJURY

A late effect code is not used with a code for a current injury or illness of the same type, with one exception. A code from category **438, Late effects of cerebrovascular disease,** is assigned as an additional code when a patient with residual effects from an earlier cerebrovascular disease is seen because of current cerebrovascular disease. For example, a patient with residual aphasia due to subdural hemorrhage two years ago who is admitted because of acute cerebral thrombosis would have the following codes assigned:

434.00 Cerebral thrombosis, without mention of cerebral infarction
438.11 Late effect of cerebrovascular disease, with speech and language deficits, aphasia

Exercise 6.6

Code the following diagnoses.

	Code(s)
1. Residuals of poliomyelitis or Late	138
2. Sequela of old crush injury to left foot or Late	906.4
3. Cerebrovascular accident two years ago with residual hemiplegia of the dominant side	438.21
4. Contracture of hip following partial hip replacement one year ago	718.45

Review Exercise 6.7

Code the following diagnoses.

	Code(s)
1. Traumatic arthritis, right ankle, following fracture, right ankle	716.17 905.4
2. Cicatricial contracture of left hand due to burn	709.2 906.6
3. Brain damage following cerebral abscess seven months ago Late	348.9 326

Review Exercise 6.7 *(continued)*

4. Flaccid hemiplegia due to old cerebrovascular accident		438.20
5. Bilateral neural deafness resulting from childhood measles ten years ago		389.12 139.8
6. Mononeuritis, median nerve, resulting from previous crush injury to right arm	or Late	354.1 906.4
7. Posttraumatic, painful arthritis, left hand	Late	716.14 908.9
8. Residuals of previous severe burn, left wrist	or Late	906.6
9. Locked-in state (paralytic syndrome) due to old cerebrovascular accident		438.50 344.81

Coding Guidelines for Operations and Procedures

CHAPTER 7

CHAPTER OVERVIEW

- The UHDDS requires all significant procedures to be reported. Significant procedures meet any one of the following conditions.
  - — The procedure is surgical in nature.
  - — It carries an anesthetic risk.
  - — It carries a procedural risk.
  - — It requires specialized training.
- Volume 3 of *ICD-9-CM* contains both a Tabular List and an Alphabetic Index for classifying procedures.
- Conventions followed in volume 3 are essentially the same as those in volumes 1 and 2.
- The operative approach is usually considered to be an integral part of a procedure. No code is assigned except in rare situations.
- Biopsies can be both closed and open. They are not all coded with a biopsy code.
- V codes are used when a procedure is canceled. There are several possible reasons for cancellation, including contraindication, patient decision, scheduling problems, and illness of key staff.
- An incomplete procedure is coded to the extent it was performed. A variety of V codes may be used.
- Different coding principles are used for shunt procedures and stent insertions.
- Computer assisted surgeries are coded for the specific diagnostic or therapeutic procedure performed along with a code from subcategory 00.3.

LEARNING OUTCOMES

After studying this chapter you should be able to:

- Locate procedure terms in the Alphabetic Index of volume 3.
- Code procedures such as surgeries, biopsies, and stent and shunt insertions.
- Code canceled and incomplete procedures.

TERMS TO KNOW

Principal procedure
procedure performed for definitive treatment (rather than for diagnostic or exploratory purposes)

Eponym
in this context, the name of the surgeon or surgeons who developed the procedure

Biopsy
the taking of tissue from a living person for microscopic study

V codes
factors influencing health status and contact with health services

REMEMBER . . . In volume 3, procedure codes consist of two digits followed by a decimal point and one or two additional digits.

INTRODUCTION

General information on volume 3 of *ICD-9-CM* is provided in this chapter, and guidelines for coding operations and procedures are discussed. Procedures specific to certain body systems will be covered in the relevant chapters of this handbook.

UNIFORM HOSPITAL DISCHARGE DATA SET FOR REPORTING PROCEDURES

The Uniform Hospital Discharge Data Set (UHDDS) requires all significant procedures to be reported. In addition, Medicare requires the reporting of any procedure that affects payment, whether or not it meets the definition of significant procedure. Other procedures may be reported at the hospital's discretion.

A significant procedure is defined as one that meets any of the following conditions:

- Is surgical in nature
- Carries an anesthetic risk
- Carries a procedural risk
- Requires specialized training

Surgery includes incision, excision, destruction, amputation, introduction, insertion, endoscopy, repair, suturing, and manipulation. Any procedure performed under anesthesia other than topical carries an anesthetic risk. Procedural risk is more difficult to define, but any procedure that has a recognized risk of inducing functional impairment, physiologic disturbance, or possible trauma during an invasive procedure is included in this group. Procedures requiring specialized training are those that are performed by specialized professionals, qualified technicians, or clinical teams specifically trained to perform certain procedures or whose services are directed primarily to carrying them out. This implies training over and above that ordinarily provided in the education of physicians, nurses, or technicians. For Medicare reporting, the surgeon who performs the procedure must be identified by a number, and the date of the procedure must also be reported. Electronic claim formats may accept up to 25 procedure codes. However, at the present time, Medicare allows the reporting of up to six procedures; if more than six have been performed, all therapeutic procedures, particularly those related to the principal diagnosis, should be reported to the extent possible. Effective January 1, 2011, Medicare expanded the number of *ICD-9* diagnosis and procedure codes it will accept and process on institutional claims.

Under the Health Insurance Portability and Accountability Act of 1996 (HIPAA), for administrative simplification purposes, standard code sets have been designated for electronic claim transactions. This regulation went into effect in 2003.

ICD-9-CM is the standard for hospitals when reporting surgery and procedures for inpatients. The American Medical Association's *Current Procedural Terminology (CPT)* and the *Health Care Procedure Coding System (HCPCS)* level II codes rather than the *ICD-9-CM* volume 3 codes are the standards for hospital reporting of outpatient procedures and physician reporting. A hospital may also code outpatient procedures using the *ICD-9-CM* system for internal or non–claim related purposes. In addition, hospitals may report *ICD-9-CM* procedure codes for outpatient services, for specific payers under contractual agreements, or as required by their state data reporting requirements.

Principal Procedure

The principal procedure as described by the UHDDS is one performed for definitive treatment (rather than for diagnostic or exploratory purposes) or one that is necessary to care for a complication. If two or more procedures appear to meet this definition, the one most related to the principal diagnosis is designated as the principal procedure. If both are equally related to the principal diagnosis, the most resource-intensive or complex procedure is usually designated as principal. When more than one procedure is reported, the principal procedure should be identified by the one that relates to the principal diagnosis. It is important to follow UHDDS definitions because principal procedures are significant in the reporting of surgical quality indicators.

FORMAT AND ORGANIZATION

Volume 3 of *ICD-9-CM* contains both a Tabular List and Alphabetic Index for classifying procedures. The format and organization discussed earlier in this handbook in relation to volumes 1 and 2 of *ICD-9-CM* also apply to volume 3.

Most chapters in the Tabular List of Procedures in volume 3 deal with a specific body system. The four exceptions are chapters 00, 13, 16, and 17. Chapter 13 classifies obstetrical procedures, and chapter 16 classifies diagnostic and therapeutic procedures not generally considered to be surgical in nature.

Chapters 00 and 17 capture a diverse group of procedures and interventions affecting all body systems. This deviation from the normal structure of *ICD-9-CM* is an attempt to accommodate new technology when there are no available slots in the appropriate body system chapters. Chapters 00 and 17 were identified as unused chapters that could be utilized to create new codes when the corresponding specific body system chapter was full. The plan was to exhaust all codes in chapter 00 first and then start populating chapter 17 when chapter 00 was no longer available.

Procedure codes consist of three or four digits, with two digits preceding a decimal and one or two digits following the decimal. With the exception of the four chapters mentioned above, the two-digit axis is the body system or site, with the digits following the decimal indicating a more specific site, the type or purpose of the procedure, or the operative technique used.

CONVENTIONS

The conventions followed in volume 3 are essentially the same as those used in the disease classification, with minor differences in certain instructional notes.

"Code Also"

This instructional note is used to indicate that an additional code should be assigned if the referenced procedure was performed. It also applies to two specific situations:

- To advise the coder that individual components of a procedure, or two procedures that might be considered as a unit, must be coded; this is expressed as "Code also any synchronous . . . ." For example:
  —13.1 Intracapsular extraction of lens
    Code also any synchronous insertion of pseudophakos (13.71)
  —42.6x Antesternal anastomosis of esophagus
    Code also any synchronous:
      esophagectomy (42.40–42.42)
      gastrostomy (43.1–43.2)

- To advise the coder that an additional code is to be assigned when certain adjunct procedures are performed, or certain equipment is used. This type of instruction is often found at the beginning of a category or subcategory and applies to all subdivisions. For example:
  —35.3 Operations on structures adjacent to heart valves
  Code also cardiopulmonary bypass [extra corporeal circulation] [heart-lung machine] (39.61)

The need to assign codes for two closely related procedures is sometimes indicated in the index by the use of slanted brackets enclosing the second code in the entry. This convention indicates that both codes must be assigned and sequenced as indicated.

LOCATING PROCEDURE TERMS IN THE ALPHABETIC INDEX

Main terms in the Alphabetic Index usually indicate the general type of procedure (for example, incision, excision, graft, implant, insertion, or removal), although a few are also indexed by the common name of the procedure, such as hysterectomy or appendectomy. Subterms introduced by the words "with" and "without" ordinarily immediately follow the main term, with a few exceptions. Other connecting words include "by," "for," and "to"; these terms are usually listed in alphabetical order.

Cross-reference terms are used in the procedure index just as they are in the Alphabetic Index of Diseases, but the volume 3 index is not as thoroughly cross-referenced as the volume 2 index. Therefore, it is often necessary to refer to a synonym or a general term to locate the appropriate code assignment.

Eponyms

Surgical procedures are sometimes identified by eponyms, usually the name of the surgeon (or surgeons) who developed the procedure. Eponyms may be indexed in any of three ways:

- Under the eponym itself:
  Davis operation (intubated ureterotomy) 56.2
- Under the main term **Operation:**
  Operation
  Davis (intubated ureterotomy) 56.2
- Under a main term or subterm(s) that describes the operation:
  Ureterotomy 56.2

When there is no entry for the eponym, the coder should refer to the main term that describes the procedure. For example, there is no index entry for the procedure "insertion of LeVeen shunt," but the code can be located by referring to **Shunt,** peritoneovascular, 54.94.

Excision of Organ or Lesion

Removal of an organ is usually listed by site under the main terms **Excision** or **Resection.** When only a lesion of the organ is removed, however, it is necessary to check the main term **Excision,** the subterm "lesion," and the more specific subterm that indicates the site of the lesion. For example, no entry for abdominal wall can be located under the main term Excision, but it can be located by referring to the subterm "lesion" under the main term Excision.

Bilateral Procedures

Some codes make a distinction to indicate if a procedure is performed unilaterally or bilaterally. This is not true for certain major procedures such as joint replacements. In these cases, the code is assigned twice when the procedure is performed on both sides. This guideline was developed primarily because joint replacement codes do not provide information that defines whether the procedure was unilateral or bilateral. The additional procedure has an impact on patient care and represents a significant use of resources. Codes for less significant procedures can also be assigned twice when the additional procedure meets similar criteria, but in most cases it is not useful to do so, particularly for minor procedures such as excision of skin lesions.

CODING OPERATIVE APPROACHES AND CLOSURES

The operative approach is ordinarily considered to be an integral part of the procedure. No code is assigned when a definitive procedure is carried out, except for the rare situation when the code for the surgery does not imply the approach. Both the Alphabetic Index and the Tabular List often instruct the coder to "omit code" when it represents an operative approach. However, this is not performed consistently enough for the coder to rely on it as the means of identifying which approach codes should not be assigned. Codes are not assigned for closure or anesthesia.

The operative approach is coded, however, when an opening into a body cavity is followed only by a diagnostic procedure such as a biopsy. For example, an exploratory laparotomy is performed for the purpose of removing an abdominal mass. When the cavity is opened, it is clear that a malignant lesion has spread through the abdominal cavity to the extent that a therapeutic resection is inappropriate. The surgeon removes samples of tissue to confirm the diagnosis and closes the abdominal incision. In this case, the laparotomy is coded and sequenced first, with an additional code for the biopsy. The reasoning behind this is that a procedure such as an exploratory laparotomy is a more significant procedure than a biopsy and therefore should be sequenced first.

Laparoscopic, Thoracoscopic, and Arthroscopic Approaches

Laparoscopic, thoracoscopic, and arthroscopic approaches are now being used for a number of procedures that were formerly carried out only by an open approach, and codes have been developed to include these techniques. Such approaches permit the removal of tissue or organs under videoscopic guidance through a very small incision. These procedures are less invasive than open surgery and usually result in less trauma to the patient, earlier discharge from the hospital, and more rapid recovery. The laparoscopic, thoracoscopic, or arthroscopic approach is not always successful, however, and it is sometimes necessary to shift to an open approach in order to complete the surgery. When conversion to an open approach becomes necessary, only the open procedure is coded; no code is assigned for the laparoscopic, thoracoscopic, or arthroscopic approach. Code **V64.41, Laparoscopic surgical procedure converted to open procedure**; code **V64.42, Thoracoscopic surgical procedure converted to open procedure**; or code **V64.43, Arthroscopic surgical procedure converted to open procedure,** is assigned as an additional diagnosis in this situation. This advice applies even when no separate code indicating this approach is provided in *ICD-9-CM*.

Other Endoscopic Approaches

Other endoscopic approaches are coded, unless the Alphabetic Index directs otherwise or the code title indicates that the procedure was performed by endoscopy. When an endoscope is passed through more than one body cavity, the code for the endoscopy identifies the most distant site. For example, the procedure identified as esophagogastroduodenoscopy is classified as **45.13, Other endoscopy of small intestine.**

Exercise 7.1

Code the following procedures. Do not assign diagnosis codes.

	Code(s)
1. Arthrotomy of right knee with partial patellectomy	77.86
2. Craniotomy Resection of brain tumor, right frontoparietal area	01.59
3. Laminectomy with excision of herniated lumbar disc	80.51
4. Exploratory laparotomy with partial resection of small intestine with end-to-end anastomosis	45.62
5. Exploratory laparotomy with appendectomy	47.09
6. Transurethral removal of ureteral calculus	56.0
7. Urethroscopy to control postoperative hemorrhage, prostate	60.94

Exercise 7.1 *(continued)*

8. Cystoscopy with left retrograde ureteral pyelogram	87.74
9. Laparoscopic cholecystectomy	51.23
10. Cholecystectomy, open, following attempt by laparoscopy	51.22 V64.41

CODING BIOPSIES

A biopsy is defined as the taking of tissue from a living person for the purpose of microscopic study. A biopsy code is not assigned when a lesion removed for therapeutic purposes is sent to the laboratory for examination, even though the term "biopsy" may be used in describing the procedure. Surgical specimens are routinely sent to the pathology laboratory for study; this is not considered a biopsy, and assigning a biopsy code is inappropriate. The two basic types of biopsies are open and closed.

Closed Biopsy

Closed biopsies are performed percutaneously by needle, by brush, by aspiration, or by endoscopy. Although most biopsy codes have been revised to identify an endoscopic biopsy, a few codes still do not make this distinction. For example, the code for biopsy of the urethra (58.23) does not indicate how it is performed; if it is done by endoscopy, codes for both the endoscopic approach and the biopsy are assigned. In this situation, the code for the endoscopy is sequenced first; it is considered the more significant procedure because it poses more risk for the patient.

In a brush biopsy, mucous or exfoliative tissue is removed by using a brush or bristle to collect cells for cytological examination. The procedure classification provides a separate code for a brush biopsy of a few anatomical locations; otherwise, the code for closed biopsy of the specified site is assigned. An aspiration biopsy collects cells for examination by aspiration; this procedure is also included in the code for closed biopsy.

Open Biopsy

When an open biopsy is performed by way of an incision, the incision is implicit in the biopsy code. When the approach is implied, as with biopsy of bone, no additional code for incision of the skin is required. When a biopsy is incidental to the removal of other tissue during a procedure, both the procedure and the biopsy are coded, with the more definitive procedure sequenced first. For example, a biopsy of the liver or pancreas may be performed when the main procedure is a colon resection or an appendectomy. When a diagnostic exploratory procedure, such as an exploratory transpleural thoracoscopy

(34.21) is performed for diagnostic purposes (more than just the operative approach) along with a biopsy (for example, thoracoscopic biopsy of the pleura, 34.20), both the biopsy and thoracoscopy are coded.

A needle biopsy for the removal of a small sample of tissue performed during an open surgical procedure is coded as a closed biopsy even though the body cavity was opened. The type of biopsy is determined by the technique used to obtain tissue for study; the terms "open" and "closed" in this connection do not refer to the surgical approach used to obtain access to an internal organ. The code for the definitive procedure is sequenced first, with an additional code for the needle biopsy. For example, a total cholecystectomy was performed by means of abdominal incision. During the course of the procedure, the pancreas was noted to be slightly enlarged, and a needle biopsy of the pancreas was performed to provide tissue for pathological examination. In this case, code **51.22 Cholecystectomy** and code **52.11, Closed (aspiration) (needle) (percutaneous) biopsy of pancreas,** are assigned as sequenced.

Occasionally, a biopsy is performed immediately before the definitive procedure is begun. This permits the pathologist to perform a rapid-frozen section examination to determine whether malignancy is present and allows the surgeon to modify the extent of surgery as necessary. The biopsy is then followed by more definitive surgery during the same operative episode. In this case, both a biopsy code and a code for the therapeutic procedure are assigned, with the therapeutic code sequenced first. For example:

- Biopsy (open) of transverse colon for frozen section, followed by transverse colectomy 45.74 + 45.26
- Open biopsy of breast tumor for rapid-frozen section; no malignancy found; lumpectomy carried out 85.21 + 85.12

Exercise 7.2

Code the following procedures. Do not assign diagnosis codes.

	Code(s)
1. Frozen-section examination of open biopsy of left breast mass followed by left radical mastectomy	85.45 85.12
2. Exploratory laparotomy with needle biopsy of pancreas	54.11 52.11
3. Open biopsy of nasal sinus	22.12
4. Needle biopsy of liver	50.11

Exercise 7.2 *(continued)*

5. Transurethral biopsy of bladder — 57.33

6. Percutaneous biopsy of prostate — 60.11

7. Endoscopic biopsy of bile duct — 51.14

CODING DIAGNOSIS-RELATED PROCEDURES

Certain procedures are performed only for very specific conditions; in these cases, care should be taken that the associated diagnosis code is also assigned. For example, a solitary kidney cannot be removed unless the patient has only a solitary kidney; therefore, the presence of this procedure code without a related diagnosis code would clearly be in error. Other examples include the following:

- Procedure: Repair of retinal detachment
  Diagnosis: Retinal detachment
- Procedure: Reduction of nasal fracture
  Diagnosis: Nasal fracture

CODING CANCELED PROCEDURES

Sometimes a decision to cancel a planned procedure is made after the patient has been admitted. In this case, a code from category V64, **Persons encountering health services for specific procedures not carried out,** is assigned to account for the cancellation; no procedure code is assigned. Without the canceled procedure code, the admission might be questioned in utilization or quality-of-care studies. Note that a code from category V64 cannot be assigned as the principal diagnosis. Planned surgery may be canceled for one of several reasons, including any of the following:

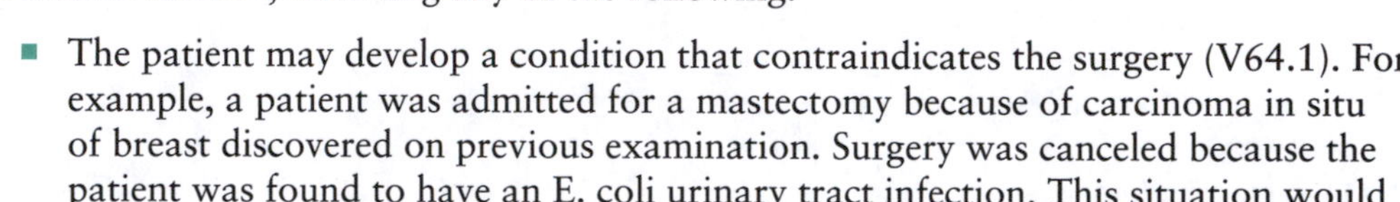

- The patient may develop a condition that contraindicates the surgery (V64.1). For example, a patient was admitted for a mastectomy because of carcinoma in situ of breast discovered on previous examination. Surgery was canceled because the patient was found to have an E. coli urinary tract infection. This situation would be coded as follows:
  Carcinoma in situ of breast 233.0
  Urinary tract infection 599.0
  due to E. coli 041.49
  Surgery canceled/contraindication V64.1
- The patient may decide not to have the planned surgery (V64.2). For example, a patient was admitted for a mastectomy because of carcinoma in situ discovered

previously. Before the procedure was begun, the patient decided to postpone the surgery in order to investigate other forms of treatment before proceeding with surgery. This situation would be coded as follows:

Carcinoma in situ of breast 233.0
Surgery canceled/patient decision V64.2

- Problems in scheduling, illness of key staff, or some other situation may necessitate the cancellation of scheduled surgery (V64.3). For example, a patient was admitted for a mastectomy because of carcinoma in situ previously discovered. Surgery was canceled because the anesthesiologist assigned to the case was involved in an auto accident and no other anesthesiologist was available. The patient was discharged, to be readmitted for the mastectomy three days later. This situation would be coded as follows:

  Carcinoma in situ of breast 233.0
  Surgery canceled/other reason V64.3

CODING INCOMPLETE PROCEDURES

Except for a code for the obstetrical procedure of failed forceps (73.3), the procedure classification makes no provision for indicating that a procedure has not been completed. When a planned procedure is begun but cannot be completed, it is coded to the extent to which it was actually performed according to the following principles:

- If incision only, code to incision of site.
- If endoscopic approach is unable to reach site, code endoscopy only.
- If cavity or space was entered, code to exploration of site.
- Code V64.x indicates that procedure codes are not completed as follows:

V64.00	Vaccination not carried out, unspecified reason
V64.01	Vaccination not carried out because of acute illness
V64.02	Vaccination not carried out because of chronic illness or condition
V64.03	Vaccination not carried out because of immune compromised state
V64.04	Vaccination not carried out because of allergy to vaccine or component
V64.05	Vaccination not carried out because of caregiver refusal
V64.06	Vaccination not carried out because of patient refusal
V64.07	Vaccination not carried out for religious reasons
V64.08	Vaccination not carried out because patient had disease being vaccinated against
V64.09	Vaccination not carried out for other reason
V64.1	Surgical or other procedure not carried out because of contraindication
V64.2	Surgical or other procedure not carried out because of patient decision
V64.3	Surgical or other procedure not carried out because of other reason

The following are examples of coding incomplete procedures:

- Patient was admitted for transurethral removal of ureteral stone. Scope was passed as far as the bladder, but the surgeon was unable to pass it into the ureter. Code the cystoscopy only.
- Patient was admitted for cholecystectomy with exploration of common duct. When the abdominal cavity was entered, extensive metastatic malignancy involving the stomach and duodenum with probable primary neoplasm in the pancreas was found. The procedure was discontinued, and the operative wound was closed. Assign only code **54.11, Exploratory laparotomy,** because that was the extent of the procedure actually performed.

- A patient was admitted for cholecystectomy. When the abdominal incision had been made, the patient suddenly developed an accelerating hypertension. Surgery was discontinued, the incision was closed, and the patient was returned to the nursing unit for care. Code only **54.0, Incision of the abdominal wall.**

When a procedure is considered to have "failed" in that it did not achieve the hoped-for result or because every objective of the procedure could not be accomplished, the procedure is coded as performed. For example, occasionally there is an almost immediate reocclusion of the coronary artery after the completion of a percutaneous coronary angioplasty, which makes it necessary to return to the operating room to perform a coronary artery bypass to correct the problem. The angioplasty might be described as a failed procedure, but, in fact, the procedure was performed and should be coded. Note that failure to achieve the therapeutic objective is not classified as a complication of the procedure.

CODING SHUNT PROCEDURES

Although shunt procedures are often identified by the name of the device (for example, Denver or LeVeen shunt), these devices are usually used for a variety of purposes. Codes are assigned on the basis of the therapeutic intent and the procedure involved rather than on the name of the shunt. Codes can be found in the index under the main terms Creation, Formation, or Shunt.

Ventriculoperitoneal shunts are inserted to drain cerebrospinal fluid to the peritoneal cavity when the normal cerebrospinal pathway is obstructed. When a procedure is described as a revision of a ventriculoperitoneal shunt, the coder must review the operative report to determine which portion of the shunt is involved. If only the peritoneal site is revised, code **54.95, Incision of the peritoneum,** is assigned. If the ventricular site is revised, code **02.42, Replacement of ventricular shunt,** is assigned. If both sites are involved in the revision, both codes should be assigned.

Sometimes, a ventriculoperitoneal shunt may undergo externalization because of recurrent infections. This procedure may be performed at bedside and involves incising the skin at the anterior chest wall. The shunt is externalized and connected to an external drainage system. Assign code **86.09, Other incision of skin and subcutaneous tissue,** for this type of procedure.

CODING STENT INSERTIONS

Intravascular stents are tubular metal implants designed to restore blood flow by reopening or enlarging a blood vessel and maintaining patency. Stents are also valuable in treating threatened or abrupt vessel closure, thus reducing the need for emergency surgery. Drug-eluting stents are a new type of stent created to address the common problem of vessel restenosis post stent insertion. Drug-eluting stent refers to a stent with an active drug (such as sirolimus, taxol, or paclitaxel) that is released in a controlled manner. Care must be taken to review the medical record documentation to determine the type of stent used. The insertion of conventional stents, drug-covered or drug-coated stents is assigned to **36.06, Insertion of coronary artery stent(s),** or **39.90, Insertion of non-drug-eluting peripheral vessel stent(s).** The insertion of drug-eluting stents is coded to **36.07, Insertion of drug-eluting coronary artery stent(s)** or **00.55, Insertion of drug-eluting stent(s) of other peripheral vessels.**

Coronary angioplasty performed by any technique is inherent in the placement of a coronary stent; the appropriate code for the angioplasty (00.66 or 36.03) is assigned with an additional code of 36.06 or 36.07 for the stent insertion. Code 39.90 or 00.55 is assigned for peripheral vessel stent insertion. Codes are provided for other intravascular stent insertions; for example, carotid artery (00.63), other extracranial arteries (00.64), and intracranial vessels (00.65).

Additional codes are used to provide information on the number of vessels treated (00.40–00.43) and the number of stents inserted (00.45–00.48) if multiple stents are inserted. These codes apply to both coronary and peripheral vessels. If the procedure involves a vessel bifurcation, code **00.44, Procedure on vessel bifurcation,** is used to identify the presence of a vessel bifurcation. Code 00.44 does not describe a specific bifurcation stent. This code may be used only once per operative episode regardless of the number of vessel bifurcations.

In addition to intravascular insertions, stents may also be inserted into other locations. For example, code 51.43 is assigned for insertion of a stent into a bile duct; if insertion is by endoscopy, code 51.87 is assigned. Code 51.98 is assigned for pancreatic transhepatic stent insertion. Code 46.87 is assigned for insertion of a colonic stent; if the insertion is performed via endoscopy, code 46.86 is assigned.

STEREOTACTIC RADIOSURGERY

Stereotactic radiosurgery is performed as a treatment for brain lesions and tumors such as acoustic neuroma, pituitary adenoma, and skull-based meningioma. It is also used for treating atriovenous malformations and has been used in the treatment of functional disorders such as Parkinson's disease, epilepsy, and intractable pain. Indications for treatment by this technique include lesions inaccessible to open surgery, medical contraindications for open surgery, elderly or very young patients, or recurrent lesions after open surgery or radiation therapy.

Treatment begins by taking the patient to the radiology department where a stereotactic head frame is placed to provide for target coordination determination. Code **93.59, Other immobilization, pressure, and attention to wound,** is assigned for placement of the head frame. Imaging studies such as CT or MRI scanning or angiography are then carried out. Computer imaging is used to develop an individual radiation dosage plan for the patient and identifying the precise location to be treated. When the imaging is complete, the patient is placed in the head frame and radiation is focused on the lesion. Subcategory **92.3, Stereotactic radiosurgery,** has been expanded by adding a fourth digit (92.30–92.39) that indicates the source of radiation.

COMPUTER ASSISTED SURGERY

Recent advances in technology have resulted in diagnostic and therapeutic procedures being performed with the assistance of computer technology. These may include computed tomography-free navigation and image-guided navigation, as well as imageless navigation. Computer assisted surgery (CAS) is an adjunctive surgical process using imaging, markers, reference frames, intraoperative sensing, and computer workstations. CAS is used to increase visualization and precise navigation with minimally invasive approaches. CAS planning involves creation of three-dimensional graphic models of the patient's anatomy. These models are then linked seamlessly to the surgical procedure through an intraoperative computer workstation.

Computer assisted surgeries are reported with the code for the specific diagnostic or therapeutic procedure performed, along with a code from subcategory 00.3, Computer assisted surgery [CAS]. Computer assisted surgery is classified on the basis of the different imaging modalities used, such as computed tomography (00.31), magnetic resonance (00.32), fluoroscopy (00.33), imageless computer-assisted surgery (00.34), multiple datasets (00.35), and other modalities (00.39).

ROBOTIC ASSISTED PROCEDURES

Robotic assisted surgery is the most recent development in minimally invasive surgery, whereby robotic tools allow surgeons to operate through small incisions using an endoscope. With robotic assistance, surgeons do not manipulate endoscopic tools with their hands. These procedures include the use of a computer console with 3-D imaging and instrumentation combined with the use of robotic arms, device(s), or system(s) at the time of the procedure. The surgeon sits at a console several feet from the operating table and uses joysticks (similar to those used in video games) to perform surgical tasks by guiding the robotic arms in a process known as telemanipulation.

Robotic assistance is classified on the basis of the approach used, such as open (17.41), laparoscopic (17.42), percutaneous (17.43), endoscopic (17.44), thoracoscopic (17.45), and other and unspecified (17.49). Examples of procedures performed with robotic assistance include prostatectomies, hysterectomies, and cholecystectomies.

Because these codes represent the use of robotic assistance but do not specify the actual surgical procedure performed, the code for the primary surgical procedure should be assigned first. For example, a total laparoscopic robotic assisted cholecystectomy would be coded as **51.23, Laparoscopic cholecystectomy,** followed by **17.42, Laparoscopic robotic assisted procedure.**

Note that although a computer console with 3-D imaging is used with robotic assisted surgery, it is not the same as computer assisted surgery (00.31–00.35, 00.39). Computer assisted surgery does not use robotic arms, devices, or other systems to perform surgical tasks (e.g., excision or resection).

Review Exercise 7.3

Code the following procedures. Do not assign diagnosis codes.

	Code(s)
1. Revision of peritoneal portion of ventriculoperitoneal shunt	54.95
2. Arthrotomy of right knee with excision of right medial meniscus and patellar shaving	80.6 77.66
3. Right frontal craniotomy with resection of osteoma of frontal bone	01.6
4. Dilation and curettage, uterus Cervical biopsies, punch Multiple vulvar biopsies	69.09 67.12 71.11

Review Exercise 7.3 *(continued)*

5. Atherectomy of iliac artery with injection of thrombolytic agent and stent insertion	17.56 99.10 39.90 00.40 00.45
6. Esophagoscopy with biopsy of esophagus	42.24
7. Submucous septectomy, nasal, and nasal septoplasty	21.5
8. Exploratory laparotomy Cholecystectomy Incidental appendectomy Intraoperative cholangiogram Common bile duct exploration with dilation of sphincter of Oddi	51.22 51.51 51.81 47.19 87.53
9. Laparoscopic appendectomy	47.01
10. Reclosure of operative wound of abdominal wall	54.61
11. Partial laparoscopic cholecystectomy	51.24
12. Craniotomy with plastic repair of encephalocele cranioplasty	02.12

Review Exercise 7.3 *(continued)*

13. Single-vessel percutaneous coronary angioplasty with use of thrombolytic agent and insertion of stent	00.66 36.06 00.40 00.45 99.10
14. Endoscopic insertion of stent in pancreatic duct	52.93
15. Removal of acoustic neuroma via Stereotactic Cobalt-60 radiosurgery Placement of head frame Computerized axial tomography of brain	92.32 93.59 87.03

Use of Supplementary Classifications

V and E Codes

CHAPTER **8**

CHAPTER OVERVIEW

- V codes and E codes follow the same format and conventions as the main classification.
- Certain V codes are used as principal diagnosis codes in specific situations.
- Aftercare management codes are generally listed first to explain the reasons for an encounter.
- V codes are used for continued care after the initial treatment of an injury or disease.
- V codes are also useful for coding admission for observation and evaluation and admission for palliative care.
- They are also used for special investigative examinations when no problem, diagnosis, or condition is identified and for screening examinations.
- V codes indicate personal history, family history, and genetic susceptibility to disease.

LEARNING OUTCOMES

After studying this chapter you should be able to:

- Locate V codes and E codes.
- Explain how and when V codes and E codes are used.

TERMS TO KNOW

Aftercare management
continued care during the healing phase or long-term care due to the consequences of a disease

E codes
codes for external causes of injury and poisoning

Palliative care
care focused on the management of pain and other symptoms of patients who are in the terminal phase of an illness

V codes
codes for factors influencing health status and contact with health services

REMEMBER . . . V and E codes are used throughout the classification.

INTRODUCTION

In addition to the main classification (001–999), two supplementary classifications are provided in *ICD-9-CM:*

- Factors influencing health status and contact with health service (V codes: V01–V91)
- External causes of injury and poisoning (E codes: E000–E999)

USING THE SUPPLEMENTARY CLASSIFICATIONS

Certain V codes are designated as the principal (or first-listed) diagnosis in specific situations; others are assigned as additional codes when it is important to indicate a history, status, or problem that may affect health care. Some V codes can be used as either the principal (or first-listed) diagnosis or as an additional code. E codes are assigned as additional codes to indicate the responsible medication for any condition described as an adverse effect of the correct use of a drug or other medicinal or biological substance. E codes are also used to report the external cause of an injury and the status (military or civilian status, for instance) of the person at the time the event occurred. E codes are also used to indicate the activity of the person seeking health care for an injury or health condition that resulted from the activity (a heart attack while shoveling snow, for example). Because V codes and E codes must be used throughout the classification, this chapter provides a general introduction to understanding such use before going on to other chapters in the handbook.

LOCATING V CODES AND E CODES

The format and conventions used throughout the main classification are also used in the indexes and tabular lists for these supplementary classifications. Index entries for V codes are included in the main Alphabetic Index (volume 2). These are the key main terms:

- Admission
- Examination
- History
- Observation
- Aftercare
- Problem
- Status

The Tabular List for V codes follows immediately after the final chapter of the main classification in volume 1.

E codes for poisoning and adverse effects of therapeutic drugs are located in the Table of Drugs and Chemicals in section 2 of volume 2. Names of drugs and other substances are listed alphabetically in the left-hand column of the table, with the E codes listed in the right-hand column arranged by intent of use. E codes that indicate the correct use of a prescribed drug are selected from the right-hand column labeled therapeutic use. Other E codes are assigned to indicate the external cause of injuries and poisoning. The use of E codes in this situation will be discussed in chapters 26–28.

V CODES

V codes are used as the principal (or first-listed) diagnosis in the following situations:

- To indicate that a person with a resolving disease or injury or a chronic condition is being seen for specific aftercare, such as the removal of orthopedic pins

- To indicate that the patient is seen for the sole purpose of special therapy, such as radiotherapy, chemotherapy, or dialysis
- To indicate that a person not currently ill is encountering the health service for a specific reason, such as to act as an organ donor, to receive prophylactic care, or to receive counseling
- To indicate the birth status of newborns

V codes are assigned as additional diagnosis codes in the following situations:

- To indicate that a patient has a history, health status, or other problem that is not in itself an illness or injury but may influence patient care. Note that the following V codes can be listed first if the fact of the history itself is the reason for admission or encounter:
  - V10.x Personal history of malignant neoplasm
  - V12.4 Personal history of disorders of nervous system and sense organs
  - V16–V19 Family history
- To indicate the outcome of delivery for obstetric patients

Admission or Encounter for Aftercare Management

Aftercare visit codes (V51–V58) are used when the initial treatment of a disease or injury has been completed but the patient requires continued care during the healing phase or for long-term consequences of the disease. The aftercare code is not assigned when treatment is directed at a current acute disease or injury. The exceptions to this rule are encounters for the sole purpose of dialysis (V56.x), chemotherapy (V58.11), immunotherapy (V58.12), or radiotherapy (V58.0). When the encounter is for the purpose of both radiotherapy and chemotherapy, both codes are assigned and either can be sequenced first. (Chapter 17 discusses the correct use of dialysis codes; chapter 25, chemotherapy codes.)

Admission for aftercare management ordinarily involves planned care, such as the fitting and adjustment of a prosthetic device (V52.x), attention to an artificial opening (V55.x), breast reconstruction following mastectomy (V51.0), or removal of an internal fixation device (V54.01). A code from category **V57, Care involving use of rehabilitation procedures,** is assigned as the principal diagnosis when the patient is admitted for the purpose of rehabilitation following previous illness or injury, with the fourth digit indicating the focus of treatment. An additional code is assigned for the residual condition requiring rehabilitation. No code for the original injury or illness that led to the disability is assigned.

Coding guidelines require that fracture codes be used only while the patient is receiving active treatment for the fracture and that subsequent encounters be reported with the use of an orthopedic aftercare code. Examples of active treatment are: surgical treatment, emergency department encounter, and evaluation and treatment by a new physician. Subcategories **V54.1, Aftercare for healing traumatic fracture,** and **V54.2, Aftercare for healing pathologic fracture,** are used to provide greater specificity in identifying the fracture site receiving routine care during the healing or recovery phase. Examples of fracture aftercare are: cast change or removal, removal of external or internal fixation device, medication adjustment, and follow-up visits following fracture treatment. These codes are particularly useful in the post acute care setting such as home health services.

There are also codes to report aftercare following surgery for neoplasms (V58.42), for injury and trauma (V58.43), following organ transplant (V58.44), and for surgery to specific body systems (V58.71–V58.78). These codes should be reported along with any other aftercare codes or other diagnosis codes to provide more detail regarding an aftercare visit.

Aftercare codes are generally listed first to explain the reason for the encounter. They can be used occasionally as additional codes when aftercare is provided during an encounter for treatment of an unrelated condition but no applicable diagnosis code is available (for example, the closure of a colostomy during an admission to treat an injury sustained in an automobile accident). Aftercare codes should be used in conjunction with any other aftercare or diagnosis code(s) to provide better detail on the specifics of an aftercare visit, unless otherwise directed by the classification. The sequencing of multiple aftercare codes is discretionary. When the patient is admitted because of a complication of previous care, the appropriate code from the main classification is assigned rather than the aftercare V code. (See chapter 29 of this handbook.)

Admission for Follow-Up Examination

A code from category V67 is assigned as the principal diagnosis or reason for encounter when a patient is admitted for the purpose of surveillance after the initial treatment of a disease or injury has been completed. For example:

- Examination following treatment of healed fracture   V67.4
- Examination following surgical excision of tumor followed by radiotherapy   V67.1

If a recurrence, extension, or related condition is identified, the code for that condition is assigned as the principal diagnosis rather than a code from category V67. For example:

- An asymptomatic patient who had a resection of the descending colon a year earlier is admitted for colonoscopy to evaluate the anastomosis and determine whether there is any recurrence of malignancy. Colonoscopy proved the anastomosis to be normal, and there was no evidence of cancer recurrence. In this case, code **V67.0, Follow-up examination, Following surgery,** is coded as the principal diagnosis, with an additional code of **V10.05, History of malignant neoplasm of large intestine,** and a code for the colonoscopy.
- An asymptomatic patient who had a resection of the descending colon a year earlier is admitted for colonoscopy to evaluate the anastomosis and determine whether there is any recurrence of malignancy. Colonoscopy showed the anastomosis to be normal, and there was no evidence of cancer recurrence. A polyp was found distal to the anastomosis, however, and it was removed; pathology examination showed it to be benign. Code **211.3, Benign polyp of colon,** is assigned as the principal diagnosis, with code **V10.05, History of malignant neoplasm, large intestine,** assigned as an additional code. In this case, no code from category V67 is assigned because a related condition was identified.
- A patient who had a colon resection for removal of carcinoma of the descending colon one year ago is now seen for follow-up examination to evaluate the anastomosis and determine whether there is any recurrence of disease. Colonoscopy showed normal anastomosis but revealed a recurrence of cancer at the primary site. Code **153.2, Malignant neoplasm of descending colon,** is assigned as the principal diagnosis. No code from category V67 is assigned.
- A patient who had surgical excision of a malignant neoplasm of the ovary one year ago, followed by chemotherapy, is admitted for follow-up examination. There is no evidence of recurrence or metastasis, and no other pathologic condition was identified. Code **V67.2, Follow-up examination following chemotherapy,** is assigned along with a code of V10.43 to indicate the history of ovarian cancer as the reason for the examination.
- A patient who had benign polyps of the colon removed one year ago is now complaining of pain in the left lower abdomen. A colonoscopy performed to determine whether there is any recurrence of colon polyps proved to be entirely normal. In this case, code **789.04, Abdominal pain, left lower quadrant,** is assigned rather than a code from category V67 because the abdominal pain was the reason for the admission.

Code **V67.51, Follow-up examination following treatment with high-risk medication, not elsewhere classified,** is assigned as the reason for encounter only when the patient is no longer on the medication.

Codes from subcategory V58.6 are assigned when the patient is currently receiving long-term anticoagulant therapy (V58.61), antibiotic therapy (V58.62), antiplatelets/antithrombotics (V58.63), nonsteroidal anti-inflammatories (V58.64), steroids (V58.65), aspirin (V58.66), insulin (V58.67), biphosphonates (V58.68), or long-term therapy for other high-risk medications that require continued monitoring and evaluation. Codes from subcategory V58.6 are assigned if the patient is receiving a medication for an extended period. For example:

- As a prophylactic measure (e.g., to prevent deep venous thrombosis)
- As treatment of a chronic condition (e.g., arthritis)
- For a disease requiring a lengthy course of treatment (e.g., cancer)

An additional code is assigned for the condition for which the medication is prescribed. Do not assign a code from subcategory V58.6 when the medication is to treat an acute illness or injury and is being given for a brief period of time (e.g., antibiotics to treat bronchitis). This subcategory is not used when medications are given for detoxification or as a maintenance program used to prevent withdrawal symptoms in patients with drug dependence. For example, long-term use of methadone for pain management would be coded with V58.69, but the use of methadone in a maintenance program to prevent withdrawal symptoms would be coded using the drug dependence code.

Code V58.83 is used to report encounters for therapeutic drug monitoring. If the drug being monitored is one that the patient has been receiving on a long-term basis, a code from subcategory V58.6 should be added. Coding guidelines do not provide a definition or time frame for long-term drug therapy. If a patient receives a drug on a regular basis and has multiple refills available for a prescription, then it is appropriate to document long-term drug use. Documentation of long-term drug use is at the discretion of the health care provider.

Admission for Observation and Evaluation

A code from category **V71, Observation and evaluation for suspected conditions not found,** is assigned when inconclusive symptoms, signs, or other evidence of disturbed physiology warrant clinical observation and evaluation but neither the suspected condition nor an alternative is identified, and no additional evaluation or treatment appears to be required at the current level of care. Outpatient referral for surveillance or for further diagnostic studies does not contradict the use of a code from this category. When a related diagnosis is established, the code for that condition is assigned instead of a code from category V71. Codes from category V29 are used for observation of a newborn. (See chapter 23 of this handbook.)

A code from category V71 can be assigned only as the principal diagnosis or reason for encounter, never as a secondary diagnosis. A code from category V71 is ordinarily assigned as a solo code, with two exceptions:

- When a chronic condition requires care or monitoring during the stay, a code for that condition can be assigned as an additional code. Codes for chronic conditions that do not affect the stay are not assigned.
- When admission is for the purpose of ruling out a serious injury, such as concussion, codes for minor injuries such as abrasions or contusions may be assigned as additional codes. This exception is based on the fact that such minor injuries in themselves would not require hospitalization.

The following examples may help the coder to better understand the use of category V71:

- A physician, family member, or law enforcement representative refers the patient for evaluation of a suspected mental disorder. None is found, and no other condition is identified. Code **V71.09, Observation for suspected mental condition,** is assigned.

- A patient is seen in the emergency department because of alleged rape. Observation and examination reveal no physical findings, such as hemorrhage or laceration. Code **V71.5, Observation following alleged rape or seduction,** is assigned as the principal diagnosis. Code V71.5 covers the collection of specimens, advice given for prophylaxis of pregnancy, and any other provision of counseling services. When physical findings suggest that a rape has occurred, code V71.5 is not assigned; the condition identified is coded and designated as the principal diagnosis. Rape is not a medical diagnosis but a matter of jurisprudence.
- The patient presents with generalized complaints involving nonspecific abdominal pain, minimal weight loss, and change of bowel habits. Because of a strong family history of colon cancer, the patient is admitted for evaluation for suspected malignancy. The presence of a neoplasm is ruled out, and no alternative diagnosis is made; it seems obvious that the symptoms reported are largely subjective. Code **V71.1, Observation for suspected malignant neoplasm,** is assigned with an additional code of **V16.0, Family history of malignant neoplasm of gastrointestinal tract.**

Note that a code from category V71 is not assigned when a patient is admitted to the observation unit of the hospital immediately following same-day (outpatient) surgery, even though the medical record may suggest that the admission is for observation. Hospitals are advised to contact their individual payers to obtain billing instructions on whether a single claim or separate claims should be submitted. If a single bill is submitted to a payer, code the reason for the surgery as the first reported diagnosis (reason for the encounter). If the patient develops complications during the outpatient encounter, including during the observation stay, code these complications as secondary diagnoses. Continue to report the reason for the surgery as the reason for the overall encounter. Additional codes are assigned for the procedures performed. However, if separate bills are submitted, then this advice would not apply. Hospitals should apply codes for the current encounter based on individual payer billing instructions.

For example:

- A patient is admitted following outpatient surgery for a unilateral direct inguinal hernia repair for "continued observation." Review of the medical record indicates that the patient was admitted to observation because he was experiencing severe nausea and vomiting.

  If a single claim is submitted: Code **550.90, Inguinal hernia, without mention of obstruction or gangrene, unilateral or unspecified (not specified as recurrent),** is assigned as the first-listed diagnosis, not a code from category V71. In addition, code **787.01, Nausea with vomiting,** is assigned as the secondary diagnosis, and code **53.01, Repair of direct inguinal hernia,** for the procedure.

  If separate bills are submitted: For the outpatient surgery bill, assign code **550.90, Inguinal hernia, without mention of obstruction or gangrene, unilateral or unspecified (not specified as recurrent),** as the first-listed diagnosis, along with the appropriate HCPCS code for the surgical procedure. For the observation bill, assign code **787.01, Nausea with vomiting,** as the first-listed diagnosis, not a code from category V71.

Category V89, Other suspected conditions not found, is another category of observation codes. Codes from subcategory V89.0, Suspected maternal and fetal conditions not found, may either be used as a first-listed or as an additional code assignment depending on the case. These codes should be used in very limited circumstances on a maternal record when an encounter is for a suspected maternal or fetal condition that is ruled out during that encounter. For example, a maternal or fetal condition may be suspected due to an abnormal test result, but the condition is not confirmed. If the condition is confirmed, code the condition instead of a code from subcategory V89.0. In addition, these codes are not for use if an illness or any signs or symptoms related to the suspected condition or problem are present. In such cases the diagnosis/symptom code is used. Other codes may be used in addition to the code from subcategory V89.0, but only if they are unrelated to the suspected condition being evaluated.

If a patient is admitted after a period in the outpatient observation unit for further evaluation unrelated to surgery, the principal diagnosis is the condition that provided the original reason for the outpatient observation. If a patient is admitted to an observation unit for a medical condition, and the medical condition worsens or does not improve, it may be necessary for the patient to be admitted to the hospital as an inpatient. In this case, the medical condition that led to the hospital admission would be the principal diagnosis.

Admission for Palliative Care

Palliative care is an alternative to aggressive treatment for patients who are in the terminal phase of an illness. Care is focused on the management of pain and other symptoms of the disease, which is often more appropriate than aggressive care when a patient is dying of an incurable illness. Code **V66.7, Encounter for palliative care,** is used to classify admissions or encounters for comfort care, end-of-life care, hospice care, and care for terminally ill patients. It may be used in any health care setting. It cannot be used as the principal diagnosis or reason for encounter; instead, the code for the underlying disease is sequenced first.

Special Investigations and Examinations

When a patient receives only diagnostic services during an episode of care, a code for the condition or problem that was chiefly responsible for the encounter is assigned first. A code from category **V72, Special investigative examinations,** is assigned as the reason for encounter only when no problem, diagnosis, or condition is identified as the reason for the examination. Codes from category V72 are rarely appropriate for inpatient coding and are never assigned as additional codes. For example:

- A patient is referred to the radiology department for a chest X-ray, with the reason for the examination identified as cough and fever, which may rule out pneumonia. The radiologist's report indicates that the X-ray is normal. The code for the cough (786.2) or the fever (780.60) is listed as the reason for the encounter. A code for pneumonia is not assigned; neither is a code from category V72.
- A patient is referred to the radiology department for a chest X-ray with the reason for the examination identified as cough and fever, rule out pneumonia. The radiologist's report confirms a diagnosis of bronchopneumonia. Code **485, Bronchopneumonia, organism unspecified,** is listed as the reason for the visit. Codes are not assigned for the cough or fever because these symptoms are implicit in the diagnosis of bronchopneumonia. No code from category V72 is assigned.
- A patient is referred to the clinical laboratory for blood work, with the reason for the examination identified as vertigo with possibly the need to rule out hypothyroidism. Code **780.4, Dizziness and giddiness,** is assigned as the reason for the visit. A code for hypothyroidism is not assigned because hypothyroidism is not an established diagnosis. Code **V72.69, Other laboratory examination,** is not assigned.
- A patient is referred to the radiology department for a chest X-ray as part of a routine physical examination. Code **V72.5, Radiological examination, not elsewhere classified,** is listed as the reason for the encounter because there are no presenting symptoms and the X-ray was not performed to rule out any suspected disease.

Patients are often referred to hospital ancillary services for preoperative evaluations that involve a variety of tests performed in various departments. Patients may also be referred for preoperative blood typing. In this situation, one of the following codes is assigned, with additional codes for the condition for which surgery is planned and for any findings related to the preoperative evaluation:

- V72.81 Preoperative cardiovascular examination
- V72.82 Preoperative respiratory examination
- V72.83 Other specified preoperative examination
- V72.84 Preoperative examination, unspecified
- V72.86 Encounter for blood typing

For example:

- A patient with the diagnosis of cholelithiasis was referred to the radiology department for a preoperative chest X-ray. Code **V72.83, Other specified preoperative examination,** should be listed as the reason for the encounter, with an additional code for the cholelithiasis. Note that a preoperative chest X-ray is coded to V72.83, not V72.82, because the physician is not looking only at the lungs but also at the heart, bronchus, and other structures in the patient's chest.

Screening Examinations

Codes from categories V73 through V82, Special screening examinations, are assigned to tests performed to identify a disease or disease precursors for the purpose of early detection and treatment for those who test positive. Screening is performed on apparently well individuals who present no signs or symptoms relative to the disease. Many V codes have been expanded to provide more specificity. For example, a screening mammogram may be performed because the patient falls into one of several high-risk categories, as stated by the physician (V76.11). However, if the physician has not documented that there is a high risk, code V76.12 would be used. If a screening examination identifies pathology, the code for the reason for the test (namely the screening code from categories V73 through V82) is assigned as the principal diagnosis or first-listed code followed by a code for the pathology or condition found during the screening exam. For example:

- A patient underwent routine mammography, which revealed no pathology. Code **V76.12, Other screening, mammogram,** is assigned.
- An asymptomatic patient undergoes a screening mammography. The radiologist reports the presence of microcalcifications. Assign code **V76.12, Other screening mammogram,** followed by code **793.81, Mammographic microcalcification.**
- A patient with a family history of breast cancer in her mother, aunt, and older sister presents for a screening mammogram because she is considered at high risk for the disease (V76.11, V16.3).

Codes Representing Patient History, Status, or Problems

Codes from categories V10 through V15 are used to indicate a personal history of a previous condition. When the condition mentioned is still present or still under treatment, or if a complication is present, a code from the series V10 through V15 is not assigned. Categories V16 through V19 indicate a family history and may be assigned when the family history is the reason for examination or treatment.

Status codes indicate that a patient is a carrier of a disease, has the sequelae or residual of a past disease or condition, or has another factor influencing health status. Categories V40 through V49 indicate that the patient has a continuing condition or health status that may influence care, such as the fact that a tracheostomy (V44.0), colostomy (V44.3), cardiac pacemaker (V45.01), or aortocoronary bypass graft (V45.81) is in place. V codes indicating status are redundant when the diagnosis code itself indicates that the status exists. For example, in the case of an acute rejection crisis of a transplanted kidney, Code **996.81, Complications of transplanted organ, kidney,** is used. As the patient's transplant status is implicit in that diagnosis, an additional Code V42.0, indicating kidney-transplant status, is not meaningful and should not be assigned.

A diagnostic statement expressed as "status post" most often refers to an earlier surgery, injury, or previous illness and usually has no significance for the episode of care. No code for the condition is assigned in this case. A personal history code can be assigned if desired. Note the important distinction between history and status codes. History codes indicate that the problem no longer exists. Status codes indicate that the condition is present.

Codes from categories V60 through V63 are used to indicate certain problems that may affect the patient's care or prevent satisfactory compliance with the recommended regimen. Housing problems, social maladjustment, and economic or job concerns are examples of situations that can affect a patient's compliance.

History, status, and problem codes ordinarily cannot be used as the principal diagnosis or reason for encounter with the following exceptions:

- Codes from categories V10 and V12–V13 (except V13.4, V13.61–V13.69, and V13.9)
- Code V15.88
- Codes from categories V16–V19

These codes can be used when the history is the reason for admission or encounter. They can be used as additional codes for any patient regardless of the reason for the encounter, but they are ordinarily assigned only when the history, status, or problem has some significance for the episode of care. For example, a history of previously treated carcinoma or a family history of malignant neoplasm may be useful in explaining why certain tests are performed. Status code V43.6x indicates that the patient has had a joint replacement, but this fact would probably be significant only if it limits the patient's movement to the extent that additional nursing care is required or when it prevents full participation in a rehabilitation program.

Genetic Susceptibility to Disease

Codes from category V84 are used to report genetic susceptibility to disease. Genetic susceptibility refers to a genetic predisposition for contracting a disease. Patients with a genetic susceptibility to disease may request prophylactic removal of an organ to prevent the disease from occurring. It is important to distinguish susceptibility from carrier state. An individual who is a carrier of a disease is able to pass it on to an offspring. Subcategory V84.0, Genetic susceptibility to malignant neoplasm, is further subdivided to identify the potential body site, such as breast (V84.01), ovary (V84.02), prostate (V84.03), endometrium (V84.04), endocrine glands (V84.05), and other (V84.09).

Codes from category V84 should not be used as principal or first-listed codes. Sequencing of category V84 codes would depend on the circumstances of the encounter as follows:

- If the patient has the condition to which he/she is susceptible, and that condition is the reason for the encounter, the code for the current condition is sequenced first, followed by the V84 code.
- If the patient is being seen for follow-up after completed treatment for this condition, and the condition no longer exists, a follow-up code should be sequenced first, followed by the appropriate personal history (V10.x–V13.x) and genetic susceptibility codes (V84.x).
- If the purpose of the encounter is genetic counseling associated with procreative management, assign first a code from subcategory V26.3, Genetic counseling and testing, followed by a code from category V84.

V Codes as Principal/First-Listed Diagnosis

V codes may be assigned as the principal or first-listed diagnosis or as secondary diagnoses. The *ICD-9-CM Official Guidelines for Coding and Reporting* contain a list of V codes that may only be a principal/first-listed diagnosis. V codes on that list may only be reported as the principal/first-listed diagnosis, except for cases in which there are multiple encounters on the same day and the medical records for the encounters are combined, or when there is more than one V code that meets the definition of principal diagnosis (e.g., a patient is admitted to home health care for aftercare and rehabilitation, and both equally meet the definition of principal diagnosis). These codes should not be reported if they do not meet the definition of principal or first-listed diagnosis.

Review Exercise 8.1

Code the following diagnoses.

	Code(s)
1. Visit to change surgical dressing	V58.31
2. Family history of polyps of the colon	V18.51
3. Status post aortocoronary bypass procedure	V45.81
4. Encounter for occupational therapy rehabilitation	V57.21
5. Adjustment of cardiac pacemaker	V53.31
6. Long-term use of anticoagulant therapy	V58.61
7. Encounter for weaning from respirator	V46.13
8. Aftercare for healing traumatic fracture of arm	V54.10
9. Screening mammogram, high-risk patient	V76.11
10. Encounter for radiation therapy	V58.0

Coding of Signs and Symptoms

Symptoms, Signs, and Ill-Defined Conditions

CHAPTER **9**

CHAPTER OVERVIEW

- Symptoms and signs are classified to chapter 16 if they point to multiple diseases or systems or if they are of an unexplained etiology.
- There are few situations in which a symptom code from chapter 16 is used as a principal diagnosis.
- Conversely, for outpatients, the symptom code is often used as the reason for the encounter.
- Codes from chapter 16 are assigned as secondary only when the sign or symptom is not integral to a condition.
- The codes for nonspecific abnormal findings are rarely appropriate for use in an inpatient setting.

LEARNING OUTCOMES

After studying this chapter you should be able to:

- Explain the difference between a sign and a symptom.
- Determine when to properly use a code from chapter 16 of the *ICD-9-CM* for a principal diagnosis.
- Determine when to properly use a code from chapter 16 for an additional diagnosis.

TERMS TO KNOW

Sign
objective evidence of disease observed by the examining physician

Symptom
subjective observation reported by the patient

REMEMBER . . . In an inpatient situation, there are often more appropriate options than the codes found in chapter 16 of the *ICD-9-CM.*
. . . For inpatients, a diagnosis described as possible, probable, and so on is considered to be an established diagnosis.

INTRODUCTION

A sign is defined as objective evidence of disease that can be observed by the examining physician. A symptom, on the other hand, is a subjective observation reported by the patient but not confirmed objectively by the physician.

Symptoms and signs are classified in two ways in *ICD-9-CM*. Those that are indicative of a condition that ordinarily affects only one body system are classified to the relevant chapter of *ICD-9-CM*. Those that can point to more than one disease or system, or that are of unexplained etiology, are classified to chapter 16 of *ICD-9-CM*.

SIGNS AND SYMPTOMS AS PRINCIPAL DIAGNOSES

Codes for symptoms, signs, and ill-defined conditions from chapter 16 of *ICD-9-CM* cannot be used as principal diagnoses or reasons for outpatient encounters when related diagnoses have been established. For example:

- Coma due to poisoning by heroin 965.01 + 780.01 + E980.0
- Syncope due to third-degree atrioventricular block 426.0 + 780.2

If the patient is an inpatient, a diagnosis described as possible, probable, and so on at the time of discharge is considered to be an established diagnosis. For example, a patient is admitted with severe generalized abdominal pain. The physician's diagnostic statement is abdominal pain, probably due to acute gastritis (535.00). Only the code for the gastritis is assigned, as the abdominal pain is integral to the probable gastritis. The words such as possible, probable, and so on are not considered to be established for outpatient visits or encounters. If there is not an established diagnosis, only whatever symptoms or signs that are available at the highest level of certainty are assigned.

There are only a few situations in which a symptom code from chapter 16 can be correctly designated the principal diagnosis:

1. When the diagnostic statement lists the symptom first, followed by two or more contrasting/comparative conditions. In this case a symptom code may be assigned as the principal diagnosis. More detail was offered in chapter 3 of this handbook.
2. When no related condition is identified and the symptom is the reason for the encounter, a code from chapter 16 of *ICD-9-CM* is assigned as the principal diagnosis even though other unrelated diagnoses may be listed. For example: A patient was admitted with tachycardia. An EKG did not provide any conclusive evidence of the type of tachycardia or of any underlying cardiac condition. The patient is also an insulin-dependent diabetic; blood sugars were monitored daily during the hospital stay. The reason for admission was tachycardia; therefore; code **785.0, Tachycardia** is the principal diagnosis. Because the diabetes was treated during the hospital stay, an additional code was assigned for the diabetes mellitus.
3. This guideline does not apply if the diagnosis is stated as a symptom due to two conditions rather than as two contrasting diagnoses. In this case, both conditions would be coded, and the symptom code would be assigned as an additional code only if it met criteria for the reporting of additional diagnoses. For example, if a diagnosis was stated as chest pain due to costochondritis and possible hiatal hernia, both the costochondritis and the hiatal hernia would be coded according to the guideline governing coding of contrasting/comparative conditions. No code for chest pain would be assigned because it is integral to both diagnoses.

4. Other situations in which codes from chapter 16 of the *ICD-9-CM* manual can be appropriately used as the principal diagnosis for an inpatient admission include the following:
   - Presenting signs or symptoms are transient, and no definitive diagnosis can be made.
   - The patient is referred elsewhere for further study or treatment before a diagnosis is made.
   - A more precise diagnosis cannot be made for any other reason.
   - The symptom is treated in an outpatient setting without the additional workup required to arrive at a more definitive diagnosis.
   - Provisional diagnosis of a sign or symptom is made for a patient who fails to return for further investigation or care.
   - A residual late effect is the reason for admission, and the Alphabetic Index directs the coder to an alternative sequencing.

Generally speaking, symptom codes classified to other chapters are not designated as principal diagnoses when a related condition has been identified. The symptom can be designated as principal diagnosis, however, when the patient is admitted for the sole purpose of treating the symptom and there is no treatment or further evaluation of the underlying disease. For example, patients with dehydration secondary to gastroenteritis are sometimes admitted for the purpose of rehydration when the gastroenteritis itself could be managed on an outpatient basis. In this case, the code for the dehydration can be designated as the principal diagnosis even though the cause of the dehydration is stated.

Note that these guidelines do not apply when coding and reporting hospital outpatient care or physician services. Outpatient encounters do not ordinarily permit the type of study that results in an established diagnosis, and treatment is often directed at relieving symptoms rather than treating the underlying condition. The highest level of certainty is reported as the reason for encounter for outpatients. This often means that a symptom code is assigned as the reason for the encounter.

SIGNS AND SYMPTOMS AS ADDITIONAL DIAGNOSES

Codes from chapter 16 are assigned as secondary codes only when the symptom or sign is not integral to the underlying condition (unless otherwise instructed by the classification) and when its presence makes a difference in the severity of the patient's condition and/or the care given. For example, many but not all patients with cirrhosis of the liver have ascites. When ascites is present, it makes a difference in the care given, and so the chapter 16 code for ascites (789.59) should be assigned as an additional code. Codes from chapter 16 are not assigned when they are implicit in the diagnosis or when the symptom is included in the condition code. Such redundant coding is inappropriate. For example:

- Abdominal pain due to gastric ulcer: No symptom code is assigned to the abdominal pain because it is integral to the ulcer.
- Coma due to diabetes mellitus: The symptom code for coma is not assigned because combination codes are provided for diabetes with associated coma.
- Patient admitted with chest pain, initially thought to be angina: Diagnostic studies did not support this and the physician's diagnosis is chest pain, probable costochondritis (733.6). The chest pain is not coded because it is implicit in the costochondritis.

ABNORMAL FINDINGS

Although categories 790 through 796 in chapter 16 are provided for coding nonspecific abnormal findings, it is rarely appropriate to assign one of these codes for acute inpatient hospital care. They are assigned only when (1) the physician has not been able to arrive at a definitive related diagnosis and lists the abnormal finding itself as a diagnosis and (2) the condition meets the Uniform Hospital Discharge Data Set (UHDDS) criteria for reporting of other diagnoses.

For example, if the physician lists a diagnosis of abnormal electrocardiographic findings without any mention of associated disease, assigning code **794.31, Abnormal electrocardiogram** (ECG) (**EKG**) would be appropriate if there was evidence of further evaluation for a possible cardiac condition. On the other hand, a coder might note an elevated blood pressure reading in the medical record, but the physician has not listed it as a diagnosis and there is no evidence of any follow-up or treatment. In this situation, assigning a code for this abnormal finding would be inappropriate.

If the coder notes clinical findings outside the normal range but no related diagnosis is stated, the coder should review the medical record to determine whether additional tests and/or consultations were carried out related to these findings or whether specific related care was given. If such documentation is present, it is appropriate to ask the physician whether a code should be assigned.

For example, a patient with a low potassium level treated with oral or intravenous potassium has a clinically significant condition that probably should be reported; the physician should be asked whether a diagnosis should be added. On the other hand, a finding of degenerative arthritis on a routine postoperative chest X-ray of an elderly patient when no treatment or further diagnostic evaluation has been carried out would not warrant a code assignment.

ILL-DEFINED CONDITIONS

The final section of chapter 16 of *ICD-9-CM* contains codes for ill-defined conditions or unknown causes of morbidity and mortality, such as senility without psychosis, asphyxia, nervousness, and sudden unexplained death. These codes should never be used when a more definitive diagnosis is available.

Review Exercise 9.1

Code the following diagnoses and procedures as statements given at the time of discharge. Do not assign E codes.

	Code(s)
1. Dysuria	788.1
Transurethral biopsy of bladder	57.33

Review Exercise 9.1 *(continued)*

2. Acute chest pain due to influenzal pleurisy	487.1
3. Gross, painless hematuria, cause undetermined	599.71
Intravenous pyelogram	57.93
Cystoscopy with control of bladder hemorrhage	87.73
4. Pyuria, intermittent, cause undetermined	791.9
5. Hyperplastic lymph node, left axilla	785.6
Biopsy, axillary lymph node	40.11
6. Elevated glucose tolerance test	790.22
7. Severe vertigo, left temporal headache, and nausea	780.4 784.0 787.02
8. Syncope, cause undetermined	780.2
9. Chest pain, probably angina pectoris	413.9

Review Exercise 9.1 *(continued)*

10. Psychogenic dysuria	306.53
11. Arteriosclerotic gangrene, left foot	440.24
12. Chronic epistaxis, severe, recurrent	784.7
Anterior and posterior nasal packing	21.02
13. Severe epistaxis due to hypertension	401.9 784.7
Nasal packing	21.01
14. Hereditary epistaxis	448.0
15. Generalized abdominal pain due to pancreatitis versus cholecystitis	789.07 577.0 575.10
16. Chronic fatigue syndrome	780.71

Coding of Infectious and Parasitic Diseases, Endocrine Diseases and Immunity Disorders, and Mental Disorders

Infectious and Parasitic Diseases

CHAPTER **10**

CHAPTER OVERVIEW

- Chapter 1 of the *ICD-9-CM* includes information on how to code infectious or parasitic diseases.
  - — The primary axis of chapter 1 is the organism responsible for the disease.
  - — When the main term for the condition is located, specific subterms always take precedence over general subterms.
- This chapter has information on coding specific infectious and parasitic diseases, including: tuberculosis, SARS, West Nile Virus, bacteremia, septicemia, SIRS, sepsis, toxic shock syndrome, and gram-negative bacterial infections.
- There is also detailed information on all aspects of HIV/AIDS coding procedures.

LEARNING OUTCOMES

After studying this chapter you should be able to:

- Code infectious and parasitic diseases.
- Assign a fifth-digit classification for tuberculosis codes.
- Explain the difference between, and be able to code properly, bacteremia, septicemia, SIRS, sepsis, and septic shock.
- Explain how to code for HIV testing, diagnosis, and treatment.

TERMS TO KNOW

Bacteremia
presence of bacteria in the bloodstream after a trauma or infection

Sepsis
SIRS due to infection; a severe case indicates organ dysfunction

Septicemia
a systemic disease associated with pathological microorganisms or toxins in the bloodstream

Septic shock
circulatory failure associated with severe sepsis

SIRS
systemic inflammatory response syndrome; a systemic response to infection or trauma with such symptoms as fever and tachycardia

REMEMBER . . . Codes from chapter 1 of *ICD-9-CM* take precedence over codes from other chapters for the same condition.

. . . Coding for HIV/AIDS is not allowed unless the diagnostic statement reports the diagnosis with absolute certainty.

INTRODUCTION

Chapter 1 of *ICD-9-CM* classifies infectious and parasitic diseases that are easily transmissible (communicable). The primary axis for this chapter is the organism responsible for the condition. Infectious and parasitic conditions are classified in one of several ways, making careful use of the index imperative. For example:

- A single code from chapter 1 is assigned to indicate the organism. For example, code 072.x is assigned for mumps. Some codes of this type use a fourth digit to indicate a site or an associated condition. For example, code 112.4 is assigned for Candidiasis of the lung.
- Combination codes frequently identify both the condition and the organism. For example:
  —Pneumonia due to *Staphylococcus aureus* 482.41
  —Orchitis due to mumps 072.0

Dual classification is also used extensively for chapter 1. For example:

- Meningitis due to actinomycosis 039.8 + 320.7
- Pneumonia in whooping cough (Bordetella pertussis) 033.0 + 484.3

Codes from chapter 1 take precedence over codes from other chapters for the same condition. For example, urinary tract infection due to candidiasis is classified to code **112.2, Candidiasis of other urogenital sites,** rather than to code **599.0, Urinary tract infection, unspecified site.** Conditions that are not considered to be easily transmissible or communicable are classified in the appropriate body-system chapter with an additional code from category 041 or 079 to assign to indicate the responsible organism. For example, codes **601.0, Acute prostatitis, and 041.01, *Streptococcus,* group A,** are assigned for acute prostatitis due to group A Streptococcus.

ORGANISM VERSUS SITE OR OTHER SUBTERM

A thorough index search is required in coding infection. When the main term for the condition has been located, a subterm for the organism always takes precedence over a more general subterm (such as "acute" or "chronic") when both subterms occur at the same indention level in the Alphabetic Index. For example, for a diagnosis of chronic cystitis due to Monilia, the Alphabetic Index provides subterms for both chronic and monilial:

Cystitis (bacillary) . . .
  chronic 595.2 . . .
  monilial 112.2

In this case, only code 112.2 is assigned because the subterm for the organism takes precedence over the subterm "chronic."

When the organism is specified but is not indexed under the main term for the condition, the coder should refer to the main term **Infection** or to the main term for the organism. For example, consider a diagnosis of cryptococcal cystitis. No subterm for cryptococcal is located under the main term **Cystitis,** but there is a main term entry **Infection,** followed by a subterm for Cryptococcus as well as a main term **Cryptococcus.** Code 117.5 is therefore assigned for this diagnosis rather than the code for cystitis.

SEVERE ACUTE RESPIRATORY SYNDROME (SARS)

There are specific codes provided for severe acute respiratory syndrome (SARS). This is a respiratory illness caused by a new, previously unrecognized coronavirus. SARS begins with a fever and may include chills, headache, and malaise. In some patients, there are also mild respiratory symptoms, dry cough, and trouble breathing. The codes are as follows:

- Contact with or exposure to SARS-associated coronavirus V01.82
- SARS-associated coronavirus infection 079.82
- Pneumonia due to SARS-associated coronavirus 480.3

WEST NILE VIRUS FEVER

Category 066.4 is used to report West Nile fever. The virus is transmitted to humans by the bite of a mosquito that has bitten an infected bird. Most healthy people infected by the virus have few symptoms or have a mild illness consisting of fever, headache, and body aches prior to recovering. In elderly patients or those with a weakened immune system, the virus may cause encephalitis, meningitis, or permanent neurological damage and be life threatening. Category 066.4 has been expanded to distinguish between West Nile Fever unspecified (066.40), with encephalitis (066.41), with other neurologic manifestation (066.42), and with other complications (066.49). This expansion will allow differentiation between the milder cases of the disease and those with more serious complications and neurological manifestations.

LATE EFFECTS

Chapter 1 provides three late effect codes for use when there is a residual condition due to previous infection or parasitic infestation:

- Late effects of tuberculosis 137
- Late effects of acute poliomyelitis 138
- Late effects of other infectious and parasitic diseases 139

As discussed earlier, the code for the residual effect is sequenced first, followed by the appropriate late effect code, except in a few instances where the Alphabetic Index instructs otherwise. A code for the infection itself is not assigned because it is no longer present. For example:

- Brain damage resulting from previous viral encephalitis (three years ago) 348.9 + 139.0
- Scoliosis due to poliomyelitis 138 + 737.43

TUBERCULOSIS

Tuberculosis is classified to categories 010 through 018, with the primary axis the site or type of tuberculosis. A fifth-digit subclassification is provided to indicate the method by which the diagnosis was determined. The fifth digit 1 should be used only when there is a specific statement in the record that no histological or bacteriological examination was performed. Fifth digit 2 indicates that an examination was performed but the method was unknown. The remaining fifth digits 3, 4, 5, and 6 identify various methods for establishing a diagnosis of tuberculosis. The use of these fifth digits is more germane to coding outpatient diagnostic workups; such information is generally present in outpatient records but is often not documented in inpatient records. Fifth digit 0, unspecified, should be assigned when the information is not available in the medical record. Two examples of fifth-digit subclassification for tuberculosis follow:

- Tuberculosis of lung, with capitation (bacilli by microscopy) 011.23
- Tuberculosis of hip (confirmed histological) 015.15

Care should be taken to differentiate between a diagnosis of tuberculosis and a positive tuberculin skin test without a diagnosis of active tuberculosis. Code 795.51 classifies the following:

- Nonspecific reaction to tuberculin skin test without active tuberculosis
- Positive tuberculin skin test without active tuberculosis
- Positive PPD
- Abnormal result of Mantoux test

BACTEREMIA, SEPTICEMIA, SIRS, SEPSIS, SEVERE SEPSIS, AND SEPTIC SHOCK

It is important for coders to understand the differences between bacteremia, septicemia, SIRS, sepsis, and severe sepsis in order to assign the proper codes.

Definitions

Bacteremia (790.7) refers to the presence of bacteria in the bloodstream after a trauma or mild infection. This condition is usually transient and ordinarily clears promptly through the action of the body's own immune system.

Septicemia generally refers to a systemic disease associated with the presence of pathological microorganisms or toxins in the blood. These toxins can include bacteria, viruses, fungi, and other organisms. Septicemia and sepsis have often been used interchangeably by physicians and by the *ICD-9-CM* classification. Code titles in the *ICD-9-CM* use the term "septicemia." That is in keeping with the international version of the *ICD-9,* on which the *ICD-9-CM* is based. So as not to confuse existing statistics, the term "septicemia" will continue to be used in the *ICD-9-CM*. However, more current terminology makes a distinction between sepsis and septicemia.

Most septicemia is classified to category 038, with fourth and fifth digits indicating the responsible organism. Staphylococcal septicemia uses the fifth digit to indicate that the infection is due to either *Staphylococcus aureus* (038.11) or other specified type of *Staphylococcus* (038.19). Other types of septicemia are classified to another organism, such as disseminated candidiasis (112.5) or herpetic septicemia (054.5). Organisms are sometimes transferred to other tissue, where they may seed infection in another site and lead to such conditions as arteritis, meningitis, and pyelonephritis. Additional codes are assigned for these manifestations when they are present.

A diagnosis of septicemia can neither be assumed nor ruled out on the basis of laboratory values alone. Negative or inconclusive blood cultures do not preclude a diagnosis of septicemia in patients with clinical evidence of the condition. A code for septicemia is assigned only when the physician makes a diagnosis of septicemia.

Systemic inflammatory response syndrome, or **SIRS,** generally refers to the systemic response to infection, trauma/burns, or other insult (such as cancer), with symptoms including fever, tachycardia, tachypnea, and leukocytosis. SIRS is classified to subcategory 995.9, Systemic inflammatory response syndrome (SIRS).

Sepsis generally refers to SIRS due to infection. **Severe sepsis** generally refers to sepsis with associated acute organ dysfunction. The coding of SIRS, sepsis, and severe sepsis requires a minimum of two codes:

- Sequence first a code for the underlying cause (such as infection or trauma), followed by
- A code from subcategory 995.9, Systemic inflammatory response syndrome (SIRS). Either the term "sepsis" or "SIRS" must be documented to assign a code from subcategory 995.9.
- In the case of severe sepsis, an additional code or codes for the associated acute organ dysfunction should be assigned.

Septic shock generally refers to circulatory failure associated with severe sepsis and therefore represents a type of acute organ dysfunction. The physician must specifically record "septic shock" in the diagnostic statement in order to code it as such.

The unusual or imprecise diagnostic reference to a site-specific or organ-specific sepsis, such as urosepsis, may require further clarification for coding purposes. For instance, the term **urosepsis** refers to pyuria or bacteria in the urine, not the blood. Unfortunately, urosepsis is sometimes stated as the diagnosis even though the condition has progressed to a septicemia in which a localized urinary tract infection has entered the bloodstream and become a generalized sepsis. Although the Alphabetic Index assigns urosepsis to code **599.0, Urinary tract infection, site unspecified,** this may or may not be what the physician intended by this diagnosis, and the coder should consult the physician if his intention is not clear.

When there is an equivocal diagnosis of this type, the coder should review the medical record to see whether there is any documentation that suggests the possibility of sepsis. If there is, the physician should be asked whether the diagnosis of urosepsis is intended to mean (1) generalized sepsis caused by leakage of urine or toxic urine by-products into the general vascular circulation or (2) urine contaminated by bacteria, bacterial by-products, or other toxic material but without other findings (599.0). With additional clarification from the physician, the Alphabetic Index provides two different codes based on the meaning of "urosepsis." The term "urosepsis, meaning sepsis" leads to code 995.91, while "urosepsis, meaning urinary tract infection" leads to code 599.0. A diagnostic statement of urinary tract infection followed by a diagnosis of septicemia usually indicates that the condition has progressed to septicemia. In such cases, it is the septicemia that should be coded.

Coding and Sequencing

Coders should be guided by the following instructions when coding sepsis, septicemia, SIRS, or septic shock. The coding of these conditions is dependent on the documentation available.

- When sepsis or severe sepsis is present on admission and meets the UHDDS definition of principal diagnosis—that is, the condition after study that necessitated the admission: Assign first the code for the underlying systemic infection (e.g., 038.xx, 112.5, etc.) followed by code **995.91, Sepsis,** or **995.92, Severe sepsis.** When there is an underlying localized infection (e.g., pneumonia, cellulitis, or nonspecific urinary tract infection) with sepsis, severe sepsis, or SIRS: Assign a code for the systemic infection (038.xx, 112.5, etc.) first, followed by code 995.91 or 995.92, followed by the code for the localized infection (e.g., pneumonia, cellulitis, etc.).
- When sepsis or severe sepsis develops after admission, the systemic infection code and code 995.91 or 995.92 are assigned as secondary diagnoses. When the documentation is not clear as to whether sepsis was present on admission, the physician must be queried for clarification to properly select the principal diagnosis.
- Subcategory 995.9 may **not** be assigned if the term "sepsis" or "SIRS" is not documented. A code from subcategory 995.9 can never be assigned as a principal diagnosis.

- Sepsis and septic shock associated with abortion, ectopic pregnancy, or molar pregnancy are classified to category codes in chapter 11 (630–639). If the infection occurs during labor, code 659.3x, Generalized infection during labor, is assigned; if the infection occurs during the puerperal period, code 670.0x, Major puerperal infection, is assigned.
- Sepsis due to a postoperative infection is coded based on the provider's documentation of the relationship between the infection and the procedure. This is similar to all postoperative complications.
- In cases of postoperative sepsis, assign first the complication code (such as **998.59, Other postoperative infection,** or **674.3x, Other complications of obstetrical surgical wounds**) followed by the appropriate sepsis codes (systemic infection code and either 995.91 or 995.92). For cases of severe sepsis, assign an additional code or codes for any acute organ dysfunction. Assign an additional code for the organism, if known. If the postoperative sepsis results in postoperative septic shock, assign code **998.02, Postoperative septic shock,** along with 995.92 as additional codes. Note that code 998.02 can never be assigned as a principal diagnosis.
- In cases of sepsis due to vascular catheter infection, assign first the appropriate complication code (such as **999.31, Infection due to central venous catheter** or **996.62, Infection and inflammatory reaction due to vascular device, implant and graft**). The appropriate sepsis codes (systemic infection and either 995.91 or 995.92) should be assigned as secondary codes, with an additional code or codes for any acute organ dysfunction for cases of severe sepsis. Assign an additional code for the organism, if known.
- Noninfectious process as the principal diagnosis that later develops infection and progresses to sepsis or severe sepsis: Assign first the code for the noninfectious condition (e.g., burn or serious injury), followed by the systemic infection and either 995.91 (sepsis) or 995.92 (severe sepsis). Assign also codes for any associated acute organ dysfunction in cases of severe sepsis.
- Sepsis or severe sepsis as the principal diagnosis, with the initiating event being a noninfectious condition: Assign first the code for the systemic infection and sepsis codes before the noninfectious condition.
- Associated noninfectious condition and sepsis or severe sepsis both meet the definition of principal diagnosis; either may be sequenced as the principal diagnosis.
- Only one SIRS code from category 995.9 should be assigned for patients with sepsis or severe sepsis associated with trauma or other noninfectious conditions. If a noninfectious condition leads to an infection resulting in sepsis or severe sepsis, assign either code 995.91 or 995.92. Do not additionally assign code 995.93 or 995.94. If an infection is the underlying cause, assign code 995.91 or 995.92.

Note carefully in the following cases the different codes that would be assigned based on the information available:

1. Streptococcal septicemia: Assign code **038.0, Streptococcal septicemia.** Code 995.91 is not assigned in this case if there is no documentation of sepsis or SIRS. Query the provider to determine whether the patient has sepsis—SIRS due to an infection.
2. Streptococcal sepsis: Assign code 038.0 first, followed by code 995.91.
3. Severe sepsis: Assign first the code for the systemic infection (038.xx, 112.5, etc.), followed by code 995.92. Additional codes are also assigned to identify the specific acute organ dysfunction (e.g., renal, respiratory, hepatic, etc.).
4. Septic shock: Assign first the code for the initiating systemic infection (e.g., 038.xx, 112.5, etc.), followed by the codes for severe sepsis (995.92) and septic shock (785.52) and for any associated acute organ dysfunction.
5. Sepsis due to a postoperative infection: Assign code **998.59, Other postoperative infection,** followed by the codes for sepsis (038.xx, 995.91).

6. Bacteremia: Assign code 790.7.
7. Postoperative septic shock: Assign code **998.59, Other postoperative infection,** followed by the codes for the systemic infection (e.g., 038.xx, 112.5, and so forth), for the postoperative septic shock (998.02), and for severe sepsis (995.92).

TOXIC SHOCK SYNDROME

Toxic shock syndrome (040.82) is caused by a bacterial infection. The symptoms include high fever of sudden onset, vomiting, watery diarrhea and myalgia, followed by hypotension and sometimes shock. It was originally reported almost exclusively in menstruating women using high-absorbency tampons. The organism isolated was *Staphylococcus aureus.* A similar syndrome has been identified in children and males infected with Group A *Streptococcus.* An additional code from chapter 1 is reported to identify the responsible organism.

GRAM-NEGATIVE BACTERIAL INFECTION

Gram-negative bacteria are a specific group of organisms with particular staining characteristics. They are clinically similar, as is the case with *Klebsiella* and *Pseudomonas,* and are thought of as a group even when the specific organism cannot be determined. Occasionally, several gram-negative organisms may be seen, but no single organism is identified as the causative agent, resulting in a diagnosis of gram-negative infection. Gram-negative infections are ordinarily more severe and require more intensive care than gram-positive infections. Again, a code is never assigned solely on the basis of gram-stain results; the assignment is based on the physician's clinical evaluation of the condition.

When the infectious organism has been identified, a specific code is often provided, such as **482.0, Pneumonia due to Klebsiella pneumoniae.** When a more general code is provided, such as that for urinary tract infection, an additional code from category 041 or 079 is assigned to indicate the responsible organism. Two examples follow:

- Pneumonia, due to anaerobic gram-negative bacteria 482.81
- Chronic pyelonephritis due to gram-negative bacteria <u>590.00</u> + 041.85

Table 10.1 provides a sampling of gram-negative and gram-positive organisms. A more complete list can be obtained from the health care organization's clinical laboratory director.

TABLE 10.1 Gram-Negative and Gram-Positive Bacteria

Gram-Negative Bacteria		Gram-Positive Bacteria
Bacteroides (anaerobic)	Hemophilus	Actinomyces
Bordetella	Klebsiella	Corynebacterium
Branhamella	Legionella	Lactobacillus
Brucella	Morganella	Listeria
Campylobacter	Neisseria	Mycobacterium
Citrobacter	Proteus	Nocardia
E. coli	Pseudomonas	Peptococcus
Enterobacter	Salmonella	Peptostreptococcus
Francisella	Shigella	Staphylococcus
Fusobacterium (anaerobic)	Trichinella vaginalis	Streptococcus
Gardnerella	Vellonella (anaerobic)	
Helicobacter	Yersinia	

DRUG-RESISTANT INFECTIONS

ICD-9-CM provides unique codes to distinguish between methicillin susceptible and methicillin resistant *Staphylococcus aureus* (MRSA) for septicemia (038.11 and 038.12), bacterial infections (041.11 and 041.12), and pneumonia (482.41 and 482.42). In addition, category V09 identifies infections that have become resistant to the drugs commonly used to treat them. The fourth digit indicates the type of drug to which the organism has become resistant; when more than one drug is specified, codes are assigned for each. Codes can be located in the Alphabetic Index by referring to the main term **Resistance.** For several drug types (V09.5, V09.7–V09.9), a fifth digit indicates whether multiple drugs of those particular types are affected.

Codes from category **V09, Infection with drug-resistant organisms,** are assigned only as additional codes and only when the physician specifically documents an infection that has become drug resistant. Such statements as "multi-drug resistant" or "(specified drug) resistant condition" or similar terminology indicate this condition. If no more specificity as to the type of drug can be obtained, code V09.9x should be assigned. For example:

- Resistant to penicillin V09.0
- Staphylococcal pneumonia resistant to penicillin and bacitracin
  482.40 + V09.0 + V09.81

It is important to distinguish colonization from infection. A patient may be referred to as being colonized or a carrier—meaning that an infectious organism (e.g., MRSA) is present on or in the body without necessarily causing illness. Colonization is not necessarily indicative of a disease process, and it may not be considered the cause of a patient's specific condition unless documented as such by the provider. A positive colonization test might be documented as "MRSA screen positive" or "MRSA nasal swab positive." *ICD-9-CM* provides codes for carrier or suspected carrier of infections as follows:

- Methicillin susceptible *Staphylococcus aureus* V02.53
- Methicillin resistant *Staphylococcus aureus* V02.54
- Other specified bacterial diseases V02.59

If a patient is documented as having both MRSA colonization and MRSA infection during a hospital admission, code **V02.54, Carrier or suspected carrier, Methicillin resistant *Staphylococcus aureus*,** and a code for the MRSA infection both may be assigned.

Exercise 10.1

Code the following diagnoses.

	Code(s)
1. Viral hepatitis (Australian antigen) with hepatitis delta and hepatic coma	070.21
2. Chronic gonococcal cystitis	098.31
3. Infectious mononucleosis with hepatitis B	075 070.30

Exercise 10.1 *(continued)*

4. Postmeasles otitis media	055.2
5. Acute scarlet fever	034.1
6. Gram-negative septicemia due to Bacteroides	038.3
7. Sepsis due to methicillin resistant *Staphylococcus aureus* (MRSA)	038.12 995.91
8. Chronic moniliasis of vulva	112.1
9. Pulmonary tuberculosis, infiltrative, moderately advanced, confirmed by bacterial culture	011.04
10. Late, latent syphilis	096
11. Herpes zoster of conjunctiva	053.21
12. Anthrax pneumonia	022.1 484.5
13. Acute empyema due to group B streptococcal infection	510.9 041.02
14. Encephalitis due to typhus	081.9 323.1

Exercise 10.1 *(continued)*

15. Acute respiratory distress due to sin nombre virus	518.82 079.81
16. Adenoviral pneumonia	480.0
17. Chronic gonococcal urethritis	098.2
18. Chronic vulvitis due to Monilia with microorganisms resistant to cephalosporin	112.1 V09.1
19. Amebic abscess of brain and lung Long-term use of antibiotic	006.5 V58.62

AIDS AND OTHER HIV INFECTIONS

Because the human immunodeficiency virus (HIV) infection has become a major health care concern, the collection of accurate and complete data on conditions associated with HIV infection is important for health care resource planning. Code 042 is assigned for all types of HIV infections, which are described by a variety of terms, such as the following:

- AIDS
- Acquired immune deficiency syndrome
- Acquired immunodeficiency syndrome
- AIDS-like syndrome
- AIDS-like disease (illness)
- AIDS-related complex (ARC)
- AIDS-related conditions
- Pre-AIDS
- Prodromal-AIDS
- HIV disease

Unconfirmed Diagnosis of HIV Infection

Code 042 is not assigned when the diagnostic statement indicates that the infection is "suspected," "possible," "likely," or "?". This is an exception to the general guideline that directs the coder to assign a code for a diagnosis qualified as "suspected" or "possible" as if it were established. Confirmation in this case does not require documentation of a positive serology or culture for HIV; the physician's diagnostic statement that the patient is HIV-positive or has an HIV-related illness is sufficient. The physician should be asked to state the diagnosis in positive terms.

Serologic Testing for HIV Infection

When an asymptomatic patient with no prior diagnosis of HIV infection or positive-HIV status requests testing to determine his or her HIV status, use code **V73.89, Screening for other specified viral disease.** When the patient shows signs or symptoms of illness or has been diagnosed with a condition related to HIV infection, code the signs and symptoms or the diagnosis rather than the screening code.

When the patient makes a return visit to learn the result of the serology test, code **V65.44, HIV counseling,** should be assigned as the reason for the encounter when the test result is either negative or inconclusive (795.71) or positive. Code V65.44 can be assigned as an additional code when counseling is provided for patients who test HIV positive. When a patient is known to be in a high-risk group for HIV infection, code **V69.8, Other problems related to lifestyle,** can be assigned as an additional code. When the test result is positive but the patient displays no symptoms and has no related complications and no established diagnosis of HIV infection, code **V08, Asymptomatic human immunodeficiency (HIV) infection status,** is assigned. Code V08 is not assigned when the term AIDS is used, when the patient is under treatment for an HIV-related illness, or when the patient is described as having any active HIV-related condition; code 042 is assigned instead.

When a patient has had contact with, or been exposed to, the HIV virus but shows no signs or symptoms of illness and has not been diagnosed with a condition related to HIV, assign code **V01.79, Contact with or exposure to communicable diseases, other viral diseases.**

There are federal and state laws with stringent regulations prohibiting the release of information. Therefore, the facility should have a reporting policy that conforms to federal law as well as the laws of the state in which it operates.

Newborns with HIV-positive mothers often test positive on ELISA and/or western blot HIV tests. This finding usually indicates the antibody status of the mother rather than the status of the newborn; antibodies can cross the placenta and remain for as long as 18 months after birth without the newborn's ever having been infected. Such inconclusive test results are also coded 795.71. (See chapter 23 of this handbook for further information on coding HIV infection in the newborn.)

Sequencing of HIV-Related Diagnoses

When a patient is admitted for treatment of an HIV infection or any related complications, code **042, Human Immunodeficiency Virus (HIV) disease,** is sequenced as the principal diagnosis, with additional codes for the related conditions. When a patient with an HIV infection is admitted for treatment of an entirely unrelated condition, such as an injury, that condition is designated as the principal diagnosis, with code 042 and codes for any associated conditions assigned as additional codes.

When an obstetric patient is identified as having any HIV infection, a code from subcategory **647.6** for **Other viral diseases** is assigned, with code 042 assigned as an additional code. If an obstetric patient tests positive for HIV but has no symptoms and no history of an HIV infection, code **V08, Asymptomatic Human Immunodeficiency Virus (HIV) infection status** would be assigned rather than 042.

Exercise 10.2

Code the following diagnoses.

	Code(s)
1. Candidiasis, of esophagus, opportunistic, secondary to AIDS-like disease	042 112.84
2. Pneumocystis carinii AIDS	042 136.3
3. Positive HIV test in patient who is asymptomatic, presents no related symptoms, and has no history of HIV infection	V08
4. Acute lymphadenitis due to ARC	042 683
5. Acute appendicitis (admitted for appendectomy) Kaposi's sarcoma of skin of chest, due to HIV infection	540.9 042 176.0
6. Kaposi's sarcoma of oral cavity AIDS	042 176.8
7. Agranulocytosis due to HIV infection	042 288.04

Exercise 10.2 *(continued)*

8. Burkitt's tumor of inguinal region associated with AIDS	042 200.25
9. Background retinopathy due to AIDS-like disease	042 362.10
10. Inconclusive HIV test	795.71

Endocrine, Metabolic and Nutritional Diseases and Immune-System Disorders

CHAPTER **11**

CHAPTER OVERVIEW

- Diabetes mellitus is the condition coders encounter most in working with chapter 3 of *ICD-9-CM*.
- Diabetes mellitus has two classification axes.
  - — The fourth digit identifies any associated complication.
  - — The fifth digit indicates type (1 or 2) and whether it is controlled or not.
- Diabetes causes many concurrent complications.
  - — These complications may be either acute or chronic.
  - — Assign as many codes as necessary to identify all the conditions.
- Codes from category 250 are not used for classification of secondary diabetes.
- Nutritional disorders classified by the *ICD-9-CM* include deficiencies of specific vitamins and minerals and obesity.
- Specific codes for cystic fibrosis identify site of manifestation involvement.
  - — There may be pulmonary, gastrointestinal, or other site involvement.
  - — Use codes together if different sites are involved.
- Hemochromatosis is a disorder of excess iron that is classified to category 275.
- Fluid overload is a component of congestive heart failure.
- Category 279 covers disorders of the immune system except HIV.

LEARNING OUTCOMES

After studying this chapter you should be able to:

- Code diabetes mellitus properly.
- Determine the fourth digit that identifies any acute or chronic complications with diabetes.
- Determine the fifth digit that indicates which type of diabetes is being coded.
- Identify the differences when coding for diabetes during pregnancy and gestational diabetes.
- Code disorders of iron metabolism.
- Code fluid overload due to congestive heart failure.
- Code nutritional disorders such as obesity.

TERMS TO KNOW

Diabetes mellitus
a chronic disorder of impaired carbohydrate, protein, and fat metabolism

Type 1 diabetes
also known as juvenile type; characterized by the body's failure to produce insulin

Type 2 diabetes
characterized by the body's production of insulin in an insufficient quantity or the body's inability to utilize such insulin

REMEMBER . . . You can use as many codes as necessary to identify all the conditions related to diabetes that a patient might be experiencing.

INTRODUCTION

This chapter covers a variety of conditions that are related in a general way. Because diabetes mellitus is a common medical problem, it is the condition coders encounter most often when working with chapter 3 of *ICD-9-CM*.

DIABETES MELLITUS

Diabetes mellitus, classified in category 250, is a chronic disorder of impaired carbohydrate, protein, and fat metabolism. The disorder is caused by either an absolute decrease in the amount of insulin secreted by the pancreas or a reduction in the biologic effectiveness of the insulin secreted. Other conditions include the term "diabetes," such as bronze diabetes (see disorders of iron metabolism below) and diabetes insipidus, but a diagnosis of diabetes without further qualification should be interpreted as diabetes mellitus.

Diabetes mellitus has two classification axes. The fourth digit identifies the presence of any associated complication, and the fifth-digit subclassification indicates both the type of diabetes and whether it is considered to be out of control. The terms "out of control" and "uncontrolled" are synonymous in this context. Sometimes the physician may indicate "poorly controlled" or "poor control." These are vague terms and do not necessarily indicate uncontrolled blood glucose levels. Obtain clarification from the physician to determine if the patient's diabetes is uncontrolled. Diabetes is classified as uncontrolled only when the physician specifically identifies it as such; this determination is not based on blood glucose levels documented in the medical record. "Uncontrolled diabetes mellitus" is a nonspecific term indicating that the patient's blood sugar level is not kept within acceptable levels by his or her current treatment regimen. Causes of uncontrolled diabetes mellitus may be noncompliance, insulin resistance, dietary indiscretion, and intercurrent illness.

Care should be taken when coding a diagnosis documented as "borderline diabetes." If the provider has confirmed a diagnosis of diabetes mellitus, the appropriate code from category 250, Diabetes mellitus, should be assigned. Otherwise, a diagnosis of "borderline diabetes" without further provider confirmation of the disease should be assigned a code from subcategory 790.2, Abnormal glucose.

Types of Diabetes Mellitus

There are two major types of diabetes mellitus: type I (or type 1) and type II (or type 2).

Type 1 diabetes mellitus may also be described as ketosis-prone, juvenile type, juvenile onset, or juvenile diabetes. It is characterized by the body's failure to produce insulin at all or by an absolute decrease in such production. These patients require regular insulin injections to sustain life and experience significant health problems when they do not follow the prescribed regimen for medication and diet. Careful monitoring is required in order to avoid serious complications. Code **V58.67, Long-term (current) use of insulin,** is not required for type 1 diabetics because these patients require insulin. However, this code may be assigned, if desired, to provide additional information. This handbook has followed this principle based on the advice published in *Coding Clinic*, Fourth Quarter 2004, p. 55.

Type 2 diabetes mellitus may also be described as ketosis resistant. Insulin is produced but either it is produced in insufficient quantity or the body is unable to utilize it adequately. Type 2 diabetic patients usually do not require insulin; they are ordinarily managed with oral hypoglycemic agents, diet, and exercise. For some patients, however, these measures are not effective, and insulin therapy may be required to control persistent hyperglycemia.

Category 250 has a fourth digit that identifies the presence of any associated complication and a fifth digit that indicates both the type of diabetes and whether the patient's status is controlled or uncontrolled. Nonessential modifiers related to "insulin dependent," "non-insulin dependent," and "adult onset" have been removed and are no longer considered for selection of the fifth digit. The type of diabetes (1 or 2) is the essential element in the selection of the fifth digit rather than whether the patient is on insulin. Note that the uncontrolled status is classified only when the physician specifically documents this status. If the medical record documentation is not clear with regard to the type of diabetes, query the physician or select the fifth digit of "0" for "unspecified." When the type of diabetes is not documented but does indicate that the patient uses insulin, the default is type 2. The fact that a patient is receiving insulin does not indicate that the diabetes is type 1.

When a type 2 diabetic patient routinely uses insulin, assign code **V58.67, Long-term (current) use of insulin.** However, code V58.67 should not be used if insulin is given temporarily to bring the patient's blood sugar under control during the encounter.

Some diabetic patients require the use of an insulin pump to receive insulin therapy. An insulin pump is a small, computerized device attached to the body that delivers insulin via a catheter. The pump may provide a continuous drip of insulin all day long, or it may also allow the patient to self-administer an insulin bolus by pushing a button. Failure or malfunction of the pump may result in underdosing or overdosing of insulin. Both of these situations are considered mechanical complications and are assigned code **996.57,**

FIGURE 11.1 Major Organs of the Endocrine System

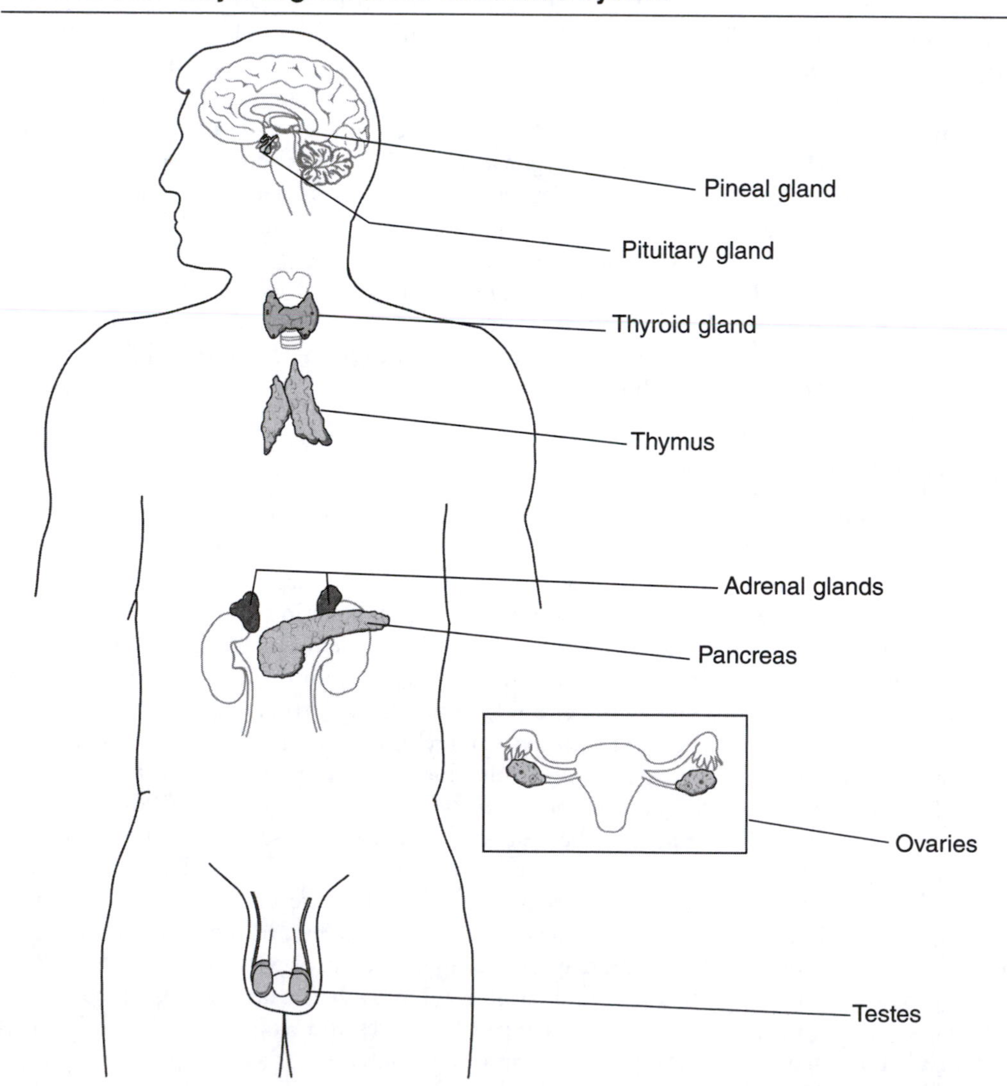

Mechanical complication due to insulin pump. When there is an overdose of insulin as a result of pump malfunction, code **962.3, Poisoning by insulins and antidiabetic agents,** is assigned as an additional code.

Secondary Diabetes

Secondary diabetes is usually the result of therapy such as the surgical removal of the pancreas or an infection. It can also be the result of an adverse effect, poisoning, or a late effect of using certain medications. Secondary diabetes is coded as follows:

- Secondary diabetes that is drug induced, chemically induced, due to the postcarcinoma state of the pancreas, or due to infection is coded to category 249, Secondary diabetes mellitus. Codes from category 250 are not assigned for secondary diabetes. For example, steroid induced diabetes mellitus due to the prolonged use of corticosteroids for an unrelated condition is coded as **249.00, Secondary diabetes without mention of complication, not stated as uncontrolled, or unspecified,** with an additional code of **E932.0, Adverse effect of therapeutic use of adrenal cortical steroids.**
- Category 249 has a fourth digit that identifies the presence of any associated complication and a fifth digit that indicates whether the patient's status is controlled or uncontrolled. The uncontrolled status is classified as such only when the physician specifically documents this status.
- Secondary diabetes mellitus that is due to pancreatectomy is coded to **251.3, Postsurgical hypoinsulinemia.** Assign a code from subcategory 249 and either code **V88.11, Acquired total absence of pancreas,** or **V88.12, Acquired partial absence of pancreas,** as additional diagnoses. For example, postpancreatectomy diabetes mellitus (lack of insulin due to surgical removal of all or part of the pancreas) is coded to 251.3, 249.00, and V88.12.

For patients with secondary diabetes who routinely use insulin, code **V58.67, Long-term (current) use of insulin,** should be assigned. However, code V58.67 should not be used if insulin is given temporarily to bring the patient's blood sugar under control during the encounter.

If the medical record documentation is not clear with regard to the type of diabetes, the Index defaults to category 250 with a fifth digit of 0 for "unspecified."

Complications and Manifestations of Diabetes Mellitus

Type 1 and type 2 diabetes mellitus, as well as secondary diabetes mellitus, can lead to a variety of complications that involve either acute metabolic derangements (249.1x–249.3x, 250.1x–250.3x), or long-term complications (249.4x–249.8x, 250.4x–250.8x). Sequencing of the diabetes mellitus and the complication or manifestation is as follows:

- Diabetes mellitus type 1 and type 2 (category 250): The code for the diabetes mellitus (category 250) is ordinarily assigned first, with an additional code for the complication or manifestation, unless the manifestation is included in the basic code. Assign as many codes from category 250 as necessary to identify all the associated diabetic conditions the patient may have.
- Secondary diabetes (category 249): The sequencing of secondary diabetes and its associated conditions should be based on the reason for the encounter. Assign as many codes from category 249 as needed to identify all of the associated conditions that the patient has. In addition, assign a code for the underlying condition that caused the diabetes. For example, a patient with secondary diabetes mellitus post-inoperable carcinoma of the pancreas is coded as **157.9, Malignant neoplasm**

of pancreas, part unspecified, and a code from category 249. If the patient is being seen by an endocrinologist for treatment of the secondary diabetes, a code from category 249 should be sequenced as the principal or first-listed diagnosis. However, if the patient is being seen for the treatment of the carcinoma of the pancreas, code 157.9 should be sequenced first.

Acute Metabolic Complications

Acute metabolic complications include ketoacidosis (249.1x or 250.1x), hyperosmolarity with or without associated coma (249.2x or 250.2x), and other coma (249.3x or 250.3x). Typical findings for patients with diabetic ketoacidosis (DKA) are glycosuria, strong ketonuria, hyperglycemia, ketonemia (blood ketone), acidosis (low arterial blood pH), and low plasma bicarbonate. Type 2 diabetics seldom develop ketoacidosis. A diagnosis of diabetic ketoacidosis should be classified as type 1 diabetes mellitus, uncontrolled (250.13). Diabetic ketoacidosis by definition is uncontrolled, and 250.13 is the default—unless the physician specifically identifies it as type 2.

Diabetes with hyperosmolarity (249.2x or 250.2x) is a condition in which there is hyperosmolarity and dehydration without significant ketosis. This condition most often occurs in patients with type 2 diabetes. Coma may or may not be present.

Diabetes with other coma (249.3x or 250.3x) includes patients with ketoacidosis who have progressed to a comatose state. This code includes hypoglycemic coma in a patient with diabetes and insulin coma, not otherwise specified.

Chronic Complications

Patients with diabetes mellitus are susceptible to one or more chronic conditions that affect the renal, nervous, and peripheral vascular systems, particularly the feet and the eyes. Onset may occur early or late in the course of the diabetes and may occur in both insulin-dependent and non-insulin-dependent patients.

Dual coding is required for this type of complication, with a code for the diabetes assigned first, followed by a code for the associated manifestation code indicating the complication. Diabetic patients often suffer several complications concurrently, in which case multiple codes from subcategories 250.4 through 250.8 are assigned, with a manifestation code assigned for each.

Renal Complications. Patients with diabetes are particularly prone to developing complications that affect the kidneys, such as nephritis, nephrosis, or chronic kidney disease. Nephritis is an inflammation of the kidney that develops slowly, over a long period of time. Nephrosis is an advanced stage of disease characterized by massive edema and marked proteinuria. Chronic kidney disease is often the ultimate progression of such conditions.

Diabetic nephropathy is coded as 249.4x or 250.4x and **583.81, Nephritis and nephropathy, not specified as acute or chronic, in diseases classified elsewhere,** or as 249.4x or 250.4x and 582.8x when the renal condition is described as "chronic glomerulonephritis." Diabetes with nephrosis or nephrotic syndrome is coded 249.4x or 250.4x and **581.81, Nephrotic syndrome in diseases classified elsewhere.** When the renal condition has progressed to chronic kidney disease, the diagnosis is sometimes stated in a way that appears to require three codes, one for the diabetes (249.4x or 250.4x), one for an interim manifestation (581.81), and one for the final or current problem (**585.x, Chronic kidney disease**). It is not necessary to code the intermediate condition, but all three codes may be assigned if the hospital prefers.

Patients who have both diabetes and hypertension may develop chronic kidney disease as a result. In this case, three codes are required: one code for the diabetes with renal manifestation, 249.4x or 250.4x; a second code from category 403 (or 404), with a fifth digit of (0) with chronic kidney disease stage I through stage IV, or unspecified, or a fifth digit of (1) with chronic kidney disease stage V or end-stage renal disease; and a third code from category 585 to indicate the specific stage of the chronic kidney disease. No other manifestation code is assigned. For example:

- Progressive diabetic nephropathy with hypertensive renal disease and chronic kidney disease stage V 250.40 + 403.91 + 585.5

Diabetic Eye Disease. Retinopathy is a common complication of diabetes. Any disease of the retina said to be due to diabetes requires a code of 249.5x or 250.5x and an additional code for the retinal complication. Nonproliferative diabetic retinopathy may be specified as mild (362.04), moderate (362.05), or severe (362.06). If the degree of severity of the diabetic retinopathy is not specified, code 362.03 should be assigned. Diabetic macular edema is only present with diabetic retinopathy; therefore, if the documentation refers to diabetic macular edema, code 362.07 must be used with a code for the diabetic retinopathy (362.01–362.06).

Senile cataracts develop more frequently in patients with diabetes, but they are not true diabetic cataracts and are not classified as ocular manifestations of the disease. A code from subcategories **366.1x, Senile cataract,** and **249, Secondary diabetes mellitus,** or **250, Diabetes mellitus,** should be assigned for senile cataracts in a diabetic patient, with sequencing depending on the circumstances of admission. Diabetic cataract (snowflake cataract, true diabetic cataract) is relatively rare. Assign codes for diabetic cataract only when the physician specifically describes the condition as such. For example:

- Diabetes mellitus with diabetic cataract 250.50 + 366.41
- Secondary diabetes mellitus with mature senile cataract 249.00 + 366.17

Diabetic Neuropathy. Peripheral, cranial, and autonomic neuropathy are chronic manifestations of diabetes mellitus. The codes for peripheral polyneuropathy are 249.6x or 250.6x and **357.2, Polyneuropathy in diabetes,** and the codes for autonomic neuropathy are 249.6x or 250.6x and **337.1, Peripheral autonomic neuropathy in disorders classified elsewhere.** Do not use the code for autonomic neuropathy unless the diagnosis is stated as such by the physician. When the neurological condition is specified, the more specific manifestation code should be assigned. Words such as "with," "with mention of," "associated with," and "in" indicate that both elements in the title must be present in the diagnostic or procedural statement. Although these terms do not necessarily indicate a cause-effect relationship, they occur together much of the time, and the classification system indicates this relationship. For example:

- Diabetic third (cranial) nerve palsy 250.60 + 378.51
- Mononeuropathy of the lower limb due to type 2 diabetes 250.60 + 355.8
- Diabetes type 1 with neuropathy 250.61 + 357.2

Diabetic Peripheral Vascular Disease. Peripheral vascular disease is a frequent complication of diabetes mellitus. Diabetic peripheral vascular disease is coded as 249.7x or 250.7x and **443.81, Peripheral circulatory disease in diseases classified elsewhere.** Although arteriosclerosis occurs earlier and more extensively in diabetic patients, coronary artery disease, cardiomyopathy, and cerebrovascular disease are not complications of diabetes and are not included in code 249.7x or 250.7x. These conditions are coded separately unless the physician documents a causal relationship.

Other Manifestations of Diabetes Mellitus. Ulcers of the lower extremities, particularly the feet, are common complications of diabetes. They may result from either diabetic neuropathy (249.6x or 250.6x) or diabetic peripheral vascular disease (249.7x or 250.7x). The code for the diabetes is assigned first, with an additional code of 707.10–707.19, 707.8, or 707.9 for any associated ulceration. If gangrene is present, code **785.4, Gangrene,** should be assigned as an additional code, with or without the intervening code for the ulcer. It is important to recognize that not all ulcers in diabetic patients are diabetic ulcers; if there is a question as to the relationship, the physician should be consulted.

Organic impotence is often the result of either diabetic peripheral neuropathy or diabetic peripheral vascular disease. It is coded first to either 249.6x/250.6x or 249.7x/250.7x, with an additional code of **607.84, Impotence of organic origin.**

Either of the preceding conditions specified as diabetic but without an indication as to whether the condition is due to neuropathy or peripheral vascular disease is coded as 249.8x or **250.8x, Diabetes with other specified manifestations,** with an additional code for the complications. Any other specified chronic manifestation that cannot be assigned to codes 250.0x through 250.7x (or 249.0x–249.7x) is also assigned to code 250.8x (or 249.8x). For example:

- Diabetes mellitus, type 1, with ulcer of great toe of right foot 250.81 + 707.15

DIABETES MELLITUS COMPLICATING PREGNANCY

Diabetes mellitus complicating pregnancy, delivery, or the puerperium is classified in chapter 11 of *ICD-9-CM*. Code 648.0x is sequenced first, with an additional code from category 249 or 250 to indicate the type of diabetes involved. Because diabetes mellitus inevitably complicates the pregnant state, is aggravated by the pregnancy, or is a main reason for obstetric care, it is appropriate to assign these codes for a pregnant diabetic patient. Assign also code **V58.67, Long-term (current) use of insulin,** if the diabetes mellitus is routinely treated with insulin.

Gestational Diabetes

A diagnosis of gestational diabetes refers to abnormal glucose tolerance that appears during pregnancy in previously nondiabetic women; it is not a true diabetes mellitus. It is thought to be due to metabolic or hormonal changes that occur during pregnancy. Patients with gestational diabetes are usually placed on a diabetic diet and sometimes require insulin therapy to maintain normal blood glucose levels during pregnancy, but the condition usually resolves during the postpartum period. Code **648.8x, Abnormal glucose tolerance,** is assigned for this condition. Assign also code **V58.67, Long-term (current) use of insulin,** if the diabetes mellitus is routinely treated with insulin. Codes 648.0x (diabetes mellitus complicating pregnancy) and 648.8x (abnormal glucose tolerance complicating pregnancy) should never be used together on the same record.

Neonatal Conditions Associated with Maternal Diabetes

Newborns with diabetic mothers sometimes experience either a transient decrease in blood sugar (**775.0, Syndrome of infant of diabetic mother**) or a transient hyperglycemia (**775.1, Neonatal diabetes mellitus**). The latter condition is sometimes referred to as pseudodiabetes and occasionally requires a short course of insulin therapy. Note, however, that these codes are assigned only when the maternal condition has actually had such an effect; the fact that the mother has diabetes in itself does not warrant the assignment of one of these codes for the newborn. When laboratory reports seem to indicate either condition, it is appropriate to check with the attending physician.

When a normal infant is born to a diabetic mother, and the infant presents no manifestations of the syndrome, assign code **V30.00, Single liveborn, born in hospital, delivered without mention of cesarean delivery,** as the principal diagnosis. Code **V18.0, Family history of certain other specific conditions, Diabetes mellitus,** should be assigned as an additional diagnosis. In addition, assign code **V29.3, Observation and evaluation of newborns and infants for suspected condition not found, Observation for suspected genetic or metabolic condition,** as an additional diagnosis for a newborn infant who requires special surveillance after being born to a diabetic mother but who lacks manifestations of infant of a diabetic mother syndrome.

Exercise 11.1

Code the following diagnoses. Do not assign E codes.

	Code(s)
1. Diabetes mellitus, type 1 Diabetic nephrosis	250.41 581.81
2. Uncontrolled secondary diabetes mellitus Snowflake cataract	249.51 366.41
3. Type 1 diabetes with ketoacidosis	250.13
4. Diabetes mellitus, type 2, out of control, with hyperosmotic, nonketotic coma	250.22
5. Diabetic Kimmelstiel-Wilson disease	250.40 581.81
6. Chronic kidney disease, stage IV due to type 1 diabetic nephrotic syndrome (Optional)	250.41 581.81 585.4
7. Impotence due to diabetic peripheral neuropathy	250.60 607.84

HYPOGLYCEMIC AND INSULIN REACTIONS

Hypoglycemic reactions can occur in both diabetic and nondiabetic patients. In a diabetic patient, hypoglycemia is coded as 249.3x or **250.3x, Diabetes mellitus with other coma,** or 249.8x or **250.8x, Diabetes with other specified complication,** if there is no mention of coma. Such reactions may occur when there is an imbalance between eating or exercise patterns and the dosage of insulin or oral hypoglycemic drugs. Hypoglycemia due to insulin may also occur in a newly diagnosed, type 1 diabetic during the initial phase of therapy while the dosage is being adjusted.

In a patient who does not have diabetes, code 251.0 is assigned for hypoglycemic coma and code 251.1 is assigned for other specified hypoglycemia if no coma is present. Code 251.2 is assigned for hypoglycemia not otherwise specified.

Hypoglycemia due to a drug used as prescribed requires an E code to indicate the responsible drug. Hypoglycemic coma or shock resulting from the incorrect use of insulin or other antidiabetic agent is coded as poisoning (962.3 + E858.0).

Exercise 11.2

Code the following diagnoses. Do not assign E codes.

	Code(s)
1. Neonatal hypoglycemia	775.6
2. Hypoglycemic coma in patient without diabetes	251.0
3. Patient with type 2 diabetes mellitus participated in a strenuous game of racquetball without adjusting his insulin dosage; he is admitted with blood sugar of 35 and is diagnosed as being hypoglycemic Hypoglycemia	250.80 V58.67
4. Type 1 diabetic developed hypoglycemia even though she had taken only the prescribed dose of insulin and did not alter her exercise or eating regimen	250.81 V58.67

CODES FOR NUTRITIONAL DISORDERS

Nutritional disorders, such as deficiency of specific vitamins and minerals, are classified in categories 260 through 269, with the exception of deficiency anemias, which are classified in the 280 through 281.9 series.

Obesity due to a specified cause, such as a thyroid disorder (240–246), is coded to the underlying condition. These codes can be assigned as the principal diagnosis when the underlying cause has not been identified; otherwise, assign code **278.00, Obesity unspecified,** or code **278.01, Morbid obesity,** as an additional code. Code **278.03, Obesity hypoventilation syndrome** (OHS), also known as Pickwickian syndrome, involves sleep-disordered breathing that causes a person to stop breathing for short periods of time while sleeping. It may be related to both obesity and neurological conditions. These codes are assigned only on the basis of the physician's diagnostic statement.

Subcategory 278.0, Overweight and obesity, requires that an additional code (V85.––V85.54) for the body mass index (BMI) be assigned, if known. BMI is a tool for indicating weight status in adults. It is a measure of weight for height. The BMI code assignment should be based on medical record documentation, which may be found in the notes of other clinicians involved in the care of the patient (e.g., a dietitian or nurse). This is an exception to the guideline that requires that code assignment be based on the documentation by the physician or any qualified health care practitioner who is legally accountable for establishing the patient's diagnosis. While BMI may be reported on the basis of another clinician's documentation, the codes for overweight and obesity should be based on the provider's documentation.

DISORDERS OF IRON METABOLISM

Hemochromatosis is the inability to rid oneself of iron that is absorbed from food in the daily diet. When iron is not excreted from the body, it can build up to four times the normal amount and reach toxic levels that accumulate in tissues of the body that affect the pancreas, liver, heart, pituitary, thyroid, and joints. When left untreated, the organs fail, causing diabetes mellitus, arthritis, cirrhosis, hypothyroidism, myocardial infarction, and neurodegenerative diseases. Hemochromatosis is known as bronzed diabetes because the excess iron shows through the skin and gives it a dark gray or bronze color.

Hereditary hemochromatosis caused by a single gene mutation is assigned to code **275.01, Hereditary hemochromatosis.** Hemochromatosis due to red blood cell transfusion occurs in severely anemic patients who have required years of transfusions. With transfusional iron overload, excess iron occurs both in the reticuloendothelial cells and parenchymal cells. In contrast with hereditary hemochromatosis, the iron is placed directly onto transferrin and from there moves to the tissues. Code **275.02, Hemochromatosis due to repeated red blood cell transfusions,** is assigned for this secondary type of hemochromatosis. Unspecified hemochromatosis is assigned to code **275.03, Other hemochromatosis.** Code **275.09, Other disorders of iron metabolism,** is assigned for other iron metabolism disorders.

FLUID OVERLOAD

Fluid overload (276.6x) is the excessive accumulation of fluid in the body. It may be caused by excessive parenteral infusion or deficiencies in cardiovascular or renal fluid volume regulation. Fluid overload is reported with code **276.69, Other fluid overload.** However, when fluid overload is a component of congestive heart failure, it is not coded separately. Transfusion associated circulatory overload (TACO) occurs when transfusion volume exceeds cardiovascular capacity; too much fluid is transfused or fluid is transfused too rapidly. Symptoms include dyspnea, hypoxemia, elevated venous pressure, and pulmonary edema. TACO is assigned to code **276.61, Transfusion associated circulatory overload.**

CYSTIC FIBROSIS

Cystic fibrosis (277.0x), also known as mucoviscidosis or cystic fibrosis of the pancreas, is a disorder of the exocrine glands that causes the accumulation of thick, tenacious mucus. It is the primary cause of pancreatic deficiency and chronic malabsorption in children. Although cystic fibrosis affects the body in a number of ways, progressive respiratory insufficiency is the major cause of illness in patients with this disease. The symptoms primarily affect the digestive and respiratory systems. In some glands, like the pancreas, the thick mucus may obstruct the pancreas, preventing digestive enzymes from reaching the intestines. The pulmonary manifestation results in mucus secretions that clog the airways and allow bacteria to multiply. Sometimes this progresses to complications such as acute and chronic bronchitis, bronchiectasis, pneumonia, atelectasis, peribronchial and parenchyma scarring, pneumothorax, and hemoptysis. Intra-abdominal complications such as meconium ileus, rectal prolapse, inguinal hernia, gallstones, ileocolic intussusception, and gastroesophageal reflux also occur.

Specific codes identify the site of manifestation involvement such as pulmonary involvement (277.02), gastrointestinal involvement (277.03), or other site involvement (277.09). These manifestation codes may be used together if different sites are involved.

If a patient is admitted due to a complication of cystic fibrosis with pulmonary involvement, such as acute bronchitis (466.0), code the complication as the principal diagnosis or first-listed code, followed by the cystic fibrosis code (277.02).

Because there is no known cure for cystic fibrosis, therapy is directed toward the complications of the disease, with the major focus on the maintenance of adequate nutritional and respiratory status. Admissions due to the cystic fibrosis itself most often occur when the patient is brought in for workup to confirm the diagnosis.

TUMOR LYSIS SYNDROME

Tumor lysis syndrome (TLS) refers to a group of serious, potentially life-threatening metabolic disturbances that can occur after antineoplastic therapy. TLS can develop spontaneously as a result of radiation therapy or corticosteroid therapy. However, it usually occurs following the administration of anticancer drugs and is often associated with leukemias and lymphomas. It is also seen in other hematologic malignancies and solid tumors. When cancer cells are destroyed, they can release intracellular ions and metabolic byproducts into the circulation, leading to TLS. Code **277.88, Tumor lysis syndrome,** is used to report spontaneous tumor lysis syndrome as well as tumor lysis syndrome following antineoplastic drug therapy. An additional E code should be assigned to identify the cause when tumor lysis syndrome is drug-induced.

CODES FOR DISORDERS OF THE IMMUNE SYSTEM

Category 279 classifies various disorders of the immune system, with the exception of conditions associated with or due to the human immunodeficiency virus (HIV), which are classified to code 042.

Review Exercise 11.3

Code the following diagnoses and procedures. Do not assign E codes.

	Code(s)
1. Hypercholesterolemia and endogenous hyperglyceridemia	272.2
2. Cystic fibrosis with mild intellectual disabilities	277.00 317
3. Thymic dysplasia with immunodeficiency	279.2
4. Congenital myxedema Inappropriate antidiuretic hormone secretion syndrome	243 253.6
5. Uninodular toxic nodular goiter with thyrotoxicosis	242.10
Unilateral thyroid lobectomy	06.2
6. Adenomatous goiter with thyrotoxicosis	242.30
Substernal thyroidectomy, complete	06.52
7. Toxic diffuse goiter with thyrotoxic crisis	242.01

Review Exercise 11.3 *(continued)*

8. Hypothyroidism, ablative, following total thyroidectomy performed three years ago	244.0
9. Cell-mediated immune deficiency with thrombocytopenia and eczema	279.12
10. Hypopotassemia	276.8

Mental Disorders

CHAPTER **12**

CHAPTER OVERVIEW

- Mental disorders are classified in chapter 5 of the *ICD-9-CM*.
- Organic brain syndrome may be coded as acute or chronic and psychotic or nonpsychotic. Organic anxiety syndrome is a psychosis and is the direct effect of a medical condition. The medical condition should be coded first.
- Dementia should be coded after the general medical condition causing it, such as Alzheimer's disease.
- Metabolic encephalopathy can manifest itself in many ways, so there is no one code for this condition.
- Schizophrenic disorders have a fourth digit indicating type and a fifth digit indicating course of illness.
- Affective disorders are characterized by mood disturbance. A fifth digit is used to illustrate severity. The fourth digit classifies disorders within this category:
    - —Depressive disorders (both single and recurrent)
    - —Manic episodes (both single and recurrent)
    - —Depressive or manic disorders that are noticeably cyclical
- Nonpsychotic mental disorders are also classified. These include:
    - —Reactions to stress (both acute and chronic)
    - —Psychophysiologic disorders
- Substance abuse and dependence are classified as mental disorders in *ICD-9-CM*.
    - —Abuse and dependence are two different conditions and should be coded differently.
    - —Alcohol dependence syndrome, drug dependence, and nondependent abuse of drugs are classified to three different categories.
    - —Therapy is secondary to the principal diagnosis of abuse or dependence.

LEARNING OUTCOMES

After studying this chapter you should be able to:

- Code a variety of mental disorders.
- Determine the difference in types of affective disorders.
- Explain the difference between substance abuse and dependence and code the conditions and therapies surrounding these two distinct conditions.

TERMS TO KNOW

Abuse
problematic use of drugs or alcohol but without dependence

Dependence
increased tolerance to drugs or alcohol with a compulsion to continue taking the substance despite the cost; often occurs with withdrawal upon cessation

Encephalopathy
general term to describe any disorder of cerebral function

REMEMBER . . . Although coding assignments for mental disorders are made according to *ICD-9-CM,* psychiatrists often state diagnoses using the somewhat different terminology found in the *Diagnostic and Statistical Manual of Mental Disorders.*

INTRODUCTION

Mental disorders of all types are classified in chapter 5 of *ICD-9-CM.*

Psychiatrists ordinarily state diagnoses in accordance with the nomenclature used in the *Diagnostic and Statistical Manual of Mental Disorders,* published by the American Psychiatric Association. Most of these codes are the same as those used in *ICD-9-CM* but the terminology may be somewhat different. Coders working with mental health records may find it useful to become familiar with this manual, but actual coding assignment is made according to the classifications in *ICD-9-CM.*

ORGANIC BRAIN SYNDROME

Organic brain syndrome is an older general term used to describe decreased mental function due to a medical disease other than a psychiatric illness. In general, organic brain syndromes cause agitation, confusion, long-term loss of brain function (dementia), and severe, short-term loss of brain function (delirium). Organic brain syndrome is common in the elderly, but it is not a part of the normal aging process. Organic brain syndrome may be either acute and reversible or chronic and irreversible.

When coding organic brain syndrome, the first step is to determine whether the condition is psychotic or nonpsychotic. Psychosis is characterized by personality derangement and loss of contact with reality. In addition it is frequently associated with delusions, illusions, or hallucinations. Neurosis, on the other hand, does not involve any gross distortion of reality or disorganization of the personality. When the diagnostic statement mentions "with dementia," "delirium," or "psychotic" or similar terms, the condition should be coded as psychotic. Unless there is clear documentation of psychosis in the medical record, however, codes indicating psychosis should not be assigned. For example:

- Organic brain syndrome psychosis associated with chronic alcoholism 291.2 + 303.90
- Organic brain syndrome, nonpsychotic, due to old concussion 310.2 + 907.0

ORGANIC ANXIETY SYNDROME

Organic anxiety syndrome is a transient organic psychosis characterized by clinically significant anxiety. It is considered to be the direct physiological effect of a general medical condition. The code for the general condition is sequenced first, with an additional code of **293.84, Anxiety disorder in conditions classified elsewhere.**

DEMENTIA IN CONDITIONS CLASSIFIED ELSEWHERE

Dementia is characterized by the development of multiple cognitive deficits such as memory impairment and cognitive disturbances such as aphasia, apraxia, or agnosia. When the cause of the dementia is not specified, the dementia is classified to subcategory 294.2, Dementia, unspecified, with the fifth digit denoting without behavioral disturbance (294.20) or with behavioral disturbance (294.21). Unspecified dementia with behavior described as aggressive, combative, or violent is classified to code 294.21. Dementia in conditions classified elsewhere is classified to subcategory 294.1x with codes to specifically identify the presence or absence of behavioral disturbances such as aggressive, violent, or combative behavior. The dementia classified in subcategory 294.1x is due to direct physiological effects of a general medical condition. When assigning codes 294.10 and 294.11, code first the underlying physical disease associated with the dementia, such as Alzheimer's disease, Parkinson's disease, or Huntington's. If the patient has a tendency to wander off, code **V40.31, Wandering in diseases classified elsewhere,** may be assigned in addition to code 294.11 or 294.21.

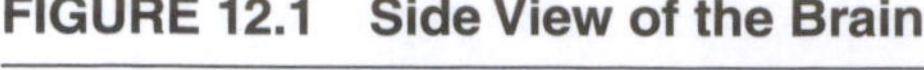

FIGURE 12.1 Side View of the Brain

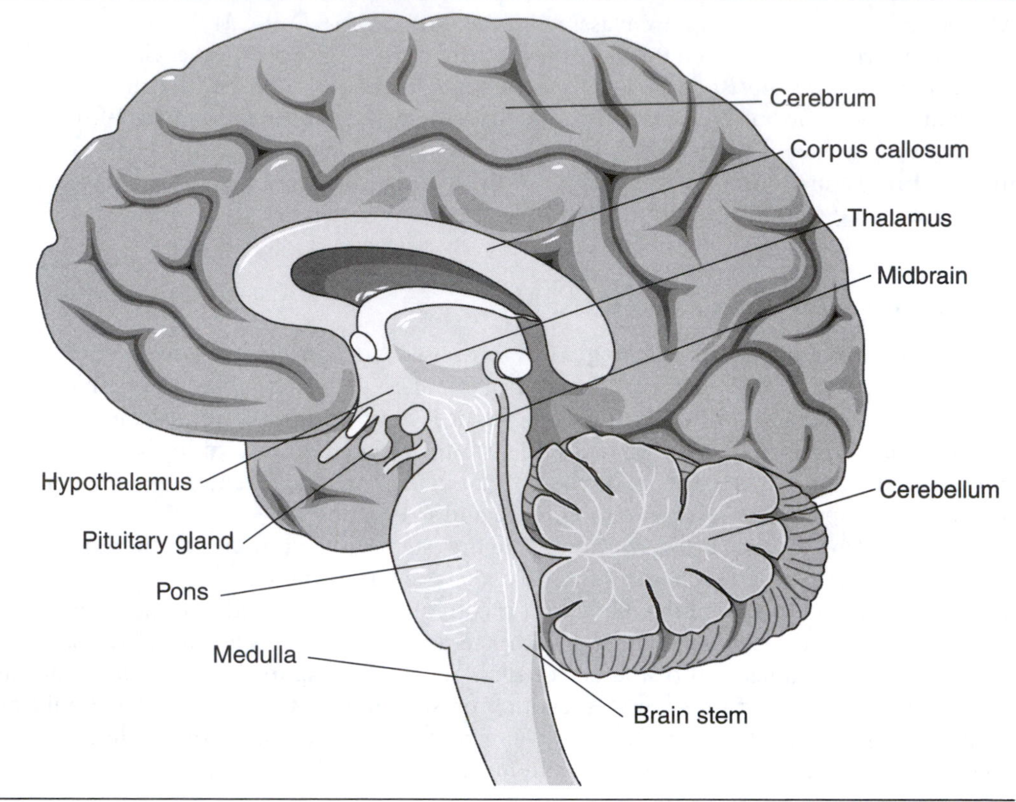

ALZHEIMER'S DISEASE

Alzheimer's disease is a process of progressive atrophy involving the degeneration of nerve cells. This degeneration leads to mental changes that range from subtle intellectual impairment to dementia with loss of cognitive functions and failure of memory. **Alzheimer's disease** is coded as **331.0.** When there is associated dementia, code **294.1x, Dementia in conditions classified elsewhere,** is assigned as an additional diagnosis. For example:

- Alzheimer's disease [without any mention of dementia] 331.0
- Dementia due to Alzheimer's disease 331.0 + 294.1x

METABOLIC ENCEPHALOPATHY

Encephalopathy is a general term used to describe any disorder of cerebral function. Metabolic encephalopathy refers to an altered state of consciousness, usually characterized as delirium. It is either hypoactive or hyperactive and transient in nature, and is essentially a reversible dysfunction of cerebral metabolism, although the delirium may be persistent. Some physicians use the term "acute confusional state" to describe this condition.

Metabolic encephalopathy can result from a wide variety of conditions, some of which affect the brain and some of which involve various body systems. Because it is a manifestation of such a variety of causes, there is no one code for this condition; code entries are located under the main term **Delirium** in the Alphabetic Index.

ALTERED MENTAL STATE

An alteration in level of consciousness not associated with delirium or with another identified condition is classified to subcategory 780.0 in chapter 16 of *ICD-9-CM*. Fifth digits are used to indicate whether it is identified as coma (780.01), transient alteration of awareness (780.02), or persistent vegetative state (780.03). Other altered mental states, such as somnolence, stupor, or states not further specified, are classified as 780.09. An altered mental status, or a change in mental status, of unknown etiology is coded to **780.97, Altered mental status.** If the condition causing the change in mental status is known, do not assign code 780.97; code the condition instead.

TRANSIENT GLOBAL AMNESIA

Transient global amnesia is a distinct form of amnesia of unknown etiology, characterized by a sudden loss of memory function. During an episode, the patient is unable to form memories or remember recent events and may ask the same question over and over because no memories of previous answers are formed. The episode usually lasts for a few hours, followed by total or near-total resolution of the memory loss, although the patient will remain amnesic for the event itself. Transient global amnesia is not psychotic in nature, and it is not considered to be due to ischemia; rather, it is a distinct cerebrovascular condition with its own code, 437.7.

SCHIZOPHRENIC DISORDERS

Schizophrenic disorders are classified in category 295, with a fourth digit indicating the type of schizophrenia. A fifth-digit subclassification is used to indicate the course of the illness as follows:

- 0 unspecified
- 1 subchronic (continuous illness for more than six months but less than two years)
- 2 chronic (continuous illness for more than two years)
- 3 subchronic with acute exacerbation (duration of illness same as subchronic but prominent psychotic features re-emergent in a patient who had been in the residual phase)
- 4 chronic with acute exacerbation (duration of illness same as chronic but prominent psychotic features re-emergent in a patient who had been in the residual phase)
- 5 in remission

Assignment of fifth digits 1 through 5 must be based on the physician's statement.

AFFECTIVE DISORDERS

Affective disorders are common mental diseases characterized by mood disturbance. Major depressive disorders are classified as episodic mood disorders under category 296 in *ICD-9-CM;* code 311 is assigned for other nonpsychotic depressive disorders.

Patients diagnosed as suffering from a major affective disorder are classified according to the type of symptoms they exhibit. Patients who experience sadness and withdrawal and lose interest in social activities or other aspects of life are classified as follows:

- 296.2x Major depressive disorder, single episode
- 296.3x Major depressive disorder, recurrent episode

Patients who exhibit symptoms of hypomania—for example, rapid speech, flight of ideas, grandiosity, and poor judgment—are classified as follows:

- 296.0x Bipolar I disorder, single manic episode
- 296.1x Manic disorder, recurrent episode

Many patients experience cyclic, recurring mood changes that result in periods of severe depression alternating with extreme elation that are beyond the normal range of mood swings. Such disorders are called bipolar or circular disorders and are classified as 296.4x through 296.6x, with the fourth digit indicating the current phase of the illness, as follows:

- 296.4x Bipolar I disorder, most recent episode (or current) manic (patient is presently in manic phase but has experienced depression in the past)
- 296.5x Bipolar I disorder, most recent episode (or current) depressed (patient is presently in depressive phase but has experienced hypomania in the past)
- 296.6x Bipolar I disorder, most recent episode (or current) mixed (patient is presently exhibiting both depressive and manic behavior)

Fifth digits are used with subcategories 296.0 through 296.6 to provide information about the current severity of the disorder, as follows:

- 0 unspecified
- 1 mild
- 2 moderate
- 3 severe, without mention of psychotic behavior
- 4 severe, specified as with psychotic behavior
- 5 in partial or unspecific remission
- 6 in full remission

Again, fifth digits 1 through 6 are assigned only when documentation of severity is included in the medical record.

Exercise 12.1

Code the following diagnoses and procedures. Do not assign E codes.

	Code(s)
1. Schizo-affective psychosis, chronic, with acute exacerbation	295.74
2. Schizophrenia, catatonic type, subchronic	295.21

Exercise 12.1 *(continued)*

3. Schizophrenia, reactive, paranoid type 295.30

   Electroshock treatment 94.27

4. Severe manic disorder, recurrent episode 296.13

5. Reactive depressive psychosis 298.0

6. Bipolar disorder, in manic phase, mild 296.41

7. Mixed bipolar affective disorder, in partial remission 296.65

NONPSYCHOTIC MENTAL DISORDERS

A variety of neurotic disorders, personality disorders, and other nonpsychotic mental disorders are classified in categories 300 through 316. These include such conditions as anxiety states, alcohol and drug dependence and abuse, adjustment to stress, and certain physiological disorders.

Reactions to Stress

ICD-9-CM provides two categories for coding transient reactions to physical or mental stress, one for an acute stress reaction and one for an adjustment or chronic stress reaction. Category 308 classifies acute reaction to stress. This condition represents a fairly severe reaction to exceptional or gross stress and may be characterized by panic, agitation, stupor, or fugue. It generally lasts for a short time, usually several hours, but occasionally can persist for days. Combat and operational stress reaction are included in this category.

Chronic reaction to stress is classified into category **309, Adjustment reaction.** These conditions are usually situation-specific and reversible. Adjustment reactions are usually less severe than acute stress reactions and last somewhat longer, although in most cases no more than a few months. The fourth-digit axis for this category is the nature of the reaction—for example, anxiety or depression. The following situations would fall into this category:

- Patient depressed over death of son (two years ago) 309.1
- Patient expresses severe anxiety over separation from husband 309.21
- Patient has just taken a new job and is having a severe anxiety adjustment to the work situation 309.23

Psychophysiologic Disorders

Two categories are provided for psychophysiologic disorders: 306 and 316. Category 306 classifies physiological malfunction arising from mental factors, with the fourth digit indicating the body system involved. For the most part, the four-digit code includes the associated symptom, and there is no need to assign an additional code. Examples of conditions that are classified in category 306 include the following:

- Psychogenic paralysis 306.0
- Psychogenic diarrhea 306.4
- Psychogenic dysmenorrhea 306.52

In assigning codes from category 306, it is important to make the distinction between these conditions and similar conditions that fall under the categories for neurotic disorders, psychoses, or organic disorders.

Category 316 classifies psychic factors associated with diseases classified elsewhere. Typical conditions that are often associated with code 316 include asthma, ulcerative colitis, and dermatitis. If such a condition is considered to be psychogenic in origin, code 316 is assigned first, followed by an additional code for the associated condition. For example:

- Psychogenic asthma 316 + 493.90
- Psychogenic paroxysmal tachycardia 316 + 427.2

Special Symptoms or Syndromes

Category 307 includes codes for a variety of special symptoms and syndromes of nonorganic origin, such as tics and specified nonorganic sleep disorders. These codes are not assigned when they are due to a mental disorder classified elsewhere or are of organic origin. Eating disorders such as bulimia nervosa (307.51) and anorexia nervosa (307.1) are included in this category. For some anorexic patients, the weight loss is so severe that it leads to malnutrition. Code 261, Nutritional marasmus, should be assigned as an additional diagnosis to further describe the severity of the patient's condition.

Exercise 12.2

Code the following diagnoses.

	Code(s)
1. Acute delirium resulting from pneumonia due to Hemophilus influenzae	482.2 293.0
2. Passive-aggressive personality	301.84
3. Depression with anxiety Conversion reaction (tremors)	300.4 300.11
4. Adolescent adjustment reaction, with severe disturbance of conduct	309.3
5. Severe involutional depression, recurrent	296.33
6. Stress reaction, psychomotor	308.2

SUBSTANCE ABUSE DISORDERS

Substance abuse and dependence are classified as mental disorders in *ICD-9-CM*. Alcohol dependence syndrome is classified in category 303, drug dependence is classified in category 304, and nondependent abuse of drugs, including both alcohol or drugs, is classified in category 305. Although the terms "abuse" and "dependence" may be used interchangeably in certain treatment programs, they are actually quite different conditions and are coded differently in *ICD-9-CM*. For both abuse and dependence codes, the fifth digit represents the pattern of use, as follows:

- 0 unspecified
- 1 continuous
- 2 episodic
- 3 in remission

The coder should not attempt to apply these digits without documentation of the pattern of use in the medical record. Such documentation should be from a provider (as defined in the *Official Guidelines for Coding and Reporting*)—the physician or any qualified health care practitioner who is legally accountable for establishing the patient's diagnosis. The designation of the pattern of drug or alcohol use or dependence requires the provider's clinical judgment. Unless the provider has documented the specific pattern of use, assign fifth digit 0 to indicate that the documentation is not specific or is unclear.

Alcohol Dependence and Abuse

Alcoholism (alcohol dependence) is a chronic condition in which the patient has become dependent on alcohol, with increased tolerance, and is unable to stop its use even with such strong incentives as impairment of health, deteriorating social interactions, and interference with job performance. Such patients often experience physical signs of withdrawal when there is a sudden cessation of drinking.

Code **303.0x, Alcohol dependence syndrome, acute alcoholic intoxication,** is assigned when a patient who is dependent on alcohol presents for care in a state of acute intoxication. If the patient presents when not acutely intoxicated, as for a rehabilitation program, the condition is classified as **303.9x, Other and unspecified alcoholism.** Because alcoholism is by definition a chronic condition, both codes are not assigned; when the diagnosis is stated as "acute and chronic alcoholism," code 303.0x covers both conditions. Although there is a code for history of alcoholism (V11.3), it is very rare for a patient with alcoholism to experience a full recovery; alcoholism in remission is ordinarily the code that should be assigned.

Alcohol abuse represents problem drinking and includes those patients who drink to excess but have not reached a stage of physical dependence on alcohol. It may include such alcohol-related conditions as temporary mental disturbance, slurred speech, blackouts, difficulty in driving, arguments with family and friends, and difficulty in the work environment. Alcohol abuse is classified as code **305.0x, Alcohol abuse.** This code is also assigned for a diagnosis of simple drunkenness.

Drug Dependence and Abuse

Drug dependence is a chronic mental and physical condition related to the patient's drug use. It is characterized by behavioral and psychological responses and also includes a compulsion to take the drug in order to experience its psychic effect or to avoid the discomfort that results from its absence. Such patients often experience physical signs of withdrawal when there is a sudden cessation of drug use. Category **304, Drug dependence,** uses a fourth digit to indicate the class of drug involved. Certain codes indicate a combination of drugs; in particular, code 304.7x is assigned when an opioid drug is involved with other drugs and code 304.8x when no opioid drug is present.

Drug abuse represents problematic use of drugs by patients who take drugs to excess but have not reached a stage of dependence. It represents use of the drug in a maladaptive pattern that may adversely affect social functioning or physical and/or mental health. Nondependent abuse drugs are classified in category 305, with the fourth digit indicating the drug involved. For both alcohol and drug dependence and abuse, fifth digits provide the pattern of use:

- 0 unspecified
- 1 continuous
- 2 episodic
- 3 in remission

Substance-Related Conditions

Patients with substance abuse or dependence often develop related physical complications or psychotic symptoms. Mental disorders related to alcohol use are classified in category **291, Alcohol-induced mental disorders;** those related to drug use are classified in category **292, Drug-induced mental disorders.**

Patients dependent on either alcohol or drugs or on a combination of the two frequently experience withdrawal symptoms and require detoxification. Symptoms and signs of withdrawal include tremulousness, agitation, irritability, disturbed sleep, anorexia, autonomic hyperactivity, seizures, and hallucinations. A severe form of withdrawal known as delirium tremens is characterized by fever, tachycardia, hypertension or hypotension, hallucinations, agitation, confusion, fluctuating mental states, and seizures. Symptoms of withdrawal usually begin after a significant decline in the blood alcohol level.

Three subcategory codes—291.0, 291.3, and 291.81—are provided for alcoholic withdrawal. Only one of these codes should be assigned, with code 291.0 taking precedence over the other two and code 291.3 taking precedence over code 291.81, as indicated by the exclusion notes. Note that fifth digits have been added to subcategory 291.8 to provide separate codes for withdrawal (291.81) and alcoholic anxiety and alcoholic mood (291.89).

When the patient is admitted in withdrawal or when withdrawal develops after admission, the withdrawal code is designated as the principal diagnosis, with an additional code for alcoholism. For example:

- Alcoholic withdrawal delirium due to acute and chronic alcoholism
  291.0 + 303.00
- Alcohol-induced psychotic disorder with hallucinations due to chronic alcoholism
  291.3 + 303.90
- Alcoholic withdrawal due to continuous chronic alcoholism 291.81 + 303.91

Drug withdrawal symptoms are coded as **292.0, Drug withdrawal.** Other mental disorders due to drug dependence or abuse are classified in the 292.1 through 292.9 series. A code should also be assigned for the dependence or abuse.

Selection of the Principal Diagnosis

The designation of the principal diagnosis for patients with either substance abuse or substance dependence depends on the circumstances of the admission, as defined in the following guidelines:

1. When a patient is admitted with a diagnosis of a substance-related psychosis, sequence the psychosis code first, followed by the alcohol or drug dependence or abuse code.
2. When a patient is admitted for the purpose of detoxification or rehabilitation or both, and there is no indication of withdrawal or other psychotic symptoms, sequence the substance abuse or dependence code as the principal diagnosis.
3. When a patient is admitted for detoxification or rehabilitation for both drug and alcohol abuse or dependence, and both are treated, either condition may be designated as the principal diagnosis.
4. When a patient with a diagnosis of substance abuse or dependence is admitted for treatment or evaluation of a physical complaint related to the substance use, follow the directions in the index for conditions described as alcoholic or due to drugs; sequence the physical condition first, followed by the code for abuse or dependence.

5. When a patient with a diagnosis of alcohol or drug abuse or dependence is admitted because of an unrelated condition, follow the usual guidelines for selecting a principal diagnosis.

Substance Abuse Therapy

Treatment for patients with a diagnosis of substance abuse or dependence consists of detoxification, rehabilitation, or both. The abuse or dependence is the principal diagnosis for a patient admitted for such programs.

Detoxification is the management of withdrawal symptoms for a patient who is physically dependent on alcohol or drugs. It is more than simple observation; it involves active management. Treatment may involve evaluation, observation and monitoring, and administration of thiamine and multivitamins for nutrition as well as other medications (such as methadone, long-acting barbiturates or benzodiazepines, or carbamazepine) as needed. The detoxification program for patients with alcohol dependence is usually continued over a four- or five-day period. Detoxification takes longer for opiates and sedatives/hypnotics, usually lasting from three weeks to a period of months, and may be carried out in either a residential or an outpatient setting. If the medical record documents detoxification as having been carried out, the code can be assigned even when no medications were actually administered.

Rehabilitation is a structured program carried out with the goal of establishing strict control of drinking and drug use. A variety of rehabilitation modalities may be utilized. These include methadone maintenance, therapeutic residential communities, and long-term outpatient drug- or alcohol-free treatments. When a patient with drug dependence is on medications for detoxification or for maintenance programs to prevent withdrawal symptoms (e.g., methadone maintenance for opiate dependence), the appropriate code for the drug dependence should be assigned, rather than code **V58.69, Long-term (current) use of other medications.**

A code for rehabilitation therapy is assigned for a patient who begins a program even when it is not completed. Category **V57, Care involving use of rehabilitation procedures,** is used for physical rehabilitation only and is not assigned for alcohol or drug rehabilitation programs.

Detoxification and rehabilitation for patients with alcohol dependence or abuse are coded as follows:

- 94.61 Alcohol rehabilitation
- 94.62 Alcohol detoxification
- 94.63 Alcohol rehabilitation and detoxification

Treatment for drug abuse or dependence is coded as follows:

- 94.64 Drug rehabilitation
- 94.65 Drug detoxification
- 94.66 Drug rehabilitation and detoxification

Many patients exhibit maladaptive use of both alcohol and drugs, and combined therapy may be used for these patients:

- 94.67 Combined alcohol and drug rehabilitation
- 94.68 Combined alcohol and drug detoxification
- 94.69 Combined alcohol and drug rehabilitation and detoxification

It is also possible to provide detoxification for either drugs or alcohol and rehabilitation for both, which would require assignment of either **94.62, Alcohol detoxification,** or **94.65, Drug detoxification,** along with **94.69** for **Combined alcohol and drug rehabilitation and detoxification.**

Psychiatric Therapy

Mental disorders other than substance abuse disorders are commonly treated with psychodynamic ("talk") therapy, drug therapy, electroconvulsive therapy, or a combination of therapeutic modes. Commonly used procedures include lithium therapy (94.22), play therapy (94.36), group therapy (94.44), and electroconvulsive therapy (ECT) (94.27). Because the diagnosis alone does not always explain the length of stay or the level of resource utilization for such patients, therapy codes are helpful in analyzing patterns of care.

Review Exercise 12.3

Code the following diagnoses and procedures.

	Code(s)
1. Paranoid alcoholic psychosis with chronic alcoholism, continuous	291.5 303.91
2. Alcoholic cirrhosis of liver Chronic alcoholism	571.2 303.90
3. Acute alcoholic intoxication, episodic	305.02
4. Marijuana dependence, used continuously	304.31
5. Acute intoxication and chronic alcoholism	303.00
Detoxification and rehabilitation	94.63

Review Exercise 12.3 *(continued)*

6. Episodic barbiturate abuse	305.42
7. Cocaine dependence, episodic	304.22
8. Amphetamine abuse, continuous	305.71
9. Dependence on barbiturate and heroin	304.70
10. Admitted because of syndrome of inappropriate secretion of antidiuretic hormone secondary to chronic alcoholism	253.6 303.90

Coding of Diseases of the Blood and Blood-Forming Organs and Diseases of the Nervous System

Diseases of the Blood and Blood-Forming Organs

CHAPTER 13

CHAPTER OVERVIEW

- Diseases of the blood and blood-forming organs are classified in chapter 4 of *ICD-9-CM*.
- Anemia is the most common condition dealt with in chapter 4.
  - It can be due to chronic or acute blood loss, chronic disease, or the use of chemotherapy. Acute blood loss anemia may occur after surgery or trauma.
  - The use of precise terminology is important in classifying anemias.
- There are a variety of codes associated with sickle-cell anemia.
  - It is important to distinguish between sickle-cell anemia and sickle-cell trait.
  - Other codes for sickle-cell include HB-SS disease and thalassemia.
- Coagulation defects are another type of disease of the blood.
  - They affect clotting time and ability.
  - An E code may be used to indicate the adverse effect of an anticoagulant medication.
  - Hypercoagulation is also a possibility.
- Diseases may decrease or increase the production of white blood cells (leukocytes). These diseases are classified according to whether the count is low or elevated.

LEARNING OUTCOMES

After studying this chapter you should be able to:

- Code the various types of anemia.
- Understand when and when not to code a coagulation defect because certain drug therapies are being used.
- Distinguish between the various diseases of the white blood cells and the various types of white blood cells.

TERMS TO KNOW

Anemia
a condition in which blood is deficient in the amount of hemoglobin in red blood cells or in the volume of red blood cells

Aplastic anemia
a condition in which there is a deficiency of red blood cells because the bone marrow is failing to produce them

Pancytopenia
a type of aplastic anemia in which red blood cells, white blood cells, and platelets are all deficient

Sickle-cell anemia
a hereditary disease of the red blood cells passed to a child when both parents carry the genetic trait

Sickle-cell trait
a condition that occurs when a child receives the trait from only one parent

Thrombocytopenia
a deficiency in platelets, the cells that are important in blood clotting

REMEMBER . . . There are a variety of conditions that can be classified as an anemia. Be sure to check with a physician if the terminology in the medical report is unspecific or misleading.

INTRODUCTION

Diseases of the blood and blood-forming organs—including bone marrow, lymphatic tissue, platelets, and coagulation factors—are classified in chapter 4 of *ICD-9-CM*. Neoplastic diseases, such as leukemia, are classified in chapter 2 of *ICD-9-CM* along with other neoplastic diseases. Diseases of the blood and blood-forming organs complicating pregnancy, childbirth, or the puerperium are reclassified in chapter 11 of *ICD-9-CM*. Anemia of pregnancy, for example, is coded 648.2x, with an additional code from chapter 4 assigned to indicate the specific type of anemia. Hematological disorders of the fetus and newborn are classified as perinatal conditions in chapter 15 of *ICD-9-CM*.

ANEMIA

The condition that coders must deal with most often in chapter 4 of *ICD-9-CM* is anemia. Anemia refers to either a reduction in the quantity of hemoglobin or a reduction in the volume of packed red cells, a condition which occurs whenever the equilibrium between red cell loss and red cell production is disturbed. A decrease in production can result from a variety of causes, including aging, bleeding, and cell destruction.

The use of precise terminology is important in classifying anemias. When a diagnostic statement of anemia is not qualified in any way, the coder should review the medical record to determine whether more information can be located in laboratory or pathology reports or in a hematology consultation before the code for an unspecified type of anemia is assigned. Remember, however, that a code should not be assigned on the basis of a diagnostic report alone; when it appears that a more specific type of anemia is present, the coder should check with the physician for concurrence.

Deficiency Anemias

Iron-deficiency anemias are classified in category 280. This type of anemia may be due to a chronic blood loss (280.0) from conditions such as chronic hemorrhagic gastrointestinal conditions or menorrhagia, or to inadequate intake of dietary iron (280.1). If the cause is unspecified, code 280.9 is assigned. Other deficiency anemias are coded in category 281, with a fourth digit indicating the specific type of deficiency such as pernicious anemia or B_{12} vitamin deficiency.

Exercise 13.1

Code the following diagnoses and procedures. Do not assign E codes.

	Code(s)
1. Anemia, hypochromic, microcytic, with iron deficiency, cause unknown	280.9
2. Macrocytic anemia secondary to vitamin B_{12} malabsorption with proteinuria	281.1

Anemia Due to Acute Blood Loss

It is important to distinguish between anemia due to chronic blood loss and anemia due to acute blood loss, because the two conditions have entirely different codes in *ICD-9-CM*. Acute blood-loss anemia results from a sudden, significant loss of blood over a brief period of time. It may occur due to trauma such as laceration, or a rupture of the spleen or other injury of abdominal viscera, where no external blood loss is noted. A diagnosis of acute blood-loss anemia should be supported by documented evidence of the condition, such as a sustained, significant lowering of the hemoglobin level and/or hematocrit.

Acute blood-loss anemia may occur following surgery, but it is not necessarily a complication of the procedure and should not be coded as a postoperative complication unless the physician identifies it as such. Many surgical procedures, such as hip replacement, routinely involve a considerable amount of bleeding as an expected part of the operation. This may or may not result in anemia; a code for anemia should be assigned only when the anemia is documented by the physician. If, in the physician's clinical judgment, surgery results in an expected amount of blood loss and the physician does not describe the patient as having anemia or a complication of surgery, do not assign a code for the blood loss.  If a postoperative blood count is low enough to suggest anemia, it is appropriate to ask the physician whether a diagnosis of anemia should be added. The coder should not assume, however, that mention of blood loss and/or transfusion during surgery is an indication that anemia is present. Blood replacement is sometimes carried out as a preventive measure. When postoperative anemia is documented without specification of acute blood loss, code **285.9, Anemia, unspecified,** is the default. Code **285.1, Acute posthemorrhagic anemia,** should be assigned when postoperative anemia is due to acute blood loss. When neither the diagnostic statement nor review of the medical record indicates whether a blood-loss anemia is acute or chronic, code 280.0 should be assigned.

Exercise 13.2

Code the following diagnoses and procedures. Do not assign E codes.

	Code(s)
1. Anemia due to blood loss from chronic gastric ulcer	280.0 531.40
2. Anemia, chronic, secondary to blood loss due to adenomyosis	280.0 617.0
3. Posthemorrhagic anemia due to acute blood loss following perforation of chronic duodenal ulcer	285.1 532.60

Anemia of Chronic Disease

Patients with chronic illnesses are often seen with anemia, which may be the cause of the health care admission or encounter. Treatment is often directed at the anemia, not the underlying condition. Codes for this type of anemia are classified as follows:

- Anemia in chronic kidney disease: 285.21 and a code from category 585, Chronic kidney disease, to indicate the stage of chronic kidney disease
- Anemia in neoplastic disease: 285.22 and the neoplasm code that is responsible for the anemia. Code 285.22 is for anemia in, due to, or with the malignancy, and not due to the antineoplastic chemotherapy drugs, which is an adverse effect.
- Anemia of other chronic disease: 285.29 and the code for the chronic condition causing the anemia

These codes may be used as the principal or first-listed diagnosis when the reason for the encounter is to deal with the anemia. On the other hand, they may be used as secondary diagnosis codes when the reason for the encounter is to deal with the underlying chronic disease or another condition. The code for the chronic condition causing the anemia should also be assigned. There is no effective therapy for anemia of chronic illness but very symptomatic patients may require a transfusion of packed blood cells.

Anemia Due to Chemotherapy

Anemia due to antineoplastic chemotherapy is classified to code **285.3, Antineoplastic chemotherapy induced anemia.** This type of anemia is rarely a hemolytic process and is not truly an aplastic process. Antineoplastic chemotherapy induced changes are generally short term and do not usually reduce the marrow cellularity to a point of aplasia. It is not necessary to additionally report the E code because the information about being an adverse effect of a chemotherapy drug is included in the anemia code. However, providers may choose to collect the E code for internal data collection purposes.

Anemia due to chemotherapy should not be confused with aplastic anemia due to antineoplastic chemotherapy, which is coded to 284.89. Anemia due to drug, where the drug is not specified, is coded to the type of anemia (or to code 285.9 if the type of anemia is not specified).

Aplastic Anemia

Aplastic anemia (284.x) is caused by a failure of the bone marrow to produce red blood cells. The condition may be congenital, but it is usually idiopathic or acquired. It may be due to an underlying disease such as a malignant neoplasm or an infection (for example, viral hepatitis). It may also be caused by exposure to ionizing radiation, chemicals, or drugs, and it often results from treatment for malignancy. Aplastic anemia due to chronic systemic disease, drugs, infection, radiation, or toxic (paralytic) is coded to **284.89, Other specified aplastic anemias.** When the type of anemia is not specified but appears to be related to a diagnosis of malignancy or treatment for malignancy, the physician should be queried to determine whether the code for aplastic anemia may be appropriate.

Pancytopenia (284.19) is a type of aplastic anemia that represents a deficiency of all three elements of the blood. When a patient has anemia (deficiency of red cells), neutropenia (deficiency of white cells), and thrombocytopenia (deficiency of platelets), only the code for pancytopenia (284.19) should be assigned. When the pancytopenia is drug induced, *ICD-9-CM* distinguishes whether it is due to antineoplastic chemotherapy (284.11) or other drug (284.12). Code **284.09, Other constitutional aplastic anemia,** would be assigned if the pancytopenia was congenital rather than due to chronic disease. Do not assign code 284.1x if the pancytopenia is due to bone marrow infiltration (284.2), hairy cell leukemia (202.4), human immunodeficiency virus disease (042), leukoerythroblastic anemia (284.2), malformations (284.09), myelodysplastic syndromes (238.72–238.75), myeloproliferative disease (238.79), or other constitutional aplastic anemia (284.09).

Exercise 13.3

Code the following diagnoses and procedures. Do not assign E codes.

	Code(s)
1. Aplastic anemia due to ionizing radiation	284.89
2. Myelophthisic anemia	284.2

Sickle-Cell Anemia and Thalassemia

In coding sickle-cell disorders, it is important to understand the difference between sickle-cell anemia or disease (282.6x) and sickle-cell trait (282.5). Sickle-cell disease is a hereditary disease of the red blood cells; the disease is passed to a child when both parents carry the genetic trait. Sickle-cell trait occurs when a child receives the genetic trait from only one parent. Patients with sickle-cell trait do not generally develop sickle-cell disease; they are carriers of the trait. When a medical record contains both the terms sickle-cell trait and sickle-cell disease, only the code for the sickle-cell disease is assigned.

Code **282.62, Hb-SS disease with crisis,** is assigned when vaso-occlusive crises or other crises are present. An additional code is assigned to report the type of crisis, such as acute chest syndrome (517.3) or splenic sequestration (289.52). If a condition such as cerebrovascular embolism occurs, a code should also be assigned to indicate its presence.

Another possible type of sickle-cell disease is sickle-cell thalassemia. Specific codes are available for sickle-cell thalassemia with crisis (282.42) or without crisis (282.41). Additional codes are assigned when the type of crisis is specified.

Thalassemia is a genetic blood disorder resulting from a defect in a gene that controls production of one of the hemoglobin proteins. There are many forms of thalassemia. Each type has many different subtypes. A person must inherit the defective gene from both parents to develop thalassemia major. Thalassemia minor occurs when the defective gene is inherited from only one parent. Persons with this form of the disorder are carriers of the disease and usually do not have symptoms. *ICD-9-CM* provides unique codes for different types of thalassemia, such as alpha thalassemia (282.43), beta thalassemia (282.44), delta-beta thalassemia (282.45), thalassemia minor (282.46), hemoglobin E-beta thalassemia (282.47), and other thalassemia (282.49). Code **282.40, Thalassemia, unspecified,** is reported when the type of thalassemia is not identified. However, thalassemia trait, not otherwise specified, is assigned to code **282.46, Thalassemia minor.**

Exercise 13.4

Code the following diagnoses. Do not assign E codes.

	Code(s)
1. Classical hemophilia	286.0
2. Hemolytic anemia, sickle-cell Hb-SS disease	282.61
3. Hereditary spherocytic, hemolytic anemia	282.0
4. Thalassemia	282.40
5. Sickle-cell crisis	282.62

COAGULATION DEFECTS

Coagulation defects are characterized by prolonged clotting time. Some are congenital in origin; others are acquired. Hemorrhagic disorder due to intrinsic circulating anticoagulants, antibodies or inhibitors (subcategory 286.5) is essentially the only condition that presents any problem to the coder. This condition results from the presence of circulating anticoagulants in the blood that interfere with normal clotting. These anticoagulants are usually inherent or intrinsic in the blood, like other coagulation defects, but occasionally may be augmented by long-term anticoagulant therapy. This condition is a relatively rare disorder, even more so when it occurs as a result of anticoagulant therapy. Subcategory 286.5 has been expanded to uniquely identify acquired hemophilia (286.52), antiphospholipid antibody with hemorrhagic disorder (286.53), and other hemorrhagic disorder due to intrinsic circulating anticoagulants, antibodies or inhibitors (286.59).

Bleeding in a patient who is being treated with Coumadin, heparin, or another anticoagulant does not indicate that a hemorrhagic disorder due to intrinsic circulating anticoagulant is present. In this situation, a code for the condition and associated hemorrhage is assigned, with an additional code of **E934.2, Anticoagulants,** to indicate the responsible medication. Code 286.5x is not assigned unless the physician specifically documents a diagnosis of hemorrhagic disorder due to circulating anticoagulants.

Heparin-induced thrombocytopenia (289.84) is one of the most severe side effects of heparin therapy. Heparin therapy is widely used to prevent and treat clotting disorders. In some people, heparin triggers autoimmune conditions of severe platelet deficiency with severe thrombotic (clot-related) complications.

Hypercoagulable states refer to a group of acquired and inherited disorders caused by increased thrombin generation. There is an increased tendency for blood clotting and there may be fibrin deposition in the small blood vessels. These disorders are divided into primary and secondary hypercoagulable states. Primary hypercoagulable states (289.81) are inherited disorders of specific anticoagulant factors. Secondary hypercoagulable states (289.82) are primarily acquired disorders that predispose to thrombosis through complex and multifactorial mechanisms involving blood flow abnormalities or defects in blood composition and of vessel walls. Examples of conditions that can cause secondary hypercoagulable states are malignancy, pregnancy, trauma, myeloproliferative disorders, and antiphospholipid antibody syndrome.

Prolonged prothrombin time or other abnormal coagulation profiles should not be coded as a coagulation defect. Code **790.92, Abnormal coagulation profile,** is assigned for this abnormal laboratory finding. If the patient is receiving Coumadin therapy, however, a prolonged bleeding time is an expected result, and therefore code 790.92 is not assigned. Note also that Coumadin is not a circulating anticoagulant; it induces anticoagulation through other mechanisms. Examples of appropriate code assignments include the following:

- Duodenal ulcer with hemorrhage due to Coumadin therapy 532.40 + E934.2
- Acute gastritis with hemorrhage due to anticoagulant therapy 535.01 + E934.2

Here are some additional case examples:

- A 50-year-old man receiving Coumadin therapy is admitted with hematemesis secondary to acute gastritis. A prolonged prothrombin time is reported, secondary to the anticoagulant effects of the Coumadin therapy. Code **535.01, Acute gastritis with hemorrhage,** is assigned; code 286.5x is not reported because no hemorrhagic disorder was identified. No code is assigned for the prolonged bleeding time because this is an expected result of Coumadin therapy. Note again that Coumadin is not a circulating anticoagulant; it induces anticoagulation through other mechanisms.
- A patient is admitted following multiple episodes of hematemesis secondary to Coumadin therapy. No significant pathology was discovered. The Coumadin is discontinued, and no recurrence of the bleeding occurs. Code **578.0, Hematemesis,** is assigned with an additional code of E934.2 to indicate Coumadin as the responsible external agent. Code 286.5x is not assigned.

DISEASES OF PLATELET CELLS

Thrombocytopenia is a deficiency in the blood cells that help the blood to clot. Post-transfusion purpura (PTP) is the recipient's response following a transfusion of blood products from an HPA-positive donor in which anti-HPA antibodies are produced that destroy the platelets. The alloantibody destroys the transfused platelets as well as the recipient's own platelets to produce a severe thrombocytopenia in HPA-negative women who were immunized during a previous pregnancy or transfusion. Code **287.41, Post-transfusion purpura,** is assigned for this rare condition. Code **287.49, Other secondary thrombocytopenia,** is assigned for secondary thrombocytopenia that is due to dilutional causes, drugs, extracorporeal circulation of blood, massive blood tranfusion, platelet alloimmunization, and other secondary thrombocytopenias.

DISEASES OF WHITE BLOOD CELLS

White blood cells (leukocytes) play an important role in the body's immune system by fighting off infection. Many different diseases can affect white blood cells. There are several different types of normal white blood cells (WBCs), including neutrophils, lymphocytes, monocytes, eosinophils, and basophils.

Diseases that may decrease production of WBCs include drug toxicity, vitamin deficiencies, blood diseases, infections (viral diseases, tuberculosis, typhoid), or abnormalities of the bone marrow; or the decrease could be cyclic (varying in severity possibly due to biorhythms). Antibodies may attack WBCs as a result of a disease or because of medications stimulating the immune system. Pooling of WBCs occurs with some overwhelming infections, heart-lung bypass during heart surgery, and hemodialysis.

Some diseases increase the production of WBCs. If all types of WBCs are affected, leukocytosis occurs. Leukocytosis can be caused by infection, inflammation, allergic reaction, malignancy, hereditary disorders, or other miscellaneous causes—for example, medications such as cortisone-like drugs (prednisone), lithium, and nonsteroidal anti-inflammatory drugs. Other illnesses target specific types of WBCs, such as neutrophilia, lymphocytosis, and granulocytosis.

Diseases of the WBCs are primarily classified on the basis of whether the WBC count is low or elevated. In addition, more specific codes are available depending on the type of blood cell affected. For example:

- Low neutrophil count or neutropenia (subcategory 288.0) is further subdivided as follows: unspecified (288.00), congenital (288.01), cyclic or periodic (288.02), drug-induced (288.03) (for example, due to chemotherapy), neutropenia due to infection (288.04), or other reasons such as immune or toxic (288.09).
- Decreased WBC counts (subcategory 288.5) are classified as follows: unspecified leukocytopenia (288.50); decreased lymphocytes or lymphocytopenia (288.51); or other decreased WBC count including basophils, eosinophils, monocytes, or plasmacytes (288.59).

FIGURE 13.1 Four Major Types of Blood Cells

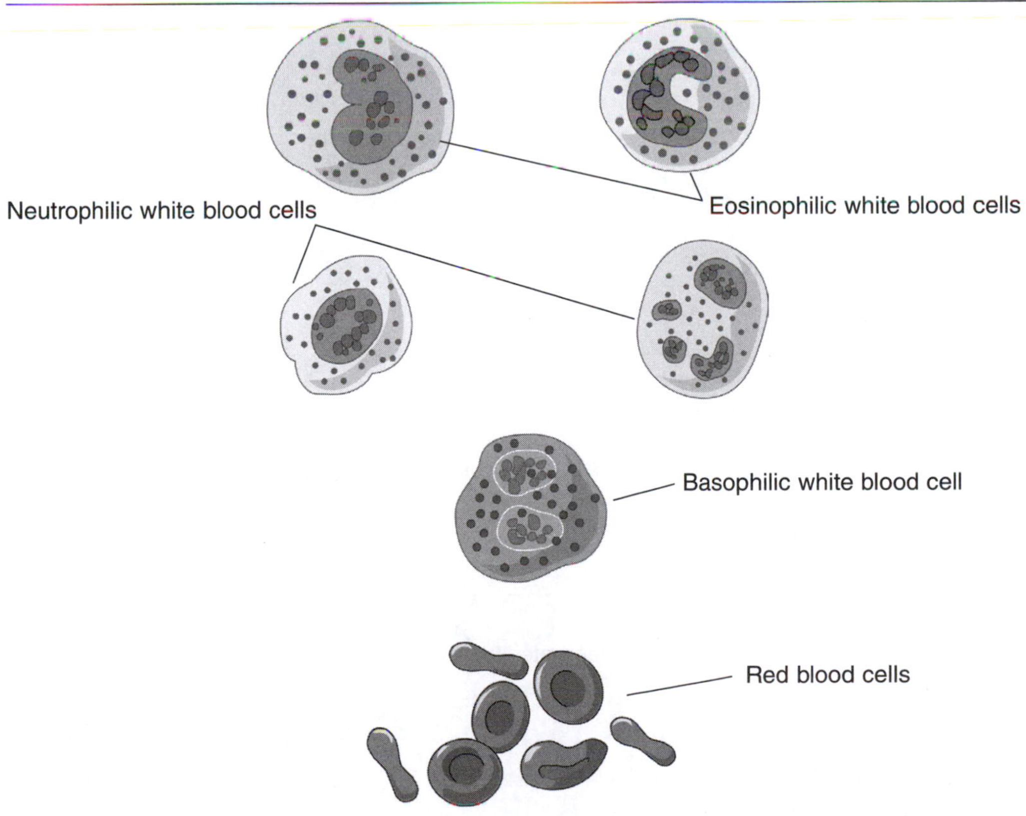

- Elevated WBC counts (subcategory 288.6), on the other hand, are classified as follows: unspecified leukocytosis (288.60); elevated lymphocytes or lymphocytosis (288.61); leukemoid reaction including basophilic, lymphocytic, monocytic, myelocytic, or neutrophilic leukemoid reaction (288.62); monocytosis (288.63); plasmacytosis (288.64); basophilia (288.65); bandemia (288.66); or other elevated WBC count (288.69).

It is important to remember that these codes should not be assigned on the basis of laboratory findings alone. Physician concurrence regarding the significance of the laboratory results should be confirmed before assigning these codes.

Review Exercise 13.5

Code the following diagnoses.

	Code(s)
1. Pancytopenia, congenital	284.09
2. Cyclic neutropenia	288.02
3. Hereditary thrombocytopenia	287.33
4. Anemia Neutropenia Thrombocytopenia Pancytopenia	284.19
5. Cervical adenitis due to *Staphylococcus aureus*	289.3 041.11
6. Autoerythrocyte sensitization purpura	287.2
7. Pernicious anemia, Addison type	281.0
8. Acute gastritis with hemorrhage, exacerbated by heparin therapy Table: heparin	535.01 E934.2

Diseases of the Nervous System and Sense Organs

CHAPTER **14**

CHAPTER OVERVIEW

- Nervous system and sense organ diseases can be found in chapter 6 of *ICD-9-CM.*
- Dual coding is often required for infectious diseases of the central nervous system.
- Pain can be coded by recording the site of the pain.
  - Codes for pain, not elsewhere classified (338), can be used for coding pain control or management.
  - If the cause is known but not treated in the encounter, code it as an additional diagnosis.
- Coders must be careful when coding seizures to epilepsy. Seizures may be caused by a variety of conditions and should be coded accordingly.
- Other diseases of the central nervous system covered in this chapter of the handbook are hemiplegia, Parkinson's disease, autonomic dysreflexia, and narcolepsy.
- Many problems of the peripheral nervous system are manifestations of other conditions.
  - These problems are assigned as additional codes.
  - Critical illness polyneuropathy and critical illness myopathy, for example, are complications of sepsis.
- Eye diseases are extremely complicated to code, and understanding the terminology and diagnostic statement completely is vital to proper coding.
- Eye diseases and conditions covered in this handbook include corneal injuries (from both light and wounding), conjunctivitis, cataracts, and glaucoma.
- Hearing loss may be coded as conductive, sensorineural, or a combination of the two.

LEARNING OUTCOMES

After studying this chapter you should be able to:

- Explain the difference between the central and peripheral nervous systems and locate the two areas in the *ICD-9-CM*.
- Understand how to code for pain.
- Explain what is needed before a code of epilepsy is assigned.
- Code for a variety of conditions of the nervous system.
- Code disorders of the eye and ear.

TERMS TO KNOW

Central nervous system
the brain and spinal cord

Conductive hearing loss
hearing loss due to a problem with a part of the ear

Peripheral nervous system
all elements of the nervous system except the brain and spinal cord

Sensorineural hearing loss
hearing loss due to a problem with the sensory part of the ear or the nerves associated with hearing

REMEMBER . . . Due to legal and personal reasons, a code of epilepsy cannot be assigned unless it is clearly diagnosed by a physician.

INTRODUCTION

Diseases of the nervous system and sense organs are classified in chapter 6 of *ICD-9-CM*. Because the nervous system is complex and difficult to comprehend, thinking of it as a two-level system may help to simplify the coding process:

- 320–349 central nervous system (brain and spinal cord)
- 350–359 peripheral nervous system (all other neural elements)

Cerebral degeneration, Parkinson's disease, and meningitis are conditions affecting the central nervous system. Polyneuropathy, myasthenia gravis, and muscular dystrophies affect the peripheral nerves. The peripheral nervous system includes the autonomic nervous system, which regulates the activity of the cardiac muscle, smooth muscle, and glands.

FIGURE 14.1 The Nervous System

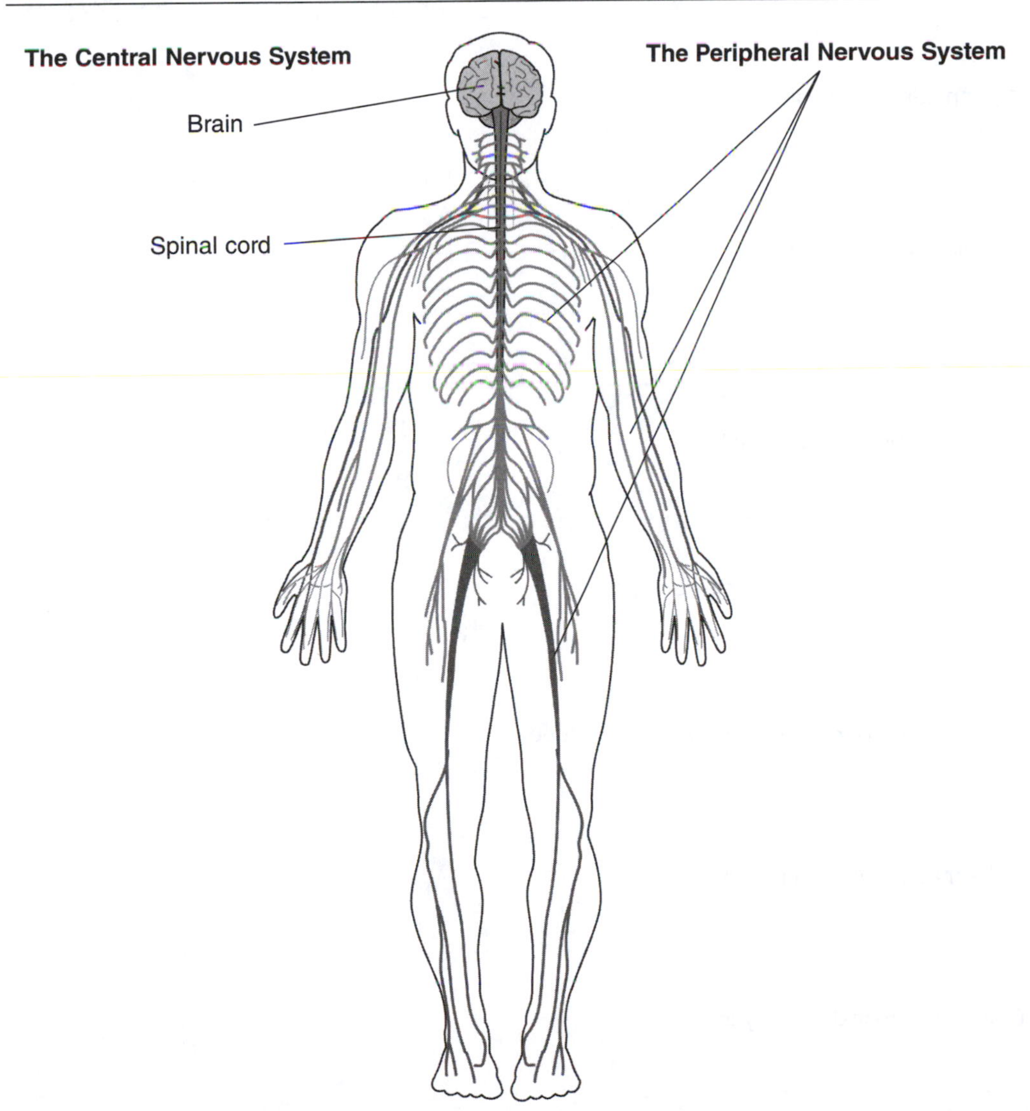

INFECTIOUS DISEASES OF THE CENTRAL NERVOUS SYSTEM

Infectious diseases of the central nervous system are classified in several ways, and it is imperative that the coder carefully follows the directions provided by the Alphabetic Index and Tabular List. Dual coding is frequently required, with the code for the underlying condition sequenced first, followed by a manifestation code. For example, meningitis sarcoidosis is classified as **135, Sarcoidosis,** with a manifestation of **321.4, Meningitis in sarcoidosis.** Bacterial meningitis due to certain organisms such as *Pneumococcus, Streptococcus,* and *Staphylococcus* is classified in categories 320 and 321, with a fourth digit indicating the responsible organism.

Exercise 14.1

Code the following diagnoses and procedures.

	Code(s)
1. Candidal meningitis	112.83
2. Influenzal encephalitis	487.8 323.41
3. Encephalitis due to rubella	056.01
4. Chronic serous otitis media, left ear	381.10
Myringotomy with insertion of drainage tube	20.01
5. Herpes zoster with meningitis	053.0
6. Staphylococcal meningitis	320.3

PAIN

Pain may be coded by reporting the site of pain. These codes may be found in the symptom chapter (e.g., headache, 784.0) or in the appropriate body system chapter (e.g., pain in limb, 729.5). Codes in category 338, Pain, not elsewhere classified, may be used in conjunction with the site of pain codes if the category 338 code provides more detail about acute or chronic pain and neoplasm-related pain unless otherwise indicated below.

The determination of whether the pain is acute, chronic, or chronic pain syndrome is dependent on the provider's documentation. There is no time frame defining when pain becomes chronic.

Encounter/Admission for Pain Control/Management

Category 338 codes may be used as the principal diagnosis or first-listed code when pain control or pain management is the reason for the admission/encounter. These encounters are typically not for diagnostic workup or treatment of the underlying condition but for management of pain. In these situations, if the underlying cause of the pain is known, report it as an additional diagnosis. An example of this is a patient with displaced intervertebral disc, nerve impingement, and severe back pain who presents for injection of steroid into the spinal canal. The injection is intended to relieve the pain, but it does not treat the displaced disc.

If the admission is for control of pain related to, associated with, or due to, a malignancy, code **338.3, Neoplasm related pain,** should be assigned. The underlying neoplasm is reported as an additional diagnosis. Because the neoplasm code will provide information regarding the specific site, an additional code for the site of pain should not be assigned.

If the admission or encounter is for a procedure to treat the underlying condition, the underlying condition should be assigned as the principal or first-listed diagnosis. For example, if a patient is admitted for a spinal fusion to treat lumbar spinal stenosis, assign code **724.02, Spinal stenosis, lumbar region, without neurogenic claudication,** as the principal diagnosis. No code from category 338 should be assigned.

Patients with chronic pain who have failed conservative therapies may undergo insertion of neurostimulators for pain control. In such cases, the appropriate pain code is assigned as the principal or first-listed diagnosis. When an admission or encounter is for a procedure aimed at treating the underlying condition, and a neurostimulator is inserted for pain control during the same admission/encounter, a code for the underlying condition should be assigned as the principal diagnosis with the pain code as a secondary diagnosis.

If the encounter is for any other reason except pain control or pain management and a related definitive diagnosis for the pain has not been established (confirmed) by the provider, the code for the specific site of pain should be assigned first, followed by the appropriate code from category 338. If the definitive diagnosis has been established, assign the code for the definitive diagnosis.

Postoperative Pain

Postthoracotomy pain and other postoperative pain are classified to subcategories 338.1 and 338.2, depending on whether the pain is acute or chronic. The default for postthoracotomy and other postoperative pain not specified as acute or chronic is the code for the acute form. Postoperative pain associated with a specific postoperative complication (such as painful wire sutures) or associated with devices, implants, or grafts left in a surgical site (such as a painful hip prosthesis) is assigned to the appropriate code(s) found in chapter 17, Injury and Poisoning. A code from category 338 is assigned as an additional code to identify acute or chronic pain.

Postoperative pain may be reported as the principal or first-listed diagnosis when the reason for the encounter or admission is postoperative pain control/management. Postoperative pain may be reported as a secondary diagnosis code when a patient presents for outpatient surgery and develops an unusual or inordinate amount of postoperative pain.

Please note that routine or expected postoperative pain immediately after surgery should not be coded.

HEADACHE

A diagnosis of headache without any further specificity is classified to chapter 16 and coded to **784.0, Headache.** However, more specific headaches are classified to **307.81, Tension headache,** or to chapter 6, Diseases of the Nervous System and Sense Organs.

Specific headaches are classified in chapter 6 as follows:

- Headache syndromes (category 339):
  —Cluster headaches and other trigeminal autonomic cephalgias (339.00–339.09)
  —Tension-type headache (339.10–339.12)
  —Posttraumatic headache (339.20–339.22)
  —Drug-induced headache (339.3)
  —Complicated headache syndromes (339.41–339.44)
  —Other specific headache syndromes (339.81–339.89)
- Migraines (category 346) require a fifth-digit subclassification to indicate whether the migraine is intractable and whether there is status migrainosus (also called status migraine). Status migrainosus generally refers to a severe migraine attack that lasts for more than 72 hours. However, the designation of status migrainosus should be confirmed by the physician before the fifth digits "2" or "3" are assigned with codes in this category.
- Headache following lumbar puncture is assigned to code **349.0, Reaction to spinal or lumbar puncture.**

EPILEPSY

Epilepsy is a paroxysmal disorder of cerebral function characterized by recurrent seizures. Coders must not assume, however, that any diagnostic statement describing convulsions or seizures should be coded to epilepsy; these conditions also occur in a number of other diseases, such as brain tumor, cerebrovascular accident, alcoholism, electrolyte imbalance, and febrile conditions. Grand mal seizures, for example, can be due to causes other than epilepsy. Because a diagnosis of epilepsy can have serious legal and personal implications for the patient, such as the inability to obtain a driver's license, a code for epilepsy must not be assigned unless the physician clearly identifies the condition as such in the diagnostic statement. When the diagnosis is stated only in terms of convulsion or seizure without any further identification of the cause, code 780.39 should be assigned. When the physician mentions a history of seizure in the workup but does not include any mention of seizures in the diagnostic statement, no code should be assigned unless there is clear documentation that the criteria for reporting the condition have been met and the physician agrees that a code should be added. Please note that the classification assigns seizure disorder and recurrent seizures to epilepsy 345.9x, whereas the main term seizure(s) is indexed to **780.39, Other convulsions.**

ICD-9-CM provides a fifth-digit subclassification for category **345, Epilepsy and recurrent seizures,** that permits identification of epilepsy as intractable when so described by the physician. Terms such as "pharmacoresistant (pharmacologically resistant)," "poorly controlled," "refractory (medically)," and "treatment resistant" are included under fifth digit 1 with intractable epilepsy. In the absence of specific statements to this effect, fifth digit 0 is assigned. The coder should not assume that the condition is intractable from general statements in the medical record.

Exercise 14.2

Code the following diagnoses and procedures. Do not assign E codes.

	Code(s)
1. Intractable epilepsy, grand mal type	345.11
Electroencephalogram	89.14
2. Psychomotor epilepsy	345.40
3. Poorly controlled Jacksonian epilepsy	345.51
4. Intractable temporal lobe epilepsy	345.41
5. Febrile convulsions, recurrent	780.31
6. Psychosensory epilepsy, partial	345.40

HEMIPLEGIA/HEMIPARESIS

Hemiplegia is paralysis of one side of the body. It is classified to category 342, with a fifth digit to indicate whether the dominant or nondominant side is affected. Hemiplegia occurring in connection with a cerebrovascular accident (CVA) often clears quickly and is sometimes called a transient hemiplegia. Hemiplegia is not inherent to an acute CVA; therefore, a code from category 342, Hemiplegia, is assigned as an additional code when it occurs. Even if it resolves without treatment, it affects the patient's care. Any neurologic deficits caused by the CVA should be reported even when they have resolved at the time of discharge. When the patient is admitted at a later time with hemiplegia, code 438.2x is assigned to indicate that the condition is a late effect of a cerebrovascular accident. (See chapter 24 of this handbook for more discussion of cerebrovascular disease.)

Examples of appropriate coding for hemiplegia follow:

- Cerebral thrombosis with transient hemiplegia that has cleared by discharge 434.00 + 342.90
- Cerebral thrombosis with hemiplegia still present at discharge 434.00 + 342.90
- Hemiplegia of dominant side due to previous CVA 438.21
- Hemiparesis due to old spinal cord injury 342.90 + 907.2

PARKINSON'S DISEASE

Parkinson's disease, also known as Parkinsonism, is a chronic, progressive disorder of the central nervous system characterized by a fine, slowly spreading involuntary tremor, postural instability, and muscle weakness and rigidity. The fourth-digit axis for category **332, Parkinson's disease,** is based on whether the disease is primary (332.0) or secondary (332.1). Secondary Parkinson's disease is often an adverse effect of the therapeutic use of medication, in which case an E code to indicate the responsible drug is assigned as an additional code. Parkinson's disease is sometimes due to syphilis and in that case is coded to **094.82, Syphilitic Parkinsonism.**

AUTONOMIC DYSREFLEXIA

Autonomic dysreflexia is a syndrome characterized by an abrupt onset of excessively high blood pressure caused by an uncontrolled sympathetic nervous system discharge in persons with spinal cord injury, usually at or above the T6 level. Anything that would ordinarily cause pain below this level may trigger a parasympathetic response resulting in bradycardia, blurred vision, and sweating. True autonomic dysreflexia is potentially life-threatening and is considered a medical emergency. Code **337.3, Autonomic dysreflexia,** is used to report this condition. It is not necessary to code each manifestation or symptom separately. Unlike most dual coding where the underlying condition is listed first, in this case the code for the dysreflexia is sequenced first, with an additional code for the underlying chronic condition that has precipitated this life-threatening condition (e.g., pressure ulcer, fecal impaction, urinary tract infection).

NARCOLEPSY

Narcolepsy is a chronic neurological disorder with inability to regulate sleep and wakefulness normally. Symptoms are excessive daytime sleepiness, sleep paralysis (paralysis upon falling asleep or waking up), cataplexy (sudden, brief episodes of paralysis or muscle weakness), and vivid hallucinations (vivid dreamlike images that occur at sleep onset). Other possible symptoms are disturbed nighttime sleep, leg jerks, nightmares, and frequent awakenings. Irresistible sleep attacks may occur throughout the day regardless of the amount or quality of prior nighttime sleep. Affected individuals may fall asleep at work or school, or while eating, talking, or driving.

ICD-9-CM distinguishes between subcategory 347.0 (narcolepsy) and 347.1 (narcolepsy in conditions classified elsewhere). When reporting subcategory 347.1, the underlying condition is coded first. In addition, fifth digits distinguish between narcolepsy with cataplexy (347.01, 347.11) and without cataplexy (347.00, 347.10).

Exercise 14.3

Code the following diagnoses.

	Code(s)
1. Parkinson's disease	332.0
2. Secondary Parkinsonism due to prescribed drug (Thorazine)	332.1 E939.1
3. Severe hypertension and pounding headache due to autonomic dysreflexia due to fecal impaction	337.3 + 560.32

DISORDERS OF THE PERIPHERAL NERVOUS SYSTEM

Disorders of the peripheral nervous system are classified to categories 350 through 359 according to the condition and the nerves involved. Many codes in this section are manifestations of other disease and are assigned as additional codes, with the underlying condition listed first.

CRITICAL ILLNESS POLYNEUROPATHY

Critical illness polyneuropathy is commonly associated with complications of sepsis and multiple organ failure. It is considered to be secondary to Systemic Inflammatory Response Syndrome (SIRS). Synonyms for critical illness polyneuropathy include neuropathy of critical illness, intensive care unit (ICU) neuropathy, and intensive care polyneuropathy. Patients with this condition show abnormal electrophysiologic changes consistent with primary axonal degeneration of motor fibers. They also demonstrate severe weakness, making it difficult to wean them from mechanical ventilation. Assign code **357.82, Critical illness polyneuropathy,** for this condition.

CRITICAL ILLNESS MYOPATHY

Critical illness myopathy is also associated with sepsis. It is a cause of difficulty in weaning patients from mechanical ventilation and prolonged recovery after illness. It is also associated with neuromuscular blocking agents and corticosteroids (in asthma and organ transplant patients), and neuropathy. Code **359.81, Critical illness myopathy,** is used to report this condition.

Exercise 14.4

Code the following diagnoses and procedures.

	Code(s)
1. Nephropathic amyloidosis	277.39 583.81
2. Interdigital neuroma, 3–4 and 4–5 interspaces, left foot	355.6
Excision of Morton's neuroma, left foot	04.07
3. Tardy palsy due to entrapment of ulnar nerve	354.2
4. Peripheral polyneuritis, severe, due to chronic alcoholism	357.5 303.90
5. Polyneuropathy in sarcoidosis	135 357.4
6. Tic douloureux	350.1

DISORDERS OF THE EYE AND ADNEXAE

The classification for diseases of the eye is very detailed, and understanding the terminology used is especially important for the coder. Terms that seem similar may have entirely different meanings. The coder should be sure to fully understand the diagnostic statement in the medical record before assigning a code.

Visual impairment (369) is classified according to severity, with the status of the better eye listed first and the lesser eye listed second in the code title. Legal blindness in the United States is defined as severe or profound impairment of both eyes. Sample codes include the following:

- Better eye, profound impairment; lesser eye, near-total impairment 369.07
- Better eye, severe impairment; lesser eye, near-total impairment 369.13

Occasionally, visual problems can cause tilting of the head, resulting in ocular torticollis or ocular-induced torticollis. Torticollis refers to abnormal head posture. Palsy of the superior or inferior oblique muscles will cause the patient to hold the head at an angle to compensate for the visual disturbance. Ocular torticollis is coded by assigning first the appropriate code for the ocular condition causing the torticollis, e.g. nystagmus (379.50), strabismus (378.9), fourth nerve palsy (378.53), etc., followed by code **781.93, Ocular torticollis.**

FIGURE 14.2 The Eye

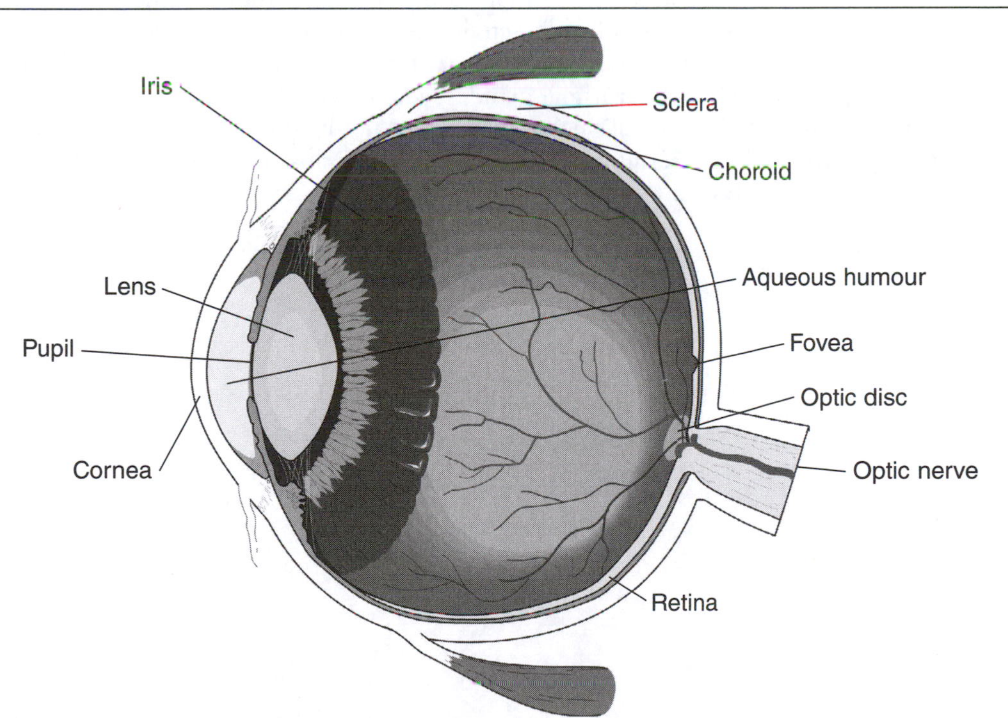

Corneal Injury

Code **370.24, Photokeratitis,** is assigned for a corneal flash burn, generally referred to as ultraviolet keratitis. This type of burn results from unprotected exposure to the sun or ultraviolet light, or, for example, the light from a welder's torch. It is always an injury; code **E926.2, Visible and ultraviolet light sources,** is assigned as an additional code.

Corneal or corneoscleral lacerations are classified in category **871, Open wound of the eyeball.** The fourth digits are assigned to indicate whether there is associated prolapse of intraocular tissue, whether it is a penetrating injury, whether it is with or without a magnetic foreign body, and whether it is related to other conditions. An E code is assigned for the external cause. Repair is classified as **11.51, Suture of corneal laceration.**

Conjunctivitis

Conjunctivitis is an inflammation of the conjunctiva that may be due to infection, allergy, or other cause. When the cause of acute conjunctivitis is a chemical or toxic agent, code 372.06 is used with an additional E code for the chemical or toxic agent. Giant papillary conjunctivitis (372.14) is an inflammation resulting from an allergic reaction to contact lenses. **Vernal conjunctivitis (372.13)** is due to an allergic reaction to pollen. Conjunctivitis due to Chlamydia is classified to 077.x or to 076.x when designated as trachoma.

Disorders of conjunctivochalasis are reported using code 372.81. This is a situation in which redundant conjunctiva lies over the lower eyelid margin and covers the lower punctum. It can create a variety of symptoms from aggravation of a dry eye at the mild stage, disruption of the normal flow of tears at the moderate state, and exposure problems of the severe stage. Treatment consists of a simple local surgical excision to relieve the symptoms. Code **370.34, Exposure keratoconjunctivitis,** is assigned for dry eye related to Bell's palsy. Code **375.15, Tear film insufficiency, unspecified,** is provided by the index for dry eye syndrome, a disorder of the lacrimal gland. Code 375.15, however, is inappropriate for the dry eye associated with Bell's palsy, which does not involve the lacrimal gland but is due to exposure to the air resulting from the inability to close the eye as a result of the acute severe facial paralysis of Bell's palsy.

Exercise 14.5

Code the following diagnoses and procedures. Do not assign E codes.

	Code(s)
1. Intermittent monocular esotropia	378.21
Recession of medial rectus muscle	15.11
2. Senile entropion, left	374.01
Repair entropion by suture technique	08.42
3. Blepharoptosis, congenital	743.61
Repair blepharoptosis, tarsal technique	08.35
4. Ectropion due to cicatrix	374.14
Blepharoplasty with extensive repair	08.44
5. Conjunctivochalasis	372.81

Cataracts

In coding cataracts the coder must avoid making assumptions about the type of cataract based on the patient's age or other conditions. A cataract in an older patient is not necessarily senile or mature; the coder should be alert to the terminology used in the diagnostic statement. Cataracts in patients with diabetes are most often senile; a true diabetic cataract is rare and its code should not be assigned unless the physician clearly identifies it as such.

Cataract extraction is coded according to the technique used. If an artificial lens is implanted at the same time the cataract is removed, codes are assigned for both procedures, with the cataract extraction sequenced first.

Exercise 14.6

Code the following diagnoses and procedures. Do not assign E codes.

	Code(s)
1. True diabetic cataract in type 1 diabetes mellitus	250.51 366.41
2. Incipient senile cataract, right eye Diabetes mellitus, type 2	366.12 250.00
Extracapsular cataract extraction, OD Intraocular lens implant insertion	13.59 13.71
3. Myotonic cataract with Thomsen's disease	359.22 366.43

Glaucoma

Glaucoma is an eye disease characterized by increased intraocular pressure that causes pathological changes in the optic disk and defects in the field of vision. Category **365, Glaucoma,** uses a fourth digit to classify glaucoma by type and a fifth digit to provide more specificity. Subcategory 365.7, Glaucoma stage, provides codes for glaucoma stages as follows: unspecified stage (365.70), mild stage (365.71), moderate stage (365.72), severe stage (365.73), and indeterminate stage (365.74). A code from subcategory 365.7 may be assigned to identify the glaucoma stage for open angle glaucoma (365.10–365.13), primary angle-closure glaucoma (365.20–365.23), corticosteroid-induced glaucoma, glaucomatous stage (365.31), pseudoexfoliation glaucoma (365.52), glaucoma associated with ocular inflammations or vascular disorders (365.62–365.63), and glaucoma associated with ocular trauma (365.65).

In order to completely describe glaucomas, two codes from category 365 are needed: one for the type (365.1–365.5) and one for the stage (365.70–365.74). Codes for the stage may not be assigned as a principal or first-listed diagnosis.

It is possible for a patient to have bilateral glaucoma, with each eye being of the same or different stages and types. These cases should be coded as follows:

- Same stage and type: Assign only one code for the type of glaucoma and one code for the stage.
- Different stages: Assign one code for the type of glaucoma and one code for the highest glaucoma stage.
- Different types and different stages: Assign one code for each type of glaucoma and one code for the highest glaucoma stage.
- Evolving stage: Assign the code for the highest stage documented.

Care should be taken not to confuse code **365.74, Indeterminate stage glaucoma,** with code **365.70, Glaucoma stage, unspecified.** Code 365.74 is used for glaucomas whose stage cannot clinically be determined, and code assignment should be based on the clinical documentation. Code 365.70 should be assigned when there is no documentation regarding the stage of the glaucoma.

Aqueous misdirection was formerly known as malignant glaucoma. There is no true malignancy associated with this type of glaucoma. It is associated with fluid buildup in the back of the eye, pushing the lens and iris forward, blocking off the drain, and thereby increasing the intraocular pressure. This condition is extremely difficult to treat and often requires surgical intervention. Code **365.83, Aqueous misdirection**, is used to report this condition.

Exercise 14.7

Code the following diagnoses and procedures. Do not assign E codes.

	Code(s)
1. Glaucoma secondary to posterior dislocation of lens	379.34 365.59
2. Exophthalmos secondary to thyrotoxicosis	242.00 376.21
3. Acute early stage narrow-angle glaucoma, OD Chronic severe stage narrow-angle glaucoma, OS	365.22 365.71 365.23 365.73
Iridectomy with scleral fistulization	12.65
4. Primary open-angle glaucoma	365.11

DEAFNESS AND HEARING LOSS

Hearing loss may be unilateral or bilateral. Most hearing loss is classified in one of three ways:

- Conductive (389.05–389.06), with decrease due to a defect in the conductive apparatus of the ear (also called conduction deafness)
- Sensorineural (389.13, 389.14, 389.17, or 389.18), with the loss due to a defect in the sensory mechanism of the ear or nerves
- Mixed conductive and sensorineural hearing loss (389.20, 389.21, or 389.22)

Hearing Devices

Three major types of hearing devices are used to overcome hearing deficits:

- Externally worn battery-powered hearing aids
- Implantable bone conduction (electromagnetic) hearing devices
- Implantable cochlear prosthetic devices

The most widely used and least expensive of these is the externally worn battery-powered hearing aid, which includes a microphone, amplifier, and controls. It is commonly used to correct mild to moderate conductive hearing loss. Fitting of the hearing aid does not require surgical intervention and is coded 95.48.

The implantable bone conduction hearing device is implanted surgically on the surface of the mastoid bone. Although its circuitry is similar to the hearing aid in that it also contains a microphone, amplifier, and controls, it produces an electromagnetic inductive coil-energy transmission rather than a battery-powered amplification of sound. This device is used primarily for patients with a conductive hearing impairment (389.0x) who cannot use the battery-powered hearing aid and for whom a cochlear implant is not a viable option.

The cochlear implant is used for persons with profound sensorineural deafness (389.1x) that cannot be mitigated by the use of a modern, powerful hearing aid. Speech and sound information are transformed into electrical signals that create a perception of sound when

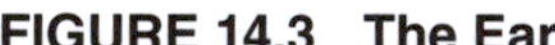

FIGURE 14.3 The Ear

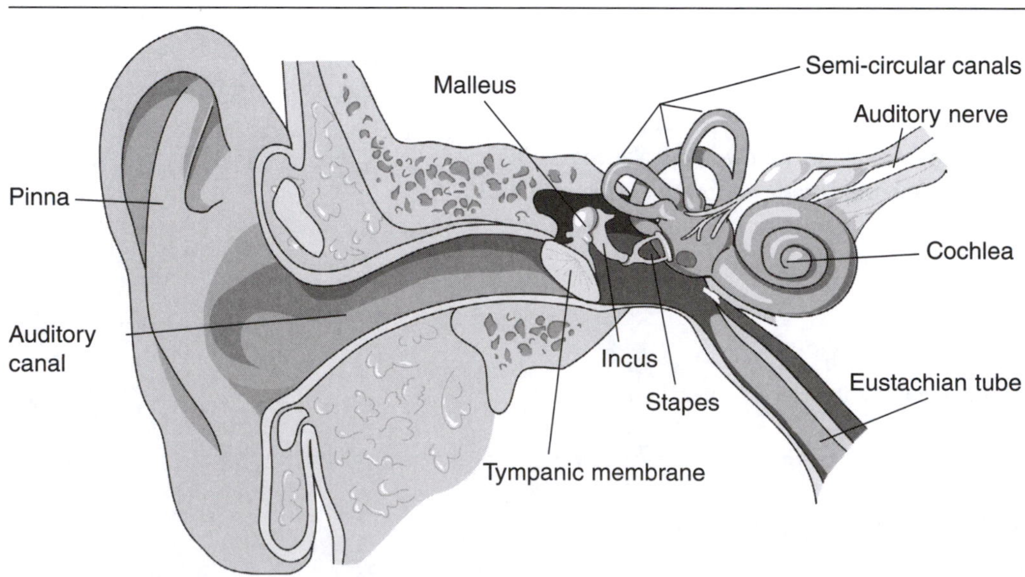

they act on the fibers of the auditory nerve within the cochlea. The cochlear prosthesis is designed to stimulate the auditory nerve in a manner that exploits the ability of the cochlea and the central nervous system to discriminate the frequency, tempo, and intensity of ambient sound in ways that help the patient to recognize source and information content.

Cochlear implants incorporate a single channel (20.97) or multiple channels (20.98) of electrical information that is transmitted to the auditory nerve via one or more electrodes within the cochlea. The codes for this procedure include implantation of a complete device, with the receiver implanted into the skull and the electrodes into the cochlea. Replacement of the complete device is also assigned to codes 20.96 through 20.98. If only the internal coils and/or electrodes are replaced, code **20.99, Other operations on middle and inner ear,** should be assigned. Repair or removal of prosthetic device or electrodes without replacement is also classified as 20.99.

Review Exercise 14.8

Code the following diagnoses and procedures. Do not assign E codes.

	Code(s)
1. Congenital external canal atresia	744.02
2. Sudden hearing loss due to chlamydial infection	388.2 079.98
Implant of electromagnetic hearing device	20.95
3. Sensory hearing loss, bilateral	389.11
4. Sensorineural deafness, bilateral	389.18
Implant of multiple-channel cochlear device	20.98
5. Perforation of tympanic membrane due to acute suppurative otitis media	382.01

Coding Diseases of the Respiratory, Digestive, and Genitourinary Systems

Diseases of the Respiratory System

CHAPTER **15**

CHAPTER OVERVIEW

- Respiratory diseases are classified in chapter 8 of *ICD-9-CM*.
- Pneumonia is a common infection that is coded several ways.

  —It is coded in combination with the responsible organism.

  —It is coded as a dual classification.
- Influenza may be coded alone or in combination with other codes.
- COPD is always caused by another condition.

  — Correct COPD classification is dependent on accurate identification of what caused the obstruction.

  — There is a NEC code for COPD without designation of what caused it.
- Asthma is classified with a fourth digit to indicate type and a fifth digit to indicate exacerbation or status asthmaticus.
- Pleural effusion is almost always integral to other diseases. Only the code for the underlying disease is assigned.
- Respiratory failure is always due to an underlying condition. Therefore, it is important to be sure that the principal diagnosis and secondary diagnosis are properly assigned.
- Acute pulmonary edema is divided into two categories.

  — Those of cardiogenic origin have codes that are related to heart failure.

  — Those of noncardiogenic origin have a variety of codes, such as drowning.
- Procedures involving the respiratory system have a large section of codes. Some of these procedures include: biopsies of the bronchus and lung, ablation, thoracoscopic, open, mechanical ventilation, and respiratory assistance not considered mechanical.

LEARNING OUTCOMES

After studying this chapter you should be able to:

- Classify the variety of pneumonia that you will encounter as a coder.
- Determine the correct coding of COPD based on the documented diagnosis.
- Know when to code for respiratory failure as the principal or secondary diagnosis.
- Know how to classify both cardiogenic and noncardiogenic acute pulmonary edemas.
- Code procedures commonly used to treat respiratory system diseases.

TERMS TO KNOW

Acute pulmonary edema
excessive fluid in the tissue and alveolar spaces of the lung

Athelectasis
a collapse of lung tissue; an integral part of pulmonary disease

Bronchospasm
a sudden constriction of the muscles in the walls of the bronchioles

COPD
chronic obstructive pulmonary disease; a general term describing conditions that result in an airway obstruction

Pleural effusion
accumulation of fluid within the pleural spaces

REMEMBER . . . You should only code for avian influenza or novel H1N1 flu if the case is confirmed. Modifiers like "suspected" are not enough to establish a classification.

INTRODUCTION

Except for neoplastic diseases and some major infectious diseases, respiratory diseases are classified in categories 460 through 519 in chapter 8 of *ICD-9-CM*. Note that *Streptococcus* and *Neisseria* are normal flora for the respiratory system; therefore, their presence does not indicate an infection unless they are seriously out of control. A respiratory infection cannot be assumed from a laboratory report alone; physician concurrence and documentation are necessary. Remember also that infectious organisms are not always identified by laboratory examination, particularly when antibiotic therapy has been started; an infection code may be assigned without laboratory evidence when it is supported by clinical documentation.

PNEUMONIA

Pneumonia is a common respiratory infection that is coded in several ways in *ICD-9-CM*. Combination codes that account for both pneumonia and the responsible organism are included in chapters 1 and 8 of *ICD-9-CM*. Examples of appropriate codes for pneumonia include the following:

- Pneumonia due to *Klebsiella* 482.0
- Pneumonia due to *Staphylococcus aureus* 482.41
- Salmonella pneumonia 003.22
- Postmeasles pneumonia 055.1
- Pneumonia with influenza 487.0

Other pneumonias are coded as manifestations of underlying infections classified in chapter 1, and two codes are required in such cases. Examples of this dual classification coding include the following:

- Pneumonia in anthrax 022.1 + 484.5
- Bronchial pneumonia in typhoid fever 002.0 + 484.8

FIGURE 15.1 The Respiratory System

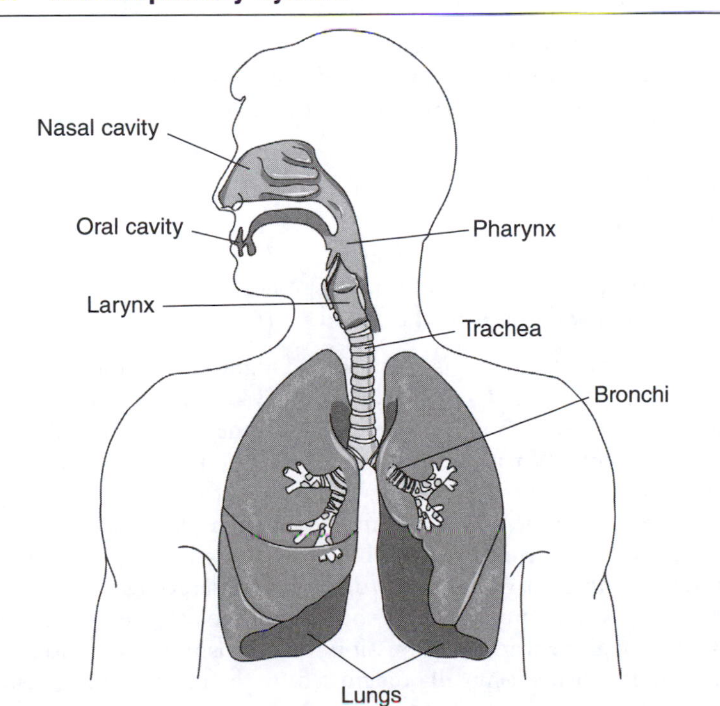

When the diagnostic statement is pneumonia without any further specification, the coder should review laboratory reports for mention of the causative organism and check with the physician to determine whether there appears to be support for a more definitive diagnosis. When the organism is not identified, code **486, Pneumonia, organism unspecified,** is assigned.

Lobar Pneumonia

A diagnosis of pneumonia that mentions the affected lobe is not classified as lobar pneumonia unless specifically documented as such by the physician. The term "lobar pneumonia" (481) is outdated; it does not refer to the lobe involved but to a particular type of pneumonia, which is usually caused by *Streptococcus* pneumoniae. If the documentation refers to "multilobar pneumonia," it simply refers to pneumonia affecting more than one lobe. Query the provider regarding the specific type of pneumonia and code accordingly based on the causal organism. Assign code **486, Pneumonia, organism unspecified,** if the provider is unable to identify the organism causing the multilobar pneumonia.

Interstitial Lung Diseases

Idiopathic interstitial pneumonias (subcategory 516.3) are a group of scarring diseases of the lung of unknown etiology with distinctive presentations, pathophysiology, and clinical course. *ICD-9-CM* provides unique codes for several specific types of idiopathic interstitial pneumonia (516.31–516.37), as well as code **516.30, Idiopathic interstitial pneumonia, not otherwise specified,** to be used when the specific type is not documented. For example:

- Idiopathic pulmonary fibrosis 516.31
- Idiopathic non-specific interstitial pneumonitis 516.32
- Acute interstitial pneumonitis 516.33
- Respiratory bronchiolitis interstitial lung disease 516.34
- Idiopathic lymphoid interstitial pneumonia 516.35
- Cryptogenic organizing pneumonia 516.36
- Desquamative interstitial pneumonia 516.37

Childhood interstitial lung disease (subcategory 516.6) is much rarer than interstitial lung disease in adults and is typically associated with respiratory distress, diffuse infiltrates on chest imaging, and abnormal lung histology. Codes for childhood interstitial lung disease include:

- Neuroendocrine cell hyperplasia of infancy 516.61
- Pulmonary interstitial glycogenosis 516.62
- Surfactant mutations of the lung 516.63
- Alveolar capillary dysplasia with vein misalignment 516.64
- Other interstitial lung diseases of childhood 516.69

Plasma cell interstitial pneumonia is an acute and highly contagious pneumonia caused by Pneumocystis carinii. It is coded as **136.3, Pneumocystosis.** This condition is frequently seen in patients with acquired immunodeficiency syndrome (AIDS) and is a major cause of death among AIDS patients. When associated with AIDS, code 042 is sequenced first with an additional code of 136.3. This type of pneumonia is not limited to patients with AIDS, however; it may develop in patients with immunocompromised states due to other causes, such as cancer, severe malnutrition, and debility. It may also occur in patients treated with certain types of immunosuppressive drugs after undergoing organ transplantation or cancer treatment. Never assume that this code should be assigned because the patient's condition is severe enough to warrant admission to the hospital. Interstitial pneumonia is classified as 136.3 only when specifically diagnosed by the physician as plasma cell pneumonia, pneumocystosis, or pneumonia caused by Pneumocystis carinii.

Legionnaires Disease

Legionnaires disease (482.84) is a type of pneumonia that is almost always caused by inhalation of aerosols that come from a contaminated water source. Legionnaires disease is often difficult to distinguish from other types of pneumonia. It is usually identified by the presence of bacteria in the sputum, by the presence of Legionella antigens in the urine, or by comparing Legionella antibody levels in two blood samples taken several weeks apart. Legionnaires disease accounts for about 4 percent of lethal nosocomial pneumonia, and about 5 to 15 percent of known cases have been fatal. Because of the serious nature and frequent incidence of this disease, a separate code is provided for greater specificity—code **482.84, Other bacterial pneumonia, Legionnaires disease.** An additional code should be assigned for the responsible organism.

Gram-Negative Pneumonia

Gram-negative pneumonia NEC is classified as **482.83, Pneumonia due to other gram-negative bacteria;** or to 482.81 when it is specified as anaerobic. When the organism has been identified, the index may provide a more specific code. As discussed earlier, a gram-negative organism is one that develops a particular type of stain on testing and is considered part of a group of organisms that require careful management. Gram-positive pneumonia, not otherwise qualified, is classified as **482.9, Bacterial pneumonia unspecified.** This type of pneumonia is far easier to treat and requires the expenditure of fewer resources than the treatment of gram-negative pneumonia.

Gram-negative pneumonia usually appears as a complication of surgery, trauma, or chronic illness such as advanced carcinoma, cardiac failure, or alcoholism. It also is a common complication of chronic obstructive pulmonary disease and frequently follows treatment with immunosuppressive drugs or use of inhalation therapy apparatus.

Findings in a debilitated, chronically ill, or aged patient that might suggest a complicating gram-negative pneumonia include the following:

- Worsening of cough, dyspnea, and reduction of oxygen level
- Fever
- Purulent sputum
- Patchy infiltrate on chest X-ray (in addition to previously noted densities caused by a primary underlying disease)
- Elevated leukocyte count

Note, however, that a diagnosis of gram-negative or other bacterial pneumonia cannot be assumed on the basis of the presence of any or all such findings; only the physician can determine the diagnosis. Such findings can, however, help document a diagnosis or could serve as the basis for a query to the doctor.

Aspergillosis

Pneumonia due to infectious aspergillosis is classified as code **117.3, Aspergillosis,** with an additional code of **484.6, Pneumonia in aspergillosis.** Allergic bronchopulmonary aspergillosis, however, occurs as an eosinophilic pneumonia caused by an allergic reaction to the aspergillosis fungus, commonly found on dead leaves, bird droppings, compost stacks, or other decaying vegetation. Code 518.6 is assigned for this allergic condition.

Aspiration Pneumonia

Aspiration pneumonia is a severe type of pneumonia resulting from the inhalation of foods, liquids, oils, vomitus, or micro-organisms from the upper respiratory tract or the oropharyngeal area. Pneumonitis due to inhalation of foods or vomitus is coded 507.0, with that due to inhalation of oils and essences as 507.1, and that due to inhalation of other solids or liquids to 507.8. Pneumonia due to aspiration of microorganisms is classified as bacterial pneumonia in categories 480 through 483. Although aspiration pneumonia usually develops from one type of aspirated material, it is possible for both the type of pneumonia coded to category 507 and that coded to the 480 through 483 series to be present concurrently. Patients transferred from a nursing home to an acute care hospital because of pneumonia are often suffering from aspiration pneumonia due to aspirated organisms, usually gram-negative bacteria.

Ventilator Associated Pneumonia

Pneumonia associated with the use of a ventilator is assigned to code **997.31, Ventilator associated pneumonia.** In addition, a code for the specific organism should also be assigned. For example, ventilator associated pneumonia due to methicillin resistant *Staphylococcus aureus* (MRSA) is coded to 997.31 and 041.12. Code 997.31 should be assigned only when the provider has documented ventilator associated pneumonia. As with all procedural or postprocedural complications, code assignment is based on the provider's documentation of the relationship between the condition and the procedure. (See chapter 29 of this handbook for further discussion of ventilator associated pneumonia.)

Exercise 15.1

Code the following diagnoses. Do not assign E codes.

	Code(s)
1. Lobar pneumonia with influenza	487.0
2. Pneumonia, left upper lobe	486
3. Klebsiella pneumonia	482.0
4. Pneumonia due to fungus	117.9 484.7
5. Acute lobar pneumonia	481
6. Perihilar viral pneumonia	480.9
7. Pneumonia due to Chlamydia	483.1

Exercise 15.1 *(continued)*

Intermittent positive-pressure breathing (IPPB)	93.91
8. Aspiration pneumonia due to aspiration of vomitus	507.0
9. Plasma cell interstitial pneumonia due to AIDS	042 136.3
10. Pneumonia due to pulmonary coccidioidomycosis	114.0

INFLUENZA

The *ICD-9-CM* classifies influenza to category 487. Influenza caused by unspecified or seasonal influenza viruses, in combination with any form of pneumonia or bronchopneumonia, is assigned a combination code, **487.0, Influenza with pneumonia.** An additional code is assigned to identify the type of pneumonia. Influenza with other respiratory manifestations such as laryngitis, pharyngitis, or respiratory infection (upper) (acute) is coded to 487.1. Influenza may also develop manifestations in body systems other than the respiratory system, such as encephalopathy and involvement of the gastrointestinal tract, which are coded to **487.8, Influenza with other manifestations.**

Subcategory **488.0, Influenza due to identified avian influenza virus,** is used to report avian influenza caused by the viruses that normally infect only birds and, less commonly, other animals. A strain of this virus has been transmitted to humans. Code 488.01 is used to report pneumonia with avian influenza virus, with an additional code to specify the type of pneumonia. Code 488.02 is used to report avian influenza virus with other respiratory manifestations. Code 488.09 is assigned for avian influenza with other manifestations.

Subcategory **488.1, Influenza due to identified 2009 H1N1 [swine] influenza virus,** is limited to influenza explicitly documented as being due to identified (novel) 2009 H1N1 virus (referred to as swine flu). This influenza was a rather virulent pandemic detected in the United States in April 2009. Code 488.11 is used to report pneumonia with identified (novel) 2009 H1N1 influenza virus. An additional code is assigned for the pneumonia. Code 488.12 is assigned for other respiratory manifestations with identified (novel) 2009 H1N1 influenza virus. Code 488.19 is assigned for other manifestations with identified (novel) 2009 H1N1 influenza virus. Codes from subcategory 488.1 should not be used for any other type of H1N1 influenza virus.

Subcategory **488.8, Influenza due to novel influenza A,** is used to report influenza due to identified novel influenza A virus. This subcategory includes influenza due to animal origin influenza virus, infection with influenza viruses occurring in pigs or other animals, and other novel influenza A viruses not previously found in humans. Similar to subcategories 488.0 and 488.1 noted above, there are combination codes to report when the influenza occurs with pneumonia (488.81), with other respiratory manifestations (488.82), and with other manifestations (488.89).

Similar to the guidelines for coding HIV infection, codes 488.01–488.09, 488.11–488.19, and 488.81–488.89 should be assigned only for confirmed cases of avian flu, identified (novel) 2009 H1N1 flu, or novel influenza A. In this context, "confirmation" does not require documentation of positive laboratory testing specific for avian influenza, identified (novel) 2009 H1N1 flu, or novel influenza A. However, "confirmation" does require provider documentation of avian influenza, identified (novel) 2009 H1N1 flu, or novel influenza A.

Subcategories 488.0, 488.1, and 488.8 are not assigned when the diagnostic statement indicates that the infection is "suspected," "possible," "likely," or "?". This is an exception to the general guideline that directs the coder to assign a code for a diagnosis qualified as "suspected" or "possible" as if it were established.

SUPRAGLOTTITIS

Supraglottitis, which is also called epiglottitis, is an acute life-threatening upper respiratory infection. It seems to occur primarily in children but can be rapidly fatal in all ages. This fatal event appears to result from an edematous epiglottis that is obstructing the airway. It is an infection of the supraglottic structures that affects the lingual tonsillar areas, epiglottic folds, false vocal cords, and the epiglottis. Because the infection covers all the supraglottic structures, the term supraglottitis is nonspecific. Categories of 464, acute laryngitis and tracheitis, the larynx, the trachea, and the epiglottis have unique subcategories; the exception of acute laryngitis, with and without obstruction, is identified at the code level. The diagnosis supraglottitis may represent any of the codes within 464. A unique code for supraglottitis is provided for cases when the term is used and a specific site of infection is not identified. These codes are as follows:

- 464.0 Acute laryngitis
  - 464.00 without mention of obstruction
  - 464.01 with obstruction
- 464.5 Supraglottitis, unspecified
  - 464.50 without mention of obstruction
  - 464.51 with obstruction

CHRONIC OBSTRUCTIVE PULMONARY DISEASE

Chronic obstructive pulmonary disease (COPD) is a general term used to describe a variety of conditions that result in obstruction of the airway. The conditions that comprise COPD are:

- Chronic obstructive asthma 493.2x
- Chronic obstructive bronchitis 491.2x
- Emphysema 492.8
- Chronic bronchitis with emphysema 491.20

The correct coding of COPD depends on the accurate identification of the specific condition responsible for the airway obstruction, as well as on whether an acute condition, such as respiratory failure, is associated with it. When the diagnosis is stated only as COPD, the coder should review the medical record to determine whether a more definitive diagnosis is documented. Code **496, Chronic airway obstruction, not elsewhere classified,** is assigned only when the medical record documentation does not specify the type of COPD being treated and a more specific code cannot be assigned.

The conditions that make up COPD and asthma may sometimes overlap. Careful review of the conditions documented is necessary for accurate code selection. It is essential to review first the index and then verify the code selection in the Tabular List. Many instructional notes under the different COPD subcategories and codes provide guidance for code selection.

The medical record documentation may reveal varying degrees of severity of COPD. All of the following terms are coded to **491.21, Obstructive chronic bronchitis, With acute exacerbation:** COPD in exacerbation; severe COPD in exacerbation; endstage COPD in exacerbation; decompensated COPD; exacerbation of COPD; and acute exacerbation of chronic obstructive bronchitis.

Acute Bronchitis with Chronic Obstructive Bronchitis

A diagnosis of acute bronchitis with chronic obstructive bronchitis is assigned to code **491.22, Obstructive chronic bronchitis with acute bronchitis.** Code **466.0, Acute bronchitis,** is not assigned as an additional code. If the documentation indicates acute bronchitis with COPD with acute exacerbation, only code 491.22 is assigned. The acute bronchitis included in code 491.22 supersedes the acute exacerbation.

Asthma

Asthma is a bronchial hypersensitivity characterized by mucosal edema, constriction of bronchial musculature, and excessive viscid edema. Manifestations of asthma are wheezing, dyspnea out of proportion to exertion, and cough. A diagnosis of wheezing alone is not classified as asthma; code 786.07 would be assigned in such a case. Asthma is classified into category 493, with a fourth digit indicating the type of asthma and a fifth digit indicating whether status asthmaticus or exacerbation is present.

Status asthmaticus is defined in slightly different ways by different authorities, but in general it represents a patient who continues extreme wheezing in spite of conventional therapy or has suffered from an acute asthmatic attack in which the degree of obstruction is not relieved by the usual therapeutic measures. Early status asthmaticus represents patients who are refractory to treatment or who fail to respond to the usual therapies; advanced status asthmaticus represents patients who show full development of an asthma attack that could result in respiratory failure, with signs and symptoms of hypercapnia (excess carbon dioxide in the blood). Fifth digit 1 is assigned for both types of status asthmaticus. Use of this fifth digit usually indicates a medical emergency for treatment of acute, severe asthma. Other terms used to describe status asthmaticus include the following:

- Intractable asthma attack
- Refractory asthma
- Severe, intractable wheezing
- Airway obstruction not relieved by bronchodilators
- Severe, prolonged asthmatic attack

The coder should never assume that status asthmaticus is present without a specific statement from the physician. However, asthma described as acute, characterized by prolonged or severe intractable wheezing, or asthma being treated by the administration of adrenal corticosteroids should alert the coder that status asthmaticus may exist and that the physician should be asked whether the diagnosis should be added.

Acute exacerbation of asthma refers to increased severity of the asthma symptoms, such as wheezing and shortness of breath. The fifth digit of "2" is used for asthma referred to as "exacerbated" or in "acute exacerbation."

Asthma characterized as obstructive or diagnosed in conjunction with COPD is classified as chronic obstructive asthma 493.2x. Other asthma is coded as 493.0x, 493.1x, 493.8x, or 493.9x. Fifth digits "0" for unspecified, "1" for status asthmaticus, and "2" indicating the asthma is in exacerbation or acute exacerbation, apply only to codes 493.0x, 493.1x and 493.9x. An asthma code with a fifth digit of "2," with acute exacerbation, may *not* be assigned with an asthma code with a fifth digit of "1," with status asthmaticus. Only the code with the fifth digit of "1" should be assigned.

A diagnosis of acute asthmatic bronchitis or asthmatic bronchitis without further specification is coded as 493.9x. If the diagnosis is stated as acute bronchitis with chronic obstructive asthma, code 493.2x is assigned. A diagnosis of chronic asthmatic bronchitis or asthmatic bronchitis with COPD is coded **493.2x, Chronic obstructive asthma.** Examples of coding for asthma include the following:

- Acute asthmatic bronchitis with status asthmaticus 493.91
- Childhood asthma 493.00
- Asthma with COPD 493.20
- Chronic asthmatic bronchitis with acute exacerbation 493.22
- Psychogenic asthma 316 + 493.90

Bronchospasm

Bronchospasm is an integral part of asthma or any other type of chronic airway obstruction, but no additional code is assigned to indicate its presence. Code **519.11, Acute bronchospasm,** is assigned only when the underlying cause has not been identified.

Exercise 15.2

Code the following diagnoses. Do not assign E codes.

	Code(s)
1. Bronchial asthma, allergic, due to house dust	493.00
2. Chronic bronchitis with decompensated COPD	491.21
3. Acute exacerbation of chronic asthmatic bronchitis	493.22
4. Acute asthmatic bronchitis	493.90
5. Chronic obstructive lung disease with acute exacerbation	491.21
6. Chronic asthmatic bronchitis	493.20
7. Obstructive asthma with status asthmaticus	493.21
8. Acute bronchitis with acute bronchiectasis	494.1

ATELECTASIS

Atelectasis reduces the ventilatory function. Minor atelectasis is an integral part of pulmonary disease and is included in the code for associated lung disease. Pulmonary collapse can be a severe problem, but mild atelectasis usually has little effect on the patient's condition or the therapy provided. Slight strands of atelectasis are often noted on X-ray reports, but this finding is generally of little clinical importance and is usually not further evaluated or treated. Code **518.0, Pulmonary collapse,** should not be assigned on the basis of an X-ray finding alone; it should be coded only when the physician identifies it as a clinical condition that meets the criteria for a reportable diagnosis.

PLEURAL EFFUSION

Pleural effusion is an abnormal accumulation of fluid within the pleural spaces. It occurs in association with pulmonary disease and certain cardiac conditions, such as congestive heart failure, or certain diseases involving other organs. It is almost always integral to the underlying disease and is usually addressed only by treatment of that condition. In this situation, only the code for the underlying disease is assigned. However, occasionally the effusion is addressed separately, with additional diagnostic studies such as decubitus X-ray or diagnostic thoracentesis. The effusion may be treated by therapeutic thoracentesis, or chest-tube drainage. When treatment is addressed only to the pleural effusion, it can be designated as the principal diagnosis; otherwise, it can be assigned as an additional code when it is further evaluated or treated. Pleural effusion noted only on an X-ray report is not reported.

Pleural effusion due to tuberculosis is classified to 012.0x unless it is due to primary progressive tuberculosis (010.1x). When pleural effusion is due to another bacterial infection, code 511.1 is assigned, with an additional code for the responsible organism. Malignant pleural effusion can occur due to impaired pleural lymphatic drainage from a mediastinal tumor (especially in lymphomas) and not because of direct tumor invasion into the pleura. Malignant pleural effusion is coded to 511.81 with the malignant neoplasm assigned as the first-listed or principal diagnosis. Traumatic effusion is classified to code 862.39 if open wound; otherwise code 862.29 is assigned.

RESPIRATORY FAILURE

Respiratory failure is a life-threatening condition that is always due to an underlying condition. It may be the final pathway of a disease process or a combination of different processes. Respiratory failure can result from either acute or chronic diseases that cause airway obstruction, parenchymal infiltration, or pulmonary edema. It can arise from an abnormality in any of the components of the respiratory system, central nervous system, peripheral nervous system, respiratory muscles, and chest wall muscles. The diagnosis is based largely on arterial blood gas analysis findings, which vary from individual to individual, depending on several factors. The coder should never assume a diagnosis of respiratory failure without a documented diagnosis by the physician. Respiratory failure is classified as acute (518.81), chronic (518.83), or acute and chronic combined (518.84). When respiratory failure follows surgery or trauma, code 518.51 is assigned when the respiratory failure is acute, and code 518.53 when the respiratory failure is acute and chronic. Other pulmonary insufficiency (including adult respiratory distress syndrome and shock lung) following trauma and surgery is assigned to 518.52.

Careful review of the medical record is required for the coding and sequencing of respiratory failure. The coder must review the circumstances of admission to determine the principal diagnosis. Code **518.81, Acute respiratory failure,** may be assigned as a principal diagnosis when it is the condition established after study to be chiefly responsible for occasioning the admission to the hospital, and the selection is supported by the Alphabetic Index and Tabular List. Respiratory failure may be listed as a secondary diagnosis if it develops after admission.

When a patient is admitted with respiratory failure and another acute condition (e.g., myocardial infarction, aspiration pneumonia, or cerebrovascular accident), the principal diagnosis will depend on the individual patient's situation and what caused the admission of the patient to the hospital. This applies whether the other acute condition is a respiratory or nonrespiratory condition. The physician should be queried for clarification if the documentation is unclear as to which one of the two conditions was the reason for the admission. The guideline regarding two or more diagnoses' equally meeting the definition of principal diagnosis (Section II, C) may be applied in situations when both the respiratory failure and the other acute condition are equally responsible for occasioning the admission to the hospital.

Example 1: A patient with chronic myasthenia gravis goes into acute exacerbation and develops acute respiratory failure. The patient is admitted due to the respiratory failure.

Principal diagnosis:	518.81	Acute respiratory failure
Secondary diagnosis:	358.01	Myasthenia gravis with (acute) exacerbation

Example 2: A patient with emphysema develops acute respiratory failure. The patient is admitted through the emergency department for treatment of the respiratory failure.

Principal diagnosis:	518.81	Acute respiratory failure
Secondary diagnosis:	492.8	Other emphysema

Example 3: A patient arrived in the hospital in acute respiratory failure. The patient was intubated, and the physician documents that the patient is being admitted to the hospital for treatment of the acute respiratory failure. The patient also has congestive heart failure.

Principal diagnosis:	518.81	Acute respiratory failure
Secondary diagnosis:	428.0	Congestive heart failure, unspecified

Some chapter-specific coding guidelines (e.g., obstetrics, poisoning, HIV, and newborn) provide sequencing direction. These guidelines would take precedence over code 518.81 when coding respiratory failure associated with a condition from one of these chapters.

Example 1: A patient is admitted to the hospital postpartum as a result of developing pulmonary embolism leading to respiratory failure.

Principal diagnosis:	673.24	Obstetrical blood-clot embolism, postpartum condition or complication
Secondary diagnosis:	518.81	Acute respiratory failure

In this example, the obstetrical code is sequenced first because there is a chapter-specific guideline (Section I, C, 11, a, 1) that provides sequencing directions specifying that chapter 11 codes have sequencing priority over codes from other chapters.

Example 2: A patient who is diagnosed as overdosing on crack is admitted to the hospital with respiratory failure.

Principal diagnosis:	970.81	Poisoning by other specified central nervous system stimulants, cocaine
Secondary diagnosis:	518.81	Acute respiratory failure
	305.60	Nondependent abuse of drugs, Cocaine abuse, unspecified

In this example, poisoning is sequenced first because there is a chapter-specific guideline (Section I, C, 17, e, 2, d) that provides sequencing directions specifying that the poisoning code is sequenced first, followed by a code for the manifestation. The acute respiratory failure is a manifestation of the poisoning. This advice is consistent with information previously published in *Coding Clinic,* First Quarter 1993, page 25.

Example 3: A patient is admitted with respiratory failure due to Pneumocystis carinii, which is due to AIDS.

Principal diagnosis:	042	Human immunodeficiency virus [HIV]
Secondary diagnosis:	518.81	Acute respiratory failure
	136.3	Pneumocystosis

In this example, the HIV is sequenced first because there is a chapter-specific guideline (Section I, C, 1, a, 2, a) that provides sequencing directions specifying that if a patient is admitted for an HIV-related condition (in this case the pneumocystis carinii), the principal diagnosis should be 042, followed by additional diagnosis codes for all reported HIV-related conditions.

In the event that instructional notes in the Tabular List provide sequencing direction, the sequencing of respiratory failure is dependent on these notes.

Example: A patient is admitted to the hospital with severe *Staphylococcus aureus* sepsis and acute respiratory failure.

Principal diagnosis:	038.11	*Staphylococcus aureus* septicemia
Secondary diagnosis:	995.92	Severe sepsis
	518.81	Acute respiratory failure

Sepsis is sequenced first in this case because there is an instructional note under code 995.92 indicating to code first the underlying infection. In addition, code 995.92 has a "use additional code" note to specify acute organ dysfunction and lists acute respiratory failure (518.81). This instruction means that respiratory failure would be a secondary diagnosis.

ADULT RESPIRATORY DISTRESS SYNDROME

Adult respiratory distress syndrome (ARDS) is an acute clinical-pathological state characterized by severe dyspnea, diffuse infiltrative lung lesions, and hypoxemia, with tachypnea and tachycardia present on physical examination. Treatment includes maintaining fluid balance, providing oxygen or ventilatory support, and treating the underlying condition. The condition is ordinarily a manifestation of an associated disease process and may occur following shock, surgery, or trauma. When it is due to infection, an additional code for the responsible organism should be assigned.

Adult respiratory distress syndrome following shock, surgery, or trauma is assigned to code 518.52. When neither trauma nor surgery is involved, it is classified as **518.82, Pulmonary insufficiency not elsewhere classified.** It is sometimes described as respiratory failure due to shock or trauma that occurs in lungs that were previously normal. It differs from respiratory failure in that pulmonary insufficiency does not imply that the respiratory system is completely unable to supply adequate oxygen to maintain metabolism and/or eliminate sufficient carbon dioxide to avoid respiratory failure. Terms such as "shock lung," "traumatic wet lung," "white lung syndrome," and "postperfusion lung" also describe this condition.

Pulmonary insufficiency is implicit in asthma and various types of chronic obstructive pulmonary disease. In these conditions, it reflects the body's inability to excrete carbon dioxide rather than its failure to provide oxygen. It is included in the codes for those conditions; no additional code is assigned.

OTHER PULMONARY INSUFFICIENCY, NEC

Pulmonary insufficiency, not elsewhere classified, is a manifestation of another disease process, somewhat like respiratory failure. Unlike respiratory failure, however, it does not imply a complete inability of the respiratory system to supply adequate oxygen to maintain metabolism and/or eliminate sufficient carbon dioxide to avoid respiratory failure. It is an integral part of any COPD code, including such specific types as chronic obstructive bronchitis (491.2x), emphysema (492.x), chronic obstructive asthma (493.2x), or COPD not elsewhere classified (496). Code 518.82 is not assigned as an additional code.

ACUTE PULMONARY EDEMA

Acute pulmonary edema is a pathological state in which there is excessive, diffuse accumulation of fluid in the tissues and the alveolar spaces of the lung. It is broadly divided into two categories that reflect the origin of the condition: cardiogenic and noncardiogenic.

Cardiogenic

Acute pulmonary edema of cardiac origin is a manifestation of heart failure and as such is included in the following code assignments:

- Left ventricular failure 428.1
- Congestive heart failure 428.0
- Hypertensive heart disease 402.9x
- Rheumatic heart disease, acute 391.x
- Rheumatic heart failure (congestive) 398.91

Pulmonary edema is not included in the codes for acute myocardial infarction (410.10–410.92), acute or subacute ischemic heart disease (411.0–411.89), or coronary atherosclerosis (414.0x or 414.8). When pulmonary edema is present along with one of these conditions, the pulmonary edema is assumed to be associated with left ventricular failure (428.1) unless the heart failure is described as congestive or decompensated, in which case code **428.0, Congestive heart failure,** is assigned. Pulmonary edema is included in codes 428.x; no additional code is assigned.

Noncardiogenic

Noncardiogenic acute pulmonary edema occurs in the absence of heart failure or other heart disease. It is coded in a variety of ways, depending on the cause. When the cause is not specified, code **518.4, Acute edema of lung, unspecified,** is assigned. Postoperative pulmonary edema is also coded as 518.4.

Postradiation pulmonary edema (postradiation pneumonia) is an inflammation of the lungs due to the adverse effects of radiation. It is coded as **508.0, Acute pulmonary manifestations due to radiation.**

Acute pulmonary edema due to fumes and vapors is coded as 506.1. Acute pulmonary edema due to aspiration of water in a near-drowning is coded to **994.1, Drowning and nonfatal submersion;** other and unspecified effects of high altitude is coded as 993.2. Acute pulmonary edema in cases of drug overdose is classified as poisoning, with code 518.4 assigned as an additional code. Any mention of drug dependence or abuse should also be coded. E codes should be assigned with any of these codes to indicate the external circumstances involved.

Chronic pulmonary edema or pulmonary edema NOS that is not of cardiac origin is coded as **514, Pulmonary congestion and hypostasis,** unless the Alphabetic Index or the Tabular List instructs otherwise.

Pulmonary edema caused by congestive overloads, such as pulmonary fibrosis (515), congenital stenosis of the pulmonary veins (747.49), or pulmonary venous embolism (415.1x), is noncardiogenic. Such conditions are assigned to code 518.4 when described as acute or to code 514 when described as chronic or not otherwise specified. Be careful not to confuse this condition with edema associated with heart disease.

BIOPSIES OF BRONCHUS AND LUNG

An endoscopic biopsy of the bronchus (33.24) involves passing an endoscope into the lumen of the trachea and bronchus, where a bit of tissue is removed for pathological study. An endoscopic biopsy of the lung (33.27) goes through the main bronchus into the smaller bronchi and lung alveoli to perform a lung biopsy. Either type of biopsy can be performed independently, or both may be performed in the same operative episode, in which case both codes are assigned. Another type of lung biopsy is the thoracoscopic biopsy. In this procedure, small incisions are made into the chest wall and a thoracoscope is inserted through the incision in order to remove specimens for pathologic examination. This is coded as a thoracoscopic lung biopsy (33.20). This code includes the thoracoscopic approach.

Bronchoalveolar lavage (BAL), also called "liquid biopsy," should not be confused with whole lung lavage. BAL is a diagnostic procedure performed via a bronchoscope under local anesthesia. It involves washing out alveoli tissue and peripheral airways to obtain a small sampling of tissue. BAL is coded to **33.24, Closed [endoscopic] biopsy of bronchus.** Whole lung lavage is a therapeutic procedure performed for pulmonary alveolar proteinosis. The procedure is performed under general anesthesia and mechanical ventilation. The lungs are lavaged by filling and emptying one lung at a time with saline solution. The second lung is usually lavaged three to seven days after the first lung. Report whole lung lavage using code **33.99, Other operations on lung.**

ABLATION OF LUNG

Tumor ablation is an alternative to surgical removal of lung lesions. Ablation can be achieved using extreme heat, freezing chemicals (cryoablation), focused ultrasound, microwaves, or radiofrequency. These procedures are typically performed by interventional radiologists using imaging guidance—such as computed tomography (CT), ultrasound, or fluoroscopy—and inserting a probe directly to the lesion.

ICD-9-CM procedure codes for ablation do not distinguish between the different energy sources used to ablate the tumor. Instead, the classification of ablation is arranged by the operative approach used, such as open (32.23), percutaneous (32.24), thoracoscopic (32.25), and other and unspecified (32.26).

BRONCHIAL THERMOPLASTY ABLATION

Code **32.27, Bronchoscopic bronchial thermoplasty ablation of airway smooth muscle,** is assigned for the bronchoscopic ablation of airway smooth muscle of the lung. A catheter is used to deliver radiofrequency energy into the airways to reduce excess airway smooth muscle that constricts in people with asthma. Reduction of airway smooth muscle lessens the area that narrows in response to external stimuli such as dust and other allergens.

THORACOSCOPIC PROCEDURES

Codes have been created to report thoracoscopic lung procedures to distinguish them from open procedures. Thoracoscopic procedures involve the creation of small incisions into the chest wall and insertion of a thoracoscope through the incision. Table 15.1 lists codes for the thoracoscopic and open approaches for some common lung procedures.

TABLE 15.1 Thoracoscopic and Open Codes for Common Lung Procedures

Procedure	Thoracoscopic Codes	Open Codes
Excision of lesion or tissue of lung	32.20	32.29
Ablation of lung lesion or tissue	32.25	32.23
Segmental resection of lung	32.30	32.39
Lobectomy of lung	32.41	32.49
Pneumonectomy	32.50	32.59
Lung biopsy	33.20	33.28
Drainage of pleural cavity	34.06	34.09
Pleural biopsy	34.20	34.24
Decortication of lung	34.52	34.51

MECHANICAL VENTILATION

Mechanical ventilation is a process by which the patient's own effort to breathe is augmented or replaced by the use of a mechanical device. Mechanical ventilation is classified as noninvasive (93.90) when delivered via a noninvasive interface like a face mask, nasal mask, nasal pillow, oral mouthpiece, or oronasal mask. Mechanical ventilation is considered continuous invasive (96.7x) when the ventilatory assistance is provided via an invasive interface such as endotracheal intubation or tracheostomy and receives mechanical ventilation in an uninterrupted fashion. An endotracheal tube can be placed orally or nasally. If either intubation or tracheostomy is performed after admission or in the emergency department of the same hospital immediately before admission, it should be reported. Intubation or tracheostomy carried out elsewhere prior to admission or in an ambulance prior to arrival at the hospital cannot be reported even though the ambulance may be operated by the same facility.

Codes for invasive mechanical ventilation indicate whether the patient was on the ventilator for fewer than 96 consecutive hours (96.71) or more than 96 consecutive hours (96.72). Continuous invasive mechanical ventilation of unspecified duration is coded to 96.70. The starting time for calculating the duration begins with one of these events:

- Endotracheal intubation performed in the hospital or hospital emergency room, followed by initiation of mechanical ventilation
- Initiation of mechanical ventilation through tracheostomy performed in the hospital or emergency room
- Admission of a patient who is already on mechanical ventilation after previous intubation or tracheostomy

A tracheal tube is often inserted to keep the tracheostomy open for attachment to the mechanical ventilator. Start counting hours on ventilation only after mechanical ventilation has actually been initiated.

It is occasionally necessary to replace an endotracheal tube because of a problem such as a leak; removal with immediate replacement is considered part of the duration and counting should continue. Patients who are started on mechanical ventilation by means of an endotracheal tube may later receive a tracheostomy through which the ventilation continues. Continue counting the number of hours the patient is on ventilation from the time the original intubation was initiated.

Once a patient's condition has stabilized and the patient no longer needs continuous ventilatory assistance, various weaning methods may be employed to allow the patient to gradually resume the work of breathing. During weaning, the patient is monitored for any evidence of cardiopulmonary instability. The period during which the weaning process takes place is counted as part of the duration time. All of the period of weaning is counted during the process of withdrawing the patient from ventilatory support. The duration includes the time the patient is on the ventilator and the weaning period. It ends when the mechanical ventilation is turned off (after the weaning period). Note that some patients do not require this weaning process.

Duration of mechanical ventilation ends with one of the following events:

- Removal of the endotracheal tube (extubation)
- Discontinuance of ventilation for patients with tracheostomy after any weaning period is completed
- Discharge or transfer while still on mechanical ventilation

Occasionally the condition of a patient who has been on ventilation earlier in the hospital stay deteriorates and a subsequent period of mechanical ventilation may be required. Use the guidelines above to calculate this additional period. In such cases, two codes from category 96.7x should be assigned.

When mechanical ventilation is utilized during surgery, it is not normally coded when it is considered a normal part of surgery. However, in the event that the physician documents that the patient has a specific problem and is maintained on the mechanical ventilator longer than expected or if the patient requires mechanical ventilation for an extended period of time postoperatively, it may be coded. If the postoperative mechanical ventilation continues for more than two days, or if the physician has clearly documented an unexpected extended period of mechanical ventilation, the mechanical ventilation may be reported separately. The hours of mechanical ventilation should be counted starting from the point of intubation.

Other types of respiratory assistance considered noninvasive mechanical ventilation are continuous positive airway pressure (CPAP, 93.90), bilevel positive airway pressure (BiPAP, 93.90), and noninvasive positive pressure ventilation (NIPPV, 93.90). Other common types of mechanical ventilation are intermittent positive-pressure breathing (IPPB, 93.91) and continuous negative-pressure ventilation (CNP, 93.99). The duration of treatment with these modalities does not affect code assignment. It is important to carefully review the documentation regarding how the mechanical ventilation was provided, because BiPAP and CPAP are considered invasive mechanical ventilation when delivered through an endotracheal tube or a tracheostomy and are coded to 96.7x.

Tracheostomy Complications

Complications of a tracheostomy are classified to subcategory 519.0 in chapter 8. Infection of a tracheostomy is classified to code 519.01, with an additional code to identify the type of infection and/or a code from category 041 to identify the organism. Mechanical complications are coded to 519.02; other complications, such as hemorrhage of tracheoesophageal fistula due to the tracheostomy, are coded to 519.09.

Review Exercise 15.3

The following exercise provides examples of conditions classified in chapter 8 of *ICD-9-CM.* Code the following diagnoses and procedures. Do not assign E codes.

	Code(s)
1. Chronic left maxillary sinusitis	473.0
Left Caldwell-Luc sinusectomy	22.61

Review Exercise 15.3 *(continued)*

2. Acute upper respiratory infection due to Pneumococcus Febrile convulsions	465.9 041.2 780.31
3. Deviated nasal septum Allergic rhinitis Ethmoidal sinusitis	470 477.9 473.2
Submucous resection of nasal septum	21.5
4. Chronic pulmonary edema	514
5. Allergic rhinitis due to tree pollen	477.0
6. Congestive heart failure with pleural effusion	428.0
7. Acute respiratory failure due to intracerebral hemorrhage	431 518.81
8. Acute pharyngitis due to *Staphylococcus aureus* Infection	462 041.11

Review Exercise 15.3 *(continued)*

9. Chronic chemical bronchitis due to inhalation of chlorine fumes	506.4
Bronchoscopy with brush biopsy of bronchus	33.24
10. Total tension pneumothorax, spontaneous, left	512.0
11. Admitted in acute respiratory failure due to acute exacerbation of chronic obstructive bronchitis	518.81 491.21
12. Acute tracheobronchitis due to respiratory syncytial virus infection	466.0 079.6
13. Gram-negative pneumonia, anaerobic	482.81
14. Adult respiratory distress syndrome, due to shock	518.52
15. Acute respiratory distress syndrome due to hantavirus infection	518.82 079.81
16. Infected tracheostomy due to staphylococcal abscess of the neck	519.01 682.1 041.10

Diseases of the Digestive System

CHAPTER 16

CHAPTER OVERVIEW

- Diseases of the digestive system are found in chapter 9 of *ICD-9-CM*.
- There are many types of GI hemorrhage that can be classified. Sometimes documentation may point to bleeding in multiple locations.
- Esophagitis is classified with digestive system codes, but esophageal varices are coded as a disease of the circulatory system.
- Combination codes are provided for ulcers that indicate bleeding, perforation, or both. Coders should look in the medical record for any indication of site.
- Special notice should be given to conditions involving diverticula because of the similarity of the conditions and names.
- Coding diseases of the biliary system involves determining the location of the calculus.
- Other biliary system conditions revolve around removal of the gallbladder.
- Codes for adhesions include both intestinal and peritoneal. However, minor adhesions are usually not coded.
- Hernias are classified by type and site, and combination codes are used to indicate associated issues. There are specific codes for the repair of particular types of hernia.
- Diarrhea can be related to a variety of conditions. It is important to check the Alphabetic Index carefully before coding.
- Other common digestive system issues covered in this chapter of the handbook are appendicitis and constipation.

LEARNING OUTCOMES

After studying this chapter you should be able to:

- Classify a variety of conditions that affect the GI tract.
- Explain the difference in the meaning of terms associated with diverticula.
- Classify diseases of the biliary system.
- Classify common digestive system conditions such as diarrhea, constipation, and appendicitis.
- Correctly code bariatric surgeries and any possible complications related to these procedures.

TERMS TO KNOW

Biliary system
a network including the gall bladder and bile ducts

Calculus
a stone comprised of minerals that forms in an organ or duct of the body

Diverticulitis
the inflammation of existing diverticula

Diverticulosis
the presence of one or more diverticula of the designated site

Diverticulum
a small pouch or sac opening from a tubular or saccular organ; considered a medical condition; the plural term is diverticula

Esophagitis
an inflammation of the lining of the esophagus

Esophageal varices
abnormally enlarged veins in the lower part of the esophagus

GI
gastrointestinal; of the stomach and/or intestines

REMEMBER . . . There are many combination codes and exclusion notes used in chapter 9 of *ICD-9-CM*.

INTRODUCTION

Diseases of the digestive system are classified in chapter 9 of *ICD-9-CM*. The coding principles presented in previous chapters of this handbook apply throughout chapter 9. In addition, particular attention should be given to the use of combination codes and to the many exclusion notes in this chapter.

GASTROINTESTINAL HEMORRHAGE

Gastrointestinal (GI) bleeding manifests itself in several ways:

- Hematemesis (vomiting of blood), which indicates acute upper gastrointestinal hemorrhage
- Melena (presence of dark-colored blood in stool), which indicates upper or lower GI hemorrhage
- Occult bleeding (presence of blood in stool that can be seen only on laboratory examination), which indicates upper or lower GI bleeding
- Hematochezia (presence of bright-colored blood in stool), which indicates lower GI bleeding

The most common causes of GI bleeding are gastric and intestinal ulcers and diverticular disease of the intestine. A diverticular hemorrhage stops spontaneously in approximately 80 percent of cases, with the other 20 percent experiencing a second or third bleeding episode. *ICD-9-CM* provides fifth digits for gastrointestinal ulcers, gastritis, angiodysplasia, duodenitis, diverticulosis, and diverticulitis to indicate whether there is associated hemorrhage. For example:

- Acute gastritis with hemorrhage 535.01
- Diverticulitis with hemorrhage 562.13
- Angiodysplasia of duodenum with hemorrhage 537.83

Codes from category **578, Gastrointestinal hemorrhage,** are not assigned when codes for bleeding of any of the sites mentioned above are available. This category is acceptable only when the physician's diagnostic statement clearly states that the bleeding is due to another condition. Patients with a recent history of GI bleeding are sometimes seen for an endoscopy to determine the site of the bleeding but do not demonstrate any bleeding during the examination. If the physician documents a clinical diagnosis based on the history or other evidence, the fact that no bleeding occurs during the episode of care does not preclude the assignment of a code that includes mention of hemorrhage, or a code from category 578 when the cause of bleeding could not be determined.

It is important to carefully review the inclusion terms in this chapter because some digestive system codes will include hemorrhage or gastrointestinal bleeding, and therefore the G.I. bleeding would not be coded separately. For example, if the physician listed "GI bleeding due to acute ischemic colitis," only code **557.0, Acute vascular insufficiency of intestine,** would be assigned because "hemorrhagic" is an inclusion term under code 557.0.

Occasionally, physician documentation may refer to GI bleeding and either single or multiple GI-related endoscopic findings such as gastritis, duodenitis, esophagitis, diverticulosis (of colon), colon polyp, and so forth. If the physician does not link the GI bleeding with any specific condition nor states that the GI bleeding is not due to these conditions, the physician needs to be queried to determine whether the GI bleeding was caused by any of the endoscopic findings. If the physician does not establish a causal relationship between the GI bleeding and the endoscopic findings, code **578.9, Hemorrhage of gastrointestinal tract, unspecified,** should be reported. In addition, codes for the GI endoscopic findings without hemorrhage should be assigned as additional diagnoses. The physician must identify the source of the bleeding and link the clinical finding from the endoscopy because the finding may be unrelated to the bleeding. The combination codes describing hemorrhage should not be assigned unless the physician identifies a causal relationship. If the documentation provides more specific information and the bleeding is linked to a specific condition, assign the appropriate combination code with bleeding.

Patients may present for a colonoscopy because of rectal bleeding. If the findings include internal and external hemorrhoids with no statement as to whether the rectal bleeding is due to the hemorrhoids, the physician should be queried to determine whether the rectal bleeding is secondary to the hemorrhoids or if the hemorrhoids are an incidental finding. If the hemorrhoids are incidental findings and unrelated to the rectal bleeding, code **569.3, Hemorrhage of rectum and anus,** should be assigned followed by codes for the hemorrhoids without mention of complication. If, however, the physician establishes a causal relationship between the bleeding and the hemorrhoids, assign code **455.2, Internal hemorrhoids with other complication,** as the first-listed diagnosis. Code **455.5, External hemorrhoids with other complication,** should be assigned as a secondary diagnosis. Do not assign the combination code for hemorrhoids with bleeding unless the physician explicitly states a causal relationship.

FIGURE 16.1 The Digestive System

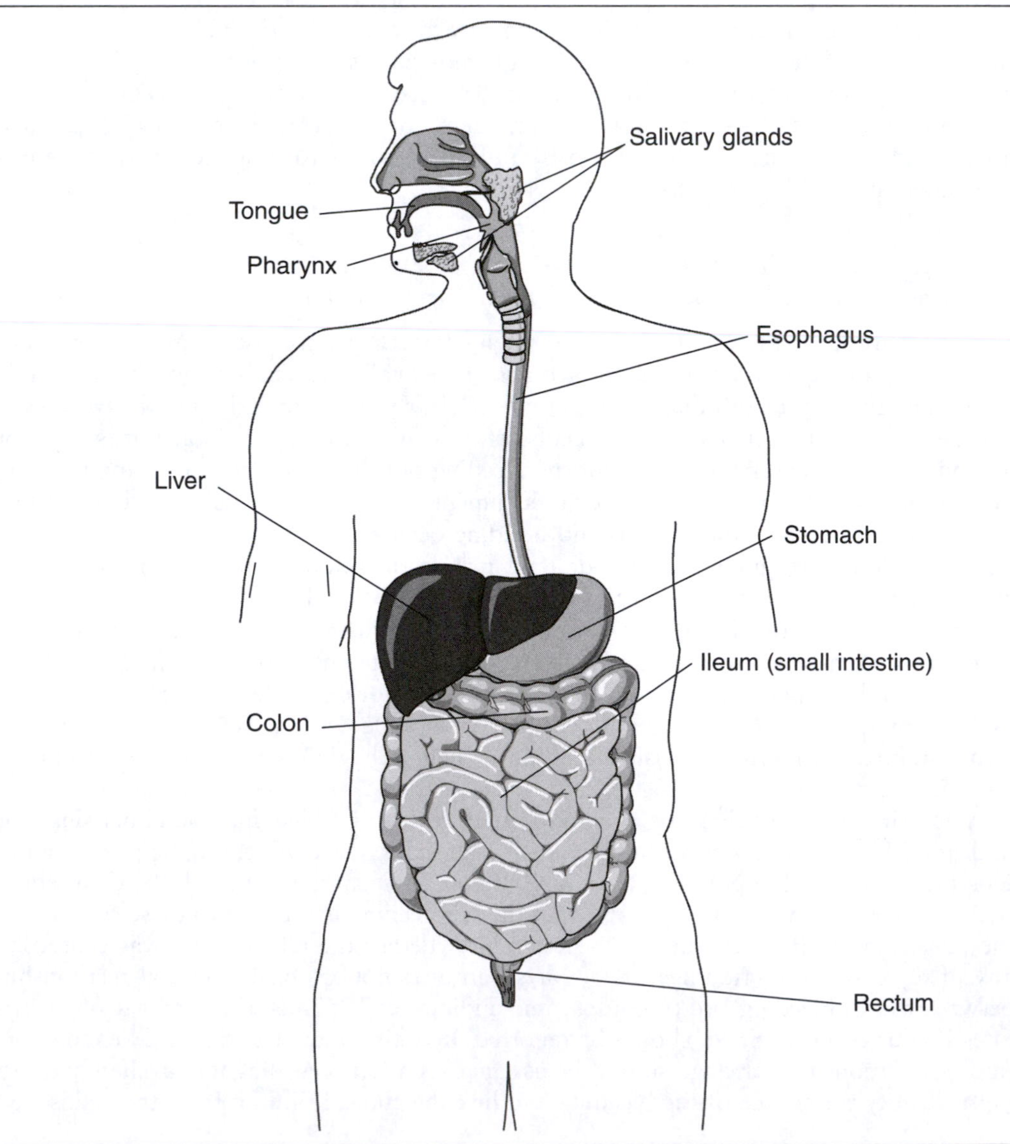

ESOPHAGITIS

Esophagitis is classified to category code 530, with a variety of specific conditions. Acute esophagitis is classified to 530.12, reflux esophagitis to 530.11, and eosinophilic esophagitis to 530.13. Ulcer of the esophagus without bleeding is classified to 530.20, whereas ulcer of the esophagus with bleeding is coded to 530.21, and dyskinesia of esophagus to 530.5. Barrett's esophagus (code 530.85) is a precancerous condition in which the normal cells of the lining of the esophagus are replaced by columnar cells.

Bleeding of the esophagus is coded as **530.82, Esophageal hemorrhage,** unless the bleeding is due to esophageal varices. Esophageal varices are not classified as a disease of the digestive system but as a disease of the circulatory system. They are coded as follows:

- Esophageal varices with bleeding   456.0
- Esophageal varices without mention of bleeding   456.1

When esophageal varices are associated with cirrhosis of the liver or portal hypertension, dual coding is required, with the underlying condition coded first. For example:

- Bleeding esophageal varices with cirrhosis of liver   571.5 + 456.20
- Bleeding esophageal varices in portal hypertension   572.3 + 456.20

Therapy for esophageal varices consists primarily of ligation (42.91) or endoscopic injection of a sclerosing agent (42.33). Diagnostic tests include esophageal motility studies classified as code **89.32, Esophageal manometry,** a test that is performed to rule out motor dysfunction of the esophagus, with particular attention to the competency of the gastroesophageal valve. Code 89.39, Other nonoperative measurements, is assigned for the pH esophageal monitoring test.

ULCERS OF THE STOMACH AND SMALL INTESTINE

Combination codes are provided for gastric, gastrojejunal, and duodenal ulcers that indicate whether there is associated bleeding, associated perforation, or both. A fifth-digit subclassification indicates the presence or absence of obstruction that limits the ability of food or fluid to pass through the outlet of the stomach or the intestinal lumen. Such obstruction may be due to spasm, swelling, edema, and/or scarring.

Ulcers of the stomach and the small intestine are often described as peptic without any further identification of the site. The coder should review the medical record for any indication of the site involved; codes from category **533, Peptic ulcer, site unspecified,** should not be used when a more specific code can be assigned. Examples of appropriate coding include the following:

- Chronic gastric ulcer with obstruction   531.71
- Acute duodenal ulcer   532.30
- Gastric ulcer with hemorrhage and perforation   531.60

DIEULAFOY LESIONS

Dieulafoy lesions are a rare cause of major gastrointestinal bleeding. When gastrointestinal bleeding is present with Dieulafoy lesions, a separate code for the gastrointestinal bleeding would not be assigned because it is an integral part of the disease. Assign code 537.84 for Dieulafoy lesion of the stomach and duodenum and code 569.86 for Dieulafoy lesion of the intestine.

Code 530.82 would be assigned for Dieulafoy lesions of the esophagus. Dieulafoy lesions of the esophagus typically cause severe bleeding. Endoscopic adrenaline injections can be used to control the bleeding.

Exercise 16.1

Code the following diagnoses and procedures. Do not assign E codes.

	Code(s)
1. Acute gastric ulcer with massive gastrointestinal hemorrhage	531.00
Exploratory laparotomy with gastric resection, partial, with Billroth I anastomosis	43.6
2. Duodenal ulcer, with obstruction, perforation, and hemorrhage	532.61
3. Penetrating gastric ulcer	531.50
Subtotal gastrectomy with esophageal anastomosis Vagotomy	43.5 44.00
4. Bleeding gastric ulcer	531.40
Billroth II gastrectomy	43.7

COMPLICATIONS OF ESOPHAGOSTOMY AND GASTROSTOMY

Complications of an esophagostomy and gastrostomy are classified in chapter 9 rather than in the 996–999 series. Code 530.86 is assigned for an infection of the esophagostomy. An additional code would be assigned to specify the infection. Code 530.87 is assigned for a mechanical complication of the esophagostomy, such as malfunction.

The mechanical complication of a gastrostomy is assigned code 536.42. Code 536.41 is assigned for an infection of the gastrostomy. Additional codes would be assigned to specify the type of infection and the responsible organism if that information is available in the medical record.

COMPLICATIONS OF COLOSTOMY AND ENTEROSTOMY

Complications of colostomy or enterostomy procedures are classified as 569.6x. Codes from postoperative complication categories 996 through 999 are not assigned. For example:

- Malfunction of colostomy 569.62
- Cellulitis of abdominal wall due to complication of enterostomy 569.61 + 682.2

DIVERTICULOSIS AND DIVERTICULITIS

A diverticulum is a small pouch or sac opening from a tubular or saccular organ, such as the esophagus, intestine, or urinary bladder. Diverticulosis indicates the presence of one or more diverticula of the designated site; diverticulitis is the inflammation of existing diverticula. A diagnosis of diverticulitis assumes the presence of diverticula; only the code for diverticulitis is assigned, as indicated in the Alphabetic Index, even when both conditions are mentioned in the physician's diagnostic statement. Examples of appropriate coding include the following:

- Diverticulosis of duodenum 562.00
- Diverticulosis and diverticulitis of duodenum 562.01
- Diverticulitis of jejunum with hemorrhage 562.03
- Diverticulitis of cecum with abscess 562.11 + 569.5

ICD-9-CM assumes diverticulosis, not otherwise specified, to be a condition of the colon.

Congenital versus Acquired Diverticula

Diverticula may be either acquired or congenital. For certain sites, *ICD-9-CM* assumes that the condition is congenital unless specified otherwise; in other sites, the presumption is that the diverticula are acquired. For example, diverticula of the colon are assumed to be acquired unless specified as congenital; but diverticula of the esophagus are assumed to be congenital unless otherwise specified. The Alphabetic Index (Volume 2) lists the following entries for diverticula of the colon and the esophagus:

Diverticula . . . 562.10 . . .
  colon (acquired) 562.10 . . .
    congenital 751.5 . . .
  esophagus (congenital) 750.4
    acquired 530.6 . . .
  Meckel's (displaced) (hypertrophic) 751.0

Acquired diverticula of the esophagus are often described by the type of diverticulum (pulsion or traction) or by the portion of the esophagus involved (pharyngoesophageal, midesophageal, or epiphrenic). These qualifications do not affect the code assignment; all are coded **530.6, Diverticulum of esophagus, acquired.** For example:

- Epiphrenic diverticula of esophagus 530.6
- Midesophageal traction diverticula of esophagus 530.6

DISEASES OF THE BILIARY SYSTEM

Acute and chronic cholecystitis without associated calculus is classified into category 575, with additional digits indicating whether it is acute (575.0), chronic (575.11), or both acute and chronic (575.12). Combination codes are assigned for cholecystitis, cholelithiasis, and choledocholithiasis to permit reporting these related conditions with a single code. These codes are presented in three groups: calculus of gallbladder (574.0–574.2), calculus of bile duct (574.3–574.5), and calculus of both gallbladder and bile ducts (574.6–574.9). Within each group, the fourth digit indicates whether there is associated cholecystitis and whether it is acute. Code 574.8 combines calculus of gallbladder and bile duct with both acute and chronic cholecystitis. Fifth digits indicate whether there is associated obstruction.

Codes **575.2, Obstruction of gallbladder,** and **576.2, Obstruction of bile duct,** are assigned only when there is obstruction but no calculi are present.

Cholesterolosis

Cholesterolosis is a condition characterized by abnormal deposits of cholesterol and other lipids in the lining of the gallbladder. In its diffuse form, it is known as strawberry gallbladder. This diagnosis is usually made by the pathologist on the basis of tissue examination and is ordinarily an incidental finding without clinical significance. It should not be coded when other gallbladder pathology is present.

Postcholecystectomy Syndrome

Postcholecystectomy syndrome (576.0) is a condition in which symptoms suggestive of biliary tract disease either persist or develop following cholecystectomy with no demonstrable cause or abnormality found on workup. A postoperative complication code from the 996 through 999 series is not assigned with code 576.0.

Cholecystectomy

A cholecystectomy (excision of the gallbladder) can be total or partial and can be performed either as an open procedure (51.21–51.22) or through a small, less-invasive laparoscopic incision (51.23–51.24). When coding a cholecystectomy, the coder should review the operative report to determine whether exploration or incision of the bile ducts was also performed for removal of stones (51.41) or for other relief of obstruction (51.42) as well as whether an intraoperative cholangiogram (87.53) was performed. Incision of the cystic duct is included in the basic procedure code.

Removal of Biliary Calculi

Biliary stones are removed in several ways. A cholecystectomy automatically removes any gallbladder calculus. Alternatively, a cholecystotomy (51.04) can be carried out for the removal of gallbladder stones without removing the gallbladder. Stones in the common duct can be removed percutaneously (51.96), by endoscopy (51.88), or by common duct exploration in connection with a cholecystectomy (51.41). Other biliary stones can also be removed percutaneously (51.98) or endoscopically (51.88).

Extracorporeal shock wave lithotripsy (98.52) destroys biliary stones without invasive surgery. The advantages of lithotripsy over conventional surgery for removal of stones include a shorter hospital stay and avoidance of the potential complications associated with surgical intervention.

Exercise 16.2

Code the following diagnoses and procedures. Do not assign E codes.

	Code(s)
1. Acute cholecystitis with calculus of gallbladder and bile duct	574.60
Laparoscopic cholecystectomy	51.23
2. Chronic cholecystitis with calculus in common duct	574.40
Cholecystectomy Common bile duct exploration with removal of common bile duct stone Intraoperative cholangiogram Incidental appendectomy	51.22 51.41 87.53 47.19
3. Biliary obstruction, extrahepatic	576.2
4. Cholecystitis, acute and chronic, with cholesterolosis	575.12
Total cholecystectomy	51.22

Exercise 16.2 *(continued)*

5. Acute cholecystitis with choledocholithiasis	574.30
6. Acute and chronic cholelithiasis with calculi in gallbladder and bile duct	574.90
7. Acute and chronic cholecystitis with gallbladder and bile duct calculus and obstruction	574.81

ADHESIONS

Intestinal and peritoneal adhesions are classified as code **568.0, Peritoneal adhesions** or as **560.81, Intestinal or peritoneal adhesions,** when obstruction is also present. These codes do not include pelvic peritoneal adhesions; such adhesions are classified as code **614.6, Pelvic peritoneal adhesion, female,** which also includes postoperative and postinfection adhesions.

Usually, minor adhesions do not cause symptoms or increase the difficulty of performing an operative procedure. When minor adhesions are easily lysed as part of another procedure, coding a diagnosis of adhesions and a lysis procedure is inappropriate. For example, there are often minor adhesions around the gallbladder that can be pushed aside easily without cutting during gallbladder surgery; coding of adhesions and/or lysis is not appropriate in such situations. Sometimes, however, a strong band of adhesions can cause obstruction or prevent the surgeon from gaining access to the organ to be removed, and a surgical lysis is required before the operation can proceed. In such cases, coding both the adhesions and lysis would be appropriate. It is important to note that coders should not code adhesions and lysis based solely on mention of adhesions or lysis in an operative report. Documentation of clinical significance by the surgeon may include, but is not limited to, such language as: numerous adhesions requiring a long time to lyse, extensive adhesions involving tedious lysis, extensive lysis, and so forth. If there is any question, the determination of whether the adhesions and the lysis are significant enough to merit coding must be made by the physician. Lysis of peritoneal adhesions can be performed by laparoscopy (54.51) or by an open procedure (54.59).

HERNIAS OF THE ABDOMINAL CAVITY

Hernias are classified by type and site, with combination codes used to indicate any associated gangrene or obstruction. With inguinal and femoral hernias, a fifth-digit subclassification indicates whether the hernia is unilateral or bilateral and whether it is specified as recurrent; that is, whether it had been repaired during a previous surgery. An incisional ventral hernia is classified as recurrent. Hernias described as incarcerated or strangulated are classified as obstructed. Careful review of the medical record and attention to instructional notes are important steps in coding these conditions. Coding examples include the following:

- Bilateral inguinal hernia with obstruction (no mention of gangrene) 550.12
- Unilateral recurrent inguinal hernia with gangrene 550.01
- Gangrenous femoral hernia, recurrent, bilateral 551.03
- Diaphragmatic hernia with gangrene 551.3
- Umbilical hernia with obstruction 552.1
- Incarcerated femoral hernia 552.00

Hernia repairs can be performed with a laparoscope inserted through a small incision or through a traditional open surgical approach. When coding hernia repair, the coder should be careful not to use a bilateral repair code when the hernia itself is described as unilateral. A unilateral repair may be done even though bilateral hernias are present, but, obviously, it is impossible to repair bilateral hernias when only one hernia exists. Repair of inguinal hernias is further subdivided according to whether the hernia is direct or indirect, even though the diagnosis codes do not make this distinction. A direct hernia is one with protrusion through the abdominal wall; an indirect hernia protrudes through the inguinal ring only. Hernia repair codes also make a distinction between simple repairs and those repairs in which a graft or prosthesis (for example, mesh) is used to reinforce the repair. In coding repair of a diaphragmatic (esophageal or hiatal) hernia, the axis for the code is whether an abdominal or thoracic approach was used.

Coding examples include:

- Repair of unilateral direct inguinal hernia 53.01
- Laparoscopic repair of unilateral direct inguinal hernia with mesh prosthesis 17.11
- Repair of bilateral indirect inguinal hernias 53.12

Exercise 16.3

Code the following diagnoses and procedures. Do not assign E codes.

	Code(s)
1. Right direct inguinal hernia and left indirect sliding inguinal hernia	550.92
Repair of right direct and left indirect inguinal hernias	53.13
2. Incarcerated left inguinal hernia	550.10
Laparoscopic left indirect inguinal herniorrhaphy with mesh prosthesis	17.12

Exercise 16.3 *(continued)*

3. Recurrent left inguinal hernia	550.91
Repair of indirect inguinal hernia, left	53.02
4. Gangrenous umbilical hernia	551.1
Repair of umbilical hernia	53.49
5. Strangulated umbilical hernia	552.1
Laparoscopic repair of umbilical hernia with mesh prosthesis	53.42
6. Reflux esophagitis secondary to sliding esophageal hiatal hernia	530.11 553.3
Repair of esophageal hiatus hernia, abdominal approach	53.75
7. Recurrent ventral incisional hernia with obstruction and gangrene	551.21

APPENDICITIS

Category **540, Acute appendicitis,** uses a fourth digit to indicate the presence of either generalized peritonitis (540.0) or peritoneal abscess (540.1). If both are listed in the diagnostic statement, only code 540.1 is assigned, as acute appendicitis often progresses to peritoneal abscess. Occasionally, an appendix ruptures during an appendectomy; this is not classified as a complication of surgery.

Category **541, Appendicitis, unqualified,** is a vague code that should not be used in an acute care facility. Additional information is almost always available in the medical record.

Surgical removal of a diseased appendix is coded **47.0x, Appendectomy.** Code **47.1x, Incidental appendectomy,** is used when the appendix is removed as a routine prophylactic measure in the course of other abdominal surgery. It should not be assigned when there is a diagnosis of significant appendiceal pathology. If the appendix is removed by means of exploratory laparotomy and no other therapeutic procedure is performed, code 47.09 should be assigned even though the appendix may not demonstrate any pathology on tissue examination. No code is assigned for the approach.

DIARRHEA

A code from categories 001 through 008 is assigned for infectious diarrhea when the organism has been identified. Code 009.2 is assigned for infectious diarrhea not otherwise specified, or described only as dysenteric diarrhea or epidemic diarrhea. Code 009.3 is provided for diarrhea presumed to be of infectious origin, but it does not apply in the United States and would be assigned only on the basis of the physician's specific statement. Check the Alphabetic Index carefully before coding, because diarrhea can be related to a variety of conditions. Symptom code 787.91 is assigned for diarrhea for which no appropriate subterm can be located. Note that the main term for diarrhea is followed by a long list of nonessential modifiers. Examples of appropriate code assignments include the following:

- Diarrhea due to Giardia 007.1
- Acute diarrhea 787.91
- Coccidian diarrhea 007.2
- Chronic ulcerative diarrhea 556.9
- Infantile diarrhea 787.91
- Functional diarrhea 564.5

CONSTIPATION

There is a single code for constipation (564.00), but there are two distinct subtypes recognized: slow transit constipation (564.01) and outlet dysfunction constipation (564.02). The slow transit results from a delay in transit of fecal material throughout the colon secondary to smooth muscle. The latter results from difficulty evacuating the rectum during attempts at defecation. Treatment for these two types is very different. The slow transit type is treated with either laxatives or surgery. Biofeedback is taught for relaxation for the outlet dysfunction constipation.

REDUCTION OF INTUSSUSCEPTION

Intussusception, primarily a disease of young children, is the prolapse of one part of the intestine into the lumen of an immediately adjacent part, resulting in intestinal obstruction. The most common therapy is reduction by using a fluoroscopically controlled hydrostatic barium enema. Air has recently become an alternative to barium as the contrast agent of choice and ionizing radiation enemas may also be used. An ultrasound-guided reduction is now being used in some institutions. In this type of reduction the condition is first diagnosed sonographically with the reduction carried out by means of a normal saline enema under ultrasound guidance. Code 96.29 is assigned for all these reductions; no additional code is assigned for either the fluoroscopic or ultrasound guidance. If these noninvasive procedures are not effective, surgical intervention may be required.

BARIATRIC SURGERY AND COMPLICATIONS

Bariatric surgery refers to procedures performed on morbidly obese patients for the purpose of weight loss. There are several types of restrictive and malabsorptive gastric procedures that are performed for weight loss when other methods have failed. Malabsorptive operations are the most common and restrict food intake as well as the amount of calories and nutrients the body absorbs. Restrictive operations restrict food intake but do not interfere with the normal digestive process.

Weight loss is usually achieved by reducing the size of the stomach (restrictive operations) with an implanted device (such as gastric banding) or through removal of a portion of the stomach, or by resecting and re-routing the small intestines to a small stomach pouch (malabsorptive operations), such as gastric bypass surgery. Although restrictive operations lead to weight loss for most patients, they are less successful than malabsorptive operations in achieving long-term weight loss.

Examples of malabsorptive procedures are the following:

- Roux-en-y gastric bypass procedure (44.39) is accomplished by creating a small stomach pouch to restrict food intake. Next, a Y-shaped section of the small intestine is attached to the pouch to allow food to bypass the lower stomach, the duodenum (the first segment of the small intestine), and the first portion of the jejunum (the second segment of the small intestine). This type of bypass reduces the amount of calories and nutrients the body absorbs. The small pouch serves as the stomach and only holds two to six ounces per serving. Initially, patients experience rapid weight loss, leveling off in 8–24 months at 20–40 percent above the ideal body weight.
- The biliopancreatic diversion (BPD) (43.89) requires excision of part of the stomach to create a small pouch. Food empties from the pouch past the pyloric valve, which regulates emptying of the stomach, into the duodenum and the last segments of the small intestine. In contrast to the roux-en-y surgery, the pyloric valve remains part of the digestive process so that "dumping" is eliminated. Dumping occurs when the pyloric valve and duodenum are bypassed and food empties directly into the small intestine. Patients may experience symptoms such as nausea and vomiting, diarrhea, and abdominal cramps as a result of dumping.
- Another type of biliopancreatic diversion (BPD) is the "duodenal switch" procedure. As with the original BPD, this operation includes stomach resection, but only the outer margin is removed, leaving a sleeve of stomach with the pylorus and beginning of the duodenum at its end. The duodenum is divided so that pancreatic and bile drainage is bypassed. The near-end alimentary limb is then attached to the beginning of the duodenum, while the common limb is created in the same way as the BPD. Three codes are required to fully describe the biliopancreatic diversion with duodenal switch: code **43.89, Other partial gastrectomy;** code **45.51, Isolation of segment of small intestine;** and code **45.91, Small-to-small intestinal anastomosis.**

Restrictive operations restrict food intake but do not interfere with the normal digestive process. Examples of restrictive bariatric procedures are gastroplasty (44.69), laparoscopic gastroplasty (44.68), vertical banded gastroplasty (44.68), laparoscopic gastric restrictive procedure or laparoscopic banding (44.95), laparoscopic revision of gastric restrictive procedure (44.96), and laparoscopic vertical sleeve gastrectomy (43.82).

Gastric bands may require periodic adjustments. When a patient is seen for adjustment of a gastric band, code **V53.51, Fitting and adjustment of gastric lap band,** is assigned as the principal or first-listed diagnosis, along with procedure code **44.98, Laparoscopic adjustment of size of adjustable gastric restrictive device.** Code **V45.86, Bariatric surgery status,** may be reported as an additional code.

Category 539, Complications of bariatric procedures, has been created to uniquely identify complications of gastric band procedures, such as infection (539.01) or other complications of gastric band procedure (539.09), complications of other bariatric procedures such as infection (539.81), and other complications of bariatric procedure (539.89). In the case of infections, additional codes are used to specify the type of infection, such as abscess or cellulitis of abdomen (682.2), or septicemia (038.0–038.9), with an additional code to identify the organism (041.00–041.9).

Occasionally, the problems due to the gastric restrictive devices may require laparoscopic removal of the device, in which case code **44.97, Laparoscopic removal of gastric restrictive device(s)**, is assigned for the procedure.

Review Exercise 16.4

Code the following diagnoses and procedures. Do not assign E codes.

	Code(s)
1. Acute ruptured appendicitis with postoperative paralytic ileus	540.0 997.4 560.1
Appendectomy	47.09
2. Acute hepatitis and early cirrhosis of the liver due to chronic alcoholism	571.1 571.2 303.90
3. Anorectal cryptitis, chronic	569.49
Cryptectomy	49.39
4. Perirectal abscess Atony of colon	566 564.89
Incision and drainage of perirectal abscess	48.81

Review Exercise 16.4 *(continued)*

5. Hepatic coma with massive ascites secondary to Laennec's cirrhosis	572.2 571.2 789.59
6. Intestinal obstruction due to peritoneal adhesive band	560.81
Extensive lysis of adhesive band	54.59
7. Diverticulosis and diverticulitis of right colon	562.11
Right hemicolectomy with end-to-end anastomosis	45.73
8. Infection of gastrostomy with abscess of abdominal wall due to *Streptococcus* B	536.41 682.2 041.02
9. Polyp of rectum	569.0
Colonoscopy with polypectomy	48.36
10. Neurogenic bowel	564.81

Diseases of the Genitourinary System

CHAPTER **17**

CHAPTER OVERVIEW

- Diseases of the genitourinary system are classified in chapter 10 of *ICD-9-CM*.
  - — They are not found in chapter 10 if they are classified by etiology.
  - — These include transmissible infections, neoplastic diseases, and conditions complicating pregnancy, childbirth, and the puerperium.
- The term "urinary tract infection" is often used by physicians when referring to conditions such as urethritis, cystitis, or pyelonephritis.
- Stress incontinence has different codes depending on the sex of the patient. When the underlying cause is known, that should be sequenced first.
- Chronic kidney disease develops in conjunction with other conditions. The sequencing of the code in conjunction with others is found in the Tabular List.
- A relationship is presumed when a patient has both hypertension and kidney disease. Codes extend to the fifth digit to cover this condition.
- Renal dialysis codes vary from admission codes to insertion of catheter without the performance of dialysis. Dialysis codes cover complications such as dialysis dementia.
- Conditions involving the prostate involve a fourth and fifth digit. Neoplasms of the prostate are not included within this category of codes.
- Other related codes covered in this chapter are prostatectomy, endometriosis, genital prolapse, dysplasia of the cervix and vulva, and endometrial ablation.
- Neoplasms of the breast are classified in chapter 2 of *ICD-9-CM*. However, not all conditions and procedures involving the breast are related to neoplasms.

LEARNING OUTCOMES

After studying this chapter you should be able to:

- Distinguish between the different conditions often referred to as urinary tract infections.
- Code for a variety of kidney diseases and their treatments.
- Explain coding for kidney disease in conjunction with hypertension and diabetes.
- Classify conditions that affect both male and female genitalia.

TERMS TO KNOW

Acute kidney failure
sudden failure of renal function following a severe insult to the kidneys

Chronic kidney disease
long-term disability of the renal function

Nephropathy
general term indicating that renal disease is present

Ureter
carries urine from the bladder to the kidneys to the bladder

Urethra
carries urine from the bladder to the outside of the body

REMEMBER . . . It is important to distinguish between chronic kidney disease, acute kidney failure, and acute kidney injury.

INTRODUCTION

Diseases of the genitourinary system are classified in chapter 10 of *ICD-9-CM,* except those that are classified by etiology, such as certain easily transmissible infections, neoplastic diseases, and conditions complicating pregnancy, childbirth, and the puerperium. Subterms should be checked carefully in the Alphabetic Index, and special attention should be given to the terms "urethra" and "ureter," which are often confused by coders.

INFECTIONS OF THE GENITOURINARY TRACT

Physicians often use the term "urinary tract infection (UTI)" when referring to conditions such as urethritis, cystitis, or pyelonephritis. Urethritis and cystitis are lower urinary tract infections; pyelonephritis is an infection of the upper urinary tract. The main term for the specific condition should be referred to the Alphabetic Index before referring to the main term **Infection.** For example, under the main term cystitis, subterms are located for diphtheritis (032.840) and chlamydial (099.53) infection. There is also a subterm for amebic cystitis that indicates dual coding (006.8 + 595.4).

When there is no subterm for the organism, the code for the condition is assigned, with an additional code from category 041 or 079 to indicate the organism. For example, there is no subterm for E. coli under the main term for cystitis; therefore codes 595.0 and 041.49 are assigned for cystitis due to E. coli.

The following examples indicate complete coding for such infections:

- Cystitis due to Trichomonas 131.09
- Acute cystitis due to Proteus infection <u>595.0</u> + 041.6
- Chronic pyelonephritis due to E. coli <u>590.00</u> + 041.49

Urinary tract infections that develop following surgery are rarely true postoperative infections and are not usually classified as such. When the operative procedure involves the urinary tract, however, it may be appropriate for the coder to ask the physician whether the infection is related to the procedure. When the infection is related to the

FIGURE 17.1 The Urinary System

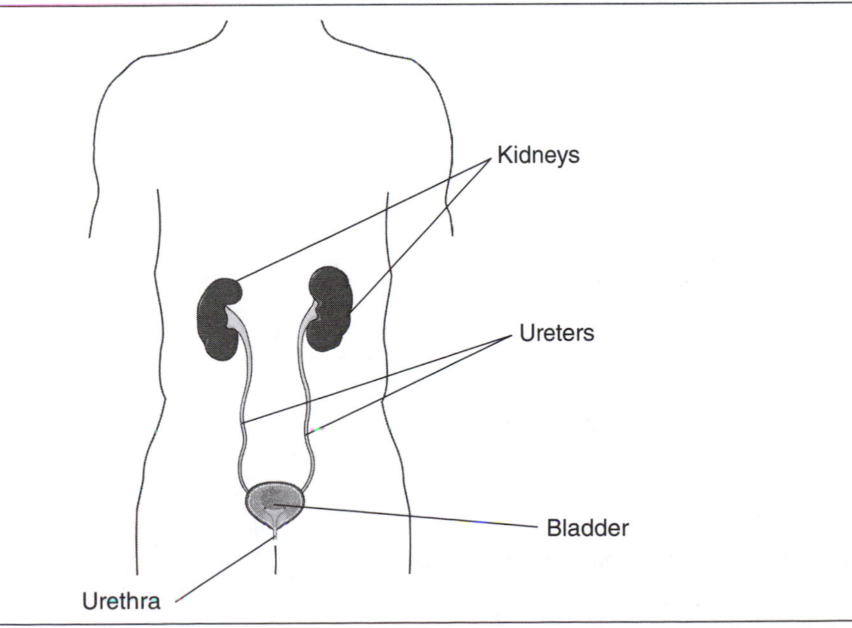

presence of an implant, graft, or device (such as an indwelling or a suprapubic catheter), code 996.6x is assigned. As with all postprocedural complications, code assignment is based on the provider's documentation of the relationship between the infection and the procedure. In the absence of documentation indicating that the infection is due to the surgical procedure, code **599.0, Urinary tract infection,** not otherwise specified, should be assigned. If the provider states that the UTI is secondary to the indwelling urinary catheter, assign code **996.64, Infection and inflammatory reaction due to indwelling urinary catheter,** and code **599.0, Urinary tract infection, site not specified.**

Exercise 17.1

Code the following diagnoses and procedures. Do not assign E codes.

	Code(s)
1. Urethral stricture due to gonorrheal infection	098.2 598.01
Urethral dilation	58.6
2. Abscess of right scrotum due to group B *Streptococcus*	608.4 041.02
Incision and drainage of scrotal abscess	61.0
3. Acute pyelonephritis due to Helicobacter pylori Infection	590.10 041.86
4. Chronic cystitis Pseudomonas infection	595.2 041.7
5. Chronic cystitis due to Monilia infection	112.2
6. Urinary tract infection due to candidiasis	112.2

HEMATURIA

Hematuria refers to blood in the urine. Gross hematuria refers to hematuria that is so plentiful that it is visible to the naked eye. Microscopic hematuria refers to blood in the urine visible only under a microscope. The *ICD-9-CM* provides separate codes for gross hematuria (599.71), microscopic hematuria (599.72), and unspecified hematuria (599.70). Many genitourinary conditions have hematuria as an integral associated symptom. For example, the medical record has a diagnostic statement of hematuria due to renal calculus but only a code of **592.0, Calculus of kidney,** is assigned. The hematuria is integral to this condition and no additional code is assigned. A certain amount of hematuria is expected following a urinary tract procedure or a prostatectomy. This is not considered a postoperative complication, and no code is assigned unless the bleeding is excessive or persistent.

Microscopic hematuria should not be confused with hemoglobinuria, which is coded as 791.2. Hemoglobinuria is an abnormal finding and refers to the presence of free hemoglobin in the urine on laboratory examination of the urine. It is reported only when the physician has indicated its clinical significance.

URINARY INCONTINENCE

Stress incontinence causes involuntary urine loss with physical strain such as coughing or sneezing. Although it occurs in both male and female patients, it occurs more frequently in women, typically as a result of physical changes brought on by earlier childbearing. Stress incontinence in female patients is coded as **625.6, Stress incontinence, female;** in male patients it is assigned code **788.32, Stress incontinence, male.** Prostate surgery is the primary cause of incontinence in men.

Urinary incontinence due to cognitive impairment, severe physical disability, or immobility is coded to **788.91, Functional urinary incontinence.**

Other types of incontinence are also classified into subcategory **788, Symptoms involving urinary system.** When more than one type of incontinence is present, it is classified as mixed incontinence (male) (female), and code 788.33 is assigned. When the underlying cause of incontinence is known, the code for that condition should be sequenced first.

Treatment for incontinence depends, to a large extent, on the particular type of incontinence present. If it is due to an intrinsic sphincter deficiency, collagen injections are sometimes carried out. Code **59.72, Injection of implant into urethra and/or bladder neck,** is assigned for this therapy.

Other treatments for incontinence are surgical in nature. Codes for repair of incontinence depend on the procedure performed. Examples of these procedure codes are:

- 59.3 Plication of urethrovesical junction
- 59.4 Suprapubic sling operation
- 59.5 Retropubic urethral suspension
- 59.6 Paraurethral suspension
- 59.71 Levator muscle operation for urethrovesical suspension
- 59.79 Other repair of urinary stress incontinence

RENAL DISEASE

Renal disease is classified into categories 580 through 593. Glomerulonephritis is a type of nephritis in which there is bilateral inflammatory change without infection. Nephrotic syndrome is a complex clinical state characterized by edema, albuminuria, and increased permeability of the glomerular capillary basement membrane. The syndrome can result from an unknown cause, or it may result from glomerulonephritis or diseases such as diabetes, systemic lupus erythematosus, hypertension, and amyloidosis. Nephropathy is a general term that indicates that renal disease is present. Infection of the kidney is classified to 590.x. Kidney disease complicating pregnancy, labor, and the puerperium is reclassified in chapter 11 of *ICD-9-CM*.

Chronic Kidney Disease and End-Stage Renal Disease

Chronic kidney disease (CKD) is considered a more current and precise term than chronic renal failure or chronic renal insufficiency. CKD develops as a complication of other diseases, such as diabetes mellitus, primary hypertension, glomerulonephritis, nephrosis, interstitial nephritis, systemic lupus erythematosus, obstructive uropathy, and polycystic kidney disease. The sequencing of the CKD code in relationship to codes for other contributing conditions is based on the conventions of the Tabular List.

Patients usually live for many years with such chronic kidney disease. When kidney involvement becomes so extensive that kidney function can no longer keep up with the body's needs, dialysis is usually required.

ICD-9-CM classifies CKD on the basis of severity. Based on the glomerular filtration rate (GFR), chronic kidney disease has been categorized into five stages. Category **585, Chronic kidney disease (CKD)**, has been expanded to the fourth-digit subcategory level for further specification of the varying stages of chronic kidney disease. The fourth-digit subcategory codes are as follows:

- 585.1 Chronic kidney disease, Stage I
- 585.2 Chronic kidney disease, Stage II (mild)
- 585.3 Chronic kidney disease, Stage III (moderate)
- 585.4 Chronic kidney disease, Stage IV (severe)
- 585.5 Chronic kidney disease, Stage V
- 585.6 End-stage renal disease
- 585.9 Chronic kidney disease, unspecified

End-stage renal disease (585.6) is a complex syndrome characterized by a variable and inconsistent group of biochemical and clinical changes that affect volume regulation, acid-base balance, electrolyte balance, excretion of waste products, and several endocrine functions. It is a progression of chronic kidney disease and is defined by clinicians as the point at which regular dialysis sessions or a kidney transplant is required to maintain life. Chronic renal failure not otherwise specified and chronic renal insufficiency are both assigned code **585.9, Chronic kidney disease, unspecified.** If both a stage of CKD and end-stage renal disease (ESRD) are documented for the same patient, only code 585.6 would be assigned.

Kidney transplant may be recommended for patients with severe CKD caused by severe, uncontrollable hypertension, infections, diabetes mellitus, or glomerulonephritis. Patients who have undergone kidney transplant may still have some form of CKD because the kidney transplant may not fully restore kidney function. Code V42.0 may be assigned with the appropriate CKD code to indicate that a CKD patient is status post kidney transplant. It is incorrect to assume that mild or moderate CKD following a transplant is a transplant failure unless it is documented as such in the medical record. If transplant failure, rejection, or other transplant complication is documented in patients with severe CKD or ESRD, code **996.81, Complications of transplanted organ, kidney,** is assigned. If a post kidney transplant patient has CKD and the documentation is unclear whether there is transplant failure or rejection, it is necessary to query the provider.

Acute Kidney Failure

Acute kidney failure (584.x) is very different from chronic kidney disease; it is not a phase of the same condition. Chronic kidney disease is a long-term inability of the kidneys to function adequately; acute kidney failure is the sudden cessation of renal function following severe insult to normal kidneys. Toxic agents, traumatic or surgical shock, tissue destruction due to injury or surgery, or a variety of other conditions can cause acute kidney failure.

Acute renal insufficiency (593.9) is considered an early stage of renal impairment, evidenced by diminished creatinine clearance or mildly elevated serum creatinine or BUN. Clinical symptoms or other abnormal laboratory findings may or may not be present but are usually minimal. Treatment varies, depending on the underlying cause, but serious attention is given to prevent its progression to renal failure. Code **997.5, Urinary complications,** is assigned if renal insufficiency is due to a procedure.

Physicians sometimes use the terms "renal insufficiency" and "renal failure" interchangeably, but the *ICD-9-CM* classifies these terms to different codes. *ICD-9-CM* classifies unspecified and acute renal insufficiency to code 593.9, whereas acute kidney failure is assigned to category 584. Chronic renal insufficiency, chronic renal failure, and unspecified chronic kidney disease are assigned to code 585.9. Unspecified renal failure is identified with code 586. It is important for the coder to be guided by the classification. If the physician uses both terms in the medical record, the physician should be queried for clarification as to the correct diagnosis.

Acute kidney injury is a phrase used by some physicians to refer to acute kidney failure. Care should be taken to determine whether the documentation refers to a traumatic injury to the kidney (which would be assigned to a code in category 866) or to a nontraumatic event, which is actually acute kidney failure. Nontraumatic acute kidney injury is assigned to **584.9, Acute kidney failure, unspecified.**

Kidney Disease with Hypertension

ICD-9-CM presumes a relationship when a patient has both hypertension and chronic kidney disease or renal sclerosis; category **403, Hypertensive kidney disease,** or category **404, Hypertensive heart and kidney disease,** should be assigned. The fifth digit indicates the stage of chronic kidney disease as follows:

- Category 403
  —Fifth digit of 0 is for "chronic kidney disease stage I through stage IV, or unspecified"
  —Fifth digit of 1 is for "chronic kidney disease stage V or end-stage renal disease"
- Category 404
  —Fifth digit of 0 is for "without heart failure and with chronic kidney disease stage I through stage IV, or unspecified"
  —Fifth digit of 1 is for "with heart failure and with chronic kidney disease stage I through stage IV, or unspecified"
  —Fifth digit of 2 is for "without heart failure and with chronic kidney disease stage V or end-stage renal disease"
  —Fifth digit of 3 is for "with heart failure and with chronic kidney disease stage V or end-stage renal disease"

Codes 403.x0, 404.x0, and 404.x1 require an additional code from 585.1–585.4, 585.9 to identify the specific stage of CKD. Codes 403.x1, 404.x2, and 404.x3 require an additional code of 585.5 or 585.6 to identify the specific stage of CKD.

Acute kidney failure is not caused by hypertension and is not included in the hypertensive kidney disease codes. When acute kidney failure and hypertension are both present, assign a code from category **584, Acute kidney failure,** with an additional code for the hypertension.

The use of codes from categories 403 and 404 does not apply in the following situations:

- The renal condition is acute kidney failure.
- The hypertension is described as secondary.
- The kidney disease is specifically stated as due to a cause other than hypertension.

Examples of appropriate codes for kidney disease with hypertension include the following:

- Hypertensive kidney disease with chronic kidney disease 403.90 + 585.9
- Hypertensive heart and kidney disease with chronic kidney disease 404.90 + 585.9
- Hypertensive heart and kidney disease with stage V chronic kidney disease and congestive heart failure 404.93 + 585.5 + 428.0
- Acute kidney failure; hypertension 584.9 + 401.9

Kidney Disease with Diabetes Mellitus

Diabetic nephropathy is coded as **250.4x, Diabetes with renal manifestations,** or **249.4x, Secondary diabetes with renal manifestations.** A manifestation code is assigned as an additional code to indicate the specific kidney condition, such as glomerulosclerosis, arteriolar nephrosclerosis, chronic interstitial nephritis, papillary necrosis, other tubular lesions, or chronic kidney disease.

Kidney disease sometimes results from both hypertension and diabetes mellitus. In this situation, the combination code from category 403 or category 404 and a code from subcategory 250.4x or 249.4x are assigned. A code from category 585 is assigned to identify the manifestation as chronic kidney disease.

Examples of appropriate codes for kidney disease due to diabetes include the following:

- Diabetic nephrosis 250.40 + 581.81
- Chronic kidney disease due to hypertension and type 1 diabetes mellitus 403.90 + 250.41 + 585.9
- Chronic kidney disease, unspecified due to type 1 diabetic nephropathy 250.41 + 585.9 (+ 583.81 optional)

In the last example, the code for the intervening nephropathy leading to chronic kidney disease can be assigned, but it is not required.

RENAL DIALYSIS

Patients with end-stage renal disease require a regular schedule of dialysis treatments to manage the symptoms arising from kidney disease. They may be admitted to the hospital or seen as outpatients for the sole purpose of dialysis. Code **V56.0, Admission for extracorporeal dialysis (hemodialysis),** or code **V56.8, Admission for other dialysis (peritoneal),** is assigned as the principal diagnosis for such admissions, with an additional code for the kidney disease. If the patient is admitted for other reasons but continues to receive dialysis therapy during the hospital stay or is known to be maintained on renal dialysis, code **V45.11, Renal dialysis status,** may be assigned as an additional code; the condition responsible for the admission is designated as the principal diagnosis. Code V56.0 may only be used as a principal or first-listed diagnosis code. If the patient is known to be noncompliant with renal dialysis, code **V45.12, Noncompliance with renal dialysis,** may be assigned.

The performance of hemodialysis requires the insertion of a venous catheter (38.95) or a totally implantable venous access device (86.07); the associated dialysis is coded **39.95, Hemodialysis.** Peritoneal dialysis is accomplished by instilling a prepared fluid into the peritoneal cavity and removing the uremic toxins along with the prepared fluid. Insertion of a Tenckhoff catheter for this purpose is coded **54.93, Creation of a cutaneoperitoneal fistula;** code **54.98, Peritoneal dialysis,** is assigned for the associated dialysis.

Patients are sometimes admitted for insertion of a catheter or a vascular access device, but no dialysis is performed during the admission. In this case, the condition is coded as the principal diagnosis, and code V56.x is not assigned. When dialysis is performed during the same episode of care, procedure code 39.95 is assigned to specify that the dialysis was actually performed during the encounter. When the admission is for fitting or adjustment of the dialysis catheter, code V56.1 is assigned for an extracorporeal catheter and V56.2 for a peritoneal catheter. If concurrent dialysis is performed, procedure code 39.95 is assigned. Some coding examples follow:

- Patient with end-stage renal disease admitted for insertion of Hickman catheter for renal dialysis (no dialysis performed) 585.6 + 38.95
- Patient with chronic kidney disease, stage V, admitted for hemodialysis V56.0 + 585.5 + 39.95
- Patient with unspecified chronic kidney disease admitted for creation of AV fistula for renal dialysis; dialysis not performed on this admission 585.9 + 39.27

Patients frequently develop complications as a result of dialysis therapy. When dialysis dementia is diagnosed, code 294.8 is assigned. Dialysis disequilibrium without associated dementia is coded to **276.9, Electrolyte and fluid disorder, not elsewhere classified.** External cause code E879.1 is assigned with any of these codes to indicate that the condition is the result of kidney dialysis. If the complication is the reason for admission, the code for the complication is sequenced first as the principal diagnosis, with an additional code for the chronic kidney disease.

It normally takes two to three months for an arteriovenous fistula to mature. A nonmaturing or nondeveloping fistula is considered a mechanical complication and is coded to **996.1, Mechanical complication of other vascular device, implant, and graft.** Primary causes of a nonmaturing fistula are narrowing of a vein or multiple competing veins. Treatment may consist of performing an arteriovenostomy to create a new arteriovenous fistula (39.27). Other treatment options may be performed by interventional radiologists—such as balloon angioplasty; revision of AV fistula; and/or closing off competing veins, which can be performed using various techniques.

Exercise 17.2

Code the following diagnoses and procedures. Assign E codes as appropriate.

	Code(s)
1. End-stage renal disease	585.6
Peritoneal dialysis	54.98
2. Dialysis disequilibrium with acute delirium	276.9 293.0 V45.11 E879.1

COMPLICATIONS OF CYSTOSTOMY

Complications of cystostomy are classified to 596.8x. Codes from postoperative complications 996 through 999 are not assigned. Code 596.81 is assigned for an infection of the cystostomy. An additional code would be assigned to specify the type of infection, such as abscess or cellulitis of abdomen (682.2) or septicemia (038.0–038.9), with an additional code to identify the organism (041.00–041.9). Mechanical complication of cystostomy, including malfunction of cystostomy, is coded as 596.82; while other complications of cystostomy, such as fistula, hernia, or prolapse, are coded as 596.83.

CYSTOSCOPY AS OPERATIVE APPROACH

Cystoscopy is used as the approach for many procedures performed in diagnosing and treating urinary tract conditions; no code is assigned for the cystoscopic approach. A transurethral approach (TUR) is indicated by the title of the procedure and is included in the code.

REMOVAL OF URINARY CALCULUS

Urinary calculi are relatively common and often pass without surgery. Several types of surgical techniques are used when intervention is necessary. Extracorporeal shock wave lithotripsy (ESWL) of the kidney, ureter, and/or bladder (98.51) reduces the stones to a slush that can be excreted over a short period of time. This code includes removal of stones from any area in the urinary system, including those in a Koch pouch. Ultrasound destruction of bladder calculi uses two codes, **57.0, Transurethral clearance of the bladder,** and **59.95, Ultrasound fragmentation of urinary stones.** Kidney stones can be removed by percutaneous nephrostomy with fragmentation (55.04) or without fragmentation (55.03). Transurethral ureteroscopic lithotripsy with fragmentation of stones (56.0) removes calculi from the ureter and renal pelvis.

A two-step procedure is sometimes used when it is necessary to manipulate a ureteral stone back into the renal pelvis in order to remove it. This procedure involves the insertion of a ureteral catheter (59.8) for manipulation, followed by either percutaneous nephrostomy with fragmentation of stones (55.04), or by extracorporeal shock wave lithotripsy (98.51).

Exercise 17.3

Code the following diagnoses and procedures. Do not assign E codes.

	Code(s)
1. Right ureteral calculus Right calyceal diverticulum Left renal cyst, solitary (acquired)	592.1 593.89 593.2
2. Impacted renal calculus with medullary sponge kidney	592.0 753.17
Extracorporeal shock wave lithotripsy of kidney calculus	98.51
3. Calculus in bladder	594.1
Lithotripsy of urinary bladder with ultrasonic fragmentation	57.0 + 59.95

PROSTATE DISEASE AND THERAPY

Diseases of the male genital organs are classified in categories 600–608, with conditions of the prostate using categories 600–602. Neoplasms of the prostate are classified as follows:

- Malignant neoplasm of the prostate 185
- Benign neoplasm of the prostate 222.2
- In situ neoplasm of the prostate 233.4

Urinary obstruction is a primary symptom of hyperplasia of the prostate. Hyperplasia of the prostate is classified to category 600 with fourth digits providing additional specificity regarding the nature of the hypertrophy. The fifth digits provide a combination code that includes the prostate condition with or without urinary obstruction as follows:

- Benign hypertrophy of prostate without urinary obstruction and other lower urinary tract symptoms (LUTS) 600.00; with urinary obstruction and other lower urinary tract symptoms (LUTS) 600.01
- Nodular prostate without urinary obstruction (excludes malignant neoplasm) 600.10; with urinary obstruction 600.11
- Benign localized hyperplasia without urinary obstruction and other lower urinary tract symptoms (LUTS) 600.20; with urinary obstruction and other lower urinary tract symptoms (LUTS) 600.21
- Cyst of prostate 600.3
- Hyperplasia of prostate, unspecified, without urinary obstruction and other lower urinary tract symptoms (LUTS) 600.90; with urinary obstruction and other lower urinary tract symptoms (LUTS) 600.91

If a patient with benign prostatic hypertrophy (BPH) has symptoms of urinary obstruction or retention, such as incomplete bladder emptying, it is allowable to use the fifth digits for "with obstruction" for the BPH code. The fifth digits were created specifically to identify that the prostatic hypertrophy is obstructing urine flow to any degree,

FIGURE 17.2 The Male Reproductive System

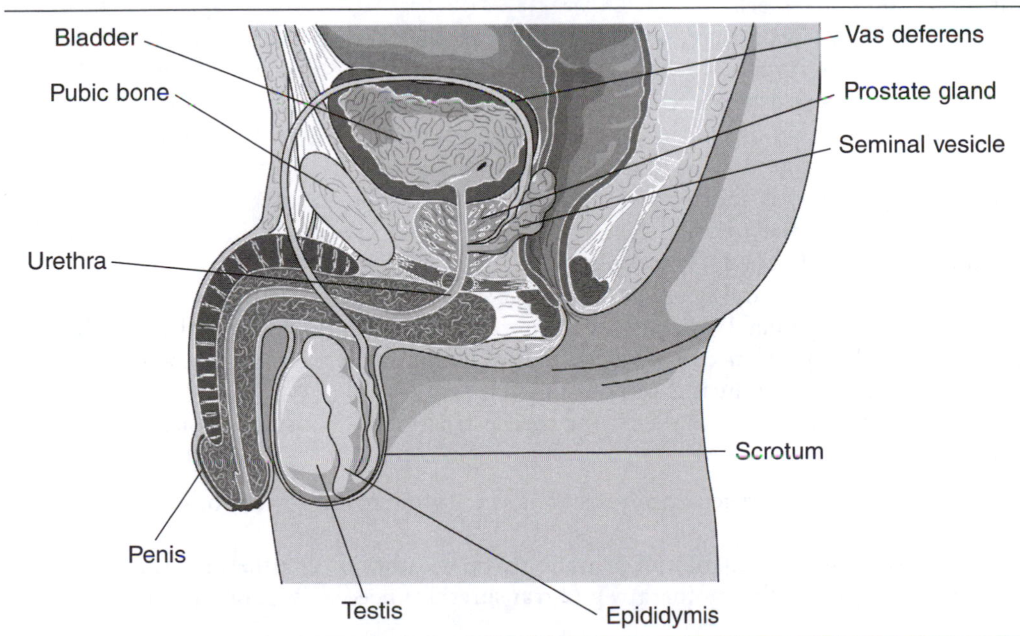

not just for complete obstruction. If a patient with BPH has symptoms of urinary incontinence, such as postvoid dribbling, the fifth digits for "with obstruction" should not be assigned unless the physician has specifically documented a urinary obstruction.

As indicated by the "use additional code" note under codes 600.01, 600.21, and 600.91, an additional code should be assigned in conjunction with the BPH code to identify other lower urinary tract symptoms, such as incomplete bladder emptying (788.21), nocturia (788.43), straining on urination (788.65), urinary frequency (788.41), urinary hesitancy (788.64), urinary incontinence (788.30–788.39), urinary obstruction (599.69), urinary retention (788.20), urinary urgency (788.63), and weak urinary stream (788.62).

Category 601 classifies inflammatory disease of the prostate as follows:

- 601.0 Acute prostatitis
- 601.1 Chronic prostatitis

Category 602 classifies other disorders of the prostate with such conditions as follows:

- 602.0 Calculus of the prostate
- 602.1 Congestion or hemorrhage of prostate
- 602.3 Dysplasia of prostate

The approach used for prostatectomy usually determines the code assigned as follows:

- 60.21 Transurethral, (ultrasound) guided laser-induced prostatectomy (TULIP)
- 60.29 Transurethral prostatectomy (TURP), other
- 60.3 Suprapubic prostatectomy
- 60.3 Transvesical prostatectomy
- 60.4 Retropubic prostatectomy
- 60.62 Cryoablation of prostate
- 60.62 Perineal (transperineal) prostatectomy

Code **60.5, Radical prostatectomy,** is assigned for radical prostatectomy regardless of the approach used. In a radical prostatectomy, the seminal vesicles and vas ampullae are excised along with the prostate. A prostatectomy performed with a radical cystectomy is coded **57.71, Radical cystectomy;** this procedure involves removal of the bladder, prostate, and seminal vessels.

In the TULIP procedure, a miniature ultrasound system is combined with a laser, which permits the surgeon to view the prostate on a television monitor. The surgeon then discharges the laser at the blockage caused by the enlarged prostate. The blockage disintegrates over a period of several weeks, passing out of the body without further intervention. The result is the same as that achieved by transurethral prostatic resection (TURP), but the hospital stay is shorter and there are fewer complications.

A "sweep" of the regional lymph nodes is often carried out in connection with a prostatectomy performed for neoplastic disease. This procedure involves removal of regional lymph nodes and lymphatic drainage of the area, skin, subcutaneous tissue, and fat. Code **40.3, Regional lymph node excision,** is assigned as an additional code when this procedure is also performed. A code for radical lymph node excision is assigned when the excision extends to the muscle and deep fascia.

Other types of therapy utilized for the destruction of prostatic tissue are coded as follows:

- Transurethral destruction of prostate tissue by microwave thermotherapy (TUMT of prostate) 60.96
- Transurethral destruction of prostate tissue by other thermotherapy; this includes radiofrequency thermotherapy and transurethral needle ablation (TUNA) 60.97

ENDOMETRIOSIS

Endometriosis is a condition in which aberrant tissue that almost perfectly resembles the mucous membrane of the uterus is found in various other sites within the pelvic cavity. A code from category **617, Endometriosis,** is assigned for this condition with a fourth digit indicating the site in which the aberrant tissue is found. For example:

- Endometriosis of the ovary 617.1
- Endometriosis of the colon 617.5
- Endometriosis of fallopian tube 617.2

GENITAL PROLAPSE

Prolapse of the vagina and/or the uterus is a relatively common condition. In coding genital prolapse, it is first necessary to determine whether the condition involves the vaginal wall, the uterus, or both; and whether the prolapse is complete or incomplete. For example:

- Uterovaginal prolapse, incomplete (uterus descends into introitus, and cervix protrudes slightly beyond) 618.2
- Uterovaginal prolapse, complete (entire cervix and uterus protrude beyond the introitus, and vagina is inverted) 618.3

Code 618.5 is assigned for prolapse of vaginal vault occurring after hysterectomy; it is not classified as a surgical complication. This condition may be due to the surgical technique or to the relaxation of supporting structures following surgery. Pelvic or vaginal enterocele, a herniation of the intestine through intact vaginal mucosa, is coded **618.6, Vaginal enterocele, congenital or acquired,** whether it is congenital or acquired. Prolapse

FIGURE 17.3 The Female Reproductive System

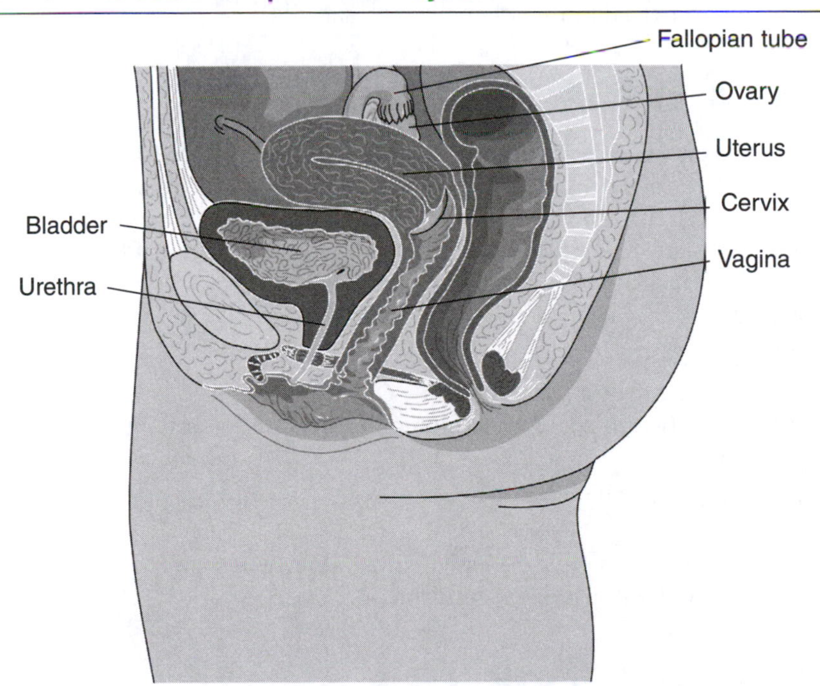

of the uterus in an obstetric patient is classified in chapter 11 of *ICD-9-CM*. Examples of appropriate coding for genital prolapse include the following:

- Prolapse of uterus (no vaginal wall involvement) 618.1
- Vaginal enterocele 618.6
- Prolapse of cervical stump 618.84
- Prolapse of gravid uterus (undelivered) 654.43

Subcategory **618.0, Prolapse of vaginal walls without mention of uterine prolapse,** has fifth digits to provide additional specificity regarding the type of vaginal prolapse, such as the following:

- 618.00 Unspecified prolapse of vaginal walls
- 618.01 Cystocele, midline
- 618.02 Cystocele, lateral
- 618.03 Urethrocele
- 618.04 Rectocele
- 618.05 Perineocele
- 618.09 Other

ENDOMETRIAL HYPERPLASIA

Endometrial hyperplasia refers to excessive proliferation of the cells of the inner lining of the uterus. It is considered a significant risk factor for endometrial cancer and requires careful monitoring. *ICD-9-CM* provides the following codes for endometrial hyperplasia:

- 621.30 Endometrial hyperplasia, unspecified
- 621.31 Simple endometrial hyperplasia without atypia
- 621.32 Complex endometrial hyperplasia without atypia
- 621.33 Endometrial hyperplasia with atypia
- 621.34 Benign endometrial hyperplasia
- 621.35 Endometrial intraepithelial neoplasia [EIN]

DYSPLASIA OF CERVIX AND VULVA

Code **622.1x, Dysplasia of cervix (uteri),** is also identified as CIN (cervical intraepithelial neoplasia). CIN I is coded to 622.11, and CIN II is coded to 622.12. Dysplasia of the cervix specified as CIN III, however, is carcinoma in situ of the cervix, and code **233.1, Cervix uteri,** is assigned. Dysplasia of the vulva is coded **624.8, Other specified noninflammatory disorders of vulva and perineum.**

Vulvar intraepithelial neoplasia (VIN) is classified as follows:

- VIN I or mild dysplasia of vulva—624.01
- VIN II or moderate dysplasia of vulva—624.02
- VIN III is classified to **233.3, Carcinoma in situ of other and unspecified female genital organs.**

A diagnosis of CIN III or VIN III can be made only on the basis of pathological examination of tissues.

Codes 795.00–795.09 would be assigned for abnormal results from a cervical cytologic examination without histologic confirmation.

ENDOMETRIAL ABLATION

Endometrial ablation is used as an alternative to hysterectomy for women with dysfunctional bleeding that does not respond to hormone therapy. It can also be used to treat women with fibroid tumors or endometrial polyps. A scope equipped with either a roller ball or a u-shaped wire is inserted into the uterus. The lining of the uterus is ablated by laser, radiofrequency electromagnet energy, or electrocoagulation. Code **68.23, Endometrial ablation,** is assigned for this procedure.

DISEASES OF THE BREAST

Neoplasms of the breast are classified in chapter 2 of *ICD-9-CM*. The coder should be aware, however, that terms such as growth, cyst, and lump do not necessarily refer to neoplastic disease. When surgery is performed, the pathology report provides more specific information to assist in code assignment. Examples of appropriate coding include the following:

- Fibrocystic disease of the breast 610.1
- Benign neoplasm of breast 217
- Benign neoplasm of skin of breast 216.5
- Gynecomastia 611.1
- Carcinoma of the male breast 175.9
- Carcinoma of the female breast 174.9

Biopsies of the breast are classified as closed (85.11) or open (85.12). When the procedure is described as an excisional biopsy, it usually refers to excision of the entire lesion rather than a simple biopsy, in which case it is coded to **85.21, Local excision of lesion of breast.** The term "lumpectomy" also describes a local excision of a breast lesion.

When surgery on the breast is performed for possible neoplasm, it is customary to perform a biopsy before the definitive surgery begins. A rapid-frozen section is reviewed by a pathologist to determine whether malignancy is present. The code for the definitive procedure is sequenced first, followed by the code for the biopsy.

With advances in cancer therapy, radical mastectomy is not performed as often as in the past because a lumpectomy or a modified radical mastectomy appears to be equally effective in most cases. The main distinction between a radical and modified mastectomy is that all or part of the pectoralis major and all of the pectoralis minor are removed in a radical mastectomy, whereas the pectoralis major is preserved in a modified radical mastectomy. Mastectomy codes (85.4x) indicate whether a procedure is performed unilaterally or bilaterally and the extent of the procedure. The coder must review the operative report carefully before assigning these procedure codes.

A **tissue expander** (85.95) is another procedure frequently carried out in conjunction with breast surgery. This tissue insertion permits a flap closure of the site making it not necessary for the patient to undergo a skin graft. Saline is usually injected into the breast expander at regular intervals following its insertion to gradually enlarge the size of the expander. Tissue expanders used in areas other than the breast are coded as **86.93, Insertion of tissue expander.**

BREAST RECONSTRUCTION

Reconstructive breast surgery is performed for a variety of reasons. Prostheses are often implanted for patients who have undergone mastectomies. Breast reconstruction can be performed immediately after the surgery or delayed to a later time. When it is known that patients will undergo postoperative radiation, reconstruction is usually delayed. When a patient undergoes a mastectomy and the reconstruction is delayed, code **V51.0, Encounter for breast reconstruction following mastectomy,** is assigned as the principal or first-listed diagnosis for the return admission for each encounter for a stage of the breast reconstruction.

If the purpose for reconstruction is to increase breast size for improved appearance, prosthetic implants are usually used. Reduction mammoplasty is sometimes performed for patients whose large breast size interferes with normal daily activities or causes significant discomfort, as well as for cosmetic reasons. When mammoplasty is performed to reduce breast size, code **611.1, Hypertrophy of the breast,** is assigned as the principal diagnosis. When the purpose of the mammoplasty is cosmetic, code **V50.1, Other plastic surgery for unacceptable cosmetic appearance,** is assigned as the principal diagnosis.

Coding examples for reconstruction include the following:

- Total reconstruction of right breast 85.70
- Flaps and microsurgical procedures 85.71–85.76, 85.82–85.85
- Nipple-areola reconstruction 85.87
- Reduction mammoplasty 85.3x

Problems related to deformity and disproportion post–breast reconstruction may require patients to seek further medical care. Contour irregularity, excess tissue in reconstructed breast, or misshapen reconstructed breast are assigned to code **612.0, Deformity of reconstructed breast.** Breast asymmetry, or disproportion between native breast and reconstructed breast, and ptosis (sagging) of native breast in relation to reconstructed breast are assigned to **612.1, Disproportion of reconstructed breast.**

Sometimes complications develop in patients who have breast implants, making removal of the implants advisable. In such cases, the code for the principal diagnosis depends on the nature of the complication. For example, if the reason for the surgery is that the implant has ruptured, the principal diagnosis code is **996.54, Mechanical complication due to breast prosthesis.** When the reason for removal is that the patient had a capsular contracture of the right breast implant, code **611.83, Capsular contracture of breast implant,** is assigned as the principal diagnosis. Code **85.94, Removal of implant of breast,** is assigned for removal of a breast implant.

Patients sometimes request removal of an implant because they are concerned that a complication might occur in the future, although there is no problem at present. In this case, assign **V52.4, Fitting and adjustment of breast prosthesis and implant.** For example:

- A patient experienced a ruptured breast implant on the left side and was admitted for removal of the implant and insertion of a new implant.
  Principal diagnosis: 996.54 Mechanical complications due to breast prosthesis
  Surgery performed: 85.93 Revision of breast implant
- A patient who had undergone a previous right mastectomy with a breast implant inserted at the time of surgery recently suffered from a painful capsule. She was admitted for removal and reinsertion of the implant.
  Principal diagnosis: 996.79 Other complication due to other internal prosthetic device
  Surgery performed: 85.93 Revision of breast implant
- A patient had undergone bilateral breast implantation three years ago and was now admitted for elective implant removal. She had no related problems but had become concerned because of newspaper reports describing illnesses associated with breast implants.
  Principal diagnosis: V52.4 Fitting and adjustment of breast prosthesis and implant
  Surgery performed: 85.94 Removal of breast implant (assign code twice to indicate procedure was performed bilaterally)

Review Exercise 17.4

Code the following diagnoses and procedures. Do not assign E codes.

	Code(s)
1. Hydronephrosis with chronic pyelitis Pyelonephritis, focal, chronic, left	591 590.00
2. Rapidly progressive chronic glomerulonephritis	582.4
3. Syphilitic epididymitis	095.8 604.91
4. Chronic prostatitis due to Proteus	601.1 041.6
5. Phimosis and balanoposthitis	605 607.1
6. Encysted hydrocele, male	603.0
Excision of hydrocele of spermatic cord	63.1
7. Benign prostatic hypertrophy with urinary obstruction	600.01 599.69
Transurethral prostatectomy	60.29

Review Exercise 17.4 *(continued)*

8. Acute and chronic cervicitis	616.0
Vaginal hysterectomy	68.59
9. Chronic pelvic inflammatory disease	614.4
Dysmenorrhea	625.3
10. Menometrorrhagia	626.2
Endometrial polyp	621.0
Corpus luteum cysts of both ovaries	620.1
Total abdominal hysterectomy	68.49
Bilateral salpingo-oophorectomy	65.61
11. Cystocele with incomplete uterine prolapse	618.2
and stress incontinence	625.6
Cystocele repair	70.51
Vaginal suspension of uterus	69.22
12. Pelvic peritoneal endometriosis	617.3

Review Exercise 17.4 *(continued)*

13. Dermoid cyst of ovary	220
Laparoscopic wedge resection of ovarian cyst	65.24
14. Infertility due to pelvic peritoneal adhesions	614.6 628.2
Hysterosalpingogram, radiopaque dye	87.83
15. Psychogenic dysmenorrhea	306.52
16. Adhesions of ovary and fallopian tubes	614.6
Laparoscopic lysis of adhesions	65.81
17. Menorrhagia	626.2
Dilatation and curettage with endometrial ablation	68.23
18. Submucous fibroid of uterus	218.0
Laparoscopically assisted vaginal hysterectomy	68.51

Coding of Diseases of the Skin and Diseases of the Musculoskeletal System

Diseases of the Skin and Subcutaneous Tissue

CHAPTER 18

CHAPTER OVERVIEW

- Diseases of the skin and subcutaneous tissue can be found in chapter 12 of *ICD-9-CM*.
- Category 692 classifies dermatitis due to plants, food, drugs, and medications in contact with skin.
- Category 693 classifies dermatitis caused by medications taken internally.
  - — The coder must determine whether the condition is an adverse effect of proper administration or a poisoning due to the incorrect use of the drug.
  - — E codes are used to classify the causation.
- Chronic ulcers of the skin are classified using the fifth digit to specify the site.
- The sequencing of the code for cellulitis is dependent on the severity of the wound and the primary goal of the treatment (for cellulitis or for the wound).
- Excision of a lesion is coded based on severity of the excision. Exclusion notes indicate that skin lesions of several areas are coded elsewhere.
- Debridement is classified as either excisional or nonexcisional (brushing, irrigating, scrubbing, or washing).
- The classification of skin grafts is dependent on the process used (artificial skin, creation of neodermis, decellularized allodermis, and so on).

LEARNING OUTCOMES

After studying this chapter you should be able to:

- Know how to classify dermatitis due to contact, food, and ingestion of drug (both correct and incorrect usage).
- Code ulcers of the skin.
- Explain how to classify cellulitis based on location and the primary goal of the treatment.
- Code procedures done on the skin, such as excisions, debridement, and grafting.

TERMS TO KNOW

Cellulitis
an infection of the skin and soft tissues resulting from some sort of break in the skin

Debridement
removal of dead, damaged, or infected tissue

REMEMBER . . . This chapter of *ICD-9-CM* includes more than just conditions of the skin. It also includes conditions of the nails, sweat glands, hair, and hair follicles.

INTRODUCTION

Chapter 12 of *ICD-9-CM* deals with conditions affecting the skin and subcutaneous tissue. The chapter is organized around the following subdivisions:

- Infections of skin and subcutaneous tissue 680–686
- Other inflammatory conditions of skin and tissue 690–698
- Other diseases of skin and subcutaneous tissue 700–709

Conditions affecting the nails, sweat glands, hair, and hair follicles are included in this chapter. Congenital conditions of skin, hair, and nails are classified in category **757, Congenital anomalies of the integument.** Neoplasms of skin are classified in chapter 2 of *ICD-9-CM*.

DERMATITIS DUE TO DRUGS

Category 692 is classified for contact dermatitis such as plants other than food and drugs and other medications in contact with skin. Category 693 is assigned for dermatitis caused by drugs and medications taken internally. This distinction does not apply to the eyelid and the ear.

In coding dermatitis caused by medicines, the coder must first determine whether the condition represents an adverse effect due to the proper administration of a drug or poisoning due to the incorrect use of the drug. When the dermatitis is due to a medication used correctly as prescribed, the dermatitis code is sequenced first, with an E code from the E930 through E949 series included to indicate the medication responsible. When the dermatitis is due to incorrect use of the drug, it is classified first as a poisoning by drugs, medicinal and biological substances (960–969) with an additional code for the dermatitis, and an E code is assigned to indicate the way in which the poisoning occurred and the

FIGURE 18.1 The Skin and Subcutaneous Tissue

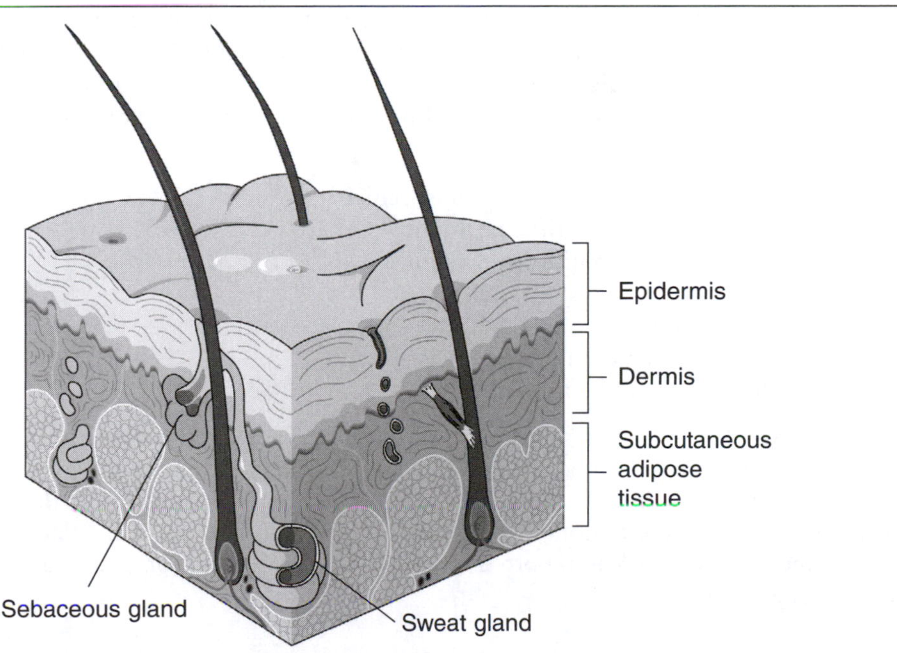

type of drug involved. (A more detailed discussion of the distinction between adverse effects and poisoning due to drugs and medications is provided in chapter 28 of this handbook.)

Correct coding examples include the following:

- Dermatitis due to allergic reaction to penicillin tablets, taken as prescribed (adverse reaction) 693.0 + E930.0
- Dermatitis due to accidental ingestion of mother's penicillin tablets (poisoning) 960.0 + 693.0 + E856

In the first example, which indicates an adverse reaction to a prescribed medication taken as directed, the code for dermatitis is sequenced first, followed by an E code to indicate that the drug responsible was penicillin. In the second example, code 960.0, Poisoning due to penicillin, is sequenced first, with an additional code to indicate that the effect of the poisoning is dermatitis and an E code to indicate that the poisoning was accidental.

Palmar plantar erythrodysesthesia (PPE), also called hand foot syndrome, is an example of a specific dermatitis that occurs as an adverse reaction to antineoplastic or biologic drugs used for cancer treatment. After the administration of chemotherapy, small amounts of the drug can leak from the capillaries, damaging tissue in the palms of the hands and the soles of the feet. The leakage results in redness, tenderness, and peeling of the palms and soles. The affected area resembles sunburn and may become dry, peel, and numb. This condition affects the hands and feet because of the increased friction and heat to which the extremities are exposed through normal use. Treatment involves reducing or stopping the drug therapy. Assign codes **693.0, Dermatitis due to substances taken internally, Due to drugs and medicines,** and **E930.7, Drugs, medicinal and biological substances causing adverse effects in therapeutic use, Antineoplastic antibiotics,** for the palmar-plantar erythrodysesthesia due to antineoplastic antibiotics.

ERYTHEMA MULTIFORME

Erythema multiforme is a skin disorder resulting in symmetrical red, raised skin areas all over the body, often resembling targets because they are dark circles with purple-gray centers. In some cases, there are severe systemic symptoms. Erythema multiforme can occur in response to medications, infections, or illness. The exact cause is unknown.

The different types of erythema multiforme and other erythematous conditions are classified as follows:

- 695.10 Erythema multiforme, unspecified
- 695.11 Erythema multiforme minor
- 695.12 Erythema multiforme major
- 695.13 Stevens-Johnson syndrome
- 695.14 Stevens-Johnson syndrome—toxic epidermal
- 695.15 Toxic epidermal necrolysis
- 695.19 Other erythema multiforme

Patients with erythema multiforme may also suffer from a variety of other associated manifestations that should be coded separately. The manifestations range from arthropathy (713.3) to corneal ulcer (370.00–370.07) to stomatitis (528.00). If the condition is drug induced, an E code should also be assigned to identify the drug. In addition, a code from subcategory 695.5 is reported to reflect the percentage of body surface involved with skin exfoliation.

ULCERS OF THE SKIN

Most chronic ulcers of the skin are classified in category **707, Chronic ulcer of skin,** with 785.4 assigned as an additional code when gangrene is present. Ulceration associated with arteriosclerosis of the extremities is classified as code **440.23, Atherosclerosis of the extremities with ulceration,** with an additional code from 707.10–707.19, 707.8, or 707.9; or if gangrene is present, to **440.24, Atherosclerosis of the extremities with gangrene.**

Subcategory **707.0, Pressure ulcers,** provides fifth digits to identify the specific site of the ulcer, such as elbow (707.01), upper back (707.02), lower back (707.03), hip (707.04), buttock (707.05), ankle (707.06), heel (707.07), and other site (707.09).

ICD-9-CM provides additional codes (707.20–707.25) to identify the stage of the pressure ulcers. The code for the site of the pressure ulcer (707.0x) should be sequenced first, followed by the code for the stage (707.2x). Codes from subcategory 707.2 apply only to pressure ulcers (707.0x). The code assignment for the pressure ulcer stage may be based on nursing documentation; however, the associated diagnosis of pressure ulcer should be coded on the basis of the provider's documentation (namely, the physician or any qualified health care practitioner who is legally accountable for establishing the patient's diagnosis, as defined in the *Official Guidelines for Coding and Reporting*).

Care should be taken not to confuse a pressure ulcer in which the stage is unspecified or not documented (707.20) with a pressure ulcer documented as unstageable (707.25). The staging of pressure ulcers takes into account the depth of tissue loss and the depth of tissue exposed. "Unstageable" refers to pressure ulcers whose stage cannot be clinically determined (e.g., the ulcer is covered by eschar or has been treated with a skin or muscle graft) as well as pressure ulcers documented as deep tissue injury but not documented as due to trauma. The assignment of the pressure ulcer stage code should be guided by clinical documentation of the stage or the terms found in the Index. The provider should be queried if the clinical term cannot be found in the Index or if there is no documentation of the stage.

Documentation of pressure ulcers may sometimes refer to "deep tissue injury." Care should be taken to review the provider documentation to determine whether the term refers to a traumatic injury (such as a contusion) or a pressure ulcer. The Alphabetic Index entry for "Injury, deep tissue" refers the coder to "*see Contusion, by site*"; whereas the entry for "Injury, deep tissue, meaning pressure ulcer" leads to code **707.25, Pressure ulcer, unstageable.**

Unfortunately, some patients may suffer from more than one pressure ulcer, and these ulcers may be at the same or different stages. These should be coded as follows:

- Same site, same stage: Assign one code for the site and one code for the stage. Example: Pressure ulcer both buttocks, both stage II 707.05 + 707.22
- Same site, different stages: Assign one code for the site and separate codes for each stage. Example: Pressure ulcer both buttocks, one stage II and one stage III 707.05 + 707.22 + 707.23
- Different sites, same stage: Assign separate codes for the sites and one code for the stage. Example: Pressure ulcer of left buttock and left elbow, both stage II 707.05 + 707.01 + 707.22
- Different sites, different stages: Assign separate codes for the sites and separate codes for the stages. Example: Stage III pressure ulcer of left buttock and stage II pressure ulcer of left elbow 707.05 + 707.23 + 707.01 + 707.22
- Evolving stage: Assign the code for the highest reported stage for that site. Example: Admitted with stage II pressure ulcer of buttocks, which advanced to stage III during encounter 707.05 + 707.23

Care should be taken to distinguish between pressure ulcers documented as "healed" (no code assigned) and "healing" (assign the appropriate code for the stage documented).

Examples of correct coding for chronic ulcers of the skin include the following:

- Pressure ulcer, sacral area, stage IV 707.03 + 707.24
- Pressure ulcer, sacral area, stage III with gangrene 707.03 + 707.23 + 785.4
- Ulcer of lower limb, except pressure ulcer 707.10–707.19
- Chronic ulcer of other specified sites 707.8
- Chronic ulcer of unspecified site 707.9

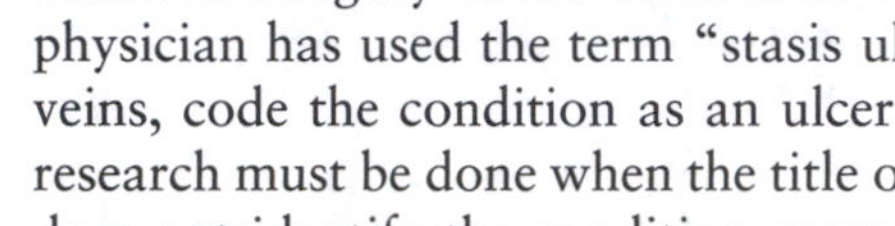

Stasis ulcers are ordinarily due to varicose veins of the lower extremities and are coded to category 454.x rather than to the categories for conditions of the skin. When the physician has used the term "stasis ulcer" but has identified a cause other than varicose veins, code the condition as an ulcer of the skin. A basic rule of coding is that further research must be done when the title of the code suggested by the Alphabetic Index clearly does not identify the condition correctly. In this case, even though the index directs the coder to a code involving varicose veins, the code should not be used when no varicosities are present.

CELLULITIS OF THE SKIN

Cellulitis is an acute, diffuse infection of the skin and soft tissues that commonly results from a break in the skin, such as a puncture wound, laceration, or ulcer. Occasionally, the break is so small that it cannot be identified by either the patient or the examining physician. Clinically, cellulitis usually presents as an abrupt onset of redness, swelling, pain, or heat in the infected area. Coders should not assume, however, that a reference to redness at the edges of a wound or ulcer represents cellulitis. The normal hyperemia associated with a wound usually extends a small distance beyond the edges of the wound rather than extending to the diffuse pattern that characterizes cellulitis.

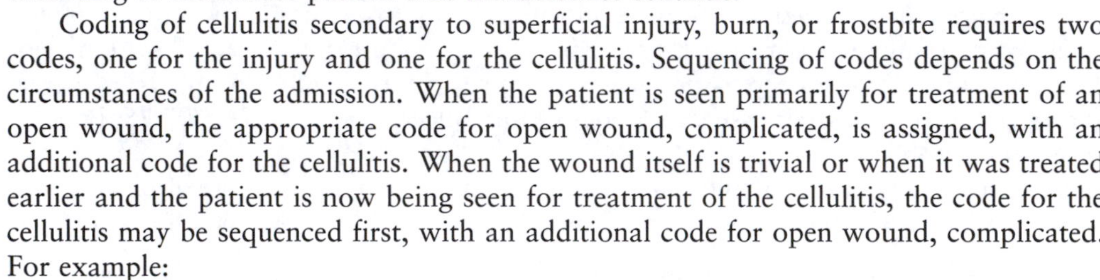

Coding of cellulitis secondary to superficial injury, burn, or frostbite requires two codes, one for the injury and one for the cellulitis. Sequencing of codes depends on the circumstances of the admission. When the patient is seen primarily for treatment of an open wound, the appropriate code for open wound, complicated, is assigned, with an additional code for the cellulitis. When the wound itself is trivial or when it was treated earlier and the patient is now being seen for treatment of the cellulitis, the code for the cellulitis may be sequenced first, with an additional code for open wound, complicated. For example:

- A patient suffered laceration of the lower leg while on a hiking trip two days ago and came to the hospital on his return. By the time he was seen, cellulitis was beginning to develop. The wound was cleansed, nonexcisional debridement was carried out, and antibiotics were started for the cellulitis.
  Principal diagnosis: 891.1 Open wound, complicated
  Additional diagnosis: 682.6 Cellulitis
  Procedure: 86.28 Nonexcisional debridement of wound, infection or burn
- A patient suffered a minor puncture injury to the finger when removing a staple at the office. Five days later, he was admitted to the hospital because of cellulitis of the finger and was treated with intravenous antibiotics. The wound itself did not require treatment, and therefore no code for injury is assigned.
  Principal diagnosis: 681.00 Cellulitis

Cellulitis of the skin is classified as code **681, Cellulitis and abscess of finger and toe,** and code **682, Other cellulitis and abscess.** Both abscess and lymphangitis are included in the codes for cellulitis of the skin. An additional code should be assigned to indicate the organism responsible, if this information is available. The responsible organism is usually *Streptococcus.*

Cellulitis may also present as a postoperative wound infection or as a result of the penetration of the skin involved in intravenous therapy. It may develop very early or may not appear until later. Note that code **958.3, Posttraumatic wound infection, NEC,** is not assigned when the infection is identified as cellulitis. For example:

- A patient had an appendectomy six days ago and is now readmitted with evidence of staphylococcal cellulitis of the operative wound.
  Principal diagnosis: 998.59 Postoperative infections
  Additional diagnosis: 682.2 Cellulitis of trunk
  Additional diagnosis: 041.10 *Staphylococcus*

Cellulitis frequently develops as a complication of chronic skin ulcers, in which case it is assigned to a code from the series 707.00 through 707.9. These codes do not include any associated cellulitis, and so two codes are required to describe these conditions. Designation of the principal diagnosis depends on the circumstances of the admission.

Cellulitis described as gangrenous is classified to code 785.4 rather than in the 681 and 682 categories when it develops as the result of either injury or ulcer. When gangrene is present, the injury or ulcer is sequenced first, with code **785.4, Gangrene,** assigned as an additional code. This practice is compatible with the usual guidelines concerning the use of chapter 16 codes as principal diagnoses and corresponds to the instructions in the Alphabetic Index.

OTHER CELLULITIS

Although cellulitis most commonly occurs in the skin and subcutaneous tissue, it also occurs in other areas. In such cases, codes from other chapters are assigned as appropriate.

Pelvic cellulitis in women is classified as an inflammatory condition and is assigned to category 614. Occasionally, pelvic cellulitis occurs following abortion, delivery, or molar or ectopic pregnancy, in which case it is classified to chapter 11 of *ICD-9-CM*. In male patients, pelvic cellulitis is coded as **567.21, Peritonitis (acute) generalized.**

EXCISION OF LESION

Excision or destruction of most skin lesions is classified as code **86.3, Other local excision or destruction of lesion or tissue of skin and subcutaneous tissue,** or as code **86.4, Radical excision of skin lesion.** Simple excisions are coded to 86.3 and involve only the skin. Code 86.3 includes both local excision and destruction carried out by cauterization, cryosurgery, fulguration, or laser beam. A radical or wide excision (86.4) goes beyond the skin and involves underlying and/or adjacent tissue. The surgeon's description should be followed carefully when assigning these codes. Notice that the exclusion notes indicate that skin lesions of several areas (for example, skin of the breast, anus, lip, eyelid, nose, ears, female perineum, scrotum, and penis) are coded elsewhere.

DEBRIDEMENT

Debridement of the skin and subcutaneous tissue is a procedure by which foreign material and devitalized or contaminated tissue are removed from a traumatic or infected lesion until the surrounding healthy tissue is exposed.

Excisional debridement of the skin (86.22) is the surgical removal or cutting away of such tissue, necrosis, or slough. It can be performed either by direct excision or by laser destruction. Depending on the availability of a surgical suite or the extent of the area involved, excisional debridement can be performed in the operating room, in the emergency department, or at the patient's bedside. Excisional debridement may be performed by a physician and/or other health care provider and involves an excisional, as opposed to a mechanical (brushing, scrubbing, washing), debridement. Use of a sharp instrument does not always indicate that an excisional debridement was performed. Minor removal of loose fragments with scissors or using a sharp instrument to scrape away tissue is not an excisional debridement. Excisional debridement involves the use of a scalpel to remove devitalized tissue. Documentation of excisional debridement should be specific regarding the type of debridement. If the documentation is not clear or if there is any question about the procedure, the provider should be queried for clarification.

Nonexcisional debridement of the skin (86.28) is the nonoperative brushing, irrigating, scrubbing, or washing of devitalized tissue, necrosis, slough, or foreign material. For example, water jet scalpel debridement is coded to **86.28, Nonexcisional debridement of wound, infection, or burn.** The use of Versajet is an example of a nonexcisional debridement. The Versajet consists of an ultra-high-pressure generator with a console and disposable attachments. A natural vacuum created by the jet stream removes tissue fragments. Specialized features allow physicians to debride traumatic wounds, chronic wounds, or other soft tissue lesions and aspirate and remove contaminants or other debris. Assign code 86.28 for Versajet debridement. Another example of nonexcisional debridement is ultrasonic debridement. Code 86.28 also includes minor snipping of tissue, such as that loosened by Hubbard tank therapy. Nonexcisional debridement may be performed by a physician or by other health care personnel.

When coding for debridement of areas other than skin, and there is no index entry or guidance provided in the Tabular List, the coder should look for other terms such as excision or destruction of lesion of that site. For example, assign code **83.39, Excision of lesion of other soft tissue,** for debridement of tendon. This code can be located in the index in the following manner:

Excision, lesion
    tendon 83.39

When coding multiple-layer debridements of the same site, the coder should assign a code only for the deepest layer of debridement. For example, sharp excision and debridement of a coccyx wound down to the fascia and including bone is coded to **77.69, Local excision of lesion or tissue of bone, other.** Debridement carried out in conjunction with another procedure is often included in the code for the procedure, but not always. Index entries and inclusion notes provide guidance for the coder.

DERMAL REGENERATIVE GRAFT

Several new technologies that are able to permanently regenerate or replace skin layers are now being used to treat severe burns. Code **86.67, Dermal regenerative graft,** is assigned for grafts using any of these technologies. Note that this code does not classify heterograft to skin (86.65) or homograft to skin (86.66). The inclusion note for code 86.67 lists biologic skin replacement systems as follows:

- Artificial skin, NOS
- Creation of "neodermis"
- Decellularized allodermis
- Integumentary matrix implants
- Prosthetic implant of dermal layer of skin
- Regenerate dermal layer of skin

Code **996.55, Mechanical complication due to artificial skin graft and decellularized allodermis,** is assigned for failure or rejection of these systems. Code 996.52 is assigned for complication of other skin graft. Status code V43.83 is assigned to indicate that the patient has an artificial skin graft.

Review Exercise 18.1

The following exercise provides examples of conditions classified in chapter 12 of *ICD-9-CM*. Code the following diagnoses and procedures.

	Code(s)
1. Varicose ulcer, lower left leg with severe inflammation	454.2
2. Pilonidal fistula with abscess	685.0
Excision of pilonidal sinus	86.21
3. Large abscess of right flank due to *Staphylococcus aureus*	682.2 041.11
Infection	
Incision and drainage of abscess, right flank	54.0

Review Exercise 18.1 *(continued)*

4. Hard corn deformity, right little toe Soft corn deformities, 3rd, 4th, and 5th toes, right	700
5. Keloid scar on left hand from previous burn or Late	701.4 906.6
Radical excision of scar	86.4
6. Chronic purulent inflamed acne rosacea of lower lip	695.3
Wide excision of chronic acne rosacea of lower lip with full-thickness graft over defect, lower lip	27.42 27.55
7. Giant urticaria	995.1
8. Contact dermatitis of eyelid	373.32
9. Seborrheic keratosis underlying the second metatarsal head, right foot	702.19
10. Cellulitis of anus	566

Review Exercise 18.1 *(continued)*

11. Acute lymphangitis, upper arm, due to group A streptococcal infection	682.3 041.01
12. Gangrenous diabetic ulcer of right foot due to peripheral circulatory disorder	250.70 707.14 785.4
13. Surgical (excisional) debridement of skin and fascia of foot	83.39
14. Infected ingrown toenail, right great toe	703.0
15. Cellulitis, buttock	682.5
16. Cellulitis of eyelid	373.13

Diseases of the Musculoskeletal System and Connective Tissue

CHAPTER **19**

CHAPTER OVERVIEW

- Diseases of the musculoskeletal system and connective tissue are covered in chapter 13 of *ICD-9-CM*.
- Classification to the fifth digit is important when coding conditions of the musculoskeletal system. This digit indicates the site involved.
- Coding back pain is often dependent on the distinction between degeneration, displacement, and the presence or absence of myelopathy.
- Arthritis can be coded independently or in a dual coding situation if it is a manifestation of another condition.
- Osteoarthritis can be further classified based on whether it is localized or generalized.
- There are stress fractures, pathological fractures, and traumatic fractures.
  - Fractures that are spontaneous are always considered pathological.
  - The fifth digit indicates the bone involved in the fracture.
  - A traumatic fracture should never be coded on the same bone as a pathological fracture.
- Coding joint replacements requires knowledge of the joint involved and whether it is a partial or total replacement.
- Coding joint revisions requires information on the removal of any joint replacement components.
- Coding spinal fusion requires knowing the anatomic portion (column) fused, the technique (approach) used (anterior, posterior, or lateral transverse), whether it is a refusion, and the number of vertebrae fused.
- Coding spinal disc prostheses requires knowledge of the type of prosthesis and the segment treated.
- Other conditions coded in this chapter include plica syndrome and fasciitis.

LEARNING OUTCOMES

After studying this chapter you should be able to:

- Explain the different types of arthritis and what to look for when coding arthritis.
- Explain the difference between pathological and traumatic fractures.
- Code joint replacements and revisions.
- Code back disorders and the variety of procedures for correcting spinal problems.

TERMS TO KNOW

Joint revision
procedure that adjusts, removes, or replaces a joint replacement component

Myelopathy
damage to the myelinated fiber tracts that carry information to the brain

Osteoarthritis
the most common form of arthritis; a degenerative joint disease

Pathological fracture
fracture that occurs in a bone weakened by disease

REMEMBER . . . There is a note at the start of chapter 13 that lists the site-specific fifth digits for classifying conditions of the musculoskeletal system.

INTRODUCTION

Chapter 13 of *ICD-9-CM* is governed by the general coding guidelines already discussed in this handbook. An understanding of the following terms may be helpful to the coder in assigning codes from chapter 13:

- Arthropathy: disorder of the joint
- Arthritis: inflammation of the joint
- Dorsopathy: disorder of the back
- Myelopathy: disorder of the spinal cord

Most arthropathies are classified in categories 710 through 719 and most dorsopathies in categories 720 through 724 in *ICD-9-CM*.

FIGURE 19.1 The Human Skeleton

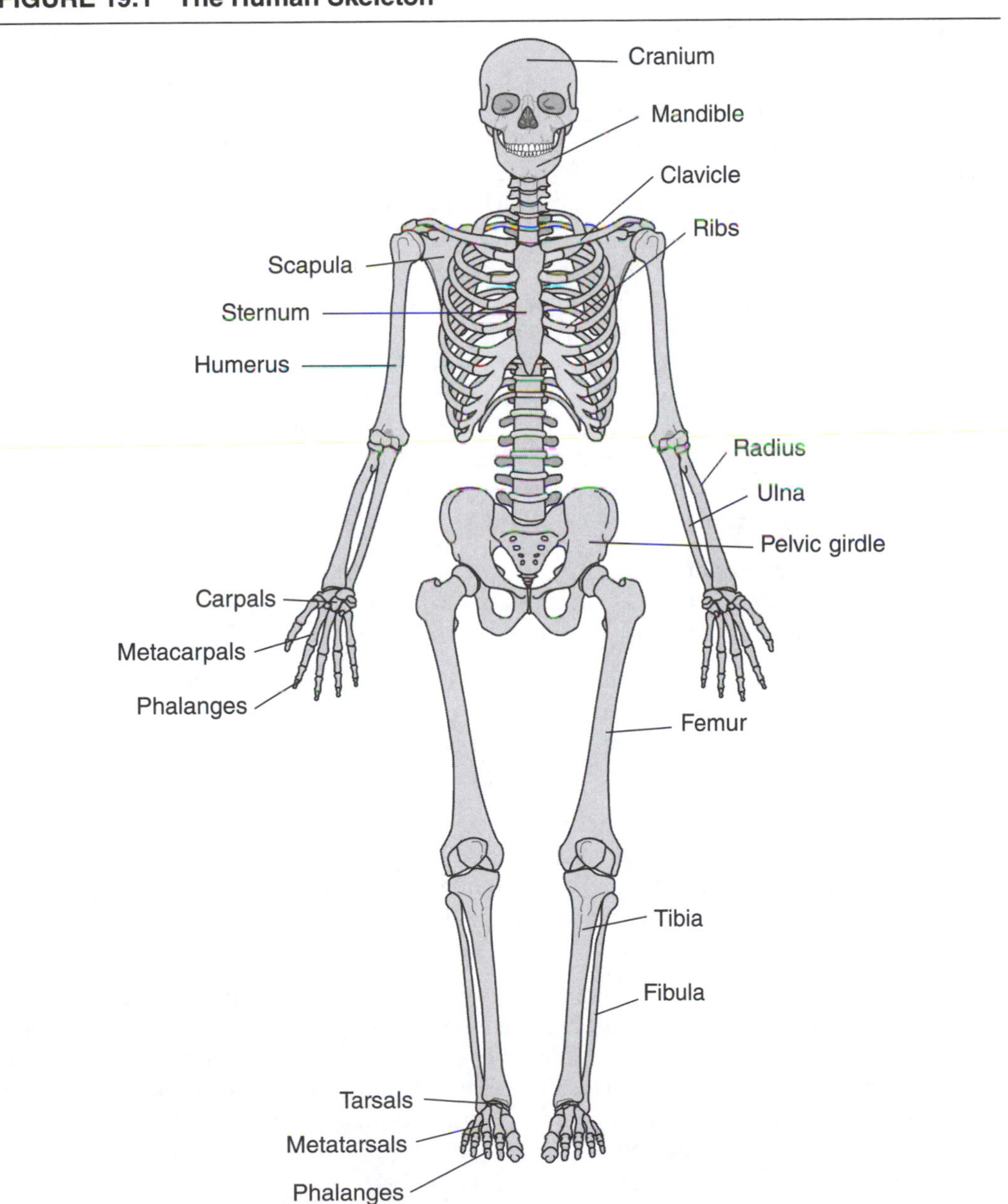

FIFTH-DIGIT SUBCLASSIFICATION

Many of the categories for diseases of the musculoskeletal system and connective tissue have fifth-digit subclassifications. A note at the beginning of chapter 13 lists fifth digits that apply to categories 711–712, 715–716, 718–719, and 730 to indicate the site involved. This note also indicates the specific bones and joints included in each fifth digit. For example, fifth digit 6 (lower leg) includes the tibia, fibula, patella, and knee joint. The fifth digits are repeated at the beginning of each of the categories and subcategories to which they apply, but the definitions are not repeated. When not all fifth digits apply to a specific subcategory, the appropriate fifth digits are displayed in brackets underneath the code title. Other categories and subcategories use different fifth digits; these are displayed as part of the code title.

BACK DISORDERS

Back pain described as lumbago or low back pain, without further qualification, is coded **724.2, Lumbago.** Back pain not otherwise specified is coded **724.5, Backache, unspecified.** Psychogenic back pain is classified under 724.5 and **307.89, Other pain disorder related to psychological factors.**

Intervertebral disc disorders are classified in category 722. Careful attention to the terminology is important in coding these conditions. Degeneration and displacement (herniation) of the disc are not the same conditions and require different codes.

The presence or absence of myelopathy is an important distinction to be made in assigning codes for certain back disorders. Myelopathy is a functional disorder and/or pathological change in the spinal cord that often results from compression. Codes for back disorders such as spondylosis and herniation of the intervertebral disc differentiate between conditions with and without myelopathy. Codes for a herniated disc without myelopathy include those with paresthesia but not paralysis. Terms that are included as **Intervertebral disc disorders with myelopathy** are classified into subcategory **722.7,** with a fifth digit used to indicate the site involved. Examples include the following:

- Herniated intervertebral disc, cervical, without myelopathy 722.0
- Herniated intervertebral disc, lumbosacral, with myelopathy 722.73
- Herniated intervertebral disc, thoracic, without myelopathy 722.11

Back pain associated with herniation of an intervertebral disc is included in the code for the herniated disc; no additional code is assigned.

Surgery for the excision or destruction of a herniated disc is classified in volume 3 of *ICD-9-CM* by the type of surgery performed. For example:

- Excision of herniated intervertebral disc 80.51
- Destruction of displaced intervertebral disc by chemonucleolysis 80.52
- Other destruction (including percutaneous suction diskectomy, automated percutaneous diskectomy, and laser destruction) 80.59
- Diskectomy with corpectomy 80.99

Code 03.09 is assigned for a laminectomy performed for the purpose of exploration or decompression of the spinal canal. Laminectomy performed for the purpose of excision of herniated disc material, however, represents the operative approach and is not coded. Occasionally after a decompression laminotomy, Mersilene stabilization may be carried out to reconstitute the intraspinous ligament. The placement of Mersilene sutures is inherent to the total procedure and should not be coded separately.

ARTHRITIS

Arthritis is the common term for a wide variety of conditions that primarily affect the joints, muscles, and connective tissue. The associated symptoms are inflammation, swelling, pain, stiffness, and mobility problems. Arthritis may occur independently, but it is also a common manifestation of a variety of other conditions, and dual coding guidelines apply. Examples include the following:

- Arthritis of the shoulder due to dicalcium phosphate crystals 275.49 + 712.11
- Charcot's arthritis due to diabetes 250.60 + 713.5
- Reiter's arthritis of hand 099.3 + 711.14

Arthritis is also associated with Lyme disease, either as a component of current disease or as a late effect. When the Lyme disease is currently active, code **088.81, Lyme disease,** and ***711.8x, Arthropathy associated with other infectious and parasitic diseases,*** are assigned. When the arthritis is a late effect of the Lyme disease, the listed codes are **139.8, Late effect of other infectious and parasitic disease,** and 711.8x.

Osteoarthritis is the most common form of arthritis; it is also called polyarthritis, degenerative arthritis, and hypertrophic arthritis. It is a degenerative joint disease, usually occurring in older people, with chronic degeneration of the articular cartilage and hypertrophy of the bone. It is characterized by pain and swelling. Codes from category **715, Osteoarthrosis and allied disorders,** are assigned except when the spine is involved when a code from 720.0–724.9 is assigned.

The primary axis for coding osteoarthritis is whether it is generalized or localized. When localized, it is further subdivided according to whether it is primary (715.1x) or secondary (715.2x). Primary osteoarthritis, also known as polyarticular degenerative arthritis, affects joints in the spine, knee, and hip, as well as certain small joints of the hands and feet. (Note that the codes for localized osteoarthritis include bilateral involvement of the same site.) A code from subcategory 715.3 is assigned for localized arthritis that is not identified as either primary or secondary. Secondary arthritis, also called monarticular arthritis, is confined to the joints of one area and results from some external or internal injury or disease. Osteoarthritis that involves multiple sites but is not specified as generalized is coded as **715.8x, Osteoarthritis involving or with mention of more than one site, but not specified as generalized.**

Rheumatoid arthritis (714.0), another fairly common type of arthritis, is an autoimmune disease that affects the entire body. Pyogenic arthritis (711.0x) is due to infection and is classified with a fifth digit indicating the joints involved. An additional code should be assigned for the responsible organism. Gouty arthritis (274.0x) is a recurrent arthritis of the peripheral joints in which excessive uric acid in the blood is deposited in the joints. If the gout is due to lead, code 984.x is assigned.

Exercise 19.1

Code the following diagnoses and procedures. Do not assign E codes.

	Code(s)
1. Acute and chronic gouty arthritis	274.01 274.02

Review Exercise 19.1 *(continued)*

2. Chronic nodular rheumatoid arthritis with polyneuropathy	714.0 357.1
3. Traumatic arthritis, left ankle, due to old traumatic dislocation Late	716.17 905.6
Compression arthrodesis, left ankle	81.11
4. Herniated intervertebral disc, L4–5	722.10
Laminectomy with excision of intervertebral disc, L4–5	80.51
5. Chronic lumbosacral sprain	724.6

DERANGEMENT

Derangement of the knee is classified to category 717; derangement of other sites is classified to category 718, with fourth digits indicating the site. Code 718.3x is assigned if the derangement is described as being recurrent. Derangement due to current injury is classified to categories 830–839, Dislocation of joint, with the fourth digit indicating the site and fifth digit indicating whether the dislocation is open or closed. Certain categories also provide fifth digits that indicate the type of dislocation.

Exercise 19.2

Code the following diagnoses. Do not assign E codes.

	Code(s)
1. Recurrent derangement of ankle	718.37
2. Recurrent derangement of knee	718.36
3. Derangement of knee due to a current fall	836.2

PATHOLOGICAL FRACTURES

Pathological fractures occur in bones that are weakened by disease. These fractures are usually spontaneous but sometimes occur in connection with slight trauma that ordinarily would not result in a fracture in healthy bone. There are many different underlying causes for pathological fractures, including osteoporosis, metastatic tumor of the bone, osteomyelitis, Paget's disease, disuse atrophy, hyperparathyroidism, and nutritional or congenital disorders.

Fractures described as spontaneous are always pathological fractures. When the fracture is described as a compression fracture, the record should be reviewed to determine whether any significant trauma has been experienced. A fall from a height, such as a diving board, with compression fracture of the spine would be classified as an injury; but a compression fracture in an older patient resulting from a slight stumble or other minor injury would probably be considered pathological, particularly when the patient also suffers from an underlying condition that frequently causes such fractures. The physician should be asked for clarification.

All pathological fractures are coded as 733.1x, with a fifth digit indicating the bone involved. Newly diagnosed pathologic fractures are reported using a code from subcategory 733.1. Subcategory 733.1 is assigned so long as the patient is receiving active treatment for the pathological fracture. Examples of active treatment are surgical treatment, emergency department encounter, and evaluation and treatment by a new physician. A pathological fracture is designated as the principal diagnosis only when the patient is admitted solely for treatment of the pathological fracture. Ordinarily, the code for the underlying condition responsible for the fracture is listed first with an additional code for the fracture. Never assign a code for both a traumatic fracture and a pathological fracture of the same bone; one or the other would be assigned. (See chapter 26 of this handbook for a discussion of coding traumatic fractures.)

Appropriate coding examples include the following:

- Fracture of tibia and major osseous defects due to senile osteoporosis 733.16 + 733.01 + 731.3
- Pathological fracture due to metastatic carcinoma of bone; ovarian cancer five years ago 733.14 + 198.5 + V10.4

STRESS FRACTURES

Stress fractures are somewhat different from pathological fractures in that pathological fractures are always due to a physiologic condition such as cancer or osteoporosis that results in damage to the bone. Stress fractures are due to repetitive force applied before the bone and its supporting tissues have had enough time to provide such force. They are usually negative in an X-ray display, and days or weeks may pass before the fracture line is visible on an X-ray. Codes from 733.10–733.19 are assigned for pathological fractures. Stress fractures are coded as follows:

- 733.93 Stress fracture of tibia or fibula
- 733.94 Stress fracture of the metatarsals
- 733.95 Stress fracture of other bone
- 733.96 Stress fracture of femoral neck
- 733.97 Stress fracture of shaft of femur
- 733.98 Stress fracture of pelvis

Additional E codes are assigned to identify the cause of the stress fracture, for example, code **E927.3, Cumulative trauma from repetitive motion.**

The term "stress reaction" is included under each code as a synonymous term for stress fracture.

REPLACEMENT OF A JOINT

Replacement of a joint is classified in category 81.5x for joints of the lower extremities and 81.8x for joints of the upper extremities. Code assignment depends on the joint involved and whether the replacement is total or partial. When coding hip replacements, if the type of bearing surface is known, it should be reported using the appropriate codes as follows: 00.74 for metal on polyethylene, 00.75 for metal-on-metal, 00.76 for ceramic-on-ceramic, and 00.77 for ceramic-on-polyethylene. If replacement also involves the placement of a bone-growth stimulator, code 78.9x is assigned as an additional code; the fourth digit indicates the site. Other examples include the following:

- Replacement of acetabulum with prosthesis 81.52
- Total ankle replacement 81.56
- Replacement of femoral head 81.52
- Partial replacement of hip 81.52
- Total elbow replacement 81.84

ICD-9-CM does not provide codes to indicate that a bilateral replacement has been carried out. The procedure code should be assigned twice when the same procedure is performed on bilateral joints.

Occasionally, a prosthesis must be removed because of infection, with a new prosthesis placed after a month or two when the infection has completely cleared. The first admission for such a problem would be coded **996.66, Infection or inflammation due to internal joint prosthesis,** with code **80.0x, Arthrotomy for removal of prosthesis,** assigned for the procedure. On the follow-up admission, the principal diagnosis would be acquired deformity of the site (category 736), with a procedure code for revision of the joint.

Anytime a joint replacement is adjusted or removed and replaced, the procedure is coded as a joint revision, which includes any removal of the joint replacement component. However, if there is removal of a joint spacer (e.g., cement), code 84.57 is also assigned. If the type of bearing surface is known, it should be reported using the appropriate code (00.74–00.77).

Codes for revision of hip replacements identify the specific joint components revised (acetabular, femoral, and acetabular liner and/or femoral head) and are assigned as follows:

- 00.70 Revision of hip replacement, both acetabular and femoral components (this includes total hip revision)
- 00.71 Revision of hip replacement, acetabular component
- 00.72 Revision of hip replacement, femoral component
- 00.73 Revision of hip replacement, acetabular liner and/or femoral head only

When the joint component of the revised hip replacement is not specified, assign code **81.53, Revision of hip replacement, not otherwise specified.**

Anytime a component of a joint has been previously replaced, the procedure would still be considered a revision even though part of the component is being replaced for the first time. For example, when a patient is admitted for conversion of a previous hemiarthroplasty to a total hip replacement, it should be reported with code **00.70, Revision of hip replacement, both acetabular and femoral components.**

Procedures for the revision of knee replacements are classified according to the joint component revised (tibial, femoral, patellar, or tibial insert) as follows:

- 00.80 Revision of knee replacement, total (all components)
- 00.81 Revision of knee replacement, tibial component
- 00.82 Revision of knee replacement, femoral component
- 00.83 Revision of knee replacement, patellar component
- 00.84 Revision of knee replacement, tibial insert (liner)

When the knee joint component being revised is not specified, assign code **81.55, Revision of knee replacement, not otherwise specified.**

Revision of joint replacements that are not elsewhere classified are assigned to code 81.59 (lower extremity) and code 81.97 (upper extremity). These codes are assigned for both partial or total revision.

Hip resurfacing involves grinding away the worn surfaces of the femoral head and acetabulum while retaining the femoral neck and majority of the femoral head. The procedure concludes with the placement of new bearing surfaces. Codes for hip resurfacing arthroplasty identify the specific joint components resurfaced (total involves both the acetabular and femoral components; partial involves femoral head or acetabulum only) as follows:

- 00.85 Resurfacing hip, total, acetabulum and femoral
- 00.86 Resurfacing hip, partial, femoral head
- 00.87 Resurfacing hip, partial, acetabulum

Category **V43.6, Joint replacement status,** can be assigned as an additional code when the presence of a joint replacement is significant in terms of patient care.

Exercise 19.3

Code the following diagnoses and procedures. Do not assign E codes.

	Code(s)
1. Primary osteoarthritis of hip	715.15
Replacement, total, of hip with ceramic-on-ceramic bearing surface	81.51 00.76
2. Bicompartmental total knee replacement	81.54
3. Partial replacement of left shoulder	81.81

SPINAL FUSION AND REFUSION

Spinal fusion is a surgical procedure whereby two or more vertebrae are fused to correct problems with the vertebrae. The vertebrae can be fused using bone grafting, genetically engineered bone substitute, and metal devices. The goal of spinal fusion surgery is pain relief after conservative treatments have failed. The procedure is indicated for spinal vertebrae injuries such as protrusion and degeneration of the cushion between vertebrae, curvature of the spine, or weak spine caused by injections or tumors.

When solid bone between two or more levels of the spine fails to develop after spinal fusion, it is called nonunion or pseudarthrosis. Symptoms may not occur until months or years after the original spinal fusion. Patients can often function relatively normally with pseudarthrosis unless problems develop such as sharp localized pain and tenderness over the fusion, progression of the deformity or disease, or localized motion in the fusion mass. Treatment for symptomatic pseudarthrosis consists of refusion. The procedure involves thorough removal of fibrous tissue from the intended fusion area and the addition of new bone graft.

Coding of spinal fusion and refusion is classified by the site fused (cervical, dorsal/dorsolumbar, lumbar, or lumbosacral), anatomic portion (anterior or posterior column), the approach or technique used (anterior, posterior, lateral, lateral transverse, or posterolateral), and the number of vertebrae fused or refused.

The structure of the spine is composed of the anterior, middle, and posterior columns. The anterior column is composed of the anterior longitudinal ligament, the anterior annulus, and the anterior portion of the vertebral body. The middle column includes the posterior longitudinal ligament, the posterior annulus, and the posterior portion of the vertebral body. The posterior column includes spinal structures that are posterior to the posterior longitudinal ligament.

During an anterior column fusion, the body (corpus) of adjacent vertebrae are fused (interbody fusion). The anterior column can be fused using an anterior, lateral, or posterior technique. For the posterior column fusion, posterior structures of adjacent vertebrae are fused (pedicle, lamina, facet, transverse process, or "gutter" fusion). A posterior column fusion can be performed using a posterior, posterolateral, or lateral transverse technique.

Traditionally, there have been three basic approaches to spinal fusion or spinal refusion: anterior, posterior, and lateral transverse. The classic anterior approach requires an incision in the neck or the abdomen, and the fusion is carried out from the front of the vertebrae through the anterior annulus. In the classic posterior approach, the incision is made in the patient's back directly over the vertebrae. Another approach is the lateral transverse, which involves an incision on the patient's side, and the vertebrae are approached through the lamina.

Table 19.1 displays the fusion and refusion codes with the corresponding spinal level, whether the code refers to the anterior or posterior column, and the technique involved.

TABLE 19.1 Fusion and Refusion Codes

Procedure Code	Spinal Level	Anterior Column	Posterior Column	Techniques
81.02	cervical	x		anterior
81.32	cervical	x		anterior
81.03	cervical		x	posterior, posterolateral
81.33	cervical		x	posterior, posterolateral
81.04	dorsal/dorsolumbar	x		anterior, anterolateral
81.34	dorsal/dorsolumbar	x		anterior
81.05	dorsal/dorsolumbar		x	posterior, posterolateral
81.35	dorsal/dorsolumbar		x	posterior, posterolateral
81.06	lumbar	x		anterior, anterolateral
81.36	lumbar	x		anterior
81.07	lumbar/lumbosacral		x	posterior, posterolateral, transverse
81.37	lumbar/lumbosacral		x	posterior, posterolateral, transverse
81.08	lumbar/lumbosacral	x		posterior
81.38	lumbar/lumbosacral	x		posterior

FIGURE 19.2 The Spinal Column

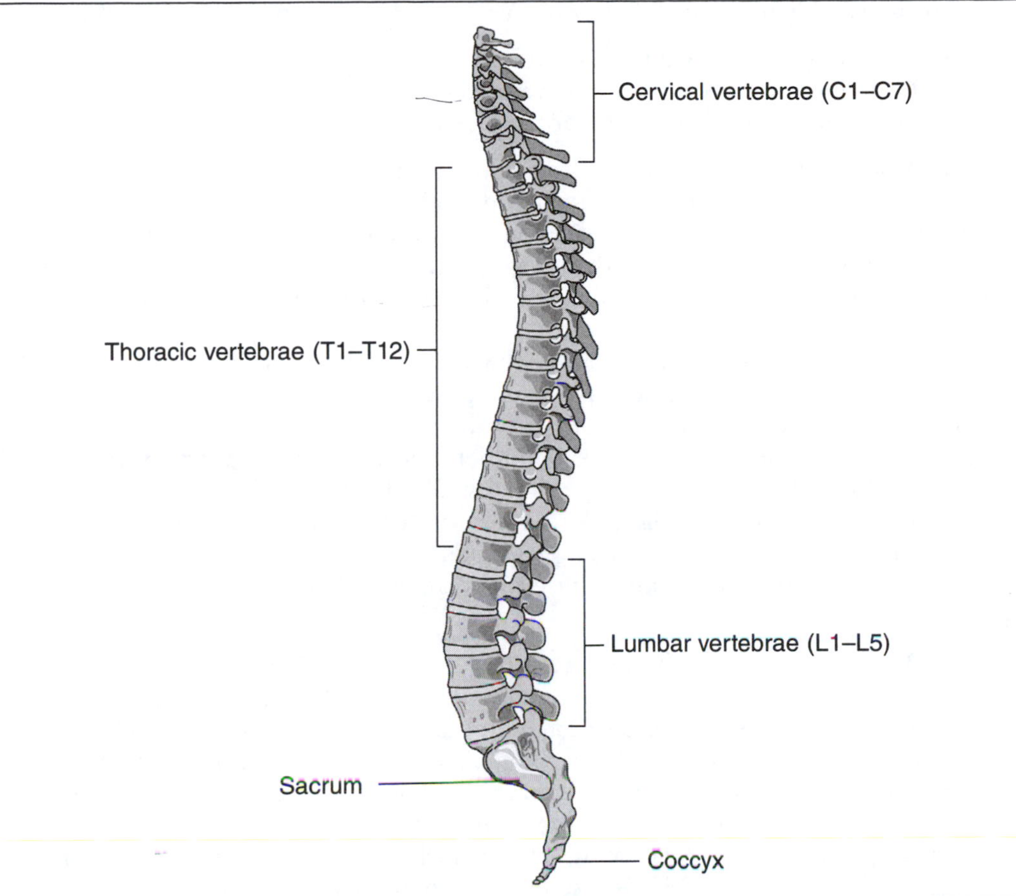

FIGURE 19.3 Section of the Spinal Column

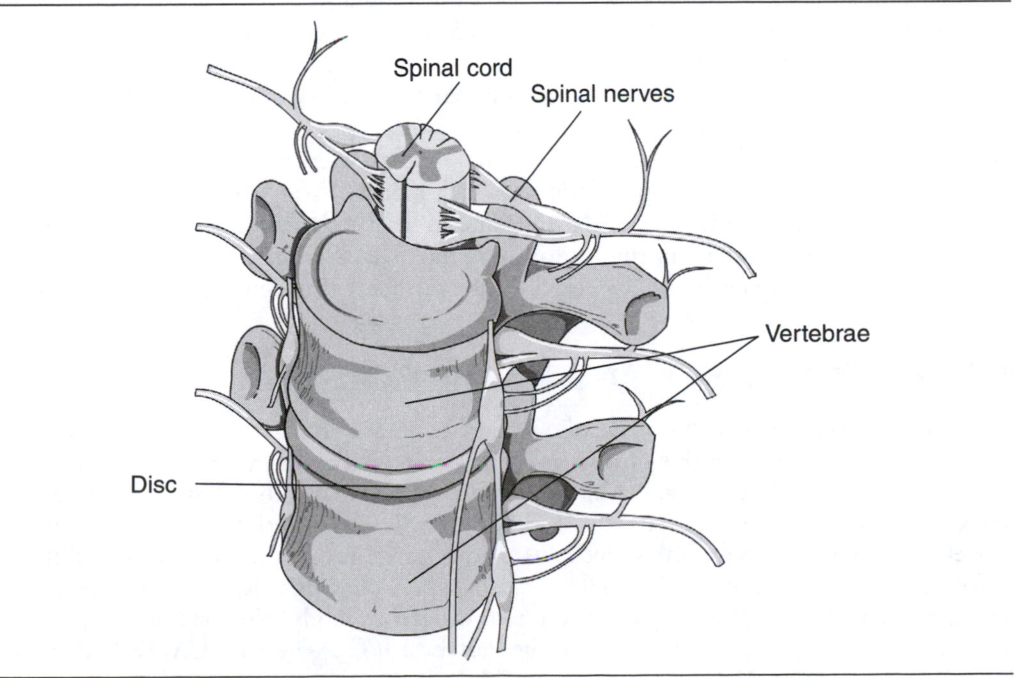

Additional codes are used to capture the number of vertebrae fused when a spinal fusion or refusion is performed. For example:

- 81.62 Fusion or refusion of 2–3 vertebrae
- 81.63 Fusion or refusion of 4–8 vertebrae
- 81.64 Fusion or refusion of 9 or more vertebrae

Occasionally, instrumentation called interbody fusion devices are used to stabilize and fuse degenerative disc spaces and to provide an immediately stable segment for fusion and relief of symptoms. These devices are also known as an interbody fusion cage, Bak cage, ray-threaded fusion cage, synthetic cage, spacer, or bone dowels. If insertion of an interbody fusion device is performed along with a spinal fusion or refusion, code 84.51 is assigned as an additional procedure code.

Synchronous excision of locally harvested bone graft is reported separately (77.70–77.79). If recombinant bone morphogenetic protein (a genetically engineered protein) is inserted to help create a bone graft substitute, assign code 84.52.

A 360-degree spinal fusion is a fusion of both the anterior and posterior portions of the spine performed through a single incision (usually via the lateral transverse approach). When coding this procedure, the coder should carefully review the documentation and first determine whether this is a fusion or refusion.

A brief explanation of common fusion and refusion procedures, with their corresponding codes, is provided below:

- ALIF (81.06 or 81.36): The anterior lumbar interbody fusion (ALIF) is an interbody fusion of the anterior and middle columns of the spine through an anterior incision, either transperitoneal or retroperitoneal. It can also be done laparoscopically.
- AxiaLIF® (81.08 or 81.38): The axial lumbar interbody fusion (AxiaLIF®) is a percutaneous fusion of the anterior column at L5–S1. An AxiaLIF® 360° refers to the combination of an AxiaLIF® procedure of the anterior column performed along with a posterior column fusion, which may include the use of pedicle screws or facet screws. The AxiaLIF® 360° is described as providing a percutaneous 360° fusion.
- DLIF (81.06 or 81.36): The direct lateral lumbar interbody fusion (DLIF) is a minimally invasive alternative to conventional spinal fusion. The DLIF is performed through a lateral approach, which allows for limited soft tissue disruption. The procedure can only be performed at L4–L5 or at higher levels and requires dissection through the psoas muscle.
- PLIF (81.08 or 81.38): The posterior lumbar interbody fusion (PLIF) involves an anterior and middle column fusion through a posterior approach.
- TLIF (81.08 or 81.38): The transforaminal lumbar interbody fusion (TLIF) involves a transverse lateral interbody fusion through a posterior approach.
- XLIF® (81.06 or 81.36): The extreme lateral interbody fusion (XLIF®) is a less invasive spinal surgery of the anterior column. The fusion may be accomplished either percutaneously or via a circular tube retractor through a lateral approach.

VERTEBROPLASTY AND KYPHOPLASTY

Percutaneous vertebroplasty is a technique used to treat vertebral compression fractures. Code 81.65 is assigned for this procedure, which involves the insertion of cement glue-like material (polymethylmethacrylate) into the vertebral body to stabilize and strengthen collapsed or crushed bone. The ARCUATE™ XP procedure is a variation of a percutaneous vertebroplasty in which an osteotome is used to cut arcs in the cancellous bone within the vertebral body. The arcs created with the osteotome then allow for dispersion of bone cement material when it is subsequently injected into the vertebral body. No bone or bone marrow is removed from, or compacted within, the vertebral body. The ARCUATE™ XP procedure is also coded to 81.65.

Percutaneous vertebral augmentation (81.66) is a procedure utilizing an inflatable balloon that is expanded in order to reestablish vertebral height in compression fractures. After the balloon is removed, the cavity is filled with polymethylmethacrylate, which hardens to further stabilize the bone. Code 81.66 includes arcuplasty, kyphoplasty, skyphoplasty, and spineoplasty.

While these procedures are similar, there is no balloon involved in the vertebroplasty, and no attempt is made to restore vertebral height to reduce the compression fractures of the vertebra.

If a vertebral biopsy is done during a kyphoplasty procedure, assign codes **81.66, Percutaneous vertebral augmentation,** and **77.49, Biopsy of bone, other.** The biopsy is not an inherent part of the kyphoplasty and should be coded separately if performed.

SPINAL DISC PROSTHESES

Minimally invasive arthroplasty procedures are being carried out as an alternative to spinal fusion. These procedures are performed to replace the degenerated disc nucleus and restore or maintain the normal function of the disc by inserting artificial disc prostheses. The prostheses are used to replace the entire spinal disc or replace the disc nucleus.

In order to properly select the procedure code for the insertion of spinal disc prostheses, it is important to determine the type of prosthesis (partial or total), as well as the spinal segment treated, such as cervical (84.61 and 84.62), thoracic (84.63), or lumbosacral (84.64 and 84.65). Note that for the thoracic spine, partial and total prostheses are included in the same code (84.63), unlike for the cervical and lumbosacral spine, where *ICD-9-CM* differentiates between partial and total disc prostheses with unique codes. If information is not available regarding the location of the spine treated, code 84.60 may be used.

Revision/replacement codes (84.66–84.69) are also available to report either the repair or the removal of the artificial disc prosthesis with the synchronous insertion of a new prosthesis. These codes specify the part of the spine treated, but they do not distinguish between partial and total prostheses.

SPINAL MOTION PRESERVATION

Patients suffering from spinal stenosis or degenerative disc disease may be treated with conservative measures, including physical therapy and pain management. When conservative care does not provide relief, surgical decompression may be an alternative treatment. Surgical decompression (03.09) involves removal of the bone and/or tissue causing pressure on the spinal cord or nerve root(s). Common surgical decompression procedures include laminotomy, laminectomy, diskectomy, foraminotomy, and medial facetectomy. The spinal segment may be deemed unstable depending on the extent of bone and tissue removed during the decompression procedure. Stabilization of the spinal segment is primarily accomplished with spinal fusion. However, new spinal motion preservation technologies have been developed to allow for spine stabilization without the motion restriction associated with fusion.

Motion preservation technologies placed in the posterior column of the spine include the following:

- Interspinous process devices (e.g., X-Stop™, Wallis®, and Coflex™ systems)
- Pedicle screw dynamic stabilization devices (e.g., Dynesys® and M-Brace™)
- Facet replacement devices (e.g., The Total Facet Arthroplasty System™ and The Artificial Facet Replacement System™)

Procedure codes in subcategory 84.8 are used for the insertion, replacement, and revision of posterior spinal motion preservation device(s). These codes include a dynamic stabilization device(s) and also include any synchronous facetectomy (partial, total) performed at the same level. If a synchronous surgical decompression (foraminotomy, laminectomy, laminotomy) is also performed, assign code **03.09, Other exploration and decompression of spinal canal,** as an additional procedure.

Subcategory 84.8 classifies spinal motion preservation procedures as follows:

- 84.80 Insertion or replacement of interspinous process device(s)
- 84.81 Revision of interspinous process device(s)
- 84.82 Insertion or replacement of pedicle-based dynamic stabilization device(s)
- 84.83 Revision of pedicle-based dynamic stabilization device(s)
- 84.84 Insertion or replacement of facet replacement device(s)
- 84.85 Revision of facet replacement device(s)

PLICA SYNDROME

Although the plica syndrome can occasionally be found in other areas, it almost always affects the knee. Plica syndrome occurs when the synovial bands that are present early in fetal development have not combined into one large synovial unit as they develop further. Patients with this syndrome often experience pain and swelling, weakness, and a locking and clicking sensation of the knee. The therapeutic goal is the reduction of the inflammation of the synovium and the thickening of the plica. Usual treatment measures hope to relieve symptoms within three months; if not, arthroscopic or open surgery to remove the plica may be required. Assign code **727.83, Plica syndrome,** for this condition and code **80.76, Synovectomy of knee,** for the surgery.

FASCIITIS

Necrotizing fasciitis is a fulminating infection that begins with severe or extensive cellulitis that spreads to the superficial and deep fascia, producing thrombosis of the subcutaneous vessels and gangrene of the underlying tissue. Group A *Streptococcus* is the most common organism responsible for this condition, but any bacteria may be the cause. Code 728.86 is assigned for this condition, with an additional code for the organism when this information is known.

Review Exercise 19.4

Code the following diagnoses and procedures. Do not assign E codes.

	Code(s)
1. Acute polymyositis Mild thoracogenic scoliosis	710.4 737.34
Muscle biopsy	83.21
2. Sclerosing tenosynovitis, left thumb and middle finger	727.05

Review Exercise 19.4 *(continued)*

3. Osteomyelitis of left distal femur due to diabetes		250.80 731.8 730.25
Sequestrectomy and excision of sinus tract, left femur		77.05 77.65
4. Adhesive capsulitis, left shoulder		726.0
5. Nonunion of fracture, left femoral neck	or Late	733.82 905.3
Inlay type iliac bone graft to nonunion of femoral neck; bone excised for graft	Excision	78.05 77.79
6. Second and third hammer toes, left		735.4
Left second and third hammer toe repair		77.56
7. Recurrent dislocation of patella		718.36
8. Deformity of left ring finger, due to old tendon injury	Late	736.20 905.8
Transfer of flexor tendon from distal phalanx to middle phalanx		82.56

Review Exercise 19.4 *(continued)*

9. Cervical spondylosis, C5–6, C6–7	721.0
Anterior column cervical spinal fusion, C5–6, C6–7	81.02 81.62
10. Right hallux valgus	735.0
Resection of hallux valgus with insertion of prosthesis	77.59
11. Bunion, left foot	727.1
Mitchell-type bunionectomy (with osteotomy of first metatarsal)	77.51
12. Dupuytren's contracture	728.6
Incision and division of palmar fascia	82.12
13. Multiple compression fractures of vertebrae and major osseous defects due to senile osteoporosis	733.13 733.01 731.3
14. Lumbar spinal stenosis Decompressive laminotomy with Dynesys stabilization system	724.02 84.82 03.09

Coding of Pregnancy and Childbirth Complications, Abortion, Congenital Anomalies, and Perinatal Conditions

Complications of Pregnancy, Childbirth, and the Puerperium

CHAPTER **20**

CHAPTER OVERVIEW

- Conditions affecting pregnancy, childbirth, and the puerperium are found in chapter 11 of *ICD-9-CM*.
  - — Codes from chapter 11 take precedence over codes from other chapters.
  - — Codes from chapter 11 are never assigned to the newborn's record.
- A fourth digit provides information regarding complications. This, paired with a fifth digit, is used to provide information regarding the episode of care (antepartum, delivery, or postpartum).
- V codes are used to indicate the outcome of the delivery.
- A normal delivery is contingent on a variety of criteria.
- Deliveries not deemed normal use as their principal code the main circumstance or complication of the delivery.
- Postpartum complications are any complications that occur throughout the six weeks following the delivery.
- There is a late effect code to use for complications that occur after the postpartum period. This code follows the codes for the condition.
- There are codes for delivery assistance procedures such as fetal head rotation, forceps delivery, vacuum extraction, episiotomy, and cesarean delivery.
- Contraceptive management and procreative management, through both admission and outpatient encounter, are covered by a series of V codes. These codes can be supplemented by additional codes if there is an underlying condition.

LEARNING OUTCOMES

After studying this chapter you should be able to:

- Code complications of pregnancy using the proper fourth and fifth digits.
- Use the proper V codes to assign the outcome of delivery.
- Code for other obstetric care besides childbirth.
- Know the difference between postpartum complications and late effects of pregnancy, childbirth, and the puerperium.
- Differentiate among the procedures assisting delivery.
- Code for contraceptive and procreative management.

TERMS TO KNOW

Antepartum
the period of pregnancy from conception to childbirth

Postpartum
the period beginning right after delivery and including the next six weeks

Puerperium
the clinical term for the postpartum period

REMEMBER . . . If the mother's record doesn't state the outcome of the delivery, look at the record of the newborn.

INTRODUCTION

Conditions that affect the management of pregnancy, childbirth, and the puerperium are classified to categories 630 through 676 and 678 through 679 in chapter 11 of *ICD-9-CM.* Conditions from other chapters of *ICD-9-CM* are usually reclassified in chapter 11 when they either complicate the obstetrical experience or are themselves aggravated by the pregnancy. Any condition that occurs during pregnancy, childbirth, or the puerperium is considered to be a complication unless the attending physician specifically documents that it neither affects the pregnancy nor is affected by the pregnancy.

When the encounter is for a condition totally unrelated to the pregnancy and the physician so documents, the code for the condition is listed first, with code **V22.2, Pregnant state, incidental,** assigned as an additional code. Chapter 11 codes take precedence over codes from other chapters, but codes from other chapters may be used as additional codes when needed to provide more specificity. Codes from chapter 11 of *ICD-9-CM* refer to the mother only and are assigned only on the mother's record. They are never assigned on the newborn's record; other codes are provided for that purpose. (See chapter 23.) Codes from categories 630 through 639 are assigned for ectopic pregnancy, molar pregnancy, and abortion. (Code assignments for these conditions are discussed in chapter 21.)

Codes from categories 640 through 676 and 678 through 679 apply throughout the entire obstetrical experience, which begins at conception and ends six weeks (42 days) after delivery. *ICD-9-CM* divides this period as follows:

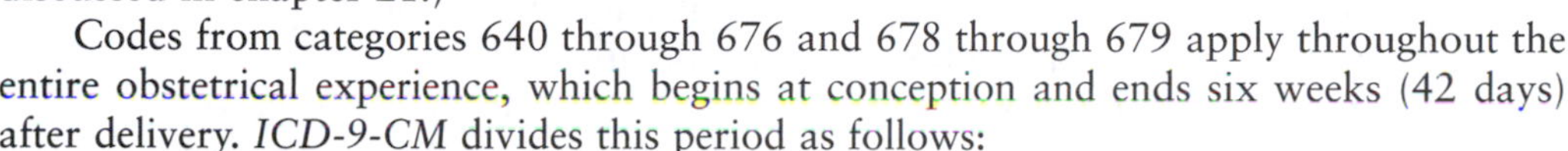

- Complications related mainly to pregnancy 640–649
- Normal delivery and other indications for care in pregnancy, labor, and delivery 650–659
- Complications occurring mainly during the course of labor and delivery 660–669
- Complications of the puerperium 670–676
- Other maternal and fetal complications 678–679

The process of labor and delivery includes three stages. The first stage begins with the onset of regular uterine contractions and ends when the cervical os is completely dilated.

FIGURE 20.1 Primary Organs of the Female Reproductive System

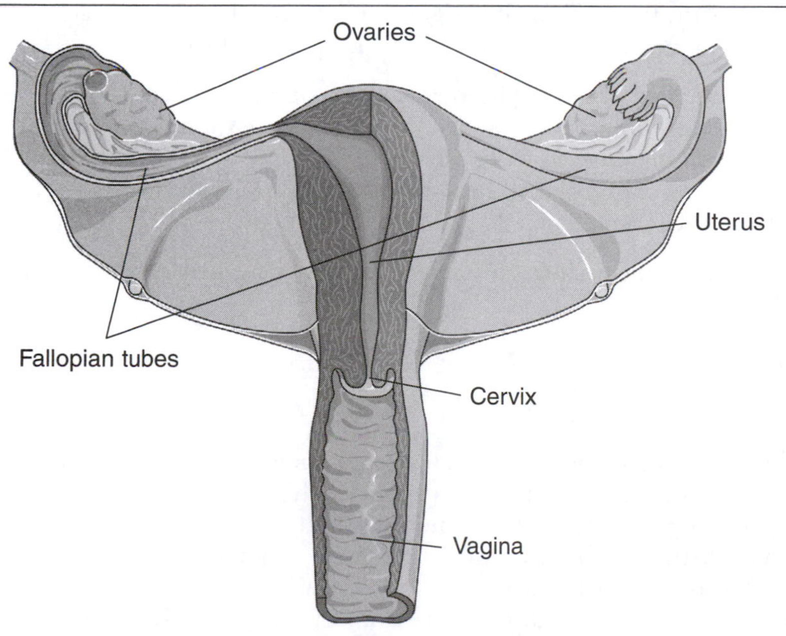

The second stage begins with complete dilation and continues until the infant has been completely expelled. The third stage begins with the expulsion of the infant and continues until the placenta and membranes have been expelled and contraction of the uterus is complete. The puerperium begins at the end of the third stage of labor and continues for six weeks.

Occasionally, a pregnancy continues for a longer term than usual gestation and is considered to be a long pregnancy. The following two codes are used when this occurs:

- 645.1x Postterm pregnancy (over 40 to 42 weeks of gestation)
- 645.2x Prolonged pregnancy (advanced beyond 42 weeks of gestation)

FIFTH-DIGIT SUBCLASSIFICATION

Categories 640 through 649, 651 through 676, and 678 through 679 use a fourth digit to provide more information regarding the type of complication. A fifth digit provides information regarding the current episode of care as follows:

- 0 unspecified as to episode of care or not applicable
- 1 delivered, with or without mention of antepartum condition
- 2 delivered, with mention of postpartum condition
- 3 antepartum condition or complication when delivery has not occurred
- 4 postpartum condition or complication when delivery occurred during a previous episode of care

The episode of care for an obstetrical patient is defined in *ICD-9-CM* as the period between admission and discharge for an inpatient or the conclusion of the current visit to the attending physician, outpatient clinic, or other health care service.

Because certain complications occur only at a given point within the obstetrical experience, only certain fifth digits are appropriate. For example, placenta previa, abruptio placentae, and antepartum hemorrhage occur only during the antepartum period. Postpartum hemorrhage, on the other hand, occurs only after delivery. In some manuals, the fifth digits that can be used with each subcategory code are listed in brackets under the code number in the Tabular List. Because multiple coding is common in this chapter, the coder must be sure that fifth-digit assignments are consistent with each other. Certain fifth-digit combinations are invalid for the same episode of care:

- 0 (for unspecified or not applicable) is inappropriate for acute hospital use, where easily accessible information always permits a more specific assignment. It cannot be used with any other fifth digit in the series.
- 1 and 2 can be used together for the same episode but not with any other fifth digit.
- 3 and 4 cannot be used together or with any other fifth digit.

Figure 20.2 illustrates the decision process for assigning fifth digits for categories 640 through 674.

OUTCOME OF DELIVERY

Because chapter 11 codes do not indicate the outcome of delivery, a code from category V27 is assigned as an additional code to provide this information whenever the patient delivers in the hospital. Fourth digits indicate both whether the outcome was single or multiple and whether liveborn or stillborn. These codes are used only on the mother's record, not the record of the newborn, and are assigned only for the episode of care during which delivery occurred. No code from category V27 is assigned when delivery

FIGURE 20.2 Decision Process for Use of Fifth Digits for Categories 640–674

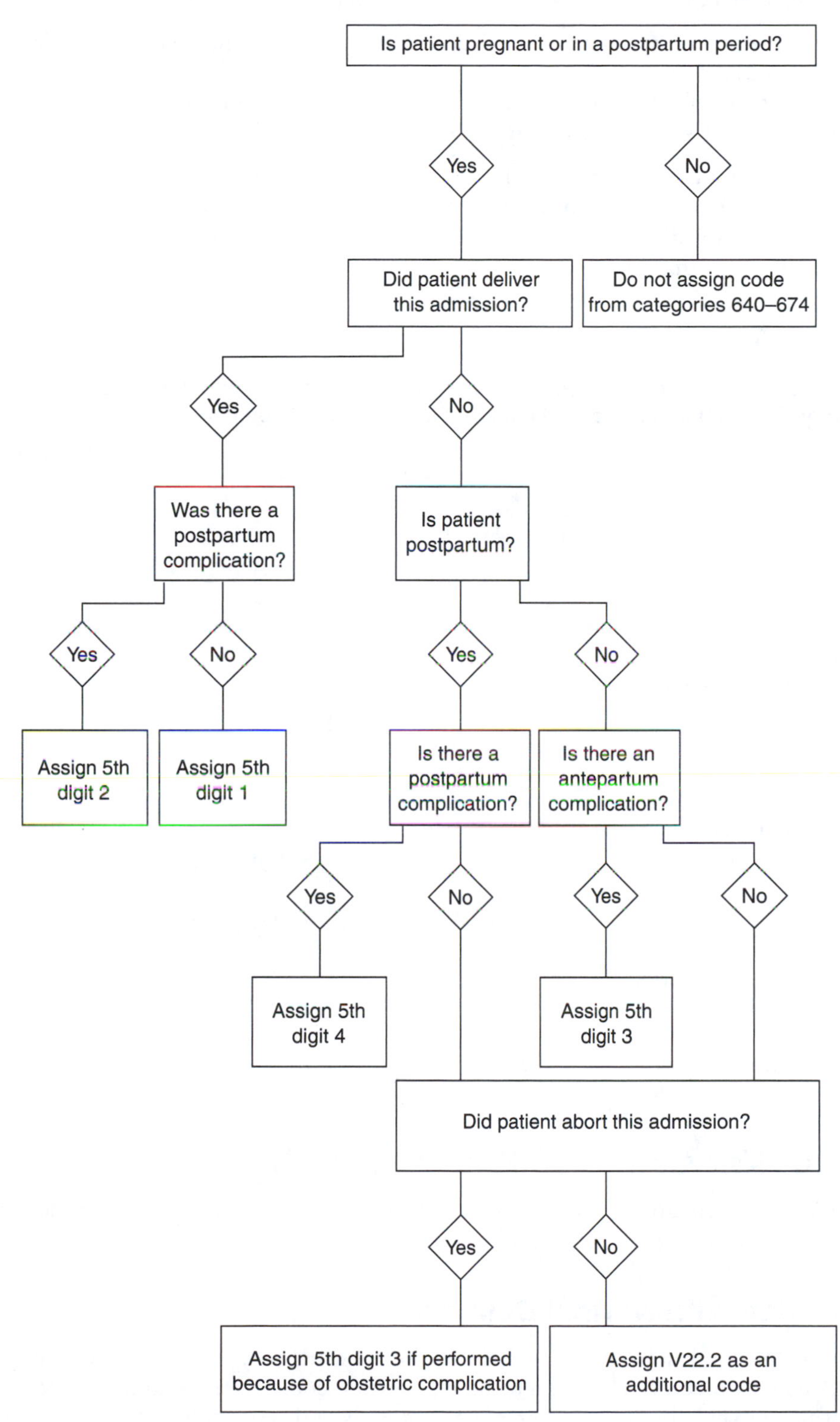

occurs outside the hospital prior to admission. Examples of appropriate use of codes from category V27 include:

- Term pregnancy, spontaneous delivery, vertex presentation; liveborn male infant 650 + V27.0
- Term pregnancy with spontaneous delivery; twin pregnancy, with one twin liveborn and one stillborn 651.01 + V27.3 + 656.41 + V91.00

To locate the code assignment for outcome of delivery, the coder should refer to the main term **Outcome of delivery** in the Alphabetic Index of Diseases and Injuries. If the mother's record does not state the outcome, the coder should refer to the newborn's record for this information.

Exercise 20.1

For the following exercise, do not assign the delivery codes; assign only the V codes for outcome of delivery. Remember that in actual practice the delivery code precedes the V code.

		Code(s)
1. Delivery of twins, both stillborn	Outcome of delivery	V27.4
2. Delivery of triplets, one stillborn	Outcome of delivery	V27.6
3. Delivery of liveborn, female infant	Outcome of delivery	V27.0
4. Delivery of single stillborn	Outcome of delivery	V27.1

SELECTION OF PRINCIPAL DIAGNOSIS

The selection of principal diagnoses for admissions for normal deliveries and other obstetric care is based on the following guidelines.

Admission with Normal Delivery

Code **650, Normal delivery,** is used only when the delivery is entirely normal with a single liveborn outcome. There can be no postpartum complications, and any antepartum complication experienced during pregnancy must have been resolved before the time of delivery. Code 650 is always the principal diagnosis. If there is any complication, code 650 cannot be assigned. Codes from other chapters may be used as additional codes, with code 650 only when the physician has documented that the conditions are not related to, and in no way complicate, the pregnancy.

All of the following criteria must be met in order for code 650 to be used correctly:

- Presentation at delivery can be only head or occipital. (Terms such as ROA, LOA, ROP, LOP, and vertex describe an occipital presentation.) Any other presentation such as breech, face, or brow disallows the use of code 650.
- Any antepartum complication must have been resolved prior to the admission.
- No abnormalities of either labor or delivery can have occurred.
- No postpartum complications can be present.
- No procedures other than the following can have been performed: episiotomy without forceps, episiorrhaphy, amniotomy (artificial rupture of the membranes), manually assisted delivery without forceps, administration of analgesics and/or anesthesia, fetal monitoring, induction of labor (in the absence of medical indications), and sterilization. If any other procedure is performed, code 650 cannot be assigned.
- Outcome of delivery must be single livebirth, V27.0. When there has been a multiple birth or stillbirth, code 650 cannot be assigned.

Examples include the following:

- A patient who had a completely normal delivery suffered a postpartum hemorrhage several hours after delivery. Code **666.12, Other immediate postpartum hemorrhage,** is assigned. Although the delivery itself was normal, complications were present during the episode of care; therefore, code 650 cannot be used.
- The prenatal history for a patient who had a completely normal delivery of a live infant indicates that she had a urinary tract infection at three months' gestation. This was treated with Bactrim on an outpatient basis. There was no recurrence of the infection during the pregnancy, and the patient had no infection at the time of delivery. In this case, code **650, Normal delivery,** is assigned.

Exercise 20.2

Write an "X" in front of each of the following circumstances of delivery that is assigned code **650, Normal delivery.**

_______ 1. Liveborn, full-term, breech presentation

_______ 2. Liveborn, premature, cephalic presentation

_______ 3. Stillborn, full-term, vertex presentation

___X___ 4. Liveborn, full-term, cephalic presentation; episiotomy with repair

_______ 5. Liveborn, full-term, vertex presentation; elective low forceps

_______ 6. Liveborn, full-term, vertex presentation; postpartum breast abscess

_______ 7. Liveborn, full-term, breech presentation changed to vertex presentation by version prior to delivery

Admission with Other Delivery

When a delivery does not meet the criteria for assignment of code **650, Normal delivery,** the principal diagnosis should correspond to the main circumstance or complication of the delivery. The principal diagnosis for a cesarean delivery should be the condition established after study that was responsible for the patient's admission. If the patient was admitted with a condition that resulted in the performance of a cesarean procedure, that condition should be selected as the principal diagnosis. If the reason for the admission/encounter was unrelated to the condition that resulted in the cesarean delivery, that condition should be selected as the principal diagnosis even if a cesarean was performed. For example:

- A patient who had a previous cesarean delivery was admitted for a second cesarean delivery. She also had type 1 diabetes mellitus. Cesarean delivery was accomplished without complication. Code **654.21, Previous cesarean delivery,** is assigned as the principal diagnosis, with an additional code of **648.01, Diabetes mellitus.** Code 250.01 would also be assigned to provide more specificity.
- A patient was admitted to the hospital in obstructed labor due to a breech presentation. Version was unsuccessful, and the patient was delivered by cesarean section several hours later. The principal diagnosis code is **660.01, Obstruction of labor due to malposition of fetus at onset of labor,** and code **652.21, Breech presentation,** is assigned as an additional code to provide more specificity.

If the patient has had a previous cesarean section, she can go through a trial of labor and experience a vaginal birth after cesarean delivery (VBAC). If the trial of labor is unsuccessful, a repeat cesarean delivery is carried out. Code 649.81 is assigned for this situation when the patient is admitted after 37 completed weeks of gestation, but before 39 completed weeks of gestation. For example:

- A 40-year-old female patient with a previous cesarean section presents to the hospital in labor at 38 completed weeks of gestation. A vaginal delivery trial is attempted, but it failed, and a classical C-section is performed without any complications. The principal diagnosis is **649.81, Onset (spontaneous) of labor after 37 completed weeks of gestation but before 39 completed weeks gestation, with delivery by (planned) cesarean section.** Codes **654.21, Previous cesarean delivery, delivered with or without mention of antepartum condition,** and **V23.82, Elderly multigravida,** are assigned as secondary diagnoses. Assign code **74.0, Classical cesarean section,** for the procedure.

Admission for Other Obstetric Care

When the admission or encounter is for obstetric care other than delivery, the principal diagnosis should correspond to the complication that necessitated the admission or encounter. If more than one complication is present, all of which are treated or monitored, any of the complication codes may be sequenced first. If no obstetric complications are present, the following guidelines govern selection of the principal diagnosis:

- If the reason for admission or encounter is not related to an obstetric condition but the patient is pregnant, code **V22.2, Incidental pregnancy,** is assigned as an additional code. This code is never assigned as the principal diagnosis and no codes from chapter 11 can be assigned.
- For routine prenatal visits when no complication is present, one of the following codes is assigned as the reason for encounter:

  V22.0 Supervision of normal first pregnancy
  V22.1 Supervision of other normal pregnancy

  These codes are assigned only as principal diagnosis and no codes from chapter 11 can be assigned.
- A code from category **V23.x, Supervision of high risk pregnancy,** can be assigned as the principal diagnosis or as an additional code; codes from chapter 11 can also be assigned. Fourth digits indicate the situation that defines the pregnancy as high risk, such as a poor obstetric history (V23.41 for history of pre-term labor, V23.42 for history of ectopic pregnancy, and V23.49 for other poor obstetric history) or grand multiparity (V23.3). An exception is that code **V23.2, Pregnancy with history of abortion,** is not assigned for a pregnant patient; code **646.3x, Recurrent pregnancy loss,** is assigned. Code **629.81, Recurrent pregnancy loss without current pregnancy,** is assigned for a patient who is not currently pregnant.
- *ICD-9-CM* also defines a high-risk pregnancy as those patients who will be 35 years of age or over or 16 years of age or less at the expected time of delivery. Codes for supervision of such patients include the following:

V23.81 Elderly primigravida
V23.82 Elderly multigravida
V23.83 Young primigravida
V23.84 Young multigravida

If the patient's age has become a complication, code 659.5x is assigned for an elderly primigravida, or code 659.6x for an elderly multigravida. Code 659.8x is assigned for a young patient whether this is the first or a later pregnancy.

- Two other V codes for supervision of other high-risk pregnancy are: **V23.85, Pregnancy resulting from assisted reproductive technology,** and **V23.86, Pregnancy with history of in utero procedure during previous pregnancy.** Code V23.85 is used to describe a current pregnancy that resulted from assisted reproductive technology (such as in vitro fertilization). Code V23.86 is used to describe a current pregnancy with history of an in utero procedure during a prior pregnancy.

  When the management of a current pregnancy is affected due to a complication of in utero surgery performed during the current pregnancy, assign the appropriate code from category 679, Complications of in utero procedures, instead of V23.86.
- Code **V23.87, Pregnancy with inconclusive fetal viability,** is assigned as the reason for an encounter to determine the viability of the pregnancy. For example, during the early weeks of pregnancy, it may be difficult for the provider to determine fetal viability. When the fetal heartbeat is not heard, an ultrasound is needed to confirm that the pregnancy is viable.
- When a patient delivers outside the hospital and is then admitted for routine postpartum care with no complications present, code **V24.0, Postpartum care and examination immediately after delivery,** is assigned as the principal diagnosis. When a postpartum complication is present, the code for that condition is designated as the principal diagnosis, and code V24.0 is not assigned.

  For example: A woman was admitted following delivery in the parking lot of the hospital. On admission, it was noted that she had sustained a first-degree perineal laceration. Code **664.04, First-degree laceration, postpartum,** is assigned rather than code V24.0.
- Occasionally, an expectant mother may visit a pediatrician to receive advice on child care or to evaluate the pediatric office. This is not a visit related to a problem with the pregnancy. Code **V65.11, Pediatric pre-birth visit for expectant mother,** may be assigned for these encounters.

Exercise 20.3

Code the following diagnoses.

	Code(s)
1. Antepartum supervision of pregnancy in patient with history of three previous stillbirths	V23.5
2. Office visit for routine prenatal care, for primigravida patient with no complications	V22.0
3. Office visit for care of elderly patient who is in the fourth month of her third pregnancy	V23.82

Exercise 20.3 *(continued)*

4. Hospital admission of patient in good condition after delivering a single liveborn infant in taxi on the way to the hospital	Admission for	V24.0
5. Admission for intravenous antibiotic therapy of patient who delivered a single liveborn at home three days ago; patient now suffering an abscess of the breast	Postpartum	675.14

FETAL CONDITIONS AFFECTING MANAGEMENT OF PREGNANCY

Codes from categories **655, Known or suspected fetal abnormality affecting management of the mother,** and **656, Other known or suspected fetal and placental problems affecting management of the mother,** are assigned only when the fetal condition is actually responsible for modifying the mother's care. Such an effect may be documented by additional diagnostic studies based on the fetal problem, additional observation, special care, or termination of the pregnancy. The fact that the fetal condition exists does not in itself justify assigning a code from these categories; this applies only when the condition affects the management of the mother's care.

For example, when fetal distress results in a decision to perform a cesarean delivery or early induction of labor in the mother, code **656.8x, Other specified fetal and placental problems,** is assigned. On the other hand, fetal distress may be noted during delivery with no change made in the mother's care. In this case, code 656.8x is not assigned because the fetal distress is not considered to have affected the management of the mother significantly, given that the only procedures performed were the administration of fluids and/or oxygen and the repositioning of the mother. This guideline also applies to code **659.7x, Abnormality in fetal heart rate or rhythm.**

Code **656.3x, Fetal distress,** is assigned when fetal metabolic acidemia is documented as affecting the management of the mother's care.

In Utero Surgery

Surgery performed in utero on a fetus is considered an obstetric encounter. Codes from chapter 15, perinatal conditions, should not be used on the mother's record to identify fetal conditions. Instead, when surgery is performed on the fetus in utero, a diagnosis code from category **655, Known or suspected fetal abnormalities affecting management of the mother,** should be assigned for the fetal condition. Procedure code **75.36, Correction of fetal defect,** is assigned for the reparative surgery.

Code **679.0x, Maternal complications from in utero procedure,** and code **679.1x, Fetal complications from in utero procedure,** describe maternal and fetal complications resulting from in utero surgery performed during the current pregnancy. Assign 679.0x or 679.1x only on the mother's record when these complications affect the management of the pregnancy. If the newborn experiences any problems or complications because of in utero procedures, assign the appropriate code from subcategory 760.6, Surgical operation on mother and fetus, on the newborn record.

Code V23.86 can be used as an additional code assignment with code 679.0x or 679.1x if the patient also has a past history of in utero surgery during a previous pregnancy.

OTHER CONDITIONS COMPLICATING PREGNANCY, CHILDBIRTH, OR THE PUERPERIUM

Some conditions inevitably complicate the obstetrical experience or are themselves aggravated by pregnancy. Hypertension, for example, is classified in category 642 during pregnancy, delivery, and the puerperium. Other designated conditions, such as urinary tract infection and liver disorders, are classified in category 646 when they complicate the obstetrical experience. Certain infectious diseases such as rubella, malaria, tuberculosis, and venereal disease are classified in category 647, and conditions such as diabetes mellitus, anemia, and thyroid dysfunction are reclassified in category 648. Conditions classifiable in categories 642 and 646 through 648 should be assumed to complicate the obstetrical experience unless the physician specifically indicates otherwise. These codes are also used when such conditions are present during childbirth or the puerperium.

For example:

- A patient, who has a history of genital herpes maintained on Valtrex, is admitted to the hospital for delivery. At the time of delivery, she is symptom free with no outbreak. Code **647.61, Infectious and parasitic conditions in the mother classifiable elsewhere, but complicating pregnancy, childbirth, or the puerperium, Other viral diseases, delivered, with or without mention of antepartum condition,** is assigned as the principal diagnosis. Code **054.10, Genital herpes, unspecified,** and code **V58.69, Long-term (current) use of other medications,** should be assigned as additional diagnoses along with the V code for the outcome of the delivery. Herpes infection during pregnancy poses a risk to the fetus and is appropriately coded as a complication of the pregnancy.

Some codes for such complications are very specific, and others are rather broad. When a code from chapter 11 describes the condition adequately, only that code is assigned. It is appropriate, however, to assign an additional code when it provides needed specificity. For example, a diagnosis of secondary diabetes or diabetes mellitus, complicating pregnancy, is coded 648.0x, but this code indicates only that the patient has diabetes mellitus. It provides no information about the type of diabetes or any complication associated with it, making an additional code from category 249, Secondary diabetes mellitus, or 250, Diabetes mellitus, useful in fully describing the patient's condition. Code **V58.67, Long-term (current) use of insulin,** may also be assigned if the diabetes mellitus is being treated with insulin. Gestational diabetes can occur during pregnancy in women who were not diabetic before the pregnancy. Gestational diabetes can complicate the pregnancy, and there is an increased risk in women with gestational diabetes to develop diabetes mellitus following delivery. Gestational diabetes is coded to 648.8x. Code V58.67 should also be assigned if the gestational diabetes is being treated with insulin. Code **V12.21, Personal history of gestational diabetes,** is assigned to indicate that a patient has a history of gestational diabetes within a previous pregnancy. On the other hand, the code for varicose veins of the legs complicating pregnancy or the puerperium (671.0x) provides complete information, and assignment of an additional code would be redundant. Code **671.2x, Superficial thrombophlebitis complicating pregnancy,** requires an additional code to specify whether the thrombophlebitis is acute or chronic, and to specify the site. Other examples of the appropriate use of these codes follow:

- Term pregnancy, delivered, spontaneous; patient has a chronic cystitis and has had recurrent bouts of acute cystitis during her pregnancy with an acute episode at time of admission <u>646.61</u> + 595.0
- Asymptomatic bacteriuria; pregnancy, near-term, undelivered 646.53
- Diabetes mellitus, type 1, out of control and in coma; intrauterine pregnancy, 28 weeks, undelivered <u>648.03</u> + 250.33

Category 649 describes certain conditions or status of the mother that affect the pregnancy, childbirth, or the puerperium. For example:

- 649.0x Tobacco use disorder complicating pregnancy, childbirth, or the puerperium
- 649.1x Obesity complicating pregnancy, childbirth, or the puerperium
- 649.2x Bariatric surgery status complicating pregnancy, childbirth, or the puerperium
- 649.3x Coagulation defects complicating pregnancy, childbirth, or the puerperium
- 649.4x Epilepsy complicating pregnancy, childbirth, or the puerperium
- 649.5x Spotting complicating pregnancy
- 649.6x Uterine size date discrepancy
- 649.7x Cervical shortening

Hypertension

Other examples show the use of codes for a patient who has both pregnancy and hypertension. Preexisting hypertension is always considered to be a complicating factor in pregnancy, childbirth, or the puerperium and is classified in category 642 as follows:

- Benign essential hypertension 642.00–642.04
- Hypertension secondary to chronic kidney disease 642.10–642.14
- Other preexisting hypertension 642.20–642.24

Patients who do not have preexisting hypertension frequently develop transient or gestational hypertension during pregnancy. This condition is essentially an elevated blood pressure and clears relatively quickly once the pregnancy is over. This condition is coded to the 642.30 through 642.34 series.

Hypertension in pregnancy sometimes leads to a pathological condition described as eclampsia or preeclampsia. When these conditions are superimposed on a preexisting hypertension, a code from subcategory 642.7x is assigned. When they arise without any preexisting hypertension, they are classified in subcategories 642.4 through 642.6.

Gestational hypertension associated with albuminuria (albumin in urine) or edema (abnormal accumulation of fluid in body tissues) or both is generally considered to be preeclampsia or eclampsia. Codes for eclampsia or preeclampsia are never assigned solely on the basis of an elevated blood pressure, an abnormal albumin level, or the presence of edema. The physician must specify the condition as eclampsia or preeclampsia before any of these codes may be assigned.

CERCLAGE OF CERVIX

Cerclage of the cervix is a surgical technique to reinforce the cervical muscle by placing sutures above the opening of the cervix to narrow the cervical canal. This procedure is used in the treatment of incompetent cervix. Cervical incompetence (654.5x), a cause of miscarriage and preterm birth in the second and third trimesters, is a condition in which the cervix begins to open and thin before pregnancy has reached term. Dilation and effacement of the cervix occurs without pain or uterine contraction in a woman with cervical incompetence. Instead of developing uterine contractions as happens in normal pregnancy, these events occur because of the weakness of the cervix, which opens under the growing pressure of the uterus as the pregnancy progresses. Cervical shortening (649.7x) is also associated with an increased risk of preterm delivery. If these changes are not delayed, rupture of the membranes and birth of a premature baby can result. The procedure usually closes the cervix through the vagina using a speculum. The transabdominal cerclage makes it possible to place the stitch exactly at the level needed. Another approach involves performing the cerclage through an abdominal incision. Patients with shortening of the cervix may benefit from cervical cerclage. The procedure can be carried out if the cervix is very short, effaced, or totally distorted.

The codes for repair of the cervical os are as follows:

- 67.51 Transabdominal cerclage of cervix
- 67.59 Other cerclage of cervix

The Shirodkar operation, transvaginal cerclage, McDonald operation, and cerclage of isthmus uteri are included in code 67.59.

POSTPARTUM COMPLICATIONS

The postpartum period, clinically termed the "puerperium," begins immediately after delivery and includes the subsequent six weeks. A postpartum complication is defined as any complication that occurs during that six-week period. One type of postpartum complication is a puerperal infection—a bacterial infection following childbirth. An estimated 2 to 4 percent of mothers who deliver vaginally may experience some form of puerperal infection. For cesarean delivery, the figure is five to ten times higher. The genital tract is the most common site of infection (e.g., endometritis: 670.1x). Other types of puerperal infections include: major puerperal infection, unspecified (670.0x), sepsis (670.2x), septic thrombophlebitis (670.3x), and other major puerperal infections, such as pelvic cellulitis (670.8x). Postpartum complications that occur during the same admission as the delivery are identified by a fifth digit 2. Fifth digit 4 is used for a postpartum complication that occurs after discharge. For example:

- A patient developed endometritis two days following cesarean section delivery while still in the hospital. Code **670.12, Puerperal endometritis, Delivered, with mention of postpartum complication,** is assigned for endometritis following delivery. This is considered a complication of childbirth and not a complication of pregnancy. In *ICD-9-CM,* there is an index entry for "endometritis, puerperal, postpartum, childbirth."
- A patient is admitted three weeks postpartum and treated for acute pyelonephritis due to E. coli infection. Code **646.64, Infections of genitourinary tract, postpartum complication,** is assigned as the principal diagnosis. Code **590.10, Acute pyelonephritis,** and code **041.4, Escherichia coli (E. coli),** are assigned as additional codes to provide specificity regarding the infection.
- A patient is admitted five weeks postpartum with acute cholecystitis and cholelithiasis. Code **646.84, Other specified complication of pregnancy,** and code **574.00, Calculus of gallbladder with acute cholecystitis without mention of obstruction,** are assigned.
- A patient who delivered via low cervical cesarean six days prior was readmitted with severe sepsis with acute kidney failure due to a methicillin resistant *Staphylococcus aureus* (MRSA) of the C-section wound. Code **674.34, Other complications of obstetrical surgical wounds,** is assigned for the postsurgical wound infection. Codes **670.24, Puerperal sepsis, postpartum condition or complication; 041.12, Methicillin resistant *Staphylococcus aureus;* 995.92, Severe sepsis;** and **584.9, Acute kidney failure, unspecified,** are also assigned for the MRSA puerperal sepsis with acute kidney failure.

Uterine atony is a condition that can complicate the delivery and is defined as failure of the uterine muscle to contract adequately after the delivery. Uterine atony can occur with or without bleeding. Code **661.2x, Other and unspecified uterine inertia,** is assigned for atony of the uterus without hemorrhage, when it occurs immediately following delivery of the baby and placenta. Assign code **666.1x, Other immediate postpartum hemorrhage,** for postpartum uterine atony with hemorrhage, when it occurs immediately following delivery of the baby and placenta. Code **669.8x, Other complications of labor and delivery,** is assigned for postpartum uterine atony without hemorrhage. For example:

- A patient developed postpartum hemorrhage due to uterine atony immediately after spontaneous vaginal delivery of twins. The B-Lynch suture was performed to control the bleeding. The B-Lynch suture is a Brace suture used to compress the uterus without compromising major vessels in cases of postpartum hemorrhage. Code **666.12, Other immediate postpartum hemorrhage, Delivered with mention of postpartum complication,** is assigned for postpartum uterine atony with hemorrhage. Code **651.01, Twin pregnancy, Delivered, with or without mention of antepartum condition,** code **V91.00, Twin gestation, unspecified number of placenta, unspecified number of amniotic sacs,** and code **V27.2, Twins, both liveborn,** are also assigned. Code **75.52, Repair of current obstetric laceration of corpus uteri,** is assigned for the B-Lynch procedure.

LATE EFFECT OF COMPLICATION OF PREGNANCY, CHILDBIRTH, OR THE PUERPERIUM

Code 677, **Late effect of complication of pregnancy, childbirth, or the puerperium,** is assigned when an initial complication of the obstetrical experience develops a sequela that requires care or treatment at a later date. This code can be used at any time after the initial postpartum period. Like all late effect codes, code 677 is sequenced after the code describing the residual condition. Examples include the following:

- A patient was admitted for repair of uterine prolapse secondary to trauma sustained during childbirth two years earlier. Code **618.1, Uterine prolapse,** is assigned first with code **677, Late effect of complication of pregnancy, childbirth, or the puerperium,** assigned as an additional code.
- A patient presented with fatigue and cold intolerance. Her history indicated that she had experienced a severe hemorrhage during delivery of a normal liveborn seven months earlier. She was diagnosed with Sheehan's syndrome and treated with replacement hormones. Code **253.2, Panhypopituitarism,** is assigned for Sheehan's syndrome, followed by code **677, Late effect of complication of pregnancy, childbirth, or the puerperium.**

OTHER FETAL PROBLEMS

Code **678.0x, Fetal hematologic conditions,** classifies several fetal blood disorders, such as fetal anemia, fetal thrombocytopenia, and fetal twin to twin transfusion. The fetus can develop anemia because the red blood cells (RBCs) are not forming properly or the RBCs are being destroyed faster than they are produced. Although rare, fetal anemia is usually caused by an incompatibility between the mother's and the fetus's red blood cells. Other causes may include a temporary slowdown of red blood cell production and/or bleeding from the fetal circulation into the maternal circulation. Fetal thrombocytopenia involves a low platelet count and can cause spontaneous bleeding, particularly into the fetal brain, resulting in acute cerebrovascular accident. Maternal-fetal immune incompatibility is usually responsible for fetal thrombocytopenia. Twin to twin transfusion occurs only in identical twins when, while still in the womb, blood moves from one twin to the other. The donor twin loses the blood and the recipient twin receives the blood. Based on the severity of the condition, both infants can experience problems. The donor twin may have too little blood, requiring a transfusion, and the recipient twin may need to have his blood reduced.

Code **678.1x, Fetal conjoined twins,** describes the incomplete anatomic separation of twins. Assign codes 678.0x and 678.1x only on the mother's record if the fetal condition affects the management of the pregnancy and is responsible for modifying the mother's care.

Exercise 20.4

Code the following diagnoses and procedures. Assign V codes where applicable.

	Code(s)
1. Intrauterine pregnancy, spontaneous delivery, single liveborn	650 V27.0
Induction of labor by cervical dilation	73.1

Exercise 20.4 *(continued)*

2. Intrauterine pregnancy, 12 weeks gestation, undelivered, with mild hyperemesis Gravidarium	643.03
3. Intrauterine pregnancy, 39 weeks, delivered, left occipitoanterior, single liveborn Primary uterine inertia	661.01 V27.0
4. Cesarean delivery of stillborn at 38 weeks gestation owing to placental infarction	656.71 V27.1 656.41
5. Intrauterine pregnancy, with pernicious anemia, not delivered	648.23 281.0
6. Intrauterine pregnancy, term Spontaneous delivery, left occipitoanterior Single liveborn	650 V27.0
Assisted spontaneous delivery	73.59
7. Intrauterine pregnancy, twins, 33 weeks Premature rupture of membranes Spontaneous delivery of premature twins, vertex presentation, both liveborn Postpartum pulmonary embolism	644.21 658.11 651.01 673.22 V27.2 V91.00
8. Premature delivery, frank breech presentation, single female liveborn First-degree tear, vaginal wall	644.21 652.21 664.01 V27.0
9. Term pregnancy, delivered, single stillborn, left occipitoanterior Terminal abruptio placentae Cord tightly around neck with compression	641.21 663.11 656.41 V27.1
10. Intrauterine pregnancy, 12 weeks; long-standing essential hypertension being monitored closely	642.03

PROCEDURES ASSISTING DELIVERY

Delivery can be assisted in a number of ways. Labor may be induced by artificial rupture of membranes (73.01) or by other surgical induction such as cervical dilatation (73.1). Artificial rupture of membranes may also be performed after labor has begun (73.09). Amnioinfusion (75.37) may also be performed. If rotation is carried out, code **72.4, Forceps rotation of fetal head,** or code **73.51, Manual rotation of fetal head,** is assigned. For a routine delivery, code **73.59, Other manually assisted delivery,** may be assigned.

Forceps Delivery and Vacuum Extraction

Forceps, vacuum extraction, or internal and combined version may also assist delivery. Codes are provided for low-forceps, mid-forceps, or high-forceps delivery. In a low-forceps, or outlet-forceps, delivery (72.0–72.1), forceps are applied to a visible fetal head after it has entered the pelvic floor. Mid-forceps (72.2x) are applied to the head during its entry into the pelvic floor, and high-forceps (72.3x) are applied to the head before it enters the pelvic brim. Breech presentations may require partial or total breech extraction (72.5x), with or without forceps to the aftercoming head. Vacuum extraction (72.7) uses a traction device rather than forceps applied to the fetal head for extraction of the fetus.

Episiotomy

Episiotomy is ordinarily performed to assist delivery; code 73.6 is assigned for a routine episiotomy. When an episiotomy is performed in connection with a forceps delivery, a combination code is provided for the type of forceps and episiotomy (72.1, 72.21, 72.31). Repair of the episiotomy is included in the episiotomy code.

Perineal Lacerations

Perineal lacerations are classified as first, second, third, or fourth degree in subcategories 664.0x through 664.3x:

- First-degree tears involve damage to the fourchette and vaginal mucosa, and underlying muscles are exposed but not torn.
- Second-degree tears include the posterior vaginal walls and perennial muscles, but the anal sphincter is intact.
- Third-degree tears extend to the anal sphincter, but the rectal mucosa is intact.
- Fourth-degree tears involve the rectal and anal mucosa.

Code 664.6x describes an anal sphincter tear complicating delivery that is not associated with a third-degree perineal laceration.

Inclusion notes for these codes indicate what is involved in each degree. When more than one degree is mentioned, only the code for the highest degree is assigned. Code **75.69, Repair of other current obstetric laceration,** is assigned for repair of an obstetrical perineal laceration. Assign code **75.62, Repair of current obstetric laceration of rectum and sphincter ani,** for suturing of an obstetric tear of the anal sphincter.

A periurethral laceration that occurs during the delivery is coded **664.81, Other specified trauma to perineum and vulva, delivered, with or without mention of antepartum condition.** Assign code 75.69 for the repair of a periurethral laceration.

Occasionally, an episiotomy extends spontaneously to become a perineal laceration or tear. In this case, assign code **73.6, Episiotomy,** along with code 75.69. Both codes are needed to completely describe this situation. For the diagnosis, assign also the appropriate code from category 664, Trauma to perineum and vulva during delivery, to specifically describe the laceration or tear.

Fetal Pulse Oximetry

Fetal oxygen monitoring provides the physician with a direct measure of fetal oxygen status when an irregular fetal heart rate is present. The intrapartum fetal oxygen monitor uses a single-use, disposable sensor that is inserted through the birth canal when one of the amniotic membranes has ruptured and the cervix is dilated over 2 centimeters. The oxygen saturation is displayed on a monitor screen as a percentage. Assign code **75.38, Fetal pulse oximetry,** for this type of fetal monitoring.

Cesarean Delivery

Cesarean delivery is an operative delivery that is carried out when, for some reason, spontaneous delivery is not possible or does not seem advisable. A **Classical cesarean section, 74.0,** removes the fetus through an incision into the upper part of the uterus using an abdominal peritoneal approach. A **Low cervical cesarean, 74.1,** uses an incision into the lower portion of the uterus, with a pelvic cavity or abdominal peritoneal incision. Other fourth digits with category 74 indicate other types of cesarean delivery.

SERVICES RELATED TO CONTRACEPTIVE MANAGEMENT

Category **V25, Encounter for contraceptive management,** is assigned as the principal diagnosis for admissions or outpatient encounters for the purpose of contraceptive management. Codes in this category cover services such as initiation of oral contraceptive measures (V25.01); counseling in natural family planning to avoid pregnancy (V25.04); insertion of intrauterine contraceptive device (V25.11); removal of intrauterine contraceptive device (V25.12); removal and reinsertion of intrauterine contraceptive device (V25.13); sterilization (V25.2); surveillance of previously implemented contraceptive measures (V25.4x); and insertion of implantable subdermal contraceptive device (V25.5). Procedure codes must also be assigned when appropriate.

Exercise 20.5

Code the following diagnoses and procedures.

	Code(s)
1. Family planning counseling	V25.09
2. Encounter for insertion of intrauterine contraceptive device	V25.11
Insertion of intrauterine contraceptive device	69.7
3. Encounter for removal of intrauterine contraceptive device	V25.12
Removal of intrauterine contraceptive device	97.71

STERILIZATION

When a patient seeks health care for the purpose of contraceptive sterilization, code **V25.2, Sterilization,** is assigned as the principal diagnosis. If there are underlying medical or psychological conditions that led to the decision to undergo sterilization, codes for these conditions may be assigned as additional diagnoses. Because sterilization may be performed as an elective procedure without any predisposing medical or psychological reasons, code V25.2 can be used as a solo diagnosis code.

When an elective sterilization procedure is performed during a hospital episode in which an obstetrical delivery has occurred, V25.2 is assigned as a secondary code, with a code from chapter 11 of *ICD-9-CM* assigned as the principal diagnosis.

Note that code V25.2 is assigned for both female and male patients for whom a contraceptive sterilization procedure is performed. Sterilization procedures for females are classified in subcategories 66.2x and 66.3x; sterilization procedures for males are classified in subcategory 63.7x.

Code V25.2 is not assigned as either a principal or a secondary diagnosis when sterilization results from other treatment or when a sterilization procedure is performed as part of the treatment for another condition. In such cases, the original condition, any complications or comorbidities, and the procedures performed are coded. For example, when a hysterectomy is performed because of injury or damage to the uterus during delivery, only the obstetrical diagnoses and procedures are coded, even though the procedure results in sterility. Code V25.2 is used only for a sterilization performed specifically for contraception; assigning it when a sterilization is incidental to other treatment is inappropriate.

Other examples of appropriate coding of situations involving sterilization follow:

- A patient with multiparity (five children) with reactive depression is admitted for elective sterilization; bilateral endoscopic ligation and division of the fallopian tubes is carried out for sterilization V25.2 + 300.4 + V61.5 + 66.22
- Term pregnancy, delivered; breech presentation; delivery by partial breech extraction; endoscopic bilateral partial salpingectomy for sterilization 652.21 + V25.2 + 72.52 + 66.29

Exercise 20.6

Code the following diagnostic statements and procedures.

	Code(s)
1. Malignant hypertension Admitted for sterilization	V25.2 401.0
Endoscopy with bilateral tubal ligation and division	66.22

Exercise 20.6 *(continued)*

2. Endometriosis of uterus Admitted for sterilization	V25.2 617.0
Bilateral partial salpingectomy for sterilization	66.39
3. Term pregnancy, with breech delivery, female infant, followed by sterilization	652.21 V25.2 V27.0
Breech extraction Bilateral partial salpingectomy	72.52 66.39
4. Elective sterilization, patient request	V25.2
Vasectomy, bilateral	63.73
5. Elective reversal of previous tubal ligation Salpingoplasty	V26.0 66.79

PROCREATIVE MANAGEMENT

A code from category **V26, Procreative management,** is assigned when a patient who is having difficulty in becoming pregnant is seen for help in correcting this problem.

Code V26.41 is assigned as the first-listed diagnosis for an encounter/visit for procreative counseling and advice using natural family planning. Couples seeking natural methods of family planning require training/counseling by a medical professional or a qualified counselor. There are five methods of natural family planning:

- Basal body temperature method
- Ovulation/cervical mucus method
- Symptothermal method
- Calendar method
- Lactational amenorrhea

Therapy for malignant neoplasms or other serious conditions can affect reproductive health and the ability to conceive. Antineoplastic drugs (e.g., alkylating agents) and radiotherapy to the pelvic area may impair ovarian and testicular function, leading to infertility. Depending on the dosage delivered and the length of treatment, healthy sperm cells and ovarian follicles can be destroyed along with cancer cells.

Code **V26.42, Fertility preservation counseling,** is assigned for encounters for advice and counseling on available options to conceive a child or maintain pregnancy before the start of cancer treatment or the surgical removal of gonads. The discussion may include whether to conceive before cancer treatment; banking of sperm, eggs, ovarian tissue, or embryos; and/or modification of surgery to spare the uterus, etc.

Code **V26.82, Fertility preservation,** is assigned for the fertility preservation encounter. These codes are not limited to those seeking advice prior to cancer treatment or gonad removal. Codes V26.42 and V26.82 may be assigned for patients having any treatment (not only cancer treatment) that may affect fertility.

Code **V26.81, Encounter for assisted reproductive fertility procedure cycle,** is assigned for patients undergoing in vitro fertilization. An additional code should be assigned to identify the type of infertility. Code V26.81 is not used for encounters for diagnostic testing prior to starting in vitro fertilization. Assign the reason for the encounter when the patient presents for diagnostic testing.

Code **V23.85, Pregnancy resulting from assisted reproductive technology,** is assigned for subsequent encounters involving antenatal supervision and/or prenatal care when in vitro fertilization has been successful.

Admission for a tuboplasty or vasoplasty to reverse a previous sterilization procedure is coded **V26.0, Tuboplasty or vasoplasty after previous sterilization.** This is performed to reverse a previous sterilization. Encounters for investigations such as sperm counts or fallopian tube insufflation are coded to **V26.2, Investigation and testing.**

ICD-9-CM provides the following codes to describe encounters for testing and counseling for genetic disease:

- V26.31 Testing of female for genetic disease carrier status
- V26.32 Other genetic testing of female
- V26.33 Genetic counseling

If the encounter is for genetic screening not associated with procreative management, assign a code from category V82.7, Genetic screening, rather than the V26.31–V26.39 code series.

SUSPECTED MATERNAL AND FETAL CONDITIONS NOT FOUND

Codes from subcategory V89.0, Suspected maternal and fetal conditions not found, are to be used in very limited circumstances on a maternal record when an encounter is for a suspected maternal or fetal condition that is ruled out during that encounter (for example, a maternal or fetal condition may be suspected due to an abnormal test result). These codes should not be used when the condition is confirmed. In those cases, the confirmed condition should be coded. These codes should not be used if an illness or any signs or symptoms related to the suspected condition or problem are present. In those cases, the appropriate codes for the diagnosis/sign or symptom should be reported instead.

Codes from subcategory V89.0 can be used with other codes, but only if they are unrelated to the suspected condition being evaluated. Codes from subcategory V89.0 may not be used for encounters for antenatal screening of the mother. For encounters for suspected fetal conditions that are inconclusive following testing and evaluation, assign the appropriate code from category 655, 656, 657, or 658.

Codes in subcategory V89.0 describe suspected fetal/maternal problems not found, as follows:

- V89.01 Suspected problem with amniotic cavity and membrane not found
- V89.02 Suspected placental problem not found
- V89.03 Suspected fetal anomaly not found
- V89.04 Suspected problem with fetal growth not found
- V89.05 Suspected cervical shortening not found
- V89.09 Other suspected maternal and fetal condition not found

Category V91 is assigned to report multiple gestation placenta status. These codes specify the number of placentas and amniotic sacs. The risk of complications will increase and the treatment plan will differ depending on the number of placentas and amniotic sacs. Subcategory V91.0 describes twin gestation placenta status; subcategory V91.1 identifies triplet gestation placenta status; subcategory V91.2 is reserved for quadruplet gestation placenta status; and subcategory V91.9 is used to describe other specified multiple gestation placenta status. Codes V91.00–V91.99 are assigned as secondary codes along with the multiple gestation codes (651x–651.9x).

Review Exercise 20.7

Code the following diagnostic statements and procedures. Assign V codes where applicable.

	Code(s)
1. Elderly primigravida (37 years old); term delivery, spontaneous, of living female infant	659.51
Outcome of delivery	V27.0
Episiotomy and repair	73.6
2. Term pregnancy, living dichorionic twins (diamniotic sacs), cesarean delivery performed because fetal distress noted prior to labor	656.81 651.01 V91.03
Outcome of delivery	V27.2
Low cervical cesarean delivery	74.1

Review Exercise 20.7 *(continued)*

3. Delivery, term birth, living child, ROA presentation	650 V27.0
Outcome of delivery	
Fetal monitoring during labor	75.34
Episiotomy and episiorrhaphy	73.6
4. Uterine pregnancy, term, delivered with obstructed labor due to transverse presentation Preexisting hypertension with mild preeclampsia, single liveborn	660.01 652.31 642.71 V27.0
Outcome of delivery	
5. Intrauterine pregnancy, near-term, delivered, spontaneous Third-stage hemorrhage with anemia secondary to acute blood loss Monochorionic twins, both liveborn, diamniotic placenta	651.01 666.02 648.22 285.1 V91.02 V27.2
Outcome of delivery	
6. Pregnancy, delivered, frank breech presentation with liveborn male infant	652.21 V27.0
Outcome of delivery	
Partial breech extraction with forceps to aftercoming head	72.51
7. Term pregnancy, delivered, spontaneous Liveborn, male infant	650 V27.0
Outcome of delivery	
Assisted spontaneous delivery	73.59
Elective sterilization following delivery	V25.2
Bilateral endoscopic ligation and crushing of fallopian tubes	66.21

Review Exercise 20.7 *(continued)*

8. Intrauterine pregnancy, with complicating incompetent cervix, undelivered	654.53
Modified Shirodkar operation	67.59
9. Gestational hypertension Pregnancy, third trimester, undelivered	642.33
10. Intrauterine pregnancy, term, delivered, right occipitoanterior, liveborn male infant Episiotomy that extended to second-degree lacerations, perineum Outcome of delivery	664.11 V27.0
Amniotomy for induction of labor Low-forceps delivery with episiotomy Repair of perineal laceration	73.01 72.1 75.69 73.6
11. Delivery, stillborn, male infant, brow presentation; obstructed labor Outcome of delivery	660.01 652.41 656.41 V27.1
Version and extraction Episiotomy and repair	73.22 73.6
12. Twin pregnancy with malposition of one fetus One liveborn twin, one stillborn, number of placenta and amniotic sacs undetermined	652.61 651.01 656.41 V27.3 V91.09
Classical cesarean section	74.0

Review Exercise 20.7 *(continued)*

13. Outpatient evaluation of fetal bradycardia	659.73
14. Postpartum uterine atony without hemorrhage occurring two weeks after delivery	669.84
15. Encounter for testing of female for genetic disease carrier status	V26.31
16. Encounter for in vitro fertilization (IVF); infertility due to obstructed fallopian tube; previous pregnancy resulting from IVF	V26.81 628.2
17. Visit for procreative counseling using natural family planning	V26.41
18. Delivery, preterm, conjoined twins; 34 weeks gestation Outcome of delivery, twins, both liveborn Classical cesarean section	678.11 644.21 V91.00 V27.2 74.0

Abortion and Ectopic Pregnancy

CHAPTER **21**

CHAPTER OVERVIEW

- Codes for pregnancy with an abortive outcome are found in categories 634–639 in chapter 11 of *ICD-9-CM.*
- The primary axis for coding abortion is the type of abortion (spontaneous, legally induced, illegally induced, or failed).
- A fifth digit is used to classify whether the abortion is complete, incomplete, or unspecified.
- A fourth digit is used to classify whether a complication is present.
- Codes are available to indicate whether maternal condition is the reason for the abortion.
- On the occasion of an inadvertent abortion, the condition that caused the admission is coded as the principal diagnosis.
- If the abortion results in a liveborn infant, the code for early onset of delivery is used.
- In cases of multiple fetuses, there are codes to indicate whether any of the fetuses were lost during the pregnancy, even if only one live birth is recorded.
- Molar pregnancies and other abnormal products of conception are also coded in the categories of the 630s.
- Codes for ectopic pregnancies have a fourth digit to indicate location and a fifth digit to indicate whether there is also an intrauterine pregnancy.

LEARNING OUTCOMES

After studying this chapter you should be able to:

- Classify abortive outcomes by type of abortion.
- Use a fifth digit to indicate whether the abortion is complete or incomplete.
- Use a fourth digit to indicate complications to the abortion.
- Understand how to code different types and occurrences of abortions (such as inadvertent and loss of fetus with remaining fetus).
- Classify abnormal products of conception (such as molar and ectopic pregnancies).

TERMS TO KNOW

Abortion
the expulsion or extraction of all or part of the placenta with or without an identifiable fetus weighing less than 500 grams or with less than an estimated 22 weeks gestational age

Biochemical pregnancy
a pregnancy that is too early to confirm, except through biochemical means, and is the earliest form of miscarriage

Ectopic pregnancy
a pregnancy in which a fertilized ovum implants and develops outside the uterus

Molar pregnancy
a condition in which an ovum within the uterus develops into a mole or benign tumor

REMEMBER . . . *ICD-9-CM* rules may be different from individual state rules when it comes to classifying abortions.

INTRODUCTION

Abortion is defined as the expulsion or extraction of all or part of the placenta or membrane with or without an identifiable fetus weighing less than 500 grams. When the fetus's weight cannot be determined, an estimated gestation of less than 22 completed weeks is considered an abortive outcome (abortion). Although requirements for fetal death reporting vary from state to state, these requirements should not be confused with *ICD-9-CM* rules for classifying abortions; they are entirely separate. If an expelled fetus weighs more than 500 grams or if the period of gestation is more than 22 weeks but less than 37 weeks, it is considered an early delivery and code **644.21, Early onset of delivery,** is assigned.

Pregnancy with abortive outcome is classified in categories 634 through 639. Note that the term "abortion" in the disease classification of *ICD-9-CM* refers to a fetal death; the codes for the abortion procedure used to terminate a pregnancy are located in volume 3. The abortion code is assigned as the principal diagnosis when the admission or encounter is for the purpose of dealing with a spontaneous abortion or performing an elective abortion. If a procedure to terminate the pregnancy is performed in the hospital, the procedure code is also required.

TYPES OF ABORTION

The primary axis for coding abortion is the type of abortion. Abortive outcome is classified by type in *ICD-9-CM* as follows:

- **Spontaneous abortion (634):** one that occurs without any instrumentation or chemical intervention
- **Legally induced abortion (635):** one performed for either therapeutic or elective termination of pregnancy (terms such as "elective abortion," "induced" or "artificial abortion," and "termination of pregnancy" are used when this type of abortion is performed)
- **Illegally induced abortion (636):** one not performed in accordance with provisions of state law or not meeting regulatory requirements in regard to the qualifications of the individual performing the abortion or to the location in which it is performed. This category is used for inpatient coding only when a patient who had an abortion performed outside the hospital is admitted to ensure that the abortion is complete or to treat a complication.
- **Failed abortion (638):** one in which an elective abortion procedure has failed to evacuate or expel the fetus and the patient is still pregnant

ICD-9-CM provides default category 637 for coding an abortion of unspecified type; the use of this code in an acute care facility is not appropriate.

FIFTH-DIGIT SUBCLASSIFICATION

A fifth-digit subclassification is used with categories 634 through 637 to indicate whether the abortion is complete or incomplete. When the patient is admitted because of spontaneous abortion, the fifth digit is based on whether it was complete or incomplete at the time of admission. Abortions performed in the hospital are not ordinarily discharged as incomplete. The fifth digits are assigned as follows:

- 0 unspecified (not stated as either complete or incomplete)
- 1 incomplete; all products of conception have not been expelled from the uterus
- 2 complete; all products of conception have been expelled from the uterus

The coder should not assume that an abortion is complete or incomplete without a specific statement by the physician or other concrete information in the medical record. The fact that a follow-up dilatation and curettage (D & C) is performed is not evidence in itself that an abortion is incomplete; the physician makes this determination on the basis of the pathology report.

When the purpose of the admission/encounter is an elective legal abortion, assign the appropriate code from category 635, Legally induced abortion, along with the fifth digit "0." Given the *Official Guidelines for Coding and Reporting* statement that the "fifth digit assignment is based on the status of the patient at the beginning (or start) of the encounter," a clearly appropriate fifth digit is not available for elective abortions at this time. Currently, the fifth digit "0" is the most appropriate choice. This selection is based on the *Coding Clinic* advice from Fourth Quarter 2011.

COMPLICATIONS ASSOCIATED WITH ABORTION

Fourth digits are used with categories 634–639 to indicate whether a complication is present and the general type of complication, such as a metabolic disorder or genital infection. The abortion code is assigned as the principal diagnosis and an additional code is assigned to provide more specificity for the complication.

- A patient was admitted with spontaneous abortion, and a D & C was performed to remove any retained products of conception. None were found but there was evidence of pelvic infection. The patient was discharged on the fourth hospital day with the infection cleared. The principal diagnosis is **634.02, Spontaneous abortion complicated by genital tract and pelvic infection.** An additional code should be assigned for the infection.

When a patient is readmitted because a complication has developed following discharge, a code from category 639 is assigned as the principal diagnosis. The same fourth digits used with the abortion codes are used and an additional code is assigned to provide more specificity regarding the complication. For example:

- A patient was readmitted one week following discharge after an abortion because she had developed endometritis. Code **639.0, Complication of genital tract and pelvic infection following abortion,** was assigned as the principal diagnosis with an additional code for the endometritis.
- A patient is admitted in renal failure one week after discharge following an abortion. Code **639.3, Complications following abortion and ectopic and molar pregnancies, Renal failure,** is assigned as the principal diagnosis.

Note that category codes 634 through 638 cannot be assigned with a code from category 639.

If the readmission is for the purpose of dealing with retained products of conception, however, a code from the 634 through 637 series is assigned along with fifth digit 1 to indicate that it was incomplete. This advice should be followed even though the patient was discharged previously with a diagnosis of complete abortion. For example:

- A patient who underwent an elective abortion one week earlier was admitted because of continued bleeding. A dilation and curettage (D & C) was performed, and the pathology report showed retained products of conception. Code **635.11, Legally induced abortion complicated by delayed or excessive hemorrhage,** is assigned. Code 639 is not assigned because the abortion was incomplete.

- Five days following discharge for spontaneous abortion, a patient is admitted with a diagnosis of infection due to retained fetal tissue. The retention of fetal tissue indicates that the abortion was not complete, and so code **634.01, Spontaneous abortion complicated by genital tract and pelvic infection, incomplete,** is assigned even though the patient was hospitalized for the abortion previously.

Exercise 21.1

Code the following diagnoses, assigning fifth-digit codes. Consider the diagnostic statements given below as the only information available in the medical record. Do not assign procedure codes.

	Code(s)
1. Failed attempted abortion complicated by hemorrhage	638.1
2. Incomplete early abortion (spontaneous)	634.91
3. Therapeutic abortion with electrolyte imbalance	635.40
4. Electively induced abortion with amniotic fluid embolism	635.60
5. Patient readmitted with bleeding due to retained placenta one week following previous hospital admission for spontaneous abortion	634.11
6. Discharge #1: Electively induced abortion	635.90
Discharge #2 (same patient): Sepsis following induced abortion during previous admission	639.0

MATERNAL CONDITION AS REASON FOR ABORTION

Codes from categories 640 through 648 and 651 through 657 can be assigned as an additional code to indicate a maternal condition that assisted in the decision to proceed with an elective abortion. Pregnancy can be terminated on a purely elective basis, however, and it is not necessary to assign a code to indicate a reason for the abortion. For example:

- A patient is admitted for elective abortion, based on her physician's advice that her severe congenital heart disease indicates that an abortion might be advisable to prevent cardiac complications. In this case, the principal diagnosis code is **635.90, Legal abortion,** and **648.53, Congenital cardiovascular disorders,** is also assigned, along with an additional code to identify the particular heart disease.
- A patient who had rubella at six weeks gestation requests abortion because of the possibility of fetal abnormality. Code **635.90, Legally induced abortion without mention of complication,** is designated as the principal diagnosis, with an additional code of **655.33, Suspected damage to fetus from viral disease in the mother.**
- A patient who is 26 weeks pregnant presents for elective termination of pregnancy due to fetal anomalies. Assign code **635.90, Legally induced abortion, without mention of complication, complete,** as the principal diagnosis. Code **655.93, Known or suspected fetal abnormality affecting management of mother, unspecified, antepartum condition or complication,** is assigned as an additional diagnosis.
- A patient is admitted with placenta previa. She does not request abortion, but after evaluating various treatment possibilities, her physician concludes that an abortion is necessary. The patient consents, and the abortion is carried out. In this case, the code for placenta previa (641.03) is sequenced first, followed by the abortion code.

INADVERTENT ABORTION

An inadvertent abortion sometimes occurs when a pregnant patient suffers major trauma or undergoes surgery for another condition. In this situation, the code for the condition that occasioned the admission is designated as the principal diagnosis, with an additional code for the abortion.

When abortion occurs because of surgery performed on the uterus for a condition unrelated to the pregnancy, the code for the condition that required surgery is sequenced first, with an additional code from category **637, Unspecified abortion,** used to indicate that an abortion occurred. For example:

- Hysterectomy was performed after a diagnosis of uterine carcinoma. When the excised uterus was examined, a six-week-old fetus was found.
  Principal diagnosis: Carcinoma of uterus 182.8
  Additional diagnosis: Unspecified abortion, complete 637.92

When abortion occurs as a result of major trauma or surgery other than on the uterus, a code for the traumatic injury or the condition that required the surgery is sequenced as the principal diagnosis. A code from category **634, Spontaneous abortion,** is assigned as an additional code. For example:

- Appendectomy was performed because of acute appendicitis with peritonitis. On second postoperative day, patient experienced an inadvertent abortion (complete).
  Principal diagnosis: Appendicitis with peritonitis 540.0
  Additional diagnosis: Spontaneous abortion 634.92

Exercise 21.2

Code the following diagnoses. Do not assign procedure codes.

	Code(s)
1. Therapeutic abortion performed because of severe reactive psychosis	635.90 648.43 298.8
2. Inadvertent abortion prompted by radiation treatment damage to fetus, necessitating termination of pregnancy	635.90 655.63 E926.9
3. Elective abortion performed because of chromosomal abnormality of fetus	635.90 655.13

ABORTION PROCEDURE RESULTING IN LIVEBORN INFANT

Occasionally, an attempt to terminate a pregnancy results in a liveborn infant. Note that a fetus that has any heartbeat, respiration, or involuntary muscle movement after expulsion is considered to be a live birth, no matter how short a time it survives. In this situation, code **644.21, Early onset of delivery,** is assigned rather than an abortion code because, by definition, an abortion cannot result in a live birth. A code for the procedure used in the attempt to terminate the pregnancy should also be assigned. For example:

- A patient delivered a liveborn infant with extreme immaturity following attempted abortion by insertion of laminaria. Code **644.21, Early onset of delivery, delivered,** is assigned, along with code **V27.0** (for the **single liveborn**) and code **69.93** (for the **insertion of the laminaria**).

LOSS OF FETUS WITH REMAINING FETUS

Occasionally, a patient with multiple gestation is admitted for what appears to be a spontaneous abortion during which one or more fetuses are expelled but one or more live fetuses remain in utero. In such cases, no code from 634 through 639 is assigned, and one of the following complication of pregnancy codes is assigned instead:

- 651.33 twin pregnancy with fetal loss and retention of one fetus
- 651.43 triplet pregnancy with fetal loss and retention of one or more fetuses
- 651.53 quadruplet pregnancy with fetal loss and retention of one or more fetuses
- 651.63 other multiple pregnancy with fetal loss and retention of one or more fetuses

MULTIPLE GESTATION FOLLOWING FETAL REDUCTION

Subcategory code 651.7 identifies multiple gestation following fetal reduction during the current pregnancy. These pregnancies are considered high risk, and there is a need to identify them, even if the pregnancy is reduced to a single fetus. For example, when the woman delivers the single newborn, these codes make it possible to identify that this was originally a multiple gestation that underwent fetal reduction. Note that subcategory 651.7 refers to fetal reduction, whereas subcategories 651.3, 651.4, 651.5, and 651.6 described in the preceding section are for spontaneous abortion or involuntary fetal loss. For example:

- A patient presented with monochorionic (monoamniotic) twin gestation complicated by inter-twin vascular communication. She underwent elective reduction of the fetus because of inter-twin vascular communication. One fetus had developed polyhydramnios. Code **651.73, Multiple gestation following elective reduction, antepartum condition or complication,** is assigned as the principal diagnosis. Code **655.83, Other known or suspected fetal abnormality, not elsewhere classified,** code **657.03, Polyhydramnios, antepartum condition or complication,** and code **V91.01, Twin gestation, monochorionic/monoamniotic** (**one placenta, one amniotic sac**) should be assigned as additional diagnoses.
- A patient with an initial twin pregnancy had previously undergone fetal reduction of one fetus because of suspected chromosomal anomalies. The patient is now admitted and delivers a normal single liveborn infant. Code **651.71, Multiple gestation following (elective) fetal reduction, delivered, with or without mention of antepartum condition,** is assigned as the principal diagnosis. Code **V27.0, Single liveborn,** is assigned to indicate the outcome of the delivery. Code **V91.00, Twin gestation, unspecified number of placenta, unspecified number of amniotic sacs,** is assigned to indicate an unknown number of placenta and amniotic sacs.

The codes for multiple gestation following fetal reduction are as follows:

- 651.70 Multiple gestation following (elective) fetal reduction, unspecified as to episode of care or not applicable
- 651.71 Multiple gestation following (elective) fetal reduction, delivered, with or without mention of antepartum condition
- 651.73 Multiple gestation following (elective) fetal reduction, antepartum condition or complication

Codes in category V91 should be assigned along with the multiple gestation codes (651.0x–651.9x) as a secondary code to specify the number of placentas and amniotic sacs, if documented in the medical record.

PROCEDURES FOR TERMINATION OF PREGNANCY

Abortion may be induced by dilatation and curettage (69.01), aspiration curettage (69.51), injection of prostaglandin or saline (75.0), insertion of laminaria (69.93), or insertion of prostaglandin suppository (96.49). *ICD-9-CM* also provides a code for hysterotomy to terminate pregnancy (74.91), but this procedure is seldom performed.

ECTOPIC AND MOLAR PREGNANCIES

Ectopic and molar pregnancies and other abnormal products of conception are classified as follows, with an additional code from category 639 when any complication occurs:

- 630 Hydatidiform mole
- 631.0 Inappropriate change in quantitative human chorionic gonadotropin (hCG) in early pregnancy

- 631.8 Other abnormal products of conception (blighted ovum)
- 632 Missed abortion
- 633 Ectopic pregnancy

A molar pregnancy occurs when a blighted ovum (631.8) within the uterus develops into a mole or benign tumor. The hydatidiform mole is a particular type of molar pregnancy and is classified separately (630) in *ICD-9-CM*. All other molar pregnancies are included in code 631.8.

Utilization of assisted technologies has resulted in an increase in multiple gestational pregnancies in which an intrauterine pregnancy may coexist with an ectopic pregnancy. An ectopic pregnancy (633) occurs when a fertilized ovum is implanted and develops anywhere outside the uterus. The fourth digit indicates the extrauterine location of the ectopic pregnancy. Fifth digits are assigned to indicate whether there is an intrauterine pregnancy in addition to the extrauterine pregnancy. The codes are as follows:

- 633.00 and 633.01 Abdominal pregnancy
- 633.10 and 633.11 Tubal pregnancy
- 633.20 and 633.21 Ovarian pregnancy
- 633.80 and 633.81 Other ectopic pregnancy

Tubal pregnancy is the most common type of ectopic pregnancy. Surgical procedures for removing a tubal ectopic pregnancy include **66.01, Salpingotomy,** or **66.02, Salpingostomy;** in both procedures, the ectopic pregnancy is removed from the tube by means of an incision into the fallopian tube. It can also be removed by salpingectomy (excision of the fallopian tube) with the ectopic pregnancy intact (66.62). Code **74.3, Removal of extratubal ectopic pregnancy,** is assigned for removal of any other type of ectopic pregnancy. For example:

- Tubal pregnancy 633.1x
  Removal of ectopic fetus from fallopian tube by salpingotomy 66.01
- Tubal pregnancy 633.1x
  Salpingectomy with removal of tubal pregnancy 66.62
- Abdominal pregnancy 633.0x
  Removal of abdominal pregnancy 74.3
- Cornual pregnancy 633.8x
  Removal of cornual pregnancy 74.3

Code 631.0 describes inappropriate change in quantitative human chorionic gonadotropin (hCG) in early pregnancy. Human chorionic gonadotropin is a hormone produced in the body during pregnancy. An hCG blood test measures the level of hCG detectable in the blood. In early pregnancy, the hCG level should double roughly every two to three days. If the hCG doubling time is slower or if the level decreases over time, this is a possible sign of miscarriage or ectopic pregnancy. If an ultrasound indicates no intrauterine pregnancy, an ectopic pregnancy must be ruled out. When no ectopic pregnancy is found, the miscarriage is confirmed.

A biochemical pregnancy is the earliest form of miscarriage. A biochemical pregnancy is a pregnancy that is too early to confirm except through biochemical means. In a biochemical pregnancy, the fertilized egg will not implant properly in the uterus, resulting in an early miscarriage. Assign code **631.0, Inappropriate change in quantitative human chorionic gonadotropin (hCG) pregnancy,** for a biochemical pregnancy.

Complications of Molar and Ectopic Pregnancy

Unlike complications of abortions, complications of ectopic and molar pregnancies are classified in category 639, whether they occur during the initial episode of care or during a later episode. When the complication occurs during an episode of care for the purpose of treating the ectopic or molar pregnancy, a code from the 630 through 633 series is sequenced first, followed by a code from category 639. When the patient is readmitted for a complication following treatment of an ectopic or molar pregnancy, assign a code from category 639 as the principal diagnosis. An additional code that describes the complication more specifically can be assigned as needed. Sample codes include the following:

- Pelvic peritonitis following ectopic tubal pregnancy (this admission) 633.1x + 639.0
- Hemorrhage following ruptured ectopic tubal pregnancy removed on previous admission 639.1

Missed Abortion

The term "missed abortion" refers to fetal death that occurs prior to the completion of 22 weeks of gestation, with the dead fetus retained for a period of time in the uterus. This condition may be indicated by a cessation of growth, hardening of the uterus, or by actual diminution in size of the uterus. Absence of fetal heart tones after they had been previously heard is also indicative of a missed abortion. The retained fetus may be expelled spontaneously, or surgical or chemical intervention may be required. For example:

- A patient in the 20th week of gestation reports that she is no longer feeling any fetal movement. The physician cannot hear any fetal heart tones, although they were present one month ago. On examination, the uterus is hard and possibly smaller than on the last visit. Code **632, Missed abortion,** is assigned.

When the period of gestation is longer than 22 weeks, retention of a dead fetus is considered a missed intrauterine death (656.4x).

Review Exercise 21.3

Code the following diagnoses. Do not assign procedure codes.

	Code(s)
1. Therapeutic abortion with embolism	635.60
2. Failed attempted induction of abortion	638.9
3. Ruptured right tubal pregnancy with peritonitis due to group A *Streptococcus*	633.10 639.0 041.01
4. Incomplete early abortion (spontaneous)	634.91

Review Exercise 21.3 *(continued)*

5. Spontaneous abortion, complete, with excessive hemorrhage	634.12
6. Electively induced abortion with liveborn	644.21 V27.0
7. Electively induced abortion complicated by shock	635.50
8. Ectopic pregnancy, right fallopian tube	633.10
9. Carneous mole	631.8
10. Hydatidiform mole	630
11. Missed abortion, 19 weeks gestation	632
12. Electively induced abortion Family problems due to multiparity	635.90 V61.5

Congenital Anomalies

CHAPTER **22**

CHAPTER OVERVIEW

- Congenital anomalies are classified in chapter 14 of *ICD-9-CM*.
- Congenital and acquired conditions are often distinguished with a parenthetical note in the main term or subterm of a condition in the Alphabetic Index.
- In a few specific cases, separate codes are provided for the congenital and acquired versions of a condition.
- Congenital anomalies are classified first by the body system involved.
- Although congenital anomalies are present at birth, they may not be recognized until later in life.
- Patient age plays no role in assigning chapter 14 codes. They can be used at any age.
- In the case of newborns, congenital conditions that may have future implications are reported even though they may not be treated during the current episode of care.
- Conditions caused by mechanical factors during gestation are coded with a fourth digit to indicate site or type.
- Conditions due to birth injury are considered perinatal and are not part of the congenital classifications.

LEARNING OUTCOMES

After studying this chapter you should be able to:

- Distinguish between congenital and acquired conditions in the Alphabetic Index.
- Code for a congenital anomaly even if the classification does not provide a specific code for it.
- Explain the relationship of patient age to codes for congenital anomalies.
- Explain the difference between congenital and perinatal deformities.

TERM TO KNOW

Congenital anomaly
abnormal condition present at birth, which may not be recognized until later in life

REMEMBER . . . There are about 4,000 congenital anomalies. Not all have been classified with a specific code.

INTRODUCTION

Congenital anomalies are classified in categories 740–759 in chapter 14 of *ICD-9-CM*. Congenital anomalies are abnormal conditions that are present at birth, although they may be recognized later. Codes from chapter 14 may be used throughout the life of the patient. If a congenital anomaly has been corrected, a personal history code should be used to identify the history of the anomaly. Codes in subcategory V13.61–V13.69 are used for congenital malformations that may still be present but do not require additional care, as well as corrected anomalies that are no longer present. Many congenital conditions can now be repaired because of medical advances, and patients are left with no residual condition.

LOCATION OF TERMS IN THE ALPHABETIC INDEX

A distinction between acquired and congenital conditions is often noted in the Alphabetic Index by a nonessential modifier associated with the main term or a subterm. When either term appears in parentheses with the main term, the alternative term can ordinarily be located as a subterm.

Note that some conditions are congenital by definition and have no acquired version; others are always considered to be acquired. For many conditions, of course, no distinction is made. When the diagnostic statement does not describe a condition as being either acquired or congenital, however, *ICD-9-CM* often makes a presumption that it is one or the other.

The following example from the Alphabetic Index demonstrates this usage:

Deformity. . .
  breast (acquired) 611.89
    congenital 757.9
  bronchus (congenital) 748.3
    acquired 519.1

In this example, the Alphabetic Index assumes that deformity of the breast without other qualification is classified as acquired, whereas deformity of the bronchus is classified as congenital if not otherwise specified. The Tabular List may offer additional guidance by means of an exclusion note. For example, the entry under category **562, Diverticula of intestine,** refers the coder elsewhere for congenital diverticulum of colon, coded **751.5, Other anomalies of intestine.** For code 751.5, the inclusion note indicates that congenital diverticulum of the colon is appropriately classified here.

ICD-9-CM provides separate codes for congenital hydrocephalus (742.3), spina bifida with hydrocephalus (741.0), acquired secondary normal pressure hydrocephalus (331.3), obstructive hydrocephalus (331.4), and acquired idiopathic normal pressure hydrocephalus (331.5).

Congenital hydrocephalus is defined as an excessive accumulation of cerebrospinal fluid (CSF) in the brain, which is present at birth. The excessive fluid leads to increased intracranial pressure and possibly brain damage. Code **742.3, Congenital hydrocephalus,** is assigned for this birth defect.

Spina bifida is a congenital anomaly involving incomplete closure of the embryonic neural tube, resulting in a spinal cord defect. Many individuals with spina bifida have an associated abnormality of the cerebellum, referred to as Chiari II malformation. In affected individuals the back portion of the brain is displaced from the skull into the upper neck. Hydrocephalus develops in approximately 90 percent of individuals with myelomeningocele/spina bifida, because the displaced cerebellum obstructs the flow of CSF. Assign code **741.0, Spina bifida, with hydrocephalus,** for this type of congenital anomaly.

Normal pressure hydrocephalus (NPH) or secondary NPH can be caused by any condition where the flow of cerebrospinal fluid is blocked, such as subarachnoid hemorrhage, head trauma, cerebral infarction, infection, tumor, or complications of surgery. Assign code **331.3, Communicating hydrocephalus,** for secondary NPH. Obstructive hydrocephalus develops secondary to a blockage in the normal circulation of CSF in the brain. In most instances, the blockage affects the third and fourth ventricles at the level of the Aqueduct of Sylvius, also referred to as an aqueductal obstruction. This can result from scarring or tumor. Assign code **331.4, Obstructive hydrocephalus,** for this acquired condition. Idiopathic normal pressure hydrocephalus (INPH) can occur without any identifiable cause. Code **331.5, Idiopathic normal pressure hydrocephalus (INPH),** is assigned for this type of acquired hydrocephalus. If the medical record documentation does not specify whether the hydrocephalus is congenital or acquired, code **331.4, Obstructive hydrocephalus,** is the default.

Congenital anomalies are classified first by the body system involved. Many congenital anomalies have specific codes in *ICD-9-CM;* others are located under such general terms as anomaly and deformity rather than under the name of the specific condition. For example:

- Congenital malposition of gastrointestinal tract 751.8
- Prader-Willi syndrome 759.81
- Congenital hiatus hernia 750.6
- Strawberry nevus 757.32
- Congenital hydrocephalus 742.3

Because approximately 4,000 congenital anomalies have been identified, it is impossible for the classification to provide a specific code for each. When the type of anomaly is specified, but no specific code is provided, the code for other specified anomaly of that type and site should be assigned. Often, only the code for unspecified anomaly of that general type or site can be assigned. When a specific code is not available, additional codes for manifestations of the anomaly should be assigned to the extent possible. Use additional secondary codes from other chapters to specify conditions associated with the anomaly.

- An eight-day-old infant is diagnosed with Finnish-type congenital nephrosis. Finnish-type congenital nephrosis is a minimal change type I nephrotic disease of childhood, occurring during the first week of life. This condition is caused by mutations in the gene for nephrin on chromosome 19. Proteinuria, hypoalbuminemia, hypogammaglobulinemia, and hyperlipidemia are common lab findings. Codes **753.3, Other anomalies of kidney,** and **581.3, Nephrotic syndrome, With lesion of minimal change glomerulonephritis,** are assigned for Finnish-type congenital nephrosis.
- A ten-month-old infant is diagnosed with cardiofaciocutaneous (CFC) syndrome. Assign code **759.89, Other specified anomalies, Other,** for cardiofaciocutaneous syndrome. Additional codes may be assigned for any manifestations of the condition as instructed by the guideline on congenital anomalies. Cardiofaciocutaneous syndrome is a genetic condition associated with mutation in four known genes: BRAF, MEK1, MEK2, and KRAS.

RELATIONSHIP OF AGE TO CODES

Codes from chapter 14 can be reported for a patient of any age. Many congenital anomalies, although actually present at birth, do not manifest themselves until later in life. In addition, many cannot be corrected and persist throughout life and these conditions may be reported for an adult patient. Patient age is not the determining factor in assigning these codes. Here are some examples:

- A patient, 30 years of age, with Marfan syndrome was admitted for a heart valve replacement and repair of an abdominal aortic aneurysm. In this case, the code for **Marfan syndrome, 759.82,** is assigned in spite of the patient's age because the condition is an inherited disorder of the connective tissue that is transmitted as an autosomal dominant trait.

- A patient, age 25, was admitted for brain surgery, which revealed a colloid cyst of the right third ventricle. In this case, code **742.4, Other specified anomaly of the brain,** is assigned because a colloid cyst of the third ventricle is always congenital and the patient's age does not influence code assignment.
- A 35-year-old patient presents with a congenital pulmonary arteriovenous malformation (AVM). Code **747.32, Pulmonary arteriovenous malformation,** is assigned because age does not affect code assignment. A pulmonary AVM is an abnormal communication between pulmonary arteries and pulmonary veins. Although these are usually congenital, they can also be acquired. In many cases, the pulmonary AVM is small and does not usually present until adulthood, even when congenital. However, in some cases AVMs can cause serious problems, and the patient can develop cyanosis, heart failure, dyspnea, and even respiratory failure.

NEWBORN WITH CONGENITAL CONDITIONS

When a diagnosis of a congenital condition is made during the hospital episode in which an infant is born, the appropriate code from chapter 14 of *ICD-9-CM* should be assigned as an additional code, with the appropriate code from the V30 through V39 series used as the principal diagnosis. (See chapter 23 of this handbook.) For example:

- Term birth, male; incomplete cleft lip on right side V30.00 + 749.12
- Term birth, male; hypospadias V30.00 + 752.61

Note that this is an exception to the guidelines for reporting other conditions. Congenital conditions that may have future health care implications are reported for newborns even though they are not further evaluated or treated during the current episode of care.

CONGENITAL DEFORMITIES VERSUS PERINATAL DEFORMITIES

Certain musculoskeletal deformities that result from a mechanical factor during gestation, such as intrauterine malposition or pressure, are classified in category **754, Certain congenital musculoskeletal deformities,** with a fourth-digit axis indicating the site or type of deformity. Conditions due to birth injury are classified as perinatal conditions in category 767 in chapter 15 of *ICD-9-CM,* with an additional code assigned to identify the specific condition whenever possible. Examples include the following:

- Bilateral congenital dislocation of hip 754.31
- Congenital dislocation of knee 754.41
- Fracture of clavicle due to birth trauma 767.2

CYSTIC KIDNEY DISEASE

There are major differences in the clinical characteristics, pathophysiology, and prognosis of the various types of congenital cystic kidney disease. This fact augments the importance of being as specific as possible about the type when assigning a code. For example, **medullary sponge kidney** (**753.17**) is relatively common and has a good prognosis, but **medullary cystic kidney** (**753.16**) can lead to chronic kidney disease. When the diagnostic statement does not indicate whether a renal cyst is congenital or acquired, *ICD-9-CM* presumes that the cyst is congenital.

CONGENITAL ANOMALIES OF UTERUS, CERVIX, VAGINA, AND EXTERNAL GENITALIA

The development of the female reproductive tract is a complex process that involves a highly orchestrated series of events, including cellular differentiation, migration, fusion, and canalization. Failure of any part of the process results in congenital anomalies. Mullerian anomalies include all congenital anomalies of the uterus, cervix, and vagina. *ICD-9-CM* provides unique codes for the spectrum of congenital uterine, cervical, and vaginal anomalies:

- 752.31 Agenesis of uterus
- 752.32 Hypoplasia of uterus
- 752.33 Unicornuate uterus
- 752.34 Bicornuate uterus
- 752.35 Septate uterus
- 752.36 Arcuate uterus
- 752.39 Other anomalies of uterus
- 752.43 Cervical agenesis
- 752.44 Cervical duplication
- 752.45 Vaginal agenesis
- 752.46 Transverse vaginal septum
- 752.47 Longitudinal vaginal septum
- 752.49 Other anomalies of cervix, vagina, and external female genitalia

OMPHALOCELE AND GASTROSCHISIS

An omphalocele is a distinct ventral wall defect. The intestines are usually covered by a membranous sac, with the intestine being exposed only if the sac ruptures. An omphalocele is commonly associated with other structural and chromosomal anomalies. Code **756.72, Omphalocele,** is assigned for a congenital omphalocele.

Gastroschisis is an anomaly involving a defect of the ventral body wall to the right of the umbilical cord insertion. This anomaly is caused by failure of the developing abdominal wall to completely close, allowing the intestines to protrude from the defect. The exposed intestines are not covered by a membranous sac. Assign code **756.73, Gastroschisis,** for congenital gastroschisis.

Review Exercise 22.1

Code the following diagnoses and procedures. Do not assign E codes.

	Code(s)
1. Polycystic kidneys, adult type	753.13
2. Hypospadias with congenital chordee	752.61 752.63

Review Exercise 22.1 *(continued)*

Repair of hypospadias and release of chordee	58.45 64.42
3. Congenital pyloric stenosis	750.5
Ramstedt procedure	43.3
4. Congenital dislocation of left hip with subluxation of right hip	754.35
Closed reduction of dislocation of both hips with immobilization in plaster casts	79.75
5. Congestive heart failure in patient with congenital interatrial septal defect	428.0 745.5
6. Posterior subcapsular cataract, OS, congenital	743.31
Intracapsular cataract extraction with peripheral iridectomy and insertion of intraocular lens prosthesis	13.19 13.71
7. Accessory fifth digit, right foot	755.02
8. Esophageal web with esophageal spasm and reflux esophagitis	750.3 530.5 530.11

Review Exercise 22.1 *(continued)*

9. Left trigger thumb, congenital	756.89
Tenolysis of flexor sheath of left thumb	82.91
10. Urachal cyst and patent urachus	753.7
11. Thoracoabdominal coarctation of aorta	747.10
12. Hallux rigidus, left	735.2
13. Down's syndrome	758.0
14. Bilateral talipes equinovarus, congenital	754.51
Heel cord lengthening	83.85
15. Unilateral cleft lip and cleft palate, complete	749.21
Rotation-advancement repair of cleft lip Repair cleft palate	27.54 27.62
16. Cystic lung, congenital	748.4
17. Shone's syndrome, with subaortic stenosis and aortic coarctation	746.84 746.81 747.10

Perinatal Conditions

CHAPTER **23**

CHAPTER OVERVIEW

- Perinatal conditions other than congenital anomalies are classified in chapter 15 of *ICD-9-CM*.
- These conditions can be found under the main term **Birth** or as a subterm under the condition's main term.
- Perinatal conditions are sequenced as the principal diagnosis but behind the appropriate V code for the birth episode.
- Codes for perinatal conditions can be used throughout the patient's life. There is no prohibition due to age.
- Conditions are coded only if they have an implication for the newborn's future care.
- Newborn immaturity and prematurity are classified via birth weight. Codes for these conditions are never assigned without a physician's clinical evaluation as indicated in the diagnostic statement.
- Newborn postmaturity is classified by length of gestation.
- The perinatal conditions in chapter 15 cover fetal distress, metabolic abnormalities, difficulties due to aspiration, and more.
- A code is assigned from V29 when a healthy infant is evaluated for a suspected condition that is not found.
- Infections specific to the perinatal period are considered congenital.
- Infections that occur after birth but within the perinatal period may or may not be classified in chapter 15.
- Codes from categories 760–763 are assigned only when a mother's condition adversely affects the newborn.
- V codes are used for routine newborn vaccination and health supervision.

LEARNING OUTCOMES

After studying this chapter you should be able to:

- Locate codes and follow general guidelines with regard to perinatal conditions.
- Use V codes to classify the birth, and use them with other codes for perinatal conditions.
- Code situations involving newborn immaturity, prematurity, and postmaturity.
- Code for evaluation and observation of newborns and infants.
- Determine what chapter to use to classify a newborn or infant infection.
- Know how and when to assign codes for maternal condition on the newborn record.

TERMS TO KNOW

Newborn immaturity
implies a birth weight less than 1,000 grams

Newborn postmaturity
a gestational period of more than 42 weeks

Newborn prematurity
implies a birth weight of 1,000–2,499 grams

REMEMBER . . . Codes from chapter 15 are never found on a maternal record, and codes from chapter 11 are never found on a newborn's record.

INTRODUCTION

Conditions other than anomalies that originate in the perinatal period are classified in chapter 15 of *ICD-9-CM* and categories 760–779. The perinatal period is defined as before birth through the 28th day following birth. The perinatal period ends on the 29th day of life because the World Health Organization considers the day of birth as "day zero" for international comparisons.

LOCATING CODES FOR PERINATAL CONDITIONS IN THE ALPHABETIC INDEX

Codes for perinatal conditions are located in the Alphabetic Index (volume 2) by referring to the main term **Birth** or to the main term for the condition and then to such subterms as "neonatal," "fetal," and "infantile." If the Alphabetic Index does not provide a specific code for a perinatal condition, assign code **779.89, Other specified conditions originating in the perinatal period,** followed by the code from another chapter that specifies the condition.

GENERAL PERINATAL GUIDELINES

Codes from chapter 15 are never used on maternal records. By the same token, codes from chapter 11, Complications of Pregnancy, Childbirth and the Puerperium, should never be reported on the newborn record.

Generally, chapter 15 codes are sequenced as the principal or first-listed diagnosis on the newborn record, except for the appropriate code from the V30 through V39 series for the birth episode. Codes from other chapters may be assigned as secondary diagnoses to provide additional detail.

The perinatal guidelines for secondary diagnoses are the same as the general coding guidelines for "additional diagnoses" (refer to chapter 3). In addition, assign codes for any conditions that have been specified by the provider as having implications for future health care needs. Assign codes from chapter 15 only for definitive diagnoses established by the provider. If a definitive diagnosis has not been established, codes for signs and symptoms may be assigned.

Sometimes a newborn may have a condition that may be either due to the birth process or community acquired. If the documentation does not specify which it is, the default code selected should be due to the birth process, and a chapter 15 code should be selected. When the condition is community acquired, do not report a chapter 15 code.

RELATIONSHIP OF AGE TO CODES

Most conditions originating during the perinatal period are transitory in nature. Other conditions that originate during the perinatal period, however, persist, and some do not manifest themselves until later in life. Such conditions are classified in chapter 15, no matter how old the patient is, and may be reported throughout the life of the patient if the condition is still present. For example:

- A 33-year-old woman was admitted for treatment of vaginal carcinoma due to intrauterine exposure to DES (diethylstilbestrol) taken by her mother during pregnancy. Code **184.0, Malignant neoplasm of vagina,** and code **760.76, Diethylstilbestrol,** are assigned because the intrauterine exposure was still an important element in the patient's condition, even though the problem did not present itself until later in the patient's life.
- An 18-year-old man was admitted for workup because he had begun experiencing respiratory problems. A diagnosis of bronchopulmonary dysplasia was made, and the patient was discharged to be seen in the physician's office in two weeks.

Code 770.7, **Chronic respiratory disease arising in the perinatal period,** is assigned because bronchopulmonary dysplasia is a congenital condition even though it may not become a problem until later in the patient's life.

CLASSIFICATION OF BIRTHS

A code from categories V30 through V39 is assigned as the principal diagnosis for any newborn. The first axis for coding is whether the birth is single or multiple; codes for multiple births indicate whether mates are liveborn or stillborn. The fourth-digit axis indicates that the birth occurred in the hospital (0) or immediately before admission to the hospital (1). Fourth digit 2 indicates that the birth took place outside the hospital and that the newborn was not admitted; therefore, it is not assigned except for an outpatient encounter. For live births in the hospital, a fifth digit indicates whether there was a cesarean delivery. Note that categories V33, V37, and V39 should not be used in the acute care hospital; the medical record will provide sufficient information to permit assignment of a more specific code.

A code from this series is assigned only on the newborn record and is assigned only for the episode in which the birth occurred. If a newborn is discharged and readmitted or transferred to another facility, the code for the condition responsible for the transfer or readmission is designated as the principal diagnosis. For example:

- A single liveborn in the hospital with an associated diagnosis of subdural hemorrhage due to birth trauma would be coded as **V30.00, Single liveborn, + 767.0, Subdural and cerebral hemorrhage,** with the V code sequenced first.
- If the infant is discharged and readmitted or transferred to another facility for treatment of the hemorrhage, the principal diagnosis for that admission would be 767.0; no code from the V30 through V39 series would be assigned.
- If the admission of an infant born outside the hospital is delayed and the newborn is admitted later because of complication, the complication code would be assigned as the principal diagnosis; no code from the V30 through V39 series would be assigned.

OTHER DIAGNOSES FOR NEWBORNS

A code from the V30 through V39 series indicates only that a birth occurred. Additional codes are assigned for all clinically significant conditions noted on the examination of the newborn. A newborn condition is clinically significant when it has implication for the newborn's future health care. This is an exception to the UHDDS guidelines.

Insignificant or transient conditions that resolve without treatment are not coded. Medical records of newborns sometimes mention conditions such as fine rashes, molding of the scalp, and minor jaundice. Because these conditions usually resolve without treatment and require no additional workup, they would not be coded. For example:

- The physician documented diagnoses of syndactyly and hydrocele on the newborn's diagnostic statement. Even though no treatment was given and no further evaluation was done during the infant's hospital stay, both of these conditions will require treatment at some time in the future, and so they are reported.
- The physician mentioned on the newborn delivery record that the infant had slight jaundice. No further evaluation was done, and the jaundice cleared by the following day. No code for jaundice is assigned.
- The pediatrician documented in the newborn medical record that the baby's heart murmur was benign and most likely due to a patent ductus arteriosus/patent foramen ovale (PDA/PFO). He ordered a cardiac consult and an echocardiogram to evaluate the PDA/PFO. Assign code **745.5, Ostium secundum type atrial septal defect,** for the PFO and code **747.0, Patent ductus arteriosus,** for the PDA. These conditions were further evaluated (e.g., cardiac consultation and echocardiogram); therefore, they can be reported.

PREMATURITY, LOW BIRTH WEIGHT, AND POSTMATURITY

Newborns delivered before full term are defined as either immature or premature and are classified in category 765 as follows:

- Immaturity (765.0x) implies a birth weight of less than 1,000 grams.
- Prematurity (765.1x) implies a birth weight of 1,000–2,499 grams.

Even when a newborn is not premature, it may be appropriate to assign a code from category **764, Slow fetal growth and fetal malnutrition.** This code does not imply prematurity but indicates that the newborn is smaller than expected for the length of gestation. A code to specify the number of completed weeks of gestation (765.20–765.29) should only be used with category 764 and codes 765.0x and 765.1x to report: (1) the number of weeks of gestation for preterm infants, (2) infants with extreme immaturity, and/or (3) infants with slow fetal growth and malnutrition. Occasionally, the obstetrician will document the gestational age in the mother's record, and the pediatrician will document a different gestational age in the infant's chart. For the newborn, the coder would assign the appropriate codes for gestational age based on the attending provider's (e.g., pediatrician's) documentation. Different providers (e.g., obstetrician and pediatrician) may use different criteria in determining weeks of gestation for the mother versus the gestational age of the infant.

To indicate the birth weight, fifth digits are assigned to codes for immaturity (765.0), prematurity (765.1), and slow fetal growth and fetal malnutrition (764.0–764.9). Note that the weight expressed by the fifth digit should be reasonably consistent with the four-digit code to which it is applied. For example, a diagnosis of immaturity would appear to be inconsistent with fifth digit 9 because a birth weight of 2,500 grams falls far outside the criteria for immaturity even though there is no indication in the manual that the heavier weight is excluded. The physician should be queried when there is a significant discrepancy.

Codes from category 764 and subcategories 765.0 and 765.1 are never assigned on the basis of birth weight or estimated gestation alone but only on the physician's clinical evaluation of the maturity of the newborn, as indicated in the diagnostic statement. For example, an infant born at hospital A at 34 weeks gestation and transferred to hospital B after 14 days for further evaluation of a congenital anomaly could still have a code for prematurity assigned as an additional diagnosis. The fifth digit for these codes is always based on birth weight, not the infant's weight at the time of transfer or readmission.

There is no time frame that limits the use of these codes; a code can be assigned as long as the physician considers the birth weight an important element of the infant's condition. For example: A 12-month-old child who was born preterm is being seen for acute bronchiolitis due to respiratory syncytial virus (RSV). The physician listed "acute bronchiolitis due to RSV, ex-26 week preemie" in the diagnostic statement. Code **466.11, Acute bronchiolitis due to respiratory syncytial virus (RSV)**, is assigned as the first-listed diagnosis. Code **765.23, 25–26 weeks of gestation,** is assigned to indicate that the child was born at 26 weeks. Codes from chapter 15 should be assigned when the provider has indicated that prematurity and gestational age are contributing conditions even though the baby is no longer premature at the time of the current encounter.

Postterm is defined as a gestational period more than 40 to 42 completed weeks. Prolonged gestation or postmaturity is defined as a gestational period of more than 42 completed weeks. Category 766 classifies a long gestation and/or high birth weight as follows:

- 766.0 Exceptionally large baby (usually implies weight of 4,500 grams or more)
- 766.1 Other "heavy for dates" infants, regardless of gestation period
- 766.21 Post-term infant
- 766.22 Prolonged gestation of infant

Codes **766.21, Post-term infant,** and **766.22, Prolonged gestation of infant,** may be assigned based only on the gestational age of the newborn. A specific condition or disorder does not have to be associated with the longer gestational period for these codes to be assigned.

FETAL DISTRESS AND ASPHYXIA

Fetal distress may be defined as signs that indicate a critical response to stress. It implies metabolic abnormalities such as hypoxia and acidosis that affect the functions of vital organs to the point of temporary or permanent injury or even death. Code 768.x is assigned for fetal distress in a liveborn, with the fourth digit indicating when it was first noted as follows:

- 768.2 First noted before onset of labor
- 768.3 First noted during labor and delivery
- 768.4 Unspecified as to time of onset

Asphyxia refers to a decreased level of oxygen delivered to the body or an organ with a buildup of carbon dioxide. Birth asphyxia occurs when an infant does not receive enough oxygen before, during, or just after birth, and it can cause decreased heart rate, decreased blood flow, and low blood pressure leading to cellular and organ damage. When the duration of the asphyxia is brief, the infant can recover without any long-lasting injury. If the time period is longer, it may lead to reversible damage, and when prolonged, irreversible injury. The codes for birth asphyxia are assigned based on whether it is severe (768.5) or mild to moderate (768.6). The codes for birth asphyxia exclude hypoxic-ischemic encephalopathy (HIE), code series 768.70–768.73.

Hypoxic-ischemic encephalopathy (HIE) is a life threatening condition that usually results from damage to the cells of the brain and spinal cord secondary to inadequate oxygen during the birth process. HIE is evidence of acute or subacute brain injury due to asphyxia. It is the most common cause of neurologic disease during the neonatal period and is associated with significant mortality and morbidity. Infants with the mild form of HIE are hyper-alert and overreact to the slightest stimulus. This stage usually lasts 24 hours or less. Infants can recover with normal neurologic function. Moderate HIE is associated with lethargy, clinical seizures, suppressed tendon reflexes, bradycardia, and periodic breathing. This stage may last from two to 14 days. A good neurologic prognosis is seen in infants who can recover within five days. Severe HIE is characterized by stupor to coma, primitive to no reflexes, variable heart rate, and apnea. Half of infants with severe HIE die. Eighty percent of those who survive have mental retardation, epilepsy, cerebral palsy, and learning disabilities. Only 10 percent survive with no neurological disability. The codes for HIE distinguish between mild, moderate, severe, or unspecified, as follows:

- 768.70 Hypoxic-ischemic encephalopathy, unspecified
- 768.71 Mild hypoxic-ischemic encephalopathy
- 768.72 Moderate hypoxic-ischemic encephalopathy
- 768.73 Severe hypoxic-ischemic encephalopathy

Subcategory 763.8 distinguishes abnormalities of heart rate or rhythm from the more serious fetal stress indicators classified in category 768:

- 763.81 Abnormality in fetal heart rate or rhythm before onset of labor
- 763.82 Abnormality in fetal heart rate or rhythm during labor
- 763.83 Abnormality in fetal heart rate or rhythm, unspecified as to time of onset

Codes for fetal distress or abnormality of heart rate and rhythm are assigned to the newborn record only when the condition is specifically identified by the physician. These codes are never assigned on the basis of other information in the newborn record.

Subcategory **770.8, Other respiratory problems after birth,** classifies respiratory problems, including apnea, cyanotic attacks, respiratory failure, hypoxia, and asphyxia, noted after birth. *ICD-9-CM* provides codes to describe other respiratory problems occurring after birth such as respiratory arrest of newborn and hypoxemia of newborn:

- 770.87 Respiratory arrest of newborn
- 770.88 Hypoxemia of newborn

FETAL AND NEWBORN ASPIRATION

Subcategory code **770.1, Fetal and newborn aspiration,** describes meconium aspiration and other types of fetal aspiration as follows:

- 770.10 Fetal and newborn aspiration, unspecified
- 770.11 Meconium aspiration without respiratory symptoms
- 770.12 Meconium aspiration with respiratory symptoms
- 770.13 Aspiration of clear amniotic fluid without respiratory symptoms
- 770.14 Aspiration of clear amniotic fluid with respiratory symptoms
- 770.15 Aspiration of blood without respiratory symptoms
- 770.16 Aspiration of blood with respiratory symptoms
- 770.17 Other fetal and newborn aspiration without respiratory symptoms
- 770.18 Other fetal and newborn aspiration with respiratory symptoms

If applicable, an additional code, 416.8, should be assigned to identify any secondary pulmonary hypertension.

Meconium aspiration in newborns occurs when the fetus gasps while still in the birth canal and inhales meconium-stained amniotic, vaginal, or oropharyngeal fluids. Massive aspiration syndrome is synonymous with massive fetal aspiration. Although meconium aspiration syndrome and massive meconium aspiration are somewhat different conditions with similar clinical presentation and course, code **770.12, Meconium aspiration with respiratory symptoms,** is assigned for both. Code 779.84 would be assigned for meconium staining.

A diagnosis of meconium in liquor is considered an abnormal finding, and code **792.3, Abnormal findings in other body substances, Amniotic fluid,** is assigned. Code 763.84 is assigned for meconium passage during delivery.

Tachypnea, wheezing, and apnea are sometimes present in meconium aspiration; these conditions may resolve over a short period or may take a more prolonged course. In the milder forms of this condition, dyspnea occurs soon after birth, lasts two or three days, and is followed by rapid recovery. Therapy includes bronchoscopic suction of meconium, oxygen administration, humidity control, and prophylactic antibiotics.

HEMOLYTIC DISEASE OF THE NEWBORN

Infants born to Rh-negative mothers often develop hemolytic disease owing to fetal-maternal blood group incompatibility. These conditions are classified in category **773, Hemolytic disease of fetus or newborn, due to isoimmunization.** Note that an indication of incompatibility on a routine cord blood test is not conclusive. Do not assign a code from category 773 on the basis of this finding alone; a diagnosis of isoimmunization or hemolytic disease requires confirmation by a positive Coomb's (direct antibody or direct antiglobulin) test.

NECROTIZING ENTEROCOLITIS

Necrotizing enterocolitis (NEC) is a severe gastrointestinal condition, which involves injury to the bowel, intestinal mucosal disruption associated with enteric feedings, infectious pathogens, and immature immune response. It is a major cause of morbidity and mortality in premature infants. Although NEC commonly affects premature infants with a birth weight of less than 1,500 grams, it can also occur in infants with low risk factors. The exact etiology of NEC is unknown; however, it is thought that the intestine of the premature infant is weakened by too little oxygen and blood flow. The infant then has an increased risk of developing NEC because of difficulty with blood and oxygen circulation, digestion, and fighting infection. When feedings are started and the food moves into the weakened area of the intestinal tract, bacteria from the food can damage the intestinal tissues. These tissues can develop necrosis and perforation, leading to acute abdominal infection. *ICD-9-CM* classifies necrotizing enterocolitis according to stage as follows:

- 777.50 Necrotizing enterocolitis in newborn, unspecified
- 777.51 Stage I necrotizing enterocolitis in newborn
- 777.52 Stage II necrotizing enterocolitis in newborn
- 777.53 Stage III necrotizing enterocolitis in newborn

PERIVENTRICULAR LEUKOMALACIA (PVL)

Periventricular leukomalacia (779.7) occurs with increasing frequency in infants with very low birth weight. It refers to necrosis of white matter adjacent to lateral ventricles with formation of cyst and is a major risk factor for cerebral palsy and other neurological disorders. Although the cause of this condition is still obscure, recent studies have associated it with intrauterine growth retardation, intrauterine infections, and pregnancies involving monozygotic twins. PVL is frequently associated with severe intraventricular hemorrhage, but it is not necessarily the cause of the problem. An additional code is reported when intraventricular hemorrhage (772.10–772.14) is associated with periventricular leukomalacia.

DISORDERS OF STOMACH FUNCTION AND FEEDING PROBLEMS

The *ICD-9-CM* separately classifies vomiting, bilious emesis, failure to thrive, and other feeding problems in newborns. Persistent vomiting in a newborn may be a sign of a very serious condition. These codes are used for newborns experiencing feeding problems (779.31), bilious vomiting (779.32), other vomiting (779.33), and failure to thrive (779.34) and are only assigned up to the 28th day of life. Codes in the main classification are used for infants and children older than 28 days. For example: A 10-day-old baby presents for weight recheck and feeding problems. Code **V20.32, Health supervision for newborn 8 to 28 days old,** is assigned, along with code **779.31, Feeding problems in newborn.**

OBSERVATION AND EVALUATION OF NEWBORNS AND INFANTS

A code from category **V29, Observation and evaluation of newborns for suspected condition not found,** is assigned when a healthy newborn or infant is evaluated for a suspected condition that is found not to be present when study is complete. These codes may be assigned as an additional code along with a code from categories V30 through V39 when the newborn is further evaluated during the hospital episode in which birth occurred.

A code from category V29 may also be assigned as the principal diagnosis for a later readmission or encounter when a code from V30 through V37 no longer applies. It is used only for healthy newborns and infants for whom no reportable condition is identified after study and is assigned only during the perinatal period of 28 days. When the newborn presents signs or symptoms of a suspected problem, or when a definite condition is identified, a code for the symptom or condition is assigned; a code from V29 is not assigned. For example:

- The physician was concerned that a newborn with a drug-dependent mother may have been adversely affected. Drug screens were carried out on the newborn, and the newborn was placed in the intensive care nursery temporarily for closer observation of potential withdrawal symptoms. Drug screens were negative. Codes **V30.00, Single liveborn,** without mention of cesarean delivery, and **V29.8, Observation for other specified suspected condition,** are assigned.

- A newborn infant was readmitted two days after discharge because of slight cyanosis and the possibility of a perinatal respiratory problem. Complete workup disclosed no problem, and the newborn was discharged without any diagnosis having been established. Code **V29.2, Observation for suspected respiratory condition,** is assigned as the principal diagnosis.
- A newborn infant was readmitted two days after discharge because of cyanosis and the possibility of a perinatal respiratory problem. The infant was diagnosed as having type I respiratory distress syndrome. Code **769, Respiratory distress syndrome,** is assigned. No code from category V29 should be assigned.

Although ordinarily no additional code is assigned when V29 is the principal diagnosis, codes can be assigned for a perinatal or congenital condition that requires continuing therapy or monitoring during the stay. Codes for congenital conditions that do not receive further evaluation or therapeutic treatment are not assigned when a newborn is admitted for observation. It would be inappropriate to assign codes in category V89, Suspected maternal and fetal conditions not found, for the newborn. This code category is only reported on the maternal record.

INFECTIONS ORIGINATING DURING THE PERINATAL PERIOD

Many infections specific to the perinatal period are considered to be congenital and may be classified in chapter 15 of *ICD-9-CM* when they are acquired before birth via the umbilicus (for example, rubella) or during birth (for example, herpes simplex). Codes are located by referring to the main term for the infection and then identifying subterms, such as "neonatal," "newborn," "congenital," or "maternal," affecting fetus or newborn. Certain perinatal infections (for example, congenital syphilis), however, may appear in chapter 1 of *ICD-9-CM,* Infections and Parasitic Diseases.

Infections that occur after birth but appear during the 28-day perinatal period may or may not be classified in chapter 15. When none of the subterms mentioned above are listed, the usual infection code is assigned. If an infection does not appear for a week or more after birth, the record should be reviewed to see whether there is any indication that it may be due to exposure to the infection rather than being congenital. Clarification should be sought from the physician when the record is not completely clear.

If a newborn has sepsis, assign code **771.81, Septicemia [sepsis] of newborn.** An additional code is assigned to identify the specific infection or the causal organism. A code from category **038, Septicemia,** should not be used on a newborn record. Code 771.81 describes the sepsis. Assign additional codes to identify severe sepsis (995.92) and any associated acute organ dysfunction (i.e., acute renal failure, acute respiratory failure, hepatic failure, septic shock, and so on), if applicable.

As mentioned in chapter 10 of this handbook, ELISA or Western blot tests of newborns with HIV-positive mothers are often positive. This result usually indicates the antibody status of the mother rather than that of the newborn. Code **795.71, Nonspecific serologic evidence of human immunodeficiency virus** (HIV), is assigned to the newborn chart because the HIV antibodies can cross the placenta into the newborn and may persist for as long as 18 months, producing a false positive test result in the newborn. The newborn may later lose these antibodies, which means that there was never any actual HIV infection.

MATERNAL CONDITIONS AFFECTING THE FETUS OR NEWBORN

Codes from categories 760 through 763 are assigned only on the newborn's record and only when the maternal condition is the cause of morbidity or mortality in the newborn. Unless there is an adverse effect, no code from this series is assigned. The fact that the mother has a related medical condition or has experienced a complication of pregnancy, labor, or delivery does not warrant assignment of a code from these categories on the newborn's record. For example:

- Term birth, living child, mother diabetic, delivered by cesarean section, is coded as V30.01. No code from the series 760 through 763 is assigned because the medical record does not document a problem affecting the newborn.
- Newborn delivered of mother addicted to cocaine showed no sign of dependence, but a drug screen was positive. In this case, code **760.75, Noxious influence affecting fetus or newborn, via placenta or breast milk, cocaine,** is assigned as an additional code on the newborn's record.
- A newborn was admitted following cesarean delivery and was diagnosed with hypermagnesemia. The provider documented that the infant had developed hypermagnesemia due to the mother's treatment with magnesium sulfate for pregnancy-related eclampsia prior to delivery. Assign codes **775.5, Other transitory neonatal electrolyte disturbances,** and **760.79, Noxious influences affecting fetus or newborn via placenta or breast milk, Other.**

When a specific condition in the infant that resulted from the mother's condition is identified, a code for that condition is assigned rather than a code from categories 760 through 763. For example, infants born to diabetic mothers sometimes experience a transient abnormally low blood glucose level (hypoglycemia), classified as **775.0, Syndrome of infant of a diabetic mother.** Others may have a transient diabetic state (hyperglycemia), sometimes referred to as pseudodiabetes, which is coded as **775.1, Neonatal diabetes mellitus.**

When these fetal or newborn conditions affect the management of the mother, codes 655.x and 656.x are assigned on the maternal record.

SURGICAL OPERATION ON MOTHER AND FETUS

Codes in subcategory 760.6, Surgical operation on mother and fetus, are used to capture newborns affected by amniocentesis, in utero procedures, surgery performed on the mother during pregnancy, and other maternal factors unrelated to the current pregnancy (i.e., mother's history of surgery not associated with pregnancy). These codes are only assigned on the newborn's record. If the management of the pregnancy is affected because of complications of in utero surgery, assign the appropriate code from category 679, Complications of in utero procedures, on the mother's record. Obstetric codes from chapter 11 should not be used on the newborn's record.

Specific codes for newborns affected by the above factors are as follows:

- 760.61 Newborn affected by amniocentesis
- 760.62 Newborn affected by other in utero procedure
- 760.63 Newborn affected by other surgical operations on mother during pregnancy
- 760.64 Newborn affected by previous surgical procedure on mother not associated with pregnancy

ENDOCRINE AND METABOLIC DISTURBANCES SPECIFIC TO THE FETUS AND NEWBORN

ICD-9-CM provides codes to describe acidosis of newborn and other neonatal endocrine and metabolic disturbances. Causes of respiratory acidosis include, but are not limited to, asphyxia, obstruction to the respiratory tract, respiratory distress syndrome, pneumonia, pulmonary edema, and/or apnea. Metabolic acidosis may be caused by renal failure, septicemia, hypoxia, hypothermia, hypotension, cardiac failure, dehydration, electrolyte disturbances, hyperglycemia, anemia, intraventricular hemorrhage, and/or metabolic disorders. The underlying cause of acidosis must be treated in order to correct the problem. The following codes are used for acidosis of a newborn and other neonatal endocrine and metabolic disturbances:

- 775.81 Other acidosis of newborn
- 775.89 Other neonatal endocrine and metabolic disturbances

INFANTILE COLIC

Code **789.7, Colic,** is assigned for infantile colic. Assign code **789.0x, Abdominal pain,** for colic in an adult or child more than 12 months old. A colicky baby is a healthy, well-fed baby who cries more than three hours a day, three days a week, for more than three weeks. The crying usually occurs at about the same time every day for no apparent reason and may be intense, with the baby having clenched fists and tensed abdominal muscles. The baby may be inconsolable. There is no known cause for colic. It may last from the first few weeks of birth through four months of age.

APPARENT LIFE THREATENING EVENT

Apparent life threatening event (ALTE) refers to an episode that may be characterized by any of the following signs: apnea, cyanosis, changes in muscle tone, and/or choking or gagging. It was previously referred to as near-miss sudden infant death syndrome (SIDS) or aborted crib death, but these terms should not be used because they imply an association between ALTE and SIDS. Code **799.82, Apparent life threatening event in infant,** is assigned for ALTE in a newborn or infant.

Because of the wide variety of presentations of the ALTE episode, signs and symptoms may be coded as additional diagnoses when:

- No confirmed or identifiable cause of the ALTE has been established, or
- When signs and symptoms are not associated routinely with the confirmed cause of the ALTE, or
- When the reporting of signs and symptoms provides additional information about the cause of the ALTE

ROUTINE VACCINATION OF NEWBORNS

Newborns are vaccinated shortly after birth against hepatitis B and varicella. When the need for vaccination is indicated during the newborn stay, codes V05.3 for hepatitis B and V05.4 for varicella may be assigned. If the newborn's vaccination is not administered because of parental refusal, assign code **V64.05, Vaccination not carried out because of caregiver refusal.** Code **99.55, Prophylactic administration of vaccine against other diseases,** would be assigned for the vaccination performed.

HEALTH SUPERVISION OF INFANT OR CHILD

Category **V20, Health supervision of infant or child,** is assigned for routine encounters of infants and children when no problem has been identified. Code **V20.2, Routine infant or child health check,** is assigned for a routine examination of an infant older than 28 days (e.g., well-baby visit) or for a routine office visit for a child. Code V20.31 is used for newborns under eight days old and code V20.32 is for newborns eight to 28 days old. Code V20.32 includes newborn weight check. If any vaccinations are administered during any of these routine examinations, assign also the appropriate prophylactic vaccine V code. Codes V20.2, V20.31, or V20.32 would not be assigned for a hospital admission.

Review Exercise 23.1

Code the following diagnoses and procedures as they would be assigned to a newborn's record. Presume that all births occurred in the hospital unless stated otherwise.

	Code(s)
1. Term birth, living male, cesarean delivery, with hemolytic disease due to ABO isoimmunization Newborn	V30.01 773.1
2. Term birth, living child Physiological neonatal jaundice Newborn	V30.00 774.6
3. Normal, full-term female, spontaneous delivery Congenital left hip subluxation Newborn	V30.00 754.32
4. Newborn, male, premature (1,400 grams) Hyaline membrane disease	V30.00 765.15 765.20 769
5. Term birth, living male Ophthalmitis of the newborn due to maternal gonococcal infection Newborn	V30.00 098.40
6. Near-term birth, living male, delivered by cesarean section with neonatal hypoglycemia Newborn	V30.01 775.6

Review Exercise 23.1 *(continued)*

7. Term birth, living child Intrauterine growth retardation	Newborn	V30.00 764.90
8. Premature birth, living female infant (1,850 grams) Withdrawal syndrome in infant due to maternal heroin addiction	Newborn	V30.00 765.17 765.20 779.5
9. Term birth, twin, with fracture of right clavicle during birth (mate stillborn)	Newborn	V32.00 767.2
10. Five-year-old child with Erb's palsy secondary to birth trauma		767.6
11. Infant with hemolytic disease due to Rh isoimmunization (patient received by transfer from other facility)		773.0
Phototherapy		99.83
12. Patient born in Community Hospital, with erythroblastosis fetalis due to ABO incompatibility; transferred immediately after birth to intensive care nursery at University Hospital for exchange transfusion and further care	Newborn	
a. Codes for Community Hospital stay		V30.00 773.1
b. Codes for University Hospital stay		773.1 99.01
13. Normal, male infant, delivered by cesarean when fetal distress was noted early in labor Fetal distress due to cord compression	Newborn	V30.01 768.3 762.5

Review Exercise 23.1 *(continued)*

14.	Newborn born on the way to the hospital and admitted directly to newborn nursery Anemia due to acute blood loss from umbilical stump		V30.1 776.5 772.3
15.	Term birth with severe sepsis due to *E. coli* caused by amnionitis	Newborn	V30.00 771.81 762.7 995.92 041.4
16.	Term birth, delivered with meconium aspiration syndrome due to prolonged labor, first stage Cord around neck of infant two times	Newborn	V30.00 770.12 763.89 762.5
17.	Term birth, living male, with partial facial paralysis	Newborn	V30.00 767.5
18.	Premature infant (1,300 grams) transferred from Community Hospital to intensive care nursery at University Hospital for supervision of weight gain	Newborn	765.15 765.20
19.	Newborn twins, #1 delivered in parking lot of hospital, #2 delivered after admission of mother	Newborn	#1: V31.1 #2: V31.00
20.	Term birth, living child; mother known to be a chronic alcoholic; newborn placed in intensive care nursing for observation for possible alcohol-related problems; none found	Observation Newborn	V30.00 V29.8
21.	Routine visit to well-baby clinic for checkup; healthy 14-day-old infant		V20.32

Coding of Circulatory System Diseases and Neoplastic Diseases

Diseases of the Circulatory System

CHAPTER **24**

CHAPTER OVERVIEW

- Circulatory disorders are classified in chapter 7 of *ICD-9-CM*.
- Rheumatic fever is classified with and without rheumatic heart disease.
- Ischemic heart disease is a general term for conditions affecting the myocardium.
  - — Myocardial infarctions are classified with a fourth digit to indicate the wall involved. They are also classified as to whether there is an ST-segment elevation. A fifth digit is used to indicate episode of care.
  - — The code for intermediate coronary syndrome includes a range of anginas.
  - — The conditions included in the category for "other forms of heart disease" include atherosclerosis.
- If a patient is admitted with stable angina (currently a rare practice), the underlying cause is the principal diagnosis.
- There are two main categories of heart failure—systolic and diastolic.
  - — A fifth digit specifies the type of failure.
  - — It is further classified by left- and right-sided failure.
- Cardiac arrest is assigned as a principal diagnosis only when a patient is pronounced dead before the underlying cause can be identified.
- An aneurysm is diagnosed and then classified according to its location.
  - — Sometimes a term is used to describe its appearance.
  - — A term may also describe its etiology.
- Nontraumatic conditions affecting the cerebral arteries are coded together.
  - — These include strokes.
  - — A fourth and fifth digit provide codes for the late effects of strokes.
- Hypertension is classified:
  - — By type (primary or secondary)
  - — By nature (benign, malignant, or unspecified)
- Hypertension can be paired with heart disease, chronic kidney disease, or both.
- Procedures for treating these conditions are varied and appear throughout this chapter of the handbook.

LEARNING OUTCOMES

After studying this chapter you should be able to:

- Classify the disorders related to the heart and the rest of the circulatory system.
- Distinguish between the different conditions regarded as ischemic heart disease.
- Classify heart failure by category and location.
- Code for a variety of procedures involving the circulatory system and the heart.

TERMS TO KNOW

Diastolic heart failure
occurs when the heart has a problem relaxing between contractions to allow enough blood into the ventricles

Systolic heart failure
occurs when the ability of the heart to contract decreases

Thrombophlebitis of a vein
a condition indicated by a clot that has become inflamed

Thrombosis of a vein
a condition indicated by the forming of a clot

REMEMBER . . . The range of circulatory disorders is broad and complex, requiring close attention to instructional terms.

INTRODUCTION

Chapter 7 of *ICD-9-CM* classifies circulatory disorders except for those that have been reclassified to chapter 11 (obstetrical conditions) or to chapter 14 (congenital anomalies). This chapter covers a broad range of conditions, many of which are commonly seen for patients admitted to acute care hospitals. Because these are complex disorders and many are interrelated, it is particularly important for the coder to be alert to all instructional terms.

FIGURE 24.1 Major Vessels of the Arterial System

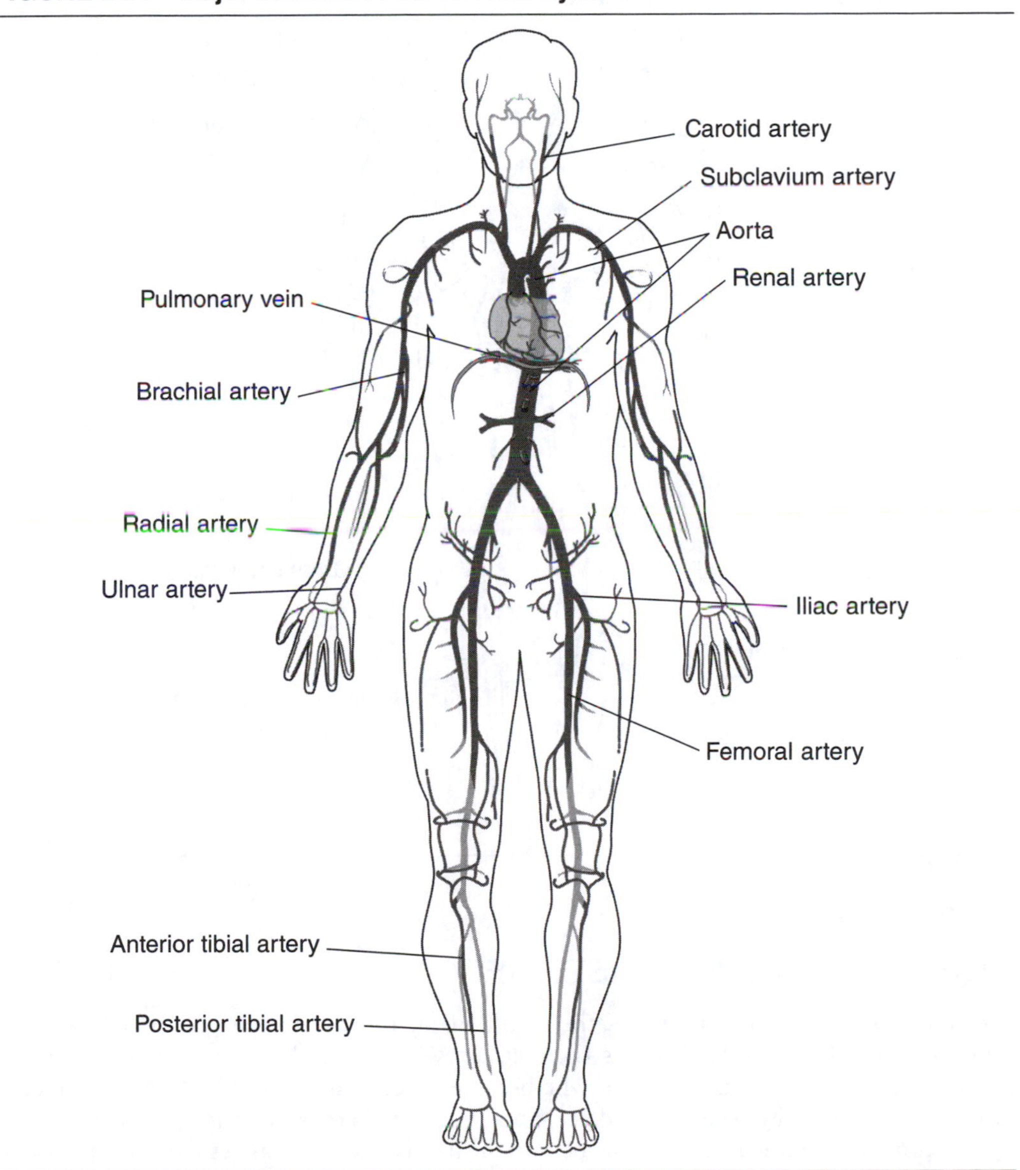

FIGURE 24.2 Major Vessels of the Venous System

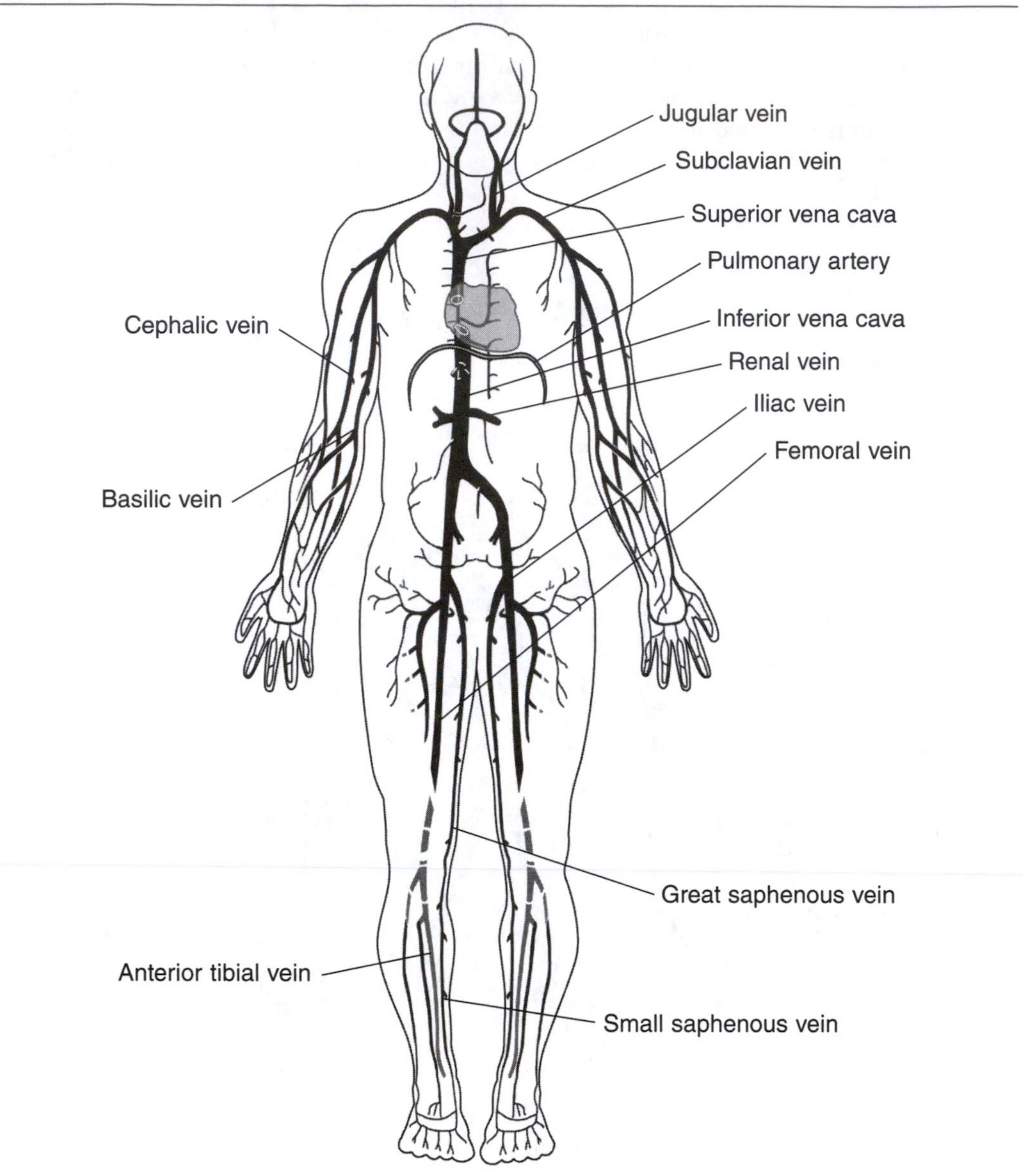

RHEUMATIC HEART DISEASE

Rheumatic heart disease occurs as the result of an infection with group A hemolytic *Streptococcus*. *ICD-9-CM* classifies rheumatic fever with and without rheumatic heart disease. The first axis distinguishes whether the fever is acute (390–392) or quiescent (393–398.99), and the second axis determines whether there is heart involvement.

Chronic rheumatic heart disease includes heart disease that has resulted from a previously active rheumatic infection. The heart valves are most often involved. *ICD-9-CM* presumes that certain mitral valve disorders of unspecified etiology are rheumatic in origin. When the diagnostic statement includes more than one condition affecting the mitral valves, one of which is presumed to be rheumatic, all are classified as rheumatic. For example:

- Mitral valve stenosis 394.0
- Mitral valve insufficiency 424.0
- Mitral valve stenosis and insufficiency 394.2

In these examples the mitral valve stenosis is presumed to be of rheumatic origin, but the mitral valve insufficiency is not. In the third example, the combination code presumes both to be rheumatic because the stenosis is presumed to be rheumatic.

ICD-9-CM presumes that a disorder affecting both the mitral and aortic valves is rheumatic in origin. Otherwise, the aortic condition is classified as rheumatic only when specifically stated as such. Examples follow:

- Aortic valve insufficiency 424.1
- Mitral valve insufficiency with aortic valve insufficiency 396.3
- Aortic valve stenosis 424.1
- Rheumatic aortic stenosis 395.0
- Mitral stenosis and aortic stenosis 396.0

A diagnosis of heart failure in a patient who has rheumatic heart disease is classified as **398.91, Rheumatic heart failure,** unless the physician specifies a different cause. However, do not make an assumption that congestive heart failure is rheumatic in nature.

FIGURE 24.3 The Interior of the Heart

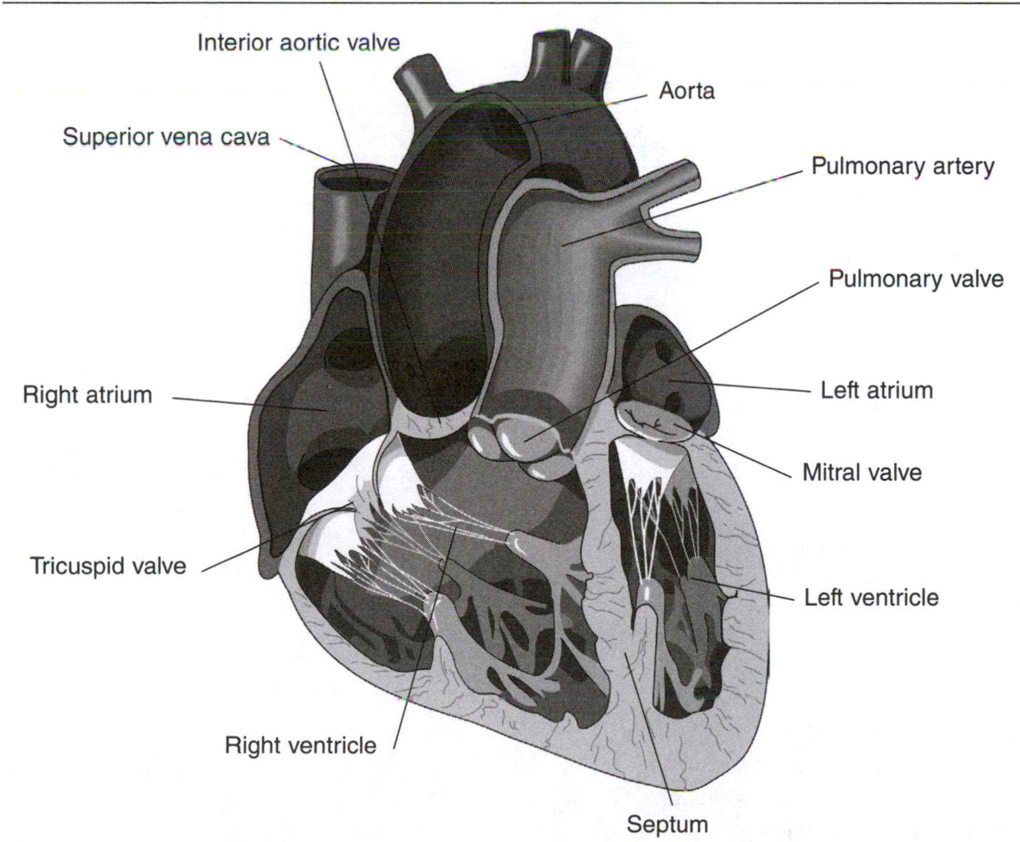

Unless *ICD-9-CM* directs the coder to assign the code for "rheumatic," it is inappropriate to assign a code for rheumatic congestive heart failure. For example:

- End-stage congestive heart failure due to rheumatic heart disease and dilated cardiomyopathy with mitral valve insufficiency 398.91 + 425.4 + 394.1
- Congestive heart failure, status post aortic valve replacement, and currently has severe mitral valve regurgitation, tricuspid valve regurgitation, and a history of aortic valve stenosis status post valve replacement 428.0 + 424.0 + 397.0 + V43.3

Exercise 24.1

Code the following diagnoses.

	Code(s)
1. Mitral regurgitation	424.0
2. Mitral valve stenosis with congestive heart failure	394.0 428.0
3. Severe mitral stenosis and mild aortic insufficiency	396.1
4. Aortic and mitral insufficiency Atrial fibrillation	396.3 427.31
5. Mitral insufficiency, congenital	746.6
6. Mitral valve insufficiency with aortic regurgitation	396.3
7. Chronic aortic and mitral valve insufficiency, rheumatic, with acute congestive heart failure due to rheumatic heart disease	398.91 396.3

ISCHEMIC HEART DISEASE

Ischemic heart disease is the general term for a number of disorders affecting the myocardium caused by a decrease in the blood supply to the heart due to coronary insufficiency. The insufficiency is usually caused by deposits of atheromatous material in the epicardial portions of the coronary artery that progressively obstruct its branches so that the lumen of the arteries become either partially or completely occluded. Other common terms for ischemic heart disease are arteriosclerotic heart disease (ASHD), coronary ischemia, coronary artery disease, and coronary arteriosclerosis (atherosclerosis).

Ischemic heart disease is classified in categories 410 through 414 as follows:

- Acute myocardial infarction 410
- Other acute and subacute forms of ischemic heart disease 411
- Old (healed) myocardial infarction 412
- Angina pectoris 413
- Other forms of chronic ischemic heart disease 414

Myocardial Infarction

Acute myocardial infarction is an acute ischemic condition that ordinarily appears following prolonged myocardial ischemia. It is usually precipitated by an occlusive coronary thrombosis at the site of an existing arteriosclerotic stenosis. Although ischemic heart disease is a progressive disorder, it is often silent for long periods with no clinical manifestations, then appears suddenly in an acute form without any intervening symptoms having been experienced.

A myocardial infarction described as acute or with a duration of eight weeks or less is classified in category **410, Acute myocardial infarction,** with a fourth digit indicating the wall involved. Codes 410.0x through 410.6x identify transmural infarctions; code 410.7x identifies subendocardial infarctions that do not extend through the full thickness of the myocardial wall. Diagnostic statements do not always mention the affected wall, but this information can almost always be found in the electrocardiographic report. A code from subcategory **410.9, Myocardial infarction, unspecified site,** should not be assigned unless no information regarding the site is documented in the medical record. Myocardial infarctions can also be classified according to whether there is ST-segment elevation (codes 410.0–410.6 and 410.8) or non-ST-segment elevation (code 410.7). If there is no information regarding whether there is ST elevation or non-ST elevation, or information regarding the site of the myocardial infarction, coders should assign code 410.9. If a myocardial infarction is documented as nontransmural or subendocardial, but the site is provided, it is still coded as a subendocardial MI. If a non-ST elevation myocardial infarction (NSTEMI) evolves to ST-elevation myocardial infarction (STEMI), assign the code for the STEMI. If STEMI converts to NSTEMI due to thrombolytic therapy, assign the code for STEMI. Be careful to note that these codes are used for documented acute myocardial infarctions and should not be confused with abnormal findings on electrocardiograms of ST-segment elevation.

A fifth-digit subclassification is provided for category 410 to indicate whether the current admission is the initial episode of care or a subsequent one for the same infarction. Note that the significant terms are "initial" and "subsequent," not "acute" and "chronic." Fifth digit 0, episode of care unspecified, is assigned only when the medical record does not contain sufficient information for a more specific assignment. Although physicians do not ordinarily use the terms "initial" or "subsequent" in the diagnostic statement, it is safe to consider an admission for infarction as the initial episode of care when the history makes no mention of a previous infarction.

Fifth digit 1 indicates the initial (first) episode of care for an infarction. It is used in both the first hospital to which a patient is admitted as well as to any other acute care facility to which the patient is transferred without an intervening discharge. For example, if a patient is admitted to Hospital A for an initial episode of care for an acute anteroseptal myocardial infarction, transferred to Hospital B for further diagnostic workup or therapy, and then transferred back to Hospital A without being discharged from acute care, code **410.11, Acute myocardial infarction, of other anterior wall, initial episode of care,** would be assigned for all three admissions.

Fifth digit 2, subsequent episode of care, is assigned when the patient is admitted for further care of the cardiac condition any time during the first eight weeks after the infarction occurred. Myocardial infarction described as chronic or with a duration of more than eight weeks is classified as **414.8, Other specified forms of chronic ischemic heart disease.**

Patients sometimes experience a second infarction involving another wall during a hospital admission for an acute myocardial infarction. In this case, both infarctions are coded according to the sites involved.

An associated postinfarction hypotension is sometimes experienced by patients with acute myocardial infarction. In this situation, the code for the infarction is sequenced first, with an additional code of **458.8, Other specified hypotension.**

Evolving Infarction

An evolving myocardial infarction sometimes precipitates right ventricular failure that progresses to congestive heart failure. The patient may then be admitted because of this precursor condition, which then progresses to an acute myocardial infarction. After study, the principal diagnosis in this situation is the infarction, with an additional code assigned for the heart failure. Additional codes should also be assigned for any mention of cardiogenic shock, ventricular arrhythmia, and fibrillation. For example:

- Congestive heart failure with acute myocardial infarction of anterolateral wall with ventricular fibrillation 410.01 + 428.0 + 427.41

Exercise 24.2

Code the following diagnoses; do not code procedures.

	Code(s)
1. A patient felt well until around 10 p.m., when he began having severe chest pain, which continued to increase in severity. He was brought to the emergency department by ambulance. There was no previous history of cardiac disease, but the EKG showed an acute anterolateral myocardial infarction, and the patient was admitted immediately for further care.	410.01
2. A patient with compensated congestive heart failure on Lasix began to have extreme difficulty in breathing and was brought to the emergency department, where he was found to be in congestive failure. Because it was felt that an impending infarction was possible, a PTCA was carried out, but the patient went on to have an acute inferolateral infarction.	410.21 428.0

Exercise 24.2 (*continued*)

3. A patient was admitted with acute anterior myocardial infarction with no history of previous infarction or previous care for this episode. During the hospital stay, he also experienced an acute anterolateral infarction.	410.11 410.01
4. A patient was admitted to Community Hospital on 3/3 with severe chest pain, which was identified as an acute anterolateral wall infarction (no history of earlier care). Patient was transferred to University Hospital later on 3/3 for angioplasty and returned to Community Hospital on 3/6 to continue recovery. Patient was discharged on 3/8.	
First admission to Community Hospital	410.01
Transfer to University Hospital	410.01
Transfer back to Community Hospital	410.01
5. The patient in the previous situation was readmitted to Community Hospital on 3/12 because he was having severe chest pains. Extension of the infarction was suspected but ruled out.	410.02

If the infarction is described as old or healed, the coder should review the medical record to determine whether the infarction is actually old and/or healed or whether the diagnosis refers to a more recent infarction still under care. A diagnosis of old myocardial infarction is usually made on the basis of electrocardiographic findings or some other investigation in a patient who is not experiencing symptoms. Code **412, Old myocardial infarction,** is essentially a history code, even though it is not included in the V-code chapter of *ICD-9-CM*. It should not be assigned when current ischemic heart disease is present and should be assigned as an additional code only when it has some significance for the current episode of care.

Other Acute and Subacute Ischemic Heart Disease

Code **411.1, Intermediate coronary syndrome,** includes conditions described as unstable angina, crescendo angina, preinfarction angina, accelerated angina, and impending myocardial infarction. These conditions occur after less exertion than angina pectoris; the pain is more severe and is less easily relieved by nitroglycerin. Without treatment, unstable angina often progresses to acute myocardial infarction.

Code 411.1 is designated as the principal diagnosis only when the underlying condition is not identified and there is no surgical intervention. Patients with severe coronary arteriosclerosis and unstable angina may be admitted for cardiac bypass surgery or a percutaneous coronary angioplasty to prevent further progression to infarction. In such cases, the code for coronary arteriosclerosis (414.0x) is assigned as the principal diagnosis, with an additional code for the unstable angina. Examples of appropriate coding follow:

- A patient was admitted with unstable angina and underwent right and left heart catheterization, which showed coronary arteriosclerosis. A coronary bypass procedure was recommended, but the patient felt he needed some time to think it over and to discuss it with his family. For this admission, the coronary arteriosclerosis (414.0x) is the principal diagnosis, with an additional code for the unstable angina.

- A patient was admitted with unstable angina and a history of myocardial infarction five years ago. She was treated with IV nitroglycerin, and the angina subsided by the end of the first hospital day. No other complications were noted, and no additional diagnostic studies were carried out. In this case, the unstable angina is the principal diagnosis.

A diagnosis of acute ischemic heart disease or acute myocardial ischemia does not always indicate an infarction. It is often possible to prevent infarction by means of surgery and/or the use of thrombolytic agents if the patient is treated promptly. If there is occlusion or thrombosis of the artery without infarction, code **411.81, Acute coronary occlusion without myocardial infarction,** is assigned. Code **411.89, Other acute and subacute forms of ischemic heart disease,** includes coronary insufficiency and subendocardial ischemia.

Postmyocardial Infarction Syndrome

Patients with acute myocardial infarction sometimes experience postmyocardial infarction syndrome (411.0) or angina described as postinfarction angina. Postmyocardial infarction, also called Dressler's syndrome, is a pericarditis characterized by fever, leukocytosis, pleurisy, pleural effusion, joint pains, and occasionally pneumonia. Except for these two conditions, no code from category 411 is assigned with a code from category 410.

Exercise 24.3

Code the following diagnoses.

	Code(s)
1. Acute myocardial infarction, inferolateral wall (initial care) Third-degree atrioventricular block	410.21 426.0
2. Acute myocardial infarction of inferoposterior wall (initial) Congestive heart failure Hypertension	410.31 428.0 401.9
3. Impending myocardial infarction (crescendo angina) resulting in occlusion of coronary artery	411.81
4. Acute coronary insufficiency	411.89

Chronic Ischemic Heart Disease

Category **414, Other forms of chronic heart disease,** includes such conditions as coronary atherosclerosis, chronic coronary insufficiency, myocardial ischemia, and aneurysm. Diagnoses of coronary artery disease or coronary heart disease without any further qualification are too vague to be coded accurately; the physician should be asked to provide a more specific diagnosis. Code **414.9, Unspecified chronic ischemic heart disease,** should rarely be assigned in an acute care hospital setting.

Code **414.0x, Coronary atherosclerosis,** includes conditions described as arteriosclerotic heart disease, coronary arteriosclerosis, coronary stricture, and coronary sclerosis or atheroma. A fifth-digit subclassification indicates the nature of the coronary artery involved. For example:

- Native coronary artery 414.01
- Autologous vein bypass graft 414.02
- Nonautologous biological bypass graft 414.03
- Artery bypass graft, including internal mammary artery 414.04
- Native coronary artery of transplanted heart 414.06
- Bypass graft (artery) (vein) of transplanted heart 414.07
- Unspecified type of bypass graft 414.05
- Unspecified type of vessel, native or graft 414.00

Physicians rarely include information regarding the type of graft in the diagnostic statement, but it is almost always available in the medical record. If the medical record makes it clear that there has been no previous bypass surgery, code **414.01, Coronary atherosclerosis of native coronary arteries,** can be assigned. If there is a history of previous bypass, code 414.02, 414.03, or 414.04 should be assigned when information indicating the material used in the bypass is available. Note that arteriosclerosis of a bypass vessel is not classified as a postoperative complication.

When atherosclerosis of a native coronary artery in a transplanted heart is identified in the diagnostic statement, code 414.06 would be assigned. Code **414.07, Coronary atherosclerosis of bypass graft (artery) (vein) of transplanted heart,** is assigned to identify atherosclerosis of a bypass graft in a transplanted heart.

A chronic total occlusion involves complete blockage of a coronary artery (414.2) that has been present for an extended period (e.g., months or years). The chronic total occlusion develops when plaque accumulates in the artery, leading to a substantial reduction in blood flow and the development of bypass collateral blood flow. Although well-developed collaterals do not completely compensate for diminished blood flow, collaterals help to preserve the viability of the myocardium and prevent resting ischemia. Patients with chronic total occlusion who present with a change in anginal status that is directly related to physical activity have an increased risk of myocardial infarction or death. Chronic total occlusion of a coronary artery may be treated with angioplasty (00.66) or stent placement, usually a drug-eluting stent (36.07). These types of obstructions are more resistant to guidewire crossing and are more difficult to treat than other types of coronary stenosis. Advanced methods in treatment have been developed to specifically handle chronic total coronary occlusions.

Code 414.2 should be used as an additional code assignment if coronary atherosclerosis (code series 414.00–414.07) is present with a chronic total occlusion of a coronary artery. Code 414.2 should not be assigned if the patient is diagnosed with acute coronary occlusion with or without myocardial infarction.

Code **414.3, Coronary atherosclerosis due to lipid rich plaque,** describes coronary atherosclerosis with the exact composition of the atherosclerotic plaque. The presence of lipid-rich atherosclerotic plaque can precipitate an acute coronary event. The identification of plaque as lipid- or non-lipid-rich is clinically significant because this information can assist interventional cardiologists in determining the correct treatment (i.e., drug-eluting stent or non-drug-eluting stent). Near infrared spectroscopy (38.23) is a new intravascular diagnostic tool that can detect and differentiate lipid-rich atherosclerotic plaque. The appropriate code for the coronary atherosclerosis (414.00–414.07) should be sequenced first, followed by code 414.3 as an additional code assignment.

Code **414.4, Coronary atherosclerosis due to calcified coronary lesion,** is assigned to describe calcified coronary lesions. These types of lesions are different from other ischemic coronary lesions. The deposits of calcium in these lesions present a rigid obstacle that puts patients at increased risk for complications, such as inadequate stent expansion, acute stent thrombosis, and restenosis, when treated by stent and angioplasty.

ANGINA PECTORIS

Angina pectoris (413.9) is an early manifestation of ischemic heart disease, although in rare instances it occurs as a result of congenital abnormalities of the coronary arteries or such conditions as aortic stenosis, valvular insufficiency, aortic syphilis, and Raynaud's phenomenon. It is characterized by chest pain, usually perceived by the patient as a sensation of tightness, squeezing, pressing, choking, burning, heartburn or gas, or an ill-defined discomfort. This type of angina can be produced by anything that increases the oxygen requirements of the myocardium, such as exercise, walking into the wind, cold weather, consumption of a large meal, emotional stress, and elevation of blood pressure. This type of pain is similar to that of unstable angina, but it is less severe, more easily controlled, and usually relieved in a predictable manner, either by rest or the administration of nitroglycerin.

Angina pectoris sometimes occurs even when the patient is at rest, apparently without any stimulation, such as during the night. This condition is referred to as nocturnal or decubitus angina and is classified as 413.0. A variant type that also occurs at rest is known as Prinzmetal angina. Angina described as angiospastic or with coronary spasm at rest is coded to **413.1, Prinzmetal angina.**

In today's health care environment, it is unlikely that a patient would be admitted to the hospital for treatment of stable angina except for the purpose of undergoing diagnostic studies to determine its underlying cause. In this case, the underlying cause, not the stable angina, is sequenced as the principal diagnosis.

Exercise 24.4

Code the following diagnoses and procedures.

	Code(s)
1. Crescendo angina due to coronary arteriosclerosis	414.00 411.1
Right and left cardiac catheterization	37.23
2. Angina pectoris with essential hypertension	413.9 401.9

HEART FAILURE

Heart failure occurs when an abnormality of cardiac function results in the inability of the heart to pump blood at a rate commensurate with the body's needs or the ability to do so only from an abnormal filling pressure. This decrease in blood supply to body tissue results in unmet needs for oxygen as well as in a failure to meet other metabolic requirements. This in turn results in pulmonary and/or systemic circulatory congestion and reduced cardiac output. Precipitating causes of heart failure include cardiac arrhythmias, pulmonary embolism, infections, anemia, thyrotoxicosis, myocarditis, endocarditis, hypertension, and myocardial infarction. All codes for heart failure include any associated pulmonary edema; therefore, no additional code is assigned. A diagnosis of acute pulmonary edema in the absence of underlying heart disease is classified with conditions affecting the respiratory system. (See chapter 15 of this handbook for more information on the respiratory system.)

There are two main categories of heart failure: systolic and diastolic. Systolic heart failure (428.2x) occurs when the ability of the heart to contract decreases. Diastolic heart failure (428.3x) occurs when the heart has a problem relaxing between contractions (diastole) to allow enough blood to enter the ventricles. Fifth digits further specify whether the heart failure is unspecified, acute, chronic, or acute on chronic.

When the diagnostic statement lists congestive heart failure along with either systolic or diastolic heart failure, two codes are required to report the specific type of heart failure: congestive, diastolic, and/or systolic. Congestive heart failure is not an inherent component of systolic or diastolic heart failure. For example:

- A patient is documented as having systolic dysfunction with acute exacerbation of congestive heart failure (CHF). It is coded as acute systolic heart failure with congestive heart failure. Code **428.0, Congestive heart failure, unspecified,** and code **428.23, Systolic heart failure, Acute on chronic,** are assigned. An acute exacerbation of a chronic condition (heart failure) is coded as acute on chronic.

ICD-9-CM's Alphabetic Index provides the following direction for systolic dysfunction with heart failure:

Dysfunction
  systolic 429.9
    with heart failure—*see* Failure, heart

Diastolic or systolic dysfunction without mention of heart failure is indexed to **429.9, Heart disease, unspecified.** It is not appropriate for the coder to assume that a patient is in heart failure when only "diastolic dysfunction" or "systolic dysfunction" is documented.

Heart failure is differentiated clinically by whether the right or left ventricle is primarily affected. Left-sided heart failure (left ventricular failure) is due to the accumulation of excess fluid behind the left ventricle. Code **428.1, Left heart failure,** includes associated conditions such as dyspnea, orthopnea, bronchospasm, and acute pulmonary edema; no additional codes are assigned. Heart failure, unspecified, is coded to 428.9. This is a vague code, however, and an effort should be made to determine whether a code from the series 428.0 through 428.4 would be more appropriate.

Right-sided failure ordinarily follows left-sided failure and is classified in *ICD-9-CM* as congestive heart failure (428.0). This code includes any left-sided failure that is present; therefore, codes 428.0 and 428.1 are not assigned for the same episode of care; code 428.0 takes precedence.

The term "congestive heart failure" (428.0) is often mistakenly used interchangeably with "heart failure." Congestion, pulmonary or systemic fluid build-up, is one feature of heart failure, but it does not occur in all patients.

Hypertensive heart failure with congestive failure is classified in category 402, with code 428.0 assigned as an additional diagnosis. If chronic kidney disease or renal sclerosis (including atrophy of kidney, contracted kidney, renal cirrhosis, or renal fibrosis) is present, a code from category 403 is assigned, and the appropriate code from 585.1–585.6, 585.9 to identify the stage of chronic kidney disease is assigned as an additional diagnosis. If hypertensive heart disease, congestive heart failure, and chronic kidney disease or renal sclerosis are all present, a code from category 404 is used, with code 428.0 and a code from 585.1–585.9. Fifth digits for category 404 indicate with or without heart failure and/or the stage of the chronic kidney disease. Further information in classifying hypertension and other associated conditions is provided later in this chapter.

Compensated, Decompensated, and Exacerbated Heart Failure

When heart failure occurs, the heart muscle commonly develops compensatory mechanisms such as cardiac hypertrophy, raised arterial pressure, ventricular dilation, or increased force of contraction. When this occurs, the heart failure may be described as *compensated*, permitting near-normal function. When these compensatory mechanisms can no longer meet the increased workload, decompensation of the heart function results; this situation is often described as *decompensated* heart failure. Code assignment is not affected by the use of these terms; the code for the type of heart failure is assigned. An exacerbation is defined as an increase in the severity of a disease or any of its symptoms. The terms "exacerbated," and "decompensated" indicate that there has been a flare-up (acute phase) of a chronic condition. For example:

- A patient with a known history of CHF is admitted with an exacerbation of diastolic congestive heart failure. Codes **428.33, Diastolic heart failure, acute on chronic,** and **428.0, Congestive heart failure, unspecified,** are assigned.

CARDIAC TAMPONADE

Cardiac tamponade, also referred to as pericardial tamponade or tamponade (423.3), is the compression of the heart caused by the accumulation of fluid inside the pericardium. Cardiac tamponade is often associated with viral or bacterial pericarditis. This condition typically occurs as a result of chest trauma, heart rupture, dissecting aortic aneurysm, cancer, cardiac surgery, renal failure, and/or acute myocardial infarction. The underlying cause of the tamponade should be coded first, followed by code 423.3.

Cardiac tamponade can be life-threatening if left untreated. The goals of therapy are to improve heart function, relieve symptoms, and treat the tamponade. This can be accomplished with pericardiocentesis (37.0) or creation of a pericardial window (37.12).

For example: A patient developed increased pericardial effusion and underwent pericardiocentesis due to rapid pericardial tamponade. Assign code **423.3, Cardiac tamponade.** For the procedure, assign code **37.0, Pericardiocentesis.**

CARDIOMYOPATHY

Cardiomyopathy (425.x) presents a clinical picture of a dilated heart, flabby heart muscles, and normal coronary arteries.

Common types of cardiomyopathy are those due to the long-term consumption of alcohol (425.5) and those described as congestive or constrictive, which are classified as code **425.4, Other primary cardiomyopathies.**

The symptoms of congestive cardiomyopathy (425.4) are essentially the same as those of congestive heart failure, and the condition is often associated with congestive heart failure. Treatment ordinarily revolves around management of the congestive heart failure, and so the heart failure (428.0–428.43) is designated as the principal diagnosis, with an additional code assigned for the cardiomyopathy.

Code **425.11, Hypertrophic obstructive cardiomyopathy,** is assigned for hypertrophic obstructive cardiomyopathy, and code **425.12, Other hypertrophic cardiomyopathy,** is reserved for hypertrophic cardiomyopathy not described as obstructive. Hypertrophic cardiomyopathy (HCM) is usually an inherited condition in which the heart muscle becomes thick without any obvious cause. Younger people usually present with a severe form of hypertrophic cardiomyopathy that is frequently asymptomatic and a leading cause of sudden cardiac death in young athletes.

Two codes may be required for cardiomyopathy due to other underlying conditions; for example, cardiomyopathy due to amyloidosis is coded **277.30, Amyloidosis, unspecified,** and **425.7, Nutritional and metabolic cardiomyopathy.** The underlying disease, amyloidosis, is sequenced first. Hypertensive cardiomyopathy should be coded to category **402, Hypertensive heart disease,** with an additional code of **425.8, Cardiomyopathy in other diseases classified elsewhere.** Assign first code **359.21, Myotonia atrophica,** with 425.8 as an additional code assignment for cardiomyopathy due to myotonia atrophica.

The term "ischemic cardiomyopathy" is sometimes used to designate a condition in which ischemic heart disease causes diffuse fibrosis or multiple infarction, leading to heart failure with left ventricular dilation. This is not a true cardiomyopathy and is coded to **414.8, Other specified forms of chronic ischemic heart disease,** when no further clarification is provided by the attending physician. A diagnostic statement of ischemic alcoholic cardiomyopathy is assigned to both code **414.8, Other specified forms of chronic ischemic heart disease,** and code **425.5, Alcoholic cardiomyopathy,** because these conditions are not related.

TAKOTSUBO SYNDROME

Takotsubo syndrome is a newly recognized reversible form of left ventricular dysfunction, seen in patients without coronary disease. Code **429.83, Takotsubo syndrome,** is assigned for Takotsubo syndrome, broken-heart syndrome, reversible left ventricular dysfunction following sudden emotional stress, stress-induced cardiomyopathy, and transient left ventricular apical ballooning syndrome. This syndrome is usually precipitated by emotional or physiological stress with sudden onset of chest symptoms, electrocardiographic changes characteristic of myocardial ischemia, transient left ventricular dysfunction, low-grade troponin elevation, and insignificant coronary stenosis by ventriculography. Patients presenting with Takotsubo syndrome are usually monitored and treated for left heart failure, intraventricular obstruction, and/or cardiac arrhythmias, if they develop. Apical ballooning syndrome previously indexed to code **429.89, Other ill-defined heart disease,** is now assigned to code 429.83.

CARDIAC ARREST

Code **427.5, Cardiac arrest,** may be assigned as a principal diagnosis only when a patient arrives at the hospital in a state of cardiac arrest and cannot be resuscitated or is resuscitated briefly and pronounced dead before the underlying cause of the arrest is identified. It may be assigned as a secondary code when cardiac arrest occurs during the hospital episode and the patient is resuscitated (or resuscitation is attempted). In this case, the code for the underlying cause is designated the principal diagnosis, with code 427.5 assigned as an additional code. Note that codes are not assigned for symptoms integral to the condition, such as bradycardia and hypotension. Cardiac arrest that occurs as a complication of surgery is coded as **997.1, Cardiac complications.** Code 669.4x is assigned for cardiac arrest complicating abortion, ectopic pregnancy, or labor and delivery. None of these codes are assigned to indicate that a patient has died. Do not code cardiac arrest to indicate the patient's death.

ANEURYSM

An aneurysm is a localized abnormal dilation of blood vessels. A dissecting aneurysm is one in which blood enters the wall of the artery and separates the layers of the vessel wall. As the aneurysm progresses, tension increases and the aneurysm is likely to rupture, which usually results in death.

Aneurysms are diagnosed primarily according to their location, such as the following:

- Aneurysm of coronary vessels 414.11
- Dissecting aneurysm of abdominal aorta 441.02
- Aneurysm of abdominal aorta with rupture 441.3
- Aneurysm of thoracic artery 441.2
- Ruptured aneurysm of thoracic artery 441.1
- Thoracoabdominal aneurysm 441.7

Occasionally, a term describing the aneurysm's appearance is used, such as "berry aneurysm" (430), or a term may describe its etiology, such as "syphilitic aneurysm of aorta" (093.0) or "traumatic aneurysm" (901.0, 901.2).

An aneurysm of a vessel may be treated by resection with anastomosis (38.3x) or replacement (38.4x), with the fourth digit indicating the vessel involved. Repair is achieved by clipping (39.51) or a variety of other procedures such as electrocoagulation, suture, or wiring (39.52). Several new procedures are now being used for aneurysm repair. Endoluminal endovascular prosthesis is a new technique for transfemoral graft placement and aneurysm exclusion in patients with abdominal aortic aneurysm. This is an alternative to open surgery, is minimally invasive, and avoids laparotomy. Hospital stays are shorter and there is less intensive postoperative management. Another technique is the use of the Corvita endovascular graft for abdominal aortic aneurysm and common iliac aneurysm. Placement of a Vanguard endograft is used for treatment of aortoiliac aneurysmal disease. The following codes are used for endovascular procedures on vessels:

- 39.71 Endovascular implantation of other graft in abdominal aorta
- 39.72 Endovascular repair or occlusion of head and neck vessels
- 39.73 Endovascular implantation of graft in thoracic aorta
- 39.74 Endovascular removal of obstruction from head and neck vessels
- 39.77 Temporary (partial) therapeutic endovascular occlusion of vessel
- 39.78 Endovascular implantation of branching or fenestrated graft(s) in aorta
- 39.79 Other endovascular repair (of aneurysm) of other vessels

Report code 00.58 along with codes 39.71 and 39.73 when intraoperative intra-aneurysm sac pressure monitoring is done in conjunction with an endovascular repair.

Code 36.91 is assigned for repair of an aneurysm of a coronary vessel, and code 37.32 is assigned for excision or repair of an aneurysm of the heart.

Code 39.77 is used for procedures in which the vessel is partially occluded via an endovascular device. This type of procedure is different from other occlusion procedures that completely occlude the vessel or permanently occlude the vessel. For example:

- The patient underwent successful placement of a temporary balloon occlusion catheter into the left internal carotid artery. During the procedure, there was no change in the patient's baseline neurological exam status throughout the 30 minutes of intra-arterial balloon inflation. Assign code **39.77, Temporary (partial) therapeutic endovascular occlusion of vessel,** for the temporary test occlusion.

Code **39.78, Endovascular implantation of branching or fenestrated graft(s) in aorta,** describes placement of a fenestrated endograft in patients who are not anatomical candidates for standard endovascular devices for repair of abdominal aortic aneurysms (AAA). Patients with short or angulated necks; aneurysmal extension into either internal iliac artery; or complex aneurysmal involvement of the juxtarenal, paravisceral, and thoracoabdominal aorta are not ideal candidates for standard endovascular repair.

These newer fenestrated endografts are customized for each individual aneurysm and are designed to extend the proximal sealing zone from the infrarenal segment to the juxta and suprarenal aorta, thereby circumventing the limitation of short or absent aortic necks.

Endovascular embolization uses particulate agents, such as gelfoam, polyvinyl alcohol and spherical embolics, coils, liquid sclerosing agents (such as alcohol and tissue adhesives), and other types of embolic materials. When coils are used, it is also referred to as coil embolization; assign code **39.79, Other endovascular repair of (aneurysm) of other vessels,** for coil embolization. For example:

- A patient had a gelfoam and coil embolization of the right lumbar artery; code 39.79 is assigned.

AORTIC ECTASIA

Aortic ectasia refers to a mild dilation of the aorta that is not defined as an aneurysm; the dilation is usually less than 3 cm in diameter. Patients with aortic ectasia do not have an aortic aneurysm. In *ICD-9-CM,* aortic ectasia is classified as follows:

- Aortic ectasia, unspecified site 447.70
- Thoracic aortic ectasia 447.71
- Abdominal aortic ectasia 447.72
- Thoracoabdominal aortic ectasia 447.73

CEREBROVASCULAR DISORDERS

Acute organic (nontraumatic) conditions affecting the cerebral arteries include hemorrhage, occlusion, and thrombosis and are coded in the 430 through 437 series. Category **433, Occlusion and stenosis of precerebral arteries,** and category **434, Occlusion of cerebral arteries,** use a fifth-digit subclassification to indicate whether there is mention of associated cerebral infarction. Fifth digit 1, indicating the presence of cerebral infarction, is not assigned unless cerebral infarction is clearly documented in the medical record and the physician has indicated a relationship between cerebral artery stenosis or occlusion and the infarction. The coder should never assume that infarction has occurred. Note that these fifth digits apply for the current episode of care only; they do not indicate that the patient has had a cerebral infarction in the past. Code **433.10, Occlusion and stenosis of precerebral arteries, carotid artery, without mention of cerebral infarction,** is used to describe carotid artery stenosis without cerebral infarction. If the documentation describes bilateral carotid artery stenosis, code **433.30, Occlusion and stenosis of precerebral arteries, multiple and bilateral, without mention of cerebral infarction,** is assigned along with code 433.10 to further describe the laterality. Assigning both codes will allow information on both the specific artery involved and the laterality to be captured.

Diagnostic statements often are not specific regarding the site or type of the cerebrovascular condition. When the diagnosis is stated as cerebrovascular accident, CVA, or stroke without any further qualification, it is important for the coder to review the medical record for more definitive information or to consult with the physician. When no further information is available, code **434.91, Cerebral artery occlusion, unspecified, with cerebral infarction,** is assigned for the diagnosis of stroke or CVA to allow for improved uniformity in coding and statistical data.

Code 434.91 is assigned for an aborted CVA when there is no further specification as to the type of CVA. Patients who present with symptoms of an acute cerebrovascular infarction and are treated with tissue plasminogen activator (tPA) have actually suffered a cerebral infarction. Although brain damage may not be demonstrated by CT scan, brain damage would be visible microscopically. The administration of tPA is coded to **99.10, Injection or infusion of thrombolytic agent.** It is effective in treating ischemic stroke caused by blood clots that are blocking blood flow to the brain. It is also effective in treating myocardial infarctions.

Code V45.88 is assigned as an additional code along with code series 433–434 (with a fifth digit of 1), or with code series 410.00–410.92. Code V45.88 captures the information that the patient is status post administration of tPA at a different facility within the past 24 hours prior to admission to the current facility.

Occasionally, a hemorrhage can occur in the brain—in the space where there is tissue death (infarction) due to the thrombolytic therapy (tPA). A cerebral hemorrhage can also occur spontaneously after the original infarct. For example:

- A patient sustained a left frontal cerebral infarction with hemorrhagic conversion. The provider documented that the patient had an acute cerebral infarct and later developed hemorrhagic conversion of the infarct. The provider stated that the hemorrhagic conversion had occurred spontaneously. Assign both code **434.91, Cerebral artery occlusion, unspecified, with cerebral infarction,** and code **431, Intracerebral hemorrhage.**
- A patient was admitted with expressive aphasia due to acute cerebral infarction. The patient was given intravenous (IV) tissue plasminogen activator (tPA) within 4.5 hours of the onset of symptoms, with significant improvement of aphasia. A brain MRI showed acute left temporoparietal infarct with asymptomatic hemorrhagic conversion. The provider stated that the hemorrhagic conversion was caused by the tPA therapy. Assign code **434.91, Cerebral artery occlusion, unspecified, with cerebral infarction,** as the principal diagnosis. Assign code **997.02, Iatrogenic cerebrovascular infarction or hemorrhage,** and code **431, Intracerebral hemorrhage,** for the cerebral hemorrhagic conversion due to the thrombolytic therapy. Code 997.02 is assigned because the hemorrhage resulted from treatment with the thrombolytic agent. Assign code **784.3, Aphasia,** and code **E934.4, Drugs, medicinal and biological substances causing adverse effects in therapeutic use, fibrinolysis-affecting drugs,** as additional diagnoses. Assign code **99.10, Injection or infusion of thrombolytic agent.**

Each component of a diagnostic statement identifying cerebrovascular disease should be coded unless the Alphabetic Index or the Tabular List instructs otherwise. For example:

- Cerebrovascular arteriosclerosis with subarachnoid hemorrhage due to ruptured berry aneurysm 430 + 437.0
- Intracerebral hemorrhage with vasogenic edema 431 + 348.5
- Cerebral amyloid angiopathy 277.39 + 437.9

A new therapy (99.75) is now being used in which a neuroprotective agent is administered directly on nerve cells to minimize ischemic injury, particularly for acute subarachnoid hemorrhage.

In the event of a postoperative stroke, assign code **997.02, Iatrogenic cerebrovascular infarction or hemorrhage.** Assign an additional code to identify the specific type of stroke/cerebrovascular accident. The general coding rule for postoperative complications is that when the complication code does not specifically identify the condition, an additional code should be assigned to more fully explain it.

Conditions classifiable in categories 430 through 437 are reclassified in subcategory **674.0x, Cerebrovascular disorders in the puerperium,** when they occur during pregnancy, childbirth, or the puerperium. Although the code title mentions puerperium, the inclusion note indicates that these conditions are included when they occur any time during the obstetrical experience. Because code 674.0x does not indicate the nature of the cerebrovascular condition, it is appropriate to assign an additional code from chapter 7 of *ICD-9-CM* for greater specificity.

Late Effects of Cerebrovascular Disease

Codes from category **438, Late effect of cerebrovascular disease,** allow for greater specificity in reporting the residual effects of stroke as follows:

- 438.0 Cognitive deficits
- 438.1x Speech and language deficits
- 438.2x Hemiplegia/hemiparesis
- 438.3x Monoplegia of upper limb
- 438.4x Monoplegia of lower limb
- 438.5x Other paralytic syndrome
- 438.6 Alternations of sensations
- 438.7 Disturbances of vision
- 438.8x Other late effects of cerebrovascular disease
- 438.9 Unspecified late effects of cerebrovascular disease

Instructions to use an additional code have been added to 438.5, 438.6, and 438.7 to indicate the specific residual condition. An additional code should also be added to 438.89 to indicate the specific late effect.

Codes from this category are assigned for any remaining deficits when the patient is admitted at a later date. Like other late effect codes, category 438 is assigned only when it is significant for the current episode of care. Code **V12.54, Personal history of transient ischemic attack (TIA), and cerebral infarction without residual deficits,** should be assigned rather than a code from category 438 when the patient has a history of a cerebrovascular infarction (CVA) with no residual conditions, a history of TIA, or a history of prolonged reversible ischemic neurological deficit (PRIND). Codes from category 438 differ from other late effect codes in two ways:

- These codes can be assigned as the principal diagnosis when the purpose of the admission is to deal with the late effect. If the admission is for the purpose of rehabilitation, however, a code from category V57 is assigned as the principal diagnosis with an additional code from category 438.
- These codes can be assigned as additional codes when a new CVA is present and deficits from an earlier episode remain. This distinction permits the identification of those deficits due to the current CVA and those remaining from an earlier episode.

Unlike other late effects, neurological deficits such as hemiplegia and aphasia due to cerebrovascular accidents are often present from the onset of the disease rather than arising after the original condition itself has cleared. Such deficits are frequently transient and are no longer present at discharge; if they have cleared by the time of discharge, codes for the deficits are still assigned. Hemiplegia is not inherent to an acute cerebrovascular accident. Therefore, it should be coded even if the hemiplegia resolves, with or without treatment. The hemiplegia affects the care that the patient receives. Report any neurological deficits caused by a CVA even when they have been resolved at the time of discharge from the hospital. For example, suppose that a patient is admitted because of subarachnoid hemorrhage with associated aphasia and hemiplegia that has cleared by the time of discharge. Even though these deficits have cleared at discharge, the following codes are assigned:

- 430 Subarachnoid hemorrhage
- 784.3 Aphasia
- 342.90 Hemiplegia

Exercise 24.5

Code the following diagnoses.

	Code(s)
1. Occlusion of right internal carotid artery with cerebral infarction with mild hemiplegia resolved before discharge	433.11 342.90
2. Hemiplegia on right (dominant) side due to old cerebral thrombosis	438.21
3. Admission for treatment of new cerebral embolism with cerebral infarction and with aphasia remaining at discharge (patient suffered cerebral embolism one year ago, with residual apraxia and dysphagia) Late	434.11 784.3 438.81 438.82
4. Cerebral thrombosis with right hemiparesis and aphasia still present at discharge	434.00 342.90 784.3
5. Cerebrovascular accident due to cerebral embolism, with infarction	434.11
6. Insufficiency of vertebrobasilar arteries	435.3
7. Admission for rehabilitation because of monoplegia of the right arm and left leg, each affecting dominant side (patient suffered a nontraumatic extradural hemorrhage one month ago) Late	V57.89 438.31 438.41
8. Quadriplegia due to ruptured berry aneurysm five years ago	438.53 344.00

HYPERTENSION

ICD-9-CM classifies hypertension by type (primary or secondary) and nature (benign, malignant, or unspecified). Categories 401 through 404 classify primary hypertension according to a hierarchy of the disease from its vascular origin (401) to the end-organ involvement of the heart (402), chronic kidney disease (403), or heart and chronic kidney disease combined (404). Primary hypertension is also described as essential hypertension, hypertensive vascular disease, or systolic hypertension.

Benign and Malignant Hypertension

Malignant hypertension is an accelerated, severe hypertensive disorder, with progressive vascular damage and a poor prognosis. It is characterized by rapidly rising blood pressure, usually in excess of 140 millimeters of mercury diastolic. Without effective treatment, malignant hypertension can lead to congestive heart failure, hypertensive encephalopathy, intracerebral hemorrhage, uremia, and even death. *ICD-9-CM* includes hypertension described as accelerated or necrotizing in the code for malignant hypertension.

The term "benign hypertension" refers to a relatively mild degree of hypertension of prolonged or chronic duration. Although malignant hypertension is almost always identified in the diagnostic statement, benign hypertension is rarely specified as a diagnosis, perhaps because the term "benign" has a different significance for the physician than it does in the classification system. Hypertension not classified as malignant would rarely be designated as the principal diagnosis, although occasionally a patient may be admitted for careful monitoring while a new medication regimen is being implemented.

Secondary hypertension (405) is the result of some other primary disease. When the condition causing the hypertension can be cured or brought under reasonable control, the secondary hypertension may stabilize or disappear entirely. The underlying cause is sequenced first, followed by the code for the hypertension. For example:

- Hypertension due to systemic lupus erythematosus 710.0 + 405.99
- Acromegaly with secondary hypertension 253.0 + 405.99

Location of Hypertensive Disease Codes

The Alphabetic Index includes a table under the main term **Hypertension** with subterms indexed in the usual manner. Three columns to the right provide codes for the malignant, benign, and unspecified versions of that type of hypertension. For example, a reference to cardiorenal hypertension provides codes for all three types of hypertension, but a reference to accelerated hypertension shows only a code for malignant hypertension because accelerated hypertension is only malignant. Codes should always be verified with the Tabular List and any instructional terms should be noted. There are also subentries for hypertensive and due to hypertension under the main term for certain other conditions.

Diagnostic statements of hypertension frequently include the terms "uncontrolled" or "controlled" or "history of." Hypertension described as "uncontrolled" is coded by its type and nature; *ICD-9-CM* does not have a code to indicate this uncontrolled status. Hypertension described as "controlled" or "history of" hypertension usually refers to an existing hypertension that is under control by means of continuing therapy. The coder should review the medical record to determine whether the hypertension is still under treatment; if so, the appropriate code from categories 401 through 405 should be assigned.

Some providers may document hypertensive urgency without further specification. When only hypertensive urgency is documented, query the provider regarding the specific type of hypertension. If, however, upon clarification the hypertension is still not further specified (e.g., malignant or benign), assign code **401.9, Essential hypertension, Unspecified.** The coder is directed to "See hypertension" when "urgency, hypertensive" is referenced in the index.

HYPERTENSIVE HEART DISEASE

Certain heart conditions are assigned to category **402, Hypertensive heart disease,** when a causal relationship is stated (due to hypertension) or implied (hypertensive). Hypertensive heart disease includes cardiomegaly, cardiovascular disease, myocarditis, and degeneration of the myocardium. Category 402 includes a fifth-digit subclassification that indicates whether heart failure is present. However, an additional code is still required to specify the type of heart failure (428.0–428.43), if known.

A cause-and-effect relationship between hypertension and heart disease cannot be assumed, however, and careful attention must be given to the exact wording of the diagnostic statement. When the diagnostic statement mentions both conditions but does not indicate a causal relationship between them, separate codes are assigned. For example:

- Congestive heart failure due to hypertension 402.91 + 428.0
- Hypertensive heart disease with congestive heart failure 402.91 + 428.0
- Congestive heart failure with hypertension 428.0 + 401.9

A causal relationship is presumed to exist for a cardiac condition when it is associated with another condition classified as hypertensive heart disease. For example:

- Hypertensive myocarditis with congestive heart failure 402.91 + 428.0
- Hypertensive cardiovascular disease with congestive heart failure 402.91 + 428.0

The coder should review the medical record for any reference to the presence of conditions such as coronary arteriosclerosis or chronic coronary insufficiency that could merit additional code assignments.

HYPERTENSION AND CHRONIC KIDNEY DISEASE

When the diagnostic statement includes both hypertension and chronic kidney disease or renal sclerosis, *ICD-9-CM* usually assumes that there is a cause-and-effect relationship. A code from category **403, Hypertensive chronic kidney disease,** is provided in the Alphabetic Index; a causal relationship need not be indicated in the diagnostic statement. A fifth digit is used with category 403 to indicate the stage of the chronic kidney disease. Note that category 403 does not include acute kidney failure, which is an entirely different condition from chronic kidney disease and is not caused by hypertension. Kidney conditions that are not indexed to hypertensive chronic kidney disease may or may not be hypertensive; if the physician indicates a causal relationship, only the code for hypertensive chronic kidney disease is assigned. Sample codes for cases of hypertensive chronic kidney disease include the following:

- Hypertensive nephropathy, benign 403.10
- Hypertensive nephrosclerosis 403.90
- Accelerated hypertension with chronic kidney disease 403.00 + 585.9
- Acute kidney failure with renal papillary necrosis and hypertension 584.7 + 401.9

HYPERTENSIVE HEART AND CHRONIC KIDNEY DISEASE

When a heart condition ordinarily coded to category 402 and a kidney condition coded to category 403 both exist, a combination code from category **404, Hypertensive heart and chronic kidney disease,** is assigned. Fifth digits are provided to indicate with or without heart failure, as well as the stage of the chronic kidney disease, as follows:

- 0 without heart failure and with chronic kidney disease stage I through stage IV, or unspecified
- 1 with heart failure and with chronic kidney disease stage IV, or unspecified

- 2 without heart failure and with chronic kidney disease stage V or end-stage renal disease
- 3 with heart failure and chronic kidney disease stage V or end-stage renal disease

An additional code (585.1–585.6, 585.9) should be used with categories 403 and 404 to identify the specific stage of chronic kidney disease.

When the diagnostic statement indicates that both hypertension and diabetes mellitus are responsible for chronic kidney disease, both the appropriate code from category 403 or 404 and code 250.4x, from the subcategory for diabetes with renal manifestations, are assigned, with sequencing optional. An additional code is assigned for the stage of chronic kidney disease (585.1–585.6, 585.9), if known.

HYPERTENSION WITH OTHER CONDITIONS

Although hypertension is often associated with other conditions and may accelerate their development, *ICD-9-CM* does not provide combination codes. Codes for each condition must be assigned to fully describe the condition. For example:

- Atherosclerosis of aorta with benign essential hypertension <u>440.0</u> + 401.1
- Coronary atherosclerosis and systemic benign hypertension <u>414.00</u> + 401.1
- Arteriosclerotic heart disease 414.00
- Arteriosclerotic heart disease with essential hypertension <u>414.00</u> + 401.9

The baroreflex system is the system that helps to regulate function of the heart, kidneys, and peripheral vasculature to maintain an appropriate blood pressure. The carotid sinus baroreflex activation device is currently the only medical device used to treat refractory hypertension. It consists of an implantable pulse generator, bilateral carotid sinus leads, and a computer programming system. The pulse generator is placed in a subcutaneous pocket in the pectoral region below the collar bone. Electrodes are placed bilaterally on the carotid arteries (two main blood pressure control points), and the leads run under the skin and connect to the pulse generator. Placement of the leads is determined by intraoperative blood pressure responses to test activations. The programming system regulates the activation energy from the device to the leads and can be adjusted based on the needs of the patient.

When the device is activated, the programming system delivers activation energy through the leads to the carotid sinus. The baroreceptors of the carotid arteries send signals through neural pathways to the brain that there is a rise in blood pressure that needs to be corrected. The brain sends signals to other parts of the body to counteract the rise in blood pressure by modulating the nervous system and hormones to dilate blood vessels and allow blood to flow more freely, reduce the heart rate, and influence fluid handling by the kidneys. This results in reduced blood pressure and workload by the heart, improved circulation, and a more optimal neurohormonal balance. The following codes are used to describe implantation, replacement, and revision of a carotid sinus stimulation device:

- 39.81 Implantation or replacement of carotid sinus stimulation device, total system
- 39.82 Implantation or replacement of carotid sinus stimulation lead(s) only
- 39.83 Implantation or replacement of carotid sinus stimulation pulse generator only
- 39.84 Revision of carotid sinus stimulation lead(s) only
- 39.85 Revision of carotid sinus stimulation pulse generator
- 39.86 Removal of carotid sinus stimulation device, total system
- 39.87 Removal of carotid sinus stimulation lead(s) only
- 39.88 Removal of carotid sinus stimulation pulse generator only

For example: A patient who is status post implantation of a carotid sinus baroreflex activation device due to refractory hypertension was admitted to have the leads adjusted and repositioned within the carotid sinus for better signal activation. Assign code **V53.39, Fitting**

and adjustment of other device, other cardiac device, as the principal diagnosis. Assign code **401.9, Essential hypertension, unspecified,** as an additional diagnosis. Assign code **39.84, Revision of carotid sinus stimulation lead(s) only,** for repositioning of the leads.

Exercise 24.6

Code the following diagnoses.

	Code(s)
1. Left heart failure with benign hypertension	428.1 401.1
2. Hypertensive cardiomegaly	402.90
3. Congestive heart failure Cardiomegaly Hypertension	428.0 429.3 401.9
4. Acute congestive heart failure due to hypertension	402.91 428.0
5. Hypertensive heart disease Myocardial degeneration	402.90
6. Acute cerebrovascular insufficiency	437.1
7. Cerebral thrombosis Moderate arterial hypertension	434.00 401.9
8. Arteriosclerotic cerebrovascular disease Hypertension, benign	437.0 401.1
9. Chronic coronary insufficiency Essential hypertension	414.8 401.9
10. Acute coronary insufficiency Hypertensive heart disease	411.89 402.90

HYPERTENSION COMPLICATING PREGNANCY, CHILDBIRTH, AND THE PUERPERIUM

Hypertension associated with pregnancy, childbirth, or the puerperium is considered to be a complication unless the physician specifically indicates that it is not. This condition includes preexisting hypertension as well as transient hypertension of pregnancy or hypertension arising during pregnancy. Hypertension complicating pregnancy, childbirth, and the puerperium is reclassified in category 642. (See chapter 20 of this handbook.)

ELEVATED BLOOD PRESSURE VERSUS HYPERTENSION

Blood pressure readings vary from time to time and tend to increase with age. Because of these variables, a diagnosis of hypertension must be made on the basis of a series of blood pressure readings rather than a single reading. A diagnosis of elevated blood pressure reading, without a diagnosis of hypertension, is assigned code 796.2. This code is never assigned on the basis of a blood pressure reading documented in the medical record; the physician must have specifically documented a diagnosis of elevated blood pressure.

True postoperative hypertension is classified as a complication of surgery, and code **997.91, Complications affecting other specified body systems, hypertension,** is assigned along with an additional code to identify the type of hypertension. However, a diagnosis of postoperative hypertension often refers only to an elevated blood pressure that reflects the patient's agitation or inadequate pain control and would be coded to 796.2. When the patient has a preexisting hypertension, only a code from categories 401 through 405 is assigned; neither preexisting hypertension nor simple elevated blood pressure is classified as a postoperative complication. Any other diagnosis of transient hypertension, except that occurring in pregnancy, or a diagnosis of postoperative hypertension not clearly documented in the medical record should be discussed with the physician to determine whether it represents an elevated blood pressure reading or a true hypertension.

ATHEROSCLEROSIS OF EXTREMITIES

Atherosclerosis of the native arteries of the extremities is classified into subcategory 440.2. Fifth digits used with subcategory **440.2, Atherosclerosis of the extremities,** indicate the progression of the disease as follows:

- Code 440.21 indicates atherosclerosis of the extremities with intermittent claudication.
- Code 440.22 indicates the presence of rest pain; it includes any intermittent claudication.
- Code 440.23 indicates a condition that has progressed to ulceration; it includes any rest pain and/or intermittent claudication.
- Code 440.24 indicates the presence of gangrene; it includes any or all of the preceding conditions. An additional code is assigned for any associated ulceration (707.10–707.19, 707.8, 707.9).

Atherosclerosis of extremities involving a graft is coded to 440.3x as follows:

- 440.30 unspecified graft
- 440.32 autologous vein bypass graft
- 440.33 nonautologous biological bypass graft

A chronic total occlusion of an artery of the extremities (440.4) develops when hard calcified plaque accumulates in an artery over an extended period of time, resulting in a clinically significant decrease in blood flow. Approximately 40 percent of patients with peripheral vascular disease (PVD) present initially with partial occlusion, which progresses to a chronic total occlusion. Intervention with angioplasty and stenting is more complex because passing a guidewire through a total occlusion is extremely difficult.

Code 440.4 should be used as an additional code assignment with subcategory 440.2x, Atherosclerosis, Of native arteries of the extremities, when a chronic total occlusion is present with arteriosclerosis of the extremities. An acute total occlusion of a peripheral artery is assigned to code series 444.21–444.22.

PULMONARY EMBOLISM

An embolus is a blood clot that usually occurs in the veins of the legs (deep vein thrombosis). Emboli can dislodge and travel to other organs in the body. A pulmonary embolism is a clot that lodges in the lungs, blocking the pulmonary arteries and reducing blood flow to the lungs and heart. Pulmonary embolic disease may be acute or chronic (longstanding, having occurred over many weeks, months, or years). In the majority of cases, acute pulmonary emboli do not cause chronic disease because the body's mechanisms will generally break down the blood clot. An acute embolus is usually treated with anticoagulants (e.g., intravenous heparin and warfarin or oral Coumadin) to dissolve the clot and prevent new ones. For acute pulmonary embolism, anticoagulant therapy may be carried out for three to six months. Therapy is discontinued when the embolus dissolves. A filter to interrupt the vena cava is another treatment option. The device filters the blood returning to the heart and lungs until the pulmonary embolism dissolves.

The tulip filter device (38.7) is indicated in cases of recent pulmonary embolism and proximal deep vein thrombosis (DVT) with a contraindication to anticoagulation, and as prophylaxis following trauma. When used on a temporary basis, complications of permanent filters (i.e., thrombosis, migration, inferior vena cava occlusion or perforation, filter fragmentation, and increased risk for DVT) can be avoided. The tulip filter device consists of four legs that form the shape of a cone. A small hook at the base of each leg is used for fixation of the device. Filter wires form the shape of tulip petals, giving the device its name. A hook at the apex of the cone allows the filter to be retrieved, although it may be used as a permanent fixture to manage thromboembolic disease. For example:

- A patient with pulmonary embolism (415.19) underwent placement of bilateral common femoral vein tulip filters. Code **38.7, Interruption of vena cava,** is assigned for insertion of the femoral tulip filter.

Code **415.19, Pulmonary embolism and infarct, Other,** is used for an acute pulmonary embolism. Code **416.2, Chronic pulmonary embolism,** is assigned for a chronic or recurrent pulmonary embolism. In addition, report code **V58.61, Long-term (current) use of anticoagulants,** along with code 416.2, or code **V12.55, Personal history of pulmonary embolism,** to describe any associated long-term use of anticoagulant therapy. This drug therapy is important to report because it influences the management of the patient.

SADDLE EMBOLI

Saddle emboli are one of the most severe forms of embolism and are associated with high mortality rates. Patient survival depends on an early diagnosis. The aorta is the most common site for a saddle embolus, but it may occur at other sites, such as the pulmonary artery.

Saddle pulmonary emboli occur at the level of the bifurcation of the pulmonary trunk and extend into the main right and left pulmonary arteries. This type of embolism is considered unstable and can fragment spontaneously or obstruct multiple distal pulmonary arteries. Assign code **415.13, Saddle embolus of pulmonary artery,** for a saddle embolus of the pulmonary artery.

Code **444.01, Saddle embolus of abdominal aorta,** is assigned for an embolus of the abdominal aorta. Code **444.09, Other arterial embolism and thrombosis of abdominal aorta,** is reserved for other emboli of the abdominal aorta.

THROMBOSIS AND THROMBOPHLEBITIS OF VEINS OF EXTREMITIES

Deep vein thrombosis and thrombophlebitis are two distinct processes, which can coexist. A patient can develop a thrombus with or without inflammation. A diagnosis of thrombosis of a vein indicates that a clot has formed; a diagnosis of thrombophlebitis indicates that the clot has become inflamed. When both thrombosis and thrombophlebitis are documented, a code from category 451, Thrombophlebitis, may be assigned with a code from category 453, Venous embolism and thrombosis.

Thrombophlebitis of the extremities is classified according to the veins involved, as follows:

- 451.0 Superficial veins of lower extremities
- 451.1x Deep veins of lower extremities
- 451.2 Unspecified veins of lower extremities
- 451.82 Superficial veins of upper extremities
- 451.83 Deep veins of upper extremities
- 451.84 Unspecified veins of upper extremities

Deep vein thrombosis (DVT), also referred to as venous thromboembolism, is a blood clot in a major vein. DVT generally involves the veins of the lower extremity, but it can also occur in the veins of the upper extremity. With the use of catheters for venous access and cardiac devices, there is increased risk of developing DVT in the upper extremities, such as the axillary, subclavian, or brachiocephalic veins. DVT can occur following orthopedic surgery, pelvic/abdominal surgery, or following prolonged inactivity (e.g., long-distance travel, bed rest due to injury or illness, and paralysis). Some individuals have a predisposition for developing blood clots due to an abnormality in their blood clotting system (e.g., Factor V mutation, Protein C or S deficiency, or lupus). Treatment involves anticoagulants to inhibit further development of blood clots or clot-dissolving drugs. In the hospital, heparin is usually administered intravenously. In some cases, a filter is placed in the vena cava to prevent emboli or clots from traveling to the heart and lungs. Following discharge, anticoagulant therapy is recommended for three to six months (or longer). High-risk patients may be maintained on anticoagulant therapy for an indefinite period. Coumadin therapy and the filter can be used to treat acute, chronic, or recurrent DVT; or the DVT may resolve over time and no active disease remain, but the therapy is continued to prevent recurrence or to manage susceptibility for recurrence. The assignment of the appropriate DVT codes should be based on provider documentation.

Venous embolism and thrombosis can be of deep vessels or superficial vessels, and it can be acute or chronic, with recurrent episodes. Recurrent deep vein thrombosis can be prevented through prophylactic anticoagulant therapy, venous stasis prevention with gradient elastic stockings, and intermittent pneumatic compression of the legs.

ICD-9-CM classifies venous embolism and thrombosis as follows:

- 453.4x Acute venous embolism and thrombosis of deep vessels of lower extremity
- 453.5x Chronic venous embolism and thrombosis of deep vessels of lower extremity
- 453.6 Venous embolism and thrombosis of superficial vessels of lower extremity
- 453.7x Chronic venous embolism and thrombosis of other specified vessels
- 453.8x Acute venous embolism and thrombosis of other specified veins

Atheroembolism is separate and distinct from atherosclerosis, thrombosis, or embolism. Thrombosis and embolism involve true clots, whereas atheroembolism involves cholesterol crystals from atheromatous plaques from vessels like the aorta or the renal artery. Atheroembolism is most commonly associated with the extremities. Category 445 is used to report atheroembolism.

OTHER CIRCULATORY CONDITIONS

In general, the coding principles applicable throughout *ICD-9-CM* apply to other sections of the *ICD-9-CM* chapter on circulatory diseases, such as categories 415 through 417 and 451 through 459, which are not discussed specifically in this handbook.

Exercise 24.7

Code the following diagnoses and procedures.

	Code(s)
1. Bleeding internal and external hemorrhoids Stasis ulcer, left lower extremity	455.2 455.5 454.0
Hemorrhoidectomy	49.46
2. Chronic venous embolism and thrombosis of subclavian veins on long-term Coumadin therapy Chronic iatrogenic hypotension	453.75 V58.61 458.29
3. Arteriosclerosis of legs with intermittent claudication	440.21
4. Postoperative infarction of pulmonary artery Saphenous phlebitis, right leg	415.11 451.0
5. Pulmonary hypertension	416.0
6. Raynaud's syndrome with gangrene	443.0 785.4
7. Esophageal varices, hemorrhagic	456.0

Exercise 24.7 *(continued)*

8. Bleeding esophageal varices due to portal hypertension	572.3 456.20
Ligation of esophageal varices	42.91
9. Arteriosclerotic ulcer and gangrene of lower leg	440.24 707.10
10. Patient was admitted with acute headache and problems with vision; condition deteriorated rapidly, and patient died within four hours of admission; final diagnosis: ruptured berry aneurysm	430
11. Dissecting aneurysm of thoracic aorta	441.01
Excision of the aneurysm with anastomosis	38.34

STATUS V CODES

ICD-9-CM provides several V codes to indicate that the patient has a health status related to the circulatory system, such as the following:

- Heart valve transplant V42.2
- Cardiac pacemaker in situ V45.01
- Aortocoronary bypass status V45.81

These codes are assigned only as additional codes and are reportable only when the status affects the patient's care for a given episode.

PROCEDURES INVOLVING THE CIRCULATORY SYSTEM

Several complex diagnostic tests have been developed for evaluating a patient's circulatory status, and several intensive procedures are currently in use for treating diseases of the circulatory system. The coronary artery bypass, used for patients with severe blockage in the coronary arteries, has been augmented by less invasive procedures, such as angioplasty. Some of these tests and procedures are described briefly in this section.

Intravascular Imaging Procedures

A new imaging technique for diagnosing intravascular vessels is known as Intravascular Vessel Imaging. This procedure utilizes a catheter-based ultrasound imaging method that allows viewing of the vessels from within. The codes for the intravascular imaging procedures are as follows:

- 00.21 Intravascular imaging of extracranial cerebral vessels
- 00.22 Intravascular imaging of intrathoracic vessels
- 00.23 Intravascular imaging of peripheral vessels
- 00.24 Intravascular imaging of coronary vessels
- 00.25 Intravascular imaging of renal vessels
- 00.28 Intravascular imaging, other specified vessel(s)
- 00.29 Intravascular imaging, unspecified vessel(s)

Diagnostic Cardiac Catheterization

Cardiac catheterization is an invasive diagnostic procedure performed for diagnosing and assessing the severity of cardiovascular disease. Codes 37.21–37.23 are assigned for this procedure and include recording intracardiac and intravascular pressures, recording tracings, obtaining blood for blood-gas testing, and measuring cardiac output. A number of other tests involve the insertion of cardiac catheters, but they are not classified as diagnostic catheterization unless a separate procedure with a report including the measurements listed in the preceding sentence has been documented.

Angiocardiography

Cardiac angiography (88.5x) is a diagnostic test ordinarily performed in conjunction with diagnostic cardiac catheterization. Ergovine provocation testing is often performed in association with coronary arteriograms to diagnose coronary spasm and is included in the code for the coronary arteriogram. Arteriography involving other arteries is classified into subcategory **88.4x, Arteriography,** with the fourth digit indicating the artery. The same codes are assigned for digital subtraction angiography, which is the same procedure as standard angiography except for the manner in which the image is detected and stored.

Intra-operative Fluorescence Vascular Angiography

Intra-operative fluorescence vascular angiography (88.59), or IFVA, is a new imaging technology that allows for real-time evaluation of the coronary vasculature and cardiac chambers during coronary artery bypass graft (CABG) procedures. It is used to assess the quality of the vascular anastomoses and patency of the graft, with results that are similar to selective coronary arteriography and cardiac catheterization. This is accomplished in less time and without the use of potentially harmful contrast material. Intra-operative fluorescence vascular angiography can be used in *noncoronary* applications, such as breast cancer surgery, pediatric micro and reconstructive surgery, and other types of tissue reconstruction. In addition, IFVA not only visualizes the coronary vasculature, but also enables intra-operative visualization of blood perfusion to the heart muscle, allowing surgeons to successfully perform transmyocardial revascularization (TMR). Assign **17.71, Non-coronary intra-operative fluorescence vascular angiography [IFVA].**

Bundle of His Study

The His bundle is part of the heart's conduction system, and a bundle of His study (37.29) records the heart's electrical activity. The technique involves introducing a transvenous electrode catheter through the femoral vein and then positioning it in the right ventricle near the tricuspid valve. Characteristic atrial, His bundle, and ventricular depolarizations are recorded and the intervals are timed. This study is frequently performed in conjunction with cardiac catheterization, in which case codes for both procedures are assigned, with the code for the cardiac catheterization sequenced first.

Electrophysiologic Stimulation and Recording Studies

Electrophysiologic stimulation and recording studies, commonly referred to as EP studies (EPS), are performed as part of the diagnosis and therapeutic management of patients with ventricular tachycardia or ventricular fibrillation, both forms of cardiac arrhythmia that carry a high risk of sudden death. The studies are also performed for patients who have unexplained syncope and palpitation or supraventricular tachycardia. After cardiac access is obtained either percutaneously or via cutdown, specialized electrophysiologic catheter electrodes are inserted and guided into position under fluoroscopy. Code **37.26, Catheter based invasive electrophysiologic testing,** is assigned for these studies. Code **37.20, Noninvasive programmed electrical stimulation** (NIPS), is assigned for noninvasive electrical stimulation.

Implant of Automatic Defibrillator/Cardioverter

The automatic implantable cardioverter defibrillator (AICD) is an electronic device designed to detect and treat life-threatening tachyarrhythmias by means of countershocks. Patients receiving this therapy have usually had one or more episodes of life-threatening arrhythmias that cannot be controlled by other therapy.

A total cardioverter defibrillator system implant (37.94) is usually performed as a single procedure. It includes the formation of a subcutaneous tissue pocket or abdominal fascia pocket, implantation or replacement of the defibrillator with epicardial patches and any transvenous leads, intraoperative procedures for evaluation of the lead signal, defibrillator threshold measurements, and tests of the implanted device with induction of arrhythmia. During the surgery to implant the AICD, the device is tested by inducing ventricular fibrillation (VF). Shocks are delivered and normal sinus rhythm is restored. A diagnosis of ventricular fibrillation is not coded when it is induced by use of a defibrillator (shocking) to make sure the AICD recognized the VF. The arrhythmia is being induced to check the functioning of the device. Assign also code **17.81, Insertion of antimicrobial envelope,** with the cardioverter defibrillator codes (37.94, 37.96, and 37.98) to provide additional information about devices used as part of the primary procedure. The antimicrobial envelope contains antibacterial agents to help provide protection from microbial colonization of the cardiac device during and immediately after placement. Coders should review the operative report for documentation indicating the placement of an antimicrobial envelope and assign the code for the primary procedure first, followed by code 17.81.

The implant is sometimes performed in two stages, however, with the leads implanted first (37.95) and the generator implanted on a subsequent day during the same hospital admission (37.96). Any extracorporeal circulation (39.61) or any other concomitant surgical procedure should also be coded. Code 37.26 is not assigned for an intraoperative EP study performed for device testing during implantation of an AICD. Code **37.79, Revision or relocation of cardiac device pocket,** includes creation of a loop recorder pocket and also creation of a pocket for an implantable, patient-activated cardiac event recorder. Insertion and relocation of both devices are included in this code.

When a patient is admitted for replacement or adjustment of an automatic cardioverter/defibrillator, code **V53.32, Automatic implantable cardiac defibrillator,** is assigned as the principal diagnosis unless the procedure is being performed because of a mechanical complication, in which case code **996.04, Mechanical complication of cardiac device, implant, and graft, due to automatic implantable cardiac defibrillator,** is assigned. Replacement of the entire system is included in the code for the initial insertion, and code **37.94, Implantation or replacement of cardioverter/defibrillator, total system (AICD)**, is assigned. When only the leads are replaced, code **37.97, Replacement of automatic cardioverter/defibrillator lead(s) only,** is assigned; when only the pulse generator is replaced, code **37.98, Replacement of cardioverter/defibrillator pulse generator only,** is assigned. Removal without replacement of the cardioverter/defibrillator and repositioning of the device are coded to 37.79.

Automatic implantable cardioverter/defibrillators sometimes require checking of the pacing thresholds or interrogation without arrythmia induction. This procedure is coded to **89.49, Automatic implantable cardioverter/defibrillator (AICD) check.** For example, a bedside check or interrogation of an AICD device is assigned to code 89.49.

Cardiac Pacemaker Therapy

Cardiac pacemaker therapy involves electrical control of the heart rate. *ICD-9-CM* codes differentiate between the insertion of temporary pacemakers and the insertion of permanent pacemakers. In a temporary pacemaker insertion (37.78), leads are inserted via a catheter and attached to an external pulse generator. This type of pacemaker is generally used for an acutely ill patient until a permanent one can be inserted. Another type of temporary pacemaker is used intraoperatively or immediately following surgery, with the leads inserted into the myocardium in an already-opened chest (39.64). No codes are assigned for insertion of the leads or for removal of a temporary or intraoperative pacemaker.

A temporary transmyocardial pacemaker in which a needle is inserted into the chest and into the myocardium with leads fed through the needle directly into the heart muscle and attached to an external pacing device is sometimes used in an effort at cardiopulmonary resuscitation. This procedure is considered an integral part of cardiopulmonary resuscitation (99.60), and no additional code is assigned. Two codes are required for the initial insertion of a permanent pacemaker. One code indicates the type of device, commonly called a pulse generator (37.81–37.83); the other indicates the insertion of the leads (37.71–37.74). Assign also code **17.81, Insertion of antimicrobial envelope,** with the permanent pacemaker codes (37.71–37.73 and 37.81–37.83) to provide additional information about devices used as part of the primary procedure.

Pacemaker leads (electrodes) can be placed either transvenously into the inside of the heart or epicardially onto the outside of the heart. In order to insert a transvenous lead into the ventricle, an incision is made in the skin and the lead is passed into the subclavian vein, down the superior vena cava, across the right atrium, and into the right ventricle. When transvenous leads are used, the pacemaker device is ordinarily placed in a subcutaneous pocket in the upper chest wall. Code 37.79 is assigned for the revision or relocation of a pocket for a pacemaker, defibrillator, or other implanted cardiac device.

No incision into the chest cavity is needed for the insertion of an epicardial lead. The most common site for the pacemaker pocket when epicardial leads are used is the abdominal wall.

There are three types of pacemaker devices on the market, each of which has a unique *ICD-9-CM* code for its insertion:

- Single chamber 37.81
- Single chamber, rate responsive 37.82
- Dual chamber 37.83

A single-chamber device uses a single lead; a dual-chamber device requires two leads, one in the atrium and one in the ventricle (37.72). It is important to be sure that the code for the lead insertion and the code for the pacemaker device are compatible because errors in this area have serious implications for reimbursement. A rate-responsive device is one in which the pacing rate is determined by physiological variables other than the atrial rate. This type of pacemaker permits patients to lead a more normal life and is strongly preferred for a potentially active patient. Physicians use various terms for this ability to respond and in many cases mention only the device number in documenting an insertion. The coding department should work with the hospital operating room staff and/or physicians to identify the devices commonly used in the facility and how they might be consistently identified in the operative report.

Total replacement of a permanent pacemaker system also requires two codes, one that identifies the replacement of leads (37.74 or 37.76) and one that identifies the replacement of the pacemaker device (37.85–37.87). When an existing pacemaker device is replaced with a new device, the type of device removed does not affect the code; only the type of new device inserted should be coded (37.85–37.87). Removal of the old device is included in the replacement code. Removal of lead(s) (electrode) without replacement is coded as 37.77 for leads and 37.89 for revision or removal of the pacemaker device.

When a patient is admitted for removal, replacement, or reprogramming of a cardiac pacemaker, code **V53.31, Fitting and adjustment of a cardiac pacemaker,** is assigned as the principal diagnosis. Reprogramming is a simple nonoperative procedure that does not require a procedure code. Physicians sometimes indicate that a patient is being admitted for battery replacement. This is something of a misnomer because pacemakers no longer use batteries and the whole device is actually replaced. When the pacemaker device is being replaced only because it is nearing the end of its expected life, code V53.31 is assigned as the principal diagnosis. When it is being replaced because of a mechanical complication of the device, diagnosis code **996.01, Mechanical complication due to cardiac pacemaker (electrode),** is assigned.

Cardiac Resynchronization Therapy

Cardiac resynchronization therapy (CRT) is a new technology similar to conventional pacemaker therapy and implantable cardioverter-defibrillators (ICDs). CRT is different because it requires the implantation of a special electrode within the coronary vein to attach the device to the exterior wall of the left ventricle. CRT treats heart failure by providing strategic electrical stimulation to the right atrium, right ventricle, and left ventricle of the heart to recoordinate ventricular contractions and improve cardiac output. CRT is also sometimes referred to as biventricular pacing. *ICD-9-CM* codes distinguish between the insertion of cardiac resynchronization pacemaker without internal cardiac defibrillator (CRT-P) and the insertion of cardiac resynchronization defibrillator, total system (CRT-D). CRT-P implantations are coded to 00.50 and CRT-D implantations are coded to 00.51. Assign also code **17.81, Insertion of antimicrobial envelope,** with the CRT codes (00.51, 00.53, and 00.54) to provide additional information about devices used as part of the primary procedure.

No additional codes are assigned for the creation of the pocket to hold the device, implantation of the device, insertion of transvenous leads as well as the lead into the coronary venous system, and intraoperative procedures to evaluate lead signals.

Over time, there may be a need to replace the lead into the left ventricular coronary venous system (00.52), replace the pacemaker pulse generator on a CRT-P (00.53), or replace the defibrillator pulse generator on a CRT-D (00.54). Code **37.75, Revision of lead [electrode],** is assigned for repositioning of the CRT-D or CRT-P lead only.

Cardiac Contractility Modulation (CCM)

The cardiac contractility modulation (CCM) system is a new treatment modality for patients with moderate to severe heart failure resulting from either ischemic or nonischemic cardiomyopathy. In cardiac contractility modulation, nonstimulatory impulses are delivered during the absolute refractory period (ARP) to enhance cardiac function and contractility. The CCM system is dissimilar to a cardiac pacemaker because the signals do not initiate a new heart beat; instead, they are intended to improve the strength of the heart.

The implantable pulse generator produces signals delivered to the heart via the pacemaker leads. Three leads are implanted in the heart: two leads are placed in the right ventricular septum, and a third lead is placed in the right atrium. The leads are connected to a pulse generator, and the generator is placed in a subcutaneous pectoral pocket. An external programmer allows medical personnel to customize the signal parameters according to the patient's specific needs. The charger allows the patient to recharge the battery of the pulse generator in the comfort of his or her home.

The implantation of the CCM system can occur alone, in the presence of an AICD, or in combination with implantation of both a CCM system and an AICD. For example:

- A patient was admitted for treatment of dilated cardiomyopathy. A combined insertion of an automatic implantable cardioverter/defibrillator with an antimicrobial envelope and a cardiac contractility modulation system was accomplished. Code **425.4, Other primary cardiomyopathies,** is assigned for the cardiomyopathy. Codes **37.94, Implantation or replacement of automatic cardioverter/defibrillator, total system [AICD]; 17.81, Insertion of antimicrobial envelope;** and **17.51, Implantation of rechargeable cardiac contractility modulation [CCM], total system,** are assigned for the procedures.

Valve Repair Procedures

In transcatheter aortic and pulmonary valve replacement, a bioprosthetic valve is delivered by catheter across the diseased native valve through the femoral artery or vein (endovascular approach) or through the apex of the heart by means of a thoracotomy incision (transapical approach). In both approaches (endovascular or transapical), a balloon valvuloplasty catheter is advanced and placed over the diseased native aortic or pulmonary valve, and a new bioprosthetic valve is put in place, destroying the native valve underneath it. While a valvuloplasty is done as part of the procedure, the purpose of the procedure is to insert a new aortic or pulmonary valve. This catheter-based technology allows for implantation of a prosthetic valve within the diseased native valve without the need for open heart surgery or cardiopulmonary bypass. The codes for transcatheter aortic and pulmonary valve replacement are as follows:

- 35.05 Endovascular replacement of aortic valve
- 35.06 Transapical replacement of aortic valve
- 35.07 Endovascular replacement of pulmonary valve
- 35.08 Transapical replacement of pulmonary valve
- 35.09 Endovascular replacement of unspecified heart valve

The MitraClip® implant is a minimally invasive, closed chest catheter-based approach for intracardiac repair of mitral regurgitation (MR) caused by valve pathology and/or left ventricular dysfunction. The procedure is performed on a beating heart and is an alternative to the open heart surgical approach. Interventional cardiologists can accomplish the procedure in the cardiac catheterization laboratory or in a hybrid operating suite under general anesthesia. The procedure does not require cardiopulmonary bypass. Insertion of the MitraClip® implant is coded to 35.97, **Percutaneous mitral valve repair with implant.**

Percutaneous Balloon Valvuloplasty

Percutaneous balloon valvuloplasty (PBPV) (35.96) is a noninvasive treatment for pulmonary valve stenosis. It involves a balloon wedge catheter that is advanced via the femoral vein into the heart and across the stenotic valve. The balloon is then inflated by hand pressure. There is no need for general anesthesia, the hospital stay is short, and no scarring results from the procedure. The code includes any nondiagnostic cardiac catheterization done as a part of the procedure.

Percutaneous Transluminal Coronary Angioplasty

Code 00.66 is assigned for percutaneous transluminal coronary angioplasty (PTCA). Codes 00.40–00.43 identify the number of vessels on which the PTCA was performed. An additional code is assigned for the thrombolytic agent administered (99.10). The codes identify the number of vessels treated as follows:

- 00.40 Procedure on single vessel
- 00.41 Procedure on two vessels
- 00.42 Procedure on three vessels
- 00.43 Procedure on four or more vessels

Code **00.44, Procedure on vessel bifurcation,** is used to describe the presence of a vessel bifurcation and is provided to capture data regarding the procedural differences between interventional procedures on a straight vessel and a vessel bifurcation. Bifurcation lesions usually involve blockages of a main coronary vessel and an adjacent side vessel, resulting in a lesion that is more complex to treat. Code 00.44 does not identify a specific bifurcation stent. This code is only used once per operative episode, irrespective of the number of bifurcations present in vessels.

Because reclosure often occurs following angioplasty, a stent is frequently inserted to prevent reclosure. In this procedure, a small stainless steel mesh stent is inserted during angioplasty to prop open the blocked coronary arteries. After the balloon has been threaded into the coronary artery and inflated to squash plaque deposits against the vessel wall, the process is repeated with a second balloon carrying the stent. Expansion of the balloon pushes the stent against the artery wall, where it remains to maintain patency. To report the insertion of stents, it is necessary to assign two codes. One code is used to identify the number of vascular stents inserted (00.45–00.48) and another code to identify the type of coronary stent (non-drug-eluting, 36.06, or drug-eluting, 36.07). These codes cannot be used alone because an angioplasty is needed to insert the stent. The codes describe the number of stents placed as follows:

- 00.45 Insertion of one vascular stent
- 00.46 Insertion of two vascular stents
- 00.47 Insertion of three vascular stents
- 00.48 Insertion of four or more vascular stents

A coronary atherectomy is a minimally invasive, catheter-based procedure used to remove plaque from arteries. This procedure is beneficial in cases where the plaque is very hard due to calcification, or where plaque has built up in a coronary artery bypass graft; the procedure is also beneficial for removing other difficult blockages. The types of mechanical atherectomy are rotational, directional, and transluminal extraction. An atherectomy can be carried out instead of, or along with, balloon angioplasty with or without stent insertion. Assign code **17.55, Transluminal coronary atherectomy,** for the atherectomy of a coronary vessel. Code also any percutaneous transluminal coronary angioplasty, stent insertion, infusion of a thrombolytic agent, and the number of vessels treated, along with the number of stents inserted.

Minor intimal tears often occur during angioplasty or the newer rotational atherectomy procedures; these are considered to be an unavoidable part of the procedure and are not classified as complications.

Percutaneous coronary intervention (PCI) (e.g., coronary angioplasty and atherectomy) involves the mechanical dilatation of the artery with compression of atherosclerotic plaque. The manner in which PCI improves luminal diameter is associated with injury to the artery, usually caused by balloon expansion. Mechanical fragmentation of plaque has been associated with distal embolization of plaque debris and vessel dissection. Studies have demonstrated that vessel dissection at the site of PCI is fairly common and can be identified angiographically in approximately 50 percent of patients immediately following PCI. In most cases, the dissection is minor and clinically insignificant and does not interfere with antegrade blood flow, nor does it affect the procedural outcome. When coding coronary dissection occurring during angioplasty or atherectomy, query the provider regarding the clinical significance of the dissection. If the provider confirms that the dissection is a complication of the procedure, assign code **997.1, Cardiac complications,** with code **414.12, Dissection of coronary artery,** to further describe the complication. If the provider indicates that the dissection is not clinically significant, do not assign a code.

Angioplasty of Non-coronary Vessels

Code **39.50, Angioplasty of other non-coronary vessel(s),** is assigned for percutaneous angioplasty of vessels other than coronary vessels. Assign code **17.56, Atherectomy of other non-coronary vessel(s),** for atherectomy of non-coronary vessels.

Codes **39.90, Insertion of non-drug-eluting, peripheral vessel stent or stents; 00.55, Insertion of drug-eluting stent(s) of other peripheral vessel(s);** or **00.60, Insertion of drug-eluting stent(s) of superficial femoral artery,** are assigned for associated placements of non-drug-eluting stents into other peripheral vessels and drug-eluting stents into the superficial femoral artery. If a thrombolytic agent is used, code **99.10, Injection or infusion of thrombolytic agent,** should be assigned as an additional code. The number of vascular stents inserted is identified with codes 00.45–00.48.

Assign code 00.61 for a percutaneous angioplasty of extracranial vessels, or code 00.62 for a percutaneous angioplasty of intracranial vessels. Additionally, assign code **17.53, Percutaneous atherectomy of extracranial vessel(s),** or code **17.54, Percutaneous atherectomy of intracranial vessel(s),** when percutaneous atherectomy of intracranial or extracranial vessels is also performed.

Assign code 00.63 for the percutaneous insertion of carotid artery stents, code 00.64 for other extracranial artery stents, and code 00.65 for intracranial vascular stents. Use codes 00.45–00.48 to report the number of stents inserted, codes 00.40–00.43 to report the number of vessels treated, and code 00.44 to report vessel bifurcation.

Coronary Artery Bypass Graft

Coronary artery bypass grafts (CABGs) are performed to revascularize the myocardium when a blockage in a coronary artery limits the blood supply to the heart. The grafts bypass the obstructions in the coronary arteries.

Coronary circulation consists of two main arteries, right and left, each with several branches, which are counted as arteries in coding aortocoronary bypass grafts:

- Right coronary artery (RCA)
  —Right marginal
  —Right posterior descending (PDA)
- Left main coronary artery (LMCA)
  —Left anterior descending branch (LAD)

—Diagonal
—Septal
—Circumflex (LCX)
—Obtuse marginal (OM)
—Posterior descending
—Posterolateral

The abbreviation CABG is commonly used to indicate a coronary artery bypass graft; separate codes are provided to indicate the type of bypass carried out.

The aortocoronary artery bypass is the one most commonly used. It brings blood from the aorta into the obstructed coronary artery, bypassing the obstruction by means of a segment of the patient's own saphenous vein, nonautologous biological material, or occasionally a segment of the internal mammary artery. The graft material used in an aortocoronary bypass does not affect code assignment. The axis for coding aortocoronary bypass grafts is the number of coronary arteries involved in the bypass (see figure 24.4):

- (Aorto)coronary bypass of one coronary artery 36.11
- (Aorto)coronary bypass of two coronary arteries 36.12
- (Aorto)coronary bypass of three coronary arteries 36.13
- (Aorto)coronary bypass of four or more coronary arteries 36.14

All coronary bypass procedures do not involve the aorta. The internal mammary-coronary artery bypass graft is accomplished by loosening the internal mammary artery from its normal position and using it as a conduit to bring blood from the subclavian artery to the occluded coronary artery. The axis for coding internal mammary-coronary artery bypass grafts is whether one or both internal mammary arteries are used, regardless of the number of coronary arteries involved:

- Single internal mammary-coronary artery bypass 36.15
- Double internal mammary-coronary artery bypass 36.16

It is rare for only one coronary artery to be bypassed, and it is also fairly common to perform both an internal mammary-coronary artery bypass and an aortocoronary bypass at the same operative episode (see figure 24.5). The surgeon's brief statement of the operation performed does not always distinguish the types of bypasses involved, which makes it necessary for the coder to refer to the body of the operative report when the statement is not clear.

FIGURE 24.4 Direct Myocardial Revascularization by Triple Aortocoronary Artery Bypass Using Autogenous Vein Grafts

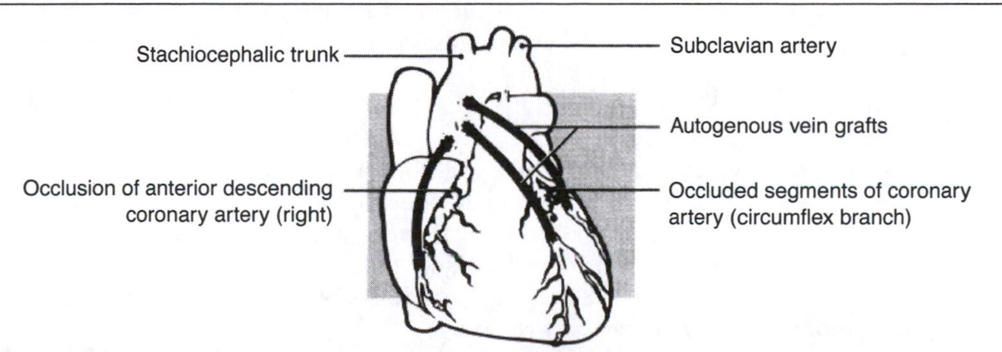

FIGURE 24.5 A Combination of Aortocoronary and Internal Mammary Artery Bypass Grafts for Myocardial Revascularization

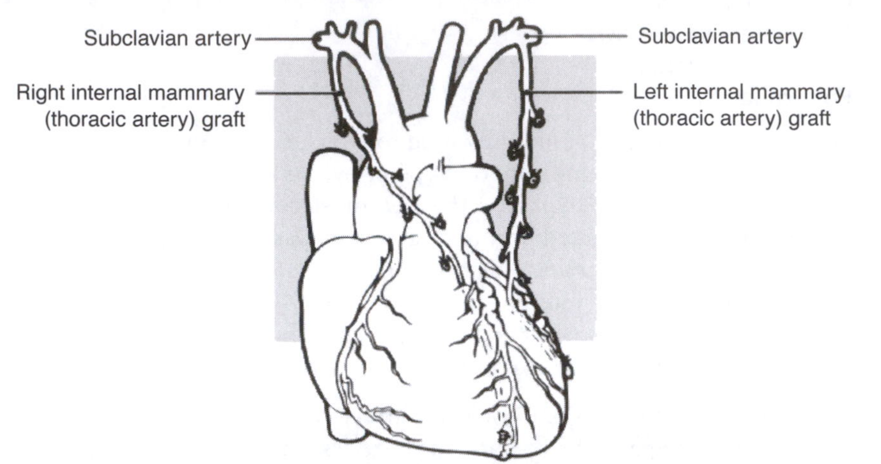

Reprinted, with permission, from *Coding Clinic for ICD-9-CM,* 4th quarter 1989. ©1989 American Hospital Association.

Other arteries are also used to bypass an obstruction in the coronary artery. Code **36.17, Abdominal-coronary artery bypass,** is used when an abdominal artery such as the gastric or gastroepiploic artery is used for the graft. Code **36.19, Other bypass anastomosis for heart revascularization,** is assigned when any other bypass anastomosis is performed.

An additional code should also be assigned for any use of extracorporeal circulation (39.61), or pressurized treatment of venous bypass graft with pharmaceutical substance (00.16). However, procedures such as hypothermia, cardioplegia, intraoperative pacing, and chest tube insertions are considered to be integral to bypass surgery; no separate codes are assigned.

In coding coronary artery bypass procedures, it is important to keep the following points in mind:

- The fact that a detached segment of the internal mammary artery is used as graft material instead of saphenous vein in performing an aortocoronary bypass does not make it an internal mammary-coronary artery bypass. The internal mammary-coronary artery bypass involves the use of the internal mammary itself as a still vascularized conduit for the blood supply and does not involve the aorta.
- When more than one coronary artery is involved in either type of graft, the anastomosis is sometimes carried out in a sequential manner, bypassing more than one artery. The mention of sequential anastomoses does not affect the code in any way.

The following examples may provide further assistance in coding coronary bypass grafts:

1. Coronary artery vascularization was carried out with four grafts: the aorta to the diagonal branch of the left coronary and in sequential fashion to the obtuse marginal branch of the circumflex, the right coronary artery, and the left anterior descending coronary artery. This procedure involved only the aorta and the coronary arteries. Because four coronary arteries were bypassed, **36.14, (Aorto)coronary bypass of four or more coronary arteries,** is assigned.
2. Grafts from the aorta to the coronary arteries were carried out by grafting the bifurcated left anterior descending system with a 1.5-millimeter section of the left internal mammary artery. The first diagonal was then grafted side-to-side with a 4-millimeter section of the saphenous vein. The obtuse marginal was then grafted

with a 4-millimeter section of the saphenous vein. The posterior descending was diffusely diseased and was grafted with a 4-millimeter section of the saphenous vein. All four grafts brought blood from the aorta to the coronary arteries. Sections of both the saphenous vein and the internal mammary artery were used for this purpose, but the materials used for the graft do not affect the code. Because four arteries (LAD, diagonal, obtuse marginal, and posterior descending) were bypassed, code **36.14, (Aorto)coronary bypass of four or more coronary arteries,** is assigned.

3. Bypass grafts were performed by bringing the left internal mammary artery to the left anterior ascending; a saphenous vein graft was then used to bring blood from the aorta to the obtuse marginal branch of the circumflex artery, to the diagonal artery, and to the proximal PDA. In this case, a single internal mammary-coronary artery bypass and three aortocoronary bypass grafts were placed (OM, diagonal, PDA). The codes assigned are **36.15, Single internal mammary-coronary artery bypass,** and **36.13, (Aorto)coronary artery bypass of three coronary arteries.** The sequence of the codes is optional.
4. The left internal mammary artery was loosened and used to bypass the left anterior descending artery; grafts of the saphenous vein were bypassed to the posterior descending artery and to the obtuse marginal branch of the circumflex. In this case, three coronary arteries were bypassed, one by an internal mammary-coronary artery bypass and two by aortocoronary bypasses. The codes assigned are **36.15, Single internal mammary-coronary artery bypass,** and **36.12, (Aorto)coronary artery bypass.**

As mentioned earlier, coronary artery bypass grafts often become occluded, sometimes because of a continuation of the arteriosclerotic disease process. Arteriosclerosis of an artery involved in a bypass graft is coded **414.02, Coronary atherosclerosis of autologous vein bypass graft,** or **414.03, Coronary atherosclerosis of nonautologous biological bypass graft.** Code **414.04, Coronary atherosclerosis of artery bypass graft,** is assigned for an artery with arteriosclerosis. (Note: If there is no mention in the medical record of the patient having undergone a bypass, code **414.01, Arteriosclerosis of native coronary artery,** should be assigned.)

Heart revascularization is also performed by other techniques. Transmyocardial revascularization can be performed by open procedure (36.31), by other transmyocardial procedures (36.32), by robot-assisted or thoracoscopic procedures (36.33), and by percutaneous or endovascular procedures (36.34). A number of other procedures such as myocardial graft using omentum, mediastinal fat, or pectoral muscles are classified in code **36.39, Other heart revascularization.**

Exercise 24.8

Code the following diagnoses and procedures.

	Code(s)
1. A patient was admitted through the emergency department complaining of chest pain with radiation down the left arm increasing in severity over the past three hours. Initial impression was impending myocardial infarction, and the patient was taken directly to the surgical suite, where percutaneous transluminal angioplasty with insertion of coronary stent was carried out on the right coronary artery. Infarction was aborted, and the diagnosis was listed as acute coronary insufficiency.	411.89 00.66 00.40 00.45 36.06

Exercise 24.8 *(continued)*

2. Saphenous vein graft was used to bring blood from the aorta to the right coronary artery, the left coronary artery, and the left anterior descending artery. Intraoperative pacemaker was used during the procedure as well as extracorporeal circulatory assistance. Bypass	36.13 39.64 39.61
3. Right and left diagnostic cardiac catheterization with bundle of His study	37.23 37.29
4. Balloon angioplasty carried out on three coronary arteries with vessel bifurcation	00.66 36.06 00.42 00.44
Insertion of two stents Extracorporeal circulation	00.46 39.61
5. Initial insertion of dual-chamber pacemaker device	37.72 37.83
6. Patient was admitted for replacement of single-chamber pacemaker device because the battery was expected to fail within a short time; device was replaced with single-chamber rate-responsive pacemaker device.	V53.31 37.86
7. Patient was admitted for replacement of displaced and protruding pacemaker device with single-chamber, rate-responsive device. Complication, mechanical	996.01 37.86
8. Catheter-based invasive electrophysiological cardiac study	37.26

Exercise 24.8 *(continued)*

9. Patient with severe coronary arteriosclerotic disease was admitted for coronary bypass (no history of previous bypass surgery). The left internal mammary artery was taken down to the left anterior descending artery, and a reverse saphenous Y graft was brought from the aorta to the distal LAD and diagonal, as well as a reverse saphenous vein graft to the obtuse marginal artery times two and distal right coronary artery.	414.01 36.14 36.15

EXCLUSION OR EXCISION OF THE LEFT ATRIAL APPENDAGE

Exclusion or excision of the left atrial appendage (LAA) is a component of most operations to treat atrial fibrillation (AF) and reduces late thromboemboli in patients with AF undergoing mitral valve surgery. LAA aneurysm is a rare anomaly, which usually presents with arrhythmia or cerebral embolism. Code 37.36 is assigned for excision, destruction, or exclusion of an LAA and includes the thoracoscopic or minithoracotomy approach. This code also includes other operative techniques, such as clipping, exclusion, oversewing, and stapling of the LAA. For example:

- Left-sided thoracoscopic stapling of the left atrial appendage 37.36

SURGICAL VENTRICULAR RESTORATION (SVR)

Surgical ventricular restoration (SVR) is a surgical technique that reshapes the heart and includes operative methods that reduce left ventricular volumes and restore elliptical shape to the left ventricle. With SVR the ventricle is not excised. For example:

- A patient developed a ventricular aneurysm and underwent surgical ventricular restoration and cardiopulmonary bypass. Code **414.10, Aneurysm of heart (wall),** is assigned as the principal diagnosis. Code **37.49, Other repair of heart and pericardium,** is assigned for the SVR, and code **39.61, Extracorporeal circulation auxiliary to open heart surgery,** is assigned for the cardiopulmonary bypass.

THORACOSCOPIC AND THORACOSCOPICALLY-ASSISTED ABLATION OF HEART TISSUE (MAZE PROCEDURE)

The maze procedure is a surgical treatment, used for atrial fibrillation, that creates lines of conduction block in the heart itself. The classic maze procedure is performed through an open chest approach, creating the lines with a scalpel by a carefully placed pattern of incisions in the heart tissue. Scar tissue (lesions) forms as the incisions heal, which creates the conduction block. There are variations called maze 1, 2, and 3, which represent different patterns of incisions. Through the years, various approaches for the maze procedure have been developed.

The open approach (37.33) is the traditional method of surgery and is performed via a median sternotomy or thoracotomy. "Cut-and-sew" was the original open technique, involving incisions into the atrial tissue followed by reconstruction of the atria. Because of the difficulties and risks associated with multiple atrial incisions, more recently a series of linear ablations are performed. There are a variety of energy sources used for ablation (e.g., radiofrequency, cryothermy, microwave, laser, and ultrasound). The energy source is delivered via a probe or a clamp instrument and can be applied at strategic locations within the heart or on the heart's surface. The creation of the incisions/ablation lines can be directly visualized with the open approach.

Endovascular (percutaneous) approaches (37.34) through peripherally inserted cardiac catheters have also been developed. Endovascular ablations have been very effective in the treatment of arrhythmias, including atrial fibrillation and atrial flutter, resulting from a single abnormal source (i.e., ectopic focus) of electrical stimulation on the right side of the heart.

The thoracoscopic approach (37.37) is the newest technique. However, what is commonly referred to as the thoracoscopic approach should more accurately be referred to as "thoracoscopically-assisted." The thoracoscope is used for illumination and visualization only, because the actual surgical ablation instruments are inserted via a mini thoracotomy or a subxiphoid incision rather than through the scope itself. Just recently, a total thoracoscopic approach has been established. As with the open approach, the thoracoscopically-assisted and total thoracoscopic techniques require opening up the pericardium. Significant dissection of the pericardial sinuses and other vital structures is required to gain access to target areas of the heart. In addition, as with the open technique, incisions can be made into the atria thoracoscopically, but most often linear ablations are done.

HEART ASSIST DEVICES

Heart circulatory support systems can provide temporary left, right, or biventricular support for patients whose hearts have failed but have the potential for recovery. The device can also be used as a bridge for patients who are awaiting a heart transplant. It involves an electromechanically driven pump the size of a human heart implanted within the abdominal wall. This system provides circulatory support by taking over most of the workload of the left ventricle. Blood enters the pump through an inflow conduit connected to the left ventricle and is ejected through an outflow conduit into the body's arterial system.

The system is monitored by an electronic controller and powered by primary and reserve battery packs worn on a belt around the waist or carried in a shoulder bag. There is also a stationary system that consists of a small bedside monitor. The controller is connected to the implanted pump by a percutaneous lead (a small tube containing control and power wires) through the patient's skin.

The implantation of a total internal biventricular heart replacement system (37.52) involves substantial removal of part or all of the biological heart. Both ventricles are resected, and the native heart is no longer intact. A ventriculectomy is included in this procedure, so it should not be coded separately. However, any associated procedures performed in conjunction with the placement of the total internal biventricular system, such as combined heart-lung transplantation (33.6) or heart transplantation (37.51), should be reported.

ICD-9-CM provides the following codes for the implantation, repair, and removal of implantable and nonimplantable single or biventricular external heart assist systems:

- 37.52 Implantation of total internal biventricular heart replacement system
- 37.53 Replacement or repair of thoracic unit of (total) replacement heart system
- 37.54 Replacement or repair of other implantable component of (total) replacement heart system
- 37.55 Removal of internal biventricular heart replacement system
- 37.60 Implantation or insertion of biventricular external heart assist system

- 37.62 Insertion of temporary non-implantable extracorporeal circulatory assist device
- 37.63 Repair of heart assist system
- 37.64 Removal of external heart assist system(s) or device(s)
- 37.65 Implant of single ventricular (extracorporeal) external heart assist system
- 37.66 Insertion of implantable heart assist system

IMPLANTABLE INFUSION PUMP AND VASCULAR ACCESS DEVICES

Implantable vascular access devices and implantable infusion pumps are two distinct catheter systems, each of which can be used to deliver drug therapy. The main difference between them is that the implantable infusion pump is self-contained and completely implanted in the body, whereas the implantable vascular access device is not a pump but a port implanted in the body to provide easy access to the vascular system. Code **86.06, Insertion of totally implantable infusion pump,** is assigned for the totally implantable infusion pump; code **86.07, Insertion of totally implantable vascular access device (VAD),** is assigned for the vascular access device.

The implantable infusion pump is surgically placed in the body, usually via laparotomy under general anesthesia. The laparotomy approach is not coded. In certain instances, a catheter is attached to the pump and inserted into an artery for direct infusion of a drug; in such cases, code **38.91, Arterial catheterization,** is also assigned. The pump is used to deliver intra-arterial drugs such as chemotherapeutic agents for patients with primary hepatomas or colon cancer with metastasis to the liver, as well as to deliver pain medication for terminal cancer patients. The pump allows the patient greater flexibility and freedom of movement while receiving treatment and also permits treatment on an outpatient basis once the pump has been inserted.

The use of an infusion pump that remains outside the body and infuses medication through a subcutaneous or venous needle is not coded. Only the procedure for placing a venous needle or catheter is coded (**38.93, Puncture of vessel, venous catheterization, NEC**). The application of this device includes the insertion of a permanent catheter.

An implantable VAD is a sterile catheter system implanted subcutaneously under local anesthesia and used for multiple purposes, such as infusion of total parenteral nutrition (TPN) and bolus injections of medication. The device is placed in central veins, such as the subclavian, rather than a peripheral vein. VADs are designed to provide repeated access to the vascular system without the trauma or complications of multiple venipuncture. The devices can be left in place for weeks or months as opposed to days and are generally placed in patients who require long-term access for chemotherapy, nutrition, or blood withdrawal.

Simple venous catheters are sterile catheter systems that provide repeated access to the vascular system for procedures such as blood withdrawal and medication or fluid administration. The catheter is inserted into a peripheral vein, such as the cephalic vein, by puncturing the skin and then taping the catheter in place. These catheters remain in place for a much shorter period of time than do VADs. Examples of simple venous catheters (also called heparin locks) include Angiocaths, Abbott catheters, and Jelco catheters. Code **38.93, Venous catheterization NEC,** is assigned for insertion of a simple catheter system. Code **86.05, Incision with removal of foreign body from skin and subcutaneous tissue,** is assigned for the removal of a vascular access device.

Central venous catheter placement with guidance is a new technology that combines electrocardiography with catheter insertion to accurately align the tip of the catheter in the correct position in the superior vena cava. For example:

- A patient had a central venous line inserted using electrocardiographic guidance. Assign code **38.97, Central venous catheter placement with guidance.**

IMPLANTABLE HEMODYNAMIC MONITOR

Codes 00.56 and 00.57 are assigned for the implantation of a hemodynamic monitoring system. The implantable hemodynamic monitoring system allows clinicians to identify early signs of volume overload before signs and symptoms of heart failure become apparent. Clinicians can then adjust treatment to prevent acute decompensated heart failure and the need for hospital admission. The device consists of two key components. A lead with a pressure sensor is placed within the right ventricle at the right ventricular outflow tract. The other component is the monitoring device, which includes pressure-sensing circuitry with memory to process and collect the data obtained by the sensor. Note that this type of sensor is physically connected by a lead to a separately implanted monitor. This differs from the implantable pressure sensor without lead, which is assigned code 38.26. Code **38.26, Insertion of implantable pressure sensor without lead for intracardiac or great vessel hemodynamic monitoring,** is used to describe the placement of a stand-alone sensor that is not physically connected to a separately implanted monitor.

INTRAVASCULAR AND INTRA-ANEURYSM PRESSURE MEASUREMENT

Code 00.58 is used for reporting the intraoperative placement of an intra-aneurysm sac pressure monitoring device. Measurement of intra-aneurysm sac pressure during endovascular repair of an abdominal or thoracic aortic aneurysm can help to detect and treat endoleaks during endoluminal grafting.

Intravascular pressure measurement of coronary arteries (00.59) provides physiological assessment of intravascular lesions. The specialized guide wire–mounted pressure sensor measures pressure and flow and can be used during diagnostic cardiac catheterization to determine the significance of a blockage in a coronary artery. Pressure wire measurement can confirm therapeutic results in coronary vessel stenting, identify culprit vessels, assist in developing an individual therapeutic strategy, and provide step-by-step guidance during complex interventional procedures. Any other diagnostic or therapeutic procedures carried out in conjunction with intravascular pressure measurement of coronary arteries are coded separately.

Code 00.67 describes intravascular pressure measurement of intrathoracic arteries (i.e., assessment of the aorta, aortic arch, and carotid arteries). Code 00.68 captures the intravascular pressure measurement of the peripheral arteries, including assessment of vessels of the arms and legs. Code 00.69 is used to report intravascular pressure measurement of other and unspecified vessels, such as the iliac, intra-abdominal, mesenteric, and renal vessels. Assign additional codes for any synchronous diagnostic or therapeutic procedures in addition to the assignment of codes 00.67, 00.68, and 00.69.

IMPLANTATION OF CARDIOMYOSTIMULATION SYSTEM

Code **37.67, Implantation of cardiomyostimulation system,** is used to report the use of a new surgical technique called dynamic cardiomyoplasty. It is a fairly complicated two-step open procedure that involves elevating the latissimus dorsi muscle, then wrapping it around the heart. A stimulator similar to a pacemaker is implanted and connected to both the heart and the wrapped muscle. There are a number of components to the procedure; all are included in code 37.67.

HEART TRANSPLANTATION

Heart transplantation is carried out when the heart is failing and doesn't respond to therapies. The main reasons for heart transplants are cardiomyopathy, severe coronary artery disease, and congenital defects of the heart. Code **37.51, Heart transplantation,** is used to report the transplantation of a heart from a donor. There is an insufficient number of organs available for transplantation to meet the need. A patient may wait months for a transplant, and many don't live long enough to receive the organ. With advances in new technology, there is now a completely implantable artificial heart available. Code **37.52, Implantation of total replacement heart system,** is used to report this procedure. Additional codes are also available to replace or repair the thoracic unit (37.53) or any other implantable component (37.54) of a total replacement heart system.

Review Exercise 24.9

Code the following diagnoses and procedures.

	Code(s)
1. Internal and external thrombosed hemorrhoids	455.1 455.4
Internal and external hemorrhoidectomy by cryosurgery	49.44
2. Varicose veins, right leg	454.9
Right greater saphenous ligation and stripping for varicosities	38.59
3. Mitral stenosis and aortic insufficiency Atrial fibrillation Hypertension	396.1 427.31 401.9
4. Abdominal aortic aneurysm Hypertensive cardiovascular disease essential	441.4 402.90
Resection of abdominal aortic aneurysm with graft replacement	38.44

Review Exercise 24.9 *(continued)*

5. Acute myocardial infarction, anterior wall (initial episode of care)	410.11
6. Renovascular hypertension secondary to fibromuscular hyperplasia, right renal artery	447.3 405.91
Renogram	92.03
7. Congestive heart failure due to hypertensive heart disease	402.91 428.0
8. Congestive heart failure End-stage dilated cardiomyopathy Permanent cardiac pacemaker in place Status	428.0 425.4 V45.01 996.09
Repair of heart assist device due to exposed wire and device malfunction	37.63
9. Cerebral occlusion, thrombotic with cerebral infarction Hypertensive cardiovascular disease	434.01 402.90
10. Hypertension Chronic kidney disease	403.90 585.9

Review Exercise 24.9 *(continued)*

11. Iatrogenic pulmonary infarction	415.11
12. Hypertensive encephalopathy due to accelerated hypertension	437.2 401.0
13. Insertion of pacemaker leads: insertion of dual-chamber pacemaker device	37.72 37.83
14. Arteriosclerosis of coronary artery (four-vessel bypass graft with saphenous vein carried out two years ago)	414.02
15. Acute pulmonary edema with left ventricular failure	428.1
16. Cerebrovascular accident, acute, with thrombosis Residual hemiplegia, right, and aphasia (at discharge) Essential hypertension	434.00 342.90 784.3 401.9
17. Severe stenosis of left main coronary arteries in patient with no previous history of bypass surgery	414.01
Aortocoronary bypass, left diagonal and left circumflex arteries with saphenous vein graft Cardiopulmonary bypass Insertion of intraoperative pacemaker	36.12 39.61 39.64

Neoplasms

CHAPTER **25**

CHAPTER OVERVIEW

- Neoplastic diseases are classified in chapter 2 of *ICD-9-CM*.
- Neoplasms are categorized by two axes.
    - — The first axis for coding is behavior (malignant, benign, carcinoma in situ, uncertain behavior, and unspecified nature).
    - — The second axis for coding is by anatomical site.
- The morphology of tumor cells is studied for classifying a neoplasm by its tissue origin.
- Neoplastic diseases are indexed by morphological type and common terms.
- The neoplasm table lists anatomical sites alphabetically. It uses behavior type to indicate the correct code.
- There are two types of malignant neoplasms.
    - — Solid neoplasms have a localized point of origin and are considered to be the primary neoplasm of the site. They often metastasize to secondary sites.
        - – The statement "metastatic to" indicates that the site of a metastatic tumor is secondary, while "metastatic from" indicates a primary site.
        - – When coding, refer to the morphology type in the Alphabetic Index.
    - — Lymphatic and hematopoietic tumors often circulate through the bloodstream and lymphatic system.
        - – These tumors do not spread to secondary sites. All sites to which they spread through circulation are considered primary.
        - – Special coding requirements are in place for Hodgkin's disease and Non-Hodgkin's lymphomas.
- Sometimes treatment can be a guide when selecting a principal diagnosis.
    - — When the treatment is directed at the primary site, the malignancy of that site is often the principal diagnosis.
    - — When it is directed at a secondary site, the malignancy of the primary site is an additional code.
    - — Admission solely for chemotherapy treatment requires a V code as the principal diagnosis.

LEARNING OUTCOMES

After studying this chapter you should be able to:

- Explain the various classifications of neoplasms.
- Locate codes for neoplastic diseases.
- Code for malignant neoplasms (both solid and hematopoietic or lymphatic).
- Code for the treatment of neoplastic diseases.

TERMS TO KNOW

Direct extension
the invasion of adjacent sites by a malignant neoplasm

Invasive
the extension of tumor cells to other adjacent sites

Metastasis
the resulting spread of invasive tumor cells

Neoplasm
a new or abnormal growth

REMEMBER . . . Morphology codes are optional but are used in tumor registries and pathology indexes.

INTRODUCTION

A neoplasm is a new or abnormal growth. In the *ICD-9-CM* classification system, neoplastic disease is classified in categories 140 through 239.

BEHAVIOR CLASSIFICATION

The first axis for coding neoplasms is behavior; the second axis is the anatomical site. *ICD-9-CM* classifies neoplasms into five behavior groups:

- Malignant 140–208
- Neuroendocrine 209
- Benign 210–229
- Carcinoma in situ 230–234
- Uncertain behavior 235–238
- Unspecified nature 239

Malignant Neoplasms

Malignant neoplasms are tumor cells that extend beyond the primary site, attaching themselves to adjacent structures or spreading to distant sites. They are characterized by relentless growth and are difficult to cure. The term "invasive" is often used to describe the extension of the tumor cells to other adjacent sites. The resulting spread is called "metastasis."

Certain types of malignant neoplasms are noted for their invasive properties (for example, malignant melanoma of the skin) and usually require excision beyond the primary site because of their potential microinvasiveness. In such cases, a biopsy finding of malignancy on tissue removed during outpatient surgery may indicate the need for more extensive surgery on an inpatient basis. When such further surgery is performed, however, the pathology report may or may not indicate further malignancy. When no further malignancy is found, the physician ordinarily documents the diagnosis as a malignancy in accordance with the findings of the initial biopsy, because that condition is the reason for admission and the primary neoplasm may, in fact, require further treatment. In this situation, the diagnosis provided by the physician should be coded even though the current pathology report does not confirm the diagnosis. A copy of the original pathology report should be obtained and filed with the current medical record if at all possible.

Neuroendocrine Tumors

Neuroendocrine tumors (category 209) arise from endocrine or neuroendocrine cells scattered throughout the body. The most common sites are the bronchi, stomach, small intestine, appendix, and rectum. These tumors are commonly classified according to the presumed embryonic site of origin, such as the foregut (bronchi and stomach), midgut (small intestine and appendix), and hindgut (colon and rectum).

A carcinoid tumor is a tumor that develops from enterochromaffin cells. These cells produce hormones that normally are found in the small intestine, appendix, colon, rectum, bronchi, pancreas, ovaries, testes, bile ducts, liver, and other organs. Carcinoid tumors are capable of producing the same hormones, often in large quantities, and can cause carcinoid syndrome (259.2). Carcinoid tumors can be found throughout the body, but the majority are found in the gastrointestinal tract. Approximately 25 percent of carcinoid tumors are found in the bronchial airways and the lung. In some cases, it may not be possible to locate the site of origin of the carcinoid tumors, although symptoms of the carcinoid syndrome may be present. Carcinoid tumors can present as a primary malignancy (codes 209.00–209.30), as a secondary or metastatic tumor (codes 209.70–209.79), or as a benign tumor (codes 209.4x–209.6x). Code V10.91 is used to describe the history of a malignant neuroendocrine tumor that has been previously excised or eradicated with no further treatment.

When multiple endocrine neoplasia (MEN) syndrome is associated with neuroendocrine tumors, code first the MEN syndrome (258.01–258.03). However, it is not assigned when the health record documentation does not support the condition. Codes from subcategory 258.0, Polyglandular activity in multiple endocrine adenomatosis, are only assigned when MEN syndrome is actually present. For example, if there is an associated endocrine syndrome, assign the appropriate additional code, such as carcinoid syndrome (259.2):

- Malignant carcinoid tumor of the stomach, Werner's syndrome, and carcinoid syndrome 258.01 + 209.23 + 259.2

Merkel cell carcinoma, also called neuroendocrine carcinoma of the skin, arises from the uncontrolled growth of Merkel cells in the skin. It is a rare skin cancer and potentially life threatening; aggressive therapy may be needed. Merkel cell carcinoma does not have a distinctive appearance and usually develops on sun-exposed skin (e.g., head, neck, and arms) as a painless, firm, flesh-colored to red or blue bump. It is diagnosed via skin biopsy. The following codes are assigned for Merkel cell carcinoma:

- 209.31 Merkel cell carcinoma of the face
- 209.32 Merkel cell carcinoma of the scalp and neck
- 209.33 Merkel cell carcinoma of the upper limb
- 209.34 Merkel cell carcinoma of the lower limb
- 209.35 Merkel cell carcinoma of the trunk
- 209.36 Merkel cell carcinoma of other sites

Benign Neoplasms

Benign neoplasms are not invasive and do not spread to either adjacent or distant sites. They may, however, cause local effects such as displacement, pressure on an adjacent structure, impingement on a nerve, or compression of a vessel and therefore require surgery. Uterine myomas, for example, may cause pressure on the urinary bladder, which results in urinary symptoms. Most benign tumors can be cured by total excision.

Carcinoma in Situ

Tumor cells in carcinoma described as in situ are undergoing malignant changes but are still confined to the point of origin without invasion of the surrounding normal tissue. Other terms that describe carcinoma in situ include "intraepithelial," "noninfiltrating," "noninvasive," and "preinvasive" carcinoma. Severe cervical and vulvar dysplasia described as CIN III or VIN III are classified as carcinoma in situ. (See chapter 17 of this handbook for more information.)

Neoplasms of Uncertain Behavior

The ultimate behavior of certain neoplasms cannot be determined at the time they are discovered, and a firm distinction between benign and malignant tumor cells cannot be made. Certain benign tumors, for example, may be undergoing malignant transformation; as a result, continued study is necessary to arrive at a conclusive diagnosis.

Neurofibromatosis refers to a group of autosomal dominant genetic disorders that cause tumors to grow along the nerves. Code **237.79, Other neurofibromatosis,** is assigned for neurofibromatosis.

Schwannomas may occur along any nerve of the body, including spinal, cranial, and peripheral nerves. Schwannomas develop all over the body except on the vestibular nerve. As the tumors grow, they compress nerves and cause pain, numbness, tingling, weakness, and other neurological symptoms. Code **237.73, Schwannomatosis,** is assigned for this condition.

Neoplasms of Unspecified Nature

Category 239 is provided for those situations in which neither the behavior nor the morphology of the neoplasm is specified in the diagnostic statement or elsewhere in the medical record. This usually occurs when a patient is transferred to another medical care facility for further diagnosis and possible treatment before diagnostic studies are completed, or when a patient is given a working diagnosis in an outpatient setting pending further study. A code from category 239 would not be used for a neoplasm treated in an acute care facility because more definitive information should always be available.

It is important not to confuse neoplasms of unspecified nature with those of uncertain behavior. The exception for coding neoplasm of unspecified nature is when coding dark areas or spots of the retina, which are referred to as neoplasms or suspected melanoma. These spots are often difficult to biopsy and must be continually evaluated. Code **239.81, Neoplasms of unspecified nature, retina and choroid,** is assigned for this condition. Because a biopsy of the retina poses a risk to the eye and is only performed if the lesion extends, there is usually no tissue biopsy to confirm the diagnosis. Therefore, code 239.81 is appropriately assigned for this condition.

Unspecified Mass or Lesion

It is incorrect to select a code from category **239, Neoplasms of unspecified nature,** when only the terms "mass" or "lesion" are used. When coding diagnoses documented as mass or lesion of a particular site, and when that site is not listed under the main terms "Mass" or "Lesion," the coder should follow the cross-references under the main term representing the documented diagnosis. If a final diagnosis is documented as "lump," and there is no index entry for the affected organ or site under "lump," look up the main term "mass" as directed by the "see also" note under the main term "lump." If there is no index entry for the specific site under "mass," look up the main term "disease." The index directs the coder to see Disease of specified organ or site for "Mass, specified organ NEC."

If a final diagnosis is documented as "lesion," and there is no index entry for the specified organ or site under the main term "Lesion," look up the main term "Disease." The index directs you to see Disease by site for "Lesion, organ or site NEC."

Exercise 25.1

By referring to the following subcategories in volume 1, match the codes in the left column with the descriptions listed in the right column. In some cases, more than one letter may be assigned to a code in the left column.

c	153.1 Transverse colon	a. Benign
d	237.2 Adrenal gland	b. Carcinoma in situ
c	172.0 Lip	c. Malignant
b	231.1 Trachea	d. Uncertain behavior
e	239.4 Bladder	e. Unspecified nature
a	210.7 Nasopharynx	
c	209.16 Sigmoid colon	

MORPHOLOGY CLASSIFICATION

Morphology of neoplasms refers to the form and structure of tumor cells and is studied in order to classify a neoplasm by its tissue origin. The tissue of origin and the type of cells that make up a malignant neoplasm often determine the expected rate of growth, the severity of illness, and the type of treatment given. Metastatic neoplasms are identified at the metastatic site by their morphology, which is different from the normal tissue at that site but the same as that at the primary site.

Morphology codes consist of a capital letter "M," followed by four digits that identify the histological type, with a slash mark and a fifth digit indicating its behavior (M0000/0). Neoplastic disease is indexed by the morphological type as well as by other common terms, with the morphology code displayed in parentheses following the index entry. Many tumor-like conditions are not classified as neoplasms, however, and therefore no morphology code is provided. Examples of such conditions are adenomatous goiter, adenosis, mass, polyp, and leukoplakia.

Behavior identification for morphology codes parallels the behavior classification in *ICD-9-CM* as follows:

- 0 Benign
- 1 Uncertain behavior, borderline malignancy
- 2 Carcinoma in situ
- 3 Malignant, primary site
- 6 Malignant, secondary site

When the diagnostic statement or pathology report indicates a behavior other than that indicated by the morphology code, the medical record information prevails. For example, the morphology code for chordoma indicates that it is malignant (M9370/3), but a malignant neoplasm code should not be assigned when the record documents the neoplasm as benign.

Use of morphology codes is optional; they are rarely used except in tumor registries and pathology department indexes. *ICD-9-CM* provides a listing of morphology codes in appendix A of volume 1.

A tumor registry is a cancer data system that provides follow-up on all cancer patients. A tumor registry documents and stores all major aspects of a patient's cancer history and treatment. The registry database includes demographics, medical history, diagnostic findings, primary site, metastasis, histology, stage of disease, treatments, recurrence, subsequent treatment, and end results. Coders may use the completed cancer staging form for coding purposes when it is authenticated by the attending physician.

Exercise 25.2

Answer the following questions either true or false.

T 1. Morphology of neoplasms refers to the study of the form and structure of the tissue and cells from which the neoplasm arises.

F 2. Metastatic neoplasms can be identified by their morphology, which is identical to the morphology of the surrounding normal tissue and cells at the metastatic site.

F 3. Morphology codes, such as M8090/3, are located in *ICD-9-CM,* volume 1, chapter 2, entitled Neoplasms.

T 4. For morphology code M8090/3, the digit 3 identifies the behavior of the neoplasm as malignant.

T 5. In hospitals and other health care settings, the use of the morphology codes (M codes) is optional, depending on the user's needs.

LOCATING CODES FOR NEOPLASTIC DISEASE

The first step in locating the code for a neoplasm is to refer to the main term for the morphological type in the Alphabetic Index of Diseases and Injuries and then to review the subentries. For some types, a specific diagnosis code is provided. For example, for a diagnosis of renal cell carcinoma, the Alphabetic Index lists the main term **Carcinoma** and the subterm "renal cell" as follows:

Carcinoma (M8010/3) . . .
  renal cell (M8312/3) 189.0

When the site is not listed as a subterm or when a specific code is not given in the index, a cross-reference to the neoplasm table in volume 2 appears. Cross-references should be followed closely; the following entries indicate the help the coder can receive when the type of neoplasm is referenced in the Alphabetic Index:

Sarcoma (M8800/3) . . .
  cerebellar (M9480/3) 191.6
  embryonal (M8991/3)—*see* Neoplasm, connective tissue, malignant . . .
  Ewing's (M9260/3)—*see* Neoplasm, bone, malignant

The neoplasm table (part of which is reproduced here as table 25.1) lists anatomical sites alphabetically on the far left. (The indention levels have the same significance as those used elsewhere in volume 2.) Columns to the right indicate the code for each behavior type for that site. To use the table, coders must first locate the anatomical site in the list, move across the page to the behavior type, and then select the appropriate code. Coders should work from the table only after taking the first step of referring to the main term for the morphological type because important information in the index could be missed, and an incorrect code could be assigned as a result. Codes from the neoplasm table should be verified in the Tabular List.

TABLE 25.1 Section of the Neoplasm Table in the Index of Diseases and Injuries

	Malignant					
	Primary	Secondary	Ca in situ	Benign	Uncertain Behavior	Unspecified
Neoplasm, neoplastic—*continued*						
alveolar—*continued*						
ridge or process—*continued*						
mucosa	143.9	198.89	230.0	210.4	235.1	239.0
lower	143.1	198.89	230.0	210.4	235.1	239.0
upper	143.0	198.89	230.0	210.4	235.1	239.0
upper	170.0	198.5	—	213.0	238.0	239.2
sulcus	145.1	198.89	230.0	210.4	235.1	239.0
alveolus	143.9	198.89	230.0	210.4	235.1	239.0
lower	143.1	198.89	230.0	210.4	235.1	239.0
upper	143.0	198.89	230.0	210.4	235.1	239.0
ampulla of Vater	156.2	197.8	230.8	211.5	235.3	239.0

Exercise 25.3

Assign both diagnosis and morphology codes to the following diagnoses.

	Code(s)
1. Bronchial adenoma	235.7 M8140/1
2. Burkitt's lymphoma of intrapelvic lymph nodes	200.26 M9750/3

Exercise 25.3 *(continued)*

3. Lipoma of breast	214.1 M8850/0
4. Giant cell leukemia	207.20 M9910/3
5. Endometrial sarcoma	182.0 M8930/3
6. Hodgkin's sarcoma	201.20 M9662/3

BASIC TYPES OF MALIGNANT NEOPLASMS

There are two basic types of malignant neoplasms:

- Solid 140–199
- Hematopoietic and lymphatic 200–208

Solid tumors have a single, localized point of origin and are considered to be primary neoplasms of that site. Solid tumors tend to spread to adjacent or remote sites, with such sites classified as secondary or metastatic neoplasms. For example, a diagnosis of carcinoma of the lung with metastasis to the brain indicates that a primary neoplasm of the lung has metastasized to a secondary site in the brain.

Lymphatic and hematopoietic neoplasms arise in the reticuloendothelial and lymphatic systems and the blood-forming tissues. These neoplasms differ from solid malignant neoplasms in several ways, including the following:

- They may arise in a single site or in several sites simultaneously.
- Tumor cells often circulate in large numbers in the bloodstream and the lymphatic system rather than remaining confined to a single site.
- Spreading to other sites in the hematopoietic and lymphatic system is not considered to be secondary but is also classified as primary neoplasm.

Because of the differences between solid and hematopoietic-lymphatic diseases, this handbook will deal with the two types of malignant neoplasms separately. Solid tumors will be discussed first and then the discussion will move on to tumors that arise in the hematopoietic and lymphatic systems.

CODING OF SOLID MALIGNANT NEOPLASMS

A solid malignant neoplasm may spread from its site of origin by either direct extension or metastasis. Direct extension is the invasion of adjacent sites; metastasis refers to the spread to distant sites and the establishment of a new center of malignancy. *ICD-9-CM* does not make a distinction between these two types of extension. The terms "metastatic" and "secondary" are generally used interchangeably.

Malignant Neoplasm of Esophagus

Category **150, Malignant neoplasm of esophagus,** presents a departure from usual *ICD-9-CM* classification principles in that the subcategories are not mutually exclusive. Because this modification appears in *ICD-9,* it has been retained in *ICD-9-CM* to maintain the compatibility of the two systems.

The purpose of this dual-axis classification is to allow the classification to accommodate the differences in terminology often encountered in medical records. For example, the same neoplasm may be identified as being in either the cervical esophagus (150.0) or the upper third (150.3), in the thoracic esophagus (150.1) or the middle third (150.4), or in the abdominal esophagus (150.2) or the lower third (150.5). Depending on the terminology used by the physician, either code can be assigned, although it would be preferable for the facility to develop a coding policy that dictates which codes will be used.

Contiguous Sites

When the point of origin cannot be determined because the neoplasm overlaps the boundaries of two or more contiguous sites, it is classified with fourth digit 8, signifying other specified sites. For example, *ICD-9-CM* provides the following codes for certain malignant neoplasms whose point of origin cannot be established and whose stated sites overlap two or more three-digit category sites:

- 140.8 Neoplasm of overlapping sites of the lip whose point of origin cannot be assigned to any other code within category 140
- 151.8 Neoplasm of stomach whose point of origin cannot be assigned to any other code within category 151
- 162.8 Neoplasm of overlapping sites of lung, bronchus, and trachea whose point of origin cannot be assigned to any other code within category 162

Exercise 25.4

Code the following diagnoses. Do not assign M codes.

	Code(s)
1. Carcinoma of cervicothoracic esophagus	150.8
2. Carcinoma of oral cavity and pharynx	149.8
3. Adenocarcinoma of rectum and anus	154.8

Basal and Squamous Cell Skin Cancers

Basal cell carcinoma (173.0–173.9 with a fifth digit 1) is the most common form of skin cancer and arises in the basal cells, which line the deepest layer of the epidermis (top skin layer). This type of skin cancer normally occurs on areas of the skin that are exposed to the sun, such as the face and neck. Long-term exposure to ultraviolet (UV) radiation from sunlight increases the risk of developing basal cell carcinoma. Avoiding the sun and using sunscreen may help to protect against basal cell carcinoma. In a few cases, contact with arsenic, exposure to radiation, open wounds that resist healing, chronic inflammatory skin conditions, and complications of burns, scars, infections, vaccinations, or even tattoos are contributing factors.

Squamous cell carcinoma (173.0–173.9 with a fifth digit 2) is the second most prevalent type of cancer. It arises in the squamous cells that make up most of the skin's upper layers (epidermis) and can occur on all areas of the body, including the mucous membranes and genitals, but is usually found on skin exposed to the sun. Individuals with fair skin, light hair, and blue, green, or gray eyes have an increased risk of developing the disease. However, anyone with a history of excessive sun exposure is at risk. Sometimes extensive sun exposure is an occupational hazard. People with a history of basal cell carcinoma are more likely to develop a squamous cell carcinoma, as are persons with an inherited, highly UV-sensitive condition such as xeroderma pigmentosum.

Neoplasms Described as Metastatic

The terms "metastatic" and "metastasis" are often used ambiguously in describing neoplastic disease, sometimes meaning that the site named is primary and sometimes meaning that it is secondary. When the diagnostic statement is not clear in this regard, the coder should review the medical record for further information. When none is available, however, the following guidelines apply.

"Metastatic To"

The statement "metastatic to" indicates that the site mentioned is secondary. For example, a diagnosis of metastatic carcinoma to the lung is coded as secondary malignant neoplasm of the lung (197.0). A code for the primary neoplastic site should also be assigned when the primary neoplasm is still present; a history code from category **V10, Personal history of malignant neoplasm,** should be assigned when the primary neoplasm has been excised or eradicated. The fourth digit of category V10 indicates the body system where the prior neoplasm occurred, and the fifth digit indicates the specific organ or site involved.

Ordinarily, no history code is assigned when the patient has had a prior benign neoplasm. The one exception is that code **V12.41, Benign neoplasm of the brain,** is assigned for a personal history of a benign brain tumor, as these can recur, are often difficult to treat, and can be life threatening.

"Metastatic From"

The statement "metastatic from" indicates that the site mentioned is the primary site. For example, a diagnosis of metastatic carcinoma from the breast indicates that the breast is the primary site (174.9). An additional code for the metastatic site should also be assigned.

Multiple Metastatic Sites

When two or more sites are described as "metastatic" in the diagnostic statement, each of the stated sites should be coded as secondary or metastatic. A code should also be assigned for the primary site when this information is available; it should be coded 199.1 when it is not.

Single Metastatic Site

When only one site is described as metastatic without any further qualification and no more definitive information can be obtained by reviewing the medical record, the following steps should be followed:

1. Refer first to the morphology type in the Alphabetic Index and code to the primary condition of that site. For example, a diagnosis of metastatic renal cell carcinoma of the lung indicates that the primary site is the kidney and the secondary site is the lung. The correct coding for this is **189.0, Renal cell carcinoma,** and **197.0, Secondary carcinoma of lung.**

   When a specific site for the morphology type is not indicated in a code entry or is not indexed, assign the code for unspecified site within that anatomical site. For example, oat cell carcinoma is indexed to **162.9, Malignant neoplasm of bronchus and lung, unspecified,** when no more specific site is stated.
2. When the morphology type is not stated or the only code that can be obtained is either 199.0 or 199.1, code as a primary malignant neoplasm, unless the site is one of the following:
   - Bone
   - Brain
   - Diaphragm
   - Heart
   - Liver
   - Lymph nodes
   - Mediastinum
   - Meninges
   - Peritoneum
   - Pleura
   - Retroperitoneum
   - Spinal cord
   - Sites classifiable to 195

Malignant neoplasms of these sites are classified as secondary when not otherwise specified, except for neoplasm of the liver. *ICD-9-CM* provides code **155.2, Malignant neoplasm of liver, not specified as primary or secondary,** for use in this situation.

Examples of coding by this two-step procedure include the following:

- Metastatic carcinoma of the lung, coded by step 2, with the primary site assigned to the lung: carcinoma of lung; secondary site not specified 162.9 + 199.1
- Metastatic carcinoma of bone, coded by step 2, with the primary site unknown and the bone as the secondary site: carcinoma, site unknown; secondary site bone 198.5 + 199.1

No Site Stated

When no site is indicated in the diagnostic statement but the morphology type is qualified as metastatic, the code provided for that morphological type is assigned for the primary diagnosis along with an additional code for secondary neoplasm of unspecified site. For example, a diagnosis of metastatic apocrine adenocarcinoma with no site specified is coded as a primary malignant neoplasm of the skin, site unspecified (173.99). An additional code of 199.1 is assigned for the secondary neoplasm. Code 173.99 is obtained by referring to the following main term and subterms in volume 2:

Adenocarcinoma (M8140/3) . . .
  apocrine (M8401/3) . . .
    unspecified site 173.99

Exercise 25.5

Code the following diagnoses. Do not assign M codes.

	Code(s)
1. Metastatic carcinoma from lung	162.9 199.1
2. Metastatic carcinoma to brain	198.3 199.1
3. Metastatic carcinoma from prostate to pelvic bone Previous prostatectomy History	198.5 V10.46
4. Metastatic carcinoma to br ain from lung Previous resection of lung with no recurrence at primary site History	198.3 V10.11
5. Metastatic carcinoma from prostate to pelvic bone	185 198.5
6. Metastatic carcinoma of brain and lung	198.3 197.0 199.1

Review Exercise 25.5 *(continued)*

7. Metastatic carcinoma of pancreas and omentum	197.8 197.6 199.1
8. Metastatic adenocarcinoma of transverse colon	153.1 199.1
9. Metastatic carcinoma of bronchus	162.9 199.1
10. Metastatic carcinoma of spinal cord	198.3 199.1
11. Metastatic carcinoma of femur	198.5 199.1
12. Metastatic carcinoma of brain	198.3 199.1
13. Metastatic serous papillary adenocarcinoma of bone	183.0 198.5
14. Metastatic infiltrating duct cell carcinoma	174.9 199.1
15. Metastatic odontogenic fibrosarcoma	170.1 199.1
16. Chondroblastic osteosarcoma of limb with metastasis	170.9 199.1

CODING OF MALIGNANCIES OF HEMATOPOIETIC AND LYMPHATIC SYSTEMS

Unlike solid tumors, neoplasms that arise in lymphatic and hematopoietic tissues do not spread to secondary sites. Instead, malignant cells circulate and may occur in other sites within these tissues. These sites are considered to be primary neoplasms rather than secondary.

Neoplasms of Lymph Nodes or Glands

Primary malignant neoplasms of lymph nodes or glands are classified in categories 200 through 202, with a fourth digit providing more specificity about the particular type of neoplasm and a fifth digit indicating the nodes involved. If the neoplasm involves lymph nodes or glands of additional sites, fifth digit 8 is assigned to indicate that the malignancy now involves multiple sites. For example, code **200.08, Reticulosarcoma-lymph nodes of multiple sites,** is assigned for a diagnosis of reticulosarcoma of intra-abdominal and intrathoracic lymph nodes; individual codes are not assigned.

When a solid tumor has spread to the lymph nodes, a code from category 196 is assigned. For example, adenocarcinoma of breast with metastasis to lymph nodes of the axilla is coded to **174.9, Malignant neoplasm of female breast,** and **196.3, Secondary metastatic neoplasm of axillary lymph nodes.** No code from categories 200 through 202 is assigned.

Lymphomas can be malignant or benign. Codes for benign lymphomas are located by referencing the site in the neoplasm table. Malignant lymphomas are located by referencing the subterms for the site under the main term **Lymphoma.** When a diagnostic statement of lymphoma does not match any subentry under **Lymphoma** in volume 2, the coder may find that the pathology report indicates the neoplasm's behavior.

Hodgkin's Disease

The same type of dual-axis classification used for esophageal neoplasms is provided for a diagnosis of **Hodgkin's disease (201.x)** and for the same reasons, that is, to maintain correlation with *ICD-9* and to take into consideration differences in terminology. One physician, for example, may describe Hodgkin's disease as **Hodgkin's paragranuloma (201.00)**,whereas a pathologist may describe it as **Hodgkin's lymphoma of mixed cellularity (201.60).**

Non-Hodgkin's Lymphomas

Non-Hodgkin's lymphomas are a heterogeneous group of malignant lymphomas that present a clinical picture that is broadly similar to Hodgkin's disease but with the absence of the giant Reed-Sternberg cells that are characteristic of Hodgkin's disease. Lymphomas develop from the lymphoid components of the immune system. The main cell found in lymphoid tissue is the lymphocyte, an infection-fighting white blood cell, of which there are two main types, B lymphocytes (B cells) and T lymphocytes (T cells). There are 30 subtypes of non-Hodgkin's lymphomas based on chemical and genetic characteristics. *ICD-9-CM* was recently updated to allow for more current classification of lymphoma based on behavior.

Marginal zone lymphomas (200.3x) are slow-growing B cell tumors that are categorized based on whether they occur outside the lymph nodes or within the lymph node. Mucosa-associated lymphoid tissue (MALT) lymphomas are extranodal marginal zone lymphomas that occur in the gastrointestinal tract, eyes, thyroid, salivary glands, lungs, and skin. Nodal marginal zone B cell lymphomas involve the lymph nodes but are less common, whereas splenic marginal lymphomas involve the spleen, bone marrow, and blood. Treatment for marginal zone lymphomas depends on the type, location, and clinical presentation.

Mantle cell lymphoma (200.4x) is an aggressive non-Hodgkin's B cell lymphoma that is frequently diagnosed as stage 4 disease and found in the gastrointestinal tract, in bone marrow, and in lymph nodes above and below the diaphragm. Treatment includes antineoplastic drugs, such as R-CHOP (rituximab, cyclophosphamide, doxorubicin, vincristine, and prednisone). Although mantle cell lymphoma is difficult to treat, combinations of chemotherapy, biological therapies, and other regimens have demonstrated increased survival rates.

Primary central nervous system (CNS) lymphoma (200.5x) is found in the brain and spinal cord. A weakened immune system increases the risk for this aggressive lymphoma and is seen in patients with acquired immunodeficiency syndrome (AIDS), history of kidney transplant, and other immunocompromised conditions. These tumors are typically limited to the cranial-spinal axis and eye without systemic involvement. Because of the diffuse nature of CNS lymphoma, radiotherapy is the standard treatment.

Anaplastic large cell lymphoma (ALCL) (200.6x) can present in two forms: systemic or cutaneous on the skin. The cutaneous type manifests as a solitary nodule or ulcerating tumor in patients without a history of concurrent mycosis fungoides (MF) or lymphomatoid papulosis (LyP) with no evidence of disease outside the skin.

Large cell lymphoma (200.7x) is the most prevalent type of non-Hodgkin's lymphoma. The disease is aggressive and occurs in the lymph nodes and extranodal sites, such as the gastrointestinal tract, testes, thyroid, skin, breast, central nervous system, and bone. Treatment with high-dose chemotherapy and stem cell/bone marrow transplantation have increased survival rates.

Peripheral T-cell lymphoma (202.7x) is a lymphoma of the T-cells circulating within the lymphatic system. Peripheral T-cell lymphoma affects organs in the body, such as the bone marrow, liver, spleen, stomach, or bowel. Peripheral T cells are aggressive and may require salvage treatment and stem cell transplantation. T-cell lymphoma, also known as cutaneous T-cell lymphoma (CTCL), affects the skin. Cutaneous lymphomas are slow growing and respond well to surgery and radiation. Treatment can occasionally include chemotherapy.

Multiple Myeloma, Other Immunoproliferative Neoplasms, and Leukemias

Multiple myeloma and other immunoproliferative neoplasms are classified in category 203, with a fourth digit indicating the particular type of neoplasm. Leukemias are classified in categories 204 through 208, with the fourth digit indicating the stage of the disease (acute, chronic, subacute). For all codes in categories 203 through 208, a fifth digit is used to indicate the status of the patient:

- 0 Without mention of having achieved remission (failed remission)
- 1 In remission
- 2 In relapse

Fifth digit 0 is assigned if the health record documentation does not indicate that the patient has achieved remission. When the provider documents that the malignancy is in remission, assign fifth digit 1. This digit is only assigned when the physician specifically describes the neoplasm as being in remission. If the patient experiences a recurrence, and the provider documents "relapse," assign fifth digit 2. A relapse or recurrence can occur any time during therapy or after completion of treatment, even months or years after remission.

Exercise 25.6

Code the following diagnoses. Do not assign M codes.

	Code(s)
1. Aleukemic myelogenous leukemia, in remission	205.81
2. Reticulum cell sarcoma of the spleen	200.07
3. Reticulosarcoma, intrathoracic	200.02
4. Intrapelvic Hodgkin's granuloma	201.16
5. Chronic myeloid leukemia	205.10
6. Plasma cell leukemia	203.10
7. Carcinoma of lung with metastatic carcinoma of intrathoracic lymph nodes	162.9 196.1
8. Mycosis fungoides of intrathoracic and intra-abdominal lymph nodes	202.18
9. Castleman's lymphoma	785.6
10. Benign lymphoma of breast	217
11. Primary central nervous system lymphoma	200.50
12. Peripheral T-cell lymphoma	202.70

SEQUENCING OF CODES FOR NEOPLASTIC DISEASES

The basic rule for designating principal diagnoses is the same for neoplasms as for any other condition; that is, the principal diagnosis is the condition found after study to have occasioned the current admission or encounter. There is no guideline that indicates a code for malignancy takes precedence. Because the principal diagnosis is sometimes difficult to determine in a patient with a malignant neoplasm, however, the thrust of treatment can often be used as a guide to selecting the principal diagnosis.

Some neoplasms are functionally active in that they may affect the activity of endocrine glands. The code for these primary neoplasms is assigned first, followed by a code for the endocrine dysfunction. For example:

- Hyperestrogenism due to carcinoma of ovary 183.0 + 256.0
- Carcinoma of ovary with hirsutism 183.0 + 704.1

Lambert-Eaton syndrome is an autoimmune disorder that is often associated with cancer, in particular small cell lung cancer, and treatment of the cancer is the first priority. When the patient presents with small cell lung cancer and Lambert-Eaton syndrome, code first the underlying malignancy. For example:

- Small cell carcinoma of the lung and Lambert-Eaton syndrome 162.9 + 358.31

Treatment Directed at Primary Site

When treatment is directed toward the primary site, the malignancy of that site is designated as the principal diagnosis unless the encounter or hospital admission is solely for the purpose of radiotherapy, chemotherapy, or immunotherapy, in which case the primary malignancy is coded and sequenced as a secondary diagnosis. For example:

- Carcinoma of sigmoid colon with small metastatic nodules on the liver; sigmoid resection of the colon carried out: 153.3 + 197.7
- Carcinoma of sigmoid colon with prior resection; admitted for chemotherapy: V58.11 + 153.3

Sometimes two primary sites are present; in this case, each is coded as a primary neoplasm. When treatment is directed primarily toward one site, the neoplasm of that site should be designated as the principal diagnosis. When treatment is directed equally toward both, either may be designated as the principal diagnosis.

Occasionally, a patient admitted for surgery to correct a nonneoplastic condition has a pathology report indicating that a microscopic focus of malignancy is also present. In this situation, the condition that occasioned the admission remains the principal diagnosis, with an additional code assigned for the malignancy. For example:

- A patient with severe urinary retention due to hypertrophy of the prostate was admitted for prostatectomy. Transurethral resection of the prostate (TURP) was carried out, and the patient was discharged with a diagnosis of benign hypertrophy of the prostate. When the pathology report was received, this diagnosis was confirmed, but a microscopic focus of adenocarcinoma was also identified. **Code 600.01, Hypertrophy (benign) of prostate with urinary obstruction and other lower urinary tract symptoms** (LUTS), is assigned as the principal diagnosis with codes **185, Malignant neoplasm of prostate,** and **788.20, Retention of urine, unspecified,** assigned as additional codes.
- A patient was admitted for treatment of endometriosis of the uterus, and a total abdominal hysterectomy was carried out. The pathology report confirmed the endometriosis but indicated that carcinoma in situ of the cervix was also present. In this case, the endometriosis was the reason for admission and remains the principal diagnosis. An additional code is assigned for the cervical neoplasm.

Treatment Directed at Secondary Site

When a patient is admitted because of a primary neoplasm with metastasis and treatment is directed solely toward the secondary site, the secondary site is designated as the principal diagnosis even though the primary malignancy is still present. A code for the primary malignancy is assigned as an additional code.

When a patient is admitted because of a primary neoplasm with metastasis and treatment is directed equally toward the primary and the secondary sites, the primary malignancy should be designated the principal diagnosis, with an additional code assigned to the secondary neoplasm.

Admission for Complications Associated with a Malignant Neoplasm

Patients with malignant neoplasms often develop complications due to either the malignancy itself or the therapy that they have received. When admission is primarily for treatment of the complication, the following guidelines govern selection of the principal diagnosis:

- When the admission/encounter is for management of an anemia associated with the malignancy, and the treatment is only for anemia, the appropriate anemia code (such as code **285.22, Anemia in neoplastic disease**) is designated as the principal diagnosis and is followed by the appropriate code(s) for the malignancy. Code 285.22 may also be used as a secondary code if the patient suffers from anemia and is being treated for the malignancy.
- When the admission/encounter is for management of an anemia associated with chemotherapy, immunotherapy, or radiotherapy, and the only treatment is for the anemia, the anemia is sequenced first. The appropriate neoplasm code should be assigned as an additional code. For antineoplastic chemotherapy induced anemia, assign code 285.3. Code E933.1, which is assigned to show the adverse effect of chemotherapy, is not necessary because code 285.3 includes the adverse effect. For example:
  —A patient with metastatic, non-small cell lung cancer of the right upper lobe developed anemia following chemotherapy. The patient presents to the oncologist for treatment of anemia of chemotherapy. Codes **285.3, Antineoplastic chemotherapy induced anemia,** and **162.3, Malignant neoplasm upper bronchus or lung,** are assigned.
- When the admission/encounter is for management of an anemia documented as "pancytopenia due to chemotherapy," code 284.11 is assigned for pancytopenia caused by cancer fighting drugs. In cancer patients, pancytopenia usually occurs due to bone marrow suppression from chemotherapy. Bone marrow suppression (a decreased ability of the bone marrow to manufacture blood cells) is a common side effect of chemotherapy. For example:
  —A patient with breast cancer of the left upper-outer quadrant developed pancytopenia following chemotherapy. The patient presents to the oncologist for follow-up of the pancytopenia. The oncologist listed chemotherapy-induced pancytopenia in his diagnostic statement. Assign code **284.11, Antineoplastic chemotherapy induced pancytopenia,** as the first-listed diagnosis. Assign code **174.4, Malignant neoplasm female breast, upper-outer quadrant,** as an additional diagnosis.
- When the admission/encounter is for management of dehydration due to the malignancy or the therapy or a combination of both, and only the dehydration is being treated (intravenous rehydration), the dehydration is sequenced first, followed by the code(s) for the malignancy.

The basic rule for designating the principal diagnosis is the same for neoplasm as for any other condition; that is, the principal diagnosis is the condition found after study to have occasioned the current admission or encounter. There is no guideline that indicates that a code for the malignancy takes precedence. Because the principal diagnosis may be difficult to determine, the focus of treatment can often be used as a guide. For example:

- A patient under treatment for prostate cancer was admitted for gross hematuria. The patient received fifteen units of blood; bladder irrigation was started and continued until the urine was clear. Code **599.71, Gross hematuria,** is assigned as principal diagnosis. Assign code **185, Malignant neoplasm of prostate,** as an additional diagnosis. In this case, the patient was admitted and treated for gross hematuria. Treatment was not directed at the malignancy.

Admission or Encounter Solely for Administration of Radiotherapy, Immunotherapy, or Chemotherapy

When a patient admission/encounter is solely for the administration of chemotherapy, immunotherapy, or radiation therapy, assign code **V58.0, Encounter for radiation therapy,** or **V58.11, Encounter for antineoplastic chemotherapy,** or **V58.12, Encounter for antineoplastic immunotherapy,** as the first-listed or principal diagnosis. When the patient receives more than one of these therapies during the same admission, more than one of these codes may be assigned, in any sequence. Because the patient is still under treatment for the malignancy even though it may have been removed surgically, an additional code for the malignancy is assigned rather than a code from category V10.

Codes from category V10 are assigned only when the primary neoplasm has been totally eradicated and is no longer under any type of treatment. This guideline applies to both solid and hematopoietic or lymphatic neoplasms, including leukemia. Note, however, that patients with leukemia are often admitted for a variety of tests or other treatment in addition to chemotherapy. If there is any question about whether the admission is for the sole purpose of chemotherapy, immunotherapy, or radiotherapy, the physician should be consulted. Codes should also be assigned for the type of radiotherapy (92.2x), immunotherapy (99.28), or chemotherapy (99.25) provided. Code 17.70 is assigned for the intravenous infusion of Clofarabine, a chemotherapeutic agent used for the treatment of pediatric patients (ages 1–21) with relapsed or refractory acute lymphoblastic leukemia.

Tumor lysis syndrome (TLS) is a group of serious, potentially life threatening metabolic disturbances that can occur after antineoplastic therapy or as a result of radiation or corticosteroid therapy. It is often associated with leukemias and lymphomas, but is also seen in other hematologic malignancies and solid tumors. Code **277.88, Tumor lysis syndrome,** is assigned with an additional E code to identify the cause when TLS is drug-induced. For example:

- A child was diagnosed with acute myeloid leukemia and admitted for chemotherapy. Chemotherapy was administered and the provider diagnosed tumor lysis syndrome secondary to antineoplastic therapy. Code **V58.11, Encounter for antineoplastic chemotherapy,** is assigned as the principal diagnosis. Codes **205.00, Myeloid leukemia, Acute, without mention of having achieved remission; 277.88, Tumor lysis syndrome;** and **E933.1, Antineoplastic and immunosuppressive drugs,** are also assigned. Code **99.25, Injection or infusion of cancer chemotherapeutic substance,** is assigned for the administration of chemotherapy.

When a patient is admitted for the purpose of radiotherapy, immunotherapy, or chemotherapy and develops complications such as uncontrolled nausea and vomiting or dehydration, the principal or first-listed diagnosis is **V58.0, Encounter for radiotherapy,** or **V58.11, Encounter for antineoplastic chemotherapy,** or **V58.12, Encounter for antineoplastic immunotherapy,** followed by any codes for the complications.

Chemoembolization is a variation of chemotherapy in which there is concurrent intra-arterial administration of a collagen particle with the chemotherapeutic agent. This arrests the vascular flow time of the chemotherapy and increases the target retention of the drug. Chemoembolization is included in code **99.25, Injection or infusion of cancer chemotherapeutic substance.** Code **38.91, Arterial catheterization,** is also assigned if the arterial line is placed during the episode of care.

New advancements in radiofrequency thermal ablation (RFA) have expanded treatment options for some cancer patients. Thermal ablative procedures utilize heat to destroy lung, liver, or renal malignancies. Minimally invasive, image-guided thermal ablation provides effective treatment of localized neoplastic disease and can also be used as an adjunct to traditional surgery, chemotherapy, and/or radiation treatment. Under radiological imaging, a needle-electrode is inserted at the site of the tumor; radiofrequency energy is then applied to destroy the tumor. Thermal ablation can be performed by three different methods: open, laparoscopic, and percutaneous. *ICD-9-CM* provides the following procedure codes to describe the various thermal ablative procedures:

- 32.23 Open ablation of lung lesion or tissue
- 32.24 Percutaneous ablation of lung lesion or tissue
- 32.25 Thoracoscopic ablation of lung lesion or tissue
- 32.26 Other and unspecified ablation of lung lesion or tissue
- 50.23 Open ablation of liver lesion or tissue
- 50.24 Percutaneous ablation of liver lesion or tissue
- 50.25 Laparoscopic ablation of liver lesion or tissue
- 50.26 Other and unspecified ablation of liver lesion or tissue
- 55.32 Open ablation of renal lesion or tissue
- 55.33 Percutaneous ablation of renal lesion or tissue
- 55.34 Laparoscopic ablation of renal lesion or tissue
- 55.35 Other and unspecified ablation of renal lesion or tissue

Laser Interstitial Thermal Therapy

Thermal therapy can be used to destroy malignancies involving the brain, breast, liver, prostate, and other organs. The energy sources come in many forms, such as laser, microwave, radiofrequency, etc. The heat source may be extracorporeal (outside the body), extrastitial (outside the tumor), or interstitial (inside the tumor).

Laser interstitial thermal therapy (LITT) is a surgical procedure in which obliteration of soft tissues in the body is performed through elevated temperatures caused by the local absorption of laser energy under magnetic resonance imaging (MRI) guidance. With this type of therapy, the energy is applied directly to the tumor rather than passing through surrounding normal tissue. The therapy encompasses the whole target but does not extend to surrounding critical structures. LITT may also be performed to remove cancerous lesions from other sites, such as head and neck, liver, breast, prostate, and lung. The following codes are specifically for LITT under guidance:

- 17.61 Laser interstitial thermal therapy [LITT] of lesion or tissue of brain under guidance
- 17.62 Laser interstitial thermal therapy [LITT] of lesion or tissue of head and neck under guidance
- 17.63 Laser interstitial thermal therapy [LITT] of lesion or tissue of liver under guidance
- 17.69 Laser interstitial thermal therapy [LITT] of lesion or tissue of other and unspecified site under guidance

When a patient is admitted for the purpose of inserting a port for later administration of chemotherapy but no chemotherapy is given during the same episode of care, the malignancy is designated as the principal diagnosis and code **V58.11, Encounter for antineoplastic chemotherapy,** is not assigned. When insertion of the port is followed by chemotherapy during the same episode of care, code V58.11 is assigned as the principal diagnosis. If an intraperitoneal catheter is inserted for the chemotherapy access, code **54.99, Other operation on abdominal wall,** is assigned with code 99.25 added if chemotherapy is administered during the episode of care.

Bacille Calmette-Guerin (BCG) is a nonspecific immunotherapy agent (99.28) used in the treatment of melanoma, cancer of the lung, soft-tissue sarcoma, carcinoma of the colon, and carcinoma of the breast. Interferon is another nonspecific immunotherapy agent used in treating malignancy. Another type of immunotherapy is interleukin-2 (IL-2), which is used to treat patients with advanced renal cell carcinoma and advanced melanoma. There is a high-dose IL-2 and a low-dose IL-2 therapy. High-dose IL-2 therapy is a hospital inpatient–based regimen usually performed in specialized treatment settings such as the intensive care unit or bone marrow transplant unit. The administration of low-dose interleukin is coded to 99.28, whereas the high-dose IL-2 is assigned code 00.15. The high-dose IL-2 therapy requires highly specialized oncology professionals because of the severity of the predictable toxicities requiring extensive monitoring. The principal diagnosis code for a patient admitted for antineoplastic immunotherapy is **V58.12, Encounter for antineoplastic immunotherapy.**

Blood brain barrier disruption (BBBD) chemotherapy (00.19) is a unique option for the delivery of drugs for the treatment of brain tumors and brain metastases. The blood brain barrier (BBB) is an impediment to the delivery of chemotherapy for central nervous system (CNS) malignancies. The BBB is the lining of the small blood vessels in the brain that prevents substances such as toxins or drugs from entering the brain. Patients receiving chemotherapy for brain tumors do not receive adequate doses because antineoplastic drugs cannot cross the BBB through conventional methods of drug delivery. An improved method for drug delivery to the CNS is the infusion of chemotherapy directly into brain arteries through disruption of the BBB. BBBD therapy delivers key drugs and other substances to the brain (i.e., rituximab, trastuzumab, antibodies, or genes), avoiding the long-term cognitive effects of radiotherapy. This technique can deliver five to ten times the concentration of the drug into the brain without the risks of neurotoxicity.

Assign code **V58.11, Encounter for antineoplastic chemotherapy,** as the principal diagnosis when the admission is for chemotherapy with infusion of a substance to disrupt the blood brain barrier. Code **00.19, Disruption of blood brain barrier via infusion (BBBD),** should be assigned for the BBBD. Assign also code **99.25, Injection or infusion of cancer chemotherapeutic substance.**

An admission for radium implant or insertion or for treatment by radioactive iodine (I-131) is not considered an admission solely for a radiotherapy session. The code for the malignant neoplasm is designated the principal diagnosis; code V58.0 is not assigned. The Viadur (leuprolide acetate) implant is used as palliative treatment for advanced prostate cancer. The device is implanted subcutaneously in the arm and delivers leuprolide acetate continuously over a period of 12 months. Leuprolide acetate lowers testosterone, a hormone that is needed by prostate cancer cells. Assign code **99.24, Injection of other hormone,** for the insertion of the viadur implant. The code for the prostate malignancy is designated as the principal diagnosis.

Intra-operative electron radiation therapy (IOERT) is a specialized, intensive radiation treatment administered during surgery directly to the cancer tumor or tumor bed. Normal tissue is protected, thereby substantially increasing the effectiveness of the treatment. The code for the malignant neoplasm is designated as the principal diagnosis; code V58.11 is not assigned. Assign code **92.41, Intra-operative radiation therapy,** for IOERT.

When the reason for the admission/encounter is to determine the extent of the malignancy or for a procedure such as paracentesis or thoracentesis, the primary malignancy or appropriate metastatic site is designated as the principal or first-listed diagnosis, even though chemotherapy or radiotherapy is administered. Because therapy such as radiotherapy and chemotherapy must be delivered at regularly scheduled intervals, it is often performed during an episode of care during which it is not the primary focus of treatment.

Malignant Neoplasm Associated with Transplanted Organ

A malignant neoplasm of a transplanted organ should be coded as a transplant complication. A code from category **996.8, Complication of transplanted organ,** is assigned as the principal diagnosis, followed by code **199.2, Malignant neoplasm associated with transplanted organ.** An additional code is assigned for the specific malignancy.

Malignant Ascites

Malignant ascites (789.51) is the abnormal buildup of fluid in the abdomen caused by malignancy. Diagnostic tests to determine the underlying cause may involve blood tests, ultrasound of the abdomen (88.76), and paracentesis (54.91). Treatment may include diuretics, therapeutic paracentesis (needle aspiration of the peritoneal cavity), or other therapies directed at the underlying cause. For example:

- A patient is admitted with pancreatic cancer with massive widespread malignant ascites. The final diagnosis is pancreatic cancer with malignant ascites and metastasis to the retroperitoneum. Therapeutic paracentesis was accomplished. Assign code **157.9, Malignant neoplasm of pancreas, part not specified,** as the principal diagnosis. Codes **789.51, Malignant ascites,** and **197.6, Secondary malignant neoplasm of retroperitoneum and peritoneum,** should be assigned as secondary diagnoses. Assign code **54.91, Percutaneous abdominal drainage,** for the paracentesis.

Malignant Pleural Effusion

Malignant pleural effusions (511.81) can occur due to impaired pleural lymphatic drainage from a mediastinal tumor (especially in lymphomas) and not because of direct tumor invasion into the pleura. The lymphoma is obstructing the drainage system, which is usually caused by disturbance of the normal Starling forces regulating reabsorption of fluid in the pleural space. The code for the malignancy is assigned first, and the code for the malignant pleural effusion is assigned as an additional diagnosis.

ENCOUNTER FOR PROPHYLACTIC ORGAN REMOVAL

For encounters specifically for prophylactic removal of breasts, ovaries, or another organ due to a genetic susceptibility to cancer or a family history of cancer, the principal or first-listed diagnosis should be a code from subcategory **V50.4, Prophylactic organ removal.** The appropriate genetic susceptibility (V84.01–V84.09) and family history (V16.0–V16.9) codes should be assigned as additional diagnoses.

If the patient has a malignancy of one site and is having prophylactic removal of another site to prevent either a new primary malignancy or metastatic disease, a code for the malignancy should also be assigned in addition to a code from subcategory V50.4.

Code V50.4x should not be assigned if the patient is having organ removal for treatment of a malignancy, such as the removal of testes for the treatment of prostate cancer. For example:

- A patient with a history of left breast carcinoma, previously treated with left breast lumpectomy and radiation therapy, was recently diagnosed with BRCA1 genetic mutation. The patient underwent bilateral prophylactic mastectomy. Code **V50.41, Prophylactic organ removal, breast,** is assigned as the principal diagnosis. Assign codes **V84.01, Genetic susceptibility to malignant neoplasm of breast; V10.3, Personal history of malignant neoplasm, breast;** and **V15.3, Other personal history presenting hazards to health, irradiation,** as additional diagnoses. Assign procedure code **85.42, Bilateral simple mastectomy.** Because the patient was previously treated for left breast cancer and was then diagnosed with the BRCA1 genetic mutation, the mastectomy is considered prophylactic.

CODING OF ADMISSIONS OR ENCOUNTERS FOR FOLLOW-UP EXAMINATIONS

Once a malignant neoplasm has been excised or eradicated, periodic follow-up examinations are carried out to determine whether there is recurrence of the primary malignancy or any spread to a secondary site. When there is no evidence of recurrence at either a primary site or a metastatic site, the appropriate code from **V67.x, Follow-up examination,** is assigned as the principal diagnosis. The fourth digit should reflect the therapy most recently carried out. The appropriate code from category V10 should be assigned as an additional code. Codes should also be assigned for any diagnostic procedures (such as endoscopy and biopsy) that are carried out.

When there is evidence of recurrence at the primary site, the code for the malignancy is designated as the principal diagnosis. For example, a primary carcinoma of the anterior wall of the urinary bladder that was previously excised but has recurred in the lateral wall is coded to **188.2, Malignant neoplasm of lateral wall of urinary bladder.**

When there is no recurrence at the primary site but there is evidence of metastasis to a secondary site, a code for secondary neoplasm of that site is assigned along with a code from category V10. No code from category V67 is assigned.

Exercise 25.7

Answer the following questions either true or false.

__F__ 1. The recurrence of an original primary malignant neoplasm that was previously removed is classified to category **V10, Personal history of malignant neoplasm.**

__F__ 2. If a primary malignant neoplasm was excised previously and the original primary site has not recurred, assign the code for the previous primary malignant neoplasm, using the appropriate code from categories 140 through 195.

__T__ 3. Whenever secondary neoplasms are present, the V code for identifying personal history of malignant neoplasm can never be sequenced as the principal diagnosis code for Uniform Hospital Discharge Data Set (UHDDS) purposes.

Review Exercise 25.8

The following exercise provides a review of the material on neoplasms presented in this handbook. For this exercise, assign procedure codes where applicable, but do not assign M codes.

	Code(s)
1. Infiltrating papillary transitional cell carcinoma of urinary bladder (neck)	188.5
Suprapubic excision of bladder tumor	57.59
2. Carcinoma of midesophagus with spread to celiac lymph nodes	150.4 196.2
Permanent gastrostomy procedure High-voltage radiotherapy	43.19 92.22
3. Malignant carcinoid tumor of small intestine	209.00
4. Carcinoma, scirrhous, left breast, outer portion	174.8
Open biopsy with frozen section followed immediately by left radical mastectomy	85.45 85.12
5. Intramural leiomyoma of uterus	218.1

Review Exercise 25.8 *(continued)*

6. Multiple myeloma	203.00
7. Carcinoma of gallbladder with metastasis to abdominal lymph nodes and liver and peritoneal implants	156.0 196.2 197.7 197.6
Exploratory laparotomy with cholecystectomy, needle biopsy of peritoneal implant, and intra-operative electron radiation therapy	51.22 54.24 92.41
8. Squamous cell carcinoma in situ, floor of mouth	230.0
Resection of lesion, floor of mouth	27.49
9. Metastatic malignant melanoma from left lateral chest wall to axillary lymph node Neoplasm	172.5 196.3
Radical excision of malignant melanoma of chest wall with radical left axillary lymphadenectomy	34.4 40.51
10. Metastatic adenocarcinoma of sacrum, prostatic in origin Previous prostatectomy History	198.5 V10.46

Review Exercise 25.8 *(continued)*

11. A 33-year-old female admitted for prophylactic removal of both breasts, with documented genetic susceptibility to breast cancer due to extensive family history of breast carcinoma Bilateral mastectomy	V50.41 V84.01 V16.3 85.42
12. Seminoma, left testis Bilateral radical orchiectomy	186.9 62.41
13. Lipoma, right kidney	214.3
14. Chronic lymphatic leukemia, in remission	204.11
15. Admitted for chemotherapy following oophorectomy on previous admission for carcinoma of ovary	V58.11 183.0 99.25
16. Brain metastasis, admitted for chemotherapy and infusion of substance to disrupt blood brain barrier	V58.11 198.3 00.19 99.25
17. Ovarian carcinoma with malignant ascites and metastasis to the peritoneal cavity	183.0 789.51 197.6

Coding of Injuries, Burns, Poisoning, and Complications of Care

Injuries

CHAPTER **26**

CHAPTER OVERVIEW

- Injuries, poisoning, and complications of trauma and of medical or surgical care are found in chapter 17 of *ICD-9-CM*.
- The primary axis for classifying injuries is the type of injury.
- The secondary axis is the anatomical site.
- The most severe cause of injury is used as the principal diagnosis.
- E codes indicate how the injury occurred, the intent (accident or intentional), the place where the injury occurred, the status of the patient at the time the injury occurred, and any activity that may have caused or contributed to the injury.
- An E code is never a principal diagnosis.
- Multiple E codes can be used. The first corresponds to the most serious diagnosis.
- Vehicle accidents involve a hierarchy when different types of vehicles are involved.
- Code child and adult abuse before the associated injuries or conditions resulting from the abuse.
- Fractures are classified into four categories based on location.
  - Three-digit categories indicate more specific sites within these groupings.
  - The fourth digit indicates an open or closed fracture.
  - The fifth digit indicates a specific bone.
- Reduction is the most common treatment for fractures. The first axis is whether the reduction is open or closed. The second axis determines if internal fixation is applied. A fourth digit indicates the bone involved.
- Fracture aftercare codes are V codes assigned for completion of treatment or routine care during the healing process.
- If dislocations accompany fractures, they are included in the fracture code.
- Internal injuries, blood vessel and nerve injuries, open wounds, and amputations are also covered in this chapter.

LEARNING OUTCOMES

After studying this chapter you should be able to:

- Use E codes to assist in the classification of an injury.
- Classify fractures up to the fifth digit.
- Code for procedures related to fractures.
- Code for open wounds and other varieties of injuries.

TERMS TO KNOW

E codes
indicate external cause of injury or poisoning; used with injury and poisoning codes

Pathological fracture
a fracture caused by bone weakening associated with conditions such as osteoporosis or neoplastic diseases

REMEMBER . . . This chapter of the *ICD-9-CM* utilizes extensive inclusion and exclusion notes, which make for some long and complicated codes.

INTRODUCTION

Chapter 17 of *ICD-9-CM* classifies injuries, poisoning, other effects of external causes, complications of trauma, and complications of medical and surgical care not classified elsewhere. Because this chapter covers such a broad range of conditions, guidelines for the coding of burns, poisoning, adverse effects, and complications of medical and surgical care will be discussed in subsequent chapters of this handbook.

Injuries are classified in the following sections:

- Fractures 800–829
- Dislocations 830–839
- Sprains and strains 840–848
- Intracranial injuries 850–854
- Internal injuries 860–869
- Open wounds 870–897
- Blood vessel injuries 900–904
- Late effects of injuries 905–909
- Superficial injuries 910–919
- Contusions 920–924
- Crushing injuries 925–929
- Foreign body entering through orifice 930–939
- Burns 940–949
- Nerve and spinal cord injuries 950–957
- Early complications of trauma 958

The primary axis for classifying injuries is the type of injury as indicated in the preceding list; the second axis is determined by the anatomical site. Inclusion and exclusion notes are used extensively in this chapter, some of them long and complex, and it is important to give careful attention to these if correct code assignments are to be made. Fourth and fifth digits are provided for many categories to indicate a more detailed anatomical site or to provide more information regarding the injury. Examples of fifth-digit subclassifications found in chapter 17 of *ICD-9-CM* are shown in table 26.1.

MULTIPLE CODING OF INJURIES

Injuries classifiable in more than one subcategory should be coded separately unless a combination code is provided. General codes for multiple injuries are provided for use when there is insufficient detail in the medical record (such as trauma cases transferred promptly to another facility). Multiple injury codes should not be assigned when documentation permits more specific code assignment.

TABLE 26.1 Fifth-Digit Subclassifications for Injuries

Category and Title		Fifth-Digit Axis
800	Fracture of vault of skull	Level of consciousness
805.0–805.1	Fracture of cervical vertebrae without mention of spinal cord injury	Cervical vertebrae involved
807.0–807.1	Fracture of rib(s)	Number of ribs involved
813	Fracture of radius and ulna	Anatomical site
864	Injury to liver	Type and severity of injury

As discussed in chapter 2 of this handbook, the word "with" and the word "and" are used in a specific way in *ICD-9-CM*. They are used a great deal in chapter 17 of the *ICD-9-CM*. The word "with" means that both sites mentioned in the diagnostic statement are involved in the injury.

The word "and" is interpreted as meaning "and/or"—that is, that either or both sites are involved. In coding injuries, mention of fingers usually takes into account the thumb, but there are a few separate codes for injuries of the thumb. Terms such as "condyle," "coronoid process," "ramus," and "symphysis" refer to the portion of the bone involved in an injury, not to the bone itself.

SEQUENCING OF INJURY CODES

If admission is due to injury and several injuries are present, the code for the most severe injury is designated as the principal diagnosis. If the diagnostic statement is not clear on this point, the physician should be asked to make this determination.

EXTERNAL CAUSE OF INJURY

As mentioned earlier in chapter 8 of this handbook, external cause of injury and poisoning codes (categories E000 and E800–E999) are used with injury and poisoning codes to provide information about how an injury occurred, the intent (accidental or intentional), the place where the injury occurred, and the status (e.g., military, civilian) of the patient at the time the injury occurred. In the case of a person who seeks care for an injury or other health condition that resulted from an activity, or when an activity contributed to the injury or health condition, activity codes (categories E001–E030) are used to describe the activity.

Injuries are a major cause of mortality, morbidity, and disability, and the cost of care related to these conditions contributes significantly to the increased cost of health care. Reporting E codes provides data for injury research and evaluation of injury-prevention strategies. E codes capture how the injury or poisoning happened (cause), the intent (unintentional or accidental; or intentional, such as suicide or assault), the person's status (e.g., civilian, military), the associated activity, and the place where the event occurred.

Although reporting external cause is optional unless mandated by state or insurance carrier regulation, health care providers are strongly encouraged to report E codes for all initial treatment of injuries. Guidelines for reporting have been developed, and providers are urged to follow these guidelines so that there is consistency in the data.

Major categories of E codes include:

- External code status
- Activity
- Transport accidents
- Poisoning and adverse effects of drugs, medicinal substances, and biologicals
- Accidental falls
- Accidents caused by fire and flames
- Accidents due to natural and environmental factors
- Late effects of accidents, assaults, or self injury
- Assaults or purposely inflicted injury
- Suicide or self-inflicted injury

The selection of appropriate E codes for injuries is guided by the Index to External Causes and by inclusion and exclusion notes in the Tabular List. The index is located in section 3 in volume 2; the Tabular List follows the section on V codes in volume 1.

External Cause Status

A code from category E000, External cause status, is assigned to indicate the work status of the person at the time the injury occurred. The status code indicates whether the injury occurred during military activity, whether a nonmilitary person was at work, or whether a student or volunteer was involved in a nonwork activity at the time of the causal event. A code from E000 should be assigned, when applicable, with other external cause codes, such as transport accidents and falls. The external cause status E codes include status codes for activities done as a hobby or for leisure and recreation, volunteer activity, and activity of off-duty military personnel. Do not assign code **E000.9, Unspecified external cause status**, if the status is not stated.

Activity Codes

Assign a code from category E001–E030 to describe an activity that caused, or contributed to, an injury, poisoning, or other health condition. These codes may be used with other external cause codes for status (E000) and place of occurrence (E849). Coders should not assign code **E030, Unspecified activity**, if the activity is not stated.

Sequencing of E Codes

An E code is never used as the principal diagnosis. If two or more events cause separate injuries, an E code should be assigned for each. If the injury is due to two or more external causes, the code for the proximal (direct) cause is listed first. For example:

- A sailor on shore leave was admitted with a fracture of the shaft of the left femur that he suffered during a fight when he stepped backwards and fell from the top of the stairs. The fall (E823.01) is the proximal cause of the fracture and the fight (E960.0) is the initiating event. The following codes should be assigned: **821.01 (Fracture, shaft of femur), E880.9 (Fall on stairs or steps), E960.0 (Unarmed fight or brawl),** and **E000.8 (Other external cause status).**
- A woman who had fractured her arm when the car she was driving hit a tree during a tornado was admitted. E908.1 is assigned for the tornado, with an additional code for the collision and status. The proximal cause was the motor vehicle accident, but the code for tornado is listed first because a cataclysmic event takes precedence.

The E code listed first should correspond to the cause of the most serious diagnosis due to external cause. This sequencing hierarchy should be followed:

- E codes for child and adult abuse take precedence over all other E codes.
- E codes for terrorism events take priority over all other E codes except child and adult abuse.
- E codes for cataclysmic events take priority over all E codes except those for child and adult abuse and terrorism. Cataclysmic events include storms, floods, hurricanes, tornadoes, blizzards, volcanic eruptions, and earth surface movements and eruptions.
- Transport accidents take priority over all other E codes except those for abuse and cataclysmic events, child and adult abuse, and terrorism.
- Activity and external cause status is assigned following all causal (intent) E codes.
- The first-listed E code should correspond to the cause of the most serious diagnosis due to an assault, accident, or self-harm, following the order of hierarchy listed above.

When a transportation accident involves more than one type of vehicle, the following order of precedence should be followed:

- Air and space transport accidents (E840–E845)
- Watercraft accidents (E830–E838)
- Motor vehicle traffic and nontraffic accidents (E810–E825)

- Railway accidents (E800–E807)
- Other road vehicle accidents (E826–E829)

For example, an accident involving both a motor vehicle and an aircraft is classified as an aircraft accident, and one that involves railway transportation equipment and a motor vehicle is classified as a motor vehicle accident. No general rule governs priority for other E codes. Exclusion notes should be followed carefully.

Transport and Vehicle Accidents

A transport accident (E800–E848) is one involving a device that is designed (or being used at the time) primarily for conveying goods or people from one place to another. A long note at the beginning of this section defines in detail just what is meant by each type of transportation and what vehicles are included.

The final digit in most of these categories indicates the role or activity of the person involved in the accident. For example, the injured person in a motor vehicle accident may be a passenger in the vehicle, a bicyclist, or a pedestrian. Definitions of these roles are provided at the beginning of each section. For example:

- Open fracture, shaft of femur (pedestrian during recreational walk struck by automobile) 821.11 + E814.7 + E001.0 + E000.8

Accidents caused by machines such as agricultural or earth-moving equipment are classified as transport accidents if the pieces of equipment were in operation as transport vehicles when the accidents occurred. Otherwise, they are classified in category E919, Accidents caused by machinery, with a fourth digit indicating the specific type of equipment.

External Cause of Injury Classified by Intent

Separate external cause codes are provided to classify the external cause of injuries resulting from accident, self-harm, or assault. If the intent is unknown, unspecified, suspected, possible, or probable, a code from categories E980 through E989, Undetermined whether accidentally or purposefully inflicted, should be assigned. When the intent of an injury or poisoning is known but the cause is unknown, use **E928.9, Unspecified accident, E958.9, Suicide and self-inflicted injury by unspecified means,** or **E968.9, Assault by other and unspecified means.** These E codes should rarely be used; medical record documentation usually provides enough detail to determine the cause of the injury.

Category E979, Terrorism, is used to identify injuries and illnesses acquired as a result of terrorism. These codes (E979.0–E979.9) follow the definition of terrorism established by the U.S. Federal Bureau of Investigation (FBI). Coders are not to classify a death or an injury as terrorist-related unless the federal government has designated the incident as terrorism.

LATE EFFECTS OF EXTERNAL CAUSES

When the condition code from the main classification is a late effect of injury, the associated E code must also indicate a late effect, as follows:

- E929.x Late effect of accidental injury
- E959 Late effect of self-inflicted injury
- E969 Late effect of injury purposely inflicted by another person

For example, a diagnosis of extensive scarring of the face due to an old burn is coded **709.2, Scar conditions and fibrosis of skin,** + 906.5 + E929.4. In this example, code 906.5 indicates that the condition is a late effect of burn of eye, face, head, and neck, and code E929.4 indicates that it is a late effect of an accident caused by fire. Code **E897, Accident**

caused by controlled fire not in building or structure, is not used because it identifies the external cause of a current injury rather than a late effect.

ICD-9-CM provides external cause category **E849, Place of occurrence,** for use as an additional code to indicate the place where an external event occurred when the place of occurrence is not implicit in the injury or poisoning code. When the place of occurrence is not specified, a code from E849 is not assigned. Note that codes from category E849 refer only to the location, not to the activity of the injured person. Separate codes are provided for the activity and status. For example:

- Fall on escalator in airport building E880.0 + E849.6
- Clothing caught fire while burning trash in backyard of home, causing burn E893.2 + E849.0 + E013.9 + E000.8

Exercise 26.1

Assign only the E codes in the following exercises.

	Code(s)
1. Closed fracture, right tibia and fibula, due to fall from bicycle while patient was working as a messenger for a delivery service	E826.1 E006.4 E000.0
2. Injury to delivery man who jumped from moving truck not on a public highway because he thought the driver was stopping	E825.1 E000.0
3. Multiple facial lacerations to military police officer driving an automobile that was in a collision with another vehicle on expressway	E812.0 E000.1 E849.5
4. Anoxic brain damage due to previous head injury, three years ago, when patient was accidentally struck by car while walking along highway Late effect of	E929.0
5. Injury received by crew member of commercial airline when he fell at takeoff Accident	E843.2 E000.0
6. Injury received by guest passenger in hot-air balloon when balloon made unexpected descent Accident	E842.6 E029.9 E000.8

Exercise 26.1 *(continued)*

7. Passenger injured when he accidentally collided with another passenger while getting off a streetcar
   Accident — E817.4, E849.5

8. Railway employee injured by accident involving collision with rolling stock
   Accident — E800.0, E000.0

9. Railway employee injured when hit by rolling stock while unloading material
   Accident — E805.0, E000.0

10. Passenger injured in accidental derailment of train
    Accident — E802.1

11. Motorcyclist injured in accidental collision with train — E810.2

CHILD AND ADULT ABUSE

Expanded codes for child and adult abuse facilitate the gathering of more specific data. Child abuse has become a major concern in the United States. National estimates indicate that approximately one to two million children in this country suffer abuse or neglect annually. Adult abuse is considered to be both underreported and underdiagnosed. Keep in mind that codes for child and adult abuse are assigned only when the physician documents abuse; coders should not interpret narrative descriptions as abuse without the physician's confirmation.

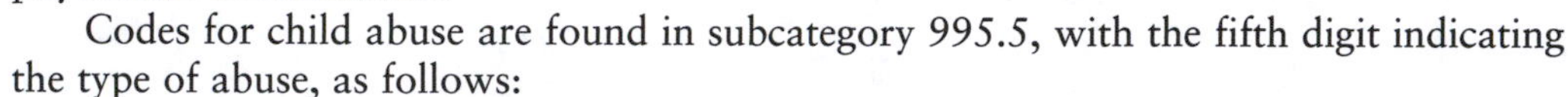

Codes for child abuse are found in subcategory 995.5, with the fifth digit indicating the type of abuse, as follows:

- Child emotional abuse 995.51
- Child physical abuse 995.54
- Child neglect 995.52
- Child sexual abuse 995.53
- Shaken infant syndrome 995.55

Adult abuse codes are provided in subcategory 995.8, with the fifth digit indicating the type of abuse:

- Adult physical abuse 995.81
- Adult emotional/psychological abuse 995.82
- Adult sexual abuse 995.83
- Adult neglect (nutritional) 995.84
- Other adult abuse and neglect 995.85

Abuse often results in physical injuries and other medical conditions. When this is the case, the abuse code is sequenced first, with an additional code for any associated injury or condition that has been documented by the physician.

When the cause of injury or neglect is intentional child or adult abuse, the E code from categories E960 through E966 and E968 through E969 should be listed as the first E code. An additional code from E967 should then be assigned to identify the perpetrator unless this information is not available. In cases of neglect, when the intent is determined to be accidental, code **E904.0, Abandonment or neglect of infants and helpless persons,** should be the first listed external injury code.

Examples of child and adult abuse include the following:

- A patient was seen in the emergency department with a diagnosis of battered woman syndrome and with a laceration of the right forehead. She reported that her husband hit her in the face because he was angry when she was late getting ready to go out to dinner. The following codes should be assigned: **995.81, Adult physical abuse, 873.42, Open wound of forehead, E960.0, Unarmed fight or brawl, E967.3, Adult battering by spouse or partner,** and **E000.8, Other external cause status.**
- A four-month-old infant was seen in the emergency department with a diagnosis of shaken infant syndrome. The baby had been unconscious for approximately two hours after being shaken vigorously by the father when he was unable to make the infant stop crying. The diagnostic statement also included diagnoses of subdural hematoma and retinal hemorrhage. The following codes should be assigned: **995.55, Shaken infant syndrome, 852.23, Subdural hematoma without mention of open intracranial wound, 362.81, Retinal hemorrhage, E967.0, Battering or other maltreatment by father,** and **E000.8, Other external cause status.**
- An elderly woman was brought to the hospital in a state of severe malnutrition. She had been living in an unlicensed care home, where she was fed only one meal per day for several months. In the hospital, a gastric feeding tube was placed and high-protein supplements were given for severe caloric deficiency malnutrition. The following codes should be assigned: **995.84, Adult neglect, 261, Nutritional marasmus, E904.1, Lack of food, E967.8, Abuse by non-related caregiver,** and **96.35, Gastric lavage.**
- A six-month-old infant with heat prostration was brought to the hospital by her parents, who had left her alone in their car while they did their grocery shopping. The parents stated that the child was asleep and they had felt that she would be all right for the short time they would be gone. The following codes should be assigned: **995.52, Child neglect, 992.53, Heat prostration,** and **E904.0, Abandonment or neglect of infant.**

Codes from category V15 are also available to indicate that a patient has a past history of psychological trauma:

- History of physical abuse, including rape V15.41
- History of emotional abuse or neglect V15.42
- History of other psychological trauma V15.49

Counseling codes for victims and perpetrators provide more specificity regarding the person receiving counseling:

- V61.11 Counseling for the victim of spousal and partner abuse
- V61.12 Counseling for the perpetrator of spousal and partner abuse
- V61.21 Counseling for victim of child abuse
- V61.22 Counseling for perpetrator of parental child abuse
- V62.83 Counseling for perpetrator of physical/sexual abuse (to be used only when the perpetrator is a person other than spouse/partner or parent)

FRACTURES

Fractures are classified in categories 800 through 829 as follows:

- Fractures of skull 800–804
- Fractures of neck and trunk 805–809
- Fractures of the upper extremity 810–819
- Fractures of the lower extremity 820–829

Three-digit categories indicate more specific sites within these broad groupings, fourth digits usually indicate whether the fracture is open or closed, and fifth digits usually indicate a more specific bone within the general site.

In an open fracture, an open wound that communicates with the bone is present. Terms that indicate open fracture include the following: "compound," "infected," "missile," "puncture," and "with foreign body."

Closed fractures do not produce an open wound. They are described by terms such as "comminuted," "depressed," "elevated," "greenstick," "spiral," and "simple." A more complete listing can be found in the note at the beginning of the coding manual's section on fractures. Any fracture not specified as open is classified as closed in *ICD-9-CM*. Occasionally, a diagnostic statement contains terms that relate to both open and closed fractures. In this case, the code for the open fracture always takes precedence. For example, a diagnosis of compound comminuted fracture uses terms that can indicate both open and closed fractures. However, such a fracture would be coded as open because the term "compound" always carries this meaning, even though the term "comminuted" by itself would refer to a closed fracture.

Skull Fractures and Intracranial Injuries

Categories 800–804 classify skull fractures by site. Fourth digits indicate whether the fracture is open or closed, whether there is associated intracranial injury, and the type of intracranial injury. Intracranial injury not associated with skull fracture is classified in categories 850 through 854, with an additional digit providing more specificity as to the type of injury and whether it was associated with an open wound.

Codes for skull fractures and intracranial injuries without skull fracture use another digit to indicate whether a loss of consciousness was associated with the injury, how long the unconscious state lasted, and whether there was a return to the preexisting level of consciousness. Because this information is rarely included in the diagnostic statement, it usually must be obtained through a review of the medical record, particularly the emergency department record and admitting note. Fifth digit 5 (with prolonged loss of consciousness without returning to consciousness) is used when an unconscious patient dies before regaining consciousness, regardless of the duration of the unconscious state.

Concussion (category 850) refers to cerebral bruising that sometimes leads to a transient unconsciousness, often followed by brief amnesia, vertigo, nausea, and weak pulse. Fourth digits (and in some instances fifth digits), provide additional specificity regarding the length of time the patient was unconscious, if any. The patient may experience severe headache and blurred vision after regaining consciousness. Recovery usually takes place within 24 to 48 hours. Patients with this type of head injury are often dazed, and the physician may have to rely on clinical findings alone to make a diagnosis of concussion.

Postconcussion syndrome (310.2) includes a variety of symptoms that may occur for a variable period of time following a concussion, sometimes as long as a few weeks. The symptoms most often associated with postconcussion syndrome are headache, dizziness, vertigo, fatigue, difficulty in concentrating, depression, anxiety, tinnitus, heart palpitations, and apathy. Any of these may cause the patient to seek treatment. Code 310.2 is ordinarily

not assigned on the initial admission for treatment of the concussion. When the patient is treated for symptoms within 24 to 48 hours of injury and the physician lists a diagnosis as postconcussion syndrome, the coder should ask the physician whether the concussion is still in the current state. If it is, it should be coded to 850.x rather than 310.2. Postconcussion headache is a part of the postconcussion syndrome. Use an additional code (339.20–339.22) to capture any associated acute or chronic posttraumatic headache along with code 310.2.

When the head injury is further described as a cerebral laceration or a cerebral contusion or when it is associated with subdural, subarachnoid, other intracranial hemorrhage, or other specified condition classifiable in categories from 851 through 854, the code for concussion is not assigned.

Vertebral Fractures

Separate subcategories are provided to distinguish fractures of the vertebra that involve spinal cord injury (806.x) from those that do not (805.x). Spinal cord injury not associated with vertebral fracture is classified into category 952. Fourth digits with categories 805, 806, and 952 indicate the vertebral site; fifth digits for categories 806 and 952 indicate the type of spinal cord injury. For example:

- 806.03 Fracture of cervical vertebral column at C1–C4 level with central cord syndrome
- 952.16 Spinal cord lesion, dorsal T7–T12, with complete lesion of spinal cord, without vertebral fracture
- 952.2 Spinal cord injury, lumbar, without vertebral fracture

Fractures of the Pelvis

Fractures of the pelvis are classified to category 808. The pelvis is formed by a group of bones (ischium, ilium, pubis, sacrum, and coccyx) that form a ring that supports the spine and connects the trunk to the lower extremities. Any or all of these bones can be fractured; fractures involving disruption of the pelvic circle are considered more severe. *ICD-9-CM* provides codes to identify multiple closed pelvic fractures with (808.43) or without (808.44) disruption of the pelvic circle. *ICD-9-CM* also provides codes for multiple open pelvic fractures with (808.53) or without (808.54) disruption of the pelvic circle.

Fractures of the Extremities

Category codes 810 through 829 classify fractures of the extremities; the fourth digit indicates whether the fracture is open or closed, and the fifth digit provides more specificity as to the portion of the bone involved. Combination codes are provided for certain sites as follows:

- Category **813, Fracture of radius and ulna,** uses a fifth digit to indicate which bone had the fracture and when both bones are involved.
- Category **811, Fracture of scapula,** uses a fifth digit to include both the glenoid cavity and the neck of the scapula.
- Category **823, Fracture of tibia and fibula,** uses a fifth digit 2 for fracture of the same site involving both tibia and fibula.

Multiple fractures of the same bone(s) classified with different fourth-digit subdivisions (bone part) within the same three-digit category are coded individually by site. For example:

- Comminuted fracture of the shaft of the right humerus with closed fracture-dislocation of right shoulder involving the greater tuberosity is coded **812.21, Shaft of humerus,** and **812.03, Greater tuberosity.**
- Closed fractures of the olecranon process of the ulna and the head and neck of the radius are coded **813.01, Olecranon process of ulna, 813.05, Head of radius,** and **813.06, Neck of radius.**

ICD-9-CM makes no provision for distinguishing between unilateral and bilateral fractures of the same site in the upper or lower limbs. An *ICD-9-CM* diagnosis code may not be reported more than once on the same encounter. This applies whether the condition is bilateral or two or more different conditions are classified to the same *ICD-9-CM* diagnosis code.

The procedure code is reported twice, however, when bilateral fracture procedures are carried out to reflect more accurately the resources used.

Chapter-specific guidelines for coding traumatic fractures and the corresponding E codes were recently updated. Key points to remember when coding traumatic fractures are as follows:

- Continue to use the acute fracture codes (800–829) while the patient is receiving active treatment for the fracture.
- Examples of active treatment are: surgical treatment, emergency department encounter, and evaluation and treatment by a new physician.
- External cause of injury codes (E codes) may be assigned while the acute fracture codes are still applicable.

Exercise 26.2

Code the following diagnoses. Do not assign E codes.

	Code(s)
1. Comminuted fracture, upper end of left tibia	823.00
2. Fracture, left ischium Fracture, left second, third, fourth, fifth, and sixth ribs	808.42 807.05
3. Closed fracture of vault of skull with subdural hemorrhage; three-hour loss of consciousness	800.23
4. Open Monteggia fracture	813.13
5. Cerebral concussion Brain stem contusion without open wound Patient unconscious for almost two hours	851.43
6. Trimalleolar fracture, left ankle	824.6

Exercise 26.2 *(continued)*

7. Closed fracture, lateral condyle, left humerus	812.42
8. Compound fracture coronoid process of mandible	802.33
9. Compound fracture, shaft of tibia and fibula, left	823.32
10. Bilateral compound depressed skull fractures Massive cerebral contusion and laceration	803.60

Pathological Fractures

Bones weakened by conditions such as osteoporosis or neoplastic disease often develop pathological fractures that occur with no trauma or only minor trauma that would not result in fracture in a healthy bone. This type of fracture is classified with musculoskeletal conditions rather than with injuries and is discussed in chapter 19 of this handbook.

Newly diagnosed pathologic fractures are reported using subcategory 733.1. Chronic pathologic fractures are included under subcategory 733.1. For example:

- A patient with a chronic vertebral pathological fracture with orders for pain medication was admitted for an unrelated condition. Code **733.13, Pathologic fracture of vertebrae,** is assigned for a chronic vertebral fracture. An aftercare code is not appropriate because these codes are limited to follow-up care during the healing or recovery phase of an acute fracture.

Subcategory 733.1 is used as long as the pathologic fracture is being managed and the patient is receiving active treatment for the fracture. Examples of active treatment are: surgical treatment, emergency department encounter, and evaluation and treatment by a new physician.

Compression Fractures

Compression fractures may be due either to disease or to trauma. The coder should search the medical record for any recent significant trauma or for any indication of concurrent bone disease that might point to pathological fracture. If the diagnosis cannot be clarified, the physician should be asked to provide further specificity.

Fractures Due to Birth Injury

Fractures due to birth injury are not classified in the injury chapter of *ICD-9-CM* but instead are classified as perinatal conditions (767.2–767.4) and are discussed in chapter 23 of this handbook.

PROCEDURES RELATED TO FRACTURES

In the treatment of fractures, the primary goal is to achieve correct bone alignment and maintain alignment until healing is completed and normal function can be restored. Procedures include open and closed reduction, simple manipulation, and application of various types of fixation and traction devices. The type of treatment depends on the general condition of the patient, the presence of any associated injuries, and the type and location of the fracture.

Reduction of Fractures

The most common fracture treatment involves moving bone fragments into as nearly normal an anatomic position as possible, with stabilization to maintain the bone in this position until it is sufficiently healed to prevent displacement. Although orthopedic surgeons now prefer to use the term "manipulation" for this procedure, the term "reduction" is still used in *ICD-9-CM*.

The first axis for coding reduction of fractures is whether the reduction is open or closed. The second axis is whether internal fixation is applied. Fourth digits indicate the bone involved.

In an open reduction, the surgeon exposes the bone by extending the open wound over the fracture or making a further incision to work directly with the bone for the purpose of restoring correct alignment. Debridement is often necessary to remove debris or other material that has entered an open fracture site. A code from category **79.6, Debridement of open fracture site,** is assigned as an additional code for debridement carried out in connection with reduction of open fracture of bones of the upper and lower extremities. Debridement is included in the codes for reduction of open fractures involving the skull, nasal and orbital bones, other facial bones, and vertebral bones.

In a closed reduction, alignment is achieved without incision to the fracture site. Debridement of the bone is not needed.

Internal Fixation

Internal fixation includes the use of pins, screws, staples, rods, and plates that are inserted into the bone to maintain alignment. When the fractured bone is in good alignment so that no manipulation is necessary, internal fixation may be used to stabilize the bone without any fracture reduction being performed. Internal fixation is also used without reduction when it is necessary to reinsert an internal fixation device because the original is either displaced or broken. An incision is made for the purpose of inserting the internal fixation wires or pins; a code from category **78.5, Internal fixation of bone without fracture reduction,** is assigned for fixation that is not associated with fracture reduction. Internal fixation can also be used with closed fracture reduction. The small incision necessary to insert the fixation device does not warrant considering the procedure to be an open reduction. Internal fixations associated with bone grafts and shortening or lengthening of bone are included in the codes for these procedures.

External Fixation

Unlike internal fixation, external fixation is ordinarily noninvasive and includes traction or immobilization by the use of casts or splints. Additional codes should be assigned for the application of an external fixator device (78.10–78.19). In addition, if the type of fixator device is known, adjunct codes should be assigned. The classification essentially recognizes three types of external fixator devices: monoplanar (84.71); ring system (84.72); and hybrid system (84.73), which includes both ring and monoplanar devices. When reduction is not carried out, however, a code from category **93.4, Skeletal traction and other traction,** is used for application of traction or a code from category **93.5** for **Other immobilization, pressure, and attention to wounds.** Code 97.88 is assigned for removal of such external immobilization devices. Although traction devices are usually applied by means of Kirschner wires or Steinmann pins, the use of these materials is not considered an internal fixation. Traction devices include the following:

- Skin traction such as tape, foam, or felt traction devices applied directly to the skin, with longitudinal force applied to the limb
- Skeletal traction into or through the bone that applies force directly to the long bones (the wires or pins are drilled transversely through the bone and exit through the skin)
- Cervical spinal traction, such as Baron's tongs, Crutchfield tongs, and halo skull traction
- Upper-extremity traction, such as Dunlap's skin traction
- Lower-extremity traction, such as Buck's extension skin traction, Charnley's traction unit, Hamilton-Russell's traction, balanced suspension traction, and fixed skeletal traction

A separate code is assigned for the application of the external fixator device called a minifixator. This complex type of external stabilization is performed under anesthesia. Holes are drilled into both proximal and distal portions of the bone, and pins are inserted through the bone and attached to the metal frame of the fixator. The pins are located internally except for the portion to which the external frame is connected. A code from subcategory **78.1, Application of external fixator device,** is assigned for this procedure in addition to any code for fracture reduction. A code from category **78.6, Removal of implanted devices from bone,** is assigned for removal of the minifixator.

ADMISSIONS OR ENCOUNTERS FOR ORTHOPEDIC AFTERCARE

Patients who have had fracture reduction usually require aftercare for removal of wires, pins, plates, or external fixation devices. In addition, patients with orthopedic injuries still in the healing stage may be seen primarily for conditions not related to the injury but with some monitoring or clinical evaluation of the injury carried out during the episode of care. Fracture aftercare codes are not assigned when treatment is directed at a current acute injury. V codes are provided for admissions or encounters for these situations, as follows:

- V53.7 Admission for fitting or adjustment of orthopedic device, such as the adjustment of an orthopedic brace or cast, or the removal or replacement of an orthopedic device
- V54.01 Encounter for removal of internal fixation device
- V54.02 Encounter for lengthening/adjustment of growth rod
- V54.89 Other orthopedic aftercare

Fracture aftercare codes (subcategories V54.0, V54.1, V54.2, and V54.8) or code V54.9 are assigned for completion of active treatment of the fracture and for routine care of the fracture during the healing or recovery phase. Examples of fracture aftercare are cast change or removal, removal of external or internal fixation device, medication adjustment, and follow-up visits following fracture treatment. Codes V54.10–V54.29 are available to provide greater specificity in identifying the fracture site being treated as well as to differentiate between traumatic (V54.1x) and pathologic fractures (V54.2x). For example:

- V54.11 Aftercare for healing traumatic fracture of upper arm
- V54.23 Aftercare for healing pathologic fracture of hip

Example 1: A patient who suffered a traumatic fracture of the left humerus a month earlier was admitted with fever and pain secondary to diverticulitis. The healing fracture was treated minimally. Principal diagnosis: 562.11, Diverticulitis; additional diagnosis: V54.11, Aftercare for healing traumatic fracture of upper arm.

Example 2: A young man who fractured the lateral malleolus of the left fibula six weeks previously was admitted for removal of the internal pins under local anesthesia. Principal diagnosis: V54.01, Encounter for removal of internal fixation device; additional diagnosis: V54.16, Aftercare for healing traumatic fracture of lower leg.

Code V54.82 is assigned for admissions or encounters involving aftercare following explantation of a joint prosthesis. Aftercare includes admissions for joint replacement surgery where it was necessary to stage the procedure, or for joint prosthesis replacement following a prior explantation of the prosthesis. There may be a medical need to remove an existing joint prosthesis (e.g., due to infection or other problem); however, it may not be possible to replace the prosthesis at the same encounter, thereby requiring a return encounter to insert a new prosthesis.

V codes are also provided to indicate an orthopedic status when it is significant for the episode of care. Orthopedic status codes include **V43.6x, Joint replacement, complete or partial, any joint; V45.4, Arthrodesis status; V88.21, Acquired absence of hip joint; V88.22, Acquired absence of knee joint;** and **V88.29, Acquired absence of other joint.** Acquired absence of joint codes (V88.2x) are assigned when a patient is awaiting implantation of a joint prosthesis. In a common scenario, the prosthesis is removed due to infection to allow the site time to heal, and the patient is readmitted before completing the joint replacement procedure. Codes in subcategory V88.2 will indicate the patient has had a prosthesis explanted; these codes can also be used when the current encounter is unrelated to implantation of a new prosthesis.

When the aftercare involves replacement of the hip joint prosthesis following previous explantation, assign code V54.82 along with code V88.21. For example:

- The patient developed an infection after a total hip replacement and was admitted for surgical treatment. At surgery, the prosthesis was removed. An antibiotic impregnated cement spacer was inserted. Because the infection had resolved, the patient was readmitted at six weeks for removal of the antibiotic spacer and revision of the total hip replacement, with insertion of a new hip prosthesis.

  For the initial admission, assign code **996.66, Infection and inflammatory reaction, due to internal joint prosthesis,** as the principal diagnosis. Code **V43.64, Organ or tissue replaced by other means, joint, hip,** should be assigned as an additional diagnosis. Assign code **84.56, Insertion of cement spacer,** and code **80.05, Arthrotomy for removal of prosthesis without replacement, hip.** For the second admission, assign code **V54.82, Aftercare following explantation of joint prosthesis,** as the principal diagnosis. Assign also code **V88.21, Acquired absence of hip**

joint. Assign code **00.70, Revision of hip replacement, both acetabular and femoral,** and code **84.57, Removal of (cement) spacer.**

Aftercare codes should be used in conjunction with any other aftercare codes or other diagnosis codes to provide better detail on the specifics of an aftercare visit, unless otherwise directed by the classification. The sequencing of multiple aftercare codes is discretionary. For example:

- A patient had an intertrochanteric hip fracture that was repaired through a total hip joint replacement. He is now receiving aftercare at the physician's office. Codes **V54.81, Aftercare following joint replacement,** and **V43.64, Organ or tissue replaced by other means, joint, hip,** are assigned for the encounter. Each code represents a different piece of information regarding the aftercare and is needed to describe the encounter fully. Code **V54.13, Aftercare for healing traumatic fracture of hip,** is not appropriate because there is no fracture; the hip has been replaced by a prosthetic joint.

Exercise 26.3

Code the following procedures; do not code diagnoses.

	Code(s)
1. Thomas splint traction	93.45
2. Open reduction and debridement of Monteggia fracture, right upper extremity, with Rush pin (internal) to stabilize ulna	79.32 79.62
3. Open reduction of fracture, ankle, with Knowles pins (internal) and two-inch screw Below-the-knee cast applied	79.36
4. Open reduction and Kirschner wire fixation (internal) of distal to main fragment, fracture of left humerus	79.31

Exercise 26.3 *(continued)*

5. Open reduction of fracture, left hip, with Jewett nail fixation	79.35
6. Reduction, fracture right humerus, with cast	79.01
7. Open reduction and internal fixation, fracture of mandible	76.76
8. Open reduction, fracture of left maxilla and	76.74
left zygomatic arch	76.72
Closed reduction, nasal bone fracture	21.71
9. Bifrontal craniotomy with elevation and debridement of compound skull fractures	02.02
Open reduction, orbital fracture	76.79
Tracheostomy (temporary)	31.1

DISLOCATIONS

Dislocation associated with fracture is included in the fracture code, and reduction of the dislocation is included in the code for the fracture reduction. Dislocation of a joint without associated fracture is classified in categories 830 through 839. The first axis is the general site, such as wrist, and the fifth digit indicates a more specific site such as midcarpal dislocation of the wrist; the fourth-digit axis indicates whether the dislocation is open or closed. Open dislocation is described by such terms as "compound," "infected," or "with foreign body;" closed dislocation is described as "complete," "partial," "simple," or "uncomplicated." When the dislocation is not specified as either open or closed, a code for closed dislocation is assigned. Reduction of dislocation not associated with fracture is coded under subcategory **79.7x, Closed reduction of dislocation,** or subcategory **79.8x, Open reduction of dislocation.** Nursemaid's elbow (832.2) is the dislocation of the elbow joint, which is usually caused by a sudden pull on the hand or arm. Medically, this condition is known as subluxation of the radial head and is most commonly seen in children under the age of five.

INTERNAL INJURIES OF THE CHEST, ABDOMEN, AND PELVIS

Internal injuries of the chest, abdomen, and pelvis are classified in categories 860 through 869, and the fourth digit indicates whether there is an associated open wound. A fifth-digit subclassification is used for certain categories within this series to provide more specificity regarding the type of injury or site. For example:

- Pneumothorax (traumatic) without mention of open wound 860.0
- Hemothorax with open wound into thorax 860.3
- Injury of duodenum without mention of open wound into cavity 863.21
- Contusion of heart without mention of open wound into the thorax 861.01

Codes 866.00–866.13 are used to describe an internal injury of the kidney caused by trauma. A nontraumatic acute kidney injury (AKI) is coded **584.9, Acute kidney failure, unspecified.**

BLOOD VESSEL AND NERVE INJURIES

When a primary injury results in minor damage to peripheral nerves or blood vessels, the primary injury is sequenced first, with additional codes from categories 950 through 957, Injury to nerves and spinal cord, and/or categories 900 through 904, Injury to blood vessels.

When the primary injury is to a blood vessel or nerve, however, the code for that injury should be sequenced first. For example, an open wound of the anterior abdominal wall with rupture of the aorta would be coded 902.0, Injury to abdominal aorta; an additional code for open wound of abdominal wall, anterior, without mention of complication, 879.2, or open wound of abdominal wall, anterior, complication, 879.3, may be assigned.

OPEN WOUNDS

Open wounds such as lacerations, puncture wounds, cuts, animal bites, avulsions, and traumatic amputations that are not associated with fracture, dislocation, internal injury, or intracranial injury are classified in categories 870 through 897. Fourth digits for categories 870 and 871, which classify open wounds of the eyeball and ocular adnexa, indicate whether the wound was a laceration or a penetrating wound. Codes for penetrating injury of these sites indicate whether a foreign body is present. The fourth digit for other codes of open wounds indicates whether a complication is present and may also indicate a more specific site. An open wound is considered to be complicated when any of the following conditions is present:

- Delayed healing
- Delayed treatment
- Foreign body in wound
- Major infection

Both cellulitis and osteomyelitis sometimes occur as complications of open wounds. Sequencing of codes for open wounds with these major infections depends on the circumstances of admission. It is important to determine whether it is the wound that is being addressed or only the resulting infection. For example, a patient who had an open wound of the hand six weeks ago might be seen because osteomyelitis has developed. In this situation, the osteomyelitis would ordinarily be designated as the principal diagnosis, with an additional code for the open wound and a fourth digit indicating that the wound is complicated. A patient who had a slight puncture wound earlier in the week might show evidence of cellulitis at the site. The wound itself did not require any attention; the reason for the encounter would be the cellulitis. In this case, cellulitis would be the principal diagnosis.

AMPUTATIONS

When listed as a diagnosis, traumatic amputation is classified as an open wound in *ICD-9-CM*. For example:

- 887.2 Traumatic amputation of arm at or above elbow
- 887.0 Traumatic amputation of arm below elbow
- 897.2 Traumatic amputation of leg at or above knee

The term "amputation" is also used for an amputation procedure, which can be performed for a variety of reasons other than the treatment of trauma. Amputation is performed by either disarticulation or cutting through the bone. Amputation procedures are classified in category **84, Other procedures on musculoskeletal system;** the third digit indicates whether amputation is of the upper or lower limb, and the fourth digit indicates the portion of the limb involved and the type of amputation. Sample codes include the following:

- Disarticulation of wrist 84.04
- Amputation through foot 84.12
- Amputation above knee 84.17
- Amputation through forearm 84.05

A below-the-knee amputation of the lower limb is through the tibia and fibula (84.15); an above-the-knee amputation is through the femur (84.17). Code 84.17 is also assigned when a below-the-knee amputation is converted into an above-the-knee amputation. A metatarsal amputation is classified as an amputation of the toe; a transmetatarsal amputation is classified as an amputation through the foot.

A revision of an amputation involves transecting the entire circumference of the bone. The length of bone transected or resected does not matter as much as the fact that the entire circumference of bone is cut through, and the revision is carried out through an existing wound (site of previous amputation). Revision of the amputation stump is coded 84.3 except for revision of a current traumatic amputation, which is classified as further amputation of the current traumatic amputation site (84.1x).

OTHER INJURIES

Superficial injuries such as blisters, abrasions, and friction burns are classified to categories 910 through 919. The fourth digit indicates a more specific site or type of injury and/or whether infection is present. When such injuries are associated with a major injury such as fracture of the same site, a code for the superficial injury is usually not assigned. Note that the term "superficial" does not refer to the severity of the injury but to the superficial structures affected, those pertaining to or situated near the surface.

The presence of a foreign body entering through an orifice is classified in categories 930 through 939. When the foreign body is associated with an open wound, it is coded as an open wound, complicated, by site. A foreign body accidentally left during a procedure in an operative wound is considered to be a complication of a procedure and is coded 998.4.

EARLY COMPLICATIONS OF TRAUMA

Certain early complications of trauma that are not included in the code for the injury are classified in category 958, **Certain early complications of trauma.** The fourth-digit axis indicates the type of complication, such as air or fat embolism, traumatic shock, or traumatic anuria. Ordinarily, codes from category 958 are assigned as secondary codes, with the code for the injury sequenced first. With today's shorter lengths of stay and increased emphasis on outpatient care, however, the complication itself may occasionally be the reason for an outpatient encounter or admission and would be the principal diagnosis in such cases.

Category 958 is not used to describe posttraumatic seroma. Assign code 729.91 for posttraumatic seroma.

Subcategory, **958.9, Traumatic compartment syndrome,** classifies compartment syndrome secondary to trauma. Acute traumatic compartment syndrome is usually a sequelae of a serious injury to the lower or upper extremities and can lead to significant motor and sensory deficits, pain, stiffness, and deformity when untreated. Acute traumatic compartment syndrome is always associated with fractures, dislocations, and/or crush injuries. Other risk factors for the development of acute traumatic compartment syndrome include vascular injuries and coagulopathy. The diagnosis is established by multiple compartment pressure readings. Traumatic compartment syndrome is coded as follows:

- 958.90 Compartment syndrome, unspecified
- 958.91 Traumatic compartment syndrome of upper extremity
- 958.92 Traumatic compartment syndrome of lower extremity
- 958.93 Traumatic compartment syndrome of abdomen
- 958.99 Traumatic compartment syndrome of other sites

Exercise 26.4

Code the following diagnoses. Do not assign E codes.

	Code(s)
1. Stab wound of abdominal wall, infected	879.3
2. Lacerations, left foot, infected	892.1
3. Traumatic amputation of left arm and hand above the elbow	887.2
4. Traumatic anuria due to injury to kidney	866.00 958.5

OTHER EFFECTS OF EXTERNAL CAUSE

Categories 990 through 995 classify other and unspecified effects of external causes resulting from exposure to heat, cold, and a variety of other conditions due to external causes that are not classifiable elsewhere in *ICD-9-CM*. Codes from these categories are not assigned when a more specific code for the effect is available. For example, colitis due to radiation therapy is coded **558.1, Gastroenteritis and colitis due to radiation,** because the effect is identified. A diagnosis of complication of radiation therapy not otherwise specified and with no further information documented in the medical record would be coded **990, Effects of radiation, unspecified.**

Codes from category 992, Effects of heat and light, should not be assigned together with codes in subcategory 780.6, Fever and other physiologic disturbances of temperature regulation. Code **992.0, Heat stroke and sunstroke,** is assigned along with additional codes to describe any associated complication of heat/sun stroke; e.g., alterations of consciousness (780.01–780.09) and/or systemic inflammatory response syndrome (995.93–995.94).

Category **995, Certain adverse effects not elsewhere classified,** is used to classify a variety of adverse effects such as anaphylactic reaction/shock, shock due to anesthesia, failed sedation during a procedure, and angioneurotic edema. For example:

- A patient was seen as an outpatient for removal of gastric polyps via esophagogastroduodenoscopy (EGD) under moderate sedation. After the polyp was removed, the patient started to regain consciousness. Code **211.1, Benign neoplasm of other parts of digestive system, stomach,** is assigned as the first-listed diagnosis. Code **995.24, Failed moderate sedation during procedure,** is assigned as an additional diagnosis.

Anaphylaxis is an immunologic reaction that affects multiple body systems. Reactions can range from mild—with hives, itchiness, swelling of eyes and lips, and some congestion—to life threatening with airway obstruction and cardiovascular collapse. Shock occurs when there is excessive fluid leakage from the blood vessels into the tissues. Anaphylactic reaction due to an adverse food reaction is coded 995.6, with a fifth digit indicating the type of food involved. For example:

- A patient with a known allergy to tree nuts presents to the emergency room with wheezing and urticaria. The patient was diagnosed with an anaphylactic reaction secondary to eating cookies containing walnuts. Assign code **995.64, Anaphylactic reaction due to adverse food reaction, due to tree nuts and seeds.** Codes from subcategory 995 are assigned for both anaphylactic reaction and/or anaphylactic shock.

Anaphylactic reaction due to drugs or medicinal substances used correctly is classified to **995.0, Other anaphylactic reaction,** with an additional code from the E930 through E949 series to indicate the responsible medicine. When the reaction is due to an incorrect use of a drug, a medicinal or biological substance, or a toxic material not chiefly medicinal, anaphylactic reaction is classified as a poisoning, with the poisoning code sequenced first and an additional code of 995.0 assigned to indicate the reaction.

Codes 995.20, 995.27, and 995.29 are assigned for unspecified, other, or allergic adverse effects, occurring secondary to medicinal substances that have been administered properly. Codes 999.41–999.59 describe allergic reactions due to serum, including blood transfusions. These codes are covered in more detail in chapter 29 of this handbook.

Code 991.6 is assigned for hypothermia with several exceptions. If it is due to anesthesia, code 995.89 is assigned; code 995.86 is used for malignant hyperthermia. When the hypothermia is not due to low temperature, code **780.65, Hypothermia not associated with low environmental temperature,** is assigned. Two codes are provided for hypothermia of the newborn: **778.2, Cold injury of newborn,** and **778.3, Other hypothermia of newborn.**

Exercise 26.5

Code the following diagnoses and assign E codes.

	Code(s)
1. Heat prostration due to salt and water depletion	992.4 E904.2
2. Frostbite, toes	991.2 E901.0
3. Radiation cataract	366.46 E926.9
4. Anaphylactic reaction due to eating peanuts	995.61

LATE EFFECTS OF INJURIES

In coding late effects of injuries, the residual condition (such as malunion, nonunion, deformity, or paralysis) is sequenced first, followed by a cause of late effect code from categories 905–909; a late effect E code is also assigned. A current injury code is never used with a late effect code for the same type of injury.

Malunion (733.81) implies that bony healing has occurred but that the fracture fragments are in poor position. Treatment of malunion ordinarily involves surgical cutting of the bone (osteotomy), repositioning the bone, and adding some type of internal fixation device with or without bone graft. Malunion is frequently diagnosed while the fracture is still in a healing state, but sometimes no surgical intervention is used in the hope that the patient may not have any functional problems as a result of the malunion.

Nonunion (733.82), on the other hand, implies that healing has not occurred and that there is still separation of the bony structures involved in the fracture. Treatment of nonunion usually involves opening the fracture, scraping away intervening soft tissue (usually scar tissue), doing a partial debridement of the bone end, and repositioning the bone. Treating nonunion of a fracture is more complicated and difficult to perform than treating a malunion.

Exercise 26.6

Code the following diagnoses and assign E codes; sequence the codes according to the principles for coding late effects.

		Code(s)
1. Paralysis of right wrist due to previous laceration of right radial nerve		354.9
		907.4
	Late	E929.8
2. Esophageal stricture due to old lye burn of esophagus		530.3
		906.8
	or Late	E929.8
3. Nonunion fracture of neck of femur suffered in a bar brawl three months ago		733.82
		905.3
	or Late	E969
4. Posttraumatic scars of face due to old accidental lacerations		709.2
		906.0
	Late	E929.8

Review Exercise 26.7

Code the following diagnoses and procedures. Assign E codes where information is provided.

		Code(s)
1. Anterior dislocation of shoulder, patient thrown from horse she was riding while working as a horse trainer		831.01 E828.2 E006.1 E000.0
Dislocation reduction		79.71
2. Fracture dislocation left humerus, surgical neck; patient caught in avalanche while on vacation skiing at mountain resort	or Dislocation	812.01 E909.2 E849.4 E003.2 E000.8
Open reduction and internal fixation with Rush pin and screws		79.31
3. Colles fracture Patient fell from chair at home		813.41 E884.2 E849.0 E000.8
Closed reduction with anterior-posterior plaster splints		79.02
4. Intracapsular fracture, neck of femur, right Patient fell from in-line skates		820.00 E885.1 E006.0 E000.8
Closed reduction with insertion of Smith-Petersen nail		79.15

Review Exercise 26.7 *(continued)*

5. Closed fractures of right femur and left ilium Fat emboli, posttraumatic Patient driving motorcycle on highway lost control and overturned	Loss of control	821.00 808.41 958.1 E816.2
Open reduction with plate fixation, right femur, with skeletal traction for ilium fracture		79.35 93.44
6. Fracture of base of skull, with right subdural hemorrhage; patient fell from parachute in a voluntary descent during military training		801.20 E844.7 E000.1
7. Posttraumatic shortening of left radius due to previous comminuted fracture of distal end of left forearm, broken in accidental crash of snowmobile	Late effect of	736.09 905.2 E929.0
8. Ruptured spleen, traumatic Severe crush injury to left kidney Traumatic shock Patient caught in heavy farm machinery that he was operating on his farm		865.04 866.00 958.4 E919.0 E849.1 E000.0
Excretory urography Splenectomy		41.5 87.73

Review Exercise 26.7 *(continued)*

9. Cerebral cortex contusion; patient died without regaining consciousness; patient had fallen from skyscraper observation tower while sightseeing	851.05 E882 E849.6 E029.9 E000.8
10. Battered wife syndrome due to severe beating of chest wall by husband Multiple contusions over trunk	995.81 922.1 E960.0 E967.3
11. Anoxic brain damage due to previous intracranial injury three years ago, when patient was accidentally struck by car while walking along highway Late effect of	348.1 907.0 E929.0
12. Comminuted fracture of the distal radius and ulna; child fell from playground equipment; initial treatment is in the physician's office	813.44 E884.0 E029.9 E000.8
Two weeks later, patient had open reduction and internal fixation (ORIF) at an acute care hospital	813.44 E884.0 79.32
Follow-up visit to the physician's office for X-rays and postoperative examination	V54.12

Burns

CHAPTER 27

CHAPTER OVERVIEW

- Categories 940–949 are assigned for all burns except sunburn and friction burns.
- Burns are first classified by general anatomical site. A fifth digit specifies the site.
- A fourth digit indicates the type of burn according to depth.
  - First-, second-, or third-degree
  - Third-degree burns can be characterized as with or without loss of body part.
- Codes are sequenced to reflect the degree of the burn. The highest degree takes precedence.
  - Multiple burns on the same site require classification of only the highest degree of burn.
  - Multiple burns at different sites require sequencing the most severe burn first and using additional codes for the burns of other sites.
- The extent of the body surface involved is estimated using the "rule of nines," and this is used to help code the burn.
- E codes are used to classify the place of occurrence as well as:
  - The cause of the burns, such as fire, electric current, and hot liquid
  - Situations such as accident, assault, and suicide
- Other injuries associated with burns often require additional codes.
- Certain preexisting conditions might have an impact on the prognosis or care of the patient. These preexisting conditions should be coded as additional diagnoses.

LEARNING OUTCOMES

After studying this chapter you should be able to:

- Understand the difference between first-, second-, and third-degree burns.
- Use a fourth digit to indicate the depth of burn.
- Properly sequence the codes of multiple burns and related conditions.
- Understand how the extent of burn is calculated using the "rule of nines."
- Identify injuries and illnesses that might be coded in association with the burns.

TERM TO KNOW

Rule of nines
a tool to help physicians estimate the amount of body surface involved in a burn

REMEMBER . . . Burns heal at different rates. It is possible to have both healed and unhealed burns for the same episode of care.

INTRODUCTION

Codes from categories 940 through 949 are assigned for current unhealed burns except sunburn and friction burns, which are classified as dermatitis and superficial injury, respectively. Nonhealing burns and necrosis of burned skin are coded as acute current burns. Sequelae (such as scarring or contracture) that remain after a burn has healed are classified as late effects (906.5–906.9). Because burns heal at different rates, a patient may have both healed and unhealed burns during the same episode of care. For this reason, it is possible to use current burn codes as well as late effect burn codes on the same record (when both a current burn and sequelae of an old burn exist).

ANATOMICAL SITE OF BURN

The first axis for classifying burns is the general anatomical site, with a fifth digit to indicate a more specific site. Category **940, Burn confined to eye and adnexa,** is an exception in that the fourth digit indicates the more specific site as well as whether the burn was due to the use of acid chemical, alkaline chemical, or other cause.

Categories 941–945 have a fifth digit for multiple specified sites; category 946 provides only codes for multiple specified burns. When coding burns, assign separate codes for each burn site. Codes for multiple sites and category 946 should only be used if the location of the burns is not documented. Category **949, Burn, unspecified,** is extremely vague and should rarely be used.

FIGURE 27.1 Skin Layers

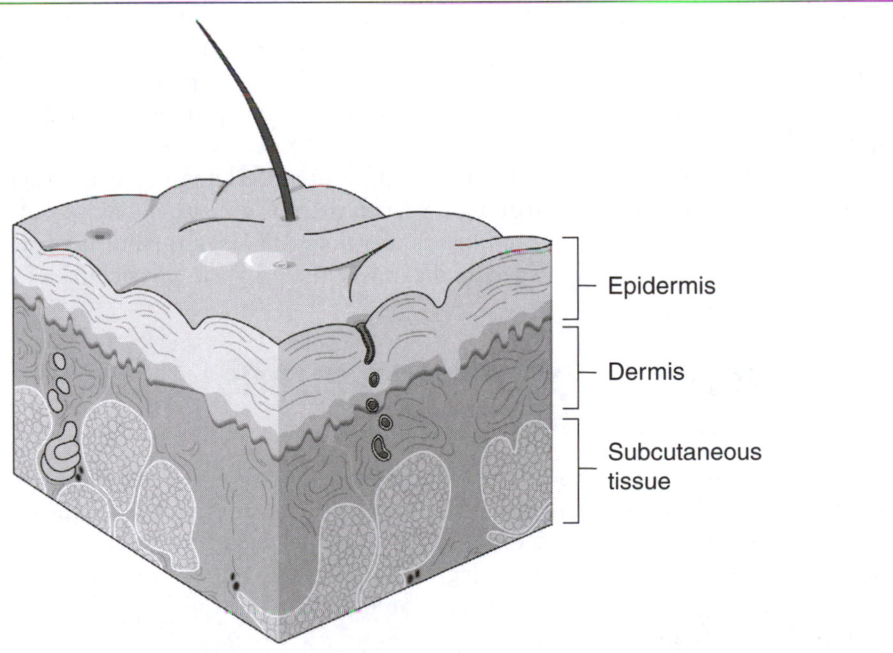

DEPTH OF BURN

For categories 941–946, the fourth digit axis indicates the type of burn according to depth or degree as follows:

- First degree (erythema)
- Second degree (blistering)
- Third degree (full-thickness involvement)
- Deep necrosis (deep third degree) without loss of body part
- Deep necrosis (deep third degree) with loss of body part

First Degree

Damage from first-degree burns is limited to the outer layer of the epidermis, with erythema and increased tenderness. First-degree burns have good capillary refill and do not represent significant injury in terms of fluid replacement needs.

Second Degree

Second-degree burns represent a partial-thickness injury to the dermis, which may be either superficial or deep. Deep second-degree burns heal much more slowly than first-degree burns and are prone to developing infection. The end result of second-degree burns may be hypertrophic scarring.

Third Degree

In third-degree burns, the dermal barrier is lost, and the presence of necrotic tissue creates fluid volume loss with systemic effects on capillaries well away from the burn site. In addition, the burn site establishes an ideal culture medium for infection, which may be life-threatening. The critical factor in healing of third-degree burns is blood supply. Areas rich in blood supply, such as hair follicles and sweat glands, have a better chance for reepithelialization.

Deep third-degree burns are characterized by an underlying necrosis with thrombosed vessels and are identified by fourth digit 5 when there is an associated loss of a body part and by fourth digit 4 when no such loss is mentioned. Codes for burns of this depth are assigned only on the basis of a specific diagnosis made by the physician.

SEQUENCING OF CODES FOR BURNS AND RELATED CONDITIONS

Burns of the same local site at the three-digit category level but of different degrees (depth) are classified according to the highest degree recorded in the diagnostic statement. A third-degree burn takes precedence over a second-degree burn, and a second-degree burn takes precedence over a first-degree burn. For example, first-degree and second-degree burns of the leg are classified as second-degree burn of limb (945.20); no code is assigned for the first-degree burn.

When coding multiple burns, sequence first the code that reflects the burn of the highest degree (most severe) with additional codes for the burns of other sites. For example, a patient is admitted with third-degree burns of the lower leg and first-degree and second-degree burns of the forearm. The following codes should be assigned:

- 945.34 Third-degree burn of leg
- 943.21 Second-degree burn of forearm

The circumstances of the admission will determine the principal diagnosis or first-listed diagnosis if a patient has both internal and external burns.

Encounters for the treatment of the late effects of burns (i.e., scars or joint contractures) should be coded to the residual condition (sequelae) followed by the appropriate late effect code (906.5–906.9). A late effect E code is also used. Code E929.4 indicates that the condition is a late effect of an accident caused by fire. Code **E897, Accident caused by controlled fire not in building or structure,** is not used because it identifies a current cause rather than a late effect.

Note that using codes in category **V51, Aftercare involving the use of plastic surgery,** is inappropriate for burn patients admitted for repair of scar tissue, skin contracture, or other sequela. For such patients, a code should be assigned for the condition being treated. Category V51 is used only for an admission for plastic surgery when there is no residual condition that can be classified elsewhere in *ICD-9-CM,* such as plastic repair for breast reconstruction of a mastectomy site.

EXTENT OF BURN

Category 948 classifies burns according to the extent of body surface involved. The fourth digit indicates the total percentage of body surface involved in all types of burns, including third-degree burns. The fifth digit indicates the percentage of the body surface involved in third-degree burns only. Because the fourth digit refers to total body surface, the fifth digit can never be greater than the total amount. For example, code 948.73 indicates that 70–79% of the body surface was involved in some type of burn; the fifth digit indicates that third-degree burns were involved in 30–39 percent of the body surface. The fifth-digit zero (0) is assigned when less than 10 percent of body surface (or when no body surface) is involved in a third-degree burn.

The extent of body surface involved in a burn injury is an important factor in burn mortality, and hospitals with burn centers need this information for evaluating patient care management and for preparing statistical data. In addition, third-party payment is often influenced by the extent of the burn. When more than 20 percent of the body surface is involved in third-degree burns, it is advisable to assign an additional code from category 948. Burn centers sometimes use a code from category 948 as a solo code because many of their patients present with such extensive and severe burns involving many sites that coding them individually is difficult.

Category 948 is based on the "rule of nines" for estimating the amount of body surface involved in a burn. Physicians may modify the percentage assignments for head and neck in infants and small children because young children have proportionately larger heads than adults. The percentage may also be modified for adults with large buttocks, abdomens, or thighs. The rule of nines establishes estimates of body surface involved as follows:

- Head and neck, 9 percent
- Each arm, 9 percent
- Each leg, 18 percent
- Anterior trunk, 18 percent
- Posterior trunk, 18 percent
- Genitalia, 1 percent

For example, based on this rule a physician can calculate that first-degree burns involve 9 percent of the body surface, second-degree burns involve 18 percent, and third-degree burns involve 36 percent. Adding these together, 63 percent of the body was involved in some type of burn. Code 948.63 (burn of any degree involving 60–69 percent of body surface, with 30–39 percent involved in third-degree burn) could then be assigned. Coders are not expected to calculate the extent of a burn, but understanding the rule of nines may help the coder recognize when burns are so extensive that the physician should be asked for additional information.

SUNBURN

Sunburn and other ultraviolet radiation burns are classified in the dermatitis category. Historically, code 692.71 was assigned for first-, second-, or third-degree sunburns. Unique codes are now available to identify more severe sunburns: code 692.75 for second-degree sunburns, and code 692.76 for third-degree sunburns. Sunburn due to other ultraviolet radiation exposure, such as a tanning bed, is classified to code 692.82.

EXTERNAL CAUSES OF BURNS

E codes, including codes from category **E849, Place of occurrence,** are assigned for burns, as discussed in the previous chapter on other injuries. The most commonly used E codes for burns are these:

- E890–E899 Accident caused by fire and flames
- E924.x Accident caused by hot substance or object, caustic or corrosive material, or steam
- E925.x Accident caused by electric current
- E968.0 Assault by fire
- E968.3 Assault by hot liquid
- E958.1 Suicide and self-inflicted injuries by burns, fire
- E958.2 Suicide and self-inflicted injuries by scald
- E929.4 Late effects of accident caused by fire
- E926.2 Visible and ultraviolet light sources, tanning beds

ASSOCIATED INJURIES AND ILLNESSES

When a burn is described as infected, two codes are required. The code for the burn is sequenced first, with code **958.3, Posttraumatic wound infection, not elsewhere classified,** assigned as an additional code. For example:

- Infected second-degree burn of abdominal wall <u>942.23</u> + 958.3

Other injuries frequently occur with burns, and other conditions are sometimes caused by burns. Examples of such injuries include the following:

- Smoke inhalation often occurs in cases of burns due to combustible products (508.2 and 987.0–987.9). Certain toxic substances from plastic products may produce hydrocyanic acid gas inhalation (987.7). Code 508.2 is assigned to describe a smoke inhalation injury not otherwise specified. Smoke inhalation is caused by inhalation or exposure to hot gaseous products of combustion and can cause serious respiratory complications. Use an additional code to identify any associated respiratory conditions, such as acute respiratory failure. Code 506.9 is assigned for smoke inhalation due to chemical fumes and vapors. When a patient presents with a burn injury and another related condition, such as smoke inhalation or respiratory failure, the circumstances of admission determine the selection of the principal or first-listed diagnosis. For example, a child who was rescued from a burning house had no obvious burns, but there was soot about his nose and mouth. The patient was intubated and ventilated for less than 48 hours because of the risk of airway edema from the smoke. The provider diagnosed smoke inhalation. Code **508.2, Respiratory conditions due to smoke inhalation,** is assigned as the principal diagnosis. Assign code **E890.2, Other smoke and fumes from conflagration,** for the external cause of the injury. The patient suffered no obvious burns but was admitted for airway management secondary to the toxic effects of smoke. Assign also codes **96.71, Continuous invasive mechanical ventilation for less than 96 consecutive hours,** and **96.04, Insertion of endotracheal tube.**

- Electrical burns, such as those caused by high-tension wires, may cause ventricular arrhythmias (427.4x) that require immediate attention.
- Traumatic shock (958.4) is often present at the time of admission or may occur later.

Preexisting conditions may also have an impact on the burn patient's prognosis and on care management and therefore should be coded as additional diagnoses when they otherwise meet criteria for reportable diagnoses. Examples of potentially harmful preexisting conditions that should be reported include the following:

- Cardiovascular disorders (such as angina, congestive heart failure, or valvular disease) may increase ischemia and precipitate myocardial infarction in a patient with extensive second-degree or third-degree burns. Pulmonary wedge monitoring (Swan-Ganz) (89.64) may be necessary in these cases.
- Asthma, chronic bronchitis, and other chronic obstructive pulmonary diseases may require ventilation therapy.
- Peptic ulcers, either gastric or duodenal, and ulcerative colitis are preexisting conditions that may lead to gastrointestinal bleeding and require treatment along with the burn.
- Preexisting kidney disease increases the risk of tubular necrosis and renal failure in patients with third-degree burns or extensive second-degree burns.
- Alcoholism may pose a threat of alcohol withdrawal syndrome, requiring prophylactic treatment for delirium tremens.
- Diabetes mellitus slows the healing process, and diabetes mellitus with stated manifestations can further complicate the management of burn cases.

Review Exercise 27.1

Code the following diagnoses, including E codes.

	Code(s)
1. First-degree burn of lower left leg and second-degree burns of left foot when adding wood to bonfire at beach resort while on vacation	945.22 945.14 E897 E029.9 E000.8 E849.4
2. First-degree burns of face and both eyes, involving cornea, eyelids, nose, cheeks, and lips, due to lye spill at home	941.12 E924.1 E000.8 E849.0
3. Burns over 38% of body, with 10% of body involved in third-degree burns and 28% involved in second-degree burns; firefighter burned in forest fire	948.31 E892 E000.0 E849.8
4. Acid burns to left cornea from nitric acid	940.3 E924.1
5. Subsequent encounter with nonhealing first- and second-degree burns of back that occurred five weeks ago when patient's clothing caught fire in kitchen accident in his home	942.24
6. Food service employee sustained first-degree and second-degree burns, thumb and two fingers, right, from kitchen fire in nursing home	944.24 E896 E015.2 E000.0 E849.7

Review Exercise 27.1 *(continued)*

7. Farm employee admitted with severe shock due to third-degree burns of back due to uncontrolled barn fire	942.34 958.4 E891.3 E000.0 E849.1
8. First-, second-, and third-degree burns of trunk; 10% first degree, 15% second degree, and 32% third degree; patient was crew member of steamship on which boiler exploded	942.30 948.53 E921.0 E000.0 E837.2
9. Severe sunburn of face, neck, and shoulders; patient spent most of the day at the beach	692.71 E926.2 E000.8 E849.8 E029.9
10. Infected friction burn of left thigh due to rope burn while water skiing at Lake Berryessa	916.1 E838.4 E002.6 E000.8 E849.8
11. First-degree burns of back of left hand due to hot tap water in home where patient was visiting	944.16 E924.2 E000.8 E849.0

Poisoning and Adverse Effects of Drugs

CHAPTER **28**

CHAPTER OVERVIEW

- A condition caused by drugs or other ingested substances can either be considered as an adverse effect or as a poisoning.
- An adverse condition is one caused by a correctly prescribed and used drug.
  - The code for an adverse effect is sequenced first.
  - An E code indicating the responsible drug follows.
- Poisoning is a condition caused by the incorrect use of a drug or other substance.
  - The code for poisoning is sequenced first.
  - This is followed by the manifestation of the poisoning.
  - Next an E code is assigned indicating the circumstances of the poisoning.
- Interactions of properly used therapeutic drugs and alcohol or non-prescription drugs are considered instances of poisoning.
- Poisoning codes and E codes for poisoning and adverse effects are found in the Table of Drugs and Chemicals in section 2 of volume 2 of *ICD-9-CM*.
- There is no limit to the number of E codes that can be used to completely describe the full list of responsible substances of a poisoning or an adverse effect.
- Acute conditions caused by alcohol or drug abuse are considered poisonings, but chronic conditions are not.
- The late effects of poisoning are dealt with in the same way as general late effects.
- The late effects of adverse reactions are coded not with a late effect E code, but with a code for the residual condition.

LEARNING OUTCOMES

After studying this chapter you should be able to:

- Differentiate between adverse effects and poisoning.
- Locate codes associated with poisoning and adverse effects.
- Assign codes for external causes of poisoning and adverse effects.
- Code for poisoning due to substance abuse.
- Code for late effects for adverse reactions and poisoning.

TERMS TO KNOW

Adverse effect
classification of a condition caused by a drug or other substance when used correctly

Poisoning
classification of a condition caused by a drug or other substance when used incorrectly

REMEMBER . . . A condition caused by the use of a drug may be classified either as an adverse effect or a poisoning. The determination is based only on whether or not the substance was correctly prescribed and properly administered.

INTRODUCTION

Conditions due to drugs and medicinal and biological substances are classified as either poisoning or adverse effects. The condition is classified as an adverse effect when the correct substance was administered as prescribed. When the substance was used incorrectly, it is classified as a poisoning (960–979). The condition may be exactly the same and the drug may be the same; the determination is based on the manner in which the substance was used. *ICD-9-CM* makes the distinction between adverse effects of drugs administered correctly and poisoning to facilitate the collection of data on adverse effects that result from the correct use of drugs and the extent to which incorrect use results in patient care problems. Note that not using the prescribed medication as frequently as prescribed or in smaller amounts is not coded as poisoning.

When the drug was correctly prescribed and properly administered, a code for the adverse effect is sequenced first, followed by an E code indicating the responsible drug or drugs (E930–E949). When the condition results from the interaction of two or more therapeutic drugs, each used correctly, it is classified as an adverse effect, and an E code is assigned for each drug involved. When the condition is a poisoning, the poisoning code is sequenced first, followed by a code for the manifestation and an E code to indicate the circumstance of the poisoning.

The adverse effects of therapeutic substances correctly prescribed and properly administered (toxicity, synergistic reaction, side effect, and idiosyncratic reaction) may be due to (1) differences among patients, such as age, sex, disease, and genetic factors, and (2) drug-related factors, such as type of drug, route of administration, duration of therapy, dosage, and bioavailability.

Harmful substances ingested or coming into contact with a person are classified as toxic effects. These are assigned to categories 980–989, Toxic effects of substances chiefly nonmedicinal as to source, except for certain localized effects that are classified to 001 through 799. For example:

- Chronic manganese toxicity   985.2 + E866.4
- Toxicity due to exposure to arsenical pesticide   985.1 + E863.4
- Toxicity due to asbestos exposure   989.81 + E866.8

Toxic effect codes should be sequenced first, followed by the appropriate code(s) to identify the result of the toxic effect. An external cause code should be assigned to indicate intent—accidental exposure (categories E860–E869), intentional self-harm (codes E950.6 or E950.7), assault (E962), or undetermined (categories E980–E9872).

A diagnostic statement of toxic effect, toxicity, or intoxication due to a prescription drug such as digitalis or lithium without any further qualification usually refers to an adverse effect of a correctly administered prescription drug. The adverse effect should be coded as such unless medical record documentation indicates otherwise. The following terms in the medical record usually indicate correct usage and identify the condition as an adverse effect:

- Allergic reaction
- Cumulative effect of drug (toxicity)
- Hypersensitivity to drug
- Idiosyncratic reaction
- Paradoxical reaction
- Synergistic reaction

When the medical record documents an error in dosage or administration, the condition should be coded as a poisoning. Terms that usually identify the condition as a poisoning include the following:

- Wrong medication given or taken
- Error made in drug prescription
- Wrong dosage given or taken
- Intentional drug overdose
- Nonprescribed drug taken with correctly prescribed and properly administered drug

The poisoning code is sequenced first, followed by the code for the manifestation. This sequencing is based on the chapter-specific guideline providing such direction. Therefore it applies even if the poisoning may have already been addressed.

For example, a patient is seen in the emergency department in a coma and acute respiratory failure due to a drug overdose. The patient undergoes a gastric lavage for the drug overdose. The patient is also intubated, connected to an invasive mechanical ventilator, and transferred to another hospital for continued toxicology management and for treatment of the acute respiratory failure. The poisoning would still be sequenced as the principal diagnosis at the receiving hospital.

Category codes 960–979 classify poisoning due to drugs and medicinal and biological substances. Subcategory code 965.6 is assigned to separately identify antirheumatics drugs that are propionic acid derivatives (965.61) and other antirheumatics drugs (965.69). The propionic acid derivatives have become widely used since they became available as over-the-counter medications.

When a condition is the result of the interaction of a therapeutic drug used correctly with a nonprescription drug or with alcohol, it is classified as poisoning. Poisoning codes are also assigned for each drug. For example, a diagnosis of coma identified as an adverse reaction to Valium taken correctly but associated with the intake of two martinis is coded as follows:

- Poisoning due to alcohol 980.0
- Poisoning due to Valium 969.4
- Coma 780.01
- Accidental poisoning by ethyl alcohol E860.0
- Accidental poisoning by benzodiazepine tranquilizers E853.2

Note that taking a lower amount or discontinuing the use of a prescribed medication is not classified as either a poisoning or an adverse reaction. Taking a larger or more frequent dosage than prescribed would be classified as a poisoning.

Figure 28.1 illustrates a process for coding poisoning and adverse effects of drugs.

LOCATION OF POISONING CODES AND E CODES ASSOCIATED WITH POISONING AND ADVERSE EFFECTS

Codes for poisoning and E codes associated with poisonings or adverse effects are located most easily by referring to the Table of Drugs and Chemicals in section 2 of volume 2 of *ICD-9-CM*. Drugs and other chemicals are listed in alphabetical order at the far left of the table, with the first column on the right listing the poisoning code for that substance and the remaining columns providing E codes for the external circumstance (accident, suicide, assault). A code from the therapeutic use column is selected for coding an adverse effect.

If a specific drug cannot be located in the table, it can usually be found by referring to the American Hospital Formulary Service (AHFS). As an example of how to use the AHFS number in locating codes in the table, consider the drug Elavil, which is not listed as such in the Table of Drugs and Chemicals. Through reference to the AHFS index, the number 28:16:04 is located and Elavil can then be located in the table under the main

FIGURE 28.1 Decision Tree for Coding Adverse Effects of Drugs or Poisoning Due to Drugs or Medicinal or Biological Substances

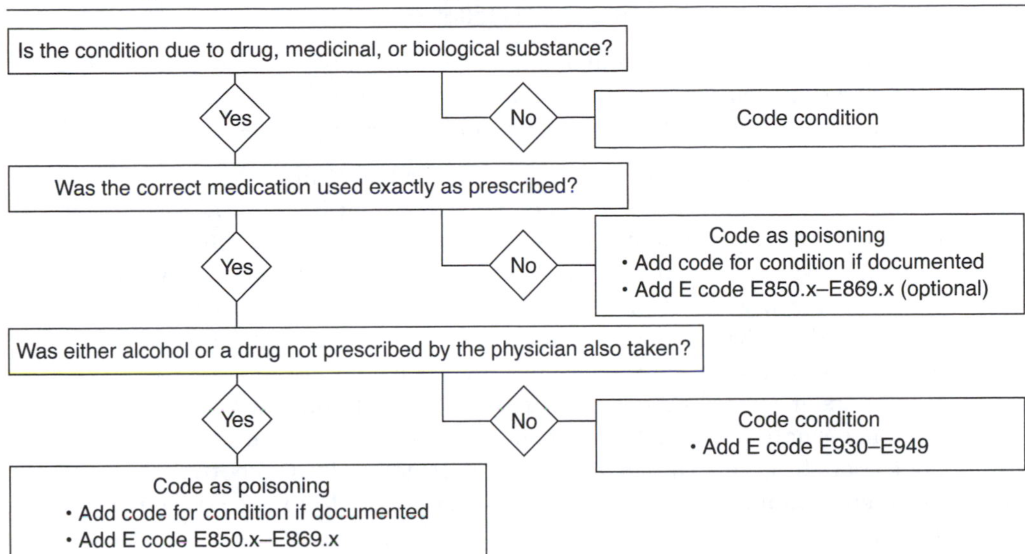

term "Drug" by referring to this number. AHFS numbers are listed in numerical order in the table. A list of AHFS numbers with the associated *ICD-9-CM* poisoning codes is also available in appendix 3 of volume 1. They are listed only by the function of the drug, not by the name of the specific drug.

The American Hospital Formulary is published by the American Society of Hospital Pharmacists. It consists of a collection of monographs on various drugs and a drug index, which is the section that will be most useful to the coder. If this publication is not available in the medical records department, it is usually available in the hospital pharmacy. The hospital pharmacist can also be a valuable source of information.

Neither a poisoning code nor an E code from the table should be assigned without verification in the Tabular List. The Table of Drugs and Chemicals is extensive and very detailed, but it does not take into account the instructional notes in the Tabular List. For example, the table lists codes from category **960, Poisoning by antibiotics,** but the exclusion note at category 960 indicates that codes from category 976 should be used for local (topical) applications or for treating eyes, ears, nose, and throat.

GUIDELINES FOR ASSIGNMENT OF EXTERNAL CAUSE CODES FOR POISONING AND ADVERSE EFFECTS

When the same E code describes the causative agent for more than one adverse reaction, assign the E code only once. When two or more drugs or medicinal or biological substances are reported as being responsible for an adverse effect, code each individually unless a combination code is listed in the therapeutic use column in the Table of Drugs and Chemicals, in which case the combination code should be assigned. For example:

- Supraventricular premature beats secondary to use of digitalis and Valium, both used as prescribed 427.61 + E942.1 + E939.4
- An infant with a high fever due to correct administration of DPT vaccine 780.63 + E948.6
- Patient suffering from dry mouth and itching as a result of taking phenobarbital as prescribed by his physician 527.7 + 698.9 + E937.0

When the external cause for a poisoning is not stated, a code for poisoning undetermined whether accidental or purposely inflicted (E980–E982) is assigned. For example, a diagnosis of coma due to codeine is coded as follows:

- Coma due to accidental poisoning due to codeine 965.09 +780.01 + E850.2
- Coma due to codeine taken in a suicide attempt 965.09 + 780.01 + E950.0
- Coma due to overdose of codeine, cause unknown 965.09 + 780.01 + E980.0

The coder should assign as many E codes as needed to completely describe all responsible substances for either an adverse effect or a poisoning. However, if the reporting format limits the number of E codes that can be used, the one most closely related to the principal diagnosis should be assigned. If complete coding would require different E codes in the same three-digit category, use the code for "Other" specified in that category; if there is no other specified code in that category, use the appropriate unspecified code in that category. If the codes are from different three-digit categories, assign the appropriate E code for other multiple drugs and medicinal substances. For example, a poisoning that resulted from ingestion of aspirin, phenobarbital, and antihistamines taken in a suicide attempt would ordinarily require E codes from three different three-digit categories. If the reporting form does not allow for assignment of all three, code **E950.4, Suicide and self-inflicted poisoning by other specified drugs and medicinal substances,** would be assigned.

Environmental Toxins

Code **E928.6, Environmental exposure to harmful algae and toxins,** describes the external cause of exposure to red tide. Karennia brevis (K. brevis) are microscopic fast-growing marine algae, which create blooms called red tides. K. brevis produces a powerful toxin called brevetoxin. When shellfish feed on K. brevis, brevetoxin becomes concentrated in the shellfish. Individuals who eat shellfish contaminated with brevetoxin develop neurotoxic shellfish poisoning. This type of food poisoning leads to severe gastrointestinal and neurologic symptoms. Assign code V87.32 to describe possible contact with and exposure to algae bloom. This code may be assigned when the patient may have been in the vicinity of algae bloom but has not developed symptoms, or when the patient may have symptoms suspicious of exposure to algae bloom, but a definitive cause of the symptoms has not been confirmed.

Environmental exposure to brevetoxin can also affect people who swim in an ocean polluted by brevetoxins or who inhale brevetoxins in the air. Symptoms can include irritation of the eyes, nose, and throat; tingling of the lips and tongue; coughing; wheezing; and shortness of breath. For example: A patient developed severe abdominal pain, vomiting, and a tingling sensation in the fingers after eating shellfish. The patient was diagnosed with neurotoxic shellfish poisoning due to red tides. Assign code **988.0, Toxic effect of noxious substances eaten as food, fish and shellfish,** and code E928.6.

Exercise 28.1

Code the following diagnoses, assuming that the drug involved was taken correctly unless otherwise specified. Assign E codes where appropriate.

	Code(s)
1. Coma due to acute barbiturate intoxication, attempted suicide	967.0 780.01 E950.1
2. Two-year-old patient ingested an unknown quantity of mother's Enovid	962.2 E858.0
3. Syncope due to hypersensitivity to antidepressant medication Table	780.2 E939.0
4. Hypokalemia resulting from reaction to Diuril given by mistake in physician's office	974.3 276.8 E858.5
5. Diplopia due to allergic reaction to antihistamine, taken as prescribed Table	368.2 E933.0
6. Lethargy due to unintentional overdose of sleeping pills	967.9 780.79 E852.9

Exercise 28.1 *(continued)*

7. Electrolyte imbalance due to interaction between lithium carbonate and Diuril, both taken as prescribed	Table	276.9 E939.8 E944.3
8. Parkinsonism, secondary to correct use of haloperidol	Table	332.1 E939.2
9. Cerebral anoxia resulting from barbiturate overdose, suicide attempt		967.0 348.1 E950.1
10. Toxic encephalopathy due to excessive use of aspirin		965.1 349.82 E980.0
11. Ataxia due to Valium (taken as prescribed) consumed with three martinis	Table, Valium; Table, alcohol	969.4 980.0 781.3 E853.2 E860.0
12. Allergic dermatitis due to bovine insulin	Table	693.0 E932.3
13. Coumadin intoxication due to accumulative effect resulting in gross hematuria	Table	599.71 E934.2

Exercise 28.1 *(continued)*

14. Severe bradycardia due to accidental double dose of digoxin	Table, digoxin	972.1 427.89 E858.3
15. Generalized convulsions due to accidental Darvon overdose		965.8 780.39 E850.8
16. Light-headedness resulting from interaction between Aldomet and peripheral vasodilating agent (both taken as prescribed)	Table	780.4 E942.6 E942.5

UNSPECIFIED ADVERSE EFFECT OF THERAPEUTIC USE

ICD-9-CM provides subcategory **995.2, Other and unspecified adverse effect of drug, medicinal and biological substance,** to identify adverse reactions when the nature of the reaction is not specified. Subcategory 995.2 was expanded to provide additional codes to describe an array of nonspecific drug allergies, hypersensitivities, and/or adverse reactions. An additional code from the E930 through E949 series is also assigned to indicate the responsible drug or biologic substance. These codes may be used in the outpatient setting, but their use for inpatient reporting is inappropriate. If the patient is exhibiting symptoms or signs, the code for that condition should be assigned. If the adverse condition cannot be identified, code **796.0, Nonspecific abnormal toxicological findings,** should be assigned. This code includes abnormal levels of heavy metals or drugs in blood, urine, or other tissues. An additional code from categories E930–E949 should be assigned to indicate the responsible substance. The code assignments for unspecified adverse effects of drugs and medicinal and biological substances are as follows:

- 995.20 Unspecified adverse effect of unspecified drug, medicinal and biological substance
- 995.21 Arthus phenomenon
- 995.22 Unspecified adverse effect of anesthesia
- 995.23 Unspecified adverse effect of insulin
- 995.27 Other drug allergy
- 995.29 Unspecified adverse effect of other drug, medicinal and biological substance

POISONING DUE TO SUBSTANCE ABUSE OR DEPENDENCE

An acute condition due to a reaction resulting from the interaction of alcohol and a drug(s) or due to a drug involved in abuse or dependence is classified as a poisoning. Additional codes are assigned for both the acute manifestation of the poisoning and the dependence or abuse. An E code to indicate the circumstances of the episode should be assigned. For example:

- Acute pulmonary edema due to accidental heroin overdose in a patient who is heroin dependent 965.01 + 518.4 + 304.00 + E850.0

Chronic conditions related to alcohol or drug abuse or dependence are not classified as poisoning. The code for the chronic condition is sequenced first, followed by a code for the abuse or dependence. For example:

- Alcoholic cirrhosis of the liver; chronic alcohol dependence 571.2 + 303.90
- Alcoholic hepatitis; chronic alcohol dependence, episodic 571.1 + 303.90
- Drug-induced depressive state due to cocaine abuse 292.84 + 305.60

Exercise 28.2

Code the following diagnoses. Assign E codes where appropriate.

		Code(s)
1. Muscle cramps of leg due to occupational use of arsenic pesticide	Table, arsenic	985.1 729.82 E863.4
2. Systemic hypocalcemia and hypokalemia due to use of lye in household chores	Table, lye	983.2 275.41 276.8 E864.2 E849.0
3. Bradycardia due to ingestion of oleander leaves	Table, oleander	988.2 427.89 E980.9

LATE EFFECTS OF POISONING

The rules discussed earlier in relation to coding late effects also apply to coding late effects of poisoning. The code for the residual condition is sequenced first, with code **909.0, Late effect of poisoning due to drug, medicinal or biological substance,** or **909.1, Late effect of toxic effects of nonmedicinal substance,** assigned as an additional code. Code E929.2 is also assigned for late effects of poisoning.

LATE EFFECTS OF ADVERSE REACTIONS TO DRUGS

ICD-9-CM does not provide a late effect E code for adverse reactions to drugs correctly administered. A code is assigned for the residual condition, with code **909.5, Late effect of adverse effect of drug, medicinal or biological substance,** assigned as an additional code. An E code (E930–E949) for the responsible drug is also assigned.

Long-term chronic effects of a prescription drug taken over a period of time—and still being taken at the time the chronic effects arise—are coded as current adverse effects. For example, steroid-induced diabetes in a patient currently taking steroids as prescribed is coded as an adverse effect (249.00 + E932.0). If the patient suffers delayed effects that arose or remain long after the medication was discontinued, code **909.5, Late effect of adverse effect of drug, medicinal or biological substance,** would be assigned as an additional code to indicate that it is a late effect. For example:

- Brain damage due to allergic reaction to penicillin (current medication) 348.9 + E930.0
- Brain damage due to allergic reaction to penicillin (use of medication discontinued six months ago) 348.9 + 909.5 + E930.0

Review Exercise 28.3

Code the following diagnoses, sequencing the codes correctly. Assign E codes.

		Code(s)
1. Extrapyramidal disease resulting from previous overdose of Thorazine in an attempted suicide six months ago	Late or Late effect of	333.90 909.0 E959
2. Bilateral neural deafness resulting from accidental overdose of streptomycin administered in physician's office two years ago	Late or Late effect of	389.12 909.0 E929.2
3. Anoxic brain damage secondary to previous accidental overdose of Nembutal nine months ago	Late or Late effect of	348.1 909.0 E929.2
4. Secondary Parkinsonism due to poisoning by lithium four years ago	Late or Late effect of	332.1 909.0 E929.2

Complications of Surgery and Medical Care

CHAPTER **29**

CHAPTER OVERVIEW

- Categories 996–999 in *ICD-9-CM* cover complications of medical and surgical care that are not already classified elsewhere.
- Not all postcare conditions are classified as complications.
  - —There must be an unexpected or abnormal occurrence.
  - —There must be a cause-and-effect relationship between the condition and the care.
  - —There must be an indication that it is a complication.
- There are several instructional notes (and in particular exclusion notes) related to complications.
- When coding, look for a subterm indicating postoperative or iatrogenic condition.
- Look to main term **Complications** if no subterms are found in the particular entry for the condition.
- Complications involving an internal device, implant, or graft are classified first. The fifth digit is used for a variety of reasons in the complications category—from specifying location to type of device or procedure.
- It is important to distinguish between admission for complications and admission for routine and scheduled aftercare.

LEARNING OUTCOMES

After studying this chapter you should be able to:

- Understand when and when not to code a condition or occurrence as a complication.
- Locate complication codes.
- Use all of the instructional notes present in *ICD-9-CM* to properly classify a condition caused by a complication of medical or surgical care.

TERM TO KNOW

Iatrogenic condition
condition resulting from the treatment of another condition

REMEMBER . . . Coders should never make assumptions with regard to complications because of the legal ramifications of these codes.

INTRODUCTION

Categories 996 through 999 are provided in *ICD-9-CM* for complications of medical and surgical care that are not classified elsewhere. Code assignment is based on the provider's documentation of the relationship between the condition and the care or procedure. Note that not all conditions that occur following surgery or other patient care are classified as complications. First, there must be more than a routinely expected condition or occurrence. For example, a major amount of bleeding is expected with joint replacement surgery; hemorrhage should not be considered a complication unless such bleeding is particularly excessive. In addition, there must be a cause-and-effect relationship between the care provided and the condition, and some indication that it is a complication, not a postoperative condition in which no complication is present, such as an artificial opening status or absence of an extremity. In some cases, this is implicit, as in a complication due to the presence of an internal device, an implant or graft, or a transplant. Code assignment for postprocedural complications is based on the provider's documentation of the relationship between the complication and the procedure. The coder cannot make this determination and should always query the provider for clarification when a postprocedural complication is not clearly documented. Note that the term "complication" as used in *ICD-9-CM* does not imply that improper or inadequate care is responsible for the problem.

No time limit is defined for the development of a complication. It may occur during the hospital episode in which the care was provided, shortly thereafter, or even years later. When it occurs during the episode in which the operation or other care was given, it is assigned as an additional code. When it develops later and is the reason for the hospital admission, it is designated as the principal diagnosis. Complications of surgical and medical care are classified in *ICD-9-CM* as follows:

- Complications that occur only in other specified body sites are classified in that chapter of *ICD-9-CM*.
- Complications that affect multiple sites or body systems are generally classified in categories 996–999.
- Complications of abortion, pregnancy, labor, or delivery are reclassified in chapter 11 of *ICD-9-CM*.

It is imperative that the coder use the index carefully and follow all instructional notes. Exclusion notes are fairly extensive in this section and often direct the coder elsewhere. There are several basic exclusions that must be observed:

- Complications of medicinal agents, such as adverse effects, complications of anesthesia, and poisoning due to medicinal or toxic agents
- Burns from local applications and irradiation
- Complications of anesthesia and other drugs
- Complications of the condition for which surgery was performed
- Specified conditions classified elsewhere, such as serum hepatitis or electrolyte imbalance
- Any condition classified elsewhere in the Alphabetic Index when described as being due to a procedure or medical care, such as postoperative psychosis or postlaminectomy syndrome. (Note that the adjective "iatrogenic" is often used to indicate that the condition is a result of treatment.)

When assigning codes in categories 996–999, Complications of Surgical and Medical Care NEC, use an additional code to identify the specific complication, but only if the additional code provides greater specificity as to the nature of the condition. If, however, the complication code fully describes the condition, no additional code is necessary. The instructional note at subcategory 996.7, Other complications of internal prosthetic device, implant, and graft, instructs the coder to "Use additional code to identify complication, such as: . . . venous embolism and thrombosis." For example:

- A patient developed thrombosis of a femoral popliteal bypass graft. Assign code **996.74, Other complications of internal (biological) (synthetic) prosthetic device, implant, and graft, due to other vascular device, implant, and graft,** with code **444.22, Arterial embolism and thrombosis, lower extremity,** for a femoral popliteal artery graft thrombosis. Both codes are required to fully describe the nature of the condition.

LOCATING COMPLICATION CODES IN THE ALPHABETIC INDEX

The coder should first refer to the main term for the condition and look for a subterm indicating a postoperative or other iatrogenic condition. For example:

Adhesion(s) . . .
  postoperative (gastrointestinal tract) . . . 568.0
    eyelid 997.9 . . .
    urethra 598.2
Colostomy . . .
  malfunction 569.69

When no entry can be found under the main term for the condition, the coder should refer to the main term **Complications** and look for an appropriate subterm, such as one of the following:

- Nature of complication, such as foreign body, accidental puncture, or hemorrhage
- Type of procedure, such as colostomy, dialysis, or shunt
- Anatomical site or body system affected, such as respiratory system
- General terms such as mechanical, infection, or graft

Examples include the following entries from the Alphabetic Index:

Complications
  postmastoidectomy . . . 383.30
Complications
  cardiac . . . 429.0
    device . . . 996.72
      infection . . . 996.61
      long-term effect 429.4
      mechanical . . . 996.00

POSTOPERATIVE CONDITIONS NOT CLASSIFIED AS COMPLICATIONS

Certain conditions resulting from medical or surgical care are residual conditions of a procedure, but no complicating factor is involved. For example, postlaminectomy syndrome often occurs following laminectomy, but it is a sequela of the procedure, not a complication. The extensive exclusion list at the beginning of the 996 through 999 series is helpful in making some of these distinctions. Other examples include:

- Postoperative intestinal or peritoneal adhesions with obstruction 560.81
- Infection of enterostomy, due to group C *Streptococcus* 569.61 + 041.03
- Postoperative pelvic adhesions 614.6

Some conditions that occur postoperatively are neither classified as complications nor have special codes to indicate that they are postoperative in nature. Pain, for instance, is coded only to the site of the pain when a code is warranted at all. Patients are frequently admitted from outpatient surgery with pain and/or nausea and vomiting, but these are common symptoms during postoperative recovery and are not coded to categories 996 through 999 unless the physician identifies them specifically as complications of the surgery. The principal diagnosis is the symptom or other condition that occasions the postoperative admission. Sometimes the patient is admitted because of a general concern rather than because of specific symptoms. Although physicians may state that the admission is for observation, this type of situation is ordinarily not coded to **V71.x, Observation and evaluation for suspected conditions not found.** If no specific condition is identified, the principal diagnosis would be admission for surgical aftercare (V58.4x).

Postoperative anemia is rarely considered to be a complication of surgery. When the physician documents postoperative anemia due to blood loss, code **285.1, Acute posthemorrhagic anemia,** is assigned, but no complication code is assigned unless the physician documents excessive bleeding as a complication. The fact that blood is administered during a surgical procedure does not indicate a postoperative anemia. Transfusions are sometimes given as a prophylactic replacement to avoid postoperative anemia. Anemia is not assigned solely because the patient received a transfusion; the physician must document the condition.

A diagnosis of postoperative hypertension often means only that the patient has a preexisting essential hypertension or an elevated blood pressure. If the physician clearly identifies it as a postoperative complication, code **997.91, Complications affecting other specified body systems not elsewhere classified, hypertension,** is assigned.

Exercise 29.1

Code the following diagnoses. Do not assign E codes.

	Code(s)
1. Postoperative pulmonary embolism	415.11
2. Postoperative pulmonary edema	518.4
3. Colostomy malfunction	569.62
4. Postleukotomy syndrome	310.0
5. Postoperative peritoneal adhesions	568.0
6. Postoperative blind loop syndrome	579.2

COMPLICATIONS DUE TO PRESENCE OF INTERNAL DEVICE, IMPLANT, OR GRAFT

Category **996, Complications peculiar to certain specified procedures,** classifies conditions that occur only because an internal device, implant, or graft is present. Complications of this type are classified first according to whether they are mechanical or nonmechanical in nature. A mechanical complication is one that results from a failure of the device, implant, or graft, such as displacement or malfunction. These are classified in subcategories 996.0 through 996.5, with a fifth digit indicating the body system and/or type of device involved. For example:

- Perforation of uterus by intrauterine contraceptive device 996.32
- Protrusion of intramedullary nail in left femur 996.49
- Mechanical complication of peritoneal dialysis catheter 996.56
- Mechanical complication of arteriovenous dialysis catheter 996.1
- Malfunction of transjugular intrahepatic portosystemic shunt (TIPS) 996.1
- Defective automatic implantable cardiac defibrillator (AICD) 996.04
- Broken vascular catheter tip 996.1
- Clotted peripherally inserted central catheter 996.1

Subcategory **996.4, Mechanical complication of internal orthopedic device, implant, and graft,** classifies a range of complications involving prosthetic joint implants. The specific mechanical complications are indicated as follows:

- 996.40 Unspecified mechanical complication of internal orthopedic device, implant, and graft
- 996.41 Mechanical loosening of prosthetic joint
- 996.42 Dislocation of prosthetic joint
- 996.43 Broken prosthetic joint implant
- 996.44 Peri-prosthetic fracture around prosthetic joint
- 996.45 Peri-prosthetic osteolysis
- 996.46 Articular bearing surface wear of prosthetic joint
- 996.47 Other mechanical complication of prosthetic joint implant
- 996.49 Other mechanical complication of other internal orthopedic device, implant, and graft

Infection and inflammatory reactions due to the presence of a device, implant, or graft that is functioning properly are classified in subcategory **996.6x, Infection and inflammatory reaction due to internal prosthetic device, implant, and graft.** Code **996.62, Infection and inflammatory reaction due to vascular device, implant and graft,** is used for infections due to arterial, dialysis, or peripheral venous catheters. Bloodstream infections due to central venous catheters should be assigned code 999.32 rather than code 996.62. Examples of central venous catheters include the Hickman catheter, peripherally inserted central catheter (PICC), portacath, umbilical venous catheter, and triple lumen catheter. Central line–associated bloodstream infections are systemic infections. Codes 999.32 and 999.33 distinguish between local and systemic infections due to central venous catheter. A local infection due to a central venous catheter is assigned code 999.33. These include exit or insertion site infections, port or reservoir infections, or tunnel infections, which are laboratory-confirmed bloodstream infections, not due to an infection at another site.

Code **996.64, Infection or inflammation due to indwelling urinary catheter,** should have additional codes for the specific infection, such as cystitis or sepsis, and for the responsible organism if that information is available. Fifth digits indicate the site and/or type of complication. For example:

- Infected pacemaker pocket 996.61
- E. coli infection due to peritoneal dialysis catheter 996.68 + 041.4
- Chronic interstitial cystitis due to indwelling catheter 996.64 + 595.1

Subcategory 996.7x classifies other complications due to the presence of internal prosthetic device, implant, and graft. This includes nonmechanical complications, such as embolism, thrombosis, fibrosis, stenosis, or pain. When the complication is documented as postoperative pain due to the presence of a device, implant, or graft left in a surgical site, an additional code is used to identify the complication, such as acute pain (338.18–338.19) or chronic pain (338.28–338.29).

Code 996.72 is assigned for occlusion of a coronary bypass graft unless it is identified by the physician as being due to arteriosclerosis. Arteriosclerotic occlusions of a coronary artery bypass graft are classified as codes 414.02 through 414.05, Coronary atherosclerosis. The fifth digit indicates the type of graft. Occlusion of the coronary artery when there is no history of bypass graft is classified as arteriosclerosis of native coronary arteries (414.01).

Subcategory 996.8, Complications of transplanted organ, is reserved for transplant complications or rejections, with the fifth digit indicating the organ involved. When infection is present, a code from category 041 or 079 should be assigned as an additional code. A transplant complication code is assigned only if the complication affects the function of the transplanted organ. Two codes are required to fully describe a transplant complication: the appropriate code from subcategory 996.8 and a secondary code that identifies the complication. For example:

- Acute graft-versus-host disease resulting from complications of bone marrow transplant 996.85 + 279.51
- Malignant neoplasm of transplanted kidney 996.82 + 199.2 + 189.0
- Lymphoproliferative disorder post intestinal transplant 996.87 + 238.77

Code 996.88 describes complications of stem cell transplants. Stem cell transplants can be performed using the patient's own stem cells (autologous stem cell transplant) or donor stem cells (allogeneic stem cell transplant). Most stem cell transplantation procedures are performed using stem cells collected from the peripheral blood. Complications can develop from a stem cell transplant, including graft-versus-host disease, stem cell (graft) failure, organ damage, cataracts, secondary cancers, and death.

Preexisting conditions or conditions that develop after the transplant are not coded as complications unless they affect the function of the transplanted organs. Posttransplant surgical complications that do not relate to the function of the transplanted organ are classified to the specific complication. For example, a postsurgical infection is coded as a postoperative wound infection, not as a transplant complication. Posttransplant patients who are seen for treatment unrelated to the transplanted organ are assigned a code from category **V42, Organ or tissue replaced by transplant,** to capture the transplant status of the patient. A code from category V42 should never be used with a code from subcategory 996.8.

For conditions that affect the function of the transplanted kidney, other than chronic kidney disease (CKD), code 996.81 should be assigned, along with a secondary code that identifies the condition. Patients with CKD following a transplant should not be assumed to have transplant failure or rejection unless it is documented by the provider. Patients who have undergone a kidney transplant may still have some form of CKD because the kidney transplant may not fully restore kidney function. Therefore, the presence of CKD alone does not constitute a transplant complication. If documentation supports the presence of failure or rejection, then it is appropriate to assign code **996.81, Complications of transplanted organs, kidney,** followed by the appropriate CKD code (585.1–585.9). For example:

- A patient with end-stage kidney disease, due to a congenital anomaly of the urinary tract, underwent deceased donor renal transplantation. Postoperatively he had persistent severe hyperkalemia, which required hemodialysis. The patient also experienced delayed graft function. Assign code **585.6, End stage renal disease,** as the principal diagnosis. Code **996.81, Complication of transplanted organ kidney,** is assigned for the delayed graft function. Assign codes **753.9, Unspecified anomaly of urinary system,** and **276.7, Hyperpotassemia,** as additional diagnoses. For the procedures, assign codes **55.69, Other kidney transplantation,** and **39.95, Hemodialysis.**

Exercise 29.2

Code the following diagnoses. Do not assign E codes.

	Code(s)
1. Leakage of breast prosthesis	996.54
2. Intrauterine contraceptive device imbedded in uterine wall Imbedding	996.32
3. Erosion of skin by pacemaker electrodes Complication	996.01
4. Bone marrow transplant with rejection syndrome Acute graft-versus-host disease Complication	996.85 279.51
5. Displaced lens implant, right eye Complication	996.53
6. Complication of transplanted intestine Malignant neoplasm of colon related to intestinal transplant	996.87 199.2 153.9

COMPLICATIONS AFFECTING SPECIFIC BODY SYSTEMS NOT CLASSIFIED ELSEWHERE

Titles for most of the codes from category **997, Complications affecting specified body systems, not elsewhere classified,** are general in nature and offer little specificity. These codes are not assigned when the Alphabetic Index provides another code, and they should not be assigned without specific documentation by the physician that the condition is a complication of the surgery. When a code from category 997 is assigned, an additional code for the condition is ordinarily assigned to provide specificity.

ICD-9-CM differentiates between cardiac complications that occur during the immediate postoperative period following any type of surgery (997.1) and long-term functional effects following cardiac surgery (429.4). Originally, the immediate postoperative period was defined as the time between the surgery and the patient's discharge from the hospital. With current changes in medical practice resulting in earlier discharges, this definition is no longer viable, and code 997.1 may be assigned for complications that occur reasonably soon after surgery, even after discharge. Code **429.4, Functional disturbance,** also classifies long-term functional effects that result from the presence of a cardiac prosthesis.

Pacemaker syndrome (429.4) sometimes occurs when a patient fitted with a ventricular pacemaker experiences decreased cardiac output during paced rhythm. This syndrome can overshadow any improvement resulting from pacemaker therapy and may actually lead to a worsening of the symptoms that were present before the pacemaker was implanted. Examples of the appropriate use of category 997 are as follows:

- Acute cholecystitis; postoperative cardiac arrhythmia (same admission) 575.0 + 997.1 + 427.9
- Heart failure following cardiac surgery performed during previous admission; patient discharged one month ago 429.4
- Heart failure on second postoperative day following surgery 997.1
- Coronary artery dissection occurring during percutaneous coronary angioplasty 997.1 + 414.12

Code **997.31, Ventilator associated pneumonia,** is assigned only when the provider has specifically documented ventilator associated pneumonia (VAP). An additional code is used to identify the specific organism involved (e.g., E. coli, code 041.49). Do not assign an additional code from categories 480–484 to identify the type of pneumonia. The coder should query the provider when the documentation is unclear as to whether the patient has a pneumonia associated with mechanical ventilation. For example:

- A patient is admitted for acute respiratory failure, intubated, and placed on mechanical ventilation. He developed VAP. Code 518.81 is assigned as the principal diagnosis. Code 997.31 is assigned as an additional diagnosis. Assign codes 96.70 and 96.04 for the mechanical ventilation and intubation.

Assign the appropriate code from categories 480–484 for a patient admitted with one type of pneumonia who subsequently develops VAP. The principal diagnosis is the code for the specific type of pneumonia (e.g., code 481, Pneumococcal pneumonia) diagnosed at the time of admission. Code 997.31 would be assigned as an additional diagnosis if the provider has specifically documented VAP.

If the patient is on a ventilator and develops pneumonia, and the documentation is not clear as to whether the pneumonia was due to the ventilator, query the physician for clarification.

Code 997.32 is assigned for postoperative aspiration pneumonia and includes chemical pneumonitis and Mendelson's syndrome when they result from a procedure. Code 507.0 is not assigned with 997.32 because 997.32 fully describes the nature of the complication.

Code 997.41 is used to report the retention of gallstones following cholecystectomy. This condition is not uncommon following a laparoscopic cholecystectomy, as gallstones may fall into the abdominal cavity, causing a later obstruction or infection. Code **997.41, Retained cholelithiasis following cholecystectomy,** is assigned in this situation.

Complications of an amputated stump are classified in subcategory 997.6 with the addition of a fifth digit indicating the type of amputated stump complication. A code from subcategories V49.6 through V49.7 is assigned to indicate the site of the amputation. Amputation stump complications are classified as follows:

- 997.60 Amputation stump complication, Unspecified complication
- 997.61 Amputation stump complication, Neuroma of amputation stump
- 997.62 Amputation stump complication, Infection (chronic)
- 997.69 Amputation stump complication, Other

OTHER COMPLICATIONS OF PROCEDURES NOT CLASSIFIED ELSEWHERE

Category **998, Other complications of surgery, not elsewhere classified,** is used to classify a miscellaneous group of postoperative complications. Additional codes are not usually required because the complication code itself provides sufficient specificity. For example:

- 998.32 Disruption of external operation (surgical) wound
- 998.82 Cataract fragments in eye following cataract surgery
- 998.01 Postoperative shock, cardiogenic

Cardiogenic shock is attributable to a weakened heart that is not able to pump enough blood to organs of the body. Causes of cardiogenic shock include myocardial infarction, pericardial tamponade, and heart failure. Assign code **998.01, Postoperative shock, cardiogenic,** for cardiogenic shock due to surgery. Postoperative infections originating in the wound, lungs, or blood/vascular catheter may lead to septic shock. Code **998.02, Postoperative shock, septic,** is assigned for postoperative septic shock. Assign code **998.09, Postoperative shock, other,** for postsurgical hypovolemic shock (the most common type of postoperative shock), which occurs when large amounts of fluids are lost because of hemorrhage or severe dehydration. For example:

- A patient developed refractory cardiogenic shock, which required temporary extracorporeal membrane oxygenation (ECMO) support, after undergoing aortic valve replacement due to severe aortic stenosis. Assign code **424.1, Aortic valve disorders,** as the principal diagnosis. Assign code **998.01, Postoperative shock, cardiogenic,** as an additional diagnosis. Assign codes **35.22, Other replacement of aortic valve,** and **39.65, Extracorporeal membrane oxygenation [ECMO],** for the procedures.

Wound dehiscence involves partial or total disruption of any or all layers of an operative wound site. Common causes of wound dehiscence include excess tension on the sutured edges, necrosis of the wound edges, seroma or hematoma causing pressure on the wound, and wound infection. *ICD-9-CM* provides codes to distinguish between disruption of internal (998.31) and external (998.32) surgical wounds as well as a disruption of a traumatic injury wound repair (998.33). For example:

- An 8-year-old had a lower leg traumatic laceration that was sutured several weeks ago. The patient was seen in the emergency department two weeks after the sutures were removed because of disruption of the wound repair. Code 998.33 is assigned for this encounter.

Subcategory **998.1, Hemorrhage or hematoma or seroma complicating a procedure,** classifies the specific complication with a fifth digit as follows:

- 998.11 Hemorrhage complicating a procedure
- 998.12 Hematoma complicating a procedure
- 998.13 Seroma complicating a procedure

Code **998.2, Accidental puncture or laceration during a procedure,** classifies inadvertent rents, tears, or lacerations that occur during surgery. *ICD-9-CM* makes a distinction between dural tears (349.31) and other types of accidental surgical punctures or lacerations (998.2). An incidental dural tear occurring during surgery is coded to 349.31 rather than 998.2.

Code **998.4, Foreign body accidentally left during a procedure,** is assigned for situations in which there is an unintended retention of a foreign object (e.g., sponge) in a patient after surgery or other procedure. The occurrence of unintended retention of objects at any point after the surgery ends should be captured regardless of setting or whether the object is removed. For example:

- At surgery, a suture broke away from the needle and the needle was lost. Multiple attempts to find it were unsuccessful. An X-ray did not reveal the needle and the chest was closed. Another X-ray showed that the needle was positioned to the right of the aortic valve. The chest was reopened but the needle still could not be located. The surgeon decided that further search for the needle would cause the patient harm, so the chest was closed, and the patient was transferred to the ICU in stable condition. Assign code **998.4, Foreign body accidentally left during a procedure.** Although the surgeon made the decision to leave the needle to avoid harm to the patient, it was not the intent of the original procedure to leave a foreign body behind.

Patients are frequently seen for continued care for postsurgical wounds that are either healing slowly or not healing at all. Code **998.83, Non-healing wound,** is assigned for such admissions or encounters.

COMPLICATIONS OF MEDICAL CARE NOT CLASSIFIED ELSEWHERE

Category **999, Complications of medical care,** is used to classify a number of specific conditions that may occur following almost any type of procedure. Codes from category 999 classify conditions that result from medical care rather than from surgery. For example:

- Generalized vaccinia following vaccination 999.0
- Air embolism following infusion 999.1
- Phlebitis following perfusion 999.2
- Acute infection following transfusion, infusion or injection of blood and blood products 999.34
- Anaphylactic reaction due to vaccination 999.42
- Anaphylactic reaction due to other serum 999.49
- Rh incompatibility reaction following transfusion 999.70

Code 999.34 describes an acute infection following a transfusion, infusion, or injection of blood and blood products. Transfusion-transmitted infections include any infectious organism (bacteria, virus, parasite, or other) transmitted through transfusion, infusion, or injection of blood or blood products—whole blood, red blood cells (RBCs), plasma, platelets, or other. Code 999.34 should be used for acute infections, not for chronic cases. In addition, if the transfusion-transmitted infection has specifically been identified as human immunodeficiency virus (HIV), assign a code for the HIV disease first.

Extravasation is the accidental infiltration of intravenously infused drugs into the surrounding tissue. Vesicants are chemically active substances that can produce blistering on direct contact with the skin or mucous membrane. Extravasation of antineoplastic drugs during cancer treatment can lead to serious complications. In milder cases, extravasation can cause pain, reddening, or irritation on the arm at the site of the infusion needle. In severe cases, tissue damage may involve tissue necrosis and lead to loss of the limb. The following codes are assigned to describe infusion complications:

- 999.81 Extravasation of vesicant chemotherapy
- 999.82 Extravasation of other vesicant agent
- 999.88 Other infusion reaction

ICD-9-CM provides codes to report transfusion reactions due to blood or blood product incompatibility as follows:

- ABO incompatibility reaction (999.60–999.69)
- Rh and other non-ABO incompatibility reaction (999.70–999.79)
- Other and unspecified incompatibility reaction (999.80, 999.83–999.85, 999.89)

These codes also provide information on the different types of hemolytic transfusion reactions, including both acute hemolytic transfusion reaction and delayed hemolytic transfusion reaction. A hemolytic transfusion reaction is a systemic response by the body to the administration of blood that is incompatible with the recipient's blood, resulting in destruction of red blood cells. This can lead to acute renal failure and/or disseminated intravascular coagulation (DIC).

Allergic reactions following blood transfusion are attributed to soluble substances in donor plasma. The most common transfusion reactions are fever, chills, pruritus, or urticaria, which can resolve without specific treatment or complications. Instructional notes in the Tabular List indicate that anaphylactic reactions due to the administration of blood are excluded from codes in subcategory 999.6, ABO incompatibility reaction due to transfusion of blood or blood products. For example:

- A patient presents with complaints of dizziness, weakness, and fatigue. The provider documented weakness and fatigue due to acute anemia due to blood loss, and the patient subsequently received two units of packed RBCs. During the administration of the second unit, she developed fever, hoarseness, and facial edema and was treated with IV Benadryl. Assign code **285.1, Acute posthemorrhagic anemia,** as the principal diagnosis. Code **999.41, Anaphylactic reaction due to administration of blood and blood products,** should be assigned as an additional diagnosis. Assign code **E934.7, Natural blood and blood products.** Assign code **99.04, Transfusion of packed cells.**

Code 999.42 is used to report anaphylactic reactions due to vaccination, and code 999.49 is reserved for anaphylactic reaction due to other serum. Although an anaphylactic reaction to vaccine is rare, it can develop when a person with preformed IgE antibodies to a vaccine constituent is given a vaccine containing that substance. These IgE-mediated reactions are usually caused by vaccine components other than the immunizing agent. Serum sickness is a reaction similar to an allergy. It involves an immune system reaction to certain medications, injected proteins used to treat immune conditions, or antiserum (the liquid part of blood that contains antibodies that help protect against infectious or poisonous substances). Codes 999.51, 999.52, and 999.59 describe other serum reactions due to the administration of blood and blood products, other serum reaction due to vaccination, and other serum reaction, respectively.

Please note that other transfusion-related problems are coded to other chapters, such as hemochromatosis due to repeated blood cell transfusions (275.02), transfusion associated circulatory overload (276.61), posttransfusion purpura (275.02), and posttransfusion fever (780.66).

COMPLICATIONS VERSUS AFTERCARE

As discussed earlier, it is important to differentiate between an admission for a complication of surgery or medical care and one for aftercare. An admission for aftercare is usually planned in advance to take care of an expected residual or to carry out follow-up activity, such as removal of pins or plates placed during earlier orthopedic surgery. Aftercare is classified into categories V50 through V58. Subcategory **V58.3, Attention to dressing and sutures,** distinguishes encounters for change or removal of nonsurgical wound dressing (V58.30), change or removal of surgical wound dressing (V58.31), and removal of sutures (V58.32). The coder must be careful not to assign complication codes for routine aftercare encounters. For example:

- Admitted for removal of pins from femur V54.01
- Admitted for replacement of knee prosthesis following explantation of infected joint prosthesis V54.81
- Patient visit for removal of cast V53.7

Exercise 29.3

Code the following diagnoses, some of which identify complications and some of which identify aftercare. Do not assign E codes or procedure codes.

	Code(s)
1. Admitted for removal of internal fixation nail that has extruded into surrounding tissue, causing severe pain Complication, orthopedic	996.49
2. Admitted for closure of colostomy	V55.3
3. Admitted for adjustment of breast prosthesis	V52.4
4. Admitted for removal of displaced breast prosthesis Complication, surgical, internal	996.54

STATUS POST

The term "status post" used in diagnostic statements is sometimes interpreted by coders to mean that there is a postoperative complication; however, the term is rarely intended to carry this meaning. It usually indicates that the patient underwent the procedure at some time in the past. The condition ordinarily would be classified in the V10 through V19 series but only when it is significant for the current episode of care.

SURGICAL OR MEDICAL CARE AS EXTERNAL CAUSE

ICD-9-CM provides two sets of E codes to indicate medical or surgical care as the cause of a complication. Codes from categories E870 through E876 are used only when the condition is stated to be due to a misadventure of medical or surgical care. Code E876.5 is assigned when the wrong operation (procedure) is performed on the correct patient and includes a wrong device implanted into a correct surgical site. Code E876.6 is assigned for performance of operation (procedure) on patient not scheduled for surgery. Code E876.7 is assigned for performance of correct operation (procedure) on wrong side/body part. Codes from categories E878 through E879 are used when the condition is described as due to medical or surgical care but without mention of misadventure. Examples include the following:

- Radiation pneumonitis due to adverse reaction to radiotherapy 508.0 + E879.2
- Sponge inadvertently left in abdomen during laparotomy 998.4 + E871.0
- Left femoral component inserted into right leg instead of right femoral component during total knee replacement 998.89 + E876.5

Because of the potential legal problems that may develop from reporting these codes, the facility should give careful thought to formulating policies and guidelines for their use. Coders should never make an assumption that there has been a misadventure; such codes should be assigned only when there is a clear-cut diagnostic statement to this effect by the physician.

Review Exercise 29.4

Code the following diagnoses. Do not assign E codes, V codes, or procedure codes.

	Code(s)
1. Infected injection site, left buttock or Complications	999.39
2. Sloughing of skin graft due to rejection of pedicle graft to right arm	996.52
3. Headache due to lumbar puncture	349.0
4. Postoperative cardiac arrest occurring in recovery room during closure of abdomen, with successful resuscitation	997.1 427.5
5. Persistent vomiting following gastrointestinal surgery	564.3
6. Air embolism resulting from intravenous infusion	999.1
7. Thrombophlebitis of antecubital vein of the upper arm resulting from intravenous infusion Postoperative	999.2 451.82

Review Exercise 29.4 *(continued)*

8. Hypovolemic shock due to surgery this morning	Postoperative	998.09
9. Persistent postoperative vesicovaginal fistula		998.6 619.0
10. Cardiac insufficiency resulting from mitral valve prosthesis, in place for three years		429.4
11. Perforation of coronary artery by catheter during cardiac catheterization	Complication	998.2
12. Displacement of cardiac pacemaker electrode	Complication, mechanical	996.01
13. Phantom limb following surgical amputation		353.6
14. Neuroma of stump following surgical amputation of left leg		997.61
15. Methicillin susceptible *Staphylococcus aureus* infection of transplanted kidney	Complication, transplant, organ	996.81 041.11

Preview of *ICD-10-CM* and *ICD-10-PCS*

Introduction to the *ICD-10-CM* and *ICD-10-PCS* Classifications

CHAPTER **30**

Nelly Leon-Chisen, RHIA

CHAPTER OVERVIEW

- *ICD-10-CM* and *ICD-10-PCS* have been developed to take the place of *ICD-9-CM.*
- The compliance date for implementation of these two classification systems in the United States is October 1, 2013.
- The change to *ICD-10* is needed for a variety of reasons.
  - — The *ICD-9-CM* classification is limited in its ability to expand to include new technology.
  - — Once a category becomes full in *ICD-9-CM,* several types of diagnoses or procedures have to be classified within the same code to save space.
  - — Many other countries in the world have already made the change. This makes it difficult to compare the health data of the United States with the rest of the world.
- Implementing *ICD-10-CM* and *ICD-10-PCS* could improve quality of care and patient safety and make the reimbursement claims process run more smoothly.
- Every application and database in which diagnosis or procedure codes are captured, stored, analyzed, or reported will use the new classification system.

LEARNING OUTCOMES

After studying this chapter you should be able to:

- Explain the improvements that make the *ICD-10* system more efficient and useful than the *ICD-9* system.
- Explain why a change to *ICD-10-CM* and *ICD-10-PCS* will be beneficial.

TERMS TO KNOW

ICD-10-CM
International Classification of Diseases, Tenth Revision, Clinical Modification; consists of diagnosis codes

ICD-10-PCS
International Classification of Diseases, Tenth Revision, Procedure Classification System; consists of procedure codes

REMEMBER . . . A successful transition to *ICD-10-CM* and *ICD-10-PCS* will require careful planning and coordination of resources.

INTRODUCTION

The *International Classification of Diseases, Tenth Revision, Clinical Modification* (*ICD-10-CM*) and the *International Classification of Diseases, Tenth Revision, Procedure Classification System (ICD-10-PCS)* have been developed as a replacement for *ICD-9-CM*. *ICD-10-CM* consists of a clinical modification of the World Health Organization's *ICD-10*. *ICD-10-CM* consists of diagnosis codes, whereas *ICD-10-PCS* consists of procedure codes. **The compliance date for implementation in the United States is October 1, 2013.** The federal regulatory update to the Health Insurance Portability and Accountability Act (HIPAA) that required the transition to both *ICD-10-CM* and *ICD-10-PCS* was published in the January 16, 2009, *Federal Register*. To download the complete rule, visit http://edocket.access.gpo.gov/2009/pdf/E9-743.pdf. This rule affects health plans, health care clearinghouses, and health care providers that transmit any electronic health information in connection with HIPAA transaction standards. A separate final rule, issued on the same day, calls for compliance with an updated version of current electronic claim transaction standards (Version 5010) on January 1, 2012. To view the electronic transaction (5010) final rule, visit http://edocket.access.gpo.gov/2009/pdf/E9-740.pdf.

RATIONALE FOR CHANGE

ICD-9-CM has been in use in the United States since 1979. Many improvements in medical practice and technology have taken place since *ICD-9-CM* was first implemented. Although *ICD-9-CM* is updated on a regular basis, the classification is limited in its ability to expand enumeration because of the physical numbering constraints contained in the current system. Some categories have vague and imprecise codes. This lack of specificity creates such problems as the inability to collect accurate data on new technology, increased requirements for submission of documentation to support claims, lack of quality data to support health outcomes, and less accurate reimbursement.

Over the years, many of the *ICD-9-CM* categories have become full, making it difficult to create new codes. Once a category is full, several types of similar diagnoses or procedures are combined under one code, or a place is found in another section of the classification for a new code. Because of a lack of space in the classification, several distinct procedures performed in different parts of the body, and with widely different resource utilization, may be grouped together under the same procedure code. The structural integrity of the *ICD-9-CM* procedure classification has already been compromised with new code numbers having been assigned to "chapter 00" and "chapter 17" when new numbers were not available within the appropriate body system chapter. More important, many other countries have already converted to *ICD-10,* making it difficult to compare the United States' health data with international data. Thus far, 138 countries have implemented *ICD-10* for mortality, and 99 countries have implemented it for morbidity reporting. *ICD-10* is available in 42 languages.

THE RAND COST-BENEFIT STUDY

A cost-benefit study commissioned by the National Committee on Vital and Health Statistics (NCVHS) from the RAND Corporation in 2003 identified the following expected benefits from the implementation of *ICD-10-CM* and *ICD-10-PCS:*

- Improvements to the quality of care and patient safety
- Fewer rejected or questionable reimbursement claims

- Improved information for disease management
- More accurate reimbursement rates for emerging technologies, and
- Better understanding of the value of new procedures

INTERNATIONAL DEVELOPMENT OF *ICD-10*

ICD-10 was released by the World Health Organization (WHO) in 1993. The WHO authorized development of an adaptation of the *ICD-10* for use in the United States. All modifications to the *ICD-10* need to conform to the WHO conventions for the *ICD*. *ICD-10* contains only diagnosis codes. Each country needs to develop its own procedure coding system.

UNITED STATES' DEVELOPMENT OF *ICD-10*

In the United States, a clinical modification of the WHO diagnosis coding system has been developed *(ICD-10-CM),* and a new, unique procedure classification system was created: *ICD-10-PCS*.

ICD-10-CM was developed under the leadership of the National Center for Health Statistics, a federal agency under the Centers for Disease Control. *ICD-10-CM* is intended as a replacement for volumes 1 and 2 of the *ICD-9-CM* (diagnosis codes).

ICD-10-PCS was developed by 3M Health Information Systems under contract to the Centers for Medicare & Medicaid Services (CMS). The *ICD-10-PCS* was designed to replace volume 3 of the *ICD-9-CM* for reporting hospital inpatient procedures.

COMPLIANCE DATE

The Department of Health and Human Services (HHS) is adopting *ICD-10-CM* and *ICD-10-PCS* as medical data code sets under HIPAA, replacing the *ICD-9-CM* volumes 1 and 2 code sets for reporting diagnoses and the volume 3 code set for reporting procedures—including the official coding guidelines—when conducting standard transactions. Because *ICD-10-PCS* codes are used only by hospitals for inpatient procedures, the *ICD-10-PCS* codes would not be used in outpatient transactions or by physicians.

Full compliance is expected for claims received for encounters and discharges occurring on or after October 1, 2013 (FY 2014). HHS believed it was in the best interests of the health care field to have a single compliance date for *ICD-10-CM* and *ICD-10-PCS* to ensure the accuracy and timeliness of claims and transaction processing. The compliance date is based on the date of discharge for inpatient claims and the date of service for outpatient claims. The date is consistent with the long-standing practice of inpatient facilities using the version of *ICD* codes in effect at the date of discharge. *ICD-10-CM/PCS* codes may not be reported before the compliance date.

A large number of provider and health plan databases and applications will be affected—every application in which diagnosis or procedure codes are captured, stored, analyzed, or reported. A successful transition to *ICD-10-CM* and *ICD-10-PCS* will require careful planning and coordination of resources. Health information coding professionals will need to become proficient in the new system. This change is welcome and long overdue because *ICD-9-CM* is no longer able to meet the pressing requirements for increased granularity and specificity in a hospital coding system.

CODE SET FREEZE

A partial code set freeze to the updating of both *ICD-9-CM* and *ICD-10-CM/PCS* codes has been put into place as follows:

- October 1, 2011: Last regular annual update to both *ICD-9-CM* and *ICD-10-CM/PCS*.
- October 1, 2012: Limited code updates to both *ICD-9-CM* and *ICD-10-CM/PCS* codes to capture new technology and new diseases.
- October 1, 2013: No updates to *ICD-9-CM*. Limited code updates to *ICD-10-CM/PCS* to capture new technology and new diseases.
- October 1, 2014: Regular updates to *ICD-10-CM/PCS* will begin.

ICD-10-CM

CHAPTER **31**

Nelly Leon-Chisen, RHIA

CHAPTER OVERVIEW

- *ICD-10-CM* consists of 21 chapters.
- E codes and V codes are incorporated into *ICD-10-CM;* in *ICD-9-CM* they are treated as supplementary classifications.
- Improvements include the ability to report laterality, the addition of a sixth and up to a seventh character, and the addition of dummy placeholders.
- *ICD-10-CM* was field tested in 2003.
    - — More than 6,000 medical records from a variety of settings were coded using both the old and new classifications.
    - — The time required to code records in *ICD-10-CM* was not greater.
    - — Those who participated favored migration to *ICD-10-CM.*
- The *ICD-10-CM* code structure is alphanumeric.
- The classification is divided into the Alphabetic Index and the Tabular List.
- The use of a dummy place holder ("x" as the fifth character) allows for further expansion without a disruption of the six-character structure. The "x" is also used in seven-character codes.
- Inclusion notes are similar to their counterparts in *ICD-9-CM,* but exclusion notes have been separated into "excludes1" and "excludes2."
- Other conventions, such as cross-reference notes, abbreviations, and punctuation, remain the same.
- Mapping between the *ICD-9* and *ICD-10* coding systems has been developed to facilitate the transition.

LEARNING OUTCOMES

After studying this chapter you should be able to:

- Describe the major differences between *ICD-9-CM* and *ICD-10-CM.*
- Explain the *ICD-10-CM* field testing process and results.
- Describe the code structure, format, and conventions of *ICD-10-CM.*

TERMS TO KNOW

Excludes1
a note specific to *ICD-10-CM* that means "not coded here"

Excludes2
a note specific to *ICD-10-CM* that means "not included here"

GEMs
General Equivalence Mappings; files in the public domain that provide information on linkages between the diagnosis codes in *ICD-9-CM* and the new *ICD-10-CM* code set and between procedure codes in *ICD-9-CM* volume 3 and *ICD-10-PCS*

Laterality
the ability to report the location of a medical condition as right versus left

REMEMBER . . . The dummy placeholder in *ICD-10-CM* is the character "x."

INTRODUCTION

The *International Classification of Diseases, Tenth Revision, Clinical Modification (ICD-10-CM)*, is the United States' modification to the World Health Organization's diagnosis coding system. In this chapter we discuss its development and field testing, as well as the structure, format, and conventions of *ICD-10-CM*.

DEVELOPMENT OF *ICD-10-CM*

In 1994 the National Center for Health Statistics (NCHS) determined that a clinical modification of the *ICD-10* would be a significant improvement worth implementing in the United States. A clinical modification was needed to include emerging diseases and more recent medical knowledge, as well as to include new concepts and expand distinctions for ambulatory and managed care encounters.

The clinical modification for *ICD-10* was developed in three phases, with the first phase being the development of a prototype with the assistance of a technical advisory panel (TAP). The next two phases consisted of enhancements to the prototype based on minutes of the ICD-9-CM Coordination and Maintenance Committee and public comments. Development of the *ICD-10-CM* was done in consultation with physician groups, professional associations (e.g., the American Hospital Association, or AHA), and other users of *ICD-9-CM*. The *ICD-10-CM* is updated on an annual basis to keep up with the changes being made to the *ICD-9-CM*. The *ICD-10-CM* is available for download at http://www.cdc.gov/nchs/icd/icd10cm.htm#10update.

The *ICD-10-CM* is in the public domain. However, neither the codes nor the code titles may be changed except through the coordination and maintenance process overseen jointly by NCHS and the Centers for Medicare & Medicaid Services (CMS).

ICD-10-CM consists of 21 chapters. The classification of external causes of injury and poisoning (E codes) and the classification of factors influencing health status and contact with health services (V codes) are incorporated within *ICD-10-CM* instead of being considered supplementary classifications, as in *ICD-9-CM*.

Major modifications in the *ICD-10-CM* include the following:

- Identification of trimesters to obstetrical codes
- Expanded diabetes, injury, alcohol/substance abuse, and postoperative complication sections
- Ability to report laterality (to specify whether a medical condition occurred on the right or left side)
- Standard definitions for "excludes" notes
- Combination diagnosis/symptoms codes
- Identification of initial encounter, subsequent encounter, and sequelae of injuries
- Expanded external causes of injuries
- Improved clinical detail
- Addition of a sixth character
- Addition of a seventh character extension in some chapters (from a maximum of five character codes in *ICD-9-CM)*

Table 31.1 provides a quick overview of the major differences between *ICD-9-CM* (volumes 1 and 2) and *ICD-10-CM*.

TABLE 31.1 Major Differences between *ICD-9-CM* and *ICD-10-CM*

Feature	*ICD-9-CM*	*ICD-10-CM*
Minimum number of digits/characters	3	3
Maximum number of digits/characters	5	7
Number of chapters	17	21
Supplemental classification	V codes and E codes	No, incorporated into classification
Laterality (right vs. left)	No	Yes
Alphanumeric vs. numeric	Numeric, except for V codes and E codes	Alphanumeric, with all codes starting with an alpha character and some codes with alpha 7th character extension
Excludes notes	Yes	Exclude 1 Exclude 2
Dummy placeholders	No	Yes: "x"

FIELD TESTING

The AHA and the American Health Information Management Association (AHIMA) conducted the world's first field test of *ICD-10-CM* in 2003. The Web-based data collection process, results tabulation, and assistance with data analysis were provided by the Health Information Management & Systems Division, School of Allied Medical Professions, and by the Medical Media Design Department, College of Medicine and Public Health, both at the Ohio State University. The field testing was conducted with the help of hundreds of health information management volunteers across the United States. The primary purpose of the study was to assess the functionality and utility of applying *ICD-10-CM* to actual medical records in a variety of health care settings and the level of education and training required by professional, credentialed coders to implement *ICD-10-CM*.

For detailed information on the study's design and a complete report of the field study, visit the *ICD-10* Resources section at www.ahacentraloffice.org.

Results of Field Testing

Over six thousand completed medical records were coded using both *ICD-9-CM* and *ICD-10-CM*. The records were obtained from a variety of settings, including: short-term acute care hospital inpatient settings, short-term acute care hospital outpatient settings, post acute care settings (home health, hospice, nursing homes, long-term care hospitals, and rehabilitation units or facilities), physician practices, clinics, community health centers, freestanding ambulatory surgery centers, and freestanding diagnostic facilities. More than 23,000 *ICD-10-CM* codes were assigned, and all chapters were represented in the test.

There was no time difference between assigning *ICD-9-CM* and *ICD-10-CM* codes for 3,616 records, or more than half of the sample. Taking longer to code with *ICD-10-CM* was expected because participants were basically unfamiliar with the coding system, had received minimal training, and lacked user-friendly coding tools. None of the participants had the opportunity to gain significant *ICD-10-CM* coding proficiency. On the other hand, the vast majority of them were highly proficient in *ICD-9-CM*.

Considering the barriers to coding productivity, it is particularly surprising that the time required to code records in *ICD-10-CM* was not greater. The availability of much-improved coding tools, more training, and increased familiarity with *ICD-10-CM* will significantly reduce the amount of time needed to code records in *ICD-10-CM*, possibly to the point whereby *ICD-10-CM* may actually require less coding time than *ICD-9-CM*.

The clinical descriptions of the *ICD-10-CM* codes were thought to be better than *ICD-9-CM*. Respondents thought the notes, instructions, and guidelines in *ICD-10-CM* were clear and comprehensive.

The testing participants favored migration to *ICD-10-CM* and thought the system should be implemented in three years or less. *ICD-10-CM* was seen to be an improvement over *ICD-9-CM*. Participants in some nonhospital settings indicated that they believed *ICD-10-CM* was much more applicable to those settings than was *ICD-9-CM*. *ICD-10-CM* codes can be applied to today's medical records in a variety of health care settings without having to change documentation practices, although improved documentation would result in higher coding specificity and therefore higher data quality in some cases.

Participants felt that a maximum of 16 hours of training would be necessary to adequately prepare coding professionals for *ICD-10-CM* coding. Participants suggested training should be provided relatively close to the implementation date (three to six months before the date).

Study Conclusion

The study concluded that the results of this field-testing project along with independent data analysis support *ICD-10-CM* as an appropriate replacement for the *ICD-9-CM* diagnosis coding system. *ICD-10-CM* represents an improvement over *ICD-9-CM* in that it reflects advances in medical care and knowledge that have occurred since the implementation of *ICD-9-CM* in 1979. *ICD-10-CM* is sufficiently flexible to accommodate medical advances, and it ensures that the systems will remain useful well into the future. Significantly, *ICD-10-CM* meets criteria established under the Health Insurance Portability and Accountability Act (HIPAA) for code set standards as well as National Committee on Vital and Health Statistics criteria for a diagnosis coding system.

Exercise 31.1

Without referring to the handbook material, answer the following questions either true or false.

__F__ 1. The *ICD-10-CM* field testing estimated 40 hours of training would be required for experienced coders.

__T__ 2. Testing included a variety of records, including hospitals, clinics, physician offices, and post acute care settings.

__F__ 3. *ICD-10-CM* codes have a maximum of five characters.

__T__ 4. A major modification to *ICD-10-CM* includes the ability to identify trimesters with obstetrical codes.

__T__ 5. The *ICD-10-CM* has improved clinical detail.

ICD-10-CM STRUCTURE, FORMAT, AND CONVENTIONS

ICD-10-CM has many similarities to *ICD-9-CM*, especially with regard to the classification format and conventions. The code structure has changed slightly to accommodate code expansion and improvements to the classification.

Code Structure

All *ICD-10-CM* codes have an alphanumeric structure, with all codes starting with an alphabetic character. The basic code structure consists of three characters. A decimal point is used to separate the basic three-character category code from its subcategory and subclassifications. The first character in *ICD-10-CM* codes is alpha; characters 2 and 3 are numeric, and characters 4–7 are alpha or numeric. Alpha characters are not case sensitive. Most *ICD-10-CM* codes contain a maximum of six characters, with a few chapters having a seventh character code extension.

Format

The *ICD-10-CM* is divided into the Index and the Tabular List. The Index is an alphabetical list of terms and their corresponding code. The Tabular List is a chronological list of codes divided into chapters based on body system or condition.

Alphabetic Index

The Alphabetic Index is divided into the Index to Diseases and Injuries and the Index of External Causes of Injury. Similar to *ICD-9-CM,* there is also a Neoplasm Table and a Table of Drugs and Chemicals. However, there is no "Hypertension" Table in *ICD-10-CM*.

The Alphabetic Index includes entries for main terms, subterms, and more specific subterms. An indented format is used for ease of reference. It is expected that a variety of vendors will develop user-friendly printed versions, as well as computer encoding programs, as they currently exist for *ICD-9-CM*. At press time, there is one printed version available with the formatting familiar to *ICD-9-CM* users.

The draft version of the Index represents each indention level by a hyphen. In general, however, the same indention pattern, as well as the same alphabetization rules in the *ICD-9-CM* Alphabetic Index (and covered in chapter 1 of this handbook), is anticipated. A new feature in the *ICD-10-CM* Index not found in the *ICD-9-CM* is the use of a dash (-) at the end of an Index entry to indicate that additional characters are required.

Tabular List

The Tabular List contains categories, subcategories, and codes. The basic code used to classify a particular disease or injury consists of three characters and is called a category. The first character of a category is a letter; the second and third characters are numbers (for example, K29, Gastritis and duodenitis). If a three-character category has no further subdivision, it is considered a code. Subcategories may be made up of four or five characters. These subcategory characters may be letters or numbers. Codes are three, four, five, six, or seven characters long, depending on whether they are further subdivided. Each level of subdivision after a category is a subcategory. The final level of subdivision is a code. The final character in a code may be either a letter or a number. For example:

- K29 Gastritis and duodenitis *(category)*
  - K29.0 Acute gastritis *(subcategory)*
    - K29.00 Acute gastritis without bleeding *(code)*
- R10 Abdominal and pelvic pain *(category)*
  - R10.8 Other abdominal pain *(subcategory)*
    - R10.81 Abdominal tenderness *(subcategory)*
      - R10.811 Right upper quadrant abdominal tenderness *(code)*

The *ICD-10-CM* uses the placeholder character "x" at certain codes to allow for future expansion. An example of this may be seen with the poisoning, adverse effect, and underdosing codes (T36–T50) and the toxic effects codes (T51–T65). For these categories, the sixth character represents the intent: accidental, intentional self-harm, assault, undetermined, adverse effect, or underdosing. For example:

T37.5x1 Poisoning by antiviral drugs, accidental (unintentional)
T37.5x2 Poisoning by antiviral drugs, intentional self-harm
T52.0x1 Toxic effect of petroleum products, accidental (unintentional)
T52.0x2 Toxic effect of petroleum products, intentional self-harm

Certain categories have an additional seventh character extension. The extension must always be the seventh character in the code. If a code is not a full six characters long, a dummy placeholder "x" must be used to fill in the empty characters when a seventh character extension is required. Seventh character extensions can be seen in chapter 19, Injury, poisoning and certain other consequences of external causes (S00–T98).

An example of the use of the dummy place holder "x" and the seventh character extension is shown here with an excerpt from the Tabular List:

T16 Foreign body in ear
Includes: foreign body in auditory canal
The following 7th character is to be added to each code from category T16
A initial encounter
D subsequent encounter
S sequela

T16.1 Foreign body in right ear
T16.2 Foreign body in left ear
T16.3 Foreign body in ear, unspecified ear

A child presents to the emergency department with a bean in the right ear. The mother has brought the child because she was not able to remove the bean at home. This encounter would be assigned code T16.1xxA. The Tabular List showed subcategory T16.1 as the descriptor best fitting this scenario. Category T16 requires a seventh character extension. Because the code subcategory has only four characters (T16.1), the dummy placeholder "x" is inserted twice to preserve the code structure before the seventh character "A" is added to report this as the initial encounter.

Exercise 31.2

Using the excerpt from the Tabular List above, select an *ICD-10-CM* code for the following scenarios:

	Code(s)
1. A child goes to the physician's office as a referral from the emergency department after having had a bean removed from the right ear.	T16.1xxD
2. A child is seen by an audiologist for an evaluation for hearing loss after having had a pen tip removed from the left ear.	T16.2xxS

Conventions

ICD-10-CM has retained several conventions already familiar to users of *ICD-9-CM,* such as instructional notes, abbreviations, cross-reference notes, punctuation marks, and relational terms ("and"). Where conventions are similar to *ICD-9-CM,* they are not further explained in this chapter.

INSTRUCTIONAL NOTES

Several different instructional notes appear in the Tabular List and the Index. These include: "inclusion" and "exclusion" notes, "code first" notes, "use additional code" notes, and "code also" notes.

Inclusion Notes

Inclusion notes are similar to their counterparts in *ICD-9-CM* in terms of the location of the notes as well as their application. The notes may include conditions for which the code number may be used. It is important to remember that the list of inclusion terms is not meant to be exhaustive.

Exclusion Notes

One of the more significant changes for *ICD-10-CM* is the clarification of the exclusion notes. There are two types of "excludes" notes—each one with a different use; but both indicate that codes excluded are independent of each other.

"Excludes1"

An "excludes1" note means "not coded here." An "excludes1" note instructs the user that the code excluded should never be used at the same time as the code above the "excludes1" note. This instruction is used when two conditions cannot occur together, and therefore both codes cannot be used together. For example:

Q03 Congenital hydrocephalus
Excludes1: acquired hydrocephalus (G91.-)

In this example the congenital form of the condition cannot be reported with the acquired form of the same condition.

"Excludes2"

An "excludes2" note means "not included here." An "excludes2" note instructs the user that the condition excluded is not part of the condition represented by the code. However, a patient may have both conditions at the same time. When an "excludes2" note appears under a code, it is acceptable to use both the code and the excluded code together. For example:

F90 Attention-deficit hyperactivity disorders
Excludes2: anxiety disorders (F40.-, F41.-)
mood [affective] disorders (F30–F39)

In this example, the "excludes2" note serves as a warning that if a patient has an anxiety disorder rather than an attention-deficit hyperactivity disorder, the user should go to categories F40–F41 rather than remain in category F90. However, if the patient has both attention-deficit hyperactivity and an anxiety disorder, a code from category F90 could be used along with a code from categories F40–F41.

"Code First" and "Use Additional Code"

"Code first" and "use additional code" notes are similar to their counterparts in *ICD-9-CM*. Certain conditions have both an underlying etiology and multiple body system manifestations. *ICD-10-CM* "code first" and "use additional code" instructional notes indicate the proper sequencing order of these conditions: etiology (underlying condition), followed by manifestation. The "use additional code" note is found at the etiology code as a clue to identify the manifestations commonly associated with the disease. The "code first" note is found at the manifestation code to provide instructions that the underlying condition should be sequenced first.

The manifestation codes usually have the phrase "in diseases classified elsewhere" as part of the code title. Codes with this phrase are never used as a first-listed or principal diagnosis code. They must be used with the underlying condition code sequenced first. An example of this convention is category F02, Dementia in other diseases classified elsewhere.

"Code Also"

"Code also" notes in *ICD-10-CM* are similar to the "use additional code" instruction found in *ICD-9-CM*. This note indicates that two codes may be required to describe a condition fully. The sequencing order will depend on the reason for the encounter and the severity of the conditions. An example of this note can be found under code **G47.01, Insomnia due to medical condition,** where the instructional note tells us to code also the associated medical condition.

ABBREVIATIONS

The following abbreviations familiar to *ICD-9-CM* users are found in *ICD-10-CM:*

- NEC—Not elsewhere classified. This represents "other specified" in the *ICD-10-CM.*
- NOS—Not otherwise specified. This represents "unspecified" in the *ICD-10-CM.*

CROSS-REFERENCE NOTES

Cross-reference notes are used in the Alphabetic Index to advise the coder to look elsewhere before assigning a code. These notes are similar to their counterparts in *ICD-9-CM.* The cross-reference instructions include:

- "See"
- "See also"
- "See condition"

PUNCTUATION MARKS

The following punctuation marks are used, and their use is similar to *ICD-9-CM:*

- Parentheses
- Square brackets
- Colons

THE RELATIONAL TERM *AND*

The use of the term "and" is similar to *ICD-9-CM*, and it means "and" or "or."

GUIDELINES

Draft guidelines have been developed and were used for the AHA-AHIMA field-testing project. The guidelines were developed by NCHS and reviewed by the remaining *ICD-9-CM* cooperating parties (AHA, AHIMA, and CMS). A revised set of guidelines was released by the *ICD-9-CM* cooperating parties in 2011. These guidelines follow as closely as possible the *ICD-9-CM* guidelines, except for any differences related to changes inherent to the *ICD-10-CM* classification (e.g., different codes, tabular instructions, etc.). The guidelines are arranged similarly to the *ICD-9-CM* Official Guidelines. Section 1 includes *ICD-10-CM* conventions. Section 2 covers general guidelines, and section 3 is devoted to chapter-specific guidelines. The chapter-specific guidelines are sequenced in the same order in which they appear in the Tabular List.

The complete 2011 version of the guidelines may be found by visiting the Web site http://www.cdc.gov/nchs/icd/icd10cm.htm#10update. Adherence to the guidelines when assigning *ICD-10-CM* diagnosis codes is required under the Health Insurance Portability and Accountability Act (HIPAA). The instructions and conventions of the classification take precedence over guidelines.

ICD-9-CM AND *ICD-10-CM* MAPPING

Mapping between the *ICD-9-CM* and *ICD-10-CM* coding systems has been developed to facilitate the transition. NCHS has released public domain reference mappings files called General Equivalence Mappings (GEMs) to facilitate linking between the diagnosis codes in *ICD-9-CM* and the new *ICD-10-CM* code set. The GEMs are formatted as downloadable "flat" text files. Each file contains a list of code pairs. The GEMs and a documentation and user's guide are available online at http://www.cdc.gov/nchs/icd/icd10cm.htm#10update.

The documentation and user's guide provides information regarding the structure and relationships contained in the mappings to facilitate correct usage. The intended audience includes all sectors of the healthcare industry that use coded data, including professionals working in health information, medical research, and informatics. The guide is divided into two sections. Section 1 is a general interest discussion of mapping as it pertains to the GEMs and includes a summary of the specific conventions and terms used in the files. There is also a discussion of the difficulties inherent in translating between the two coding systems. Section 2 will be of interest to coding experts, researchers, claims processing personnel, software developers, and others directly involved in mapping applications. This section gives detailed information on using the GEMs files, and a glossary provides a reference list of the terms and conventions used in the mapping and their definitions. Appendix A contains tables describing the technical details of the file formats.

The GEMs are a comprehensive translation dictionary that can be used to accurately and effectively translate any *ICD-9-CM*–based data, including data for:

- Tracking quality
- Recording morbidity/mortality
- Calculating reimbursement
- Converting any *ICD-9-CM*–based application to *ICD-10-CM/PCS*

The GEMs can be useful for projects in which it may be necessary to convert large data sets from *ICD-9-CM* to *ICD-10-CM* or from *ICD-10-CM* to *ICD-9-CM*. However, the GEMs are not a substitute for learning how to use *ICD-10-CM* or for selecting *ICD-10-CM* codes.

Review Exercise 31.3

Code the following diagnoses using *ICD-10-CM*.

	Code(s)
1. Influenza with gastroenteritis	J11.2
2. Acute cholecystitis with cholelithiasis and choledocholithiasis	K80.62
3. Meningitis due to *Salmonella* infection	A02.21
4. Otomycosis, right ear	B36.9 H62.41
5. Cataract associated with galactosemia	E74.21 H28
6. Alcoholic gastritis due to chronic alcoholism	K29.20 F10.20
7. Diverticulitis of colon with intestinal hemorrhage	K57.33
8. Acute and chronic appendicitis	K35.80 K36
9. Subacute and chronic pyelonephritis	N10 N11.9
10. Acute and chronic cervicitis	N72

ICD-10-PCS

Nelly Leon-Chisen, RHIA

CHAPTER **32**

CHAPTER OVERVIEW

- *ICD-10-PCS* is a replacement for volume 3 of *ICD-9-CM,* but as an entirely new classification system bears little resemblance to it.
- Improvements include unique codes for each procedure and the ability to expand the classification to add new technology items in the future.
- All codes have an alphanumeric structure, no decimal points, and seven characters.
- *ICD-10-PCS* is divided into 16 sections relating to the general type of procedure.
- Codes in the Medical and Surgical Section specify the section, body system, root operation, body part, approach, device, and qualifier.
- *ICD-10-PCS* is divided into Index, Tables, and List of Codes.
- Guidelines and mapping files have been developed to facilitate the transition to *ICD-10-PCS.*

LEARNING OUTCOMES

After studying this chapter you should be able to:

- Discuss the main objectives in the development of *ICD-10-PCS.*
- Explain its major modifications.
- Explain its structure, format, and conventions.
- Discuss the differences between *ICD-10-PCS* and *ICD-9-CM,* volume 3.

TERMS TO KNOW

Approach
the fifth character in the code in the Medical and Surgical Section; the way the procedure site is reached (for example: open or percutaneous)

Qualifier
the seventh character in the code in the Medical and Surgical Section; it carries additional information for that particular procedure

Root operation
the third character in the code in the Medical and Surgical Section corresponding to the objective of the procedure; in this section alone there are 31 possible objectives

REMEMBER . . . In the alphanumeric structure of *ICD-10-PCS*, don't confuse the letters "O" and "I" with the numbers "0" and "1."

INTRODUCTION

The *International Classification of Diseases, Tenth Revision, Procedure Classification System* (*ICD-10-PCS*) is the procedure classification system developed as a replacement for volume 3 of the *ICD-9-CM*. In this chapter we discuss its development and field testing as well as the structure, format, and conventions of *ICD-10-PCS*.

DEVELOPMENT OF *ICD-10-PCS*

In 1992 the U.S. Health Care Financing Administration (HCFA, now the Centers for Medicare & Medicaid Services, or CMS) funded a preliminary design project for a replacement for volume 3 of the *ICD-9-CM*. In 1995 HCFA awarded a three-year contract to 3M Health Information Systems (HIS) to complete the development of a procedure coding replacement system. The new system was called *ICD-10 Procedure Coding System (ICD-10-PCS)*. The first year of the 3M contract involved the completion of the first draft of the system. The second year was devoted to external review and limited informal testing; and the third year consisted of formal independent review and testing. *ICD-10-PCS* was completed in 1998 and has been updated annually by 3M HIS since then. The goal of the revisions is to keep current with medical technology and coding needs.

A Technical Advisory Panel (TAP) was convened to provide extensive input into the development process. The TAP included representatives from the American Health Information Management Association (AHIMA), the American Hospital Association (AHA), and the American Medical Association. Many other medical specialty organizations also contributed to the development of *ICD-10-PCS*.

The four main objectives in the development of *ICD-10-PCS* were these:

- *Completeness:* All substantially different procedures should have a unique code.
- *Expandability:* The structure of *ICD-10-PCS* should allow for the easy incorporation of unique codes as new procedures are developed.
- *Multiaxial:* The structure of *ICD-10-PCS* should be multiaxial, with each code character having the same meaning within a specific procedure section and across procedure sections, whenever possible.
- *Standardized methodology: ICD-10-PCS* should include unique definitions for the terms used, with each term having a specific meaning.

The guiding principles that were followed in the development of *ICD-10-PCS* are these:

- Diagnostic information is not included in the procedure description.
- Explicit "not otherwise specified" (NOS) options are not provided.
- "Not elsewhere classified" (NEC) options are provided on a limited basis.
- All possible procedures are defined regardless of the frequency of occurrence. If a procedure could be performed, a code was created.

The initial drafts of *ICD-10-PCS* were widely distributed to all major physician specialty societies as well as being made available to the general public. Feedback from the extensive review was used to modify *ICD-10-PCS*. The lack of NOS codes was one of the most frequent concerns raised by the reviewers. It was felt that the medical record documentation might lack sufficient specificity to support the detail required by *ICD-10-PCS*. Modifications were made to the classification to address this concern.

There are 16 sections in *ICD-10-PCS* representing nearly 72,000 codes. *ICD-10-PCS* uses a table structure that permits the specification of a large number of codes on a single page in the Tabular division. The combined Tables and Index divisions of *ICD-10-PCS* represent nearly half the size of the Tabular List and Index in the World Health Organization's *ICD-10* diagnosis coding manual.

Major modifications in the *ICD-10-PCS* include the following:

- All codes have a unique definition.
- *ICD-10-PCS* affords users the ability to aggregate codes across all essential components of a procedure.
- *ICD-10-PCS* provides users with extensive flexibility.
- New procedures and technologies are easily incorporated.
- Code expansions do not disrupt systematic structure.
- *ICD-10-PCS* makes limited use of the NOS and NEC categories.
- All terminology is precisely defined and used consistently across all codes.
- No diagnostic information is included in the code.

Table 32.1 provides a quick overview of the major differences between *ICD-9-CM* (volume 3) and *ICD-10-PCS.*

As part of the continuous updating of the *ICD-10-PCS,* revisions are made yearly to streamline the classification and keep current with new technology changes being made in the *ICD-9-CM* procedure coding. The 2012 version is available on the CMS Web site at www.cms.hhs.gov/ICD10.

FIELD TESTING

There have been two field-testing projects—a formal one and an informal one. An informal test was conducted in October 1996 with the assistance of the AHA and the AHIMA. Health information professionals volunteered for training and then coded a sample of records from their institutions using *ICD-10-PCS.* Problems, questions, and suggestions were addressed to the *ICD-10-PCS* project staff at 3M Health Information Systems.

The formal testing of *ICD-10-PCS* was conducted in 1997–98 by HCFA (now CMS) using contractors. The contractors were two Clinical Data Abstraction Centers (CDACs): DynKePRO in York, Pennsylvania, and FMAS in Columbia, Maryland. The CDACs coded a sample of 5,000 medical records using *ICD-10-PCS.* Any questions or concerns noted by the CDAC coders were forwarded to the 3M project staff. This interaction resulted in revisions to the final draft of *ICD-10-PCS.* The second phase of the test included a subset of 100 medical records recoded blindly with both *ICD-9-CM* and *ICD-10-PCS.* The systems were compared on ease of use, time needed to identify codes, number of codes required, problems identifying codes, and strengths and weaknesses of each system.

TABLE 32.1 Major Differences between *ICD-9-CM* and *ICD-10-PCS*

Feature	*ICD-9-CM*	*ICD-10-PCS*
Minimum number of digits/characters	3	7
Maximum number of digits/characters	4	7
Decimal point	Yes	No
Alphanumeric or numeric	Numeric	Alphanumeric
Includes notes	Yes	No
Excludes notes	Yes	No
Embedded meaning of characters	No	Yes, multiaxial structure, with each code character having the same meaning within the specific procedure section and across procedure sections to the extent possible

For detailed information on the development of *ICD-10-PCS* and a complete report of the testing study, visit the CMS Web site at www.cms.hhs.gov/ICD10 and click on the *ICD-10-PCS* link.

Results of Field Testing

The CDAC coders were able to use *ICD-10-PCS* easily. They found that a medical dictionary or an anatomy textbook was occasionally needed because of the added detail in *ICD-10-PCS*. The CDACs felt that the initial *ICD-10-PCS* training manual would need to be strengthened with additional examples before it could be used on a national level. Both CDACs felt that, once coders were familiar with *ICD-10-PCS*, the result would be improved accuracy and efficiency of coding. The users found the system to be so well organized and well structured that codes could easily be found in the correct section of the Tables without using the Index. It was felt that *ICD-10-PCS* was an improvement over *ICD-9-CM* because of its greater specificity. The major strength identified was the system's detailed structure. This level of detail would allow users to more precisely recognize and report the procedures performed.

ICD-10-PCS STRUCTURE, FORMAT, AND CONVENTIONS

ICD-10-PCS is an entirely new classification system bearing little resemblance to *ICD-9-CM* volume 3 classification format or conventions.

Code Structure

All *ICD-10-PCS* codes have an alphanumeric structure, with all codes made up of seven characters and no decimal points. It is important to distinguish between "character" and "value" before we go any further. Each character in a code is an axis of classification that represents an aspect of the procedure. A value is one of the 34 letters or numbers that can be selected to represent one of the characters in an *ICD-10-PCS* code. These values are made up of digits 0–9, or the letters A–H, J–N, and P–Z. The letters "O" and "I" are not used so as not to be confused with the digits "0" and "1."

The classification is divided into 16 sections relating to the general type of procedure. The first character of each *ICD-10-PCS* code specifies the section. Within each section, the second through seventh characters have a standard meaning—but may have different meanings across sections. *ICD-10-PCS* is divided into the sections displayed in table 32.2.

TABLE 32.2 *ICD-10-PCS* Sections and Their Corresponding Character

Character	Section	Character	Section
0	Medical and Surgical	8	Other Procedures
1	Obstetrics	9	Chiropractic
2	Placement	B	Imaging
3	Administration	C	Nuclear Medicine
4	Measurement and Monitoring	D	Radiation Oncology
5	Extracorporeal Assistance and Performance	F	Physical Rehabilitation and Diagnostic Audiology
6	Extracorporeal Therapies	G	Mental Health
7	Osteopathic	H	Substance Abuse Treatment

The majority of the procedures that would normally be reported in an inpatient setting can be found in the Medical and Surgical Section. Therefore, the following discussion regarding the component characters of a code refers strictly to the Medical and Surgical Section. Within this section, the seven characters have the following meaning (see also figure 32.1, "Structure of Codes in the Medical and Surgical Section"):

Section: The first character in the code always refers to the section. The number "0" represents the Medical and Surgical Section.

Body System: The second character indicates the general physiological system or anatomical region involved (e.g., gastrointestinal). For additional detail, some traditional body systems have been assigned multiple categories. For example, the circulatory system has been subdivided into heart and great vessels, upper arteries, lower arteries, upper veins, and lower veins.

Root Operation: The third character refers to the root operation. The root operation specifies the objective of the procedure (e.g., resection). In the Medical and Surgical Section, there are 31 different root operations. Each root operation is precisely defined in the classification. The definitions are easily found in the Tables. Mastering the definitions of these root operations is the key to "building" a code in *ICD-10-PCS*. Root operations include terms such as "alteration," "bypass," "change," "creation," "dilation," "excision," "resection," "fusion," "insertion," "occlusion," and "repair." The complete list of root operations in the Medical and Surgical Section is included in table 32.3.

FIGURE 32.1 Structure of Codes in the Medical and Surgical Section

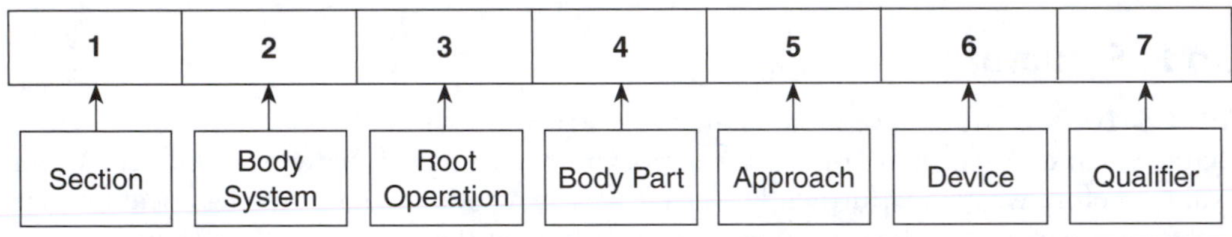

Table 32.3 *ICD-10-PCS* Root Operations and Their Corresponding Character

Character	Root Operation	Character	Root Operation
0	Alteration	J	Inspection
1	Bypass	K	Map
2	Change	L	Occlusion
3	Control	M	Reattachment
4	Creation	N	Release
5	Destruction	P	Removal
6	Detachment	Q	Repair
7	Dilation	R	Replacement
8	Division	S	Reposition
9	Drainage	T	Resection
B	Excision	V	Restriction
C	Extirpation	W	Revision
D	Extraction	U	Supplement
F	Fragmentation	X	Transfer
G	Fusion	Y	Transplantation
H	Insertion		

Some of the root operations listed in table 32.3 may not necessarily coincide with terminology used by physicians in their documentation. However, because many of the terms used to construct *ICD-10-PCS* codes are defined within the system, the physician is not expected to use the terms used in *ICD-10-PCS* code descriptions. Instead, it is the coder's responsibility to determine to what root operation the documentation in the medical record equates in the *ICD-10-PCS* definitions. The coder is not required to query the physician when the correlation between the documentation and the defined *ICD-10-PCS* terms is clear.

Body Part: The fourth character indicates the specific part of the body system or anatomical site where the procedure was performed (for example, appendix). Within *ICD-10-PCS,* body part values may refer to an entire organ (e.g., liver) or to specific portions of an organ (e.g., liver, right lobe). If a procedure is performed on a portion of a body part that does not have a separate body part value, the value corresponding to the whole body part value should be selected. For example, a procedure that is done on the alveolar process of the mandible would get coded to the whole—the mandible body part.

Approach: The fifth character refers to the technique or approach used to reach the procedure site (e.g., open). There are seven approaches in the Medical and Surgical Section:

- Open
- Open endoscopic
- Percutaneous
- Percutaneous endoscopic
- Via natural or artificial opening
- Via natural or artificial opening endoscopic
- External

As with root operations, each approach is precisely defined in the classification. Refer to table 32.4 for the approaches in the Medical and Surgical Section along with their corresponding value and definition.

Device: The sixth character is used only to specify devices that remain after the procedure is completed and does not include materials that are incidental to a procedure such as sutures or clips. When there is no device involved in the procedure, the letter "Z" representing "none" is used as the sixth character to complete the code structure.

Qualifier: The seventh character indicates a qualifier. A qualifier has a unique meaning within individual procedures. This position within the code is used to provide additional information. When there is no qualifier, the seventh character is the letter "Z" to complete the code structure.

The number of values used in an axis of classification differs as needed. This means that within different axes of the classification, there may be unique values. For example, the body part axis will have more values than the approach axis because there are more body parts than surgical approaches.

As with words in their context, the meaning of any single value is a combination of its axis of classification and any preceding values on which it may be dependent. For example: The meaning of a body part value in the Medical and Surgical Section is always dependent on the body system value. For example, the body part value "0" in the Central Nervous body system specifies Brain, and the body part value "0" in the Peripheral Nervous body system specifies Cervical Plexus.

Format

The *ICD-10-PCS* is divided into Index, Tables, and List of Codes. Codes can be located in alphabetical order within the Index. The Index will refer to a specific location within the Tables, but the Index will generally not specify the complete code, except for rare instances. The complete code can be obtained only by referring to the Tables. The List of Codes allows for direct lookup of each code, with a short description of each code being provided.

Table 32.4 Medical and Surgical Section Approaches

Value	Approach	Definition
X	External	Procedures performed directly on the skin or mucous membrane and procedures performed indirectly by the application of external force through the skin or mucous membrane
0	Open	Cutting through the skin or mucous membrane and any other body layers necessary to expose the site of the procedure
3	Percutaneous	Entry, by puncture or minor incision, of instrumentation through the skin or mucous membrane and/or any other body layers necessary to reach the site of the procedure
4	Percutaneous endoscopic	Entry, by puncture or minor incision, of instrumentation through the skin or mucous membrane and/or any other body layers necessary to reach and visualize the site of the procedure
7	Via natural or artificial opening	Entry of instrumentation through a natural or artificial external opening to reach the site of the procedure
8	Via natural or artificial opening endoscopic	Entry of instrumentation through a natural or artificial external opening to reach and visualize the site of the procedure
F	Via natural or artificial opening with percutaneous endoscopic assistance	Entry of instrumentation through a natural or artificial external opening to reach and visualize the site of the procedure, and entry, by puncture or minor incision, of instrumentation through the skin or mucous membrane and any other body layers necessary to aid in the performance of the procedure

Alphabetic Index

The Index is arranged in alphabetical order based on the type of procedure being performed (e.g., resection) or the body site (e.g., accessory cephalic vein) where the procedure is performed. Unlike *ICD-9-CM,* the *ICD-10-PCS* Index does not generally provide a complete code (with a few exceptions), but it will point to the Tables by specifying the first three or four characters of the code. It is not required to consult the Index first before proceeding to the Tables to complete the code.

For example, "appendectomy" may be looked up by "appendectomy," by "resection, appendix," or "excision, appendix." The term "Appendectomy" has two reference notes as follows:

Appendectomy
see Excision, Gastrointestinal System 0DBJ
see Resection, Gastrointestinal System 0DTJ

The first four characters of the code (in this example, "0DBJ" or "0DTJ") can be used to locate the corresponding table to find the remaining three characters to complete the code. The difference between the two entries above is that a partial appendectomy would be the "excision" entry and a total appendectomy would be the "resection."

Tables

The *ICD-10-PCS* Tables, unlike the *ICD-9-CM* Tabular List, is a division composed of grids or tables specifying the valid combinations of characters that make up a procedure code. Figure 32.2 shows a portion of the Tables.

FIGURE 32.2 Excerpt from *ICD-10-PCS* Tables

Section **O** Medical and Surgical *Body System* **D** Gastrointestinal System *Operation* **T** Resection: Cutting out or off, without replacement, all of a body part			
Body Part	*Approach*	*Device*	*Qualifer*
1 Esophagus, Upper **2** Esophagus, Middle **3** Esophagus, Lower **4** Esophagogastric Junction **5** Esophagus **6** Stomach **7** Stomach, Pylorus **8** Small Intestine **9** Duodenum **A** Jejunum **B** Ileum **C** Ileocecal Valve **E** Large Intestine **F** Large Intestine, Right **G** Large Intestine, Left **H** Cecum **J** Appendix **K** Ascending Colon **L** Transverse Colon **M** Descending Colon **N** Sigmoid Colon **P** Rectum **Q** Anus	**0** Open **4** Percutaneous Endoscopic **7** Via Natural or Artificial Opening **8** Via Natural or Artificial Opening Endoscopic	**Z** No Device	**Z** No Qualifier
R Anal Sphincter **S** Greater Omentum **T** Lesser Omentum	**0** Open **4** Percutaneous Endoscopic	**Z** No Device	**Z** No Qualifier

The top portion of each table contains a description of the first three characters of the procedure code. In this particular example "0DT" refers to the Medical and Surgical Section (0) of the gastrointestinal body system (D), and a root operation of resection (T). The root operation (resection) is followed by its definition.

The lower portion of the table has four columns representing the valid combinations of values for the four through seven positions. Basically, the user "builds" a code based on the values across each row on the grid. Columns list the body part, approach, device, and qualifier for the code. Within a table, valid codes include all combinations of choices in characters 4 through 7 contained in the same row of the table.

Using the sample table to build a code for an appendectomy would result in the combination of characters shown in figure 32.3.

In other words, the code for an open appendectomy is 0DTJ0ZZ. Conversely, if this were a laparoscopic instead of open appendectomy, then the code would be 0DTJ4ZZ. The difference between the two procedures is the approach, which is represented by the fifth character. An open approach is reported with the character "0" in the fifth position, whereas a laparoscopic approach is reported with the character "4" (percutaneous endoscopic) in the fifth position.

FIGURE 32.3 Sample Grid for Building a Code for an Appendectomy

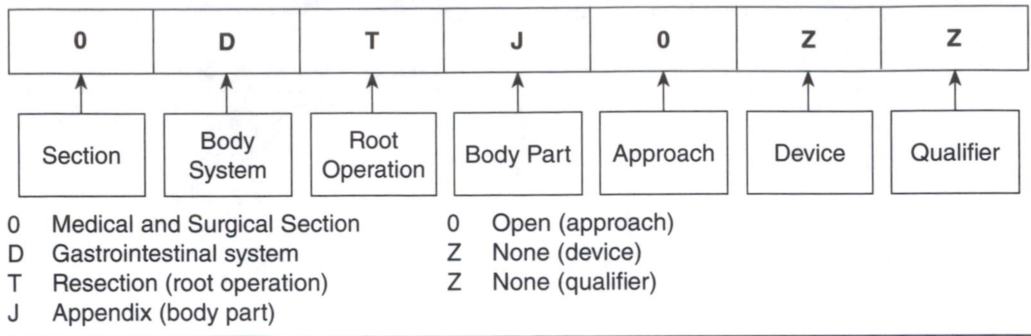

0 Medical and Surgical Section
D Gastrointestinal system
T Resection (root operation)
J Appendix (body part)
0 Open (approach)
Z None (device)
Z None (qualifier)

Exercise 32.1

Identify the *ICD-10-PCS* approach value used for each of the procedures below.

Procedure	Approach Value
1. Appendectomy	0 Open
2. Laparoscopic cholecystectomy	4 Percutaneous endoscopic
3. Adenoidectomy	X External
4. Bronchoscopy	8 Via natural or artificial opening endoscopic
5. Laparoscopic-assisted hysterectomy	0 Open

List of Codes

The *ICD-10-PCS* List of Codes displays all valid codes in alphanumeric order. Each entry begins with the seven-character code, followed by the full text description. A set of rules is used to produce standardized, complete, and easy-to-read code descriptions. At press time the List of Codes was not included in the published *ICD-10-PCS* manual, but it can be found online at the following Web site: http://www.cms.gov/ICD10/.

GUIDELINES

ICD-10-PCS guidelines have been developed by the cooperating parties (AHA, AHIMA, CMS, and the National Center for Health Statistics) in collaboration with the 3M Health Information Systems *ICD-10-PCS* project staff. The most recent version can be found on the CMS Web site at www.cms.hhs.gov/ICD10. Click on the 2012 *ICD-10-PCS* and GEMS link in the left-hand column and select the PDF link titled "2012 Official ICD-10-PCS Coding Guidelines."

The guidelines are divided into three categories: Conventions, Medical and Surgical Section, and Other Medical- and Surgical-related Sections. Guidelines within the Medical and Surgical Section are further grouped by body system, root operation, body part, approach, and device guidelines. The guidelines are numbered sequentially within each category for ease of reference.

ICD-9-CM AND *ICD-10-PCS* MAPPING

To facilitate the transition from *ICD-9-CM* to *ICD-10-PCS*, mapping between the two coding systems has been developed. CMS has released updated public domain reference mappings of *ICD-10-PCS* and *ICD-9-CM* volume 3. The General Equivalence Mappings (GEMs) are used to facilitate linking between the procedure codes in *ICD-9-CM* volume 3 and the new *ICD-10-PCS* code set. The GEMs are formatted as downloadable "flat" text files, each of which contains a list of code pairs.

In addition, a documentation and user's guide has been made available online at http://www.cms.gov/ICD10/11b15_2012_ICD10PCS.asp#TopOfPage.

The documentation and user's guide provides information on the structure and relationships contained in the mappings to facilitate correct usage. The intended audience includes, but is not limited to, professionals working in health information, medical research, and informatics. The guide is divided into two sections. General interest readers may find section 1 useful. Those who may benefit from the material in both sections 1 and 2 include clinical and health information professionals who plan to directly use the mappings in their work. A glossary provides a reference list of the terms and conventions used in the mapping along with their definitions. Software engineers and IT professionals interested in the technical details of the file format will find this information in appendix A of the user's guide.

Exercise 32.2

Using the excerpt of the table shown in figure 32.2, select the appropriate *ICD-10-PCS* code for the following procedures.

	Code(s)
1. Open resection of the upper esophagus	0DT10ZZ
2. Laparoscopic resection of descending colon	0DTM4ZZ
3. Open sigmoidectomy	0DTN0ZZ

Review Exercise 32.3

Assign *ICD-10-PCS* codes for the following procedures.

	Code(s)
1. Laparoscopic excision of right ovarian cyst	0UB04ZZ
2. Diagnostic dilatation and curettage	0UDB7ZX
3. Below knee amputation, right leg	0Y6H0Z3
4. Laparoscopic right oophorectomy	0UT04ZZ
5. Rectal polyp fulguration	0D5P8ZZ

Preparing for *ICD-10-CM* and *ICD-10-PCS*

CHAPTER **33**

Nelly Leon-Chisen, RHIA

CHAPTER OVERVIEW

- Individuals and provider organizations should start preparing for the *ICD-10* implementation now.
- It is necessary for coding professionals to review anatomy and physiology because they will play a larger role in the coding process within the new classification systems.
- There are a variety of tools available from the government and the other cooperating parties that can assist in preparing for the new classifications.

LEARNING OUTCOMES

After studying this chapter you should be able to:

- Take action to begin your own preparation for *ICD-10-CM* and *ICD-10-PCS.*
- Locate information about the new classification systems online.

TERMS TO KNOW

HIM professionals
health information management professionals; individuals working in medical coding and other related health care fields

Cooperating parties
the American Hospital Association (AHA), American Health Information Management Association (AHIMA), Centers for Medicare & Medicaid Services (CMS), and the National Center for Health Statistics (NCHS); work to ensure and disseminate reliable and consistent information to users of *ICD-9-CM* and *ICD-10-CM/PCS*

REMEMBER . . . It is not too early to begin preparation for the new classification systems.

INTRODUCTION

Although the compliance date for national implementation of *ICD-10-CM* and *ICD-10-PCS* is not until October 1, 2013, individuals and provider organizations must start preparing now. Health information management (HIM) professionals are expected to take a leadership role in their respective organizations in the transition process. In this chapter we list preparations individuals can begin to make. The next chapter discusses implementation issues to be considered by provider organizations.

CHECKLIST

Preparations for HIM/coding staff:

- Use assessment tools to identify areas of strength/weakness in the biomedical sciences (e.g., anatomy and pathophysiology).
- Brush up on or expand your knowledge of anatomy and physiology based on the assessment results. *ICD-10-CM* and *ICD-10-PCS* have the ability to provide greater specificity, and you need to be ready to select the more specific code.
- Keep current on the status of *ICD-10* issues by reading articles, attending conferences, or visiting the *ICD-10* Web sites of the cooperating parties:

  American Hospital Association (AHA)
  http://www.ahacentraloffice.com/ahacentraloffice_app/ICD-10/ICD-10.jsp

  American Health Information Management Association (AHIMA)
  http://www.ahima.org/ICD10/default.aspx

  National Center for Health Statistics (NCHS)
  http://www.cdc.gov/nchs/icd/icd10cm.htm

  Centers for Medicare & Medicaid Services (CMS)
  http://www.cms.gov/ICD10
- Sign up for the free CMS service to receive e-mail notifications when the information on its *ICD-10* page changes or is updated by visiting this link: https://subscriptions.cms.hhs.gov/service/subscribe.html?code=USCMS_608.
- The *ICD-10* chapters in this handbook are a good place to start familiarizing yourself with the coding structure, terms, and concepts related to the new classifications. There are also introductory programs, including audioseminars, from the AHA.
- Learn the fundamentals of the *ICD-10-CM* and *ICD-10-PCS* systems.
- Review the coding structure, organization, coding conventions, and unique features of *ICD-10-CM* and *ICD-10-PCS* by downloading the classification from the NCHS and CMS Web sites.
- Review the *ICD-10* fact sheets available on the CMS Web site.
- Review the *ICD-10-CM* and *ICD-10-PCS* guidelines and become familiar with new concepts such as definitions of root operations and approaches.
- Analyze and practice applying the *ICD-10-CM* and *ICD-10-PCS* coding guidelines.
- Understand the *ICD-10* final rule and its implications to your coding position.
- Begin learning about the general equivalence mappings (GEMs) between *ICD-9-CM, ICD-10-CM,* and *ICD-10-PCS.*

Preparations for HIM department management staff:

- Participate as a member of the *ICD-10* Steering Committee.
- Conduct *ICD-10* awareness training throughout the organization.
- Complete an information systems assessment inventory for the department.
- Identify training and budgeting issues for the department.
- Determine physician documentation areas requiring improvement.
- Identify areas in coding and documentation requiring operational and policy changes.
- Identify gaps in health record documentation.

Implementation Issues for *ICD-10-CM* and *ICD-10-PCS*

CHAPTER **34**

Nelly Leon-Chisen, RHIA

CHAPTER OVERVIEW

- All providers will be required to make the transition to *ICD-10-CM*.
- Only hospitals will need to implement *ICD-10-PCS*.
- Most of the implementation costs for HIM departments will be for training coding personnel.
- Information systems will also be affected by the implementation of the new classification system.
- Every electronic transaction requiring an *ICD-9-CM* code will need to be changed.
- Both commercial and homegrown/proprietary software will be affected.
  - Many commercial vendors will provide changes required by new regulations as part of their maintenance program at no extra cost to providers.
  - Most homegrown systems are found in large research hospitals or hospital billing departments. Many hospitals that use homegrown systems are moving to commercial products.
- It is not too early to begin preparing and making decisions about data conversion from *ICD-9-CM*.

LEARNING OUTCOMES

After studying this chapter you should be able to:

- Explain how the implementation of *ICD-10-CM* and *ICD-10-PCS* will impact providers.
- Discuss different actions that can be taken to prepare for the implementation.

TERM TO KNOW

Homegrown/propriety system
custom-built reporting and billing systems created by an individual provider to meet specific needs

REMEMBER . . . *ICD-10-CM* and *ICD-10-PCS* will require more knowledge of anatomy and physiology than *ICD-9-CM*.

INTRODUCTION

For institutional providers, implementation of new coding systems involves primarily two types of costs: coder training and information system changes. Hospitals need to plan for the transition to *ICD-10-CM* for both inpatient and outpatient services and to *ICD-10-PCS* for inpatient services. All other providers, such as physicians, home health agencies, skilled nursing facilities, and post acute care settings, will be affected by a change to *ICD-10-CM* only—because *ICD-10-PCS* is being implemented solely for hospitals to report inpatient services.

Implementation will require careful coordination, planning, and budgeting involving the expertise of many different individuals. An interdisciplinary implementation team will need to be convened to develop an implementation plan and lead the organization's efforts. The team should have executive sponsorship and be required to provide periodic reports on its progress.

PERSONNEL TRAINING

Personnel at multiple levels within hospitals will require training. The level and depth of training will depend on the individual's role. Training will need to include support staff, such as coders and billers, as well as any others involved in coding or reviewing coding information. Some users will require minimal awareness training, while others will need to attend training seminars to gain in-depth knowledge of the new coding guidelines, rules, and definitions. Hospitals will need to work with their medical staff to ensure that the appropriate documentation is available to support the new coding system. *ICD-10-PCS* code selection requires that more specific and detailed physician documentation be available in the health record. This greater level of specificity may also require that coders and billers expand their knowledge of medical terminology, anatomy and physiology, and disease processes.

Loss of productivity may be expected as coders take time away from coding to familiarize themselves with the new coding system. Many hospital coders already attend approximately 16 hours of training during the year to keep their coding skills current. It is assumed that these training costs will be replaced by costs associated with learning to use *ICD-10-CM* and *ICD-10-PCS*. However, whereas current training for *ICD-9* is spread throughout the year, training for *ICD-10* is likely to require bigger blocks of time. Coding productivity will also suffer until coders become proficient in the new system. It is anticipated that the in-depth training of coding professionals will occur between six and nine months before the compliance date.

INFORMATION SYSTEM ISSUES

A change to *ICD-10-CM* and *ICD-10-PCS* also requires extensive modifications to information systems. Virtually every system in which diagnosis and procedure codes are stored or processed will be affected. Issues vary from software changes to data-field expansion, timing, and data-conversion planning. Hospitals and other providers will need to perform an inventory of existing databases and information systems to determine the impact on their operations. Collaboration among departments will be necessary to identify these systems. A systems inventory should be conducted to determine where databases exist, what software is available, and whether the software is from a commercial vendor or a homegrown or proprietary program unique to the provider facility. Senior management and information systems staff should be made aware of the imminent transition to a new coding system so that remediation plans are put into place and future expansions in software and hardware are made while taking into consideration the needs of a coding change. Some providers have started making changes to their systems, and some of their commercial vendors have already done some of the work. The amount of work required for a successful transition will vary among providers depending on level of automation, number of applications requiring change, and number of vendors involved.

Commercial Software

Hospitals use a combination of purchased software and in-house-developed applications. Physician offices also rely on purchased software, although some may have homegrown programs. The software applications that will require modification encompass functions such as code assignment, health records abstraction, aggregate data reporting, utilization management, clinical systems, billing, claim submission, groupers, and other financial functions. In essence, every electronic transaction requiring an *ICD-9-CM* code would need to be changed. These changes include software interfaces, field-length formats on screens, report formats and layouts, table structures holding codes, expansion of flat files, coding edits, and significant logic changes.

A migration to new coding systems such as *ICD-10-CM* and *ICD-10-PCS* is a regulatory change. Most large health information system (HIS) vendors build the costs of regulatory changes into their user maintenance fees, so providers may not necessarily expect to incur additional costs for programming changes related to *ICD-10*. However, providers anticipate that, as a result of increased maintenance costs, they will see maintenance fees go up in the future.

Most maintenance contracts have a clause that covers regulatory changes. Some proactive providers have already been working with their commercial vendors to determine their system's capability for accepting new codes. Many large HIS vendors have indicated that they are ready to accept *ICD-10-CM* codes (because of Canadian or other international implementations), or that the field lengths have already been increased in anticipation of a migration to *ICD-10-CM* and *ICD-10-PCS*.

Homegrown/Proprietary Software

There is some variation across hospitals and other providers in the area of homegrown/proprietary software. The majority of hospitals have been moving away from homegrown systems in the last few years because of the expense and lack of sufficient information systems and technology personnel to maintain a homegrown system. University-based or large research centers may have more proprietary systems built for a specific application or research project than would be found in small- or medium-sized urban or rural hospitals.

Large hospital systems may have commercial applications, but they may also have proprietary billing systems or billing edits specific to their hospitals. Some of the homegrown systems may have smaller databases built by a department using a PC-based application and using Excel or Access.

Several different software applications use *ICD-9-CM* codes. Examples of hospital software applications that would be affected by a change to *ICD-10-CM* and *ICD-10-PCS* may be found in figure 34.1.

Small- to medium-sized stand-alone hospitals may have fewer applications, and fewer people to work with, than large acute care hospitals. However, some of the same basic clinical and financial systems would be affected. For example, a smaller stand-alone hospital with a single hospitalwide system from one vendor, with centralized coding in a single department and paper records, may find that the *ICD-10* implementation will

FIGURE 34.1 Examples of Hospital Applications Affected by the Migration to *ICD-10-CM* and *ICD-10-PCS*

- Accounting Systems
- Advance Beneficiary Notice (ABN) Software
- Billing System
- Birth Defect Registries
- Case Management System
- Claims Submission
- Clinical Data Reporting
- Clinical Department Systems (including Lab, EKG, Radiology, Surgical Scheduling, Physical Therapy, Occupational Therapy, Speech Therapy, etc.)
- Clinical Protocols
- Clinical Reminder Systems
- Compliance Checking Systems
- Databases
- Decision Support Systems
- DRG Grouper
- Electronic Prescribing
- Electronic Processing Systems (to submit claims to clearinghouse)
- Encoder Software
- Financial Systems
- Hospital Information System (HIS)
- Inpatient Rehabilitation Facility-Patient Assessment Instrument (IRFPAI) Data Collection System
- Interface Engines
- Managed Care (HEDIS) Reporting Systems
- Medical Necessity System
- Medical Record Abstracting System
- Minimum Data Set (MDS) Collection System
- OASIS System
- Outpatient Code Editor (OCE)
- Pharmacy Systems
- Physician Credentialing System
- Present on Admission (POA) Systems
- Provider Profiling
- Quality Management Reports
- Registration and Scheduling
- Research Databases
- State Birth Registration Systems
- State Death Registration Systems
- State Reporting Systems (e.g., California hospitals, which report all their *ICD-9-CM* codes to the state of California)
- Test Ordering System
- Utilization Management

mean working with that single vendor and training the coders in one department. On the other hand, hospitals within a larger health system that has grown over time as more hospitals have been acquired—each with different software vendors, departments, and processes—will obviously have a more complex implementation process that will affect more people, more departments, and more systems.

Hardware

During the transition period, information systems software will have to support *ICD-9-CM* as well as *ICD-10-CM* and *ICD-10-PCS* coding systems, therefore potentially requiring additional data storage space. Some hospitals have already started expanding the field size for the diagnosis and procedure fields based on the HIPAA Transaction Standard Notice of Proposed Rulemaking that mentioned *ICD-10* as a possibility for the future.

Neither the field-size expansion nor the larger number of codes is considered to be a problem with today's systems. It would not be a huge increase since it is a small pocket compared to the rest of the database. Validation rules may take up more room in the system, but experts don't anticipate requiring more CPU or disk space. From a technology perspective, it is considered that 20 years ago the larger field size and more codes would have been a problem; but disk capacity is inexpensive now, and CPUs are cheaper too.

DATA CONVERSION ISSUES

Providers will have to make decisions regarding the need to convert existing *ICD-9-CM* data. After conducting an inventory of the applications utilizing *ICD-9-CM* codes, a cost/benefit analysis should be performed to determine which databases would need to be converted. More than likely, a combination of old data conversion on an as-needed basis, with some up-front conversion immediately before implementation of *ICD-10,* would work best.

Other providers may consider it easier to run a report in *ICD-9-CM* and a separate report in *ICD-10-CM* or *ICD-10-PCS,* and then to add up both reports manually—therefore negating the need to perform a full conversion of the database.

TESTING AND VALIDATION

As changes are made to systems to handle the reporting of *ICD-10* codes, plans should also be developed to test and validate these system changes. Conceptually, the changes made to internal systems must ultimately be recognized and interpreted in the same way by the external entities or trading partners that are looking at the data. The systems must first be tested and validated internally; if successful, this validation will be followed by external testing.

External testing will require communicating with health plans and scheduling dates to conduct the testing. Various production scenarios should be used during the testing period. Ensure that the production scenarios reflect real-world situations; i.e., typical billing scenarios that reflect the most common types of claims.

In terms of validation, consider the results that should be achieved from a reimbursement perspective. Validate that the results would yield reimbursement results similar to those achieved by using *ICD-9-CM.* Be sure that health plans demonstrate they are processing the claim using *ICD-10* information rather than relying on the GEMs to convert an *ICD-10* code back to an *ICD-9-CM* code and then processing the claim for payment.

The items in the following checklist should be considered in anticipation of the migration to *ICD-10.*

CHECKLIST

The following checklist is excerpted from the American Hospital Association's *Regulatory Advisory* dated February 27, 2009, *Adoption of ICD-10-CM and ICD-10-PCS.* To view the complete advisory, visit the AHA's Central Office ICD-10 Resource Center: http://www.ahacentraloffice.com/ahacentraloffice_app/ICD-10/ICD-10.jsp.

- Obtain a senior management level "sponsor" for *ICD-10* related activities.
- Create *ICD-10* awareness throughout the organization. This includes educating senior management, information systems personnel, clinical department managers, and medical staff on the upcoming transition to *ICD-10.*
- Work with senior management regarding the potential budgetary, administrative, and operational implications of making the transition to *ICD-10.*
- Conduct a detailed assessment of staff education needs.
- Identify key players in your organization who should be part of your *ICD-10* implementation team.

- Identify an *ICD-10* team leader.
- Assess the impact of the change to the new coding systems and identify key tasks and objectives. Major tasks may include creating an implementation planning team, identifying and budgeting for required information system changes, and assessing and budgeting clinician and code set user education.
- Assess the impact of coding changes on strategic goals for electronic health records and other information technology.
- Develop an inventory of existing databases and systems likely to be affected by a transition to *ICD-10-CM* and *ICD-10-PCS.*
- Determine which systems use homegrown, proprietary, and custom-made software.
- Consult with your existing software vendors to determine their awareness of *ICD-10* and their plans for upgrades.
- Determine whether your current contractual agreements with vendors will cover a change to *ICD-10.*
- Consider *ICD-10* readiness in any future system improvements, such as plans for an electronic health record.
- Start working with your medical staff to improve medical record documentation. There are tangible benefits that can be gained, even with *ICD-9-CM.*
- Watch for upcoming American Hospital Association educational sessions on *ICD-10* by visiting the AHA's Central Office Web site: www.ahacentraloffice.org.

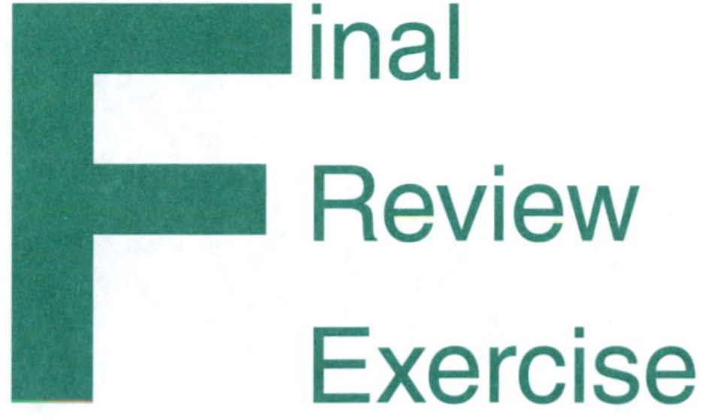

Final Review Exercise

At press time additional guideline changes were anticipated for October 1, 2011, implementation. These changes may affect code assignment in this section.

Please visit http://www.ahacentraloffice.org for updated guidelines.

Final Review Exercise

The final review exercise draws on concepts presented throughout this handbook. Read each brief summary below and assign codes for all diagnoses and procedures, including E codes for external causes and locations of occurrence as needed. For purposes of this assignment, accept narrative statements (for example, conditions, procedures, or other therapy) as though listed in a diagnostic statement.

In day-to-day practice, many hospitals have opted through their internal coding policies not to collect data on noninvasive diagnostic services performed in the inpatient setting, such as X-rays and electrocardiograms (EKGs). To provide answers that are as complete as possible, however, codes for these minor diagnostic services have been included in the answer key. The answer key begins on page 529 of the *with Answers* version of this handbook. If you are using the *without Answers* version, ask your instructor for the answer key.

1. A patient was admitted with complaint of a dull ache and occasional acute pain in the right calf. Examination revealed swelling and redness of the calf as well as a slight fever. The patient gave a history of having been on Premarin therapy for the past 20 years and stated that she has always followed the doctor's instructions for its use. Venous plethysmography revealed the presence of a thrombus. The estrogen therapy dosage was modified, and the patient was discharged with a diagnosis of acute deep vein thrombosis of the calf and thrombophlebitis due to supplemental estrogen therapy. She will be seen in the office in one week and will be followed regularly over the next several months.

2. A patient was admitted to the hospital because he was suffering acute abdominal pain. He was also found to be intoxicated, and his medical history indicated that he has been alcohol dependent for several years with periods of binging every three to four months. The current binge apparently started three days ago. The abdominal pain proved to be due to acute pancreatitis, and he was treated with nasogastric suction, administration of IV fluids, and pain control. The patient was observed for possible withdrawal reaction with standby orders; multiple vitamins were given.

3. A patient with a four-year history of anorexia nervosa was seen in the physician's office because of significant weight loss over the past three months, going from 82 pounds down to 53 pounds. She was admitted to increase body weight and to be given nutritional counseling because of her severe malnutrition.

4. A patient was admitted through the emergency department following a fall from a ladder while painting his house. He had contusions of the scalp and face and an open intertrochanteric fracture of the femur. The fracture site was debrided, and an open reduction with internal fixation was carried out.

5. A patient who underwent a modified radical mastectomy of the left breast six months earlier because of carcinoma now has metastasis to the bone. She was admitted for a transfusion of packed cells to treat aplastic anemia, probably due to her treatment by chemotherapy. She was discharged with a hemoglobin of 11.5 and will be followed as an outpatient.

6. A patient was admitted for cholecystectomy because of chronic cholecystitis. Before she went to the operating room the next morning, nursing personnel noted that she had apparently developed a urinary infection, and laboratory tests confirmed a diagnosis of urinary tract infection due to E. coli. Because of the infection, the surgery was canceled, antibiotic therapy was instituted, and the patient was discharged on the third hospital day to continue antibiotic therapy at home. She will be seen in the physician's office in three weeks, and surgery will be rescheduled.

7. A patient who recently underwent an oophorectomy because of adenocarcinoma of the ovary was admitted to the hospital for chemotherapy. Shortly after administration of the therapy, the patient developed a fever and chills and on the second day she had a productive cough. Chest X-rays indicated an acute pneumonia, and sputum culture was positive for *Klebsiella.* Antibiotics were administered, and the patient was discharged on the fifth hospital day.

8. A patient who had noticed significant abdominal enlargement over a period of several weeks without a change in her dietary habits was admitted for exploratory laparotomy. Surgery revealed a large malignant ovarian tumor, and the left ovary was resected. The pelvic cavity was explored thoroughly for any evidence of metastatic spread, but none was noted. Chemotherapy treatments were started on the day prior to discharge, and the patient was scheduled to continue therapy on an outpatient basis.

9. A patient who had undergone surgery for carcinoma of the breast two months earlier has since been on a program of chemotherapy. On a routine office visit yesterday, the physician noted that she had become severely dehydrated as a result of this program, and she was admitted for IV therapy for rehydration. Her regular chemotherapy session was carried out on the third day.

10. A patient was admitted with abdominal pain and complaints of melena noted for the past two days. Examination revealed an acute diverticulitis of the colon. Laboratory studies reported a significant hypokalemia. The provider documented hypokalemia, and the patient was placed on oral potassium. Bleeding from the diverticulitis subsided within a few days on conservative treatment, and the patient was discharged to be followed on an outpatient basis.

11. A patient was admitted with complaints of severe joint pain affecting the hands and hips. The physician's diagnosis indicated rheumatoid arthritis with sympathetic inflammatory myopathy.

12. A patient who was two months pregnant contracted rubella. On her next prenatal visit to the doctor's office, it was decided to admit the patient for therapeutic abortion because of the probability of abnormality of the fetus. Complete abortion was carried out by D & C.

13. Increasing fetal distress was noted during labor. The patient was transferred to the surgical suite, where a classical cesarean delivery was performed. A full-term normal male was delivered.

14. A patient was admitted with systolic heart failure, acute on chronic, congestive heart failure, and unstable angina. The unstable angina was treated with nitrates, and IV Lasix was administered to manage the heart failure. Both conditions improved, and the patient was discharged to be followed on an outpatient basis.

15. A patient was admitted for observation and evaluation for possible intracranial injury following a collision with another car while he was driving to work. Patient had minor bruises on the upper back and abrasions of the skin of the upper extremity. The bruises did not appear to need any treatment; the abrasions were swabbed with disinfectant and Neosporin was applied. Intracranial injury was ruled out.

16. A patient was brought to the emergency department following a burn injury experienced in a fire at the garage where he works. He was admitted and treated for first-degree and second-degree burns of the forearm and third-degree burn of the back.

17. A patient was admitted because of suspected carcinoma of the colon. Exploratory laparotomy was carried out, and a significant mass was discovered in the sigmoid colon. The sigmoid colon was resected and end-to-end anastomosis accomplished. Small nodules were noted on the liver, and a needle biopsy of the liver was performed during the procedure. The pathology report confirmed adenocarcinoma of the sigmoid colon with metastasis to the liver.

18. A patient was discharged following prostate surgery with an indwelling catheter in place. He was readmitted with urinary sepsis due to methicillin resistant *Staphylococcus aureus* (MRSA) due to the presence of the catheter. The physician confirmed the diagnosis of sepsis due to MRSA. The catheter was removed and the patient started on antibiotic therapy. The patient's condition improved over several days, and he was discharged without an indwelling catheter.

19. A patient six months pregnant was diagnosed as having an iron-deficiency anemia and was admitted for packed-cell transfusion.

20. A patient was admitted with occlusion of the carotid artery, and carotid endarterectomy was carried out with extracorporeal circulation used throughout the procedure.

21. A patient was admitted in a coma due to acute cerebrovascular thrombosis with cerebral infarction; the coma cleared by the fourth hospital day. Aphasia and hemiparesis were also present. The aphasia had cleared by discharge, but the hemiparesis was still present.

22. A patient was admitted with severe abdominal pain that began two days prior to admission and progressed in severity. Esophagogastroduodenoscopy (EGD) revealed an acute gastric ulcer, but no signs of hemorrhage or malignancy were noted. The provider documented acute gastric ulcer, and the patient was put on a medical regimen, including a bland diet, and was advised not to take aspirin.

23. A patient with type 1 diabetes mellitus seriously out of control was admitted for regulation of insulin dosage. The patient had been in the hospital four weeks earlier for an acute ST elevation myocardial infarction of the inferoposterior wall, and an EKG was performed to check its current status.

24. A patient who was treated seven weeks ago at Community Hospital for an acute anterolateral myocardial infarction is now admitted to University Hospital for surgical repair of an atrial septal defect resulting from the previous infarction. Following thoracotomy, the defect was repaired with a tissue graft; cardiopulmonary bypass was used during the procedure. The patient was discharged in good condition, to be followed as an outpatient.

25. A patient with bilateral mixed conductive and sensorineural hearing loss was admitted for cochlear implantation. A multiple-channel implant was inserted, and the patient was discharged, to be followed as an outpatient.

26. A patient who underwent a kidney transplant three months ago is admitted for biopsy because of an increased creatinine level discovered on an outpatient visit. Percutaneous biopsy revealed chronic rejection syndrome. The patient was discharged on a modified medication regimen, to be followed closely as an outpatient.

27. A patient was admitted with a fracture of the shaft of the right femur. Closed reduction was carried out and skeletal traction applied.

28. A patient who has had recurrent attacks of angina was seen in his physician's office because he felt that the anginal attacks seemed to be occurring more frequently and to be more severe and more difficult to control. He had not had a thorough evaluation previously, and bypass surgery had not been recommended in the past. He was admitted to the hospital for diagnostic studies to determine the underlying cause of this unstable angina. He underwent combined right- and left-heart catheterization, which revealed significant atherosclerotic heart disease. He was advised that coronary artery bypass surgery was indicated, but he did not want to make a decision without further discussion with his family. He was discharged on antianginal medication and will be seen in the doctor's office in one week.

29. The patient discussed in the preceding case returned to the hospital for bypass surgery. Reverse saphenous vein grafts were brought from the aorta to the obtuse marginal and the right coronary artery; the internal mammary artery was loosened and brought down to the left anterior descending artery to bypass this obstruction. The gastroepiploic artery was used to bypass the circumflex. Extracorporeal circulation and intraoperative pacemaker were used during the procedure.

30. A patient was brought to the hospital by ambulance after a fall from the scaffolding while working on the construction of a new bank building. He had struck his head and experienced a brief period of unconsciousness (less than one hour). On examination, he was found to have an open skull fracture with cerebral laceration and contusion. The skull fracture was reduced after debridement and the patient was transferred to the intensive care unit, where he stayed for four days. He was discharged on the tenth day in good condition, advised to avoid any strenuous activity and to see his physician in one week.

31. A patient was admitted for corrective surgery for a keloid of the left hand due to a burn experienced in a brush fire one year ago. Radical excision of the scar was carried out, and the defect was covered with a full-thickness graft taken from the upper arm. The patient was discharged in good condition, to be seen in the physician's office in two weeks.

32. A patient was brought to the emergency department by ambulance at 1 a.m. by her husband, who stated that they had been to a dinner party at a friend's home earlier in the evening. His wife had two martinis before the meal and several glasses of wine with the meal. At bedtime she took Valium that her physician had ordered prn for nervousness and inability to sleep. Shortly thereafter, the husband noticed that she appeared to be somewhat stuporous and became worried about her condition and brought her to the emergency department. The provider documented accidental overdose secondary to valium taken with alcohol.

33. A patient was admitted to the hospital with an admitting diagnosis of acute hip pain. There was no history of trauma; she stated that she had simply stood up from her chair, immediately experienced acute pain in the left leg, and fallen back into the chair. She has had osteoporosis for several years and is also a known diabetic. An X-ray revealed a fracture of the lower third of the shaft of the femur. A routine preoperative chest X-ray showed a few strands of atelectasis and a small cloudy area that may have represented mild pleural effusion. A cast was applied to the leg to immobilize the fracture. Her blood sugars were monitored and remained normal throughout the stay. The physician documented spontaneous fracture secondary to osteoporosis.

34. A patient with a five-year history of emphysema was brought to the hospital's emergency department in acute respiratory failure. Endotracheal intubation was carried out in the emergency department and the patient placed on mechanical ventilation. She was then admitted to the ICU, where she remained on the ventilator for three days and then was taken off the ventilator without a weaning period. She was discharged on the fifth hospital day.

35. A patient in acute respiratory failure was brought to the hospital by ambulance with ventilator in place. In the ambulance, an endotracheal tube was inserted into the patient. He had a long history of congestive heart failure, and studies confirmed that he was in congestive failure, with pleural effusion and acute pulmonary edema. The patient was treated with diuretics, and his cardiac condition was brought back into an acceptable range. He continued on ventilation for four days and was weaned on the fifth day. The physician was questioned regarding the reason for the admission, and she indicated that the patient was admitted for the acute respiratory failure.

36. A fourteen-year-old student was referred by the school health department for professional evaluation of a suspected mental disorder. According to the school counselor, he did not communicate well with other students and had demonstrated what the counselor felt was generally antisocial behavior. No evidence of mental disorder was found, and no other diagnosis to explain the student's apparent problems was identified.

37. A patient with hypertensive and diabetic end-stage renal disease who is on chronic dialysis is admitted because of dialysis disequilibrium (electrolyte imbalance).

38. A patient who has had arteriosclerotic disease of the right lower extremity with intermittent claudication for three years recently progressed to ulceration, and is now admitted with ulceration and gangrene of the toes of the right foot resulting from the arteriosclerosis. A transmetatarsal amputation of the right toes was performed, and the patient left the operating room in good condition.

39. A two-year-old child with a severe cough was admitted to the hospital with a history of having experienced malaise, loss of appetite, and cough for several days. In addition to the cough, he was experiencing some shortness of breath, and a chest X-ray showed an acute pneumonia. Sputum cultures showed B. pertussis. He was started on IV antibiotics and became afebrile on the fifth hospital day. A repeat chest X-ray was negative on the sixth hospital day, and the cough had partially cleared. He was discharged on the eighth day to be cared for at home and followed as an outpatient.

40. A ten-year-old boy was admitted because of severe cellulitis of the left leg. He had gone on a hiking trip in the nearby forest with his Scout troop a week earlier and now has a painful reddened area on the left leg. He stated that there was a good deal of thorny brush and that he had several minor thorn punctures but had experienced no problem with them. The day before admission he had developed a painful swollen area that had become worse during the night. A diagnosis of cellulitis due to *Streptococcus* A was made and antibiotics were administered. The wound itself was evaluated but did not appear to need specific treatment. The area on the leg progressively healed. The patient was discharged to continue the antibiotic series at home and will be seen in the office in one week.

41. An unconscious diving instructor was admitted with concussion and a skull fracture and subdural hematoma after diving from a high diving board and hitting the side of the pool. Drainage of the subdural space was carried out by incision and the fracture reduced. The patient left the operating room in fair condition but died the following day.

42. A patient was admitted because of increasing confusion and memory loss, which his family was unable to deal with. The patient was disoriented and unable to furnish any information. He was diagnosed as having senile dementia with Alzheimer's disease and was transferred to a nursing home.

43. Newborn twin girls, both living, were delivered in the hospital at 35 weeks, with extreme immaturity and weight of 850 grams for twin #1 and 900 grams for twin #2. Both were transferred to the neonatal intensive care nursery with a diagnosis of extreme immaturity.

44. A patient with a long history of angina pectoris came to the emergency department complaining of increasing anginal pain that he could not relieve with nitroglycerin and rest. The pain had occurred again about an hour ago and has been increasing in severity. Cardiac catheterization done recently showed some occlusion of the right coronary artery. It was decided to go ahead with a percutaneous transluminal coronary angioplasty, using a thrombolytic agent, in the hope of averting what appeared to be an impending myocardial infarction. The procedure was carried out without incident and the infarction was averted, but the patient did have an occlusion of the coronary artery.

45. A patient was admitted to the hospital with unstable angina that had been increasing in severity since the previous day. He was placed on bed rest and telemetry, and IV nitroglycerin was administered. An EKG showed some paroxysmal tachycardia as well, and so IV heparin was added to his medication program. His angina returned to its normal status, and the tachycardia was not shown on repeat studies at the end of one week. The patient was discharged to be seen by a visiting nurse over the next two weeks to supervise his medication regimen, and an appointment with his physician was made for two weeks later.

46. A patient who had been HIV positive for several years was seen in his physician's office with skin lesions over his back suggestive of HIV-related Kaposi's sarcoma. He was admitted for incisional biopsy, which confirmed the diagnosis.

47. A patient was admitted through the emergency department with acute right flank pain and was taken to surgery for removal of a ruptured appendix. At the time of the appendectomy, generalized peritonitis was observed along with some suspicious nodules on the head of the pancreas. A needle biopsy was performed while the abdomen was open; a diagnosis of carcinoma of the pancreas head was made on the basis of the pathological examination.

48. A patient with a long history of type 1 diabetes mellitus was admitted in hyperosmolar coma with blood sugars out of control. Modification of the insulin regimen was instituted and the patient was monitored carefully throughout her stay. The coma cleared on the first hospital day, and the patient was brought into control over the next four days. In addition to this acute metabolic condition, she also had a diagnosis of diabetic nephropathy, with the complication identified as nephrotic syndrome. The patient was discharged on a modified insulin regimen and will be followed by a visiting nurse until the diabetes stabilizes.

49. A patient was admitted with severe stage III pressure ulcer on the left buttock, with extensive necrotic tissue and gangrene. She was taken to the operating room, where the surgeon carefully excised the necrotic tissue. The ulcer site was then treated with antibiotic ointment and gauze bandage, and the patient was returned to the nursing unit, where the wound was monitored carefully and additional antibiotic treatment was administered. By the fourth day, healing was beginning to close the area, but treatment was continued until discharge on the seventh day. The family was advised to use an egg crate mattress and to turn the patient regularly. The patient was scheduled for an outpatient visit in one week.

50. A patient with a diagnosis of end-stage renal disease due to type 1 diabetes mellitus was admitted for her first hemodialysis session. A central venous catheter was placed and hemodialysis carried out. Patient tolerated the procedure well and will continue receiving hemodialysis on a regular schedule.

ANSWERS TO FINAL REVIEW EXERCISE

1. 451.19 Thrombophlebitis of femoral vein
   453.42 Acute venous embolism and thrombosis of deep vessels of distal lower extremity
   V07.59 Use of other agents affecting estrogen receptors and estrogen levels
   E932.2 Therapeutic use of estrogen
   89.58 Plethysmogram

   Comment: Because the physician listed deep vein thrombosis and thrombophlebitis in the diagnosis, assign codes for both conditions. Because this condition is an adverse effect of estrogen use, an E code for the medication is assigned.

2. 577.0 Acute pancreatitis
   303.00 Acute alcoholic intoxication in alcoholism, unspecified
   94.62 Alcohol detoxification

   Comment: The condition responsible for the admission was the acute pancreatitis. No code is assigned for the abdominal pain because it is integral to the acute pancreatitis. The observation for withdrawal, standby orders, and administration of multiple vitamins are sufficient to code detoxification, but no withdrawal delirium occurred and so only the code for acute intoxication in alcoholism is assigned. The designation of the pattern of drug or alcohol use or dependence requires the provider's clinical judgment. Unless the provider has documented the specific pattern of use, assign fifth digit 0 to indicate the documentation is not specific or is unclear.

3. 307.1 Anorexia nervosa
   261 Severe malnutrition

   Comment: Code 261, Nutritional marasmus, should be assigned as an additional diagnosis for the severe malnutrition. For some anorexic patients, the weight loss is so severe that it leads to malnutrition. Code 261 further describes the severity of the patient's condition.

4. 820.31 Open pertrochanteric fracture, intertrochanteric section
   920 Contusion of face and scalp
   E881.0 Fall from ladder
   E849.0 Home
   E000.8 Other external cause status
   E016.9 Other activity involving property and land maintenance, building and construction
   79.35 Open reduction with internal fixation
   79.65 Debridement

   Comment: When several injuries are present, the most severe is designated as the principal diagnosis.

5. 284.89 Other specified aplastic anemia
   198.5 Secondary malignant neoplasm of bone
   E933.1 Adverse effect of antineoplastic and immunosuppressive drugs
   V10.3 History of malignant neoplasm of breast
   V45.71 Acquired absence of breast
   99.04 Transfusion of packed cells

   Comment: The complication of anemia is designated the principal diagnosis because it is the condition that occasioned admission to the hospital and is the thrust of treatment. Code 285.3, Antineoplastic chemotherapy induced anemia, is not assigned because it excludes aplastic anemia due to antineoplastic chemotherapy. A code is assigned for the metastasis to the bone and a history code to indicate the previous breast malignancy. Code E933.1 includes the chemotherapy as the external cause (adverse effect) of the aplastic anemia.

6. 575.11 Chronic cholecystitis
   599.0 Urinary tract infection, due to
   041.49 E. coli
   V64.1 Surgery not carried out because of contraindication

   Comment: The principal diagnosis does not change because the planned treatment was not carried out; therefore, the cholecystitis is the principal diagnosis. Code V64.1 is assigned to indicate that the planned surgery was canceled because of a contraindication, which was the urinary tract infection.

7. V58.11 Encounter for antineoplastic chemotherapy
   183.0 Malignant neoplasm of ovary
   482.0 Klebsiella pneumonia
   99.25 Injection or infusion of cancer chemotherapeutic substance
   87.44 Routine chest X-ray

   Comment: When a patient is receiving therapy for neoplastic disease, a code for that condition is assigned rather than a history code, even though resection may have been performed previously. Because the patient was admitted solely for chemotherapy, V58.11 remains the principal diagnosis even though the patient remained in the hospital because of the pneumonia. Code 183.0 is assigned as an additional code rather than a history code because the patient is still under treatment.

8. 183.0 Malignant neoplasm of ovary
   65.39 Unilateral oophorectomy
   99.25 Chemotherapy

   Comment: When adjunct therapy such as radiotherapy or chemotherapy is given during an admission in which definitive surgery was performed, the code for the neoplasm is designated as the principal diagnosis and no code from category V58 is assigned. No code is assigned for the laparotomy because it is the operative approach for the oophorectomy.

9. 276.51 Dehydration
   174.9 Malignant neoplasm of breast, unspecified
   E933.1 Adverse effect of antineoplastic and immunosuppressive drugs
   99.25 Chemotherapy

Comment: Because this admission was for the sole purpose of treating the dehydration, a complication of the chemotherapy, dehydration is designated the principal diagnosis, with an additional code for the malignant neoplasm. Even though she received chemotherapy during her hospital stay, the admission was not solely for that purpose and so V58.11 is not assigned.

10. 562.13 Diverticulitis of colon with hemorrhage
    276.8 Hypopotassemia

    Comment: The presence of melena indicates there is bleeding. The fifth digit 3 is used to indicate the diverticulitis is the cause of the hemorrhage. No code is assigned for the abdominal pain as it is implicit in the diagnosis. The low potassium was treated and therefore is a reportable diagnosis.

11. 714.0 Rheumatoid arthritis
    359.6 Symptomatic inflammatory myopathy in diseases classified elsewhere

    Comment: No code for the joint pain is assigned because it is a characteristic component of rheumatoid arthritis. An instructional note at code 714.0 indicates that code 359.6 should be assigned when this type of myopathy is also present.

12. 635.90 Legally induced abortion, unspecified
    655.33 Suspected damage to fetus from viral disease in mother
    69.01 D & C for termination of pregnancy

    Comment: The fifth digit 0 is assigned for elective legal abortion. Given the *Official Guidelines for Coding and Reporting* statement that the "fifth digit assignment is based on the status of the patient at the beginning (or start) of the encounter," there isn't a clearly appropriate fifth digit available at this time. However, given the choices, the fifth digit 0 is the most appropriate. This selection is based on the *Coding Clinic* advice from Fourth Quarter 2011. Because the fetal condition was responsible for modifying the treatment of the mother, the code for it is assigned to explain the rationale for the abortion. Fifth digit 3 is assigned because this is an antepartum condition.

13. 656.81 Fetal distress
    74.0 Classical cesarean section
    V27.0 Single liveborn

    Comment: In this case, the fetal distress affected the management of the mother, leading to the decision to deliver by cesarean.

14. 428.23 Systolic heart failure, Acute on chronic
    428.0 Congestive heart failure
    411.1 Intermediate coronary syndrome

    Comment: Because both conditions equally meet the criteria for principal diagnosis, either may be listed first.

15. V71.4 Observation following other accident
    922.31 Contusion of back
    913.0 Abrasion without mention of infection
    E812.0 Motor vehicle accident involving collision with another vehicle, driver

    Comment: When the patient is admitted for observation for a possible serious injury such as an intracranial injury, the V71 code is assigned as the principal diagnosis even when minor injuries are present. In this case, the purpose of admission was to observe the patient; the minor injuries would not have required hospital admission. Additional codes are assigned for the minor injuries.

16. 942.34 Third-degree burn of back
    943.21 Second-degree burn of forearm
    E891.3 Burning caused by conflagration
    E849.3 Industrial place and premises
    E000.0 Civilian activity done for income or pay

    Comment: When several burns are present, the burn of the highest degree takes precedence; therefore, the third-degree burn of the back is designated as the principal diagnosis. When more than one degree of burn occurs at the same site, only the code for the highest degree is assigned; therefore, only the second degree of the forearm is coded.

17. 153.3 Malignant neoplasm of sigmoid colon
    197.7 Malignant neoplasm of liver, specified as secondary
    45.76 Sigmoidectomy
    50.11 Needle biopsy of liver

    Comment: No code is assigned for the exploratory laparotomy because it is the operative approach for the sigmoidectomy. End-to-end anastomosis is included in the code for the colon resection. A needle biopsy performed during open surgery is coded as a closed biopsy.

18. 996.64 Urinary sepsis due to indwelling urinary catheter
    038.12 Methicillin resistant staphylococcal septicemia, *Staphylococcus aureus* septicemia
    995.91 Sepsis
    599.0 Urinary tract infection, site not specified
    E879.6 Other procedures without mention of misadventure at the time of procedure as the cause of abnormal reaction of patient or of later complication, Urinary catheterization
    97.64 Removal of indwelling catheter

    Comment: This infection was due to the presence of the indwelling catheter and is coded as an infection of that device. The physician also confirmed the diagnosis of sepsis. Code 038.12 is assigned for *Staphylococcus aureus* sepsis instead of code 038.9. Code 995.91 is assigned along with code 038.12 to further describe sepsis.

19. 648.23 Anemia complicating pregnancy
    280.9 Iron-deficiency anemia, unspecified
    99.04 Transfusion of packed cells

    Comment: Code 648.23 from chapter 11 is assigned as the principal diagnosis because the anemia is complicating the pregnancy. Fifth digit 3 is assigned as this is an antepartum complication. Code 280.9 is also assigned to provide greater specificity as to the type of anemia.

20. 433.10 Occlusion of carotid artery, without mention of cerebral infarction
    38.12 Endarterectomy of other vessel of head and neck (carotid artery)
    39.61 Cardiopulmonary bypass (extracorporeal circulation)

    Comment: Fifth digit 0 is assigned because there is no mention of infarction associated with the carotid occlusion. The carotid artery is included in the surgery code for "other vessels of head and neck." An instructional note with category 38 indicates that an additional code of 39.61 should be assigned when extracorporeal circulation is used during the endarterectomy.

21. 434.01 Cerebral thrombosis with cerebral infarction
    780.01 Coma
    784.3 Aphasia
    342.90 Hemiplegia, affecting unspecified side

    Comment: A code for coma is assigned because it is not integral to a diagnosis of cerebral thrombosis. Codes are assigned for aphasia and hemiparesis because a code is appropriate for any neurological deficits that occur, even when they have resolved by discharge. These manifestations are coded because they affect the patient's care. Fifth digit 0 is assigned for the hemiparesis because there is no mention of whether the hemiparesis affected the dominant or nondominant side.

22. 531.30 Acute gastric ulcer without mention of hemorrhage or perforation
    45.13 Esophagogastroduodenoscopy

    Comment: No code is assigned for the abdominal pain because it is integral to gastric ulcer.

23. 250.03 Diabetes mellitus, type 1, out of control
    410.32 Inferoposterior myocardial infarction, subsequent episode of care
    89.52 Electrocardiogram

    Comment: Fifth digit 3 is used to indicate that the diabetes mellitus was out of control. A patient admitted four weeks after an acute myocardial infarction will always require clinical evaluation; in this case, a specific diagnostic study was performed also. Fifth digit 2 indicates that this is a subsequent admission for the infarction.

24. 429.71 Acquired cardiac septal defect
    410.02 Subsequent episode of care for anterolateral myocardial infarction
    35.61 Repair of septal defect with tissue graft
    39.61 Cardiopulmonary bypass

    Comment: Although seven weeks have elapsed since the infarction, it is coded and reported (subsequent episode). A code for infarction is assigned through the eighth week following its occurrence. It required continuing evaluation and monitoring during the stay. Fifth digit 2 is assigned to indicate that this is a subsequent episode of care for this infarction. No code is assigned for the thoracotomy because it is the operative approach for the repair.

25. 389.22 Mixed hearing loss, bilateral
    20.98 Implantation of multiple-channel cochlear prosthetic device

    Comment: Because a combination code including both types of hearing loss is provided, only code 389.2 is assigned rather than individual codes for the hearing loss.

26. 996.81 Complication of transplanted kidney
    55.23 Closed biopsy of kidney

    Comment: Transplant rejection is coded as a complication of the transplanted organ. A percutaneous biopsy is a closed biopsy.

27. 821.01 Closed fracture of shaft of femur
    79.05 Closed reduction of fracture of femur without internal fixation

    Comment: When the diagnostic statement does not indicate whether the fracture is open or closed, *ICD-9-CM* classifies it as closed. Application of skeletal traction is included in the code for closed reduction, and no additional code is assigned.

28. 414.01 Arteriosclerosis of native coronary artery
    411.1 Unstable angina
    37.23 Combined right- and left-heart catheterization

    Comment: When the purpose of admission for a patient with unstable angina is to determine the underlying cause, the code for the underlying condition is designated as the principal diagnosis. Because this patient has not had a bypass surgery in the past, the arteriosclerosis is of a native coronary artery.

29. 414.01 Arteriosclerosis of native coronary artery
    36.12 Aortocoronary bypass of two coronary arteries
    36.15 Single internal mammary-coronary artery bypass
    36.17 Abdominal-coronary artery bypass
    39.61 Cardiopulmonary bypass
    39.64 Intraoperative cardiac pacemaker

    Comment: Four coronary artery bypass grafts were placed, two of which were aortocoronary, one an internal mammary-coronary artery, and one an abdominal-coronary bypass. Codes are assigned for the cardiopulmonary bypass and the intraoperative pacemaker.

30. 803.62 Open skull fracture with cerebral laceration and contusion, with brief loss of consciousness
    E881.1 Fall from scaffolding
    E849.3 Industrial place and premises (building under construction)
    E000.0 Civilian activity done for income or pay
    E016.2 Activities involving building and construction
    02.02 Elevation of skull fracture fragments

    Comment: *ICD-9-CM* provides a combination code that includes both the fracture and the cerebral lacerations and contusions. Debridement of compound (open) fracture of the skull is included in the code for fracture reduction.

31. 701.4 Keloid scar
    906.6 Late effect of burn of hand
    E929.4 Late effect of accident caused by fire
    86.4 Radical excision of skin lesion
    86.61 Full-thickness skin graft to hand

    Comment: The residual keloid is sequenced first, with code 906.6 indicating that it is a late effect of a burn of the wrist and hand. Because the condition is a late effect, the E code must also be a late effect code. No code is assigned for excision of skin for the graft because the exclusion note for 86.91 indicates that it is not to be used when skin for the graft is excised during the same episode of care in which the graft is applied.

32. 980.0 Poisoning by ethyl alcohol
    969.4 Poisoning by Valium
    780.09 Other alteration of consciousness (stupor)
    E860.0 Accidental poisoning by alcoholic beverage
    E853.2 Accidental poisoning by benzodiazepine-based tranquilizer (Valium)
    E849.0 Home

Comment: Although the Valium was used correctly, the fact that alcohol was also taken during the same period of time makes this a poisoning. Because two substances were involved, two poisoning codes and two E codes are assigned. Either poisoning code can be designated as principal diagnosis.

33. 733.15 Pathological fracture of other specified part of the femur
    733.00 Osteoporosis, unspecified
    250.00 Diabetes mellitus, unspecified type
    93.53 Application of cast
    87.44 Routine chest X-ray
    88.26 Other skeletal X-ray of pelvis and hip

    Comment: Spontaneous fractures such as this are always classified as pathological. Although the osteoporosis was not treated, it is the underlying cause of the fracture and a code is needed for complete coding. No codes are assigned for the atelectasis or possible pleural effusion because these represent X-ray findings only, without further evaluation or treatment. The diabetes was monitored and so a code is assigned.

34. 518.81 Acute respiratory failure
    492.8 Emphysema
    96.71 Continuous mechanical invasive ventilation for less than 96 consecutive hours
    96.04 Insertion of endotracheal tube

    Comment: Acute respiratory failure associated with chronic pulmonary disease, such as emphysema, can be designated as the principal diagnosis. The patient was on mechanical ventilation only three days, a total of less than 96 hours. A code is assigned for the tube insertion because it was performed in the emergency department of the hospital with immediate admission.

35. 518.81 Acute respiratory failure
    428.0 Congestive heart failure
    96.72 Continuous mechanical ventilation for 96 hours or more

    Comment: When a patient is admitted with respiratory failure and another acute condition (e.g., congestive heart failure), the principal diagnosis will not be the same in every situation. Selection of the principal diagnosis will depend on the circumstances of admission. In this instance, the physician had to be queried to determine whether the congestive heart failure or the respiratory failure was responsible for the admission. Pleural effusion and acute pulmonary edema are part of congestive heart failure, and no additional codes are assigned for these conditions. Time counting for mechanical ventilation begins at time of admission when the ventilator is already in use. No code is assigned for the endotracheal tube insertion because it was done in the ambulance and cannot be reported by the hospital.

36. V71.02 Observation for possible mental disorder, adolescent antisocial behavior
    94.08 Other psychologic evaluation and testing

    Comment: It is appropriate to use category V71 when a patient is seen for evaluation and no diagnosis is made. If the suspected diagnosis or a related diagnosis had been established, including a significant symptom, the code for that condition would be assigned rather than the code from category V71.

37. 276.9 Electrolyte and fluid disorders, not elsewhere classified

403.91 Hypertensive chronic kidney disease with chronic kidney disease stage V or end-stage renal disease

585.6 End-stage renal disease

250.40 Diabetes mellitus with renal manifestations

V45.11 Renal dialysis status

E879.1 Other procedures without mention of misadventure at the time of procedure as the cause of abnormal reaction of patient or of later complication, Kidney dialysis

Comment: When end-stage renal disease is the result of both hypertension and diabetes mellitus, both diabetes and hypertension are coded because they are responsible for the condition (403.xx and 250.4). Because the patient has hypertensive end-stage renal disease and is on chronic dialysis, codes 403.91 and 585.6 are assigned. Code E879.1 is assigned to indicate the external cause.

38. 440.24 Atherosclerosis of the extremities with gangrene

707.15 Ulcer of other part of foot

84.12 Amputation through foot

Comment: Code 440.24 includes gangrene. An additional code may be assigned for the ulceration. A transmetatarsal amputation is coded as amputation through the foot as indicated in the Alphabetic Index and in the inclusion note for code 84.12.

39. 033.0 Whooping cough due to B. pertussis

484.3 Pneumonia in whooping cough

87.44 Routine chest X-ray

Comment: Whooping cough is the condition resulting from infection by B. pertussis. When pneumonia is associated with whooping cough, both the Alphabetic Index and the instructional note indicate that dual codes must be assigned, with the code for whooping cough sequenced first.

40. 682.6 Cellulitis of leg

891.1 Open wound of leg, complicated

041.01 Bacterial infection due to group A *Streptococcus*

E920.8 Accident caused by other specified piercing instrument (thorn)

E849.8 Other specified place (forest)

E001.0 Activities involving walking, marching and hiking on level or elevated terrain

E000.8 Other external cause status

Comment: In this case, the minor puncture wounds did not require treatment at the time they occurred and would not have required hospital care; therefore, the cellulitis is designated as the principal diagnosis. The wounds were evaluated, however, and so a code for the injury is assigned. Because of this infection, the open wound is classified as complicated.

41. 803.25 Closed skull fracture with subdural hematoma

E883.0 Accident from diving into water (swimming pool)

E849.4 Place of recreation or sport

E002.1 Activities involving springboard and platform diving

E000.0 Civilian activity done for income or pay

02.02 Elevation of skull fracture fragments

01.31 Incision and drainage of subdural space

Comment: The subdural hematoma is included in code 803.25. No code is assigned for concussion when there is skull fracture with intracranial injury. Fifth digit 5 is used because the patient was unconscious on admission, never regained consciousness, and expired the following day. Two procedure codes are needed, one for the fracture reduction and one for the incision and drainage of the hematoma.

42. 331.0 Alzheimer's disease
    294.10 Dementia in disease classified elsewhere without behavioral disturbance

    Comment: When dementia is associated with Alzheimer's disease, the code for Alzheimer's disease is sequenced first, followed by code 294.10.

43. Twin #1: V31.00 Liveborn twin, mate liveborn, born in hospital without mention of cesarean delivery
    765.03 Extreme immaturity, weight 750–999 grams
    765.28 35–36 Completed weeks of gestation

    Twin #2: V31.00 Liveborn twin, mate liveborn, born in hospital without mention of cesarean delivery
    765.03 Extreme immaturity, weight 750–999 grams
    765.28 35–36 Completed weeks of gestation

    Comment: A code from categories V30–V39 is always designated as the principal diagnosis for the episode in which birth occurs. A fifth digit is assigned to indicate whether the delivery was by cesarean; in this case, it was not. An additional code is assigned to indicate extreme immaturity, with a fifth digit indicating the weight.

44. 411.81 Coronary occlusion without myocardial infarction
    00.66 Percutaneous transluminal coronary angioplasty (PTCA)
    00.40 Procedure on single vessel
    99.10 Injection or infusion of thrombolytic agent

    Comment: The code for intermediate artery syndrome (411.1) is not assigned when a code from 411.8x is also assigned. Code 00.66 is assigned for the PTCA, with code 00.40 indicating that the PTCA was done on a single vessel. The infusion of a thrombolytic agent is reported separately using code 99.10.

45. 411.1 Intermediate coronary syndrome
    427.2 Paroxysmal tachycardia, unspecified
    89.52 Electrocardiogram

    Comment: In this case, no studies were done to identify the underlying pathology and no surgical intervention was undertaken. Therefore, the unstable angina is the principal diagnosis. Typically, tests such as EKGs, X-rays, and laboratory tests are not coded in the inpatient setting.

46. 042 Human immunodeficiency virus (HIV) disease
    176.0 Kaposi's sarcoma of skin
    86.11 Biopsy of skin and subcutaneous tissue

    Comment: When the patient is admitted for treatment of a condition due to HIV infection, the code for the infection is designated as the principal diagnosis, with an additional code for the related condition.

47. 540.0 Acute appendicitis with generalized peritonitis
    157.0 Malignant neoplasm of pancreas, Head of pancreas
    47.09 Appendectomy
    52.11 Closed (percutaneous) biopsy of pancreas

    Comment: The code for the appendicitis is designated the principal diagnosis because it was clearly the condition that occasioned the admission. The code for the malignant neoplasm is also assigned, but there is no guideline that suggests that a malignancy takes any precedence in a situation of this type. A needle biopsy done in the course of an open surgical procedure is coded as a closed biopsy.

48. 250.23 Diabetes mellitus, type 1, with hyperosmolarity, out of control
    250.43 Diabetes mellitus, type 1, out of control, with nephropathy
    581.81 Nephrotic syndrome in disease classified elsewhere

    Comment: The code for diabetes mellitus with hyperosmolarity includes the associated coma. Although a diagnosis of diabetic nephropathy was also established during this episode of care, it was the coma that occasioned the admission; therefore, it is designated as the principal diagnosis. Both diabetes codes use fifth digit 3 to indicate that it is type 1 and that it was also out of control.

49. 707.05 Pressure ulcer, buttock
    707.23 Pressure ulcer, stage III
    785.4 Gangrene
    86.22 Excisional debridement

    Comment: The code for gangrene must be sequenced following the code for the ulcer because it is a chapter 16 code (symptom) and the responsible condition is identified.

50. V56.0 Admitted for extracorporeal dialysis
    250.41 Diabetes mellitus, type 1, with renal manifestation
    585.6 End-stage renal disease
    39.95 Hemodialysis
    38.95 Venous catheterization for renal dialysis

    Comment: Code V56.0 is the principal diagnosis because this admission was solely for the purpose of dialysis. The fact that the venous catheter was inserted does not affect principal diagnosis assignment when the catheterization is followed by dialysis. A code for the diabetes mellitus is assigned with fourth digit 4 to indicate the presence of a kidney complication and fifth digit 1 to indicate that it is type 1 and not described as being out of control. The end-stage renal disease is the manifestation of the diabetes and the condition for which the dialysis is performed. Procedure codes are assigned for both the catheter insertion and the hemodialysis.

Appendix A: Reporting of the Present on Admission Indicator

Nelly Leon-Chisen, RHIA

Reporting of the Present on Admission Indicator

Nelly Leon-Chisen, RHIA

The present on admission (POA) indicator is a data element required for Medicare claims reporting. The POA indicator provides information on whether a diagnosis was present at the time of a patient's admission. The Medicare POA requirement applies to all diagnosis codes involving inpatient admissions to general acute care hospitals (except for critical care access hospitals, Maryland waiver hospitals, long-term care hospitals, cancer hospitals, and children's inpatient facilities). Some states (e.g., Maryland) have additional regulatory requirements for POA reporting. State guidelines for public health and quality reporting may differ from the national Medicare reporting requirements. In addition, several commercial health plans require POA reporting by contractual agreement with the hospital.

It is important that the POA indicator be reported correctly because it is significant in quality-of-care reporting and analysis and potentially significant for medicolegal and reimbursement issues. A select number of hospital-acquired conditions are not recognized by the Medicare severity-adjusted diagnosis-related group (MS-DRG) system if the condition is the only complication/comorbidity (CC) or major complication/comorbidity (MCC).

The POA indicator should be reported for principal and secondary diagnosis codes and external cause of injury codes based on a review of the provider's documentation. Distinguishing between preexisting conditions and complications enhances the use of administrative data for outcomes reporting. Secondary diagnoses may be chronic illnesses that have been in existence for some time, or they may have developed after admission. Unless the POA indicator is reported, it is not easy to determine the difference between preexisting conditions and complications when analyzing only the *ICD-9-CM* codes.

DEFINITION

The term "present on admission" means "present at the time the order for inpatient admission occurs." Conditions or adverse events that occur prior to an inpatient admission would be considered to be present on admission, including any conditions occurring in the emergency department, observation, clinic, or outpatient surgery prior to inpatient admission.

DOCUMENTATION

The usefulness of POA data for quality-of-care, medicolegal, and reimbursement issues is dependent on the provider's accurate and complete medical record documentation. A provider in this context means the physician or any qualified health care practitioner who is legally accountable for establishing the patient's diagnosis, similar to the definition used for code assignment. The coder should not include documentation from nurses or other allied health professionals who are not legally accountable for establishing the patient's diagnosis (except for the reporting of pressure ulcer staging and body mass index).

The provider must resolve any inconsistent, missing, conflicting, or unclear documentation before the appropriate POA indicator may be selected. Resolving inconsistencies may necessitate querying the provider for clarification.

There is no required time frame as to when a provider must identify or document a condition to be present on admission. In some clinical situations, it may not be possible for a provider to make a definitive diagnosis (or a condition may not be recognized or reported by the patient) for a period of time after admission. In some cases it may be several days before the provider arrives at a definitive diagnosis. This does not mean that the condition was not present on admission. Determination of whether the condition was present on admission is based on the applicable POA guideline or the provider's best clinical judgment.

GUIDELINES

Guidelines for the selection of POA indicators are included in the *ICD-9-CM Official Guidelines for Coding and Reporting* as appendix I. The POA guidelines are not intended to replace any guidelines in the main body of the official guidelines, nor are they intended to provide guidance on when a condition should be coded. Rather, the POA guidelines are intended to show how to apply the POA indicator to the final set of diagnosis codes already selected.

The guidelines are not intended to be a substitute for a provider's clinical judgment as to whether a condition was or was not present on admission. Issues related to the linking of signs and symptoms, timing of test results, or findings should be referred to the provider for clarification.

REPORTING OPTIONS

There are five options for reporting all diagnoses:

Code	Definition
Y	Yes (present at the time of inpatient admission)
N	No (not present at the time of inpatient admission)
U	No information available in the record (documentation is insufficient to determine if condition is present on admission)
W	Clinically undetermined (provider is unable to clinically determine whether condition was present on admission)
Unreported/not used (or 1 for Medicare)	Exempt from POA reporting. (This option is the only circumstance in which the POA field is left blank. The condition must be on the list of *ICD-9-CM* codes for which this field is not applicable.)

Conditions Present on Admission

Assign "Y" as the POA reporting option for the following circumstances:

- Condition explicitly documented as being present on admission
- Condition diagnosed prior to inpatient admission (e.g., hypertension, diabetes mellitus, and asthma)
- Condition diagnosed during the admission but clearly present (but not diagnosed) before admission (e.g., patient with a lump in her breast is admitted and has a biopsy, and the pathology report reveals carcinoma of the breast)

- Condition diagnosed as possible, probable, suspected, or rule out at the time of discharge and—based on signs, symptoms, or clinical findings—suspected during admission (e.g., patient admitted with chest pain, transferred to another facility, discharged as possible myocardial infarction)
- Condition that developed during an outpatient encounter prior to a written order for inpatient admission (for example, patient falls while in the emergency department, sustains a fracture, and is subsequently admitted as an inpatient)
- Condition diagnosed as impending or threatened based on symptoms or clinical findings that were present on admission (e.g., a patient with a known history of coronary atherosclerosis is now admitted for treatment of impending myocardial infarction; the final diagnosis is documented as "impending" myocardial infarction)
- Condition reported with a combination code, and all parts of the combination code are present on admission (e.g., patient with diabetic nephropathy is admitted with uncontrolled diabetes)
- Condition reported with the same *ICD-9-CM* code representing two or more conditions during the same encounter, and all conditions were present on admission. For example, bilateral fracture of the same bone, same site, and both fractures are present on admission.
- Chronic condition, even if it is not diagnosed until after admission (e.g., lung cancer diagnosed during hospitalization)
- Condition in which the final diagnosis includes comparative or contrasting diagnoses, and both are present or suspected at the time of admission (e.g., patient admitted with severe abdominal pain, nausea, and vomiting, with the admitting diagnosis of acute pyelonephritis versus diverticulum of the colon; patient discharged home)
- Infection codes that include the causal organism, if the infection (or signs of the infection) is present on admission, even though the culture results may not be known until after admission (e.g., patient admitted with severe cough, fever, and congestion whose culture of sputum reveals Staphylococcal infection; diagnosed with Staphylococcal pneumonia)
- Congenital condition (e.g., congenital megacolon), except for categories 740–759, Congenital anomalies, which are on the exempt list
- Condition present at birth or that develops in utero, including conditions that occur during delivery (e.g., injury during delivery)
- External cause of injury or poisoning that occurred prior to inpatient admission (e.g., patient fell out of bed at home)
- A pressure ulcer that is present on admission but worsens to a higher stage during the hospitalization

Conditions Not Present on Admission

Assign "N" as the POA reporting option for the following circumstances:

- Condition the provider explicitly documents as not present at the time of admission (e.g., patient develops a vascular catheter infection a few days after the insertion of the catheter)
- Condition reported as an inconclusive final diagnosis based on signs, symptoms, or clinical findings that were not present on admission (e.g., patient develops fever after surgery, and final diagnosis includes "possible postoperative infection")
- Condition diagnosed as impending or threatened and based on symptoms or clinical findings that were not present on admission (e.g., patient is admitted to the hospital for prostate surgery and postoperatively develops chest pain, and the final diagnosis includes "impending myocardial infarction")
- Condition reported with a combination code, and any part of the combination code is not present on admission (e.g., obstructive chronic bronchitis with acute exacerbation, and the exacerbation is not present on admission)

- Condition reported with the same *ICD-9-CM* code representing two or more conditions during the same encounter, and any of the conditions were not present on admission. For example, dehydration with hyponatremia is assigned to code 276.1, but only one of these conditions is present on admission.
- External cause of injury or poisoning that occurs during inpatient hospitalization (e.g., patient falls out of hospital bed during hospital stay, or patient experiences an adverse reaction to a medication administered after inpatient admission)

Unclear Documentation

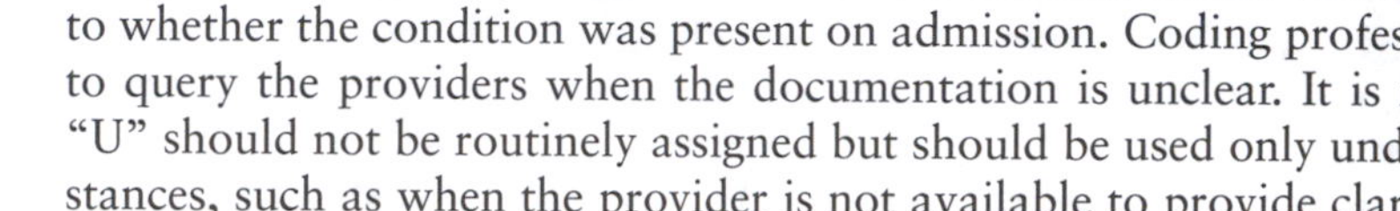

Assign "U" as the POA indicator when the medical record documentation is unclear as to whether the condition was present on admission. Coding professionals are encouraged to query the providers when the documentation is unclear. It is important to note that "U" should not be routinely assigned but should be used only under very limited circumstances, such as when the provider is not available to provide clarification.

Conditions Clinically Undetermined

Assign "W" as the POA indicator when the medical record documentation indicates that it cannot be clinically determined whether the condition was present on admission. For example, a patient is admitted in active labor and, during the stay, a breast abscess is noted when she attempts to breast feed. The provider is unable to determine if the abscess was present on admission.

It is important to distinguish between the reporting options "U" and "W." For example, if the provider is queried and is not able to determine whether the condition was present on admission, report using "W." In contrast, if the documentation is not available and the provider is not queried, or the provider is not available to provide a response, report using "U." Coders should make every attempt to limit the number of "U" options reported as this may potentially be construed as an error or treated as "N" for Medicare payment purposes.

Conditions Exempt from POA Reporting

A list of categories and codes exempt from the POA requirement may be found in the *ICD-9-CM Official Guidelines for Coding and Reporting* as part of appendix I. These codes are exempt because they indicate circumstances regarding the health care encounter or factors influencing the health status but do not represent a current disease or injury or are always present on admission. Examples include late effect codes, personal and family history codes, and need for vaccination V codes.

The Medicare reporting option for exempt conditions is "1." However, the reporting requirements of other systems vary, and the POA field may be left blank or the POA indicator may be unreported for exempt conditions. The codes and categories on the exempt list are the only codes that are exempt from POA reporting. The list of exempt codes is updated every year based on the new codes implemented for the year.

Special Considerations

For obstetrical patients, whether or not delivery occurs during the current hospitalization does not affect assignment of the POA indicator. The determining factor for POA assignment is whether the pregnancy complication or obstetrical condition described by the code is present at the time of admission. If the obstetrical code includes information that is not a diagnosis, do not consider that information in the POA determination.

Newborns are not considered to be admitted until after birth; therefore, any condition that is present at birth or that develops in utero is considered to be present at admission.

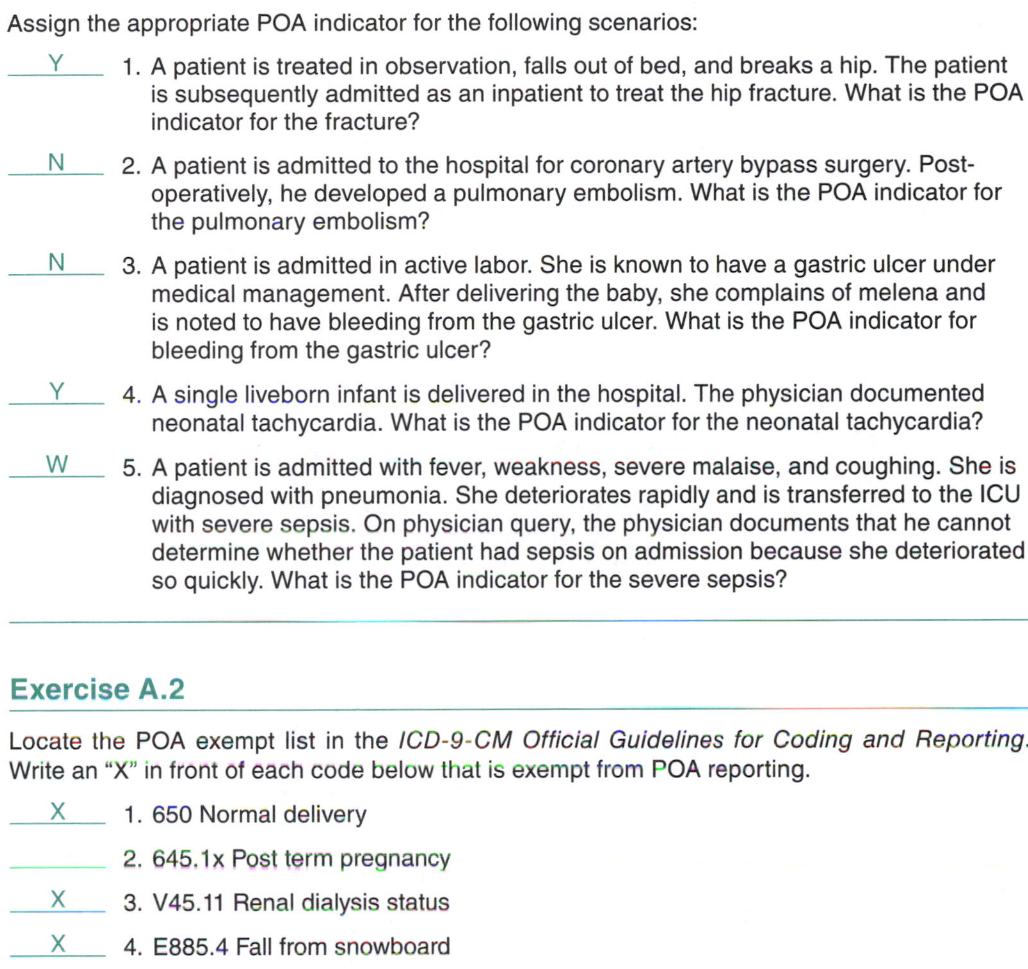

Exercise A.1

Assign the appropriate POA indicator for the following scenarios:

__Y__ 1. A patient is treated in observation, falls out of bed, and breaks a hip. The patient is subsequently admitted as an inpatient to treat the hip fracture. What is the POA indicator for the fracture?

__N__ 2. A patient is admitted to the hospital for coronary artery bypass surgery. Postoperatively, he developed a pulmonary embolism. What is the POA indicator for the pulmonary embolism?

__N__ 3. A patient is admitted in active labor. She is known to have a gastric ulcer under medical management. After delivering the baby, she complains of melena and is noted to have bleeding from the gastric ulcer. What is the POA indicator for bleeding from the gastric ulcer?

__Y__ 4. A single liveborn infant is delivered in the hospital. The physician documented neonatal tachycardia. What is the POA indicator for the neonatal tachycardia?

__W__ 5. A patient is admitted with fever, weakness, severe malaise, and coughing. She is diagnosed with pneumonia. She deteriorates rapidly and is transferred to the ICU with severe sepsis. On physician query, the physician documents that he cannot determine whether the patient had sepsis on admission because she deteriorated so quickly. What is the POA indicator for the severe sepsis?

Exercise A.2

Locate the POA exempt list in the *ICD-9-CM Official Guidelines for Coding and Reporting*. Write an "X" in front of each code below that is exempt from POA reporting.

__X__ 1. 650 Normal delivery

_____ 2. 645.1x Post term pregnancy

__X__ 3. V45.11 Renal dialysis status

__X__ 4. E885.4 Fall from snowboard

_____ 5. E987.1 Falling from high place, man-made structure

Appendix B: Case Summary Exercises

Janatha R. Ashton, RHIA, MS

Contents

About This Appendix

The case summary exercises in this appendix are based on the actual health records of both inpatients and outpatients. The patients described often have multiple conditions that may or may not be related to the current episode of care. Some exercises include several episodes of care for the same patient in various settings.

HOW TO USE THIS APPENDIX

The case summary style of the exercises requires you to consider the patient's condition as well as all relevant information provided: medical history, reason for admission or encounter, laboratory results, procedures performed, and the diagnoses listed. In all exercises, you need to apply pertinent coding principles and official coding guidelines in making code assignments and designating the principal diagnosis and procedure for each episode of care.

Each exercise includes a brief summary and a diagnosis statement that should be read carefully. You may assume that all diagnoses and procedures that are mentioned and that should be coded have been approved by the patient's physician. Be sure to sequence the principal diagnosis first.

After referring to the appropriate volume or volumes of *ICD-9-CM,* fill in the codes that you think should be assigned (including any appropriate E codes) in the space provided after each case summary. For inpatient care and the outpatient and ambulatory care settings, assign and sequence codes according to the *Official Guidelines for Coding and Reporting.*

The sequence of this appendix corresponds to chapters 9 through 29 of the handbook and progresses from simpler to more difficult areas. It is recommended that you will have read all of the chapters (1–29) of the handbook before you begin doing the case summary exercises in this appendix. You may, however, complete the exercises in any order after you have learned the basic coding principles and understand how to apply official coding guidelines.

ABOUT THE ANSWER KEY

A separate answer key is provided in appendix C of the *with Answers* version of the handbook. (Ask your instructor for the answer key if you are using the *without Answers* version.) The key lists the appropriate codes for each exercise, with the codes for the principal diagnosis and principal procedure sequenced first. Explanatory comments discuss why certain codes are appropriate while others are not and why some conditions listed in the case summaries are not coded at all. They also indicate how principal diagnosis and procedure codes were designated and which symptoms are inherent to certain conditions and so are not coded separately.

In day-to-day practice, many hospitals have opted through their internal coding policies not to collect data on noninvasive diagnostic services performed in the inpatient setting, such as X-rays and electrocardiograms (EKGs). To provide answers that are as complete as possible, however, codes for these minor diagnostic services have been included in the answer key.

For outpatient encounters, *ICD-9-CM* procedure codes are typically not reported when a claim is submitted. According to the Health Insurance Portability and Accountability Act (HIPAA) Standards for Electronic Transactions (published in the *Federal Register,* vol. 65, no. 160, p. 50325, August 17, 2000), "The use of *ICD-9-CM* procedure codes is restricted to the reporting of inpatient procedures by hospitals." However, a hospital may choose to collect *ICD-9-CM* procedure codes for internal or non–claim-related purposes. In addition, hospitals may report procedure codes for outpatient services for specific payers under contractual agreements or as required by their state data reporting requirements. For these reasons, *ICD-9-CM* procedure codes have been included in outpatient case scenarios in this appendix. Sequencing of the procedure code(s) is discretionary.

The codes and comments in the answer key reflect the latest *ICD-9-CM Official Guidelines for Coding and Reporting* (effective October 1, 2010). At press time, a revised set of guidelines was expected to be available for October 1, 2011. Please visit www.ahacentraloffice.org for guideline revisions. Specific guidelines are referenced in parentheses by section and guideline number.

Symptoms, Signs, and Ill-Defined Conditions

B1

1. **Inpatient admission:** The patient, an elderly man, was admitted through the emergency department for severe urinary retention. In the emergency department, it was also determined that his hypertension was accelerated (210/105). He had been hospitalized three months earlier for identical problems, and he said he had not taken any of his medications since the last hospitalization. The urinary retention was relieved by placement of a Foley catheter. Medications were started, and the hypertension improved rapidly. The patient was evaluated for the extent of benign prostatic hypertrophy. Transurethral resection of the prostate was recommended, but it was refused by the patient.

   Discharge diagnoses: (1) Malignant hypertension, (2) acute urinary retention secondary to benign hypertrophy of the prostate, (3) noncompliance with treatment program.

   Codes: ______________________________

2. **Inpatient admission:** The patient was admitted for recurrent epistaxis that did not respond to nasal packing in the emergency department. He was status post myocardial infarct seven weeks earlier. An EKG was performed to evaluate the status of the MI. The patient also suffered from a deviated nasal septum. Multiple attempts were made to stop the bleeding with more packing, but none were successful for more than a few hours. Therefore, the following procedures were performed: (1) anterior and posterior nasal packing, (2) ethmoidal artery ligation, (3) septoplasty. He was transfused with two units of packed cells during the operation.

   Discharge diagnoses: (1) Severe and recurrent epistaxis, (2) post myocardial infarct, (3) deviated nasal septum.

   Codes: ______________________________

3. **Inpatient admission:** The reason for the patient's admission was substernal chest pain with some arm involvement. A right and left heart catheterization and combined right and left selective coronary angiography and arteriography (Judkins technique), as well as pulmonary angiography, were performed. No coronary artery disease or pulmonary embolus was found.

   Discharge diagnosis: Chest pain without occlusive coronary artery disease.

   Codes: ______________________________

4. **Inpatient admission:** The patient, a 19-year-old man, was transferred from another hospital with intractable headache. The accompanying CT scan was normal, but clinical symptomatology was suggestive of subarachnoid hemorrhage. Lumbar puncture, cerebral arteriogram, and cerebral MRI were all normal. When the findings were discussed with the patient, he became increasingly belligerent. Although his headaches were only somewhat improved, he refused further treatment and was discharged for follow-up with his own physician.

   Discharge diagnosis: Headaches of undetermined etiology.

   Codes: ______________________________

   ____

5. **Inpatient admission:** The patient has a known diagnosis of prostatic cancer. He started having fevers approximately one week earlier. The fevers did not respond to outpatient antibiotics. Blood and urine cultures showed no growth. He was admitted for workup of the fevers with possible prostatic abscess formation. There were no obvious signs of infection or abscess on a transrectal ultrasound of the prostate. A radioisotope bone scan of the body revealed no skeletal metastases. The antibiotic therapy was changed, and he was given an IV push. He improved and was discharged.

   Discharge diagnoses: (1) Fever of unknown origin, (2) cancer of the prostate.

   Codes: ______________________________

   ____

6. **Inpatient admission:** The patient, a 2-year-old infant, had an acute onset of fever and some shaking chills at home. He was thought to have experienced a febrile seizure and was admitted for workup and treatment. There was some infiltrate in the right lung per chest X-ray. All laboratory work was within normal limits. He was observed during his stay. No problems were noticed, and he remained afebrile after the first day. He was discharged for office follow-up.

   Discharge diagnosis: Rule out febrile seizure.

   Codes: ______________________________

   ____

7. **Inpatient admission:** The patient was admitted through the emergency department with possible acute cholecystitis. She had severe abdominal pain and a markedly elevated white count. A gallbladder ultrasound, cholecystogram, and intravenous pyelogram were all normal. The next day her pain was almost gone, and the white blood count dropped to nearly normal. It was not felt worthwhile to continue the workup.

   Discharge diagnoses: (1) Abdominal pain, (2) leukocytosis.

   Codes: ______________________________

   ____

8. **Inpatient admission:** The patient, an obese male, was admitted with generalized abdominal pain suggestive of early appendicitis, although he had a normal white count and normal differential. An intravenous pyelogram and X-ray of the lower gastrointestinal tract with barium enema were negative. All laboratory studies were normal. He improved while in the hospital without a definite cause for his pain ever being identified. He was placed on a low-fat, 1,500-calorie diet prior to discharge.

   Discharge diagnoses: (1) Abdominal pain of undetermined origin, generalized (2) obesity.

   Codes: ____

   ____

9. **Inpatient admission:** This patient with type 2 diabetes was admitted for evaluation of elevated liver function tests. An abdominal ultrasound showed cholelithiasis. The hepatitis profile was negative. Her sugars stayed within the low normal range throughout hospitalization. At discharge, the physician was unable to determine whether the abnormal liver functions were due to diabetes mellitus or cholelithiasis.

   Discharge diagnosis: Abnormal liver function secondary to either diabetes mellitus or cholelithiasis.

   Codes: ____

   ____

10. **Inpatient admission:** The patient, a woman with type 1 diabetes, was admitted because of increased swelling of the right foot that was determined to be an abscess. *Staphylococcus aureus* grew from the abscess. She is now scheduled to undergo an incision and drainage of the foot abscess. Her course in the hospital otherwise was essentially unremarkable. The foot gradually improved with antibiotic therapy, hyperbaric oxygen therapy, and daily whirlpool therapy.

    Discharge diagnoses: (1) Abscess right foot, (2) type 1 diabetes mellitus.

    Codes: ____

    ____

11. **Inpatient admission:** The child was admitted with a fever and lethargy. The admitting diagnosis was "rule out sepsis." When admitted, he was responsive but lethargic. The physical examination was within normal limits except for the left ear drum, which was reddened. He was placed on intravenous antibiotics after the full septic workup was complete. Improvement was evident by the next day, when he was alert, active, and started on feedings. He became afebrile and was discharged on oral antibiotics for otitis media, with sepsis ruled out.

    Discharge diagnoses: (1) Fever, (2) otitis media.

    Codes: ____

    ____

12. **Inpatient admission:** The patient, a 10-month-old male, presented with acute stridor and respiratory distress. His mother felt that he had possibly choked on a peach. Nothing was seen on chest X-ray. A rigid bronchoscopy ruled out foreign body, but the findings were consistent with croup. He was discharged on medication to follow up with his pediatrician in one week.

    Discharge diagnosis: Croup.

    Codes: ____________________

    ____

Infectious and Parasitic Diseases

B2

1. **Inpatient admission:** This HIV-positive patient was admitted with skin lesions on the chest and back. Biopsies were taken, and the pathologic diagnosis was Kaposi's sarcoma. Leukoplakia of the lips and splenomegaly were also noted on physical examination.

   Discharge diagnoses: (1) HIV infection, (2) Kaposi's sarcoma, back and chest, (3) leukoplakia, (4) splenomegaly.

   Codes: ____

   ____

2. **Inpatient admission:** The patient underwent an outpatient laparoscopic-assisted cholecystectomy for cholecystitis and was admitted the next day because of a flare-up of chronic hepatitis C. The chronic hepatitis C was secondary to intravenous drug use. With medication, the chronic hepatitis C was controlled, and the woman was discharged.

   Discharge diagnoses: (1) Chronic hepatitis C, (2) IV drug dependence.

   Codes: ____

   ____

3. **Inpatient admission:** An elderly male patient with a history of benign hypertension became extremely febrile the day before admission. On admission he was extremely lethargic with a possible septic urinary tract infection. He was pan cultured and started on IV antibiotics and fluids. Pseudomonas showed in the urine culture. The next day, his mind was quite clear and the fever defervesced from an initial 104.6 to 99.0 degrees. However, he had gross hematuria. As the IV fluids were decreased, he resumed his usual hypertensive state. By the third hospital day, the urine had cleared and he was discharged on oral antibiotics, with septicemia ruled out.

   Discharge diagnoses: (1) Urosepsis due to Pseudomonas, (2) gross hematuria, (3) benign essential hypertension.

   Codes: ____

   ____

4. **Inpatient admission:** The patient, with arteriosclerotic coronary heart disease and type 2 diabetes mellitus, came in with symptoms that were felt to represent sepsis. She was placed on antibiotics, and the symptoms improved. ST- and T-wave changes were evident on an EKG. The patient's glucose showed marked elevation, thought to be secondary to the sepsis. The blood sugars were brought under control with insulin adjustment and an appropriate diet.

   Discharge diagnoses: (1) Arteriosclerotic coronary heart disease, (2) uncontrolled type 2 diabetes mellitus, (3) questionable sepsis.

   Codes: ____________________

5. **Outpatient clinic visit:** The HIV-infected patient was suffering from an acute lymphadenitis due to his HIV infection. The glands in the neck area were most affected. Antibiotics were prescribed, but the patient refused antiretroviral treatment at this time. He was of the opinion that his religion would eventually make antiretroviral medication unnecessary. Another problem was his narcotic dependency. He was encouraged to continue participation in both the narcotic addiction and HIV support groups.

   Diagnoses: (1) Acute lymphadenitis secondary to HIV infection, (2) narcotic dependence, (3) refusal of medication due to religious reasons.

   Codes: ____________________

6. **Inpatient admission:** The patient was admitted for the removal of a tympanostomy tube due to tympanic membrane perforation with otitis media. The physician documents that the patient had previously undergone placement of ventilation tubes for recurrent otitis media and that the otitis media has been determined to be due to MRSA. Documentation also indicates MRSA colonization on the nasal swab.

   Diagnoses: (1) Otitis media, (2) perforated tympanic membrane, (3) MRSA infection, (4) MRSA colonization, (5) removal of ventilation tubes.

   Codes: ____________________

Endocrine, Metabolic and Nutritional Diseases and Immune-System Disorders

B3

1. **Inpatient admission:** The patient was admitted for an evaluation of her adrenal malfunction. She had a 4-year history of hypertension and hypokalemia with evidence of primary aldosteronism. A CT scan of the abdomen also suggested a left adrenal mass. She was discharged and was to return for a left adrenalectomy the following week.

   Discharge diagnoses: (1) Probable adrenal mass, left, (2) hypertension and hypokalemia probably due to primary aldosteronism.

   Codes: ______________________________

   ____

2. **Inpatient admission:** The patient was admitted for severe malnutrition and hematuria secondary to amyotrophic lateral sclerosis. Because of her malnutrition, a nasogastric feeding tube was placed under fluoroscopy. During her stay, the hematuria cleared spontaneously, and she was discharged to home care.

   Discharge diagnoses: (1) Malnutrition, (2) hematuria secondary to amyotrophic lateral sclerosis.

   Codes: ______________________________

   ____

3. **Inpatient admission:** The patient fell at home and was unable to get up. Neighbors found him several hours later, and he does not remember any circumstances surrounding the event. Blood sugars were monitored, and a diagnosis of diabetes mellitus was given. It became rapidly evident to the attending physician that, even with dietary restriction, the patient would need insulin therapy to lower it. Insulin therapy was started. The only other positive finding was beta-*Streptococcus* group B, which grew from the urine culture and was treated with oral antibiotics.

   Discharge diagnoses: (1) New onset type 2 diabetes mellitus, out of control, (2) urinary tract infection with beta-*Streptococcus*.

   Codes: ______________________________

   ____

4. **Outpatient clinic visit:** The patient with type 2 diabetes was status post-cadaveric kidney and pancreatic transplants. He was being seen for follow-up of a recent below-the-knee amputation and a nonhealing gangrenous ulcer on his left foot secondary to diabetic peripheral vascular disease. The operative site was healing very nicely, and there was no evidence of infection.

   Diagnoses: (1) Status post left foot amputation, (2) status post kidney and pancreas transplants, (3) diabetes mellitus.

   Codes: ____________________

5. **Inpatient admission:** The patient, an elderly woman with type 2 diabetes mellitus, developed hypoglycemia at the nursing home and was symptomatic. In the emergency department, her decreased blood sugar was treated with intravenous D5W. A urinary tract infection was also present and was treated with antibiotics. The urine culture grew *Klebsiella,* sensitive to Cipro. She then developed mild congestive heart failure, probably secondary to the hypoglycemic reaction, which responded to oxygen and rest. Her Diabeta was restarted at a lower dosage.

   Discharge diagnoses: (1) Congestive heart failure secondary to hypoglycemia, (2) type 2 diabetes mellitus, (3) urinary tract infection.

   Codes: ____________________

6. **Inpatient admission:** The patient, a woman with a diagnosis of cell-mediated immune deficiency with thrombocytopenia and eczema, was admitted for incision and drainage of a foot abscess. Her course in the hospital was essentially unremarkable. The foot gradually improved with hyperbaric oxygen therapy and daily whirlpool therapy. *Staphylococcus aureus* grew from the abscess.

   Discharge diagnoses: (1) Abscess right foot, (2) cell-immune deficiency with thrombocytopenia and eczema.

   Codes: ____________________

7. **Inpatient admission:** The patient, a young male with type 1 diabetes, was brought in a comatose state to the emergency department by friends. He was admitted in ketoacidosis and was resuscitated with saline hydration via insulin drip. After regaining consciousness, he reported that the morning of admission he was experiencing nausea and vomiting and decided not to take his insulin because he had not eaten. He was treated with intravenous hydration and insulin drip. By the following morning, his laboratory work was within normal range and he was experiencing no symptoms.

   Discharge diagnoses: (1) Diabetic ketoacidosis, (2) juvenile-type diabetic.

   Codes: ____________________

8. **Inpatient admission:** A patient with type 1 diabetes mellitus seriously out of control was admitted for regulation of insulin dosage. He has a recently abscessed right molar, which was determined, in part, to be responsible for the elevation of his blood sugar. The patient had been in the hospital four weeks earlier for an acute myocardial infarction of the inferoposterior wall, and an EKG was performed to check its current status.

   Discharge diagnoses: (1) Myocardial infarction, (2) abscessed tooth, (3) uncontrolled type 1 diabetes mellitus.

   Codes: ____

   ____

Mental Disorders

B4

1. **Outpatient clinic visit:** The patient was seen to evaluate his progress in dealing with his long-standing alcoholism. In addition, he had a passive-aggressive personality and was dependent on Librium. He was actively participating in Alcoholics Anonymous and stated he would continue to participate. He apparently now had some alcoholic liver damage and was referred to an internist for further investigation of that condition.

   Diagnoses: (1) Alcohol dependence, episodic, (2) passive-aggressive personality disorder, (3) drug dependence, Librium, (4) alcoholic liver damage.

   Codes: ____

   ____

2. **Outpatient clinic visit:** The patient, a young female, was brought in by her sister. She has had periods of severe depression for many years. Her medications consisted of Lithium, Synthroid, and Midrin for depression, hypothyroidism, and migraine headaches, respectively. During the past week, however, she became manic, running all her credit cards to the limit, getting inappropriately involved in a woman's suicide attempt, quitting her job, and trying to take over the pulpit at church. On the day of the clinic visit, she threatened to strike the telephone repairman with a lead pipe. She was to be admitted for Lithium adjustment.

   Diagnoses: (1) Bipolar disorder, manic type, (2) hypothyroidism, (3) migraine headaches.

   Codes: ____

   ____

3. **Inpatient admission:** The woman was brought in by police for observation of a suspected mental condition. They found her roaming the streets, and she seemed disoriented and confused. She was treated for scabies, body lice, and cellulitis of the right foot. Her mental status cleared rapidly. The only psychiatric disorder found was moderate mental retardation.

   Discharge diagnoses: (1) Moderate mental retardation, (2) scabies, (3) body lice, (4) cellulitis, right foot.

   Codes: ____

   ____

4. **Outpatient clinic visit:** This 59-year-old male patient with a history of paranoid schizophrenia has had constant conflict with his family and coworkers for years. His wife reported that he was in danger of losing his job because he threatened his supervisor's life. He recently spent the night in jail after an altercation with a neighbor. Medication was prescribed, and he was to return for follow-up in one week.

   Diagnosis: Schizophrenia, paranoid type, chronic with acute exacerbation.

   Codes: ______________________________

   ____

5. **Outpatient clinic visit:** An 18-year-old teenage patient was described by his mother as having recent periods of depression, in addition to self-mutilation, temper tantrums, and stealing from neighbors. He has a history of type 1 diabetes and sometimes refuses to take his insulin or follow his diet. His speech, best described as "baby talk," had also become worse during the previous two months. A prescription was to be written for his depression.

   Diagnoses: (1) Depression, (2) borderline personality disorder, (3) delayed speech development, (4) juvenile-type diabetes mellitus, (5) self-mutilation.

   Codes: ______________________________

   ____

6. **Inpatient admission:** The patient was brought to the emergency department by the police and admitted to psychiatric service. Police requested an evaluation after the man was disorderly and aggressive at the scene of an automobile accident in which he was involved. He is admitted with a diagnosis of probable dementia.

   Diagnoses: diagnoses: (1) Organic brain syndrome with presenile dementia, (2) probably Alzheimer's disease with dementia.

   Codes: ______________________________

   ____

7. **Inpatient admission:** A patient with a four-year history of anorexia nervosa was seen in the physician's office because of significant weight loss over the past three months, going from 82 pounds down to 53 pounds. She was admitted to increase body weight and to be given nutritional counseling because of her severe malnutrition.

   Diagnoses: (1) Anorexia nervosa, severe malnutrition

   Codes: ______________________________

   ____

8. **Inpatient admission:** The patient was admitted with possible pyelonephritis. Her complaints were bilateral flank pain and chills. An intravenous pyelogram was normal. Within two days of admission, the character of her pain changed somewhat in that it became primarily epigastric and in the right upper quadrant. The physician documented in the progress notes that significant features of conversion hysteria were present and accounted for the patient's symptoms. On the third hospital day, the patient's IV was discontinued, liver function tests were rechecked, and antibiotics were discontinued. Later that day, she left abruptly, saying she would not return.

   Discharge diagnoses: (1) Abdominal pain, (2) conversion disorder.

   Codes: ______________________________

9. **Psychiatry clinic visit:** The HIV-infected patient, who had a long history of cocaine addiction, started using cocaine again. Several months ago he was admitted for treatment of pneumocystis carinii pneumonia. Presently, severe depression brought him in to the clinic. He and the physician had an extensive discussion about returning to Narcotics Anonymous and also beginning the AIDS support group. A prescription for Prozac was given for his depression.

   Diagnoses: (1) Depression, (2) cocaine addiction, (3) HIV infection.

   Codes: ______________________________

Diseases of the Blood and Blood-Forming Organs

B5

1. **Inpatient admission:** The patient had a congenital aplastic anemia that had been responding well to treatment. She was admitted for observation following a full-mouth extraction for multiple dental caries with pulp exposure and pyorrhea in outpatient surgery. She had only minimal bleeding following surgery. However, it was believed to be necessary to admit her for monitoring. She was discharged the next day with her blood counts remaining at acceptable levels.

   Discharge diagnosis: Aplastic anemia.

   Codes: ______________________________

   ____

2. **Inpatient admission:** The patient, who had sickle cell anemia, presented to the emergency department with a 2- to 3-day history of severe right leg and arm pain. After she was admitted, parenteral narcotics were administered and the pain improved. The blood counts returned to a stable level within 24 hours.

   Discharge diagnosis: Sickle cell pain crisis.

   Codes: ______________________________

   ____

3. **Inpatient admission:** The patient was an elderly woman visiting her physician with complaints of heart palpitations. A routine office evaluation revealed significant anemia. She had not been eating well because she had recently moved from her home of 30 years. After admission to the hospital, a cardiology consultation suggested that the palpitations were probably due to the anemia. During the gastrointestinal workup, mild gastritis was revealed. After a transfusion of two units of packed cells, her hemoglobin returned to normal range. The patient was discharged to the nursing home with a prescription for Zantac to control her gastritis.

   Discharge diagnoses: (1) Nutritional anemia, (2) gastritis.

   Codes: ______________________________

   ____

4. **Inpatient admission:** The patient had locally advanced bladder cancer. He had excellent response to chemotherapy treatments administered prior to admission, with only a small amount of residual disease noted in the bladder. He was admitted with increasing nausea, anorexia, fevers, and constipation. His calcium levels were found to be elevated. A slight decrease was achieved with IV hydration, and it continued to fall with IV pamidronate. Because he was asymptomatic, further workup was not indicated, and he was discharged.

   Discharge diagnoses: (1) Hypercalcemia, (2) bladder cancer.

   Codes: ____

   ____

5. **Inpatient admission:** The patient was diagnosed with Coombs' negative hemolytic anemia 4 years previously. Since diagnosis, her disease course waxed and waned. During some bouts, she had 15 to 20 blood transfusions of 2 to 3 units of packed red blood cells each. This admission was for splenectomy. The plan also called for removing a kidney stone, which was identified on her preadmission workup. Both surgeries, total splenectomy and pyelolithotomy, were performed without incident. Her postoperative recovery also went smoothly.

   Discharge diagnoses: (1) Hypersplenism secondary to hemolytic anemia, (2) stone, left kidney.

   Codes: ____

   ____

6. **Inpatient admission:** A 50-year-old man receiving Coumadin therapy is admitted with hematemesis secondary to acute gastritis. A prolonged prothrombin time is reported, secondary to the anticoagulant effect of the Coumadin therapy.

   Discharge diagnoses: (1) Acute gastritis.

   Codes: ____

   ____

7. **Outpatient visit:** A patient with breast cancer is given chemotherapy in the outpatient setting. A week later the patient presents with chemotherapy related anemia, which requires a procrit injection.

   Diagnoses: (1) Breast cancer, (2) anemia.

   Codes: ____

   ____

Diseases of the Nervous System and Sense Organs

B6

1. **Ophthalmology clinic visit:** The HIV-infected patient complained of difficulty focusing while reading. His examination revealed no evidence of retinopathy. He did have early presbyopia for which "drugstore readers" were recommended.

   Diagnoses: Presbyopia and HIV infection.

   Codes: ______________________________

   ____

2. **Inpatient admission:** The patient was under medical management for long-standing, moderate stage primary open-angle glaucoma, as well as age-related bilateral macular degeneration. Three days previously, an abnormally high intraocular pressure developed. The patient was treated successfully as an outpatient. The next day, another pressure spike occurred and the patient was admitted for further management. He was treated medically for two days, and both the pressure and visual acuity improved sufficiently for discharge.

   Discharge diagnoses: (1) Acute primary open-angle glaucoma, moderate stage, (2) macular degeneration, (3) intraocular pressure.

   Codes: ______________________________

   ____

3. **Inpatient admission:** The patient previously suffered anterior dislocation of the left hip, which was reduced; however, this was followed by numbness and weakness in the left femoral nerve distribution. Evaluation indicated that she would benefit from surgery. A left femoral nerve external neurolysis was carried out successfully.

   Discharge diagnosis: Mononeuritis, femoral nerve.

   Codes: ______________________________

   ____

4. **Inpatient admission:** The patient, a teenager, was admitted for evaluation and control of his intractable seizures. On days one, three, and four, seizures were recorded per video EEG. His video EEGs were consistent with epileptiform discharges of right temporal lobe origin. Dilantin and phenobarbital dosages were adjusted, and the patient was discharged in satisfactory condition.

   Discharge diagnosis: Partial complex epilepsy localized to the right temporal lobe.

   Codes: ______________________________

   ____

5. **Ambulatory surgery:** The patient was brought in for surgical intervention of a mature, symptomatic cataract in the left eye and high intraocular pressures despite medical therapy. Procedures performed were an external trabeculectomy and phacoemulsification with posterior chamber intraocular lens placement.

   Discharge diagnoses: (1) Advanced primary open-angle glaucoma, severe stage, (2) cataract, left eye.

   Codes: ______________________________

   ____

6. **Inpatient admission:** The patient, an 18-month-old infant, was admitted with right orbital cellulitis. He was started on antibiotics and seemed to be improving. However, the day after admission a slight exophthalmos was noticed. A CT scan showed increasing edema of the eye orbit with filling of ethmoid sinuses. The medications were changed. A right endoscopic complete ethmoidectomy was performed because the ethmoid sinuses were filled on the right side. The infant improved and was discharged in satisfactory condition.

   Discharge diagnoses: (1) Right orbital abscess, (2) exophthalmos, (3) orbital edema, (4) acute ethmoidal sinusitis.

   Codes: ______________________________

   ____

7. **Inpatient admission:** The elderly male patient, a type 1 diabetic, developed weakness of the right arm and leg. The weakness worsened and he finally fell and was unable to move. When brought to the emergency department, he was able to speak but unable to use his right arm or leg. A consultation after admission suggested either an acute left-sided cortical stroke or TIA. Diagnostic radiographic procedures were scheduled; however, he completely recovered and was able to ambulate with no neurological deficits within 24 hours of admission. He was discharged and will have a workup performed for cerebrovascular insufficiency as an outpatient.

   Discharge diagnoses: (1) Probable transient ischemic attack, (2) diabetes mellitus.

   Codes: ______________________________

   ____

8. **Inpatient admission:** The patient, an elderly female nursing home resident, was under medical management for chronic senile dementia and postherpetic neuralgia. She also had a history of renal cyst. She was admitted with nausea and emesis which cleared after several days. She also complained of increasing nasal sinus congestion and headache. She was treated with antibiotics and decongestants for sinusitis. Recovery was uneventful, and she was returned to the nursing home for further care.

   Discharge diagnoses: (1) Postherpetic neuralgia, (2) sinusitis, (3) chronic senile dementia.

   Codes: ____

   ____

9. **Neurology clinic visit:** The patient, a 23-month-old child, has congenital mitral stenosis. After a cardiac catheterization 6 months earlier, she had a large middle cerebral artery infarct. She is being followed for left arm paralysis, residuals of the cerebrovascular accident. She appeared to be making progress with weekly physical therapy. The muscle strength, tone, and stretch reflexes were improved, but she had some decrease in light touch sensation.

   Diagnoses: (1) Paralysis, left arm, (2) congenital mitral stenosis.

   Codes: ____

   ____

10. **Inpatient admission:** An 80-year-old patient with metastatic bone cancer from lung was admitted as an inpatient due to significant abdominal and hip pain. She was admitted for pain control with radiotherapy. The patient's pain was well controlled with radiotherapy, and the patient was discharged in good condition.

    Discharge diagnoses: (1) Metastatic bone cancer, (2) abdominal and hip pain, (3) radiotherapy.

    Codes: ____

    ____

Diseases of the Respiratory System

B7

1. **Inpatient admission:** The patient, a 51-year-old woman with acute respiratory failure secondary to an acute exacerbation of chronic obstructive bronchitis, was brought to the emergency department by emergency medical services. In the emergency department, she was intubated and placed on mechanical ventilation. On admission, it soon became apparent that she had suffered severe, irreversible hypoxic encephalopathy. On day 5, she was weaned from the ventilator and extubated; however, significant neurological function was never regained. In accordance with her advance directive, tube feedings were discontinued. She became febrile and dyspneic. Antibiotics were started to provide comfort and relief of her pneumonia. She expired on day 13.

   Discharge diagnoses: (1) Acute respiratory failure secondary to chronic obstructive bronchitis, (2) pneumonia, (3) encephalopathy.

   Codes: ______________________________

   ____

2. **Inpatient admission:** The elderly patient came to the emergency department complaining of shortness of breath and nausea. It was apparent that she was suffering from congestive heart failure and respiratory failure, and she was admitted for immediate treatment of the acute respiratory failure. Before any diagnostic work could be accomplished, she died.

   Discharge diagnoses: (1) Acute respiratory failure, (2) congestive heart failure.

   Codes: ______________________________

   ____

3. **Inpatient admission:** The patient was admitted after visiting the emergency department for shortness of breath, chest pain, hypoxia, and a white cell count of 32,600. The patient had a history of chronic obstructive pulmonary disease. Interstitial infiltrate at the right middle and lower lobes of the lung was seen on chest X-ray. Sputum culture grew Streptococcal pneumoniae. He tolerated the antibiotics, and the symptoms improved significantly.

   Discharge diagnoses: (1) Right lower lobe pneumonia due to Streptoccal pneumoniae, (2) acute exacerbation of chronic obstructive lung disease.

   Codes: ______________________________

   ____

4. **Inpatient admission:** The patient, a young man, came to the emergency department after being ill for at least three weeks. He initially had a head cold and sore throat, followed by fever, difficulty swallowing, chills, and brown sputum. Because of severe lymphadenopathy in the neck, as well as other stated symptomatology, he was admitted. A huge left tonsil confluent with the surrounding tissues and covered with exudate was also noted on the physical examination. This appeared to represent a peritonsillar abscess and severe tonsillitis. A throat culture showed a heavy growth of beta-*Streptococcus* group C. Intravenous antibiotics were given with success, and he was discharged.

   Discharge diagnoses: (1) Severe tonsillitis with beta-*Streptococcus* group C, (2) probable left peritonsillar abscess.

   Codes: ______________________________

5. **Inpatient admission:** The type 1 diabetic patient was admitted with a right heel ulcer that had failed a number of outpatient therapies. Also, because the patient was hypoxic on admission with a history of COPD, he was given supplemental oxygen. He coughed up sputum, and a chest X-ray showed a mild increase in interstitial markings. Consequently, he was treated for acute bronchitis with erythromycin, which provided good results. Gradually, the foot ulcer healed. But the hypoxia persisted, and an increase in his oxygen therapy was helpful. He was to be followed by home health services.

   Discharge diagnoses: (1) Diabetic foot ulcer, right heel, (2) acute bronchitis, (3) diabetes mellitus, (4) history of COPD.

   Codes: ______________________________

6. **Inpatient admission:** The patient, a man in extremely poor health due to chronic obstructive pulmonary disease and chronic alcoholism, was admitted for severe shortness of breath, a PO2 of 42, abdominal pain, and what appeared to be impending delirium tremens. He was placed on Ventolin and Solu-Medrol. Librium was also given to prevent delirium tremens. A colonoscopy was done because of a past history of polyps, with no recurrence found. It was felt that the patient had mild colitis. On discharge, he was no longer dyspneic at rest. He was to start taking Zantac for colitis and to continue Solu-Medrol.

   Discharge diagnoses: (1) Chronic lung disease with acute bronchospasm, (2) impending delirium tremens, (3) alcohol dependence, (4) colitis, (5) history of colon polyps.

   Codes: ______________________________

7. **Inpatient admission:** The patient, a 13-month-old infant, had two apnea alarms within the past few hours. After the last discharge from this hospital for apnea, an apnea alarm was ordered. Because of continued alarms, the mother returned the infant to the hospital. The infant was placed on a cardiac apnea monitor with event record mode and on continuous bioximeter. There were no alarms noted during hospitalization. She was discharged home with an apnea monitor with event record mode in place.

   Discharge diagnosis: Rule out apnea.

   Codes: ______________________________

   ____

8. **Inpatient admission:** The patient, a 3-year-old male toddler, was admitted for evaluation of fever, cough, and persistent pulmonary interstitial infiltrate. A chest tube was placed for drainage. The child's condition was consistent with pneumonia and aspiration of mucus. On the day after chest tube insertion, the chest X-ray was clear, and the chest tube was pulled. He was placed on aspiration precautions and antibiotics. He was to be followed up as an outpatient.

   Discharge diagnosis: Pneumonia secondary to aspiration of mucus.

   Codes: ______________________________

   ____

9. **Inpatient admission:** The patient, a 5-year-old male, was seen as an outpatient for asthmatic bronchitis without improvement. He was admitted for further treatment and on physical examination was also found to have suppurative otitis media. After being placed in a croup tent and treated with antibiotics, his temperature gradually returned to normal, and he improved.

   Discharge diagnoses: (1) Asthmatic bronchitis, (2) acute suppurative otitis media.

   Codes: ______________________________

   ____

10. **Inpatient admission:** The patient was admitted after she developed progressive dyspnea and wheezing, intractable to ambulatory care management. The provisional admitting diagnosis was status asthmaticus. Her history showed that she was status post mastectomy for breast cancer and still had some residual lymphedema in the left upper extremity. In the hospital, she received low-flow oxygen, antibiotics, bronchodilators, and IV steroids, as well as her usual medications for hypertension and hypothyroidism.

    Discharge diagnoses: (1) Status asthmaticus, (2) hypertension, (3) hypothyroidism, (4) status post breast cancer with lymphedema.

    Codes: ______________________________

    ____

11. **Inpatient admission:** The patient, an elderly woman, was known to have congestive heart failure, arteriosclerotic heart disease, and chronic obstructive pulmonary disease. She developed increased shortness of breath, dyspnea on exertion, temperature elevation, and productive cough. These problems were felt to represent congestive failure and pneumococcal pneumonia. She was admitted for cultures, IV antibiotics, pulmonary toilet, and increased diuresis. Her initial chest film showed congestive heart failure and bilateral lung infiltrates. In discussing this case with the pulmonary consultant, the physician felt it was wise to transfer the patient to another hospital so that both pulmonary and cardiology staff could work together with this patient.

    Discharge diagnoses: (1) Arteriosclerotic heart disease, (2) congestive heart failure, (3) pneumococcal pneumonia, (4) chronic obstructive lung disease.

    Codes: ____________________

    ____

12. **Inpatient admission:** The patient, a 94-year-old man with known arteriosclerotic coronary artery disease and exacerbation of end-stage chronic obstructive bronchitis, was admitted with a provisional diagnosis of acute respiratory failure. He was treated with IV antibiotics and pulmonary toilet. Although his long-term prognosis was poor, he was improved upon discharge.

    Discharge diagnoses: (1) Arteriosclerotic coronary artery disease, (2) end-stage chronic obstructive bronchitis, (3) angina, (4) acute respiratory failure.

    Codes: ____________________

    ____

13. **Inpatient admission:** The patient, a 5-week-old infant, had been discharged from the hospital several weeks before without any complaints. She was now admitted through the emergency department, where she was found to be febrile and lethargic and to have a weak cry. Dry mucous membranes were also noted. The admission diagnosis was "rule out sepsis." She was given STAT respiratory treatment and IV fluids, followed by intravenous antibiotics. Urine cultures grew enterococcus. Blood cultures were negative. Sputum cultures grew Mycoplasma pneumoniae. She gradually improved and was weaned from the oxygen tent. She improved rapidly and was discharged 3 days following admission.

    Discharge diagnoses: (1) Right lower lobe pneumonitis due to Mycoplasma pneumoniae, (2) fever, (3) dehydration, (4) urinary tract infection.

    Codes: ____________________

    ____

14. **Inpatient admission:** The patient, an 18-month-old male, was admitted with reactive airway disease versus viral pneumonia. His symptoms of wheezing and congestion had become increasingly worse over the past few days. He had been healthy since birth except for congenital pulmonary stenosis, which was evaluated during this admission. He was placed on medications and oxygen. Blood culture and viral panel were negative. He was to be followed by the pulmonary clinic.

    Discharge diagnoses: (1) Acute exacerbation of reactive airway disease, (2) mild pulmonary stenosis.

    Codes: ______________________________

    ____

Diseases of the Digestive System

B8

1. **Inpatient admission:** This patient underwent a gastric bypass 3 weeks earlier and is now admitted because of continuous vomiting and severe dehydration. Radiologic and laboratory studies provided no indication of problems with the previous surgery or other abnormalities. Rehydration was accomplished. On close observation, it appeared that she was eating too fast and too much.

   Discharge diagnoses: (1) Exogenous morbid obesity with recent gastric bypass, (2) dehydration due to continuous vomiting.

   Codes: ______________________________

   ____

2. **Inpatient admission:** The elderly nursing home patient was admitted with aspiration pneumonitis. She was unable to swallow or eat as a result of a stroke, which occurred 2 months earlier. She was experiencing progressive aspiration and weight loss. It was hoped that anchoring a feeding tube would alleviate the situation. Therefore, an esophagogastroduodenoscopy for percutaneous endoscopic gastrostomy with placement of a feeding tube was performed.

   Discharge diagnoses: (1) Difficulty swallowing secondary to cerebrovascular accident, (2) impending malnutrition, (3) aspiration pneumonia.

   Codes: ______________________________

   ____

3. **Inpatient admission:** The patient was transferred in from facility A, where he experienced 12 hours of hematemesis requiring transfusions with 14 units of red blood cells and 6 units of fresh-frozen plasma. Upon admission to facility B, a gastroscopic examination revealed a 4-by-2-centimeter gastric ulcer with visible vessels. He was taken to the operating room, where a hemigastrectomy with Billroth I anastomosis of the duodenum was performed.

   Discharge diagnosis: Bleeding gastric ulcer.

   Codes: ______________________________

   ____

4. **Inpatient admission:** The patient's admitting diagnosis was acute pancreatitis. Findings on a CT scan performed prior to admission were consistent with acute and chronic pancreatitis and pancreatic duct calculi. Multiple stones were noted on endoscopic retrograde cholangiopancreatography (ERCP); one of them was big enough to occlude the pancreatic duct. There was generalized stenosis of the pancreatic duct. During ERCP, a stent was put in place to bypass the area of obstruction. The patient improved immediately. Extracorporeal shock wave lithotripsy (ESWL) then achieved partial fragmentation of the stone. Because of abdominal pain, a second ESWL was required and, again, achieved only partial fragmentation of the stone. The patient underwent another ERCP, which identified multiple stones and pancreatic duct stenosis with occlusion of the previously placed stent. During the procedure, the obstructed area was passed through, but there was still a 2-millimeter area of pancreatic duct stenosis. A balloon was inserted to dilate this area endoscopically. There were multiple stones, and the occluded stent was removed and replaced with a new one beyond the area of obstruction.

   Discharge diagnoses: (1) Acute and chronic pancreatitis, (2) pancreatic calculi.

   Procedures: (1) ERCP with pancreatic duct stent insertion, (2) ESWL (pancreatic stone) on two separate occasions, (3) ERCP with prolonged dilation of pancreatic duct and removal of occluded stent and replacement with a new single-pigtail stent.

   Codes: ____________________

   ____

5. **Outpatient visit:** The patient came in complaining of severe abdominal pain. Abdominal scout film showed scoliosis and some degenerative changes in the lumbar spine. However, an abdominal CT scan showed extensive diverticulosis involving the descending and sigmoid portions of the colon, with obvious evidence of diverticulitis.

   Diagnosis: Diverticulitis.

   Codes: ____________________

   ____

6. **Inpatient admission:** The 86-year-old woman was admitted with rectal bleeding. She was also massively dehydrated, with a BUN of 124. On admission, some IV fluids and transfusions of whole blood were administered because her initial hemoglobin was 9.5 and later dropped to 7.4. On colonoscopy, multiple ulcers of the rectum, consistent with ulcerative proctitis, were found and biopsies were taken. The tissue was negative for neoplastic disease, and the patient was started on steroid enemas, with resolution.

   Discharge diagnoses: (1) Rectal bleeding, (2) dehydration, (3) acute blood loss anemia, (4) ulcerative proctitis.

   Codes: ____________________

   ____

7. **Inpatient admission:** The patient, a 20-year-old female, presented to the emergency department complaining of bilateral arm and shoulder pain, "yellow eyes," and dark urine. The emergency department evaluation revealed profound jaundice with markedly elevated liver-function tests. The patient was admitted for further evaluation. A gallbladder ultrasound was negative for gallstones. Hematological studies indicated sickle cell disease, which could be contributing to the jaundice. Because the liver function gradually improved, it was felt that she could be further evaluated as an outpatient for probable acute hepatitis B.

   Discharge diagnosis: Jaundice secondary to sickle cell disease versus acute hepatitis B.

   Codes: ____________________

   ____

8. **Inpatient admission:** The patient was admitted for evaluation of guaiac-positive stools. All sites that could be visualized on esophagogastroduodenoscopy were within normal limits except a small area in the gastric fundus, which was biopsied. A colonoscope was then inserted to 35 centimeters and diverticula were noted. Because of narrowing resulting from edema due to diverticulitis, it was not possible to pass the scope farther. The tissue report showed benign acute and chronic gastritis but no ulcer.

   Discharge diagnoses: (1) Occult blood in stool of undetermined origin, (2) diverticulosis with diverticulitis of colon, (3) acute and chronic gastritis.

   Codes: ____________________

   ____

9. **Inpatient admission (episode 1):** Because the patient had a 20-year history of severe ulcerative colitis, he was admitted for surgical intervention. A total abdominal colectomy with ileostomy was performed. The postoperative recovery was without incident.

   Discharge diagnosis: Ulcerative colitis.

   Codes: ____________________

   ____

   Inpatient admission (episode 2): Three months after surgery, the patient was again admitted for an endorectal pull-through with formation of a loop ileostomy. This procedure was further treatment for the long-standing and intractable ulcerative colitis.

   Discharge diagnosis: Ulcerative colitis.

   Codes: ____________________

   ____

   Inpatient admission (episode 3): Four months following the second surgery, the patient was admitted for ileostomy closure. He had no symptoms of ulcerative colitis. The postoperative course was uneventful.

   Discharge diagnosis: Status post ileostomy closure.

   Codes: ____________________

   ____

10. **Inpatient admission:** The patient experienced rectal pain for several months due to a 2.5-centimeter mass on the anterior rectal wall. A transanal excision of the mass was performed, and a frozen section revealed an inflammatory lesion without evidence of malignancy. The final pathology report showed the tissue to represent a granuloma of the rectum.

    Discharge diagnosis: Rectal granuloma.

    Codes: ______________________________

    ____

11. **Inpatient admission:** The patient, a woman with chronic right upper-quadrant abdominal pain, was admitted for possible pancreatitis after two episodes of vomiting clear fluid. Pain medications were started and a nasogastric tube was placed, with intermittent suction. The NG tube was pulled three days after admission, and the patient was discharged to follow up with her physician one week later.

    Discharge diagnosis: Pancreatitis.

    Principal procedure: Insertion, nasogastric tube.

    Codes: ______________________________

    ____

12. **Inpatient admission:** The patient, a man with a long history of alcohol dependence with resultant alcoholic cirrhosis, was admitted with red, coffee-ground hematemesis. An emergent esophagogastroduodenoscopy revealed bleeding esophageal varices, which were sclerosed. No problems were identified in the stomach or duodenum. He was transfused with multiple units of packed cells and fresh-frozen plasma, and yet the bleeding continued. He was returned to surgery, and an esophagoscopy was performed to sclerose the bleeding esophageal varices a second time.

    Discharge diagnoses: (1) Upper gastrointestinal bleed, (2) esophageal varices, (3) Laennec's cirrhosis, (4) alcohol dependence in remission.

    Principal procedure: Control of esophageal bleeding.

    Codes: ______________________________

    ____

13. **Inpatient admission:** The patient, a 35-year-old male, was admitted for possible gastritis. He had undergone a cadaveric renal transplant for end-stage renal disease secondary to focal membranous glomerulonephritis two years earlier. On endoscopic examination of the lower esophagus and stomach, patchy erythemas were seen in the stomach and biopsies were taken. A linear erosion was noted at the gastroesphageal junction. The impression was mild reflux esophagitis and mild antral duodenitis. As his dietary intake improved, his physical condition improved as well.

    Discharge diagnoses: (1) Reflux esophagitis, (2) duodenitis.

    Codes: ______________________________

    ____

14. **Inpatient admission:** The patient recently underwent an ultrasound that showed a filling defect in the gallbladder, thought to probably represent a cholelithiasis. It was felt that the woman's symptoms were suggestive of cholecystitis and that cholecystectomy was in order. On admission, a laparoscopic cholecystectomy with lysis of adhesions around the gallbladder was carried out, followed by an intraoperative cholangiogram. A proctologist was consulted due to the presence of persistent rectal pain. A mild anal fissure was identified on flexible sigmoidoscopy. A needle biopsy of the liver was performed due to an abnormal liver function study times 3. The pathology report indicated that the liver tissue was normal.

    Discharge diagnoses: (1) Chronic cholecystitis and cholelithiasis, (2) anal fissure, (3) abnormal liver function studies.

    Codes: ____________________

    ____

15. **Inpatient admission:** The male patient came in complaining of headache, nausea, vomiting, and chest pain. The impression on admission was possible coronary artery disease and probable viral gastroenteritis. Only a small, sliding hiatal hernia was found on air contrast upper GI. No ischemia was found on cardiac evaluation. The patient gradually improved and was discharged two days later to follow up with his family physician in one week for gastroenteritis and further evaluation of the hiatal hernia.

    Discharge diagnoses: (1) Probable viral gastroenteritis, (2) hiatal hernia.

    Codes: ____________________

    ____

16. **Inpatient admission:** The patient, a woman with a long history of Crohn's disease, was admitted with abdominal cramping, vomiting, and diarrhea of sudden onset. Admitting orders included all current medications for Crohn's disease. Her amylase was 241 on admission, and she had a slightly elevated white blood count. Both returned to normal with treatment for pancreatitis, and the abdominal problems also slowed down. She was to be followed as an outpatient.

    Discharge diagnoses: (1) Pancreatitis, (2) Crohn's disease.

    Codes: ____________________

    ____

17. **Physician office visit (episode 1):** The patient, an elderly woman, came in for severe epigastric abdominal pain. She had some nausea but no vomiting. She was referred for further studies to rule out cholecystitis and localized ulcer perforation.

    Diagnosis: Possible cholecystitis and/or perforated gastric ulcer.

    Codes: ______________________________

    ____

    Inpatient admission (episode 2): An ultrasound was negative and an upper GI failed to yield a diagnosis. Therefore, the patient was admitted for further evaluation because of the continued severity of her abdominal pain. An exploratory laparotomy was performed and immediately revealed a perforated appendix lying in a subhepatic space with abscess. An appendectomy was performed. The abscess cleared postoperatively with administration of high doses of intravenous antibiotics.

    Discharge diagnosis: Appendicitis with perforation and subhepatic abscess.

    Codes: ______________________________

    ____

18. **Inpatient admission:** The patient was admitted with vague abdominal pain, and a workup was carried out. All laboratory findings were within normal limits, except for a slightly elevated white blood count. The patient requested transfer to another hospital close to his home for further evaluation. The patient was transferred with a working diagnosis of diverticulitis versus colon tumor.

    Discharge diagnosis: Diverticulitis versus tumor of colon.

    Codes: ______________________________

    ____

19. **Inpatient admission:** The patient, an 8-year-old boy, was brought in from school because of persistent vomiting with accompanying abdominal pain. He was admitted for observation and monitoring of vital signs. Laboratory work was within normal limits, vital signs remained stable, the abdomen remained flat and soft, and there was no muscle guarding or tenderness. He was discharged the following day in an improved condition.

    Discharge diagnoses: (1) Persistent vomiting, (2) abdominal pain.

    Codes: ______________________________

    ____

20. **Inpatient admission:** The patient had a history of recurrent infections in the perianal area. He was seen 2 days earlier in the physician's office for a perianal abscess and anal fistula. The prescribed medication and enemas did not alleviate the situation, and so he was admitted for surgical intervention. In surgery, an anal fistulotomy was performed with drainage of the perianal abscess. The patient responded to further treatments of antibiotics and diet and was to be followed in the office.

    Discharge diagnoses: (1) Perianal abscess, (2) anal fistula.

    Codes: ______________________________

    ____

21. **Inpatient admission:** The patient is status post heart transplantation 6 months earlier. Since then, he had been admitted numerous times for fever and diarrhea, presumably due to cytomegalovirus. On this occasion, he was admitted for further evaluation of fever and diarrhea. Stool and blood cultures were negative. A single, shallow erosion in the right colon was viewed and biopsied on colonoscopy. Internal, bleeding hemorrhoids were also visualized. The pathology report showed moderate, nonspecific, chronic colitis with no diagnostic evidence of cytomegalovirus. Chronic colitis was determined to be the cause of the patient's symptomatology. The patient was also followed by endocrinology for his diabetes, and no changes were recommended in his medication. His diarrhea improved, medication and diet were prescribed for bleeding hemorrhoids and chronic colitis, and he was released.

    Discharge diagnoses: (1) Chronic colitis, (2) bleeding internal hemorrhoids, (3) diabetes mellitus, type 1, (4) status post heart transplant.

    Codes: ______________________________

    ____

22. **Inpatient admission:** The patient had undergone cardiac transplantation about 3 years earlier. On this occasion, he came to the emergency department with a 3-day history of right lower quadrant pain. The white blood count was elevated, and a small bowel X-ray examination showed some dilated small bowel loops but no free air. He was admitted, and an abdominal ultrasound showed a mass measuring about 5 by 5 by 4 centimeters, which was presumed to be an appendiceal cyst. He underwent an ultrasound-directed right lower quadrant aspiration; only a few drops of material were collected for diagnostic examination. Blood cultures were sterile, leukocytosis improved, and he remained afebrile with gradually decreasing pain. He was discharged on antibiotics and was to return in a few weeks for an interval appendectomy.

    Discharge diagnoses: (1) Probable appendiceal cyst, (2) status post cardiac transplantation.

    Procedure performed: Ultrasound-directed aspiration of appendiceal mass.

    Codes: ______________________________

    ____

Diseases of the Genitourinary System

B9

1. **Inpatient admission:** The patient, an 83-year-old woman, came in through the emergency department complaining of fever, confusion, and lethargy. Urine and blood cultures were positive for E. coli. Sepsis and urinary tract infection were diagnosed. The patient slowly responded to IV antibiotic therapy, but she began to experience vomiting episodes with abdominal pain. These episodes were probably related to her hiatal hernia with reflux esophagitis. The vomiting seemed to improve with medications and diet. The patient was discharged one week following admission on oral Keflex and Zantac to follow up as an outpatient.

   Discharge diagnoses: (1) Urinary tract infection, (2) gram-negative sepsis secondary to diagnosis 1, (3) hiatal hernia with reflux esophagitis.

   Codes: ____

   ____

2. **Inpatient admission:** The patient was admitted for abnormal uterine bleeding. An ultrasound performed prior to admission suggested a possible bicornuate uterus. Because of her morbid obesity, a hysteroscopy with dilation and curettage was performed. Findings indicated a single cavity without any septum, polyps, or submucous fibroids. The patient was seen by the dietitian and discharged on a 1,500-calorie diet to reduce her weight.

   Discharge diagnoses: (1) Morbid obesity, (2) abnormal uterine bleeding, (3) BMI 46.2.

   Codes: ____

   ____

3. **Inpatient admission:** The patient, a young man with hypertensive heart disease and nephrosclerosis, was admitted for placement of an arteriovenous fistula in his left wrist to prepare for hemodialysis. Hemodialysis was needed owing to chronic kidney disease.

   Discharge diagnoses: (1) Hypertensive heart disease and nephrosclerosis, (2) chronic kidney disease.

   Codes: ____

   ____

4. **Inpatient admission:** The patient had a history of frequent episodes of severe chronic interstitial cystitis. Despite previous treatment, she has had no resolution of her symptoms. She was admitted for and received a cystectomy and ileoureterostomy.

   Discharge diagnosis: Severe, chronic interstitial cystitis.

   Codes: ____

5. **Inpatient admission:** The patient had chronic kidney disease secondary to malignant hypertension and was status post insertion of a left arteriovenous fistula 6 months earlier. He presented with exacerbation of his renal condition and was admitted for evaluation and hemodialysis. His medications were adjusted, and he received hemodialysis twice during this admission. His condition stabilized, and he was discharged in an improved state.

   Discharge diagnoses: (1) End-stage renal disease associated with malignant hypertension, (2) exacerbation of kidney disease.

   Codes: ____

6. **Inpatient admission:** The patient had end-stage renal disease and chronic kidney disease secondary to malignant hypertension. He was admitted for a cadaveric renal transplant. He underwent renal hemodialysis prior to transplant. The left donor kidney was placed in the right iliac fossa. Postoperative recovery was uneventful.

   Discharge diagnosis: End-stage renal disease resulting from malignant hypertension.

   Codes: ____

7. **Inpatient admission:** The patient became ill the day before admission with nausea, vomiting, dysuria, and hematuria. Initial laboratory work included a urinalysis report of RBCs too numerous to count, and a repeat urinalysis the following day reported the same results. On cystoscopy and retrograde pyelogram, hydronephrosis of the right kidney and possibly some secondary hydronephrosis with obstruction of the ureteropelvic junction were seen. Spontaneously, the hematuria and other symptoms cleared. The patient was to be referred to a urologist for follow-up.

   Discharge diagnosis: Hematuria and hydronephrosis possibly due to idiopathic ureteropelvic obstruction.

   Codes: ____

8. **Physician office visit (episode 1):** The patient, an elderly man, has had carcinoma of the bladder with numerous recurrences. On his annual bladder checkup, an obstructive prostate with urinary retention was present, but no evidence of a recurrence of the carcinoma was found. He was to be admitted for further evaluation of the prostatic obstruction.

   Diagnoses: (1) Prostatic obstruction with urinary retention, (2) no evidence of recurrence of bladder carcinoma.

   Codes: ______________________________

   Inpatient admission (episode 2): On cystoscopy, a mild urethral stricture and an obstructive prostate with urinary retention were found. The urethra was dilated, and the patient underwent transurethral prostatectomy without complication. The pathology report showed benign prostatic hypertrophy.

   Discharge diagnoses: (1) Urethral stricture secondary to benign prostatic hypertrophy, (2) urinary retention, (3) history of carcinoma of the bladder.

   Codes: ______________________________

9. **Inpatient admission:** The nursing home patient had frequent urinary tract infections and numerous courses of antibiotics. The most recent urine culture grew a Pseudomonas aeruginosa, resistant to all oral antibiotics. The patient was therefore admitted for IV antibiotic therapy. Significant in her history was the placement about 3 years earlier of a cardiac pacemaker for conduction defects. It was working satisfactorily during her hospitalization. Because the cultures continued to show Pseudomonas after IV antibiotics were given, a cystoscopy was performed. The patient still had a bladder infection with erythema of the bladder wall. Urine cultures were obtained at that time, and the report was a high colony count of Pseudomonas that was then susceptible to oral antibiotics. She was discharged on oral Cipro.

   Discharge diagnoses: (1) Bladder infection, resistant to oral antibiotics, (2) pacemaker in situ.

   Codes: ______________________________

10. **Inpatient admission:** The patient was experiencing heavy, abnormal uterine bleeding and abdominal pain. On vaginal examination, there was bright red blood in the vagina and the left adnexa was enlarged. The woman was admitted and taken to surgery, where an exploratory laparotomy revealed a left follicular ovarian cyst. While the surgeon was examining the left ovary, the cyst spontaneously ruptured. An ovarian cystectomy was performed without complication. The postoperative course was uneventful, and the patient was discharged.

    Discharge diagnosis: Ruptured left follicular ovarian cyst.

    Codes: ______________________________

11. **Inpatient admission:** The male patient was admitted with severe colic secondary to a left ureteral calculus. A cystoscopy was performed, and a stone extracted. On retrograde pyelography, no stone was seen in the ureter or kidney. However, the pathology report indicated that only a small fragment of the stone was retrieved. Postoperatively, the patient did well at first but then began having severe colic again. He was returned to surgery for another cystoscopy. The remainder of the stone was located in the distal left ureter and extracted. The postoperative course was uncomplicated.

    Discharge diagnosis: Left ureteral calculus.

    Codes: ______________________________

    ____

12. **Inpatient admission:** The patient, a woman with insignificant past medical and surgical history, was the sister of a patient with end-stage renal disease secondary to hypertension. She was to be a living related kidney donor for her brother. She was prepared for surgery the day of admission, but due to her brother's active hepatitis C infection, the surgery was canceled.

    Discharge diagnoses: (1) Kidney donor, (2) procedure canceled.

    Codes: ______________________________

    ____

13. **Inpatient admission:** The patient was previously evaluated and found to be a suitable kidney donor for his 8-year-old son. A total unilateral left donor nephrectomy was performed without complication, and the patient was discharged.

    Discharge diagnosis: Donor nephrectomy.

    Codes: ______________________________

    ____

14. **Inpatient admission:** The patient, a young woman, was admitted with a 2-day history of dysuria, frequency, and urgency, with onset of severe flank pain on the evening prior to admission. A laboratory workup confirmed pyelonephritis, and she was immediately started on intravenous medications and fluid. Urine cultures grew Enterobacter aerogenes, which was sensitive to several antibiotics.

    Discharge diagnoses: (1) Pyelonephritis, (2) abdominal and flank pain.

    Codes: ______________________________

    ____

15. **Inpatient admission:** The patient was admitted for a hysterectomy. Prior to admission, a diagnostic workup showed extensive endometriosis involving the uterus, ovaries, and fallopian tubes. Because the patient had asthma, she was seen by the pulmonary consult service and cleared for surgery. A total abdominal hysterectomy and a bilateral salpingo-oophorectomy were performed without complication. Postoperatively, the patient did well and was discharged.

    Discharge diagnoses: (1) Endometriosis of uterus, ovaries, and fallopian tubes, (2) asthma.

    Codes: ______________________________

    ____

16. **Inpatient admission:** The patient, a young woman, was admitted for treatment of a persistent, symptomatic right adnexal mass. The cystic mass was about 5 centimeters and presumed to be ovarian in origin. An exploratory laparotomy was performed, with right ovarian cystectomy. Pathologic findings confirmed a follicular cyst. The patient's postoperative course was unremarkable, and she was discharged.

    Discharge diagnosis: Follicular cyst, right ovary.

    Codes: ______________________________

    ____

Diseases of the Skin and Subcutaneous Tissue

B10

1. **Inpatient admission:** A female patient was admitted for treatment of an open wound of the scalp with cellulitis of the scalp and left ear. The wound was the result of a cut from a tree limb 2 days before admission. The accident occurred while she was on vacation mountain climbing. Excisional debridement of the area was carried out in the operating room, and the patient was treated with antibiotics during her 2-day stay. She was discharged on oral antibiotics in an improved condition.

   Discharge diagnosis: Cellulitis of scalp and ear secondary to laceration.

   Codes: ______________________________

2. **Inpatient admission:** The patient, a young man with spina bifida of the lumbar region, was admitted for excision of a sacral pressure ulcer. He had a ventriculoperitoneal shunt in place on the right side for hydrocephalus. The lesion was successfully fulgurated without complication.

   Discharge diagnoses: (1) Stage III pressure ulcer, sacrum, (2) lumbar spina bifida, (3) status post placement of a ventriculoperitoneal shunt for hydrocephalus.

   Codes: ______________________________

3. **Inpatient admission:** The female patient was admitted from the nursing home with a large stage III sacral pressure ulcer, which was treated with excisional debridement and a flap-graft closure. She had chronic lymphocytic leukemia, which required transfusions with three units of whole blood. She was stabilized and returned to the nursing home.

   Discharge diagnoses: (1) Pressure ulcer, sacrum, (2) chronic lymphocytic leukemia.

   Codes: ______________________________

4. **Inpatient admission:** The patient, an elderly man, had an acute onset of swelling, erythema, and tenderness in the left anterior neck. He was admitted for evaluation and IV antibiotic therapy, with provisional diagnoses of thyroiditis and cellulitis. A CT scan showed a large, mixed density, soft-tissue mass in the left lower neck compatible with cellulitis. The mass appeared to involve the soft tissue of the neck but not the thyroid gland. Abscess formation could not be excluded, although none was directly visualized. His symptomatology responded well to antibiotic therapy.

   Discharge diagnoses: (1) Cellulitis, (2) possible abscess.

   Codes: ______________________________

   ____

5. **Inpatient admission:** The patient's admitting diagnoses were abdominal pain and ventral wall hernia. The woman presented for hernia repair. At the time of surgery, she was noted to have numerous midabdominal adhesions, mostly in the area of a previous midline scar. Sharp lysis of the extensive adhesions was undertaken, and then the hernia was repaired. Postoperatively, the patient did very well.

   Discharge diagnoses: (1) Ventral wall hernia, (2) abdominal adhesions.

   Codes: ______________________________

   ____

6. **Inpatient admission:** The patient was admitted for intravenous antibiotic treatment of cellulitis of the left leg secondary to a minor scratch. By the third hospital day, the erythema was much improved. During the entire hospitalization, the patient, a known drug abuser, exhibited considerable drug-seeking behavior and requested narcotics, especially IV morphine. All narcotics were discontinued on the third hospital day, and he exhibited no withdrawal symptoms. He was discharged for follow-up in the physician's office.

   Discharge diagnoses: (1) Cellulitis, left leg, (2) drug abuse, (3) scratch, left leg.

   Codes: ______________________________

   ____

Diseases of the Musculoskeletal System and Connective Tissue

B11

1. **Inpatient admission:** The patient had experienced increasingly severe pain in his left arm, left shoulder, and neck for 2 months. A magnetic resonance imaging performed prior to admission showed evidence of a C6-C7 disk herniation. His only other health problem was benign hypertension, controlled with medications. He was admitted for a cervical laminotomy and diskectomy, which was performed by oblique, muscle-splitting incision. His postoperative course was unremarkable, and he was discharged after 2 days.

   Discharge diagnoses: (1) Cervical disk herniation, (2) benign essential hypertension.

   Codes: ______________________________

   ____

2. **Outpatient encounter (episode 1):** The patient's complaints were neck pain that radiated into both arms, hand pain with numbness and clumsiness, and electric shock-type pains down her body when she bent down. A magnetic resonance imaging scan showed marked spinal stenosis at C3-C4 and C5-C6. She was to be admitted for repair of the spinal stenosis.

   Diagnosis: Spinal stenosis.

   Codes: ______________________________

   ____

   Inpatient admission (episode 2): The patient was admitted for repair of spinal stenosis. A laminectomy with fusion of C3-C4 and C5-C6 was carried out with a graft of bone excised from the iliac crest.

   Discharge diagnosis: Severe cervical spine stenosis.

   Codes: ______________________________

   ____

3. **Inpatient admission:** The patient, a 33-year-old woman, had a history of low back pain. She recently developed intractable left sciatic pain and paresthesia. Lumbar magnetic resonance imaging procedures, performed prior to admission, showed progressive lumbosacral disk herniation on the left. She was also receiving medications for gastric ulcers and asthma, and these were continued during the hospital stay. A lumbosacral microdiskectomy was performed for a protruded lumbosacral disk herniation, which also had a subligamentous extrusion. The patient recovered with resolution of symptoms and was discharged to follow up with her physician in 1 week.

   Discharge diagnoses: (1) Lumbosacral disk extrusion, (2) gastric ulcers, (3) asthma.

   Codes: ____________________

   ____

4. **Inpatient admission:** The teenage patient had complained of left hip pain for the past 3 weeks. The pain started after a fall that occurred while he was playing basketball with friends. X-rays revealed a grade I, slipped capital femoral epiphysis of the left hip. The hip was pinned percutaneously, and the postoperative course was uneventful.

   Discharge diagnosis: Slipped femoral epiphysis, left hip.

   Codes: ____________________

   ____

5. **Inpatient admission:** An emergency open repair of a right rotator cuff tear was performed on this patient after she was crushed between a sliding patio door and its frame at her apartment. Exploration revealed a torn right rotator cuff and ruptured deltoid muscle, right shoulder. Repair of the rotator cuff tendon and repair of the ruptured deltoid muscle were accomplished. The patient recovered and was discharged to follow-up in 1 week.

   Discharge diagnoses: (1) Tear, right rotator cuff, (2) rupture, deltoid muscle.

   Codes: ____________________

   ____

6. **Inpatient admission:** The patient, status post cadaveric renal and pancreas transplants with type 2 diabetes and diabetic peripheral angiopathy, had a nonhealing ulcer on his left heel that had been debrided 3 weeks earlier. He came to the emergency department complaining of a 3-day history of left foot pain, fever, and foul-smelling discharge from the ulcer. He was admitted, and a left below-the-knee amputation was performed.

   Discharge diagnosis: Diabetic gangrene of the left foot.

   Codes: ____________________

   ____

7. **Inpatient admission:** The patient, an elderly man with chest pain, was admitted to rule out acute myocardial infarct. Two weeks prior to admission, he had a respiratory infection that caused excessive coughing. On evaluation, there was no evidence of cardiac problems, and his chest pain was believed to be due to costochondritis secondary to excessive coughing.

   Discharge diagnosis: Costochondritis.

   Codes: ______________________________

   ____

8. **Inpatient admission:** The patient, an elderly woman, had severe pain in her left hip. The pain started after a hip fracture 5 years ago, when she was injured in an automobile accident. Her admission diagnoses were traumatic arthritis and ankylosis of the left hip. She also had a pacemaker and was a type 2 diabetic. A total hip replacement was performed without complication.

   Discharge diagnoses: (1) Arthritis and ankylosis secondary to old hip fracture, left side, (2) diabetes mellitus.

   Codes: ______________________________

   ____

9. **Inpatient admission:** The patient's right knee had bothered him for several months. He had a very painful chronic, indolent, septic prepatellar bursa. It was treated with many antibiotics, cleared up, and then recurred. He was currently admitted for surgical intervention. The site was incised and drained, and then the prepatellar bursa was partially excised. He was referred for physical therapy on discharge.

   Discharge diagnosis: Septic joint, right knee.

   Codes: ______________________________

   ____

10. **Inpatient admission:** For 2 weeks, the patient had been complaining of left sciatica and had failed outpatient management with bed rest and pain medications. A magnetic resonance imaging procedure confirmed L5-S1 disk herniation on the left. She was hospitalized at complete bed rest with conservative management and pain medications as needed. She received good pain relief with IV pain medication and an epidural steroid injection. She was discharged for physical therapy follow-up.

    Discharge diagnosis: Intractable pain secondary to herniation of the L5-S1 disk, with S1 radiculopathy.

    Codes: ______________________________

    ____

11. **Inpatient admission:** The patient was admitted with traumatic arthritis and ankylosis of the left hip due to an old fracture of the femoral neck. She was in good health except for suffering mild arteriosclerotic cardiovascular disease. X-rays were taken before surgery to evaluate the extent of this problem, but it was felt that it did not contradict the planned surgery. Both the femoral head and acetabulum of the left hip were replaced with a prosthesis. The surgery and postoperative course were without complication. She was transferred to a nursing home for rehabilitation therapy.

    Discharge diagnoses: (1) Arthritis and ankylosis, left hip, (2) arteriosclerotic cardiovascular disease.

    Codes: ______________________________

    ____

12. **Inpatient admission:** The patient, a 12-year-old female, had a history of scoliosis secondary to neurofibromatosis, type 1, and had been treated with a brace for 4 years. She was now admitted for surgical repair of the progressive scoliosis. A posterior lumbar fusion of T2-L3 using Izola instrumentation and iliac crest bone grafting was performed. Her postoperative course was uneventful.

    Discharge diagnosis: Scoliosis secondary to neurofibromatosis, type 1.

    Codes: ______________________________

    ____

Complications of Pregnancy, Childbirth, and the Puerperium

B12

1. **Inpatient admission (episode 1):** The patient was admitted with pregnancy at term. A repeat low transverse cervical cesarean section and elective bilateral tubal ligation were performed. A 3,300-gram male infant was delivered, with Apgar scores of 9 and 10. The postoperative course was unremarkable. On day 3, the mother's staples were removed, and both the mother and baby were discharged.

   Discharge diagnoses: (1) Term pregnancy delivered, (2) elective tubal ligation.

   Codes: ____

   ____

   Inpatient admission (episode 2): The patient underwent a cesarean section 7 days earlier. She had an infection in the operative wound at the time she was admitted through the emergency department with a temperature of 101 degrees and minimal drainage of the incision. IV Kefzol was started, but she continued to spike up to a temperature of 101.8 degrees. The antibiotic therapy was changed, and the patient defervesced.

   Discharge diagnosis: Postoperative wound infection.

   Codes: ____

   ____

2. **Inpatient admission:** This type 1, controlled diabetic was status post a low transverse cesarean delivery 12 days earlier. The day before admission, she noticed a large amount of bloody discharge from her wound. She was taken to the operating room, where the wound was opened and a very large hematoma was evacuated. The wound was drained and packed. Three days later, a secondary wound closure was accomplished.

   Discharge diagnoses: (1) Postpartum hematoma, (2) diabetes mellitus.

   Codes: ____

   ____

3. **Inpatient admission:** The patient, a 39-year-old female, gravida II, para 1, was admitted in active labor at 39 weeks gestation. She was dilated to 5 centimeters approximately 6 hours following admission. Pitocin augmentation was started, and she progressed to complete dilation. Outlet forceps were used. There was no episiotomy, but there was a second-degree perineal laceration that was repaired with 3-0 Dexon. A male infant was delivered weighing 2,835 grams, with Apgar scores of 9 and 9. The patient had indicated before delivery that she desired a sterilization procedure. Following delivery, a laparoscopic bilateral tubal ligation was accomplished.

   Discharge diagnoses: (1) Delivery at term, (2) perineal laceration, (3) elective sterilization.

   Codes: ______________________________

   ____

4. **Inpatient admission:** The admitting diagnoses were intrauterine pregnancy at 29 weeks gestation, premature labor, premature rupture of membranes times 12 days, and chorioamnionitis. An ultrasound performed after admission revealed a vertex right occiput transverse presentation with a compound presentation of a fetal hand. Because the patient had a temperature of 101.4 degrees, chorioamnionitis was presumed and antibiotics were started. On a subsequent examination, the fetus was found to be presenting vertex left occiput anterior with right hand compound presentation. The right hand was reducible and was pushed up toward the left side of the fetal body. Following a prolonged second stage, a female infant with Apgar scores of 5 and 7 was delivered spontaneously over an intact perineum. A prior cesarean section scar was found to be intact with no lacerations.

   Discharge diagnoses: (1) Delayed delivery following premature rupture of membrane, (2) chorioamnionitis.

   Codes: ______________________________

   ____

5. **Inpatient admission:** The patient, gravida II, para 1, was admitted in labor with a 27-week pregnancy. The fetus was in a complete breech position. Labor ceased within a few hours after admission, but the patient was observed closely because she has a history of recurrent pregnancy loss. By the second day, contractions recurred and she rapidly progressed to complete dilation. Because the breech presentation resulted in obstruction, an emergent low cervical cesarean section was performed, and a living female infant was delivered. The postpartum course was uneventful, and the patient was discharged in good condition on the third postoperative day.

   Discharge diagnosis: Preterm delivery, complicated by breech presentation.

   Codes: ______________________________

   ____

6. **Inpatient admission:** The patient, gravida II, para 1, was admitted at 37 weeks gestation with spontaneous rupture of membranes and contractions every 2 to 3 minutes. She has a history of congenital heart block with pacemaker. Because there was no descent, even though she was pushing adequately, three attempts at forceps delivery were made with no success due to cephalopelvic disproportion. Because of failure of forceps due to bony pelvic obstruction, a primary low transverse cesarean section was performed. A live single male was delivered. The postoperative course was uneventful.

   Discharge diagnosis: Cesarean delivery of term, live infant complicated by bony pelvis and cephalopelvic disproportion and failed forceps.

   Codes: ______________________________

7. **Inpatient admission:** The patient was admitted with an intrauterine pregnancy at 34 weeks gestation in preterm labor. The labor ceased spontaneously, and she was discharged the next day.

   Discharge diagnosis: Preterm labor.

   Codes: ______________________________

8. **Inpatient admission:** The patient, at 10 weeks gestation, was admitted for severe dehydration due to hyperemesis gravidarum. The patient had glaucoma (which the physician stated did not affect the pregnancy), and treatment with eye drops was continued during the patient's stay. She responded well to IV fluid hydration and antiemetics.

   Discharge diagnoses: (1) Hyperemesis gravidarum with dehydration, (2) glaucoma.

   Codes: ______________________________

9. **Inpatient admission:** The patient was admitted for Prostin termination of a nonviable fetus at 27 + 4 weeks gestation. An ultrasound prior to admission showed severe renal malformations in the dysmorphic fetus. A pediatric urology consult concluded fetal nonviability secondary to severe oligohydramnios, enlarged kidneys, and a nonoperable candidate. A Prostin capsule was placed intravaginally, and the patient went on to have a spontaneous vaginal delivery of a stillborn female. The patient was discharged the following day.

   Discharge diagnoses: (1) Spontaneous vaginal delivery of stillborn fetus with multiple congenital anomalies (pregnancy), (2) oligohydramnios.

   Codes: ______________________________

10. **Inpatient admission:** When admitted, this woman, with triplet gestation at 28 weeks, was thought to have had premature rupture of membranes. She was placed on magnesium sulfate after rupture of membranes was ruled out. Tocolysis and fetal monitoring were continued until she underwent spontaneous rupture of membranes 1 week later. She had a rapid vaginal delivery with liveborn triplets.

    Discharge diagnosis: Spontaneous vaginal delivery of liveborn triplets.

    Codes: ____________________

11. **Inpatient admission:** The patient, a 44-year-old female, gravida I, para 0, was admitted for termination of an intrauterine fetal death. On a routine office visit 10 days earlier, no fetal heart beat was heard. An ultrasound confirmed the suspicions. She chose termination of the pregnancy rather than waiting for a spontaneous delivery and was admitted. A Pitocin drip was started and some contractions were obtained, but the cervix remained unchanged. Dilation and curettage were performed, and she was discharged that afternoon.

    Discharge diagnoses: (1) Intrauterine fetal death at 23 weeks, (2) macerated fetus, (3) elderly primigravida.

    Codes: ____________________

12. **Inpatient admission:** The 14-year-old patient (gravida I, para 0) is pregnant at 25 weeks gestation. She was admitted with abdominal pain and questionable labor. On examination she was 50 percent effaced and tight fingertip dilated with cephalic presentation. She was placed on Terbutaline. By the next day, she was without discomfort or contractions and was discharged.

    Discharge diagnosis: Premature labor.

    Codes: ____________________

13. **Inpatient admission:** The young patient, gravida I, para 0, ab 0, at 43 weeks gestation presented in labor and labored poorly but succeeded in reaching 4 to 5 centimeters. Augmentation with Pitocin resulted in no change after several hours, and a primary lower uterine segmental cesarean section was performed due to prolonged labor, with birth of a 7-pound, 5-ounce female. The patient did well after delivery and was discharged on the fourth postoperative day.

    Discharge diagnoses: (1) Postterm, intrauterine pregnancy, (2) failure to progress in labor, with prolonged first stage.

    Codes: ____________________

14. **Inpatient admission:** The patient, gravida II, para 1, was admitted at approximately 25 + 2 weeks gestation with a history of contractions for 24 hours. She was contracting every 4 to 6 minutes. An ultrasound showed an intrauterine fetal death of one triplet but that the other two were progressing normally. The contractions stopped and then started again. The patient was given magnesium sulfate for tocolysis but contracted through the magnesium and was placed on Ritadrine. Because she then developed a fever with suspected chorioamnionitis and was in active labor, a primary low cervical cesarean section delivered three male infants, two liveborn and one fetal death. Postoperatively, she did well on antibiotics.

    Discharge diagnoses: (1) Cesarean delivery of monochorionic triplets (two liveborn and one fetal death) at 25 + 2 weeks, (2) chorioamnionitis.

    Codes: ____________________

    ____

15. **Inpatient admission:** The young patient in the 37th week of gestation was admitted with contractions occurring every few minutes. The cervix was 25 percent effaced with a 6-centimeter dilation. Although she had undergone a previous cesarean section, she wished a trial at vaginal delivery. The membranes were artificially ruptured. Six hours later, she was tried on Pitocin augmentation and within the hour progressed to complete dilation and began pushing. She pushed for 2 hours and was unable to progress satisfactorily. She was taken to surgery, where a repeat low cervical cesarean section was performed for cephalopelvic disproportion. A healthy, single, liveborn female was delivered. The postpartum course was uneventful.

    Discharge diagnoses: (1) Intrauterine pregnancy at term, (2) previous cesarean section, (3) cephalopelvic disproportion, (4) borderline midpelvis.

    Codes: ____________________

    ____

16. **Inpatient admission:** The patient, in her 25th week of gestation, was transferred from another hospital with complete effacement, complete dilation, and occasional contractions. She underwent a primary low cervical cesarean section with preoperative diagnoses of preterm labor, advanced cervical dilation, and failed magnesium tocolysis. Findings included a live male infant weighing 880 grams. The patient's postoperative course was uneventful except for the occurrence of hemorrhoids, which were successfully treated with suppositories.

    Discharge diagnoses: (1) Intrauterine pregnancy at 25 weeks, (2) preterm labor.

    Codes: ____________________

    ____

17. **Inpatient admission:** The patient was admitted in active labor at term. She had multiple sclerosis, which had been exacerbated by the pregnancy. In the delivery room, she spontaneously delivered a liveborn female infant over a midline episiotomy without complication.

    Discharge diagnoses: (1) Spontaneous vaginal delivery of term, live female, (2) multiple sclerosis.

    Codes: ____________________

18. **Physician office visit:** The patient came in for her routine prenatal checkup. She was a primigravida in her first trimester. There were no complications.

    Diagnosis: Normal pregnancy at 10 weeks.

    Codes: ____________________

19. **Physician office visit:** The patient came in for her routine prenatal checkup. She was a primigravida in her first trimester. She complained of hyperemesis. She had been unable to eat and had lost 2 pounds since her last visit. Medication was prescribed. She was to call the office immediately if there was no improvement within 12 hours. She was to be rescheduled for a return visit the following week.

    Diagnosis: First trimester pregnancy complicated by hyperemesis gravidarum.

    Codes: ____________________

20. **Inpatient admission:** The patient was admitted in labor with an estimated 39-week gestation. When she was approximately 7 to 8 centimeters dilated, an amniotomy was performed that revealed meconium-stained liquor. She rapidly progressed to complete cervical dilation. Fetal distress necessitated delivery. The infant's head was visible and in the occiput anterior position. Low forceps were applied, a midline episiotomy was performed, and the infant was successfully delivered. The midline episiotomy was repaired.

    Discharge diagnoses: (1) Term delivery of liveborn infant, (2) meconium-stained liquor, (3) fetal distress.

    Codes: ____________________

21. **Inpatient admission:** The patient, a young woman with estimated gestation of 29 weeks, was admitted for gestational diabetes. It was felt that close monitoring of her blood sugars was in order and the possibility of starting insulin should receive consideration. Throughout her stay, she had no problems or complications. She was maintained on an 1,800-calorie diet. Her blood sugars were borderline abnormal, and a trial at diet control was to be instituted before further consideration was given to the use of insulin.

    Discharge diagnoses: (1) Gestational diabetes, (2) intrauterine pregnancy, 29 weeks.

    Codes: ______________________________

    ____

22. **Inpatient admission:** The patient, with an estimated 36-week gestation, was admitted in labor. Her prenatal course was uncomplicated, except for mild preexisting hypertension. The labor was also uneventful, and the membranes spontaneously ruptured. A 7-pound, 3-ounce viable male was delivered. The delivery was spontaneous and vaginal, with a midline episiotomy, which extended into a third-degree laceration. The laceration was sutured. Following delivery, the mother was stable, with no apparent complications.

    Discharge diagnoses: (1) Spontaneous vaginal delivery of term male infant, (2) third-degree perineal laceration.

    Codes: ______________________________

    ____

23. **Inpatient admission:** The patient, with an estimated gestation of 39½ weeks, presented with spontaneous rupture of the membranes and irregular contractions. Her previous pregnancy was delivered by cesarean section. At first, labor failed to progress despite irregular contractions, and she was started on Pitocin. She then moved ahead with labor and pushed for approximately 45 minutes. The baby was delivered spontaneously, with the help of a midline episiotomy. A third-degree laceration was sutured and the episiotomy was closed.

    Discharge diagnoses: (1) Term pregnancy delivered of liveborn male infant, (2) previous cesarean section, (3) third-degree laceration.

    Codes: ______________________________

    ____

Abortion and Ectopic Pregnancy

B13

1. **Inpatient admission:** The patient was at 10 weeks gestation with an intrauterine pregnancy. She believed this pregnancy to be the result of a rape and did not wish to carry it to term. A complete abortion was accomplished with a dilation and curettage. There were no complications.

   Discharge diagnoses: (1) Elective abortion, (2) history of rape.

   Codes: ____________________

   ____

2. **Inpatient admission:** The patient at 12 weeks gestation wished to have the pregnancy terminated following studies showing the fetus to be anencephalic. An intrauterine saline injection produced an incomplete abortion. This was followed by a dilation and curettage.

   Discharge diagnosis: Therapeutic abortion secondary to fetal abnormality.

   Codes: ____________________

   ____

3. **Inpatient admission:** The patient was admitted following a spontaneous abortion, which she experienced earlier in the day. On examination, it appeared that the abortion was incomplete, and she was bleeding heavily. A dilation and curettage was performed.

   Discharge diagnosis: Incomplete spontaneous abortion.

   Codes: ____________________

   ____

4. **Obstetrics clinic visit:** The patient had an elective abortion performed at another facility 2 days earlier. She came in because of pelvic pain, fever, and a nonbloody discharge. She was given antibiotics.

   Diagnosis: Acute endometritis following abortion.

   Codes: ____________________

   ____

5. **Obstetrics clinic visit:** The 35-year-old patient wished to electively terminate a pregnancy because of her hyperthyroidism, which has been difficult to control. She was at 10 weeks gestation. A complete abortion resulted from the aspiration curettage.

   Diagnoses: (1) Therapeutic abortion, complete, (2) hyperthyroidism.

   Codes: ______________________________

   ____

6. **Inpatient admission:** The young patient was transferred in from another hospital, where she had been treated for a cerebrovascular accident. She was making a good recovery at the other hospital until yesterday, when she became agitated and aggressive and complained of abdominal pain without significant findings on examination. Her husband suggested the possibility of pregnancy, and an HCG assay confirmed the condition. After a series of discussions with the patient and family, it was decided to proceed with an abortion. She was admitted here for the abortion. A complete abortion was accomplished with aspiration curettage. Her mental status improved, and she was discharged.

   Discharge diagnosis: Elective abortion, complete, secondary to cerebrovascular accident.

   Codes: ______________________________

   ____

7. **Inpatient admission:** The patient, known to be in early pregnancy, was admitted with acute abdominal pain. Ultrasound revealed a tubal pregnancy. The tubal pregnancy was removed, and the patient was discharged the next day in good condition. She was to be seen in the doctor's office in 2 weeks.

   Discharge diagnosis: Ectopic pregnancy.

   Codes: ______________________________

   ____

Congenital Anomalies

B14

1. **Inpatient admission:** The 27-year-old patient was admitted for a pacemaker implant for her atrioventricular heart block, presumably congenital. A dual-chamber synchronous pacemaker was inserted and the atrioventricular transvenous leads were sewn inside her heart. She was kept on bed rest until she was stable and then discharged.

   Discharge diagnosis: Atrioventricular heart block, probably congenital in origin.

   Codes: ______________________________

2. **Inpatient admission:** The patient, an infant, was admitted for repair of bilateral undescended testes. In the operating room, he underwent bilateral orchiopexies. On the second postoperative day, a diffuse ileus was visualized on a KUB. The infant began vomiting secondary to the ileus. A nasogastric tube was placed, and he was maintained on nasogastric suction and IV hydration for the following 2 days. On postoperative day four, the tube was removed, and the patient was discharged. The postoperative ileus extended this admission by 2 days.

   Discharge diagnoses: (1) Undescended testes, (2) postoperative ileus, secondary to bilateral orchiopexies.

   Codes: ______________________________

3. **Inpatient admission:** The patient, a 6-week-old infant, was admitted for evaluation of a fever. She was placed on IV antibiotics, and blood cultures grew out coagulase-negative *Staphylococcus*. Because a murmur was noticed on physical examination, an echocardiogram was done. This revealed physiologic peripheral branch pulmonary artery stenosis and a small left-to-right atrial shunt, most likely a patent foramen ovale.

   Discharge diagnoses: (1) Coagulase-negative Staphylococcal sepsis, (2) peripheral pulmonary artery stenosis, (3) patent foramen ovale.

   Codes: ______________________________

4. **Inpatient admission:** The patient, a 2-month-old infant, was referred for evaluation of a faulty airway. The mother reported that he had had noisy breathing since birth and that it had worsened recently. Severe to moderate laryngomalacia was identified on a flexible bronchoscopy. A supraglottostomy with repair of the larynx was performed without complication during the procedure or afterward. The patient received antibiotics postoperatively and was discharged in good condition.

   Discharge diagnosis: Laryngomalacia.

   Codes: ______________________________

   ____

5. **Inpatient admission:** The patient, a 14-year-old male, had congenital honeycomb lung and type 1 diabetes. On admission, congestive heart failure was present. His breathing was labored, and lower extremity edema was evident. Recently, his oxygen requirements increased dramatically, he ran intermittent fevers, and he consumed large amounts of liquids. With diuretics, significant reduction of the pitting edema was achieved. Antidepressants were added to his medications to help his agitation and anxiety. Humidified oxygen mask, alternating percussion, and postural drainage helped his breathing. The insulin dosage and type were adjusted. He was discharged on a diabetic diet in stable condition.

   Discharge diagnoses: (1) Heart failure, (2) honeycomb lung, (3) type 1 diabetes mellitus, (4) depression.

   Codes: ______________________________

   ____

6. **Inpatient admission:** This 4-year-old patient has a diverticulum of the left ventricle. She had a pulmonary artery band 4 years ago for another congenital defect. Shortly after the surgery, she suffered a stroke and now has a residual paralysis of the right arm. She required feeding by nursing staff as the right side is dominant. Currently, she was admitted with labored breathing and shortness of breath. Her lungs showed infiltrates on chest X-ray, and sputum culture showed presence of *Klebsiella*. She was placed on antibiotics and oxygen for pneumonia, and she slowly improved. During this admission, her congenital problem was reevaluated by diagnostic testing. She was discharged in satisfactory condition.

   Discharge diagnoses: (1) Klebsiella pneumonia, (2) monoplegia, (3) diverticulum, left ventricle.

   Codes: ______________________________

   ____

7. **Inpatient admission:** The patient, a 2-year-old male, had congenital bilateral clubfoot and atretic spinal cord at level T11-L4. He needed a walker to ambulate, using mostly the upper extremities to get around. He was admitted for repair of a left tibial torsion. A tibial rotational osteotomy was performed, with insertion of pins. He was placed in a splint postoperatively and was changed to a long leg cast the next day. The patient was discharged subsequently to follow up with the orthopedic surgeon in 1 week.

   Discharge diagnosis: Atretic spinal cord at T11-L4 with left tibial torsion.

   Codes: ______________________________

   ____

8. **Inpatient admission:** The patient, a 20-month-old infant, was admitted for correction of a left talipes equinovarus clubfoot. Shortly after admission, she started running a fever and it became apparent that she had acute otitis media. She was placed on antibiotics and discharged. Surgery was to be rescheduled at a later date.

   Discharge diagnoses: (1) Talipes equinovarus, left, (2) bilateral otitis media.

   Codes: ______________________________

   ____

9. **Inpatient admission:** The patient, a teenage male, was referred by his orthodontist for surgical correction of multiple congenital deformities. Examination revealed maxillary hypoplasia and maxillary asymmetry. He was found to have an excessive crossbite, with the maxillary midline several millimeters to the right. Surgical correction was indicated, and the plan was to perform both maxillary and mandibular osteotomies to achieve the amount of movement needed. During surgery, it was possible to move the maxilla into its desired position without a mandibular osteotomy being performed. Postoperatively, he did very well, and the occlusion was good.

   Discharge diagnoses: (1) Maxillary hypoplasia, (2) maxillary asymmetry, (3) excessive crossbite.

   Procedure performed: Segmental maxillary osteotomy.

   Codes: ______________________________

   ____

10. **Inpatient admission:** Inpatient admission: The patient, a 10-month-old infant, had congenital extrahepatic biliary atresia. She was admitted for a liver transplant workup and at admission was in liver failure. The workup included a chest X-ray, KUB, Doppler ultrasound of liver, and EKG, as well as an upper GI endoscopy of the esophagus, stomach, and duodenum.

    Discharge diagnoses: (1) Extrahepatic biliary atresia, (2) placed on liver transplant list, stage II.

    Codes: ______________________________

    ____

Perinatal Conditions

B15

1. **Inpatient admission:** The patient, a preterm, newborn male triplet (1,720 grams), was delivered by cesarean section, as were the other two liveborn mates. He initially required supplemental oxygen and a nasal prong CPAP for transient tachypnea. He was weaned 5 hours after birth. The 1-minute Apgar score was 6 and the 5-minute score was 8. He was also treated for diaper dermatitis. A circumcision was performed prior to discharge.

   Discharge diagnoses: (1) Premature male triplet, (2) transient tachypnea, (3) diaper dermatitis.

   Codes: ______________________________

   ____

2. **Inpatient admission:** The patient, a one-day-old, 2,200-gram infant, was born prematurely at 34 weeks gestation. She was transferred from another hospital for evaluation of a congenital diaphragmatic hernia. Just before transfer, intubation was necessitated by some respiratory distress. The ventilatory support was continued for 3 days. When she was stabilized, the diaphragmatic hernia was repaired with an abdominal approach, and the hernia sac was excised. The infant progressed rapidly and was discharged on the second postoperative day.

   Discharge diagnoses: (1) Prematurity, (2) diaphragmatic hernia, (3) respiratory distress.

   Codes: ______________________________

   ____

3. **Inpatient admission:** The patient, a newborn female infant, was delivered spontaneously at term. She was noticed to be jaundiced on the initial screening labs. The total bilirubin was increased and she was started on phototherapy under bilirubin lights. She progressed rapidly and was discharged to home with the mother.

   Discharge diagnoses: (1) Term female newborn, (2) neonatal jaundice.

   Codes: ______________________________

   ____

4. **Inpatient admission:** The patient, a preterm male infant, was delivered vaginally at approximately 29 weeks gestation. He weighed 1,855 grams at birth. Initially, he did well but on the evening of birth was noted to have dusky spells when feeding. During that night, he developed tachypnea. Due to abnormal heart sounds, tachypnea, and dusky spells, an echocardiogram was performed. It showed a patent foramen ovale. The next day, the patient did well and was released to follow up with a pediatric cardiologist on an outpatient basis.

   Discharge diagnoses: (1) Premature, single, male newborn, (2) patent foramen ovale.

   Codes: ____________________

5. **Inpatient admission:** The patient, a newborn preterm male infant delivered by cesarean section, weighed 2,300 grams at birth and had Apgar scores of 8 and 9. Shortly after birth, an increased respiratory rate, effort, and grunting required that he be placed on oxygen. A classical hyaline membrane disease then developed, consistent with his 32- to 33-week gestational age and size. An umbilical artery catheter was placed immediately to allow ease in administration of IV fluids and medication. A right pneumothorax, identified on chest X-ray, was immediately needle aspirated, and a chest tube was placed. Subsequently, he was transferred to the newborn intensive care nursery at another hospital.

   Discharge diagnoses: (1) Prematurity, (2) hyaline membrane disease, (3) spontaneous right pneumothorax.

   Procedures performed: (1) Umbilical artery catheter placement, (2) right chest tube placement, (3) right lung aspiration.

   Codes: ____________________

6. **Inpatient admission:** The patient was delivered prematurely by cesarean section and weighed 1,750 grams. She had multiple problems including microcephaly and congenital heart disease. This newborn was transferred to another hospital for further evaluation and intensive pediatric care.

   Discharge diagnoses: (1) Prematurity, (2) microcephaly, (3) congenital heart disease.

   Codes: ____________________

7. **Inpatient admission:** The patient, a 6-day-old female, was admitted with respiratory distress, wheezes, and a heart murmur. She was intubated on admission and improved on the ventilator. She was extubated 48 hours later. Respiratory syncytial viral bronchiolitis was diagnosed. Other treatment included antibiotics and aerosols. An echocardiogram indicated a ventricular septal defect. She was to return at a later date for further evaluation.

   Discharge diagnoses: (1) Respiratory syncytial viral bronchiolitis, (2) ventricular septal defect.

   Codes: ______________________________

   ____

8. **Inpatient admission:** The patient, an 11-month-old male infant, had congenital cytomegalovirus infection. Because of distorted, loud, and rattling breathing, he was admitted for evaluation of his hypertrophied tonsils and adenoids. Treatment for congenital cytomegaloviral infection was continued throughout the admission. In surgery, a microrigid laryngoscopy, microrigid bronchoscopy, and adenotonsillectomy were performed. No abnormalities were noted on laryngoscopy or bronchoscopy. The patient's postoperative course was uncomplicated.

   Discharge diagnoses: (1) Hypertrophied adenoids and tonsils, (2) congenital cytomegalovirus infection.

   Codes: ______________________________

   ____

9. **Inpatient admission:** The patient, an 11-month-old male, was found to have a dysplastic kidney on the right side. Because the kidney was not functioning, he was admitted to have it removed. A right, simple nephrectomy was performed. The procedure was uncomplicated, as was the postoperative course. The pathology report showed the kidney to be both dysplastic and multicystic.

   Discharge diagnosis: Right multicystic dysplastic kidney.

   Codes: ______________________________

   ____

10. **Inpatient admission:** The patient, a 7-pound, 6-ounce male infant, was delivered to a 31-year-old woman (gravida II, para 0-1) at 43 weeks gestation. The mother's pregnancy was uncomplicated, labor lasted 24 hours, and the delivery was spontaneous. Apgar scores were 5 and 7. Due to transient tachypnea and a continued oxygen requirement, the infant was taken to the special care nursery. His overall condition improved rapidly with oxygen and adjustments in body fluids.

    Discharge diagnoses: (1) Postterm newborn male, (2) transient tachypnea of the newborn.

    Codes: ______________________________

    ____

11. **Inpatient admission:** The patient, a 3-week-old male, was admitted through the emergency department with a 3-day history of upper respiratory tract infection. Following admission, he was observed not breathing for short periods. Antibiotics were started for the URI, and he was observed closely. He had been followed in the outpatient clinic for failure to thrive. All evaluative workups were negative, and no active disease other than the respiratory infection was found. The upper respiratory infection cleared, but the apneic episodes continued. He was to be transferred to the children's hospital for more detailed studies of his apneic episodes and failure to thrive.

    Discharge diagnoses: (1) Failure to thrive, (2) upper respiratory tract infection, (3) apnea.

    Codes: ______________________________

    ____

12. **Inpatient admission:** The infant patient was born in the hospital to a 36-year-old primigravida woman at an estimated 34 weeks gestation. The mother's pregnancy was complicated by maternal hypertension and gestational diabetes. The infant was delivered by a primary cesarean section due to fetal distress resulting from the mother's failure to progress. The infant was placed on oxygen by nasal prong following birth in response to fetal distress. The oxygen was removed when heart rate, breathing, and blood gases returned to normal. The infant's blood sugars were low following birth, and an infusion of intravenous glucose was initiated until the blood sugars stabilized.

    Discharge diagnoses: (1) Premature newborn male with birth weight of 1,880 grams, (2) transient hypoglycemia.

    Codes: ______________________________

    ____

13. **Inpatient admission:** The patient, a preterm male infant, was born the day before admission in another hospital. He weighed 2,608 grams and had Apgar scores of 7 and 9. He was noted to have elevated temperature. WBCs were also elevated. He was transferred here for investigative studies. A urinary tract infection was confirmed with a urine culture that was positive for E. coli, and the infection was treated with intravenous antibiotics. Left hydronephrosis was confirmed by renal ultrasound. Suspected septicemia was ruled out when all blood cultures were negative prior to institution of antibiotic therapy.

    Discharge diagnoses: (1) Urinary tract infection, (2) congenital hydronephrosis, (3) prematurity.

    Codes: ______________________________

    ____

Diseases of the Circulatory System

B16

1. **Inpatient admission (episode 1):** The reason for this woman's admission was repair of a 4.7-centimeter infrarenal abdominal aortic aneurysm. She also had arterial hypertension. Because of her strong family history of aneurysms, she wished to have her aneurysm removed on an elective basis rather than waiting for it to follow its natural course. An infrarenal excision of the aortic aneurysm, open approach, was performed using a 16-millimeter Dacron graft replacement. The procedure was successful, and the patient was discharged on the fifth postoperative day.

   Discharge diagnoses: (1) Infrarenal abdominal aortic aneurysm, (2) arterial hypertension.

   Codes: ______________________________

   ____

   Physician office visit (episode 2): The patient presented for routine follow-up examination of an abdominal aortic aneurysm repair with graft replacement. She was doing well, with only mild discomfort. The midline incision was well healed. Femoral and distal pulses were palpable bilaterally. She was to return again in 3 months.

   Diagnosis: Status post aortic aneurysm.

   Codes: ______________________________

   ____

2. **Inpatient admission:** The patient was admitted for workup of right carotid artery stenosis. A carotid duplex performed as an outpatient at another facility showed 80 percent stenosis on the right and 40 percent on the left. A nonselective carotid arteriography, conducted the day after admission, showed only a 50 percent stenosis of the right common carotid artery. The external carotids were found to be small, but there was no significant internal carotid disease on either side. Therefore, because the patient was asymptomatic, it was felt that surgery would present a higher risk of stroke than treating her medically.

   Discharge diagnosis: Carotid artery disease.

   Codes: ______________________________

   ____

3. **Inpatient admission:** This patient was admitted for repair of a left carotid stenosis. Two months earlier, an endarterectomy of a right carotid stenosis had been performed. Six months earlier, she had suffered a cerebral hemorrhage that resulted in both apraxia and difficulty in swallowing, both of which required additional nursing assistance. The left endarterectomy was successfully accomplished and the patient was discharged on the fourth hospital day.

   Discharge diagnoses: (1) Left carotid stenosis, (2) residuals of old cerebrovascular accident.

   Codes: ______________________________

   ____

4. **Inpatient admission:** The patient was admitted with recurrent unstable angina that could not be controlled with sublingual nitroglycerin. On left cardiac catheterization with coronary arteriography, a narrowing in the left anterior descending coronary artery and a stenotic area in an intermediate branch were identified. A successful percutaneous transluminal coronary angioplasty (PTCA) of both vessels was carried out.

   Discharge diagnosis: (1) Unstable angina secondary to coronary arteriosclerosis, (2) chronic total occlusion of coronary artery.

   Codes: ______________________________

   ____

5. **Inpatient admission:** The patient received his first pacing system 15 years earlier because of congenital complete heart block and severe bradycardia. At the time of admission, he was experiencing these conditions again, plus fatigue secondary to pacemaker malfunction. He was admitted for insertion of a new generator and atrial lead. He was prepped for surgery. The old pacemaker was removed, new leads were inserted, and a new dual-chambered pacing device was inserted as a replacement. The postoperative period was uncomplicated.

   Discharge diagnosis: Malfunctioning pacemaker.

   Codes: ______________________________

   ____

6. **Inpatient admission:** The patient came to the emergency department because she was unable to speak well. She was admitted because she appeared to be somewhat aphasic. Following admission, she was found to be in atrial fibrillation. A CT scan of the head showed only some probable old defects, and the aphasia was thought to probably be due to a recent cerebral embolus. By the fifth day, she was stable and able to go home. The aphasia had cleared, and the fibrillation was controlled with medication.

   Discharge diagnoses: (1) Cerebral embolism, (2) atrial fibrillation.

   Codes: ______________________________

   ____

7. **Inpatient admission:** The patient was admitted for severe aortic valve stenosis and calcification and left ventricular hypertrophy. The aortic valve was replaced. The patient was successfully weaned from the cardiopulmonary bypass machine. An intraoperative echocardiogram revealed appropriate functioning of the prosthesis.

   Discharge diagnoses: (1) Aortic stenosis and calcification, (2) left ventricular hypertrophy.

   Codes: ____________________________

8. **Inpatient admission:** The admission diagnoses were aortic and mitral insufficiency. The patient also had HIV infection. A bacterial endocarditis, involving the aortic and mitral valves, had developed 5 months before admission and was treated and resolved with antibiotics. Procedures performed were: mitral valve repair with Carpentier ring and aortic valve repair with #21 St. Jude prosthesis, with cardiopulmonary bypass during the procedure. The patient improved considerably during the next 2 days with medications and was transferred to the rehabilitation hospital.

   Discharge diagnoses: (1) Aortic and mitral insufficiency, (2) HIV infection.

   Codes: ____________________________

9. **Inpatient admission:** The patient was admitted with atypical chest pain and aching of the left upper extremity. Following admission, she had episodic visual blurring and dizziness. A myocardial infarction was ruled out. Neurological checks were unremarkable, except for a questionable small infarct in the left occipital lobe. Her aspirin therapy was increased, and within 2 days she was fully ambulatory and asymptomatic.

   Discharge diagnoses: (1) Atypical chest pain of unclear etiology, (2) transient ischemic attacks.

   Codes: ____________________________

10. **Inpatient admission:** The patient, a young woman, was admitted with pain and edema in the left leg, which had started 2 days earlier when she drove home from Florida without stopping. Findings on a CT scan of the pelvis were consistent with thrombosis. She was discharged on Coumadin.

    Discharge diagnosis: Iliac vein thrombosis on the left, acute.

    Codes: ____________________________

11. **Inpatient admission:** The patient was brought to the hospital emergency department with burning, low sternal, epigastric pain. While in the ED, she developed respiratory distress and subsequent acute myocardial infarction with cardiopulmonary arrest. She was resuscitated and maneuvers involved in this included intubation and defibrillation. Chest X-rays confirmed pulmonary edema and congestive heart failure. EKGs confirmed acute subendocardial myocardial infarction in progress. The patient was then admitted and remained on the ventilator for approximately 24 hours, with gradual improvement. She was transferred to another hospital for further workup and treatment.

    Discharge diagnoses: (1) Acute myocardial infarction, (2) pulmonary edema, (3) congestive heart failure, (4) cardiopulmonary arrest.

    Codes: ______________________________

    ____

12. **Inpatient admission:** The patient was admitted for evaluation of a 3-month history of fever, fatigue, and headaches. She received consultation from the rheumatology service, which recommended biopsy of the temporal arteries. The left temporal artery was negative for inflammation. The right temporal artery, however, showed inflammation of the intima. The histologic picture was compatible with arteritis. Prednisone was given, and the headaches subsided.

    Discharge diagnosis: Right temporal arteritis.

    Codes: ______________________________

    ____

13. **Inpatient admission:** The patient was admitted for treatment of a stroke. She has a history of type 2 diabetes. The major manifestations were ptosis on the right, moderate expressive aphasia, and a slow shuffling gait. On a CT scan of the head, a low-density area at the posterior limb of the left internal capsule and the left posterior parietal subcortical white matter was seen. No hemorrhage was viewed. Gradually, the manifestations improved and then resolved. The patient also had a midfoot ulcer that required bedside debridement (using a Versajet) by the physician. She was discharged to be followed up by a home health nurse.

    Discharge diagnoses: (1) Cerebrovascular accident of a thromboembolic source, (2) type 2 diabetes,(3) diabetic foot ulcer.

    Codes: ______________________________

    ____

14. **Inpatient admission:** The patient had a 3-month history of progressive cyanosis of the fingers and toes. Due to sudden and dramatic progression of symptoms, she was admitted. A right upper-extremity arteriogram revealed complete absence of arterial flow to all proximal phalanges. The findings were thought to be consistent with vasculitis. A vascular biopsy was performed to confirm this diagnosis. The report indicated changes consistent with chronic inflammation and necrotizing vasculitis. On vascular surgery consultation, it was felt that her gangrene would demarcate without surgical intervention. There was gradual improvement in pain, and she was switched to oral medications.

    Discharge diagnoses: (1) Necrotizing vasculitis, (2) digital gangrene.

    Codes: ____

    ____

15. **Inpatient admission:** The patient was transferred from another hospital for evaluation of a possible recurrent pulmonary embolism and left lower-extremity pain and swelling determined to be DVT (prior to transfer). A pulmonary arteriogram confirmed a left pulmonary embolus, and heparin was started. Mammograms were taken to evaluate a right breast lump with discharge, which was found on physical examination. The finding was a suspicious density of her right breast. The patient was to be referred to the gynecology clinic for follow-up of this problem after discharge. All medications were adjusted, and she showed much improvement.

    Discharge diagnoses: (1) Deep venous thrombosis, right leg, (2) recurrent pulmonary embolism, (3) lump, right breast.

    Codes: ____

    ____

16. **Inpatient admission:** The patient, who had peripheral vascular disease, came in for a second opinion about possible reconstruction of right femorotibial occlusive disease. An angiogram demonstrated a peroneal vessel that would allow reconstruction. Following an evaluation, he was scheduled to undergo the procedure. However, because he had no other significant diseases or active cardiac ischemia, he was felt to be low risk for a distal reconstruction. The patient was discharged prior to the procedure due to the development of an upper respiratory infection. The procedure was to be rescheduled in 2 weeks.

    Discharge diagnoses: (1) Right femorotibial occlusion, (2) URI.

    Codes: ____

    ____

17. **Inpatient admission:** The patient was admitted with probable acute myocardial infarction. He was admitted to the critical care unit and also found to be in atrial fibrillation. He was given several medications. A cardiology consultation confirmed an acute inferolateral myocardial infarction on echocardiogram, and the patient was transferred to another hospital for cardiac catheterization.

    Discharge diagnoses: (1) Acute myocardial infarction, (2) atrial fibrillation.

    Codes: ______________________________

    ____

18. **Inpatient admission:** The patient, an elderly man, was transferred from a nursing home. He had had left-sided hemiplegia since suffering a cerebral thrombosis about 3 months earlier. He was doing well until the day of admission. A CT scan of the head showed an acute cerebral hemorrhage. He was treated and improved somewhat but then had increased problems secondary to extension of the bleeding. Another CT scan showed a large hematoma in the right basal ganglia. With consultation, it was decided that only supportive care was needed, and the patient was returned to the nursing home.

    Discharge diagnoses: (1) Acute cerebral hemorrhage, (2) right basal ganglia hematoma, (3) previous cerebral thrombosis with residual left-sided hemiplegia.

    Codes: ______________________________

    ____

19. **Inpatient admission:** The patient, a female resident of a nursing home, was transferred because of nausea and vomiting. She also suffered from type 1 diabetes mellitus and arteriosclerotic cardiovascular disease. An upper GI X-ray showed esophageal obstruction. She was then admitted with provisional diagnoses of esophageal obstruction versus hiatal hernia versus esophagitis. A gastroscopy was performed, and a partial obstruction due to stricture to the level of the distal esophagus was viewed and dilated. The patient improved without further symptoms. Her blood sugar levels rose to 500 on the third day of admission, and the diabetes was diagnosed as out of control. Her insulin was increased twice in an attempt to lower her blood sugar to baseline. The long-term outlook was not good inasmuch as the patient was not a candidate for definitive surgery. The esophageal stricture was thought to have resulted from a previous cerebrovascular accident.

    Discharge diagnoses: (1) Esophageal stricture, (2) arteriosclerotic cardiovascular disease, (3) uncontrolled diabetes mellitus, type 1.

    Codes: ______________________________

    ____

20. **Inpatient admission:** The patient was admitted through the emergency department with substernal chest pain, thought to represent unstable angina. He got pain relief with nitroglycerin. The next morning he asked to be discharged because he had no insurance and could not afford to be in the hospital. Because his physician did not agree with his decision, the patient signed himself out against medical advice. He promised to see the cardiologist immediately and take his medications.

    Discharge diagnosis: Angina, probably unstable.

    Codes: ______________________________

    ____

21. **Inpatient admission:** The patient was admitted with recurrent chest pain, which could not be controlled with medications and ultimately resulted in an anterior AMI. On combined right and left cardiac catheterization with coronary cineangiography, a narrowing in the left anterior descending coronary artery and stenoses in the left circumflex and distal right coronary artery were found. A successful three-vessel coronary artery bypass graft was carried out. The left internal mammary was used to bypass the left anterior descending, and a reverse segment of saphenous vein graft was used to bypass the left circumflex and distal right coronary arteries.

    Discharge diagnoses: (1) Anterior acute myocardial infarction, (2) coronary arteriosclerosis.

    Procedure: Three-vessel coronary artery bypass graft.

    Codes: ______________________________

    ____

22. **Inpatient admission:** The patient was admitted for a planned exploratory laparotomy and a possible excision of a cystic mass in the pelvis. Shortly after admission, however, she developed bigeminy. The anesthesiologist believed that she should not have surgery. The surgery was canceled, and she was referred back to her internist.

    Discharge diagnoses: (1) Bigeminy, (2) pelvic mass.

    Codes: ______________________________

    ____

23. **Inpatient admission:** The patient, an elderly woman, had a rather sudden onset of severe pleuritic chest discomfort that brought her to the emergency department. She had been undergoing a series of radiation therapy treatments for history of endometrial carcinoma. She was admitted for further evaluation. A pulmonary angiogram confirmed the diagnosis of pulmonary embolism in the right lower lobe. She was treated with heparin and later Coumadin. Coumadin was to be continued on discharge. The patient was to return for her regular radiation therapy treatment as scheduled.

    Discharge diagnoses: (1) Pulmonary embolism, (2) history of endometrial carcinoma of the uterus.

    Codes: ______________________________

    ____

24. **Inpatient admission:** The patient was transferred from another hospital for treatment of an acute inferior myocardial infarction. She also suffered from hypercholesterolemia and benign hypertension; treatment of these conditions was continued during the hospital stay. A left cardiac catheterization with coronary angiogram and arteriography was performed and revealed coronary arteriosclerosis. It was determined that she would benefit from a percutaneous transluminal coronary angioplasty. The angioplasty was performed on the left coronary artery. She tolerated the procedure well and was to continue her medical treatment after discharge.

    Discharge diagnoses: (1) Acute inferior myocardial infarction, (2) coronary arteriosclerosis, (3) hypercholesterolemia, (4) benign essential hypertension.

    Codes: ______________________________

    ____

Neoplasms

B17

1. **Inpatient admission:** The elderly woman's admitting diagnosis was carcinoma of the stomach with metastasis to the ovaries. An exploratory laparotomy was performed for the purpose of excising the gastric tumor, but it was so densely attached to other structures that it could not be resected. However, a total abdominal hysterectomy and bilateral salpingo-oophorectomy were accomplished and the patient returned to her room in fair condition. Palliative systemic chemotherapy infusions were given. On the third postoperative day, a large right pleural effusion developed, and a chest tube was placed for drainage. Cytology for malignant cells in the pleural effusion was negative. The patient remained stable and wanted to return to her home. The chest tube was removed before discharge.

   Discharge diagnoses: (1) Carcinoma of the stomach metastatic to the ovaries, (2) pleural effusion.

   Codes: ____________________

   ____

2. **Inpatient admission:** The patient underwent a hemicolectomy and splenectomy a year earlier for excision of a primary adenocarcinoma of the colon. Recently, he developed abdominal pain. He was admitted with a questionable liver lesion. An ultrasound of the liver, a CT scan of the abdomen, and an exploratory laparotomy with needle biopsy of the liver were performed. The findings indicated inoperable adenocarcinoma of the liver.

   Discharge diagnosis: Adenocarcinoma of the colon metastatic to the liver, unresectable.

   Codes: ____________________

   ____

3. **Inpatient admission:** The patient was admitted through the emergency department with severe shortness of breath. She had a history of left upper lobe, non-small cell carcinoma, which had been treated with radiation. Recently, a recurrence in the left supraclavicular area of the lung was found, and she received palliative radiation therapy. She also had a history of severe chronic obstructive bronchitis and had used home oxygen for several years. Her medications were increased for the chronic obstructive pulmonary disease, and she improved sufficiently for discharge.

   Discharge diagnoses: (1) Chronic obstructive pulmonary disease with acute exacerbation, (2) recurrent non-small cell lung cancer.

   Codes: ____________________

   ____

4. **Inpatient admission:** On a previous admission, the patient was diagnosed with poorly differentiated papillary serous cystadenocarcinoma of the ovary. She was admitted for, and received, her fifth chemotherapy treatment with Taxol and Cisplatin.

   Discharge diagnosis: Papillary serous cystadenocarcinoma, stage III.

   Codes: ____________________

   ____

5. **Inpatient admission:** The patient was seen in the outpatient clinic, where an X-ray revealed compression fractures of T6 and T8. He gave no history of trauma. He was admitted for further evaluation to determine the etiology of the pathologic fractures. Bone marrow aspirate and biopsies revealed multiple myeloma. During the stay, he went into fluid overload and developed some chest heaviness with runs of ventricular tachycardia. The tachycardia necessitated his transfer to cardiac level II to rule out myocardial infarction. Myocardial infarct was ruled out, and he was discharged after stabilization. He was to be followed up by the oncology clinic.

   Discharge diagnoses: (1) Multiple myeloma, (2) compression fractures, T6 and T8, (3) fluid overload, (4) tachycardia.

   Codes: ____________________

   ____

6. **Physician office visit:** The 63-year-old patient made her annual visit to her gynecologist. She had no complaints. Examination revealed a 6- to 7-centimeter mass at the vaginal apex. She was to be scheduled for an exploratory laparotomy.

   Diagnosis: Vaginal mass.

   Codes: ____________________

   ____

7. **Inpatient admission:** The patient was admitted for workup of an abdominal mass. An esophagogastroduodenoscopy with ultrasound of the abdomen demonstrated a complex cystic solid mass in the pancreas, which had invaded the portal vein. The mass was most consistent with carcinoma of the pancreas. The patient refused colonoscopy, biopsy, and surgery. Therefore, she was discharged with medication and was to follow up with her local physician for palliative treatment of carcinoma.

   Discharge diagnosis: Probable carcinoma of the pancreas with extension to the portal vein.

   Codes: ____________________

   ____

8. **Inpatient admission (episode 1):** The patient had a rapidly progressing, drug-resistant, primitive melanotic neuroectodermal tumor (PNET) metastatic to the left femur. He was admitted for fixation of a pathologic fracture of the left femur. An open reduction with internal fixation of the left proximal femur with intramedullary nail insertion was performed.

   Discharge diagnoses: (1) PNET metastatic to the femur, (2) pathologic fracture, neck of the left femur.

   Codes: ______________________________

   ____

   Inpatient admission (episode 2): The patient was readmitted for management of a right-sided pleural effusion. A thoracentesis was accomplished, and he had some relief of his breathing. Cytology confirmed the pleural effusion as malignant. A closed biopsy of the lung confirmed metastasis to the lung. The patient improved and was discharged to follow up in his physician's office.

   Discharge diagnoses: (1) Malignant pleural effusion, (2) PNET metastatic to the left femur and right lung.

   Codes: ______________________________

   ____

   Inpatient admission (episode 3): The patient was again admitted, this time for terminal care. The admission diagnosis was severe hypoxemia. He has massive bilateral pulmonary metastases. It was hoped that he could be relieved by chest tube drainage; however, it was obvious from his chest X-ray that removing a small amount of lung fluid would not affect the overall clinical situation. He had significant hemoptysis the second day of hospitalization and was in a comatose state until his death that evening.

   Discharge diagnoses: (1) Hypoxemia and hemoptysis secondary to malignant pleural effusion, (2) coma, (3) primitive melanotic neuroectodermal tumor metastatic to the left femur and lungs.

   Codes: ______________________________

   ____

9. **Inpatient admission:** The patient was admitted for chemotherapy. She had ovarian papillary serous cystadenocarcinoma, stage III. Three months earlier, diaphragmatic and omental masses were positive as well. She received Taxol and Cisplatin without difficulty. She was to return in 3 weeks for her next treatment.

   Discharge diagnosis: Stage III papillary serous cystadenocarcinoma with metastases to the diaphragm and omentum.

   Codes: ______________________________

   ____

10. **Inpatient admission:** The patient was admitted for removal of an abdominal aortic aneurysm. When the abdomen was opened, carcinoma of the esophagus was found. Because the patient was elderly and the aneurysm was small, the surgeon decided not to repair it or to excise the neoplasm. Prior to discharge, a percutaneous endoscopic gastrostomy tube was inserted to ensure adequate caloric intake. The patient recovered without difficulty and was discharged to home with family.

    Discharge diagnoses: (1) Aortic aneurysm, (2) carcinoma of esophagus.

    Codes: ______________________________

    ____

11. **Outpatient visit:** The patient complained of dyspnea on exertion, moderate night sweats, and intermittent fevers. On routine chest X-ray, a mass was visualized in the mediastinum. He was to be scheduled for a CT scan.

    Diagnosis: Probable neoplastic disease.

    Codes: ______________________________

    ____

12. **Inpatient admission (episode 1):** The patient was admitted for evaluation of a mediastinal mass. On CT scan of the thorax, a large mass was identified in the anterior superior portion. Multiple pulmonary nodules were also seen. Needle biopsies of nodules in the lungs, obtained during an exploratory thoracotomy, were positive for yolk sac tumor. The first of a series of five chemotherapy treatments was administered prior to discharge.

    Discharge diagnosis: Yolk sac tumor of mediastinum with metastases to both lungs.

    Codes: ______________________________

    ____

    Inpatient admission (episode 2): This admission was for a second cycle of chemotherapy for the yolk sac tumor of the mediastinum. The patient had minimal nausea and vomiting and was discharged following his treatment.

    Discharge diagnosis: Yolk sac tumor of mediastinum with metastases to lungs.

    Codes: ______________________________

    ____

13. **Inpatient admission:** The female patient had suffered from melanoma for a number of years. She had a primary resection 10 years ago without recurrence, but 1 year ago, melanoma was discovered in her axilla. She had axillary dissection, but a few months later presented with sacral pain, which bone scan revealed to be left femoral neck and right midfemur sites of metastasis. She had hepatic and adrenal metastases as well. She was admitted for the fifth course of chemotherapy, which was given.

    Discharge diagnosis: Metastatic melanoma left and right femur, liver, and adrenal gland.

    Codes: ____

    ____

14. **Outpatient clinic visit:** The patient, an elderly woman, returned to the clinic for follow-up of her right malignant ileal plasmacytoma. On a recent MRI, it was evident that the neoplasm, which was previously irradiated, had grown. Although she had failed current radiotherapy, there was no evidence that the neoplasm had spread outside its original location. She was started on medication and was to be scheduled for pelvic MRI.

    Diagnosis: Malignant ileal plasmacytoma.

    Codes: ____

    ____

15. **Inpatient admission:** The female patient had had abdominal pain for several months and infertility for 3 years. On hysterosalpingogram taken before admission, a right tubal occlusion and questionable uterine myoma were visualized. She was admitted for a myomectomy. During the procedure, multiple adhesions were noted from the tubes to a previous myomectomy site, and lysis was carried out. It was felt that the constriction of the tubes by the adhesions might be the cause of the infertility. On the third postoperative day, the staples were removed and the patient went home.

    Discharge diagnoses: (1) Symptomatic leiomyoma, (2) infertility, (3) adhesions.

    Codes: ____

    ____

16. **Inpatient admission:** The patient was admitted for treatment of a moderately differentiated adenocarcinoma of the endometrium. The diagnosis was made after a diagnostic D & C performed a month earlier. She was taken to surgery, where a laparotomy was performed through a midline incision. Exploration revealed no palpable nodes. A total abdominal hysterectomy and bilateral salpingo-oophorectomy were performed without incident or complication. Frozen section of the myometrium showed only minimal invasion at less than one-third of the depth. The postoperative course was benign, and the patient was discharged.

    Discharge diagnosis: Adenocarcinoma of the endometrium, moderately well differentiated, with minimal myometrial invasion.

    Codes: ____

    ____

17. **Outpatient surgery (episode 1):** The patient had a persistent left lung infiltrate on X-ray and subsequently had left pleural effusion. Thoracentesis and bronchoscopy with brush biopsy of the lung were performed. Tissue studies yielded no diagnosis. The patient was to be admitted for further evaluation.

 Diagnosis: Left pleural infiltrate on X-ray, pleural effusion.

 Codes: ______________________________

 ____

 Inpatient admission (episode 2): The patient was taken to surgery, where a thoracoscopy with decortication and pleural biopsy were performed. The final specimen report showed moderately differentiated epidermoid carcinoma of the lung. The patient's first course of deep radiation therapy was given prior to discharge.

 Discharge diagnosis: Primary carcinoma of lung.

 Codes: ______________________________

 ____

18. **Inpatient admission:** The patient developed right-sided tinnitus 2 years earlier, followed by a precipitous loss of hearing on the right side. A preadmission MRI scan identified a large acoustic neuroma. Because hearing on the right was totally lost, it was decided to excise the neuroma using a radiosurgical technique. The tumor was dissected completely. There were no postoperative complications, and the patient was discharged in satisfactory condition.

 Discharge diagnosis: Acoustic neuroma on the right.

 Codes: ______________________________

 ____

19. **Inpatient admission:** The patient, an elderly woman, was transferred from a nursing home with left hemiparesis and a diagnosis of suspected brain tumor. She underwent a CT-guided stereotactic biopsy without complications. The frozen-section diagnosis was glioblastoma. She was to come back for radiation therapy the following week, and in the meantime she was to be transferred back to the nursing home for further management. She had continued left hemiparesis, which prevents her from being managed at home.

 Discharge diagnoses: (1) Primary glioblastoma, right temporal lobe, (2) left hemiparesis.

 Codes: ______________________________

 ____

20. **Inpatient admission:** The patient, an elderly woman, entered the hospital with a history of weight loss, anorexia, dysphagia, and rectal bleeding. She had also fallen many times at home. A fecal impaction was diagnosed from an abdominal CT scan following admission. Preparation for colonoscopy took about 3 days, and when the colonoscopy was finally accomplished, the impaction had cleared and no abnormalities were seen. A hiatal hernia was found on esophagogastroduodenoscopy, and two meningiomas were identified on magnetic resonance imaging of the head. She was started on Zantac for the hiatal hernia. It seemed that most of her generalized symptoms were secondary to the fecal impaction. The falling episodes are most likely related to the meningiomas, although they showed no mass effect. Neurological consultation was to be obtained as an outpatient. The patient was discharged on stool softeners for prevention of fecal impaction and Zantac for hiatal hernia.

    Discharge diagnoses: (1) Meningiomas, (2) fecal impaction, (3) hiatal hernia.

    Codes: ______________________________

    ____

21. **Inpatient admission:** The patient was admitted with severe back pain. He had prostate cancer excised 3 years ago. An MRI performed prior to admission showed metastasis to the S1, S2, and S3 areas of the spine. A fine-needle aspiration biopsy of the sacrum was performed, and the report confirmed that metastatic adenocarcinoma, consistent with a prostatic primary, was strongly positive. A bilateral scrotal orchiectomy was performed without complication. Megavoltage radiation treatments were started, and the pain came under control with intravenous morphine. The patient was discharged with pain well controlled on oral medications.

    Discharge diagnosis: Metastatic prostate cancer.

    Codes: ______________________________

    ____

22. **Inpatient admission:** This 14-year-old patient was admitted to the hospital with a diagnosis of glioblastoma multiforme. The patient is now admitted to undergo a blood brain barrier disruption and intra-arterial chemotherapy via the right internal carotid artery and, two days later, via the right basilar artery.

    Discharge diagnosis: Glioblastoma multiforme, admit for chemotherapy.

    Codes: ______________________________

    ____

Injuries

B18

1. **Inpatient admission:** The patient was struck in the face with a softball during a game with friends 2 weeks earlier with no loss of consciousness. The result was severe compound fractures of the nasal sinus, ethmoid sinus, and frontal sinus bones. The fractures were debrided, and open reduction was carried out. Initially, the postoperative course was uneventful, and the nasal packs, sutures, and nasal splint were removed. However, on the eighth day, the patient became confused and combative. A lumbar puncture was grossly positive for submeningitis. Again, improvement was rapid with antibiotics and intravenous steroids.

   Discharge diagnoses: (1) Compound nasal, ethmoid, and frontal sinus fractures, (2) postoperative meningitis.

   Procedures: Open reduction of compound fractures of the nasal, ethmoid, and frontal sinus bones.

   Codes: ____________________

   ____

2. **Inpatient admission:** The patient, an elderly woman, fell backward into the bathtub at home. She was admitted with possible compression fractures of the lumbar spine. She had had several similar falls in the past due to frequent transient ischemic attacks. X-rays of the spine showed some degenerative disk disease of L4 and L5, but there were no fractures. She was treated for pain and released after 2 days.

   Discharge diagnoses: (1) Lumbar sprain injury to back, (2) probable transient ischemic attack.

   Codes: ____________________

   ____

3. **Inpatient admission:** The patient was carrying a bicycle up an outside stairway at his house when he fell from the stairway into the alley. An X-ray of the lumbosacral spine taken in the emergency department showed an L4 fracture, and X-ray of the upper arm revealed a nondisplaced fracture of the shaft of the humerus. An L4-L5 bilateral foraminotomy with fusion, a bone graft (obtained from the iliac crest) to L4-L5 facet joints, and placement of drains in the back and hip were performed. The fracture of the humerus was treated with application of a sling and immobilization for 5 days.

   Discharge diagnoses: (1) Fracture, L4, (2) nondisplaced fracture, humerus.

   Codes: ____________________

   ____

4. **Inpatient admission:** The patient was admitted following a fall from a ladder at home, in which she sustained numerous injuries. X-rays showed a nondisplaced fracture of the right humeral neck. A splint was applied, but no other treatment was required. There were contusions on her forehead, thighs, and knees, as well as small abrasions of her forehead and right thigh. The patient received pain medications because of the contusions. The abrasions were superficial and healed without treatment and without evidence of infection.

   Discharge diagnoses: (1) Nondisplaced fracture, right humerus, (2) contusions of forehead, thighs, and knees, (3) abrasions on forehead and right thigh.

   Codes: ______________________________

   ____

5. **Inpatient admission:** The patient was admitted with diagnoses of probable rib fractures and pneumonia. She slipped and fell in the bathtub of her home while taking a shower about 4 days before admission and had experienced increasingly severe upper back and neck pain. Just prior to admission, she began running a fever, felt short of breath, and developed inspiratory chest wall pain. No rib fractures were identified on chest X-ray, but right upper lobe pneumonia was evident. Sputum culture grew *Klebsiella*. The patient was started on antibiotics and the pneumonia improved. Back pain was relieved by pain medication and bed rest.

   Discharge diagnoses: (1) Right upper lobe pneumonia, (2) cervical and thoracic back strain.

   Codes: ______________________________

   ____

6. **Emergency department visit:** The patient and her husband had been drinking heavily, became intoxicated, and had an argument when they got home. During the argument, he shoved her and she fell against the corner of the water bed, striking her left upper back and chest. She came to the emergency department complaining of severe pain and difficulty breathing. She was found to have subcutaneous emphysema due to the fractures of the ninth and tenth ribs. The ribs were strapped and she was given a prescription for pain medication. She was released to be followed as an outpatient.

   Diagnoses: (1) Fractured left ribs, ninth and tenth posteriorly, (2) subcutaneous emphysema, (3) alcohol intoxication.

   Codes: ______________________________

   ____

7. **Inpatient admission:** The patient, an elderly woman, was admitted following a fall off her porch at home. A femoral intertrochanteric fracture was diagnosed in the emergency department, and she was admitted. An open reduction with internal fixation was carried out. As anticipated, postoperative transfusions for blood loss were required during surgery. The blood loss resulted in a drop in hemoglobin and hematocrit, which were monitored daily. Her postoperative recovery went smoothly, and she was transferred to the skilled nursing unit for rehabilitation.

   Discharge diagnoses: (1) Closed fracture, right femur, (2) acute blood loss anemia.

   Codes: ______________________________

   ____

8. **Inpatient admission:** Three weeks before admission, the patient sustained a perilunate dislocation along with closed fractures of the metacarpal and proximal phalanx bones of the left hand in an accident. The accident occurred when he went to sleep at the wheel and the dump truck he was driving for his civilian job overturned in the median of the interstate; no other vehicles were involved. Immediately after the accident, the patient was seen in a local emergency department, where the metacarpal fracture was reduced and casted and the proximal phalanx was reduced and splinted. The perilunate dislocation was not reduced at that time. He was now admitted to this hospital, where a closed reduction of the perilunate dislocation was carried out after X-rays confirmed there was no fracture and the phalangeal and metacarpal fractures remained in good alignment. A short arm cast was applied, and he was discharged.

   Discharge diagnoses: (1) Closed right perilunate dislocation, (2) healing fractures of the metacarpal shaft and proximal phalanx on the right.

   Codes: ______________________________

   ____

9. **Inpatient admission:** The patient fell from a tree that he was pruning on his commercial farm. He was able to drive himself to the hospital, but it was apparent on admission that his left arm was fractured. He underwent an open reduction and internal fixation of a fracture of the proximal humerus and an open reduction and internal fixation of the comminuted fractures of the radial and ulnar shafts. He recovered without incident and was discharged to follow up in 1 week.

   Discharge diagnoses: (1) Comminuted left radius and ulnar shaft fractures, (2) displaced left proximal humerus fracture.

   Codes: ______________________________

   ____

10. **Inpatient admission:** The patient fell in her apartment after tripping over her cat. She was brought in by ambulance and admitted with a fracture of the shaft of the femur. An open reduction with internal fixation was performed. A postoperative fever developed, and a chest X-ray showed severe atelectasis. Respiratory therapy gave instructions on incentive spirometry, antibiotics were initiated, and the patient was discharged to a nursing home.

    Discharge diagnoses: (1) Closed fracture, femur, (2) postoperative fever and atelectasis.

    Codes: ____

    ____

11. **Inpatient admission:** The patient was admitted after a box fell on his head at the garage where he works. A CT scan of the head was negative for any abnormalities, but hourly neurological checks were made to rule out an intracranial injury. No injury was found. A small abrasion on his right arm, where the box scraped the skin, was cleansed and Neosporin applied.

    Discharge diagnosis: Observation for possible intracranial injury.

    Codes: ____

    ____

12. **Inpatient admission:** The patient, a 7-year-old male, sustained a high-velocity gunshot wound in a drive-by shooting. He was brought to the emergency department with a massive hemorrhage from the left groin due to the gunshot wound. He also sustained lacerations of the femoral artery and vein, in addition to a bullet lodged in the femur. The patient was immediately taken to surgery. The following procedures were performed: (1) left iliac to femoral artery bypass graft with reverse saphenous vein graft, (2) left iliac to femoral vein bypass graft with vein graft, (3) removal of bullet from the femur, (4) insertion of pins and traction of fracture, left femur.

    Discharge diagnoses: (1) Lacerations of left common femoral artery and femoral vein, with massive hemorrhage, (2) gunshot wound to left groin with high-velocity rifle, (3) bullet lodged in femur, (4) open subtrochanteric fracture of left femur.

    Codes: ____

    ____

13. **Inpatient admission:** The patient, a 10-year-old boy, was admitted through the emergency department after being struck by an automobile while riding his bicycle in the street in front of his home. His injuries were fractures of the left tibia and fibula, a 4-centimeter laceration and superficial abrasions on the left side of head, and a 1-centimeter-deep laceration on the right earlobe. The fractures were reduced and a Rush rod was placed in the left tibia. The earlobe and head lacerations were sutured.

    Discharge diagnoses: (1) Simple fractures, left tibia and fibula, (2) right ear laceration, (3) left parietooccipital laceration.

    Codes: ______________________________

14. **Emergency department visit (episode 1):** The patient had been drinking heavily in recent weeks. While visiting the area, he reduced his alcohol intake during the past 24 hours and suffered a seizure. In the emergency department, he seemed to be normal. No neurological or physical abnormalities were noted, and he was released after receiving Dilantin.

    Diagnosis: Seizure, probably due to decrease in alcohol consumption.

    Codes: ______________________________

    Inpatient admission (episode 2): The patient returned to his room at a local motel, had another seizure, and then fell in the bathroom. He was again brought to the emergency department and found to have a dislocated shoulder. Several attempts were made to replace the shoulder to its proper position. Because this reduction was not successful, he was admitted. With medications to control alcohol withdrawal and seizures along with IV fluids, he became mentally clear. A closed reduction of the dislocated shoulder was performed. The injury became a difficult management problem because the patient would not leave the orthopedic appliance on, and the next day a heavy plaster cast was placed on the shoulder to ensure correct positioning and activity reduction.

    Discharge diagnoses: (1) Alcohol withdrawal seizure, (2) left shoulder dislocation.

    Codes: ______________________________

15. **Emergency department visit (episode 1):** The 14-year-old patient was brought to the emergency department with severe pain and swelling of his left ankle. He sustained the injury when he fell off his skateboard on the school playground. An X-ray showed a simple trimalleolar fracture of his left ankle. The fracture was reduced, and he was placed in a long leg cast.

    Diagnosis: Severe pain and swelling, left ankle, associated with trimalleolar fracture.

    Codes: ______________________________

Orthopedic clinic visit (episode 2): The patient was status post trimalleolar fracture of the left ankle. He had been in the cast since sustaining the injury 3 weeks earlier. He had no complaints regarding the fracture, but he had worn down the cast. The cast breakdown extended the length of the sole of the foot. The long leg cast was removed, and the skin was intact. X-rays showed a healing fracture with no change in the reduction. Therefore, he was placed back into a short leg walking cast.

Diagnosis: Aftercare, healing left trimalleolar fracture.

Codes: ____________________

____

Orthopedic clinic visit (episode 3): The patient is status post trimalleolar fracture of the left ankle. The fracture now appears to be well healed. The cast was removed. There is no swelling or redness. No additional follow-up is anticipated.

Diagnosis: Aftercare, status post left trimalleolar fracture.

Codes: ____________________

____

16. **Inpatient admission:** The patient fractured her left knee several years earlier when she was thrown off a horse. Since then she had undergone realignment and debridement procedures of the undersurface of the patella. At the time of admission, she was severely disabled with multiple effusions, pain, crepitation, and inability to bear weight on the leg. She was taken to surgery and underwent an uneventful total patellectomy. The knee was immobilized with a cast, and she was discharged.

    Discharge diagnosis: Left patellofemoral arthritis.

    Codes: ____________________

    ____

17. **Inpatient admission:** The woman suffered a displaced fracture dislocation of her right ankle. The injury happened when she jumped off her front porch in an attempt to catch her fleeing dog. She underwent an open reduction and internal fixation of the fracture and was treated with elevation, bed rest, analgesics, and antibiotics. She was released in stable condition.

    Discharge diagnosis: Trimalleolar fracture dislocation, right ankle.

    Codes: ____________________

    ____

18. **Inpatient admission:** The patient was shopping at a retail food warehouse when a gallon can of tomatoes fell on his head from a shelf about 15 feet overhead. He was briefly unconscious and disoriented. X-rays of his skull showed a depressed parasagittal skull fracture with considerable parasagittal depression. He was admitted and taken to surgery, where a craniectomy was performed, with elevation of the depressed skull fracture.

    Discharge diagnosis: Depressed skull fracture.

    Codes: ______________________________

    ____

19. **Inpatient admission:** The patient fractured her left patella when she suffered a fall into a hole while playing golf on a public course. She was taken to surgery, where an open reduction and internal fixation were performed without complication. By the second postoperative day, she was ambulatory on crutches and ready for discharge.

    Discharge diagnosis: Closed fracture, left patella.

    Codes: ______________________________

    ____

20. **Physician office visit:** The patient went to see his physician after falling off a moving motorcycle. He complained of leg pain, and the physician noted swelling in the right lower extremity. The physician felt that a fracture of the tibia was probable and referred the patient for X-ray to confirm or rule out. For reasons unknown, the patient did not report to the hospital radiology department and did not return to see the physician as instructed.

    Diagnosis: Suspected fracture, right tibia.

    Codes: ______________________________

    ____

Burns

B19

1. **Inpatient admission:** The patient, on a family outing, sustained flash burns when his clothing caught fire. Someone had thrown gasoline onto the park cooking grill on which he was cooking. He suffered second-degree burns to the face, neck, and upper chest, with some first- and second-degree burns on the left forearm. All in all, 12 percent of the total body surface area was burned. The wounds were treated with antibiotics and pain medications. Physical therapists debrided the burned areas and provided hydrotherapy. The wounds continued to heal, and the patient was discharged.

   Discharge diagnoses: (1) Second-degree burns, face, neck, and upper chest, (2) first- and second-degree burns, left forearm, (3) 12 percent of body surface affected by burns.

   Codes: ______________________________

   ____

2. **Inpatient admission:** The patient was brought to the emergency department after being burned. He had been burning brush at his commercial farm when a gust of wind moved the fire to his tractor. There was an explosion, and he caught fire. He was treated with IV fluids, antibiotics, and pain medications. All in all, 14 percent of the total body surface was affected by the burns, of which 4 percent was third degree. He was transferred to a burn treatment center for surgical debridement and skin grafting.

   Discharge diagnoses: (1) First- and second-degree burns of the face, right ear, right forearm, and right thumb. (2) Third-degree burns of the left hand.

   Codes: ______________________________

   ____

3. **Inpatient admission (episode 1):** The patient was admitted with burns of her right hand and fingers up to the wrist. She had reached into hot water, not realizing the temperature, while canning in her kitchen. She was taken to surgery, where an excisional debridement of the burns was carried out. A split thickness skin graft was applied over the dorsum and volar aspects of the hand. The postoperative recovery was without infection or other complication.

   Discharge diagnosis: Second- and third-degree burns, right hand and fingers (3 percent of total body surface burned, 2 percent affected by third degree).

   Codes: ______________________________

   ____

Physician office visit (episode 2): Both the burns and the surgical site on this woman's hand seem to be healing nicely. There was no evidence of infection. The area was rebandaged. Antibiotics were continued, and she was to return the following week.

Diagnosis: Second- and third-degree burns, right hand and fingers.

Codes: ______________________________

____

Poisoning and Adverse Effects of Drugs

B20

1. **Inpatient admission:** The patient, a 33-year-old male, was admitted through the emergency department after an overdose of Dilantin. His gait was ataxic and he had nausea, vomiting, and blurry vision. His Dilantin level was 48. He had AIDS-related complex (ARC), well documented from previous hospitalizations. He also had posttraumatic seizure disorder, which resulted from an intracranial injury received in a 1987 motor vehicle accident. On questioning, he admitted taking an additional 400 milligrams of Dilantin the day of admission. Over the next 4 days, the Dilantin level gradually decreased to 16.1, and the regular dosage was restarted. It was clear that the current dosage was adequate in preventing seizures without significant side effects.

   Discharge diagnoses: (1) Dilantin toxicity, (2) HIV positive, (3) posttraumatic seizure disorder.

   Codes: ______________________________

   ____

2. **Outpatient clinic visit:** The patient came in because of a new rash on his trunk. The thrush, previously diagnosed and being treated with Dapsone, is improving.

   Diagnoses: (1) Skin rash due to an allergic reaction to Dapsone taken internally as prescribed, (2) thrush.

   Codes: ______________________________

   ____

3. **Inpatient admission:** The patient underwent an autologous bone marrow transplantation for choriocarcinoma 13 days earlier. He was readmitted 4 hours after discharge with a rash, which changed character to an urticarial type of eruption. A skin biopsy revealed superficial perivascular infiltrate consistent with urticaria. The patient had been started on Vancomycin the morning prior to admission. Vancomycin was discontinued, and the urticaria cleared spontaneously.

   Discharge diagnoses: (1) Vancomycin allergy with an urticarial reaction, (2) choriocarcinoma.

   Codes: ______________________________

   ____

4. **Inpatient admission:** The patient, a 73-year-old male, was admitted for upper and lower gastrointestinal endoscopy for gastrointestinal bleeding. The preoperative evaluation showed a heart rate on three occasions of 35, 36, and 37. The patient normally had a heart rate in the upper 40s and had never had one in the 30s. The procedure was canceled due to his bradycardia, and a cardiac evaluation was to be obtained prior to rescheduling. The slow heart rate may have been a reaction to atropine because it occurred shortly after administration of the drug.

   Discharge diagnoses: (1) Gastrointestinal bleed, (2) slow heart rate due to atropine correctly administered.

   Codes: ______________________________

   ____

5. **Inpatient admission:** The patient, a 46-year-old with AIDS, was recently discharged after workups for fever and weight loss, which were negative. He was readmitted because of histoplasmosis. Amphotericin B was started, and he tolerated the treatment well. Because the patient needed to continue treatment with this medication at home over a fairly long period of time, a Hickman catheter was inserted as a vascular access device to facilitate administration. He also had severe granulocytopenia, thought to be due to AZT (AHFS 8:18), which was discontinued.

   Discharge diagnoses: (1) Acquired immunodeficiency syndrome, (2) disseminated histoplasmosis, (3) granulocytopenia, possibly due to AZT.

   Codes: ______________________________

   ____

6. **Inpatient admission:** The patient was admitted in an altered mental state, showing some confusion as well as ataxia, jaundice, and dizziness. Her husband reported that he felt that the problem related to a massive overusage of an herbal tea given to her by a "healer." She was told to use about a tablespoon per day in a cup of tea but instead had been drinking about a gallon a day. She had a fibroid mass diagnosed about 1 year earlier but refused conventional treatment. Instead, she was trying to cure it with the tea. After checking with the Poison Control Center, it was determined that the phenylbutazone in this particular brand of tea was probably what was causing her problems. Her mental status returned to its baseline state within 48 hours, and the other problems related to herbal tea consumption disappeared in the same time frame. The presence of a huge uterine mass was confirmed on CT scan, and surgery was offered but refused.

   Discharge diagnoses: (1) Central nervous and digestive system problems secondary to herbal tea intoxication, (2) uterine mass.

   Codes: ______________________________

   ____

7. **Inpatient admission:** The patient, a young man, collapsed on the street after leaving a bar. An ambulance brought him to the emergency department in severe respiratory distress, which escalated to respiratory failure. He was intubated, ventilatory support was initiated, and he was admitted. Respiratory arrest ensued. He died within 3 hours of admission. Autopsy findings indicated lethal levels of Valium, cocaine, marijuana, and ephedrine.

   Discharge diagnosis: Respiratory failure secondary to overdoses of multiple substances.

   Codes: ____

8. **Inpatient admission:** The patient was admitted for a transurethral resection of the prostate for benign prostatic hypertrophy. He was taken to the operating room, but immediately following the induction with general anesthesia, atrial fibrillation developed. The procedure was canceled, and the atrial fibrillation treated. It was determined that the arrhythmia was due to the anesthetic.

   Discharge diagnoses: (1) Benign prostatic hypertrophy, (2) atrial fibrillation secondary to anesthesia.

   Codes: ____

9. **Inpatient admission:** The patient was admitted with nausea and vomiting for the past 24 hours. He was found to have an elevated digoxin level, and after adjustment of dosage, the level came down and the nausea and vomiting ceased. On questioning, he seemed to be taking the digoxin correctly. A new prescription was written, and the patient's digoxin level was to be monitored.

   Discharge diagnosis: Digoxin toxicity.

   Codes: ____

10. **Inpatient admission:** The patient was admitted with asthma, which had become intractable to management on an ambulatory care basis. The medications consisted of antibiotics, bronchodilators, and IV steroids. Unfortunately, her stay was prolonged because of an allergic reaction to two of the medications. Solu-Medrol (AHFS 68:04) and prednisone caused jitteriness and anxiety to the extent that Lorazepam was necessary.

    Discharge diagnoses: (1) Severe asthma, (2) medication allergy.

    Codes: ____

11. **Inpatient admission:** The patient came to the outpatient area with swelling and discoloration of the right arm. She was admitted with a provisional diagnosis of axillary vein thrombosis. A venogram of the right arm showed nearly complete obstruction of the axillary vein with an intraluminal clot. She gave a history of having started on birth control pills recently, and it was felt that the drug (Orval) was the cause of the thrombosis. She was taken off the birth control pills and started on IV anticoagulation. When discharged, her prothrombin time was in the therapeutic range, and the arm pain and edema were better.

    Discharge diagnosis: Right axillary vein thrombosis.

    Codes: ______________________________

    ____

12. **Inpatient admission:** The patient, an elderly woman, was admitted with shortness of breath, dyspnea on exertion, fever, and productive cough. These problems were felt to represent pneumonia. She was admitted for cultures and intravenous antibiotics. A chest film showed bilateral lung infiltrates. Erythromycin and Bactrim were given intravenously. However, diarrhea resulted. These drugs were discontinued; when she was switched to Ceftin, her condition showed rapid improvement.

    Discharge diagnoses: (1) Pneumococcal pneumonia, (2) diarrhea.

    Codes: ______________________________

    ____

13. **Inpatient admission:** The patient, a young woman, was brought to the emergency department via ambulance. She was suffering from acute alcohol intoxication. She admitted, however, that she had also ingested a handful of Compazine and Advil (an ibuprofen), thinking they were vitamins and aspirin. In the emergency department, she was treated with charcoal and Narcan and admitted for observation. A psychiatric consultation was obtained, and the psychiatrist deemed the patient stable and not dangerous to herself or others. The patient agreed to obtain drug and alcohol treatment and was discharged.

    Discharge diagnoses: (1) Acute alcohol intoxication, (2) multiple substance overdose, Compazine, Advil, and alcohol.

    Codes: ______________________________

    ____

14. **Inpatient admission:** The patient was admitted with subdural hematoma that appeared to be related to the anticoagulation she had been on for some time. She underwent an initial CT scan of the brain, which confirmed the subdural hematoma. She had been on chronic Coumadin therapy and had also been taking aspirin as prescribed by her physician for a left lower-extremity deep venous thrombosis. Her Coumadin and aspirin were held, and the prothrombin time was measured on a daily basis. The Coumadin was adjusted, and the aspirin was discontinued. Her condition at discharge was good.

    Discharge diagnoses: (1) Subdural hematoma secondary to medications, (2) chronic deep venous thrombosis, left leg.

    Codes: ______________________________

    ____

15. **Inpatient admission:** The patient fractured her left patella when she fell down her basement steps. An open reduction was performed with internal fixation. During recovery, she had problems with nausea, vomiting, and urinary retention secondary to morphine administration. The pain medication was changed to Demerol, and the symptoms subsided by the second day. The patient was discharged in satisfactory condition the same day.

    Discharge diagnoses: (1) Closed fracture, left patella, (2) allergic reaction to morphine.

    Procedure: Open reduction of patellar fracture with internal fixation.

    Codes: ______________________________

    ____

Complications of Surgery and Medical Care

B21

1. **Inpatient admission:** The patient was suffering an acute rejection episode involving her cadaveric renal transplant. She had undergone the transplant 3 months earlier for end-stage renal disease (ESRD) due to focal glomerulonephritis. An ultrasound-guided biopsy of the transplanted kidney was performed, and it was deemed suitable for her to go home after a pulse of steroids.

   Discharge diagnosis: Kidney transplant rejection.

   Codes: ____________________

   ____

2. **Inpatient admission:** The admitting diagnosis was revision of hip arthroplasty. The patient had undergone a total left hip arthroplasty 5 weeks earlier for osteoarthritis. The prosthesis worked well until the previous week, when she heard a pop. X-rays taken on admission showed a superior displacement of the left acetabular cup, which continued to migrate proximally despite bed rest. The left acetabular component of the prosthesis was revised with a 60-Ganz plate. Three days after surgery, the patient had a hemoglobin of 10.9 and was transfused with two units of packed cells. Hemoglobin count improved, and the patient was discharged on the fifth postoperative day.

   Discharge diagnoses: (1) Superior displacement, left acetabular cup prosthesis, (2) acute blood loss anemia.

   Codes: ____________________

   ____

3. **Inpatient admission:** The patient was admitted for removal of a left knee prosthesis, which had caused persistent pain since it was placed 3 years earlier. A recurrent thrombophlebitis was also present in the right lower extremity and was currently being treated with Coumadin. The left knee prosthesis was revised, and there was necrotic tissue of the bone ends (tibia and fibula), which was debrided. Components of the prosthesis were noted to be loosened, and the prosthesis was replaced. Physical therapy was started, and the patient was discharged on antibiotics.

   Discharge diagnoses: (1) Necrosis, bone, (2) malfunctioning left knee prosthesis, (3) thrombophlebitis, right leg.

   Codes: ____________________

   ____

4. **Inpatient admission:** Two months before admission, the patient completed 37 X-ray therapy treatments following resection of his tongue for removal of primary squamous cell carcinoma. He was admitted for evaluation and therapy of spontaneous extraoral drainage from an exposed bone plate of the left mandible. After debridement of the affected site, he was discharged for follow-up care at the referring hospital.

   Discharge diagnosis: Osteoradionecrosis of left mandible.

   Codes: ______________________________

   ____

5. **Inpatient admission:** The patient underwent a laryngoscopy with biopsy in the ambulatory surgery area, and a primary neoplasm of the false vocal cords was confirmed. In the recovery room, she developed acute respiratory insufficiency and was placed on oxygen. Because of the severity of the respiratory insufficiency, she was admitted. By the third hospital day, her blood gases returned to normal, and she was discharged.

   Discharge diagnoses: (1) Carcinoma of vocal cords, (2) postoperative respiratory insufficiency.

   Codes: ______________________________

   ____

6. **Inpatient admission:** The patient was admitted because of a displaced T tube, which was partially out of the common bile duct. The T tube was blocked by a malignant tumor of the pancreas, which caused the tube to move out of position. The patient was transferred to another hospital for care.

   Discharge diagnoses: (1) T tube partially out of common duct, (2) tumor, head of pancreas.

   Codes: ______________________________

   ____

7. **Inpatient admission:** The admission diagnoses were possible uterine septum and adnexal mass. Laparoscopy revealed a left ovarian cystic mass, which was thought to be an endometrioma. A uterine septum was confirmed on hysteroscopy. In the course of evaluation, a perforation of the left uterine horn occurred. Laparotomy was performed, and the cystic mass was excised from the ovary. The abdominal cavity was copiously irrigated, and the uterine perforation repaired. Pathologic findings identified the cystic mass as a dermoid cyst of the ovary.

   Discharge diagnoses: (1) Dermoid cyst, left ovary, (2) uterine septum, (3) inadvertent puncture, left uterine horn.

   Codes: ______________________________

   ____

8. **Inpatient admission:** The patient underwent a cystoscopy, retrograde pyelogram, and passage of a stone basket up the left ureter the day before admission. After release, she experienced terrible pain in the ureteral area and had to be readmitted for pain control. A repeat intravenous pyelogram was normal, and laboratory studies were all within normal limits. By the end of the second day, her pain was controlled with oral medications, and she was discharged.

   Discharge diagnosis: Postoperative pain of undetermined cause.

   Codes: ______________________________

   ____

9. **Inpatient admission:** The patient underwent a cold conization of the cervix and fractional dilatation and curettage for postmenopausal bleeding in the outpatient surgery center. The surgery was uncomplicated, and the operative site was dry at the conclusion of the procedure. An examination of tissue rendered a pathologic diagnosis of severe cervical dysplasia, CIN-III. Within 2 hours postoperatively, there was excessive bleeding and a vaginal pack was placed. She bled through the pack and was then admitted for suture repair of site of the previous cervical biopsy. Postoperatively, she remained dry with no further problems and was discharged in good condition.

   Discharge diagnoses: (1) Severe cervical dysplasia, CIN-III, (2) postoperative bleeding.

   Codes: ______________________________

   ____

10. **Inpatient admission:** The patient had a subtrochanteric stress fracture of the left femur, which had been repaired with pin insertion 3 weeks earlier. She returned with an infection of the operative wound site. A wide excisional debridement of the infection site of the soft tissue was carried out. No definite infection could be demonstrated within the bone. Cultures of the operative wound grew *Staphylococcus aureus,* sensitive to everything, and the patient was maintained on IV antibiotics until discharge.

    Discharge diagnosis: Deep soft tissue infection, left thigh.

    Codes: ______________________________

    ____

11. **Inpatient admission:** The patient underwent a cervical diskectomy and fusion last year. The pain improved for a few months but has recurred. He was readmitted for further surgery. A left C3-C4, C5-C6, and C6-C7 posterior cervical decompressive laminectomy with foraminotomy was performed. There was considerable postoperative pain, well out of proportion to what would be expected for this surgery. He remained in the hospital the week following surgery, primarily to receive intramuscular pain medications.

    Discharge diagnoses: (1) Cervical spondylosis, (2) severe postoperative back pain.

    Codes: ______________________________

    ____

12. **Inpatient admission:** A month earlier, the patient had undergone open reduction and internal fixation of a traumatic fracture of the left femur. She came to the emergency department with a severe and deep infection of the left thigh. She was admitted and taken to surgery immediately, where a wide excisional debridement of the infection was carried out and hardware was removed. Cultures of fixation pins grew *Staphylococcus aureus,* and she was maintained on IV Oxacillin. She was to continue antibiotics at home after discharge.

    Discharge diagnosis: Staphylococcal infection due to orthopedic fixation device.

    Codes: ______________________________

    ____

13. **Inpatient admission:** This acutely ill patient was admitted with fever, weakness, and chills. He had undergone a bilateral herniorrhaphy 4 days before admission. He is now experiencing some urgency on urination and dysuria. On admission to the hospital, the operative incisions were slightly red and tender and the abdomen somewhat distended. Blood cultures and wound cultures revealed a heavy growth of *Staphylococcus aureus,* which also grew on a urine culture. Enterococcus faecalis also grew on the urine culture. The chills and fever receded with IV antibiotics. It was believed that the patient's problems represented postoperative complications of the herniorrhaphy.

    Discharge diagnoses: (1) Postoperative sepsis and urinary tract infection, (2) postoperative wound infection.

    Codes: ______________________________

    ____

Appendix C: Case Summary Exercises Answer Key

Janatha R. Ashton, RHIA, MS

At press time additional guideline changes were anticipated for October 1, 2011, implementation. These changes may affect code assignment in this appendix.

Please visit http://www.ahacentraloffice.org for updated guidelines.

Contents

Symptoms, Signs, and Ill-Defined Conditions

C1

1. **Codes:** 600.01, 788.20, 401.0, V15.81, 57.94.

   Comments: Codes for symptoms, signs, and ill-defined conditions such as urinary retention (788.20) are not used as a principal diagnosis when a related definitive diagnosis (prostatic hypertrophy) has been established. However, as indicated by the "use additional code" note at code 600.01, an additional code should be assigned in conjunction with the benign prostatic hypertrophy code to identify other lower urinary tract symptoms (LUTS).

2. **Codes:** 784.7, 470, 410.92, 21.04, 21.02, 21.88, 99.04, 89.52.

   Comments: Following the UHDDS definition of principal diagnosis, epistaxis is the condition established after study to be responsible for occasioning the admission of the patient to the hospital for care. Because no related condition was identified, the symptom code from chapter 16 (volume 1 of *ICD-9-CM*) can be designated as the principal diagnosis. Deviated nasal septum is not designated as principal because epistaxis is not specified as being due to this condition. Although the myocardial infarct is qualified as status post, it occurred 7 weeks ago and is therefore within the 8-week acute phase. For code 410.92, the fifth digit 2 is assigned for the subsequent episode of care.

3. **Codes:** 786.51, 37.23, 88.54, 88.56, 88.43.

   Comments: Because no underlying etiology for the substernal chest pain was identified, the symptom is designated as the principal diagnosis.

4. **Codes:** 784.0, 03.31, 88.41, 88.91.

   Comments: No cause for the headache was determined because subarachnoid hemorrhage was ruled out through testing. Therefore, the symptom is the principal diagnosis.

5. **Codes:** 780.60, 185, 88.79, 92.18.

   Comments: (1) Because the etiology of the fever was never determined, the symptom is the principal diagnosis. (2) Prostatic cancer was not the reason for admission and was not treated. Because it was further evaluated by the ultrasound, it is coded and reported as an additional condition.

6. **Code:** 780.31.

Comments: (1) The "rule out" wording in the final diagnosis means that febrile seizure was suspected. Suspected conditions that have not been ruled out at the time of discharge are coded as if confirmed for inpatients. (2) A separate code for fever 780.60 is not necessary because code 780.31 includes the fever. (3) Although infiltrate was noticed on the right lung X-ray, no further mention was made of it, and apparently it was not considered significant. (Abnormal findings are not coded and reported unless the physician indicates their clinical significance.)

7. **Codes:** 789.00, 288.60, 88.74, 87.59, 87.73.

Comments: The symptom, abdominal pain, is the principal diagnosis because no underlying etiology was identified. Leukocytosis should be coded as an additional diagnosis.

8. **Codes:** 789.07, 278.00, 87.64, 87.73.

Comments: (1) No cause for the abdominal pain could be determined; therefore, it is designated as the principal diagnosis. (2) Although obesity was not responsible for admission, it is coded because it was clinically evaluated and treatment was started.

9. **Codes:** 790.6, 250.00, 574.20, 88.76.

Comments: The diagnostic statement represents a symptom followed by contrasting/comparative diagnoses (Section II[E]). The symptom is coded and sequenced first, followed by codes for the contrasting/comparative diagnoses. Code 790.6, Other abnormal blood chemistry, should be assigned for the abnormal liver function. It can be located in the index by looking up Findings, abnormal, liver function test. Code 794.8, Nonspecific abnormal results of function studies, liver, is not appropriate because it is intended for other types of tests (such as a liver scan) and not for blood tests for assessing liver function.

10. **Codes:** 682.7, 041.11, 250.01, 86.04, 93.32, 93.59.

Comments: The symptom, swelling of the foot, is not coded because the swelling was determined to be an abscess. Code 682.7 is assigned as the principal diagnosis. The abscess is not stated as due to the diabetes; therefore, code 250.01 is the appropriate code choice. Incision with drainage is the principal procedure because it was performed as treatment for the abscess. Code 93.59 is assigned for the oxygenation of the surgical wound.

11. **Code:** 382.9.

    Comments: Fever is a symptom and should not be sequenced as the principal diagnosis because the related definitive diagnosis of otitis media has been established as the underlying etiology (Section II[A]). Fever is an inherent part of otitis media and does not require a separate code assignment.

12. **Codes:** 464.4, 33.23, 87.44.

    Comments: The symptoms, stridor and respiratory distress, are integral to the diagnosis of croup and are not coded separately.

Infectious and Parasitic Diseases

C2

1. **Codes:** 042, 176.0, 528.6, 789.2, 86.11.

   Comments: Code 042 is assigned for all HIV infections. When the purpose of the admission is to treat the HIV infection or HIV-related conditions, code 042 is designated as the principal diagnosis.

2. **Codes:** 070.54, 304.90.

   Comments: (1) Although an outpatient procedure was performed for cholecystitis, the reason for admission, per the UHDDS definition of principal diagnosis, is chronic hepatitis C. (2) Some payers may require that related outpatient services provided within 72 hours of admission be combined into the inpatient claim and reported as additional codes. If so, it is important to determine the payer policy regarding what services should be combined. For example, Medicare considers services to be related when the same *ICD-9-CM* diagnosis is applicable to both the outpatient service and inpatient admission. In this case, the reasons for the outpatient surgery and the inpatient admission were unrelated and therefore not coded.

3. **Codes:** 599.0, 041.7, 599.71, 401.1.

   Comments: (1) Although physicians may use the terms "septic" and "urosepsis" to mean sepsis, the physician has ruled out septicemia in this case, and, therefore, no septicemia code is assigned. (2) The instruction with code 599.0, "Use additional code to identify organism . . . ," must always be followed when the organism is known. (3) Because hematuria is not integral to a urinary tract infection, it is coded.

4. **Codes:** 038.9, 995.91, 414.00, 250.02, V58.67, 89.52.

   Comments: (1) The admission was necessitated by signs and symptoms of sepsis, which was never ruled out and, therefore, is the principal diagnosis (guideline Section II [H]). The guideline for sepsis [Section I, C(1)(b)(1)(a)] indicates that if sepsis is present on admission and meets the definition of principal diagnosis, the underlying systemic infection code (in this instance 038.9) should be assigned as the principal diagnosis, followed by code 995.91, Sepsis, as required by the sequencing rules in the Tabular List. (2) Diabetes is coded to uncontrolled when so stated by the physician. Code V58.67 is assigned because the patient is on insulin therapy. (3) No code is assigned for ST- and T-wave changes on the EKG because they represent abnormal findings that were not treated or further evaluated.

5. **Codes:** 042, 683, 304.90, V62.6.

   Comments: Code 042 is assigned for all HIV infections and is designated as the reason for encounter when the patient was seen for HIV infection or a related condition. Code V62.6 may be assigned to show the refusal of medications for religious reasons.

6. **Codes:** 382.9, 041.12, V02.54, 20.1.

   Comments: (1) Code 382.9 is assigned to identify the otitis media. (2) Because the physician has documented that the patient has both a MRSA infection and is a carrier of MRSA, codes 041.12 and V02.54 should both be assigned. (3) Assign code 20.1 to show the removal of the tubes.

Endocrine, Metabolic and Nutritional Diseases and Immune-System Disorders

C3

1. **Codes:** 255.8, 255.10, 276.8, 401.9, 88.01.

   Comments: (1) Either of the interrelated diagnoses, adrenal mass (255.8) or aldosteronism (255.10), can be designated as the principal diagnosis because the patient was admitted for evaluation of adrenal malfunction (Section II[B]). (2) Under Mass, specified site, the Alphabetic Index to Diseases (volume 2 of *ICD-9-CM*) directs the coder to a disease of specified organ or site, which results in code 255.8, Other specified disorder of adrenal glands.

2. **Codes:** 261, 335.20, 599.70, 96.6.

   Comments: (1) Admission was necessitated by malnutrition, not the underlying amyotrophic lateral sclerosis. Therefore, malnutrition, the condition requiring placement of a feeding tube, is the principal diagnosis. (2) Because the malnutrition is specified as severe, it is assigned to code 261.

3. **Codes:** 250.02, 599.0, 041.02, E888.9, E849.0, E000.8.

   Comments: The condition, after study, that necessitated admission was newly diagnosed diabetes out of control. Type 2 diabetic patients often require insulin to bring blood sugar down to an acceptable level, but this does not mean that the diabetes has become insulin dependent. Code V58.67, Long-term (current) use of insulin, is not appropriate because the insulin therapy was just started and there is no information about long-term use.

4. **Codes:** V67.09, 250.70, 443.81, V42.0, V42.83, V49.75.

   Comments: The reason for encounter was for follow-up examination following surgery (V67.09). Code V49.75 indicates the status post below-the-knee amputation—the reason why the follow-up was necessary. Other codes represent conditions that required consideration in evaluating the patient's current status.

5. **Codes:** 250.80, 428.0, 599.0, 041.3.

   Comments: Diabetic hypoglycemia without mention of coma is assigned to subcategory 250.8, not 251.0 or 251.2.

6. **Codes:** 682.7, 279.12, 041.11, 86.04, 93.32, 93.59.

   Comments: The admission was necessitated by the foot abscess. Therefore, the foot abscess is designated as the principal diagnosis. Codes 287.5 and 692.9 are not assigned for the thrombocytopenia and eczema in this case because immunodeficiency with thrombocytopenia and eczema is specifically indexed to code 279.12, Wiskott-Aldrich syndrome. Therefore, the thrombocytopenia and eczema are considered inherent to this syndrome and should not be coded separately.

7. **Codes:** 250.33, V58.67.

   Comments: Patients with diabetic ketoacidosis who have progressed to a comatose state are assigned to subcategory 250.3. No additional code is assigned for ketoacidosis. The fifth digit 3 signifies uncontrolled, which is appropriate because diabetic ketoacidosis by definition is uncontrolled. Code V58.67 is not required for type 1 diabetics because these patients require insulin. However, this code may be assigned, if desired, to provide additional information. This handbook has followed this principle based on the advice published in *Coding Clinic,* Fourth Quarter 2004, p. 55.

8. **Codes:** 250.03, 522.5, 410.32, V58.67.

   Comments: (1) Diabetes mellitus type 1 out of control is assigned to subcategory 250.0. The fifth digit 3 signifies the uncontrolled status of the diabetes. Code V58.67 is not required for type 1 diabetics because these patients require insulin. However, this code may be assigned, if desired, to provide additional information. (2) The abscessed tooth is significant as a possible etiology of the out-of-control diabetes and was also under treatment during this admission (penicillin-V). Code 522.5 should be assigned as an additional diagnosis. (3) Code 410.32 is assigned for the MI, which is less than 8 weeks old and was evaluated during this admission. The fifth digit 2 indicates that this is a subsequent episode of care.

Mental Disorders

C4

1. **Codes:** 303.92, 304.10, 301.84, 571.3.

   Comments: The fifth digit 2 is assigned for the long-standing alcoholism, which was documented by the physician as episodic. The fifth digit 0 is assigned to subcategory 304.1 because the pattern of Librium dependence is not specified.

2. **Codes:** 296.40, 244.9, 346.90.

   Comments: (1) The fifth digit 0 is assigned to subcategory 296.4 because the status of the manic bipolar disorder is not specified. No code assignment is necessary for depression because depression is a component of bipolar disorder. (2) Although not psychiatric conditions, both hypothyroidism and migraine headaches are coexisting conditions under treatment and should be coded.

3. **Codes:** 318.0, 133.0, 132.1, 682.7.

   Comments: (1) Although the scenario indicates that the patient was admitted for observation (subcategory V71.0), a condition (moderate mental retardation) is identified as the etiology for the patient's disorientation and confusion. No code is assigned for observation in the presence of a confirmed condition (Section I C18(d)(6)). (2) All the nonpsychiatric conditions meet the UHDDS definition of additional diagnoses. They were diagnosed and treated; therefore, codes are assigned.

4. **Code:** 295.34.

   Comments: Schizophrenia, paranoid type, is assigned to subcategory 295.3. The status of this condition is specified as chronic with acute exacerbation, which is identified with the fifth digit 4. One of the fifth digits printed at the beginning of category 295 must be assigned with each subcategory code.

5. **Codes:** 311, 301.83, 315.39, 250.01, 300.9, V58.67.

   Comments: (1) Because medication was prescribed for the patient's depression, depression is sequenced first. (2) Code V58.67 is not required for type 1 diabetics because these patients require insulin. However, this code may be assigned, if desired, to provide additional information. This handbook has followed this principle based on the advice published in *Coding Clinic,* Fourth Quarter 2004, p. 55.

6. **Codes:** 331.0, 294.11.

   Comments: Alzheimer's disease with dementia is coded as follows: the code for Alzheimer's disease is sequenced first, and code 294.11, Dementia in conditions classified elsewhere, is added. The disorderly and aggressive behavior is classified as behavioral disturbance, and the fifth digit 1 is used with code 294.1 to indicate this.

7. **Codes:** 307.1, 261.

   Comments: Code 261, Nutritional marasmus, should be assigned as an additional diagnosis for the severe malnutrition. For some anorexic patients, the weight loss is so severe that it leads to malnutrition. Code 261 further describes the severity of the patient's condition.

8. **Codes:** 300.11, 789.09, 87.73.

   Comments: Codes for symptoms, signs, and ill-defined conditions from chapter 16 of volume 1 of *ICD-9-CM* (789.0x) are not to be used as principal diagnoses when a related definitive diagnosis has been established (Section II[A]). The physician indicated that the symptomatology was due to hysterical conversion disorder (definitive diagnosis), and code 300.11 is assigned as the principal diagnosis. The fifth digit 9 is assigned for the abdominal pain identified at multiple sites.

9. **Codes:** 311, 042, 304.20.

   Comments: Depression was responsible for the clinic visit and is sequenced as the reason for encounter. The HIV infection contributed to the patient's depression, but it was the depression that was the reason for admission.

Diseases of the Blood and Blood-Forming Organs

C5

1. **Code:** 284.01.

   Comments: (1) Dental caries and pyorrhea are the reasons for the outpatient encounter; however, aplastic anemia represents the reason for inpatient admission, per the UHDDS definition of principal diagnosis. (2) Some payers may require that related outpatient services provided within 72 hours of admission be combined into the inpatient claim and reported as additional codes. If so, it is important to determine the payer policy regarding what services should be combined. For example, Medicare considers services to be related when the same *ICD-9-CM* diagnosis is applicable to the outpatient service and the inpatient admission.

2. **Code:** 282.62.

   Comments: Pain is a symptom integral to sickle cell crisis. Therefore, a separate code assignment for the pain is not necessary.

3. **Codes:** 281.9, 535.50, 785.1, 99.04.

   Comments: (1) Although palpitations were the reason for admission, the underlying cause was determined to be anemia (Section II[A]). Anemia is sequenced as the principal diagnosis. (2) In addition, code 785.1 is assigned to identify palpitations that are not inherent in anemia and were worked up by cardiology as a significant condition.

4. **Codes:** 275.42, 188.9.

   Comments: (1) Although the primary site of the neoplasm had been treated, residual disease was still present and under treatment; therefore, code 188.9 should be assigned. (2) Nausea, anorexia, fevers, and constipation are inherent to hypercalcemia and are not coded.

5. **Codes:** 289.4, 283.9, 592.0, 41.5, 55.11.

   Comments: (1) The spleen was removed because of hypersplenism, which is a further manifestation of hemolytic anemia. Hypersplenism is the principal diagnosis because it was the reason for admission and the condition to which the thrust of treatment was directed. (2) No specific treatment was addressed to the anemia, but it is related to the hypersplenism and therefore is coded. (3) Splenectomy and pyelolithotomy are both therapeutic procedures; however, splenectomy is designated as the principal procedure because it is related to the principal diagnosis.

6. **Codes:** 535.01, V58.61.

   Comments: Code 535.01 is assigned for the acute gastritis with hemorrhage. No code is assigned for the prolonged bleeding time.

7. **Codes:** 285.3, 174.9.

   Comments: (1) Code 285.3 is assigned to identify anemia due to chemotherapy. (2) Code 174.9 is assigned to show the current breast cancer. (3) It is not necessary to additionally report the adverse effect E code because the information about its being an adverse effect of a chemotherapy drug is included in the anemia code. However, providers may opt to collect the E code for purposes of internal data collection.

Diseases of the Nervous System and Sense Organs

C6

1. **Codes:** 367.4, 042.

   Comments: (1) Presbyopia is designated as the reason for encounter because it was chiefly responsible for the services received. (2) The HIV infection was not specified as causing the presbyopia and was not treated. Nevertheless, it is documented as a coexisting condition.

2. **Codes:** 365.11, 362.50, 365.72.

   Comments: (1) Glaucoma is coded and sequenced as the principal diagnosis following the UHDDS definition. (2) High intraocular pressure is integral to glaucoma and is not coded. (3) Macular degeneration is under current medical management and meets the UHDDS definition of additional diagnosis. (4) Code 365.72 is assigned for the glaucoma stage.

3. **Codes:** 355.2, 905.6, 04.49.

   Comments: (1) Mononeuritis is the condition necessitating admission of the patient to the hospital for surgery. (2) Dislocation is not coded because it is a previous condition no longer under treatment, but a code indicating that the mononeuritis is a late effect of the dislocation is assigned.

4. **Codes:** 345.41, 89.19.

   Comments: In the Alphabetic Index to Diseases (volume 2 of *ICD-9-CM*), the coder should reference Epilepsy, localization related (focal) (partial), with complex partial seizures. The fifth digit 1 is assigned because the seizures are described as intractable.

5. **Codes:** 365.11, 366.9, 365.73, 12.64, 13.41, 13.71.

   Comments: (1) Either the glaucoma or the cataract could be designated as the first-listed diagnosis because both were present on admission and both were treated (Section II[C]). The procedure performed for the definitive treatment of cataract is sequenced as the first procedure. (2) Code 365.73 is assigned for the glaucoma stage.

6. **Codes:** 376.01, 376.30, 461.2, 22.63, 87.03.

   Comments: (1) The principal diagnosis is orbital cellulitis/abscess because this was the condition necessitating admission. (2) Orbital edema is integral to orbital cellulitis and should not be coded separately. However, exophthalmos is not integral to orbital cellulitis and should be coded. (3) Ethmoidal sinusitis qualified as acute is assigned code 461.2.

7. **Codes:** 435.9, 250.01, V58.67.

   Comments: (1) Acute cerebrovascular attack was ruled out and therefore is not coded. (2) Arm and leg paralysis were transient, focal neurological deficits that completely cleared during the hospitalization. No code assignments are required. (3) The "probable" condition necessitating admission was TIA. Conditions described as probable on discharge are coded as though confirmed. (4) A code is assigned for diabetes even though no specific treatment was given because it is a condition that always requires clinical evaluation when any other medical problem is present. (5) Code V58.67 is not required for type 1 diabetics because these patients require insulin. However, this code may be assigned, if desired, to provide additional information. This handbook has followed this principle based on the advice published in *Coding Clinic,* Fourth Quarter 2004, p. 55.

8. **Codes:** 473.9, 053.19, 290.0.

   Comments: Although postherpetic neuralgia and chronic senile dementia were also present, the condition determined to be responsible for admission was sinusitis. No code is assigned for the renal cyst because it was qualified as "history of" and was not further evaluated or treated during the patient's stay.

9. **Codes:** 438.30, 746.5.

   Comments: Code 438.30, Monoplegia, identifies a late effect of the previous stroke. In coding late effects of cerebrovascular disease, a combination code identifies both the residual and the late effect; therefore, only code 438.30 is required. Because this residual was the reason for her visit, code 438.30 is listed as the reason for the encounter.

10. **Codes:** 338.3, 198.5, 162.9, 92.29.

    Comments: (1) Code 338.3 is assigned to pain documented as being related, associated, or due to cancer, primary or secondary malignancy, or tumor. This code is assigned regardless of whether the pain is acute or chronic. It may be assigned as the principal or first-listed code when the stated reason for the admission/encounter is documented as pain control/pain management. The underlying neoplasm should be reported as an additional diagnosis. (2) Code 92.29 is assigned to identify that the radiation was administered.

Diseases of the Respiratory System

C7

1. **Codes:** 518.81, 491.21, 348.1, 486, 96.72, 96.04.

   Comments: (1) Respiratory failure was responsible for admission and is designated as the principal diagnosis. (2) The patient was intubated in the emergency department and maintained on mechanical ventilation until day 5, more than 96 hours. Code 96.72 is assigned as the principal procedure.

2. **Codes:** 518.81, 428.0.

   Comments: Code 518.81, Acute respiratory failure, may be assigned as a principal diagnosis when it is the condition established after study to be chiefly responsible for occasioning the admission to the hospital, and the selection is supported by the Alphabetic Index and Tabular List. However, chapter-specific coding guidelines (obstetrics, poisoning, HIV, newborn) that provide sequencing direction take precedence. Whether the respiratory failure is due to or associated with an underlying respiratory condition does not have any bearing on the sequencing of respiratory failure. When a patient is admitted with respiratory failure and another acute condition, the principal diagnosis will depend on the circumstances of admission. In this case, the patient was admitted for immediate treatment of the acute respiratory failure and, therefore, it is sequenced as the principal diagnosis. Code 428.0, Congestive heart failure, is sequenced as an additional diagnosis.

3. **Codes:** 481, 491.21, 799.02.

   Comments: (1) Streptococcal pneumoniae is the causative organism. Because this organism is specified in the title of code 481, an additional code assignment from the 041 category would be incorrect. (2) Code 491.21 is assigned for exacerbated chronic obstructive pulmonary disease. Chronic obstructive pulmonary disease is one of the conditions that would require clinical evaluation even if no further treatment were given. Therefore, it is listed as an additional code. (3) Code 799.02, Hypoxemia, is assigned as an additional diagnosis for the hypoxia because it is not inherent in pneumonia.

4. **Codes:** 034.0, 475.

   Comments: Both tonsillitis and peritonsillar abscess were present at admission. Both conditions were treated, and both meet the criteria for principal diagnosis. Either tonsillitis or peritonsillar abscess can be sequenced as the principal diagnosis (Section II[C]).

5. **Codes:** 250.81, 707.14, 491.22, 799.02, V58.67.

   Comments: (1) In the Alphabetic Index to Diseases (volume 2) under Ulcer, diabetes, lower limb, heel, codes 250.8 [707.14] are listed. Consequently, 250.81 is designated as the principal diagnosis with an additional code of 707.14. (2) Code 491.22 includes acute bronchitis and chronic obstructive pulmonary disease. (3) Code 799.02 is assigned for the hypoxia, which is not inherent in COPD. (4) Code V58.67 is not required for type 1 diabetics because these patients require insulin. However, this code may be assigned, if desired, to provide additional information. This handbook has followed this principle based on the advice published in *Coding Clinic,* Fourth Quarter 2004, p. 55.

6. **Codes:** 496, 291.0, 303.90, 558.9, V12.72, 45.23.

   Comments: (1) Code 496 includes acute bronchospasm. (2) Impending delirium tremens are coded to 291.0, even though they did not occur. See the main entry, Impending, delirium tremens, in the Alphabetic Index to Diseases (volume 2 of *ICD-9-CM*). (3) Both conditions were present on admission and both were treated; either could be designated as the principal diagnosis. (4) Code V12.72 is assigned because the history of polyps was the reason for the colonoscopy.

7. **Codes:** 786.03, 89.67.

   Comments: "Rule out apnea" remained as a probable diagnosis on discharge. On inpatient discharges, suspected conditions are coded as though confirmed.

8. **Codes:** 507.0, 34.04, 87.44.

   Comments: After study, the condition found to be chiefly responsible for the admission of the patient for care was aspiration pneumonia. Code 507.0 includes both the aspiration and the pneumonia.

9. **Codes:** 493.90, 382.00.

   Comments: Asthmatic bronchitis without further specification as to type is assigned to code 493.90.

10. **Codes:** 493.91, 457.0, 401.9, 244.9, V10.3.

    Comments: The asthma is coded with the fifth digit 1 to indicate status asthmaticus. Status asthmaticus is usually considered to be present when the condition does not respond to treatment on an ambulatory basis. However, the physician must document status asthmaticus before a fifth digit 1 can be assigned.

11. **Codes:** 428.0, 481, 496, 414.00, 87.44.

Comments: (1) Either congestive heart failure or pneumococcal pneumonia could be designated as the principal diagnosis because both were present on admission and attention was directed to both conditions (Section II[C]). (2) Code 414.00, Arteriosclerosis of unspecified type of vessel, native or graft, is assigned because it is not clear that there has been no previous bypass surgery.

12. **Codes:** 518.81, 491.21, 414.00.

Comments: Respiratory failure is listed as the principal diagnosis because it is the reason for the admission. A code should not be assigned for angina because it does not meet criteria for reporting additional diagnoses. Code 414.00, Arteriosclerosis of unspecified type of vessel, native or graft, is assigned because it is not clear that there has been no previous bypass surgery.

13. **Codes:** 483.0, 276.51, 599.0, 041.04.

Comments: (1) Any of the conditions could have been designated as the principal diagnosis according to symptoms on admission and treatment rendered. All conditions meet the criteria for additional diagnoses (Section II[C]) except for fever, which is integral to pneumonia. (2) Based on the documentation, a code from category 771 would not be assigned. According to the *Official Guidelines for Coding and Reporting,* Section I (C)(15)(a)(3), if a newborn has a condition that may be either due to the birth process or community acquired and the documentation does not indicate which it is, the default is due to the birth process. In this case, the infant had previously been discharged in good condition and developed the pneumonitis later, which would mean that it was a community-acquired condition. According to the official guidelines, if a newborn has a community-acquired condition, a code from chapter 15 should not be assigned. Code 483.0 is assigned rather than code 486 because the organism was identified.

14. **Codes:** 493.92, 747.31.

Comments: Viral pneumonia was ruled out and should not be coded. The coder can reference Disease, reactive airway, in the Alphabetic Index to Diseases (volume 2 of *ICD-9-CM*), which leads to the note, "see Asthma." Although the asthma had not reached the status asthmaticus stage, it has become exacerbated. Congenital pulmonary stenosis is coded because it probably is involved in the reactive airway disease and would have received clinical evaluation during the stay.

Diseases of the Digestive System

C8

1. **Codes:** 564.3, 276.51, 278.01.

   Comments: Although the vomiting is not specified as due to the gastric surgery, the Tabular List and Alphabetic Index to Diseases (volumes 1 and 2 of *ICD-9-CM*) instruct the coder to assign 564.3 for any vomiting following gastrointestinal surgery.

2. **Codes:** 507.0, 438.82, 787.20, 783.21, 43.11.

   Comments: (1) Aspiration pneumonia is sequenced as the principal diagnosis. (2) Because no code exists for impending malnutrition, code 783.21 is assigned to identify loss of weight, the precursor condition. (3) Dysphagia is the late effect of the previous cerebrovascular accident. (4) As indicated by the "use additional code" note at code 438.82, an additional code is assigned to identify the type of dysphagia. Because the type of dysphagia has not been further specified other than as difficulty swallowing, code 787.20 is assigned.

3. **Codes:** 531.40, 43.6, 44.13.

   Comments: The ulcer is unspecified as acute or chronic, with hemorrhage and without mention of obstruction. Code 531.40 is assigned to identify the bleeding gastric ulcer to the greatest degree of specificity available.

4. **Codes:** 577.0, 577.1, 577.8, 52.93, 52.98, 98.59.

   Comments: Because the patient had both acute and chronic pancreatitis and separate subterms exist in the Alphabetic Index to Diseases (volume 2 of *ICD-9-CM*) at the same indention level for acute and chronic, both 577.0 and 577.1 are assigned, with 577.0 sequenced first as the acute condition. Both the pancreatic calculi and the obstruction are included in code 577.8.

5. **Codes:** 562.11, 88.01, 88.19.

   Comments: (1) After study, diverticulitis was determined to be the reason for encounter. Diverticulosis is included in the diverticulitis code. (2) No codes are assigned for scoliosis or degenerative changes in the lumbar spine because they represent incidental findings on X-ray.

6. **Codes:** 556.2, 569.3, 276.51, 285.1, 48.24, 99.03.

Comments: (1) Ulcerative proctitis is sequenced as the principal diagnosis because the workup and treatment were directed at identifying and treating the cause of the bleeding. (2) Rectal bleeding (569.3) and acute blood loss anemia (285.1), further manifestations of ulcerative proctitis, are also coded because both meet criteria for additional diagnoses. Dehydration was treated and, therefore, is also coded.

7. **Codes:** 782.4, 070.30, 282.60, 88.74.

Comments: When a symptom (782.4) is followed by contrasting or comparative diagnoses (070.30 and 282.60), the symptom should be sequenced first (*Official Guidelines for Coding and Reporting,* Section II [E]).

8. **Codes:** 792.1, 535.00, 535.10, 562.11, 45.16, 45.23.

Comments: (1) No cause for the blood in stools was determined; therefore, the symptom is the principal diagnosis. The code is referenced in the Alphabetic Index to Diseases (volume 2 of *ICD-9-CM*) under the main entry, Findings, abnormal, without diagnosis. (2) When diverticulitis is present, it is understood that diverticulosis also exists, and an additional code for the latter condition is unnecessary. (3) Two endoscopic procedures were performed, EGD and colonoscopy. Code 45.16 includes both biopsy and EGD, and the colonoscopy is coded to 45.23. Additional procedure codes are unnecessary for esophagoscopy and gastroscopy because the titles indicate that these approaches were used. When an endoscope is passed through more than one area of the body, the procedure is coded to the farthest site only.

9. **Codes (episode 1):** 556.9, 45.83, 46.20.

Comments: (1) The condition necessitating admission and surgery was ulcerative colitis. (2) Colectomy is the definitive treatment for colitis and is therefore designated as the principal procedure.

Codes (episode 2): 556.9, 48.41, 46.01.

Comments: (1) More extensive surgery was required to further control the patient's ulcerative colitis. Colitis is, again, the condition necessitating admission. (2) Endorectal pull-through is the definitive treatment for ulcerative colitis and is therefore the principal procedure.

Codes (episode 3): V55.2, 46.51.

Comments: (1) The ulcerative colitis responded to the previous surgeries and was no longer present; therefore, it is not coded. (2) The sole purpose for the third admission is ileostomy closure, V55.2. Ileostomy closure is listed in the Alphabetic Index to Procedures (volume 3 of *ICD-9-CM*) under Closure, ileostomy, or Closure, artificial opening, intestine, small.

10. **Codes:** 569.49, 48.35.

    Comments: The condition, established after study, that necessitated the admission of the patient to the hospital for care was rectal granuloma. Although the lesion was not initially identified, the physician was able to further specify the condition as granuloma following excision and pathologic examination.

11. **Codes:** 577.0, 96.07.

    Comments: (1) Pain and vomiting are not coded because they are integral to pancreatitis. (2) Although the pancreatitis is not qualified as acute or chronic, code 577.0 is assigned because this is the code provided in the Alphabetic Index to Diseases (volume 2 of *ICD-9-CM*) for pancreatitis that is not further specified.

12. **Codes:** 571.2, 456.20, 303.90, 42.33, 42.33, 99.04, 99.07.

    Comments: (1) Code 456.20 is a combination code for esophageal varices with bleeding. Because code 456.20 is italicized, it cannot be sequenced as the principal diagnosis. The coder should follow the instructional note under subcategory 456.2 to "code also underlying cause." (2) Code 571.2 identifies Laennec's cirrhosis as the etiology of the bleeding esophageal varices. (3) The varices were endoscopically sclerosed two times, the first time when an EGD was performed (42.33) and again by esophagoscopy (42.33). Code 42.33 can be found in the Alphabetic Index to Procedures (volume 3 of *ICD-9-CM*) under Control hemorrhage, esophagus, endoscopic, or under the main term Sclerotherapy. (4) Codes for the EGD and esophagoscopy are not assigned because these procedures were performed only as the approach to the more definitive procedure for control of hemorrhage. (5) Fifth digit 0 is assigned to subcategory 303.9 because there was no documentation of the pattern of use (i.e., continuous, episodic, or in remission).

13. **Codes:** 530.11, 535.60, V42.0, 44.14.

    Comments: (1) Either esophagitis or duodenitis can be designated as the principal diagnosis because both are consistent with the reason for admission, both were identified during the hospitalization, and both were treated (Section II [B]). (2) The previous kidney transplant is coded because it was significant in the patient's current care and treatment.

14. **Codes:** 574.10, 565.0, 790.6, 51.23, 50.11, 87.53, 45.24.

    Comments: (1) Code 574.10 includes both cholecystitis and cholelithiasis. (2) Adhesions and lysis of adhesions are not coded because adhesions were not listed as a discharge diagnosis. Lysis of adhesions is fairly common in cholecystectomy surgery and is not coded unless the significance was specified by the physician. Although the biopsy of the liver was normal, the physician still felt that there was an abnormality in the liver function lab studies, so this was coded.

15. **Codes:** 008.8, 87.62.

Comments: (1) The reason for admission was possible coronary artery disease and probable gastroenteritis. Possible coronary artery disease was ruled out by diagnostic evaluation and is not coded. (2) The principal diagnosis is viral gastroenteritis. Probable diagnoses at the time of discharge are coded as though confirmed. (3) No code is assigned for the hiatal hernia because it is an incidental X-ray finding for a condition that was not treated or evaluated further during the current encounter and therefore is not reportable. This is consistent with the advice published in *Coding Clinic,* First Quarter 2000, p. 6.

16. **Codes:** 577.0, 555.9.

Comments: Patient's symptomatology and treatment were related to pancreatitis. Sequence pancreatitis as principal diagnosis. Crohn's disease, a coexisting condition, is coded because it was also treated.

17. **Codes (episode 1):** 789.06, 787.02.

Comments: Only symptoms can be coded for this visit because questionable diagnoses are coded as if established only for hospital inpatients. Conditions are coded to the highest level of certainty on physician office visits. Either abdominal pain or nausea can be sequenced as the reason for the encounter.

Codes (episode 2): 540.1, 47.09.

Comments: The patient's symptomatology was explained by the definitive finding of appendicitis with perforation. Abdominal pain and nausea are inherent to appendicitis and should not be coded separately. Perforation and peritonitis are both included in code 540.1.

18. **Codes:** 562.11, 239.0.

Comments: When diagnoses are stated in a comparative or contrasting manner, both conditions are coded and sequenced according to the circumstances of admission. In this instance, either condition is consistent with abdominal pain, and either can be sequenced as the principal diagnosis (*Official Guidelines for Coding and Reporting,* Section II [D]).

19. **Codes:** 536.2, 789.00.

Comments: Vomiting, not otherwise specified, is coded as a symptom (787.03); however, when qualified as "persistent," it is classified to code 536.2. Persistent vomiting can be referenced in the *ICD-9-CM*'s Index to Diseases under Vomiting, uncontrollable.

20. **Codes:** 566, 565.1, 49.01, 49.11.

Comments: Although code 49.11 includes both anal fistulotomy and drainage of anal abscess, drainage of perianal abscess has a specific code assignment separate from that for anal fistulotomy. Code 49.01 is assigned as the principal procedure for perianal abscess drainage.

21. **Codes:** 558.9, 455.2, 250.01, V42.1, V58.67, 45.25.

Comments: (1) Chronic colitis is designated as the principal diagnosis because it is the condition, established after study, that necessitated admission. (2) A previous heart transplant is significant to the current care and treatment of the patient. It is referenced in the Alphabetic Index to Diseases (volume 2 of *ICD-9-CM*) under Status, transplant, heart, V42.1. (3) Code V58.67 is not required for type 1 diabetics because these patients require insulin. However, this code may be assigned, if desired, to provide additional information. This handbook has followed this principle based on the advice published in *Coding Clinic,* Fourth Quarter 2004, p. 55. (4) The biopsy was performed during the colonoscopy and is, therefore, a closed biopsy. The combination code (45.25) should be assigned.

22. **Codes:** 543.9, V42.1, 45.25, 88.74, 87.63.

Comments: (1) Probable appendiceal cyst is coded as though confirmed. (2) The fact that the patient had a transplanted heart is important during all subsequent medical care. It is referenced under Status, transplant, heart, in the Alphabetic Index to Diseases (volume 2 of *ICD-9-CM*). (3) Aspiration of appendiceal mass for diagnostic examination can be referenced in the Alphabetic Index to Procedures (volume 3) under Biopsy, intestine, large, closed. The reference for Biopsy, appendix, refers only to an open biopsy of the appendix and should not be assigned. A review of the procedural Tabular List (volume 3 of *ICD-9-CM*) indicates that code 45.25 is the appropriate code for a closed biopsy.

Diseases of the Genitourinary System

C9

1. **Codes:** 038.42, 995.91, 599.0, 553.3, 041.49, 530.11.

   Comments: (1) Although sepsis and UTI were both present on admission, the thrust of treatment (IV antibiotics/one-week stay) and symptomatology (fever, confusion, lethargy) were most related to the sepsis. Sepsis is sequenced as the principal diagnosis. (2) Because E. coli grew in both urine and blood cultures, code 038.42 is assigned for sepsis. (3) The guideline for sepsis [Section I, C(1)(b)(1)(a)] indicates that if sepsis is present on admission and meets the definition of principal diagnosis, the underlying systemic infection code (in this instance 038.42) should be assigned as the principal diagnosis, followed by code 995.91, Sepsis, as required by the sequencing rules in the Tabular List. (4) Code 041.49 identifies the causative organism for the urinary tract infection (code 599.0).

2. **Codes:** 626.9, 278.01, V85.42, 69.09.

   Comments: (1) Bicornuate uterus was ruled out and is not coded. (2) Hysteroscopy is the usual approach to the definitive procedure, dilation and curettage, and should not be coded.

3. **Codes:** 404.90, 585.9, 39.27.

   Comments: (1) When a patient is admitted for placement of a fistula for future dialysis, the condition is coded as the principal diagnosis rather than V56.0. Code V56.0 is used when the patient is admitted for the sole purpose of performing dialysis. (2) Hypertensive heart disease, kidney disease, and chronic kidney disease must be classified to the combination code 404.90, with the fifth digit indicating with or without heart failure and the stage of the chronic kidney disease. An additional code 585.1–585.4, 585.9, would also be assigned to identify the specific stage of the chronic kidney disease.

4. **Codes:** 595.1, 57.6, 56.51.

   Comments: (1) A urinary cystectomy, not specified as complete, radical, or total, is assigned to code 57.6, as indicated in the Alphabetic Index to Procedures (volume 3 of *ICD-9-CM*). (2) Either procedure can be sequenced as the principal procedure because both are definitive procedures related to the principal diagnosis.

5. **Codes:** 403.01, 585.6, V45.11, 39.95.

   Comments: Code 403.01 is a combination code that encompasses the malignant kidney hypertension and the patient's chronic kidney disease. There is no additional code available to indicate the exacerbation of the kidney failure. Acute kidney failure is not an exacerbation of chronic kidney disease; it is essentially a different condition. Category 403 has fifth digits to identify the stage of the chronic kidney disease. An additional code 585.5 or 585.6 would also be assigned to identify the specific stage of the chronic kidney disease. In this instance, because the patient was specified to have end-stage renal disease, assign code 585.6. Because the patient was not admitted solely for renal dialysis, code V56.0 is not assigned. Assign code V45.11 to identify that the patient is a dialysis patient.

6. **Codes:** 403.01, 585.6, 55.69, 00.93, 39.95.

   Comments: Code 403.01 is a combination code that encompasses malignant kidney hypertension, end-stage renal disease, and chronic kidney disease. Code 585.6 is assigned to identify the end-stage renal disease. Code 00.93 is assigned to identify that the transplant is from a cadaver. In addition, the organ transplant procedure (55.69) is reported separately.

7. **Codes:** 593.4, 591, 599.70, 87.74.

   Comments: (1) Ureteropelvic obstruction is designated as the principal diagnosis because it is suspected, after study, to be the underlying cause of the urinary symptoms. (2) No code is assigned for the cystoscopy because volume 3 of *ICD-9-CM* provides only code 87.74 for cystoscopy for retrograde pyelogram.

8. **Codes (episode 1):** 600.91, 788.20, V10.51.

   Comments: (1) The patient had not had any recurrence of carcinoma of the bladder. Therefore, code V10.51 is assigned for history of bladder cancer. (2) Code 788.20 is assigned as an additional code as indicated by the "use additional code" note at code 600.91.

   Codes (episode 2): 600.01, 788.20, V10.51, 60.29, 60.95.

   Comments: (1) Code 600.01 is assigned because the pathology report provided a more specific diagnosis for the prostatic condition and was confirmed by the physician in the discharge diagnosis. (2) No code is assigned for the urethral stricture because it is included in code 600.01, Prostatic hypertrophy with urinary obstruction.

9. **Codes:** 595.9, 041.7, V09.91, V45.01, 57.32.

Comments: (1) The cystoscopy specified the urinary tract infection to be of the bladder; therefore, code 595.9 is assigned instead of 599.0. (2) V09.91 shows that the Pseudomonas was resistant to multiple oral antibiotics of unspecified types.

10. **Codes:** 620.0, 65.29.

Comments: (1) The exclusion note with code 54.11, Exploratory laparotomy, states, "Excludes exploration incidental to intra-abdominal surgery—omit code." Code 54.11, therefore, is not assigned. (2) The procedure (cystectomy) is referenced in the Index to Procedures (volume 3 of *ICD-9-CM*) under Excision, lesion, ovary.

11. **Codes:** 592.1, 56.0, 56.0, 87.74.

Comments: (1) Because the cystoscopic calculus extraction (code 56.0) was repeated, the code is assigned twice to identify two separate surgical procedures. (2) The procedure, extraction of ureteral calculus, is located in the Index to Procedures (volume 3 of *ICD-9-CM*) under the main entry Removal, calculus, ureter, without incision.

12. **Codes:** V59.4, V64.3.

Comments: (1) Code V59.4 is indexed in the Alphabetic Index to Diseases (volume 2 of *ICD-9-CM*) under the main entry Donor and code V64.3 is indexed under Procedure (surgical) not done NEC. (2) Because it is the brother's condition and not the donor's that necessitated the decision to cancel the procedure, code V64.3, not V64.1, is assigned.

13. **Codes:** V59.4, 55.51.

Comments: Code V59.4 is indexed in the Alphabetic Index to Diseases (volume 2 of *ICD-9-CM*) under the main entry Donor.

14. **Codes:** 590.80, 041.85.

Comments: (1) All symptoms are integral to pyelonephritis and are not coded. (2) Because the organism is not identified in the title of code 590.80, code 041.85 is added to provide further specificity.

15. **Codes:** 617.0, 617.1, 617.2, 493.90, 68.49, 65.61.

Comments: (1) Any of the category 617 codes could have been designated as the principal diagnosis (*Official Guidelines for Coding and Reporting,* Section II[B]). (2) Total abdominal hysterectomy (68.49) and bilateral salpingo-oophorectomy (code 65.61) are assigned for the procedures performed.

16. **Codes:** 620.0, 65.29.

Comments: (1) In accordance with the exclusion note with code 54.11, Exploratory laparotomy is not coded because it is incidental to the cystectomy. (2) Cystectomy is listed in the Alphabetic Index to Procedures (volume 3 of *ICD-9-CM*) under the main entry Excision, lesion, ovary.

Diseases of the Skin and Subcutaneous Tissue

C10

1. **Codes:** 873.1, 682.8, 380.10, E004.0, E000.8, 86.22.

   Comments: Complicated open wound is sequenced as the principal diagnosis based on the circumstances of admission. Also, treatment was directed primarily toward the open wound (excisional debridement). Code E004.0, Mountain climbing, rock climbing and wall climbing, is assigned to indicate the activity that contributed to the patient's injury. Code E000.8 is assigned for the external cause status to demonstrate that the patient was engaged in a leisure activity.

2. **Codes:** 707.03, 707.23, 741.03, V45.2, 86.3.

   Comments: (1) Pressure ulcer of the sacrum is assigned to code 707.03. Code 707.23 identifies the stage of the pressure ulcer. (2) Both hydrocephalus and spina bifida are included in code 741.0, with the fifth digit 3 indicating the lumbar region. (3) The ventriculoperitoneal shunt is present but did not require attention (V45.2). (4) Fulguration of skin of any site is assigned to code 86.3.

3. **Codes:** 707.03, 707.23, 204.10, 86.22, 86.70, 99.03.

   Comments: (1) Debridement specified as excisional is coded 86.22. (2) Flap graft is synonymous with pedicle graft of skin. This can be found in the Alphabetic Index to Procedures (volume 3 of *ICD-9-CM*) under Graft, skin, flap—see Graft, skin, pedicle.

4. **Codes:** 682.1, 88.38.

   Comments: Category 682 includes both cellulitis and abscess. The thyroiditis is not coded because it was ruled out.

5. **Codes:** 553.20, 568.0, 53.59, 54.59.

   Comments: (1) The express reason for admission was hernia repair; therefore, the hernia is sequenced as the principal diagnosis. (2) Abdominal adhesions are coded because they required extensive lysis before attention could be directed to the hernia repair and were documented as a discharge diagnosis.

6. **Codes:** 682.6, 305.90.

   Comments: No code is assigned for the minor injury (scratch on leg) because it has progressed to cellulitis, and the cellulitis is coded instead.

Diseases of the Musculoskeletal System and Connective Tissue

C11

1. **Codes:** 722.0, 401.1, 80.51.

   Comments: Hypertension, although under control, is coded because it is a coexisting chronic, systemic condition that meets the UHDDS definition of additional diagnosis.

2. **Codes (episode 1):** 723.0, 88.93.

   Comments: The symptoms (pain, numbness, and clumsiness) are integral to the diagnosis of spinal stenosis and therefore are not coded. Code 88.93 is assigned for the magnetic imaging of the spine.

   Codes (episode 2): 723.0, 81.02, 81.63, 77.79.

   Comments: Three procedure codes are assigned to fully describe the operative episode during this admission. Code 81.02 identifies the fusion using bone graft. Subcategory 81.0 requires that an additional code be used to report the total number of vertebrae fused. Since four vertebrae (C3, C4, C5, and C6) were fused, code 81.63 is assigned. Code 77.79 identifies the excision of bone from the iliac crest to be used as bone graft material.

3. **Codes:** 722.10, 531.90, 493.90, 80.51.

   Comments: The terms "extrusion" and "protruded" do not affect the code assignment for the intervertebral disk displacement. Follow the note to "see Displacement, intervertebral disc" in the Alphabetic Index to Diseases (volume 2 of *ICD-9-CM*), which is located with the entries for Extrusion, or Protrusion, intervertebral disc. Because asthma and ulcers are under current treatment and meet the UHDDS definition of additional diagnoses, they are assigned codes as coexisting conditions.

4. **Codes:** 820.01, E888.8, E849.4, E007.6, E000.8, 78.55.

   Comments: (1) Because this is a current slipped epiphysis (the result of a fall), it is coded to the injury and poisoning chapter (chapter 17 of *ICD-9-CM*). The diagnosis is referenced in the Alphabetic Index to Diseases (volume 2 of *ICD-9-CM*) under the entry Slipped, epiphysis, traumatic, current. A note with the entry instructs the coder to "see Fracture, by site." (2) Code E007.6 identifies the activity that the patient was doing at the time of the injury. E000.8 shows the status of the patient; the patient was performing an activity that was not for pay. (3) There was no reduction of the slipped epiphysis, but an internal fixation device was applied (78.55).

5. **Codes:** 840.4, 840.8, E918, E849.0, E000.8, 83.63, 83.87.

Comments: Either condition (rotator cuff tear or ruptured deltoid muscle) can be sequenced as the principal diagnosis because both injuries were present on admission, both were surgically corrected, and both meet the UHDDS definition of principal diagnosis (Section II[B]). E000.8 shows the status of the patient.

6. **Codes:** 250.70, 443.81, 707.14, 785.4, V42.0, V42.83, 84.15.

Comments: (1) When a diabetic complication is the reason for admission, the code from category 249 or 250 should be assigned as the principal diagnosis, followed by the appropriate codes for the manifestations. Code 785.4 appears in italics following subcategory 250.7 in the Alphabetic Index to Diseases (volume 2 of *ICD-9-CM*) under Diabetes, diabetic, gangrene. Code 785.4 should be sequenced following the appropriate code from subcategory 250.7. A code for the peripheral angiopathy (443.81) is also assigned. (2) The nonhealing foot ulcer is a result of the diabetic peripheral angiopathy; therefore, subcategory code 250.7 is assigned to indicate diabetic complication. Codes identifying the patient as status post renal and pancreas transplants are significant to the current episode of care and should be coded. Codes from category V42 are referenced under the main entry Status in the Alphabetic Index to Diseases (volume 2 of *ICD-9-CM*).

7. **Codes:** 733.6, 786.2.

Comments: Costochondritis is assigned as the principal diagnosis because suspected conditions are coded as confirmed diagnoses for inpatients. Code 786.2 is assigned for the excessive coughing, which is the underlying cause of the costochondritis. No code is assigned for the chest pain, which is integral to the costochondritis.

8. **Codes:** 716.15, 718.55, 250.00, V45.01, V15.51, 905.4, E929.0, 81.51.

Comments: (1) The residuals or manifestations of late effects of injuries should be sequenced first, followed by appropriate codes to identify the nature of the late effects. Either arthritis or ankylosis can be designated as the principal diagnosis because the conditions were equally responsible for the admission. (2) Code V15.51 is assigned to show the history of traumatic hip fracture. (3) E929.0 is a late-effect external cause of injury code. Because a late effect of a fracture (905.4) was assigned, it should be accompanied by a late-effect E code. No code from the 00.74–00.77 series is assigned because the type of bearing surface for the hip replacement is not known.

9. **Codes:** 711.06, 83.5.

Comments: (1) Subcategory code 711.0 is referenced under Septic, joint, or Arthritis, arthritic, septic, in the Alphabetic Index to Diseases (volume 2 of *ICD-9-CM*). The fifth digit 6 is assigned for the knee. The knee is part of the lower leg according to the complete set of fifth digits printed at the beginning of the chapter. (2) A separate code is not assigned to identify the incision and drainage of the knee because it is integral to the procedural process for the bursectomy.

10. **Codes:** 722.10, 03.92, 99.23.

    Comments: Intractable pain and radiculopathy are integral to the underlying disease and are therefore not coded.

11. **Codes:** 718.55, 716.15, 905.3, 429.2, 440.9, V15.51, E929.9, 81.51.

    Comments: (1) Either ankylosis or arthritis could be designated as the principal diagnosis because both were equally responsible for the admission (Section II[B]). (2) Ankylosis and arthritis are late effects of the previous hip fracture, 905.3 and E929.9. (3) The instruction with code 429.2 should be followed to arrive at an additional code for arteriosclerosis, 440.9. (4) Code V15.51 is assigned to show the history of traumatic hip fracture. (5) Replacement of both the femoral head and acetabulum is classified as a total hip replacement, 81.51. No code from the 00.74–00.77 series is assigned because the type of bearing surface for the hip replacement is not known.

12. **Codes:** 237.71, 737.43, 81.08, 77.79, 81.64.

    Comments: Scoliosis secondary to neurofibromatosis is indexed as 237.71, with code 737.43 following in brackets. This dual coding convention requires that the codes be sequenced in this order, with the neurofibromatosis code designated as the principal diagnosis in this case. Code 81.08 requires an additional code to report the number of vertebrae fused. In this instance, ten vertebrae were fused and therefore code 81.64 has been assigned.

Complications of Pregnancy, Childbirth, and the Puerperium

C12

1. **Codes (episode 1):** 654.21, V27.0, V25.2, 74.1, 66.39.

   Comments: The *Official Guidelines for Coding and Reporting,* Section I (C)(11)(b), provide guidance on the selection of the principal or first-listed diagnosis in obstetrical encounters. In cases of cesarean delivery, the principal diagnosis should be the condition established after study that was responsible for the patient's admission. If the reason for the admission/encounter was unrelated to the condition necessitating the cesarean delivery, that condition should be selected as the principal diagnosis, even if a cesarean was performed. The fact that the patient had a previous cesarean delivery (654.21) is therefore assigned first. The summary does not indicate any other condition requiring cesarean delivery. Code V25.2 is assigned to indicate that a tubal ligation was performed for elective sterilization. To indicate the outcome of delivery (i.e, single, multiple birth), code V27.0 is assigned.

   Code (episode 2): 674.34.

   Comments: The postoperative wound infection is classified to chapter 11 of *ICD-9-CM* because it represents a complication of the postpartum period and is related to an obstetrical wound. The fifth digit on subcategory 674.3 is assigned to 4 to signify that delivery did not occur during this episode of care and that the wound infection represents a postpartum complication.

2. **Codes:** 674.34, 648.04, 250.01, V58.67, 75.91, 54.61.

   Comments: The fifth digits on codes 674.34 and 648.04 indicate that this episode of care represents a postpartum complication with delivery occurring prior to this admission. Code 648.04 is assigned because diabetes invariably either complicates the pregnancy or is itself complicated by the pregnancy. Code 250.01 is assigned with 648.04 to provide additional information about the type of diabetes. Code V58.67 is not required for type 1 diabetics because these patients require insulin. However, this code may be assigned, if desired, to provide additional information. This handbook has followed this principle based on the advice published in *Coding Clinic,* Fourth Quarter 2004, p. 55.

3. **Codes:** 669.51, 664.11, V27.0, V25.2, 72.0, 75.69, 66.29.

   Comments: No complication was given that would account for the application of outlet forceps; therefore, 669.51 is assigned. V25.2 shows that the tubal ligation was performed for the purpose of voluntary sterilization.

4. **Codes:** 644.21, 658.21, 654.21, 658.41, 652.81, V27.0, 73.59, 88.78.

Comments: (1) Premature labor is designated as the principal diagnosis because it necessitated admission. (2) Ruptured membranes did not necessitate admission because they had been ruptured for 12 days. Code 658.21 indicates a delayed delivery. Note, however, that there is considerable leeway in designating the principal diagnosis for obstetric cases and either code 644.21 or 658.21 is acceptable. (3) Although there was malpresentation of the fetus, it was reducible and did not result in obstructed labor, and so code 660.1 is not assigned.

5. **Codes:** 644.21, 660.01, 652.21, 646.31, V27.0, 74.1

Comments: In this case the breech position resulted in the need for a cesarean delivery. Although the code resulting in a cesarean delivery is ordinarily listed as the principal diagnosis, in this case the threatened early delivery was the reason for admission and therefore is listed first. Code 646.31 is assigned for a patient with a history of recurrent pregnancy loss who is pregnant; code V23.2 is not assigned. Code 629.81 would be assigned for a patient with a history of recurrent pregnancy loss who is not currently pregnant.

6. **Codes:** 660.11, 653.41, V27.0, V45.01, 74.1, 73.3.

Comments: (1) The condition that required the cesarean delivery was the obstruction due to bony pelvis and cephalopelvic disproportion. Code 653.41 was assigned as an additional code per the instructional note listed in *ICD-9-CM*'s Tabular List (volume 1 of *ICD-9-CM*) under subcategory code 660.1. (2) The congenital heart block was under control by the pacemaker and so no code is assigned for the condition, but a status code indicating that the patient had a pacemaker is assigned. (3) A procedure code is assigned to indicate the failed forceps prior to the cesarean delivery.

7. **Code:** 644.03.

Comments: The fifth digit 3 includes the antepartum condition and indicates that delivery did not occur during this episode of care.

8. **Codes:** 643.13, 276.51, 365.9.

Comments: (1) Code 643.13 is used instead of 643.03 due to the presence of the metabolic disturbance; code 276.51 (dehydration) is assigned to add specific information on the nature of the metabolic disturbance. (2) A code is assigned for the glaucoma because it was treated, but it did not complicate the pregnancy. Every condition that may coexist with pregnancy is not necessarily a complication of the pregnancy nor affected adversely by the pregnancy.

9. **Codes:** 656.41, 655.81, 658.01, V27.1, 88.78, 96.49.

Comments: (1) Code 655.81 is referenced under the main term Pregnancy, management affected by, abnormality, fetus, specified NEC. (2) Code 658.01 is referenced under Pregnancy, complicated by, oligohydramnios.

10. **Codes:** 644.21, 651.11, V27.5, V91.10, 73.59, 75.34.

Comments: (1) Because rupture of membranes was ruled out, code 658.21 cannot be assigned. However, she went into labor and delivered one week after admission; code 644.21 should be assigned. (2) Code V91.10 is assigned to indicate that this was a triplet gestation with the number of placenta and amniotic sacs unspecified. (3) Code 73.59 can be assigned for the uncomplicated obstetrics delivery.

11. **Codes:** 656.41, 659.51, V27.1, 69.01, 88.78.

Comments: The principal diagnosis and reason for admission are intrauterine fetal death. The cause of the fetal death appears to be the age of the mother; therefore, code 659.51 is assigned to identify elderly primigravida, which includes women who will be 35 years of age or older at the expected date of delivery. The macerated fetus is not a complication of pregnancy, labor, or delivery and is not coded.

12. **Codes:** 644.03, 659.83.

Comments: Premature labor after 22 weeks but before 37 completed weeks gestation is coded to subcategory 644.0. The fifth digit 3 shows that the condition represents a complication of pregnancy and that delivery had not yet occurred. Code 659.83 is assigned for complication of pregnancy in a female less than 16 years of age at expected date of delivery (the patient is 14 years old). The fifth digit 3 shows that this is an antepartum condition or complication.

13. **Codes:** 662.01, 645.21, V27.0, 74.1.

Comments: (1) The fifth digit 1 indicates an antenatal complication; it also indicates that delivery occurred during this episode of care. (2) Code 645.21 indicates the postterm pregnancy.

14. **Codes:** 644.21, 656.41, 651.11, 658.41, V27.6, V91.11, 74.1, 88.78.

Comments: (1) The patient was admitted in early labor with a 25-week gestation (644.21). (2) One triplet was dead (656.41). (3) It was a triplet pregnancy (651.11). (4) She developed suspected chorioamnionitis (658.41). Suspected conditions on inpatient admissions should be coded as though confirmed. (5) The outcome of delivery was triplets, two liveborn and one fetal death (V27.6). (6) Code V91.11 is assigned to show that this was a triplet gestation with only one placenta (monochorionic).

15. **Codes:** 660.11, 653.41, 654.21, V27.0, 74.1, 73.09.

Comments: The obstructed labor due to cephalopelvic disproportion is designated as the principal diagnosis because it necessitated the performance of a cesarean section for delivery.

16. **Codes:** 644.21, 671.82, 455.6, V27.0, 74.1.

    Comments: The hemorrhoids occurred following delivery. Therefore, the fifth digit 2 is assigned with subcategory 671.8. An additional code of 455.6 is assigned to specify the type of venous complication because the specific venous complication (hemorrhoids) is not adequately described by code 671.8x alone.

17. **Codes:** 648.91, 340, V27.0, 73.6.

    Comments: Multiple sclerosis represents a nonobstetrical condition complicating the pregnancy. Code 648.91 is assigned with an additional code of 340 to further specify the complication.

18. **Code:** V22.0.

    Comments: This is the only code assignment necessary because no complications are present.

19. **Code:** 643.03.

    Comments: Because there is a complication, a code from the V22 category is not assigned. Instead, the complication of hyperemesis is coded, and the fifth digit 3 is assigned to show an antenatal complication without delivery.

20. **Codes:** 656.31, 656.81, 72.1, V27.0, 73.09.

    Comments: (1) Subcategory 656.3 indicates that fetal distress is present; subcategory 656.8 is assigned for meconium-stained liquor. (2) Code 72.1 includes both low forceps and episiotomy. Episiotomy closure is also included in the 72.1 code. (3) 73.09 instead of 73.01 is assigned for the amniotomy because the patient was already in the first stage of labor when the procedure was performed.

21. **Code:** 648.83.

    Comments: Gestational diabetes is coded to subcategory 648.8, not 648.0, because it is not true diabetes. The fifth digit 3 indicates an antepartum complication without delivery during this episode of care.

22. **Codes:** 664.21, 642.01, V27.0, 75.69, 73.6.

    Comments: (1) Either the preexisting hypertension or the perineal laceration can be assigned as the principal diagnosis. Note that the essential hypertension complicating pregnancy is coded to 642.0x rather than to unspecified. (2) Code 75.69 identifies the repair of the third-degree perineal laceration. Assign code 73.6 to identify the episiotomy. Both codes are needed to completely describe the repair. The instructional note at subcategory 75.6 indicates "code also episiotomy if performed (73.6)."

23. **Codes:** 654.21, 664.21, V27.0, 75.69, 73.6.

Comments: (1) Codes 654.21 and 664.21 include a fifth digit of 1 to show that these complications were present before the completion of delivery. (2) Code 75.69 identifies the repair of the third-degree perineal laceration. Assign code 73.6 to identify the episiotomy. Both codes are needed to completely describe the repair. The instructional note at subcategory 75.6 indicates "code also episiotomy if performed (73.6)."

Abortion and Ectopic Pregnancy

C13

1. **Codes:** 635.90, V61.7, E960.1, 69.01.

   Comments: (1) An elective abortion is classified in *ICD-9-CM* to legally induced abortion, category 635. The fifth digit 0 is assigned for an elective legal abortion because it is the most appropriate fifth digit available at this time. (2) Procedure code 69.01 is assigned to identify a D & C for termination of pregnancy. Use of code 69.02 is not appropriate because it is assigned only for a D & C following delivery or abortion. (3) V15.41 can be added to show the reason for the abortion, but it is not required.

2. **Codes:** 635.90, 655.03, 75.0, 69.02.

   Comments: (1) A therapeutic abortion is classified in *ICD-9-CM* to legally induced abortion, category 635. The fifth digit 0 is assigned for an elective legal abortion because it is the most appropriate fifth digit available at this time. (2) When a code from chapter 11 of *ICD-9-CM* is assigned to indicate the reason for an abortion, as was 655.03, the fifth digit 3 is assigned. (3) In this case, code 69.02 is correctly assigned because the D & C was performed after the abortion was accomplished by intrauterine injection.

3. **Codes:** 634.11, 69.02.

   Comments: (1) The abortion was spontaneous (634), complicated by excessive bleeding (634.1), and incomplete (634.11). (2) Code 69.02 is assigned because the procedure was performed after termination of the pregnancy.

4. **Codes:** 639.0, 615.0.

   Comments: Codes in the 639 category are to be used when the complication itself was responsible for an episode of medical care, the abortion having been dealt with at a previous episode. This woman aborted prior to her visit and was seen for a complication, endometritis. Code 615.0 is assigned as an additional code to provide more specificity regarding the complication.

5. **Codes:** 635.90, 648.13, 242.90, 69.51.

   Comments: (1) A therapeutic abortion is classified in *ICD-9-CM* to legally induced abortion, category 635. The fifth digit 0 is assigned for an elective legal abortion because it is the most appropriate fifth digit available at this time. (2) The reason for the abortion was thyroid dysfunction (648.13). When a code from chapter 11 of *ICD-9-CM* is added to an abortion code to explain the reason for the abortion, the fifth digit 3 is assigned. (3) Code 242.90 provides further specificity to the nonobstetrical complication, hyperthyroidism (648.13).

6. **Codes:** 635.90, 674.03, 69.51.

   Comments: (1) A therapeutic abortion is classified in *ICD-9-CM* to legally induced abortion, category 635. The fifth digit 0 is assigned for an elective legal abortion because it is the most appropriate fifth digit available at this time. (2) The reason for the abortion was an acute cerebrovascular accident (674.03). Note also that the title of code 674.03 reads, Cerebrovascular disorder in the puerperium; however, the inclusion note instructs that the code may be assigned during pregnancy, childbirth, or the puerperium. (3) When a code from chapter 11 of *ICD-9-CM* is added to an abortion code to explain the reason for the abortion, the fifth digit 3 is assigned.

7. **Codes:** 633.10, 66.02.

   Comments: Ectopic pregnancies are classified by site. Removal of a tubal ligation not otherwise specified is coded to 66.02, Salpingostomy. See the nonessential modifier in the Alphabetic Index to Procedures (volume 3 of *ICD-9-CM*) for Removal, ectopic fetus, fallopian tube.

Congenital Anomalies

C14

1. **Codes:** 746.86, 37.83, 37.72.

   Comments: (1) Congenital anomaly codes apply to both pediatric and adult patients; patient age does not preclude the use of these codes. The heart block is suspected to be congenital in origin and is coded as confirmed. (2) The insertion of the pacemaker is assigned to code 37.83, and the insertion of the leads is assigned to code 37.72.

2. **Codes:** 752.51, 997.49, 560.1, E878.8, 62.5, 62.5, 96.07, 87.79, 97.59.

   Comments: (1) Code 752.51 does not indicate that the disease condition was bilateral; however, disease codes may be assigned only once per episode of care. (2) The procedure was bilateral; therefore, the procedure codes are assigned two times because code 62.5 does not specify bilateral.

3. **Codes:** 038.19, 995.91, 745.5, 747.31, 88.72.

   Comments: (1) The causative bacteria for the sepsis, Staphylococcus, is specified in the title of code 038.19. An additional code from category 041 for Staphylococcus would not be assigned. The guideline for sepsis [Section I, C(1)(b)(1)(a)] indicates that if sepsis is present on admission and meets the definition of principal diagnosis, the underlying systemic infection code (in this instance 038.19) should be assigned as the principal diagnosis, followed by code 995.91, Sepsis, as required by the sequencing rules in the Tabular List. (2) Pulmonary artery stenosis is assumed to be congenital unless specified as acquired. (3) Foramen ovale is always congenital in nature.

4. **Codes:** 748.3, 31.69, 33.23.

   Comments: (1) Laryngomalacia is considered to be a congenital condition whether specified as such or not. Code 748.3 is the only code available to identify this condition. (2) The supraglottostomy is not coded because it is only the opening of the operative site. The supraglottis is part of the larynx.

5. **Codes:** 428.0, 748.4, 250.01, 311, V58.67.

   Comments: (1) Honeycomb lung can be acquired or congenital. Documentation must specify congenital to appropriately assign code 748.4. Honeycomb lung is significant to the care of a patient under treatment for congestive heart failure. (2) The symptoms mentioned (i.e., edema, labored breathing) are integral to the diagnosed conditions.

6. **Codes:** 482.0, 746.89, 438.31, 87.44, 93.96.

   Comments: (1) Diverticulum of the left ventricle is always a congenital defect and should be assigned to code 746.89. Code 438.31 identifies the monoplegia as a late effect of the earlier stroke.

7. **Codes:** 736.89, 754.70, 742.59, 77.37, 78.57, 93.53, 93.54.

   Comments: (1) Atretic spinal cord is always classified as congenital, but clubfoot is presumed to be congenital unless it is described as acquired. The coder should check the Index carefully before assigning a code. (2) Code 742.59 is referenced in the Alphabetic Index to Diseases (volume 2 of *ICD-9-CM*) under the main entry Atresia, atretic, organ or site NEC—see Anomaly, specified type NEC, or the main entry Anomaly, specified type NEC, spinal cord (742.59).

8. **Codes:** 754.51, 382.9, V64.1.

   Comments: (1) The clubfoot is listed as the reason for the admission and is therefore listed as the principal diagnosis. Clubfoot can be classified as either congenital or acquired, but *ICD-9-CM* presumes it to be congenital unless specified otherwise. (2) Surgery was canceled because of a contraindication (V64.1), namely, the otitis media.

9. **Codes:** 524.27, 524.03, 524.11, 76.65.

   Comments: (1) Any of the conditions can be listed as the principal diagnosis in accordance with official coding guidelines (Section II[B]). (2) Although the surgeon did not perform an osteotomy on the mandible, a code from category V64 is not assigned. The mandibular surgery was found to be unnecessary but was not a canceled procedure. (3) The maxilla hypoplasia and asymmetry are located in chapter 9 (diseases of the digestive system) rather than in chapter 14 (congenital anomalies) of *ICD-9-CM* (volume 1).

10. **Codes:** 751.61, 572.8, 45.13, 88.74, 87.44, 87.79, 89.52, 87.62.

    Comments: (1) Both conditions were present on admission and both necessitated the workup for liver transplant. Either condition can be sequenced as the principal diagnosis in accordance with official coding guidelines (Section II[B]). (2) *ICD-9-CM* presumes that biliary atresia is congenital unless specified otherwise.

Perinatal Conditions

C15

1. **Codes:** V34.01, 765.16, 765.20, 770.6, 691.0, 64.0, 93.90.

   Comments: (1) V34.01 is the principal diagnosis because the liveborn triplet was born on this admission by cesarean section. A code from categories V30–V39 is assigned as the principal diagnosis when the infant is delivered during the current admission. (2) A fifth digit of 6 is assigned to subcategory 765.1 to identify the birth weight of the newborn. Code 765.20 is assigned because of the additional note to identify the number of weeks of gestation (unspecified in this case). (3) Codes are not assigned for the Apgar scores.

2. **Codes:** 756.6, 765.18, 765.27, 770.89, 53.7, 96.71.

   Comments: (1) Because the patient was admitted at one day old, no code from the V30-V39 series is assigned. (2) The principal diagnosis is the reason for admission, congenital diaphragmatic hernia. (3) Code 765.18 is assigned for the prematurity and birth weight. Code 765.27 is assigned because of the additional note to identify the number of weeks of gestation (34 weeks in this case). (4) Intubation is not coded because it was performed at the other hospital. (5) Mechanical ventilation was continued for less than 96 consecutive hours, hence code 96.71.

3. **Codes:** V30.00, 774.6, 99.83.

   Comments: (1) V30.00 is the principal diagnosis because the infant was born by spontaneous vaginal delivery during this admission. (2) An additional code is assigned for the jaundice because it was identified as a problem and required treatment.

4. **Codes:** V30.00, 765.17, 765.25, 745.5, 88.72.

   Comments: (1) V30.00 is the principal diagnosis because the infant was delivered vaginally on this admission. (2) The prematurity and birth weight are identified by the use of codes 765.17 and 765.25. (3) A separate code is not assigned to identify tachypnea because this is integral to patent foramen ovale, code 745.5.

5. **Codes:** V30.01, 765.18, 765.27, 769, 770.2, 33.93, 34.04, 38.91, 87.44.

   Comments: (1) V30.01 is the principal diagnosis because the infant was born by cesarean section on this particular admission. (2) The prematurity and birth weight are identified by the use of codes 765.18 and 765.27. (3) Hyaline membrane disease is always a congenital condition and should be classified only to code 769. (4) Pneumothorax is classified to code 770.2 only when it occurs during the perinatal period.

6. **Codes:** V30.01, 765.17, 765.20, 746.9, 742.1.

   Comments: (1) V30.01 is the principal diagnosis because the infant was born by cesarean section on this admission. (2) Congenital heart disease, not otherwise specified, is assigned to code 746.9.

7. **Codes:** 771.89, 466.11, 745.4, 96.04, 96.71, 88.72.

   Comments: Although bronchiolitis occurred during the perinatal period, there is no code to identify it as such. Code 466.11 is assigned. Other infections acquired 28 days after birth should be classified to the usual infection code or directed by the exclusion note for category 771. No code from the V30-V39 series is assigned because the infant was not born during this admission.

8. **Codes:** 474.10, 771.1, 28.3, 33.23, 31.42.

   Comments: (1) The condition that occasioned admission is hypertrophy of the tonsils and adenoids. (2) Code 771.1 is referenced in the Alphabetic Index to Diseases (volume 2 of *ICD-9-CM*) under Infection, cytomegalovirus, congenital, and the code is assigned because treatment was continued during the hospital stay. (3) The symptoms (i.e., distorted, loud, and rattling breathing) are integral to hypertrophied tonsils and adenoids and should not be coded separately.

9. **Codes:** 753.15, 753.19, 55.51.

   Comments: (1) Dysplastic kidney and multicystic kidney are congenital conditions always classified to chapter 14 of *ICD-9-CM* no matter how old the patient is. (2) Two separate codes are assigned to appropriately identify a dysplastic and multicystic kidney, 753.15 and 753.19. (3) Dysplastic kidney is sequenced as the principal diagnosis because it was the reason for admission.

10. **Codes:** V30.00, 766.22, 770.6, 93.96.

    Comments: (1) V30.00 is the principal diagnosis because the infant was born vaginally on this admission. (2) Codes are not assigned for the Apgar scores. (3) Code 766.22 is referenced under Prolonged gestation infant (more than 42 completed weeks gestation).

11. **Codes:** 771.89, 465.9, 779.34, 770.81.

    Comments: Upper respiratory infection was the reason for admission and should be sequenced as the principal diagnosis in accordance with the UHDDS definition. A code from subcategory 771.8 is assigned because the infection occurred during the first 28 days after birth. Code 465.9 is assigned to further specify the type of infection. Code 779.34 is assigned rather than 783.41 because this child is a newborn (not a child more than 28 days old).

12. **Codes:** V30.01, 765.17, 765.27, 775.6, 768.3, 93.96.

    Comments: (1) Code 775.6 is referenced in the Alphabetic Index to Diseases under Hypoglycemia, neonatal (volume 2 of *ICD-9-CM*). Gestational diabetes is not a true diabetes and is insufficient for the use of code 775.0, Syndrome of "infant of diabetic mother." (2) The mother's hypertension, diabetes, and failure to progress at labor were complications of her delivery and are not coded on the newborn record unless there is an adverse effect to the newborn. (3) Fetal distress was first noted in labor and was treated with oxygen and further monitoring following birth. Code 768.3 is assigned as an additional diagnosis code.

13. **Codes:** 771.82, 041.49, 765.19, 765.20, 753.29, 88.75.

    Comments: (1) Code 771.82 is referenced in the Alphabetic Index to Diseases (volume 2 of *ICD-9-CM*) under Infection, urinary, newborn. Code 041.49 is added to show E. coli as the causative organism. Only the combination code is assigned when that code fully identifies the diagnostic condition involved; therefore, code 599.0 is not assigned. (2) The premature infant weighed 2,608 grams at birth (765.19). Code 765.20 is required to identify the number of weeks of gestation. In this case, it was unspecified. (3) Congenital hydronephrosis was noted. (4) No code from the V30–V39 series is assigned because the infant was born in another hospital.

Diseases of the Circulatory System

C16

1. **Codes (episode 1):** 441.4, 401.9, V17.49, 38.44.

   Comments: The V17.49 identifies the family history of aneurysms and explains why the repair was performed on an elective basis.

   Code (episode 2): V67.09.

   Comments: V67.09 is assigned because the patient was seen, after the initial care was completed, for the purpose of determining whether there were any problems related to the surgery.

2. **Codes:** 433.10, 433.30, 88.41.

   Comments: Although only carotid artery disease was documented on discharge, arteriography indicated the specific condition to be stenosis. Assigning both 433.10 and 433.30 allows the capture of information on both the specific artery involved (433.10) and the laterality (433.30).

3. **Codes:** 433.10, 438.81, 438.82, 787.20, 38.12.

   Comments: (1) The residual apraxia and difficulty in swallowing represent late effects of the previous cerebrovascular accident. They are reportable as they required additional nursing care. (2) As indicated by the "use additional code" note at code 438.82, code 787.20 is assigned to show the type of dysphagia, which in this case is difficulty in swallowing, NOS. Only code 433.10 should be assigned for the left carotid stenosis. Code 433.30 is not assigned because the right carotid stenosis is no longer present because it was previously treated with an endarterectomy.

4. **Codes:** 414.00, 411.1, 414.2, 00.66, 00.41, 37.22, 88.57.

   Comments: (1) Angina is a symptom of coronary arteriosclerosis and should be sequenced as an additional diagnosis. (2) The physician documented chronic total occlusion of coronary artery; therefore, code 414.2 should be assigned as an additional diagnosis. (3) Two vessels were repaired with the angioplasty. Therefore, the appropriate code assignment for PTCA is 00.66, as well as code 00.41 to indicate that the PTCA was performed on two vessels.

5. **Codes:** 996.01, 746.86, 427.89, 37.87, 37.76.

Comments: (1) The reason the patient had a pacemaker is to compensate for a heart block and bradycardia. These conditions are also the reasons why he had a new pacemaker inserted. Therefore, both conditions are coded as secondary diagnoses. (2) Fatigue is not coded because it is integral to severe bradycardia.

6. **Codes:** 434.10, 784.3, 427.31, 87.03.

Comments: The reason for admission was aphasia, which after study was found to be due to a cerebral embolus. Therefore, the embolus is the principal diagnosis. Aphasia is coded because it affected patient care even though it had cleared at the time of discharge.

7. **Codes:** 424.1, 429.3, 35.22, 39.61, 88.72.

Comments: (1) Aortic valve stenosis and calcification are both assigned to 424.1. (2) The term "intraoperative," as used in describing the echocardiogram, does not affect the code assignment for 88.72. (3) Note that 35.2 includes a note to code also 39.61, cardiopulmonary bypass, if the procedure was performed.

8. **Codes:** 396.3, 042, 35.24, 35.22, 39.61.

Comments: (1) A synthetic prosthesis was utilized (code 35.24), not tissue (35.23). (2) An additional code is needed, per the instruction with 35.24 and 35.22, for the cardiopulmonary bypass (39.61).

9. **Codes:** 786.59, 435.9.

Comments: (1) A diagnosis of atypical chest pain not otherwise specified is classified to code 786.59. Had the diagnosis been "chest wall pain," it would have been classified to code 786.52. (2) Transient ischemic attacks should not be confused with "transient residuals" of an acute cerebrovascular accident. (3) The neurological symptoms did not appear until after admission. Sequence chest pain as the principal diagnosis in accordance with the UHDDS definition.

10. **Codes:** 453.41, 88.38.

Comments: The symptoms of pain and edema in the leg are integral to the iliac vein thrombosis and should not be coded separately.

11. **Codes:** 410.71, 428.0, 427.5, 99.62, 96.04, 96.71, 87.44.

Comments: (1) Cardiopulmonary arrest and cardiac arrest are both coded to 427.5. (2) Cardiopulmonary arrest is not designated as the principal diagnosis. When a patient in cardiac arrest is resuscitated in the emergency department and admitted with the condition prompting the cardiac arrest known, the condition causing the cardiac arrest is sequenced first. (3) Pulmonary edema is an integral part of congestive heart failure and should not be coded separately.

12. **Codes:** 446.5, 38.21.

    Comments: Headaches are integral to inflammation of the temporal artery and are not coded separately.

13. **Codes:** 434.11, 250.80, 707.14, 784.3, 374.30, 781.2, 86.28, 87.03.

    Comments: (1) Thromboembolic cerebrovascular accident is specified only with code 434.11, Cerebral embolism with cerebral infarction. Under Thromboembolism in the Alphabetic Index to Diseases (volume 2 of *ICD-9-CM*), the coder is directed to "see Embolism." (2) Codes are assigned for aphasia, ptosis of eyelid, and gait abnormality. Report any neurological deficits caused by a CVA even when they have been resolved at the time of discharge from the hospital. (3) A Versajet debridement is coded to 86.28. The fact that the procedure was performed by the physician does not make it excisional.

14. **Codes:** 447.6, 785.4, 38.21, 88.49.

    Comments: Gangrene (785.4) represents a further manifestation of vasculitis (447.6) and should be coded separately.

15. **Codes:** 453.40, 415.19, 611.72, 88.43, 87.37.

    Comments: (1) Either pulmonary embolism or DVT could be sequenced as the principal diagnosis. The patient was admitted for further evaluation and treatment of both conditions (*Official Guidelines for Coding and Reporting,* Section II[C]). (2) The right breast lump is not considered an incidental finding. Although it was not treated, it was identified and workup begun, with the patient being referred for further follow-up.

16. **Codes:** 444.22, 465.9, V64.1, 88.48.

    Comments: Peripheral vascular disease is further specified as femorotibial occlusive disease. The coder is directed to the Alphabetic Index to Diseases (volume 2 of *ICD-9-CM*) to look under Occlusion, arteries of extremities, lower (444.22).

17. **Codes:** 410.21, 427.31, 88.72.

    Comments: Although the patient had both acute myocardial infarction and atrial fibrillation, the reason for admission was acute myocardial infarction. Following the UHDDS definition for principal diagnosis, code 410.21 is sequenced first.

18. **Codes:** 431, 438.20, 87.03, 87.03.

Comments: (1) The reason for admission was acute cerebral hemorrhage (431). (2) There was an extension of the cerebral hemorrhage, and a hematoma developed in the right basal ganglia, also coded 431 so that no additional code assignment is required. (3) There is a left-sided residual hemiplegia, which is a late effect of a previous cerebral thrombosis (438.20). (4) In reporting, the scan would be coded twice, with different dates indicated. (5) Codes from category 438 can be assigned as an additional code when a new CVA is present and deficits from an earlier episode remain.

19. **Codes:** 438.89, 530.3, 429.2, 440.9, 250.03, V58.67, 42.92, 44.13, 87.62.

Comments: (1) The stricture is a late effect of a previous CVA (438.89); codes from category 438 can be assigned as the principal diagnosis when the purpose of the admission is to deal with the late effect. Code 530.3 is also assigned to provide greater specificity. No code is assigned for the nausea and vomiting because these symptoms are a common finding with esophageal stricture. (2) The note with code 429.2 instructs the coder to assign an additional code to identify the presence of arteriosclerosis (440.9). (3) Uncontrolled diabetes, type 1, without complication is assigned code 250.03 to identify it as uncontrolled. Code V58.67 is not required for type 1 diabetics because these patients require insulin. However, this code may be assigned, if desired, to provide additional information. This handbook has followed this principle based on the advice published in *Coding Clinic*, Fourth Quarter 2004, p. 55.

20. **Codes:** 411.1, V15.81.

Comments: (1) Because angina is documented at discharge as probably unstable, code 411.1 should be assigned. (2) The patient signed himself out against medical advice (AMA). Code V15.81 indicates noncompliance with medical treatment.

21. **Codes:** 410.11, 414.00, 36.12, 36.15, 37.23, 88.54.

Comments: (1) The left internal mammary was used to bypass the left anterior descending, equaling one bypass (36.15). (2) A segment of saphenous vein graft was used to bypass the left circumflex and distal right coronary arteries, equaling two aortocoronary bypasses (36.12). (3) The cardiac catheterization and angiography were combined right and left procedures.

22. **Codes:** 789.30, 427.89, V64.1.

Comments: (1) The reason for admission was pelvic mass. Even though the treatment plan was not carried out, it should still be sequenced as the principal diagnosis (*Official Guidelines for Coding and Reporting,* Section II[F]). The complication, bigeminy, developed after admission and is sequenced as a secondary diagnosis. (2) V64.1 shows that the planned procedure was canceled due to a contraindication.

23. **Codes:** 415.19, 182.0, 88.43.

    Comments: Endometrial carcinoma of the uterus is no longer present; however, the site is still under active treatment. Therefore, code 182.0 is assigned rather than a code from category V10.

24. **Codes:** 410.41, 414.00, 272.0, 401.1, 00.66, 00.40, 37.22, 88.53.

    Comments: Both the transferring hospital and this facility will assign code 410.41 as both hospitals rendered care during the initial episode of the acute myocardial infarct. Code 00.66 is assigned for the PTCA, as well as code 00.40 to indicate that the PTCA was performed on a single vessel.

Neoplasms

C17

1. **Codes:** 151.9, 198.6, 511.9, 68.49, 65.61, 34.04, 99.25, 97.41.

   Comments: (1) Code 54.11 is not assigned because the exploratory laparotomy was the approach for the total abdominal hysterectomy and bilateral salpingo-oophorectomy. (2) Even though pleural effusion developed following surgery, the physician did not identify it as a complication of the surgery; therefore, no code from the 996–999 series is assigned.

2. **Codes:** 197.7, V10.05, 50.11, 54.11, 88.74, 88.01.

   Comments: (1) A "history of" code is assigned for the adenocarcinoma of the colon because it had previously been excised. (2) The liver is specified as the secondary site because the neoplasm spread to it from the colon. The patient was admitted with a questionable liver lesion, which after study was diagnosed as a liver metastasis and therefore assigned as the principal diagnosis. (3) The exploratory laparotomy is coded because it was not followed by definitive surgery. (4) Even though the biopsy was performed during the laparotomy, a needle biopsy of the liver is considered a closed biopsy.

3. **Codes:** 491.21, 162.3.

   Comments: (1) The thrust of treatment was toward the chronic obstructive pulmonary disease, and it is therefore designated as the principal diagnosis. Because the chronic obstructive pulmonary disease is described more specifically in the body of the record as chronic obstructive bronchitis with acute exacerbation, code 491.21 is assigned rather than 496. The fifth digit indicates the acute exacerbation. (2) Recurrence of a neoplasm is coded as a primary neoplasm of that site, and a code from the V10 category is not assigned.

4. **Codes:** V58.11, 183.0, 99.25.

   Comments: The sole reason for admission was to receive chemotherapy; therefore, code V58.11 is designated as the principal diagnosis. A code is also assigned for the neoplasm under treatment.

5. **Codes:** 203.00, 733.13, 276.69, 427.1, 41.31.

   Comments: (1) Although the compression fractures might appear to be the reason for admission, the purpose was clearly to determine the cause of these apparently spontaneous fractures. Diagnostic studies revealed that the underlying problem was the multiple myeloma. (2) Fifth digit 0 is assigned to indicate that there was no mention of having achieved remission. Subcategory 203.0 is located under the main entry Myeloma in the Alphabetic Index to Diseases (volume 2 of *ICD-9-CM*).

6. **Code:** 625.8.

   Comments: A mass is not classified to the neoplasm chapter (chapter 2 of *ICD-9-CM*) unless it has been evaluated and determined to be neoplastic.

7. **Codes:** 157.9, 198.89, 45.13, 88.76.

   Comments: (1) Suspected carcinoma that is under treatment as if proven is coded as confirmed. (2) Once a primary neoplasm spreads/extends beyond the boundary of the organ where it originated into an adjacent structure, it is coded as a secondary neoplasm. Metastatic neoplasms of veins are coded to neoplasms of connective tissue as directed in the Alphabetic Index to Diseases (volume 2 of *ICD-9-CM*).

8. **Codes (episode 1):** 733.14, 198.5, 199.1, 79.35.

   Comments: (1) Although the Alphabetic Index to Diseases (volume 2 of *ICD-9-CM*) under Tumor, melanotic, neuroectodermal, directs the coder to "see Neoplasm, by site, benign," this neoplasm is obviously a malignant form because it has metastasized. (2) The primary site is not identified, nor is guidance provided by the Alphabetic Index. Therefore, code 199.1 for an unknown primary site is assigned. (3) The pathologic fracture is designated as the principal diagnosis because it was the reason for admission and the thrust of treatment was directed toward it.

   Codes (episode 2): 197.0, 198.5, 199.1, 511.81, 34.91, 33.26.

   Comments: The malignant pleural effusion is assigned to code 511.81. In addition, when coding malignant pleural effusion, code first the malignant neoplasm, if known. Code 199.1 is assigned to indicate that the primary malignancy has not been identified.

   Codes (episode 3): 197.0, 199.1, 198.5, 511.81, 786.30, 780.01, 799.02, V66.7, 87.44.

   Comments: Although hypoxemia and hemoptysis are related to the pleural effusion, neither is routinely present with this condition; nor is coma integral to the diagnosed conditions. Therefore, symptom codes are assigned as additional diagnoses. V66.7, Encounter for palliative care, is assigned as a secondary code because this patient was admitted for terminal care. Code V66.7 may not be used as a principal diagnosis;

rather, the underlying disease, such as carcinoma, is sequenced first. Palliative care is an alternative to aggressive treatment for patients who are in the terminal phase of their illness. Palliative care is focused toward management of pain and symptoms.

9. **Codes:** V58.11, 183.0, 198.89, 197.6, 99.25.

   Comments: The sole reason for admission is for administration of chemotherapy; therefore, V58.11 is the principal diagnosis. Additional codes are assigned for the neoplastic disease under treatment; codes from category V10 are not assigned when treatment is still in progress.

10. **Codes:** 441.4, 150.9, 43.11, 54.11.

    Comments: (1) Even though the initial treatment plan was not carried out, the principal diagnosis remains code 441.4 because the abdominal aneurysm was the condition that occasioned the admission (Section II[F]). (2) When only one site for a neoplasm is mentioned, it is assumed to be primary in the absence of any other information to the contrary.

11. **Codes:** 786.6, 786.09, 780.60, 780.8, 87.44.

    Comments: Suspected conditions are not coded in the ambulatory care setting; therefore, only codes for the presenting symptoms and the mass identified on X-ray are assigned.

12. **Codes (episode 1):** 164.2, 197.0, 33.26, 34.02, 99.25, 87.41.

    Comments: (1) Even though chemotherapy was administered, the admission was not solely for this purpose and, therefore, code V58.11 is not assigned; procedure code 99.25 shows that chemotherapy was administered. (2) Yolk sac tumor is located by referring to Tumor, yolk sac, in the Alphabetic Index to Diseases (volume 2 of *ICD-9-CM*), then referring to the neoplasm table. (3) A code is assigned for the exploratory thoracotomy because no definitive surgery was associated with it.

    Codes (episode 2): V58.11, 164.2, 197.0, 99.25.

    Comments: This admission was for the sole purpose of providing chemotherapy; therefore, code V58.11 is the appropriate principal diagnosis code. The addition of the neoplasm codes indicates the conditions requiring the therapy.

13. **Codes:** V58.11, 198.5, 197.7, 198.7, 99.25.

    Comments: The sole reason for this admission was to provide chemotherapy. Codes are assigned for the current metastatic neoplasms; the history code is not assigned because the recurrent secondary neoplasms are the same type of neoplasm as the earlier neoplasms. No code is available to show that there was a former secondary site in the axilla.

14. **Code:** 203.80.

Comments: Plasmacytoma is referenced in the Alphabetic Index to Diseases (volume 2 of *ICD-9-CM*) under its name. This is a malignant form of plasmacytoma; therefore, the subentry "malignant" is referenced. Going to the neoplasm table directly, without first referencing the name of the neoplasm in the index, would have resulted in an incorrect code assignment of 152.2.

15. **Codes:** 218.9, 614.6, 628.2, 68.29, 65.89.

Comments: (1) The myoma of the uterus is the principal diagnosis because it was the reason for admission; the lysis of the adhesions was secondary to the excision of the myoma and was required in order to remove the leiomyoma. (2) Dual coding is required for the infertility associated with peritubal adhesions.

16. **Codes:** 182.0, 68.49, 65.61.

Comments: The endometrium and myometrium are both parts of the uterus and code 182.0 is assigned for both; no additional code for secondary neoplasm is assigned. The exploratory laparotomy is the operative approach for the hysterectomy and salpingo-oophorectomy; therefore, code 54.11 is not assigned.

17. **Codes (episode 1):** 511.9, 793.19, 34.91, 33.24, 87.44.

Comments: (1) The pleural effusion was the reason for the encounter. (2) A code is assigned for the abnormal X-ray finding because the physician felt it to be significant and listed it as a diagnosis. (3) The brush biopsy of the lung is coded to 33.24 rather than 33.27 according to the exclusion note for 33.27 and the inclusion note for 33.24.

Codes (episode 2): 162.9, 34.52, 34.20, 92.22.

Comments: (1) This admission was for further evaluation of the patient's condition, and surgery for the malignancy was performed. (2) Although radiation therapy was begun during the hospital stay, it was not the purpose for this admission; therefore, code V58.0 is not assigned, and code 92.22 indicates the type of radiation provided. (3) Code 34.52 is assigned for the thoracoscopic decortication of the lung, and code 34.20 is assigned for the thoracoscopic pleural biopsy.

18. **Codes:** 225.1, 04.07.

Comments: The behavior of an acoustic neuroma is benign according to both the instructions with the main entry and the morphology code (M9560/0) in the Alphabetic Index to Diseases (volume 2 of *ICD-9-CM*). The hearing loss is integral to the neuroma, and so no additional code is assigned.

19. **Codes:** 191.2, 342.90, 01.13.

Comments: The hemiparesis is not considered a late effect of the glioblastoma because glioblastoma is a current condition under treatment. Late effect is defined as "the residual effect that remains after the termination of the acute phase of an illness or injury."

20. **Codes:** 560.32, 225.2, 553.3, V15.88, 45.23, 45.13, 88.01, 88.97.

Comments: Fecal impaction is designated as the principal diagnosis because it was felt to account for most of the admitting symptoms. Both the hiatal hernia and the meningiomas were diagnosed as the result of further evaluation of the patient's symptoms, with both conditions further evaluated and/or treated during this admission. Code V15.88, History of fall, is assigned because of the patient's history of having fallen at home many times. This code is for patients who have fallen in the past and may be more susceptible to falling in the future. It also includes the concept of a person at risk for falling.

21. **Codes:** 198.5, 338.3, V10.46, 62.41, 77.49, 92.24.

Comments: (1) The narrative indicates that there are secondary sites in the spine (198.5). (2) The primary site (prostate) was removed in 1986, and because there is no mention of any recurrence, history code V10.46 is assigned. (3) Radiotherapy was begun on this admission, but it was not the sole purpose of the admission and so code V58.0 is not assigned. (4) Code 338.3 is assigned as an additional diagnosis because the admission was for management of the neoplasm, and the pain associated with the neoplasm is also documented.

22. **Codes:** V58.11, 191.9, 00.19, 99.25.

Comments: (1) Code V58.11 is assigned as the principal diagnosis because the patient was admitted for chemotherapy, which was administered through the blood brain barrier for quicker absorption. (2) Both the blood brain barrier disruption and the administration of chemotherapy should be assigned for the procedures.

Injuries

C18

1. **Codes:** 801.51, 322.9, E917.0, E849.4, E007.3, E000.8, 02.02, 03.31.

   Comments: (1) Compound fractures are open by definition. (2) When each of the fractured bones is referenced under the main term Fracture, there is an instruction to "see Fracture, skull, base." When the subterm "open" is referenced under this entry, code 801.5 is displayed; fifth digit 1 is assigned to indicate that there was no loss of consciousness. When the subterm "sinus" is referenced under the main term Fracture, the names of each of the sinuses involved appear in parentheses as nonessential modifiers and the same code is displayed. (3) The E849 code indicates that the accident occurred in a place for recreation. (4) Code E007.3 identifies the activity the patient was involved in at the time of the injury (softball), and E000.8 identifies the patient's status, which in this case is "other" because the sport was not played for income. (5) There is no index entry for submeningitis and so the code for meningitis, not otherwise specified, is assigned. Although the diagnosis states that the meningitis is postoperative, there is no statement to indicate that the meningitis was due to the surgery itself, and so no code from the 996–999 series is assigned. (6) Debridement is included in the reduction of compound fracture of the skull; the exclusion note refers only to debridement of the skull, not otherwise specified.

2. **Codes:** 847.2, 435.9, E885.9, E849.0, E013.0, E000.8, V15.88, 87.29.

   Comments: (1) The compression fractures were ruled out; therefore, no codes are assigned. (2) The "probable" transient ischemic attack is coded as an established diagnosis because it is listed as a final diagnosis for an inpatient admission, and the summary strongly implies that the fall was probably due to another such attack. (3) The radiology report contained incidental findings of degenerative disk disease that was not treated or further evaluated; therefore, no code is assigned for this condition. (4) Code E013.0 identifies the activity, and code E000.8 identifies the patient's status. (5) Code V15.88, History of fall, is added because the patient has had several similar falls in the past. (6) Although the fractures were located in the lumbar area, the summary does not specify the area included in the X-ray.

3. **Codes:** 805.4, 812.21, E880.9, E849.0, E001.0, E000.8, 81.08, 81.62, 77.79, 87.24, 88.21, 93.59.

   Comments: (1) The vertebral fracture is the more serious injury and received the major thrust of treatment; therefore, it is designated as the principal diagnosis. (2) Code 81.08 includes foraminotomy, fusion, and use of bone graft. Code 81.62 is used to indicate the number of vertebrae fused. Code 77.79 is assigned to identify the harvesting of bone from the iliac crest for use as a bone graft. (3) The spinal X-ray is coded because it was done in the emergency department immediately before admission and is related to the principal diagnosis.

4. **Codes:** 812.01, 920, 924.00, 924.11, E881.0, E849.0, E016.9, E000.8, 88.21, 93.54.

   Comments: The fracture is obviously the most severe injury and is therefore designated as the principal diagnosis. Because the fracture was not displaced, no reduction was required. No codes are assigned for the abrasions because they required no further evaluation, and no definitive treatment was directed to them.

5. **Codes:** 482.0, 847.0, 847.1, E885.9, E849.0, E013.0, E000.8, 87.44.

   Comments: (1) The condition responsible for admission, after study, was found to be pneumonia. The back strain occurred four days prior to admission and probably would not have required hospital admission if it had been the only problem. (2) The pneumonia was described in the narrative as being due to *Klebsiella;* pneumonia of a lobe of the lung is not "lobar" pneumonia.

6. **Codes:** 807.02, 958.7, 305.00, E886.9, E849.0, E000.8.

   Comments: The fractured ribs were the reason for the emergency department encounter. Although the alcoholism was not further evaluated or treated, it was closely related to the trauma and should be coded.

7. **Codes:** 820.21, 285.1, E882, E849.0, E000.8, 79.35, 99.03.

   Comments: (1) The fracture is described as intertrochanteric in the narrative and so the more specific code is assigned. (2) The surgery resulted in only an expected amount of blood loss. However, treatment was rendered (transfusions) and monitoring continued (hemoglobin and hematocrit). This situation meets the UHDDS definition of additional diagnosis and should be assigned to code 285.1. However, code 998.11 is not assigned because the blood loss was an expected outcome and not a complication of the surgery.

8. **Codes:** 833.09, 815.03, 816.01, E816.0, E849.5, E000.0, 88.23, 79.73.

   Comments: (1) The lunate bone is in the wrist. (2) Although three weeks old, the fractures have not healed and are current injuries, and the patient is receiving active treatment for the fracture. (3) Code E816.0 is referenced in the Index to External Causes (volume 2 of *ICD-9-CM*) under the entry Accident, motor vehicle, not involving collision—see categories E816–E819. Subcategory code E816 requires that a fourth digit be assigned from the fourth digits printed at the beginning of the motor vehicle nontraffic accidents section to indicate the role of the victim, in this case the driver of the motor vehicle.

9. **Codes:** 812.00, 813.23, E884.9, E849.1, E016.1, E000.0, 79.31, 79.32.

   Comments: A comminuted fracture is a closed-type fracture according to the descriptors included at the beginning of the fractures (800-829) section in the Tabular List of Diseases (volume 1, chapter 17, of *ICD-9-CM*). The narrative provides more specificity as to the location of the fractures, and so the more specific codes are assigned. Either fracture could have been designated as the principal diagnosis because both are essentially equal in severity (Section II[B]).

10. **Codes:** 821.01, 518.0, 997.39, E885.9, E849.0, E000.8, 79.35, 87.44.

    Comments: (1) The information in the narrative is used to assign a more specific code for the fracture. (2) Assign codes 518.0 and 997.39 because the fever and atelectasis were specified as postoperative. Postoperative atelectasis is often an incidental radiographic or physical finding that is frequently a self-limiting condition, in which case it would not be coded or reported. In this case, it was associated with fever and required further diagnostic (e.g., chest X-ray) and therapeutic workup (e.g., incentive spirometry).

11. **Codes:** V71.3, 913.8, E916, E849.3, E000.0, 87.03.

    Comments: The purpose of the admission was to determine whether the patient had suffered any kind of intracranial injury; this was ruled out. Even though there was a minor injury that did not require hospital admission, the observation code is still assigned as the principal diagnosis. This situation is consistent with the inclusion note with category V71, "cases that present some symptoms or evidence of an abnormal condition which required study, but which after examination and observation show no need for further treatment or medical care."

12. **Codes:** 904.0, 904.2, 879.5, 820.32, E965.4, E000.8, 39.25, 39.25, 78.55, 77.15.

    Comments: (1) Because the hemorrhage was life threatening, either blood vessel laceration could represent the principal diagnosis (Section II[B]). (2) Code 879.5 is assigned to indicate a complicated open wound of the groin; the retention of a foreign body (bullet) makes this a complicated wound. The injury was not incidental to the fracture (did not occur secondary to the fracture) but occurred in addition to the fracture as a result of the gunshot wound.

13. **Codes:** 823.82, 873.0, 872.01, E813.6, E849.5, E006.4, E000.8, 79.16, 18.4, 86.59.

    Comments: (1) No code is assigned for the superficial abrasions because they are associated with a more severe injury at the same site. (2) A simple fracture is a closed type according to the descriptors included at the beginning of the fractures section (800-829) in the Tabular List of Diseases (volume 1, chapter 17, of *ICD-9-CM*). (3) An open wound of the earlobe is coded as open wound of auricle. (4) No code from the E849 series is used with a code from E813 because the motor vehicle accident code includes location.

14. **Code (episode 1):** 780.39.

    Comments: Code 780.39 is the appropriate code assignment for this encounter. "Probable" conditions are not coded in the outpatient setting.

    Codes (episode 2): 831.00, 291.81, 780.39, E888.9, E849.6, E000.8, 79.71, 93.53.

    Comments: Because attempts to reduce the dislocation were unsuccessful in the emergency department, the patient was admitted. Therefore, shoulder dislocation is the principal diagnosis.

15. **Codes (episode 1):** 824.6, E885.2, E849.4, E006.0, E000.8, 88.28, 79.06.

    Comments: (1) A simple fracture is closed. (2) Application of cast is included in the code for fracture reduction; no additional code is assigned.

    Codes (episode 2): V54.16, 88.28, 97.12.

    Comments: The fracture is healing, and the patient was seen solely for cast change.

    Codes (episode 3): V54.16, 97.88.

    Comments: The fracture has healed, and the patient is seen solely for removal of cast.

16. **Codes:** 716.16, 905.4, V15.51, E929.3, 77.96.

    Comments: The current arthritis is a late effect of the previous fracture and is therefore coded as traumatic arthritis. A late effect E code is also assigned because a late effect code for the original injury was assigned in the main classification. Code V15.51 is assigned to show a history of traumatic fracture.

17. **Codes:** 824.6, E882, E849.0, E004.9, E000.8, 79.36.

    Comments: A fracture dislocation is coded to fracture. A displaced fracture is a closed fracture.

18. **Codes:** 800.02, E916, E849.6, E000.8, 87.17, 02.02.

    Comments: (1) The patient was briefly unconscious following the injury, 800.02, requiring fifth digit 2. (2) The accident occurred in a retail food warehouse, E849.6. (3) Code 01.25, craniectomy, is excluded with code 02.02 because craniectomy is the operative approach.

19. **Codes:** 822.0, E883.9, E849.4, E006.2, E000.8, 79.36.

    Comments: Although the fracture was closed (822.0), an open reduction procedure with internal fixation was performed (79.36).

20. **Codes:** 729.5, 729.81, E818.2.

    Comments: Conditions are coded only to the highest level of certainty in the physician office setting. Therefore, codes are assigned only for the symptoms of leg pain and swelling. No code is assigned for the possible tibial fracture.

Burns

C19

1. **Codes:** 943.21, 941.29, 942.22, 948.10, E894, E849.4, E015.1, E000.8, 93.33, 86.28.

   Comments: (1) Because the patient had first- and second-degree burns on the forearm, only the highest degree is coded, 943.21. (2) Code 948.10 is assigned to identify 12 percent of the total body surface that was affected by first- and second-degree burns, with no third-degree burns. (3) E codes are assigned with injury codes. (4) Code E894 indicates that the cause was the ignition of highly flammable material. E849.4 indicates that the injury took place in a park. (5) Code 86.28, Nonexcisional debridement, is assigned because there was no cutting of tissue.

2. **Codes:** 944.30, 941.29, 943.21, 944.22, 948.10, E919.0, E899, E849.1, E016.9, E000.0.

   Comments: (1) The first- and second-degree burns are coded to second degree only: face and ear, 941.29; right forearm, 943.21; thumb, 944.22. (2) The third-degree burns to the left hand are coded 944.30. The third degree is sequenced first because it reflects the highest degree of burns. (3) Fourteen percent of the body was affected by burns (subcategory 948.1), of which 4 percent was affected by third degree. The fourth digit 0 is assigned because there was less than 10 percent third-degree burn. (4) E919.0 indicates that the accident was caused by farm machinery; E899 indicates a fire secondary to explosion.

3. **Codes (episode 1):** 944.38, 948.00, E924.0, E849.0, E015.9, E000.8, 86.62, 86.22.

   Comments: (1) For burns of more than one degree of the same site, code to the most severe, subcategory 944.3. To identify multiple sites of wrist and hands, assign code 944.38. (2) The wrist does not have to be affected in order to assign this code because the title of section 944 in chapter 17 of volume 1 of *ICD-9-CM* reads, "Burn of Wrist(s) and Hand(s)." The word "and" in the title of a code in this chapter means "and/or."

   Code (episode 2): 944.38.

   Comments: The remaining burns have not healed and are still under treatment; therefore, code 994.38 is assigned for a current condition under treatment.

Poisoning and Adverse Effects of Drugs

C20

1. **Codes:** 966.1, E980.4, 781.2, 787.01, 368.8, 042, 345.90, 907.0, E929.0.

   Comments: (1) The Dilantin poisoning code (966.1) is designated as the principal diagnosis, with additional codes for the manifestations. (2) The seizure disorder (345.90) is a late effect (907.0) of the previous head injury. The E code (E929.0) shows a late effect of a previous automobile accident.

2. **Codes:** 693.0, E931.8, 112.0.

   Comments: The reason for this outpatient encounter is the skin rash, which is an adverse reaction to the therapeutic use of Dapsone. The E code indicates the medication responsible for the adverse reaction. The thrush is a continuing problem that is also coded.

3. **Codes:** 708.0, 186.9, E930.8, 86.11.

   Comments: (1) The manifestation of the adverse reaction (urticaria) was responsible for admission. (2) Choriocarcinoma is referenced under its name, as a main entry, in the Alphabetic Index to Diseases (volume 2 of *ICD-9-CM*). The code for an unspecified site, male patient, is 186.9. (3) The E code indicates the medication responsible for the adverse reaction.

4. **Codes:** 578.9, 427.89, E941.1, V64.1.

   Comments: (1) The gastrointestinal bleed remains the principal diagnosis even though the planned treatment was not carried out (Section II[F]) because of the adverse reaction to the atropine. (2) Slow heart rate is bradycardia (427.89). (3) This adverse reaction is referenced in the Table of Drugs and Chemicals (volume 2 of *ICD-9-CM*) under the "Atropine, Therapeutic Use" column, E941.1. (4) Code V64.1 is assigned to indicate that the planned treatment was not carried out because of a contraindication due to the bradycardia.

5. **Codes:** 042, 115.90, 288.03, E931.7, 86.07.

   Comments: (1) Even though histoplasmosis is stated as the current problem, it is related to the patient's AIDS, which is appropriately designated as the principal diagnosis. (2) Adverse reaction to AZT is referenced in the Table of Drugs and Chemicals (volume 2 of *ICD-9-CM*) under "drug (AHFS List) 8:18, therapeutic use, E931.7." If the specific drug is not listed in the Table of Drugs and Chemicals, the American Hospital Formulary Service formulary index should be referenced for the number corresponding to the drug. Then the Table of Drugs and Chemicals in *ICD-9-CM* can be referenced for that number under the term "drug."

6. **Codes:** 965.5, 780.97, 781.3, 782.4, 780.4, E850.5, 625.8, 88.01.

   Comments: (1) The poisoning code is sequenced as the principal diagnosis, with additional codes for each of the individual manifestations. (2) Phenylbutazone is referenced in the Table of Drugs and Chemicals (volume 2 of *ICD-9-CM*) under "phenyl, butazone, poisoning, 965.5" and "accidental, E850.5." (3) The uterine mass is not further identified as to type and so code 625.8 is assigned. (4) Code 780.97 is assigned for the altered mental status; a psychosis code is not assigned without further documentation of the patient's condition.

7. **Codes:** 969.4, E853.2, 970.81, E854.3, 969.6, E854.1, 971.2, E855.5, 518.81, 96.71, 96.04.

   Comments: (1) When multiple drugs are responsible for a poisoning, each is assigned a separate code. (2) Any one of the poisoning codes could have been designated as the principal diagnosis (*Official Guidelines for Coding and Reporting,* Section II[B]). (3) Respiratory distress has evolved to acute respiratory failure as the manifestation of the poisoning, but the poisoning codes must be sequenced first. (4) The patient was intubated but remained on ventilatory support for less than 96 hours, and so the code is 96.71.

8. **Codes:** 600.00, 427.31, E938.4, V64.1.

   Comments: The development of a complication (atrial fibrillation, 427.31), an adverse reaction to anesthesia (E938.4), does not change the principal diagnosis. Even though the planned TURP was not carried out, the benign hypertrophy of the prostate was the condition responsible for the admission (*Official Guidelines for Coding and Reporting,* Section II[F]).

9. **Codes:** 787.01, E942.1.

   Comments: No code from category 995.2 is assigned because the manifestations of this adverse reaction, nausea and vomiting, are specified. A code from category 995.2 is assigned when no manifestations are listed.

10. **Codes:** 493.91, 300.00, E932.0.

    Comments: (1) Asthma (493.9) is assigned a fifth digit of 1 to indicate status asthmaticus, supported by the statement that it was "intractable" and could not be cared for on an outpatient basis. (2) The allergy to Solu-Medrol and prednisone resulted in an anxiety state that represents an adverse reaction to drugs that were administered correctly. (3) Solu-Medrol is not listed under its name in the Table of Drugs and Chemicals (volume 2 of *ICD-9-CM*). It is referenced under the AHFS list number by going to the subentry "Drug, AHFS List." When the specific drug is not listed in the Table of Drugs and Chemicals, the AHFS formulary index should be referenced for the number corresponding to the drug. Then the Table of Drugs and Chemicals in *ICD-9-CM* can be referenced for that number under the term "drug." (4) Prednisone, which is located in the Table of Drugs and Chemicals, and Solu-Medrol carry the same E code.

11. **Codes:** 453.84, E932.2, 88.67.

    Comments: (1) The axillary vein thrombosis is an adverse reaction to Orval. (2) The E code for Orval can be located in the Table of Drugs and Chemicals (volume 2 of *ICD-9-CM*) by referencing "contraceptives (oral)."

12. **Codes:** 481, 787.91, E931.9, E930.3.

    Comments: (1) The admitting symptoms are all integral to a diagnosis of pneumococcal pneumonia. (2) Diarrhea represents an adverse reaction to erythromycin and Bactrim. Separate E codes are assigned for each drug. (3) Bactrim is not listed in the Table of Drugs and Chemicals (volume 2 of *ICD-9-CM*); the AHFS formulary index should be referenced for the number corresponding to the drug (AHFS 8:40). Then the Table of Drugs and Chemicals in *ICD-9-CM* can be referenced for that number under the term "drug."

13. **Codes:** 969.1, 965.61, 980.0, 305.00, E853.0, E850.6, E860.0.

    Comments: (1) A poisoning code should be sequenced as the principal diagnosis because it is unlikely that alcohol intoxication alone would have required inpatient attention. (2) This represents an accidental poisoning by Compazine and Advil because the patient thought she was taking vitamins and aspirin. (3) There is no entry for Advil in the Table of Drugs and Chemicals (volume 2 of *ICD-9-CM*), but there is one for ibuprofen. (4) Code 305.00 is assigned for acute alcohol intoxication without a diagnosis of alcoholism.

14. **Codes:** 432.1, 453.50, V58.61, E934.2, E935.3, 87.03.

    Comments: (1) The subdural hematoma is an adverse reaction involving both Coumadin and aspirin. Therefore, E codes are assigned for each drug from the therapeutic use column of the Table of Drugs and Chemicals (volume 2 of *ICD-9-CM*). (2) Code V58.61 is assigned for the long-term use of Coumadin (anticoagulant).

15. **Codes:** 822.0, E880.9, E849.0, 787.01, 788.20, E935.2, 79.36.

    Comments: Nausea and vomiting (787.01) and urinary retention (788.20) represent adverse reactions to morphine (E935.2). These symptoms developed after admission, and the fracture of the patella remains the principal diagnosis.

Complications of Surgery and Medical Care

C21

1. **Codes**: 996.81, 55.23, 88.75.

   Comments: (1) Code V42.0 should not be assigned as it is redundant. The status of kidney transplant is evident in the code for kidney transplant rejection (996.81). (2) Whereas a patient who has undergone kidney transplant may still have some form of chronic kidney disease (the kidney transplant may not fully restore kidney function), ESRD and focal glomerulonephritis should not be coded because there is no mention of these conditions being present during the current admission.

2. **Codes:** 996.42, 285.1, 00.71, 99.04.

   Comments: (1) Displacement of an orthopedic device is classified as a mechanical complication. In the Alphabetic Index to Diseases (volume 2 of *ICD-9-CM*) under the main term Displacement, the coder is directed to "see complications, mechanical" under the subterm "internal prosthesis." (2) Acute blood loss anemia is an expected outcome of hip surgery. The condition should not be coded as a complication unless stated as such by the surgeon. (3) Code 00.71 is assigned for the revision of the hip replacement acetabular component. A code from series 00.74–00.77 would be assigned as an additional code if the type of bearing surface for the revised hip replacement is known.

3. **Codes:** 996.66, 996.41, 451.2, V43.65, V58.61, 00.80, 77.67, 88.26, 93.39.

   Comments: In the left leg, there was a mechanical complication (loose components) of the prosthesis (996.41) as well as a nonmechanical complication, necrosis (996.66). Either 996.66 or 996.41 could be designated as the principal diagnosis. Code V43.65 is assigned as an additional code to identify the affected prosthetic joint, per the instructional note under subcategory 996.4. Code V58.61 is assigned to show the long-term use of Coumadin.

4. **Codes:** 526.89, V10.01, E879.2, 76.2.

   Comments: (1) Osteoradionecrosis is an example of a complication classified elsewhere in *ICD-9-CM,* as outlined in the exclusion note at the beginning of the 996-999 series. (2) Because the primary site of the neoplasm is no longer present or under active treatment, code V10.01 is assigned. (3) Code E879.2 is assigned to identify the adverse effects of radiation therapy.

5. **Codes:** 518.52, 161.1, 31.43, 93.96.

   Comments: (1) Postoperative respiratory insufficiency is an example of a complication classified elsewhere in *ICD-9-CM,* as specified in the exclusion note at the beginning of the 996-999 series. (2) The principal diagnosis is the condition necessitating admission as an inpatient, postoperative respiratory insufficiency. (3) Most insurance payers also require codes for the ambulatory surgery and the condition for which it was performed to be assigned when patients are admitted from the outpatient surgery unit.

6. **Codes:** 996.59, 157.0.

   Comments: Code 996.59 is assigned for a complication of a prosthetic device, which includes a prosthetic implant in the bile duct. Displacement of a device is a mechanical complication.

7. **Codes:** 220, 752.35, 998.2, E870.0, 65.29, 69.41, 68.12, 54.21.

   Comments: (1) A dermoid cyst is benign per instructions in the Alphabetic Index to Diseases (volume 2 of *ICD-9-CM*) under Cyst, dermoid. (2) Therapeutic procedures are sequenced before diagnostic procedures. When there is more than one therapeutic procedure, the one most closely related to the principal diagnosis (in this case, 65.29) is sequenced first. (3) Endometrioma was ruled out by pathologic diagnosis of the dermoid cyst. Conditions that have been ruled out are not coded. (4) Accidental puncture or laceration during a procedure is coded 998.2.

8. **Codes:** 338.18, 788.0, 87.73, 592.1, 56.0, 87.74.

   Comments: (1) Pain following surgery is not a complication of surgery and should not be classified as such. Assign code 338.18, Other acute postoperative pain, as the principal diagnosis because the stated reason for the admission is documented as postoperative pain control. (2) The narrative indicates that the pain was in the ureteral area; therefore, code 788.0 should be assigned for the abdomen rather than code 789.0x. Code 788.0 is assigned to provide greater specificity regarding the location of the postoperative pain. (3) Because the surgery was performed the preceding day at the same facility, the diagnosis and procedure codes for the outpatient encounter are added. Some payers (e.g., Medicare) require that related outpatient services provided within 72 hours of an inpatient admission be combined in the same claim.

9. **Codes:** 998.11, 233.1, 627.1, 67.69, 67.2, 69.09.

   Comments: (1) The principal diagnosis is postoperative bleeding, the reason for inpatient admission. No additional code is required to describe postoperative bleeding. (2) A diagnosis of CIN-III with severe dysplasia of the cervix is coded to 233.1. (3) Additional codes are assigned for the postmenopausal bleeding, which was the reason for the original outpatient surgery, and for the dilatation and curettage as well as the suture of the cervix because they were performed within a brief period of time before admission. Some insurance payers may not require this additional coding. Some payers may require the provider to submit a separate bill for the outpatient procedure rather than combine it into the inpatient bill.

10. **Codes:** 998.59, 041.11, 86.22.

    Comments: The postoperative wound infection was of the soft tissue incision site only, not of the site of pin insertion into the bone. Therefore, code 998.59 is assigned rather than 996.67. Code 86.22 is assigned for the wide excisional debridement of the postoperative wound infection of the soft tissue.

11. **Codes:** 721.0, 724.5, 338.18, 03.09.

    Comments: Code 338.18, Other acute postoperative pain, is assigned to identify an unusual amount of postoperative pain. This is not coded as a postoperative complication. Code 721.0 is coded for additional specificity to identify the site of the pain.

12. **Codes:** 996.67, 041.11, V15.51, 86.22, 78.65.

    Comments: Because the infection resulted from the presence of an orthopedic device, code 996.67 instead of code 998.59 is assigned. Code 86.22 is assigned for the wide excisional debridement of the deep infection of the thigh. Code V15.51 is assigned to show a history of a traumatic fracture.

13. **Codes:** 998.59, 997.5, 599.0, 041.11, 041.04, 038.11, 995.91, E878.8.

    Comments: Because the UTI is specified as a postoperative complication due to two organisms, four codes (997.5, 599.0, 041.11, 041.04) are necessary to appropriately identify this condition. Codes 998.59 and 041.11 identify postoperative wound infection. Codes 998.59, 038.11, and 995.91 identify postoperative sepsis. Code 995.91 is assigned in accordance with the Tabular List instructions for category 038. Because postoperative complications are specified, code E878.8 is assigned to identify the external cause as surgical procedure. Either code 997.5 or 998.59 can be sequenced as the principal diagnosis because both conditions were present on admission and were treated (*Official Guidelines for Coding and Reporting*, Section II[B] and Section II[C]).

Index

U